I0592002

Matías Romero

Coffee and India-rubber Culture in Mexico

Matías Romero

Coffee and India-rubber Culture in Mexico

ISBN/EAN: 9783337227609

Printed in Europe, USA, Canada, Australia, Japan

Cover: Foto ©ninafisch / pixelio.de

More available books at **www.hansebooks.com**

BERKELEY
LIBRARY
UNIVERSITY OF
CALIFORNIA

COFFEE AND INDIA-RUBBER CULTURE IN MEXICO

PRECEDED BY

GEOGRAPHICAL AND STATISTICAL NOTES

ON MEXICO

BY

MATIAS ROMERO

G. P. PUTNAM'S SONS

NEW YORK AND LONDON

The Knickerbocker Press

1898

Copyright, 1898
BY
MATIAS ROMERO

INTRODUCTION.

When, after serving five years, from 1868 to 1871, as Secretary of the Treasury in Mexico under President Juarez's administration, I was obliged to resign, my health being so greatly broken down as to make it impossible for me to continue discharging the duties of that responsible, and at the time, very difficult office, feeling that if I remained in the City of Mexico, I could not regain my health as I would be subject to continual mental excitement, I made up my mind to live in the country and occupy my time in agricultural pursuits. Before deciding what branch of agriculture I should follow, I made a tour of inspection to the most favored regions of Mexico and found that india-rubber and coffee raising seemed to be the most promising and profitable undertakings.[1] The place which I thought best adapted to both of these products was the district of Soconusco, one of the counties of

[1] I take the following from an article entitled " Settlement of the Mexico-Guatemala Boundary Question," that I published in vol. xxix., No. 2, 1897, of the *Bulletin of the American Geographical Society*, of New York :

" The office of Secretary of the Treasury of Mexico was, until recently, the most difficult of administration, because, the Federal Treasury being in a state of chronic bankruptcy, it was impossible to pay on demand all its obligations, and the Secretary had to distribute the daily receipts in the best way he could ; so that all creditors presented their claims to him, thus placing in his hands almost all the details of that office, which, added to several other causes, too numerous to specify here, increased considerably the Secretary's labors. Therefore, a hard-working and conscientious man, holding that office, had to work eighteen hours every day, as long as he was able to do so, and that at a place nearly 8000 feet above the level of the sea, where the decreased atmospheric pressure seriously affects the nervous system, and does not permit of prolonged and constant mental labor.

" I remember that the Emperor Napoleon, believing, during the French intervention, and while Maximilian was in Mexico, that there was no Mexican capable of managing the finances of the country, sent to Mexico, for that purpose, two French officials, who were doubtless expert financiers, and who, being naturally very anxious to please Napoleon, expecting promotion at home if successful, worked very hard to satisfy him, with the result that after a few months one of them, M. Bonnefons, returned home very sick and soon afterward died, and his successor, M. Mantenant, returned to France insane. I have had occasion to notice that even young and strong men suffer severely after a few months of prolonged mental work, from what Mexican

the State of Chiapas, in southeastern Mexico, bordering on Guatemala, and I concluded to settle there and apply myself to coffee and india-rubber culture.

In the meanwhile, coffee raising had attained considerable development in Guatemala, the Guatemalan coffee being very highly esteemed in foreign markets, and I determined to make a tour of inspection in Guatemala and examine the principal coffee plantations, in order to learn what was the best way to make a plantation and keep it productive. I, of course, tried, during this time, to collect all the information I possibly could about these two branches of agricultural industry.

Finally I undertook to make a coffee plantation in the high lands of Soconusco—located from four to five thousand feet above the level of the sea—as, in my opinion, a temperate zone is the proper one for that tree ; and another for india-rubber in the lower lands of the district, which are warm, damp and marshy. I acquired some experience by these experiments and I made a study of the subject, not only in coffee plantations in Mexico and Guatemala, but in other countries where I un-

doctors call brain anæmia, and which, if the patient does not cease working or leave the city, it generally has an early and fatal termination.

" After having worked very hard in Washington during the French intervention in Mexico, from 1861 to 1867, as the official representative of my country, I was called by President Juarez, on my return home on the 15th of January, 1868, to the Treasury Department, and I remained in that office up to June 10, 1872, working as hard, if not harder than any of my predecessors, so that I am surprised that I did not succumb to the severity of my labors. It is true I was then young, and, owing to my regular habits, I was physically vigorous ; but the labor imposed upon me was enough to kill anybody. In the early part of 1872, I could not sleep, nor digest and assimilate my food, and altogether I was in such a condition that a few months more of such work would certainly have ended my life. I found myself under the necessity, therefore, of retiring from the Cabinet, which I did, availing myself of the close of the session of the Mexican Congress, especially dedicated to approve the appropriations for the following fiscal year and to vote the taxes to defray them. I also desired to afford President Juarez an opportunity to appoint new men to his Cabinet, as he had inaugurated a new Presidential term on the 1st of December, 1871, and it was customary to make on such occasions a total or partial change of Cabinet.

" I realized that to restore my health it would be necessary for me to lead for some years a hygienic life and to avoid excessive mental labor, and as this would not have been possible had I remained in the City of Mexico, I made up my mind to live in the country, devoting my time and energies to agricultural pursuits, since, having no fortune, I had to earn my living by my own work. I visited several desirable places in Mexico, and finally decided to settle in a place quite remote from the Capital, because I did not desire to return to public life, for which I had never had any inclination. I selected the town of Tapachula, the county seat of the District of Soconusco, in the State of Chiapas, adjoining Guatemala, located on the Pacific slope, because it was one of fine agricultural resources and of great promise ; and, early in 1873, I settled there, bought some public land and started a coffee plantation in the high lands, and one of india-rubber in the low ones, and did some commercial business, buying coffee for export, and importing agricultural implements and commodities."

derstood coffee raising was also very prosperous, like the Island of Ceylon, in the East Indies, and Brazil, which is now and has been for many years, the largest producer of coffee in the world.

When I considered that I had mastered the subject as thoroughly as I could without having any technical education for the purpose, having acquired only practical information and accepted such principles as my common sense made clear to me, I thought that I would give the benefit of my experience to other people, both in and out of Mexico, who might desire to engage in this industry. I wrote, therefore, a little manual on coffee culture on the southern coast of the State of Chiapas. The knowledge I gained in making a plantation allowed me to acquire practical experience on this subject, so that my opinions there expressed are well-grounded and perfectly correct so far as the southern coast of the State of Chiapas is concerned. In each locality, the conditions vary according to the position of the mountains, the prevailing winds, the rainfall and other circumstances which produce various meteorological phenomena affecting materially the climate ; it would be difficult, therefore, to give rules in detail which would apply absolutely to all localities, as what is desirable in one may be very objectionable in another affected by different climatological conditions.

For that reason, I confined my study to the southern district of Chiapas, which I knew quite well, and tried to verify my theories by what I had learned of coffee planting in other places, and especially in Ceylon, as I had found books which stated in a very clear and concise manner the system prevailing there of planting coffee—information which I found was very difficult to obtain from other countries, including even Brazil. I published in Mexico three editions of my manual, correcting and adding to each new one—the last one being published in July, 1874. There was, at the time, no interest in coffee culture and very little attention was therefore paid to my manual. By the advice of a friend, I placed in a bookstore about fifty copies on sale, and four or six years later, only two or three had been sold.

When the price of coffee began to rise considerably, especially after 1890, the culture of coffee received a great impetus, and the plantations were very much extended, the price became very lucrative, as it was sold at the plantation as high as 35 cents a pound in silver ; that, of course, was a great stimulus to increase its production. However, during the year 1897 the price fell considerably, as it was sold, I believe, at 12 cents a pound in silver at the plantation, that being still a remunerative price. When the interest in coffee-raising was at its height in Mexico, the Mexican Government made, in 1893, a fourth edition of my manual, but it was merely a republication of the former one, without any change at all. Since the third edition of that book was published, a great deal of interest has been awakened in the culture of coffee and I have received innumerable requests for copies of the manual from various sections of Mexico, and also from young men in the United States who, having heard of the great profits of coffee raising, are disposed to undertake coffee planting in Mexico. I have therefore concluded, in the interest of that industry and its development in Mexico, to publish an English translation of my manual.

My public duties for the last eighteen years have not allowed me much time to make new studies on coffee culture, but the interest I take in coffee raising has made me read all that came in my way on the subject ; and I also made in 1896 special visits to the new coffee districts in the State of Oaxaca, Mexico, to study their conditions. I am very sorry that I have not the time indispensable to revise this edition, and have to publish it as it came out in Spanish, several years ago. To understand it well the reader must bear in mind that it was written in Soconusco County, State of Chiapas, nearly a quarter of a century ago.

I am very sorry that my present engagements have prevented me from revising this paper up to date ; that is, changing such views expressed in the same as my experience has taught me not to be entirely correct, at least in so far as other regions outside of the southern coast of Chiapas are concerned, as that would require more time than I can afford, and in my inability to do that work, I prefer to use the paper I wrote long ago, exactly in the shape in which it then came out. Since that time, all circumstances and conditions of coffee raising have materially changed. The price of land has increased twenty times, as a caballeria, which was worth $50 in 1874, has been recently sold at $1000 ; wages have gone up twice or three times higher than they were then, and all the estimates of the costs and expenses to be approximate to present conditions would be required to be at least triple, and in some cases even this figure would not represent the exact cost. Besides, any mistake, especially in the selection of a site for a coffee plantation, may cause very serious losses, in the shape of increased expenses for planting and keeping it, and reduced receipts caused by small crops.

In 1893 and 1894 I was involuntarily drawn into a controversy with an American gentleman, who advocated the low lands of the Isthmus of Tehuantepec as the best suited for coffee and india-rubber culture, and in that correspondence I expressed some views concerning that subject in other regions than the southern coast of Chiapas, which contained some ideas formed since the book was written. I append to this paper that correspondence.

When I settled in Soconusco it was a wild county, which on account of its distance from the capital of the Republic, its isolation from the rest of the State of Chiapas, and the unsettled condition which often prevailed in Mexico, had made it almost an independent principality, ruled with an iron hand by an unscrupulous and

irresponsible local chieftain, who had been able to overpower all opposition. I tried to obtain his support for the development of the country,
and he seemed to give it to me cheerfully, and I worked earnestly for
the purpose of establishing the supremacy of the Federal government
and the Federal laws which amply guarantee personal and property
rights, and I succeeded in having Federal troops and Federal judges
sent there for that purpose. His antagonists, however, availed themselves of the opportunity of his losing power to drive him out of the
place, and he, with the natural suspicion of ignorant men, thought I
was the cause of his overthrow, and that I had been working for it, and
decided to get rid of me at any cost. Besides, the then President of
Guatemala, General J. Rufino Barrios, who suspected my going to Soconusco with some scheme hostile to his country and himself,[1] assisted
the Soconusco leader against me, and both plotted against my life, but
I was saved in an almost miraculous manner. My coffee plantation
had before, and while I was making it, been partially destroyed by

---

[1] The following extract from my paper on the "Settlement of the Mexico-Guatemala Boundary Question," just quoted, states the nature of my relations with General
Barrios, the President of Guatemala, while I was in Soconusco:

"Public men in Guatemala are generally very suspicious, and especially were
they so when Mexico was concerned, and when they saw me living as a farmer in a
very humble frontier town adjoining their country, they imagined that I must have
some hostile designs against Guatemala, and that my farming was only a pretence to
cover my hidden designs. General J. Rufino Barrios became President very soon after I settled in Soconusco, and he, as well as most of the persons around him, thought
that I had gone there either with the purpose of attempting to make myself dictator
or ruler of Guatemala, or to work for the annexation of that country to Mexico, which
had been for some time the great bugbear of Guatemalan statesmen. Judging by what
they had sometimes seen in their own country, they imagined that a man who had been
Secretary of the Treasury of Mexico for five years was, or ought to be, a millionaire,
and consequently they thought it an absurd idea that he should try to earn his living
by honest labor.

"Although I had been warned of this danger, I did not at the time fully realize
its gravity, because I did not know how suspicious of Mexico and how hostile to her
the people of Guatemala were, and I tried to allay their fears by going myself to the
City of Guatemala to make the acquaintance of its public men and to inform them of
my reasons for having settled in Soconusco, and of my purposes for the future; but,
judging me by the standard of their own views and principles, as it is natural for people to do, this act of mine probably only served to confirm them in their suspicions.

"General Barrios himself, whom I met in the City of Guatemala, before becoming President, treated me with the greatest duplicity. At the same time that
he pretended to be a friend of mine, and in some ways acted as such, probably in
order the better to deceive me by inspiring me with confidence in his sincerity,
—as when he sent me his power of attorney, authorizing me to draw upon his funds
in bank and attend to his private affairs, especially to a farm he had in Soconusco,—
he actually believed me to be his rival, and therefore his worst enemy, and he did all
he could against my person and property, but always in an underhand manner, so as
not to appear personally responsible."

neighboring Guatemalan Indians, encouraged, I was sure, although I could not prove it, by President Barrios, under the plea that I was making it in Guatemalan territory.

My sudden departure from Soconusco made me abandon and lose everything I had there. I, therefore, did not see grown the trees I had planted, but they grew well and yielded a large amount of fruit, of which a relative of mine availed himself, who made out of that plantation a large fortune, and finally bought from me the land occupied by the plantation at about the price of land there when the purchase was made.

In the several trips of inspection which I made in Mexico, I was careful to study coffee culture in every district I visited, and I published in the newspapers the result of my studies in the shape of articles relating to each district. They were finally reprinted in a book on the State of Oaxaca, which I published in Barcelona in 1886. It would take a great deal of space to publish them here, and they do not contain, so far as rules for coffee culture are concerned, any more information than appears in my manual on the subject.

As Mexico is so little known in the United States, I thought it convenient for the benefit of the readers in this country that I should precede my manual with another paper on "Geographical and Statistical Notes on Mexico," which I have just published, and which to an American reader gives more recent information than I have seen collected in any single book in the English language.

WASHINGTON, January 31, 1898. M. R.

MONEY, WEIGHTS AND MEASURES.

Before Mexico adopted the metric decimal system we used the old Spanish weights and measures.

The measures used in this book are those in vogue in Soconusco when this manual was written, namely: the vara as a unit of linear measure, which is 2.75 English feet or about 33 inches; and for land measure the Cuerda, which is a square of 25 varas on each side or 625 sq. varas, the Caballeria, which has 609.408 varas or 105¾ acres and the square league which is a square of 5,000 varas on each side or 25,000,000 sq. varas and equal to 4339.4 acres. The pounds are also the Mexican pounds equal to 1.014 English pounds.

The Mexican dollar was divided into eight parts, each of them called a *real*. The *real*, which was 12½ cents, was divided into two halves called *medios*, and each *medio* was divided into two halves called *cuartillas*, and each *cuartilla* was divided into two halves called *octavos*.

In Mexico we use the thermometer with the Centigrade scale, and the way in which this scale can be reduced to the Fahrenheit scale used in this country is well known.

CONTENTS.

x   **Contents.**

Contents.

Contents.

Contents.

Contents.

Contents

Contents.

INDIA-RUBBER CULTURE IN MEXICO . 371

GEOGRAPHICAL AND STATISTICAL NOTES
ON MEXICO

GEOGRAPHICAL AND STATISTICAL NOTES ON MEXICO.[1]

(Corrected to June 30, 1897.)

FOR a long time past I have felt the need of a short treatise containing geographical and statistical information about Mexico, to answer the many queries received on that subject by the Mexican Legation in Washington. A statistical abstract about Mexico, such as most nations publish every year, is greatly needed, especially now when the attention of business men and young men is awakening to the possibilities of Mexico. It was partly with the purpose of supplying that need that I prepared this article, which will, I hope, at least serve

[1] This article first appeared in the *Bulletin of the American Geographical Society of New York* of December 31, 1896. A club of the City of Washington requested me, in January, 1888, to deliver a lecture on Mexico, and, as I had not time to prepare one, I consented to give an informal talk on the subject, which I did on January 16th of that year. Most of my talk was taken down by a stenographer, and was the basis of the article which appeared in the *Bulletin of the American Geographical Society of New York*. That Society did me the honor of electing me one of its honorary members, at the request of Honorable Frederick A. Conkling, on January 25, 1870, and I have ever since felt that I owed it a debt which I could only pay by sending it a contribution about Mexico. The pressure of my official duties in Washington on the one hand, and my inability to treat properly the many subjects connected with a description of Mexico, added to the difficulty of compressing them into a few pages; on the other, delayed that work much longer than I desired or expected. I have added considerably to this article in the present edition, especially in that part which embraces statistical information about Mexico, and I am sure that in so far as concerns the fulness of that information and the most recent data, my article stands above any previous publication on the subject.

to call attention to that country, and awaken a desire for reading other and better monographs and books on Mexico written by more competent men. I have borrowed from the descriptions of others, especially in what appears under the heading of Geology, Geography, and Fauna.

PART I.

GEOGRAPHY

I. GEOGRAPHY.

LOCATION, BOUNDARIES, AND AREA.

Location.—Mexico is situated between 14° 30′ 42″ and 32° 42′ north latitude, and between 86° 46′ 8″ and 117° 7′ 31″ 89 longitude west of the meridian of Greenwich, embracing therefore 18° 11′ 18″ of latitude and 30° 21′ 23″ 89 of longitude. It has an area of 767,326 square miles. It is bounded on the north by the United States of America, on the southeast by Guatemala and Belize, on the south and west by the Pacific Ocean, and on the north and east by the Gulf of Mexico and the Carribean Sea.

Boundary with the United States.—The boundary with the United States is fixed by the treaties of February 2, 1848, and December 30, 1853, and begins at the mouth of the Rio Grande River on the Gulf of Mexico, follows the river for 1136 miles, beyond El Paso, Texas, to the point where it strikes parallel 31° 47′ north latitude, and from there runs along said parallel for a distance of one hundred miles, and thence south to parallel 31° 20′ north latitude ; from there west along this parallel as far as the 111th meridian of longitude west of Greenwich ; thence in a straight line to a point on the Colorado River, twenty English miles below the junction of the Gila ; thence up the middle of the said River Colorado to the intersection with the old line between Upper and Lower California, and thence to a point on the Pacific Ocean, distant one marine league due south of the southernmost point of the Bay of San Diego ; the total distance from El Paso to the Pacific being 674 miles. The whole extent of the boundary line between the two countries is 1833 miles.

The boundary line with the United States runs from southeast to northwest, the mouth of the Rio Grande being in 25° 57′ 14″ 74″ north latitude ; while the line reaches on the Pacific latitude 32° 32′ 1″ 34″ ; the point where the boundary line strikes the Colorado River is farther north, reaching 32° 42′ of north latitude. Mexico has, therefore, on the western, or Pacific side, 6° 34′ 46″ 20″ of latitude more than on the eastern or the Gulf of Mexico side.

Boundary with Guatemala.—The boundary with Guatemala is fixed by the treaties of September 27, 1882, and April 1, 1895, and runs from a point on the Pacific coast three leagues distant from the upper mouth of the River Zuchiate, and thence, following the deepest channel thereof, to the point at which it intersects the vertical plane which crosses the highest point of the volcano of Tacaná, and distant twenty-five miles from the southernmost pillar of the gate of Talquian, leaving that gate in the territory of Guatemala ; the determinate line by the vertical plane defined above until it touches the River Zuchiate at the point of its intersection with the vertical plane which passes the summit of Buenavista and Ixbul ; the determinate line by the vertical plane which passes the summit of Buenavista, determined by the astronomical observations, and the summit of the Ixbul hill from where it intersects the former to a point four kilometres beyond said hill ; thence to the parallel of latitude which crosses the last-named point, and thence eastward until it reaches the deepest channel of the Chixoy up to its junction with the Usumacinta River, following that river until it reaches the parallel situated twenty-five kilometres to the south of Tenosique in Tabasco, to be measured from the principal square of that town ; the parallel of latitude referred to above, from its intersection with the deepest channel of the Usumacinta, until it intersects the meridian which passes at one third of the distance between the centres of the Plazas of Tenosique and Sacluc, this distance being calculated from Tenosique ; from this meridian, from its intersection with the parallel above mentioned to the latitude of 17° 49' ; and from the intersection of this parallel with the latter meridian indefinitely toward the east.

The southern end of the Guatemalan line on the Pacific is in 14° 24' north latitude, while the northern end, on the Caribbean Sea, is in 17° 49' north latitude, being a difference of 3° 25' in favor of the latter. The calculated length of the southern boundary is 642 miles.

Boundary with Belize.—To the southeast of Yucatan extends the territory of Belize, occupied by a British settlement under a permit granted to them by the Spanish Government to cut wood within the limits mentioned in the treaty concluded between the Kings of Great Britain and Spain on November 3, 1783, and amended on July 14, 1786.

British Honduras, according to Mr. George Gil, F.R.G.S., in his book, " British Colonies," published in London in 1896, was declared a separate colony of Great Britain, under a Lieutenant-Governor subordinate to the Governor of Jamaica, in the year 1862, previous to which time it had been a dependency of Jamaica. In 1884 a Governor and Commander-in-Chief was appointed, by Letters Patent, and thus the colony became independent of Jamaica. On April 30, 1859, Great

Britain signed a treaty with Guatemala, within whose boundaries most of British Honduras was situated, defining the boundary of that colony.

The limits between Mexico and Belize are defined by a treaty signed at the City of Mexico on July 8, 1893, and ratified by the Mexican Senate on April 19, 1897, and begin at the mouth of Bocalarchica— a strait which separates the State of Yucatan from Ambergris Key and adjacent islands, runs along the centre of the channel between said islands and the mainland, in a southeasterly direction, until it reaches the parallel 18° 9′ north latitude; thence northwesterly at an equal distance between two keys marked on the map annexed to the treaty, to meet the parallel 18° 10′ north latitude; thence, turning toward the west, along the neighboring bay, as far as 88° 2′ west meridian, thence toward the north until it reaches the parallel 18° 25′ north latitude, thence it runs toward the west as far as meridian 88° 28′ 32″ north, this point being the mouth of the Hondo River; thence following its deepest channel, passing to the west of Albion Island and running up the Arroyo Azul until the latter stream crosses the meridian of the Garbutt Falls at a point north of the boundary lines of Mexico, Guatemala, and British Honduras; and from that point following the meridian of Garbutt Falls, running in a southerly direction up to 17° 49′, north latitude which is the boundary line between Mexico and Guatemala, leaving the so-called Snoska or Xnobba River in a northerly direction and in Mexican territory.

Cession of Mexican Territory to the United States.—Mexico has ceded to the United States, by the treaty of Guadalupe-Hidalgo of February 2, 1848, and the Gadsden Treaty of December 30, 1853, 930,590 square miles, comprising over one-half of her former territory. The same cession is considered in the United States under three heads—first under the boundary treaty signed in Washington on April 25, 1838, between the United States of America and the Republic of Texas, under which Texas was annexed to the United States in 1845; second, under the cession of the Guadalupe-Hidalgo Treaty, and the third under the Gadsden Treaty.

As Mexico did not recognize the independence of Texas until the treaty of Guadalupe-Hidalgo was signed, we consider that she only gave her consent to that annexation by said treaty, and therefore that the cession of territory made then to the United States embraced also Texas.

Mr. S. W. Lamoreaux, former Commissioner of the General Land Office, published in 1896 a map of the United States, which contained in detail the different sections of territory annexed to the same in different periods from France, Spain, Mexico, and Russia, where the Mexican annexations are clearly defined. From official data of that office, I take the following figures representing the area of each of the Mexican cessions:

First, annexation of Texas, which embraces in whole or in part the following States and Territories:

	Sq. Miles.	
Texas	265,780	
Colorado, in part	18,000	
Kansas, in part	7,766	
New Mexico	65,201	
Oklahoma	5,740	
Total		362,487

Second, cession by the Guadalupe-Hidalgo Treaty, embracing in whole or in part the following States and Territories:

	Sq. Miles.	
Arizona	82,381	
California	157,801	
Colorado, in part	29,500	
Nevada	112,090	
New Mexico	42,000	
Utah	84,476	
Wyoming, in part	14,320	
Total		522,568

Third, cession by the Gadsden Treaty, containing additions to the following Territories:

	Sq. Miles.	
Arizona	31,535	
New Mexico	14,000	
Total		45,535
Grand Total in Square Miles		930,590

General Characteristics.—Mexico is bounded on the east by the long curve of the Gulf of Mexico and by the Caribbean Sea, and its eastern coast is 1727 miles long; on the west it is washed by the Pacific Ocean, its coast describing the arc of a still larger circle, for a length of 4574 miles; but after passing the latitude of the City of Mexico, about the meridian 19° of north latitude, going south, the continent makes a decided turn towards the east, the Gulf of Mexico forming the northern border, and the Pacific Ocean the southern border.

Mexico has the shape of a cornucopia, with its narrowest end tapering toward the southwest, its convex and concave sides facing the Pacific and the Atlantic, respectively, and its widest end toward the north, or the United States. I look forward to the time, which I do not think far distant, considering our continuity of territory to the United States and our immense elements of wealth, when we shall be able to provide the United States with most of the tropical products, such as sugar, coffee, tobacco, india-rubber, etc.,[1] which they now import from several other countries.

The widest portion of Mexico is, therefore, its northern extremity, or its boundary with the United States. The narrowest point is the Isthmus of Tehuantepec, about one hundred miles from one ocean to the other; and after passing it the country expands again to the south-east towards Yucatan and Chiapas until it reaches the boundary with Guatemala and Belize.

Yucatan resembles but little in its configuration Mexico proper, as it is a level country formed by coral reefs and beds, and whose ruins show it to have been the seat of a high civilization and an advanced people.

Although the greater part of Mexico is on the North American continent proper, as the Isthmus of Panama divides North from South America, a large portion of it lies in Central America. Geographically speaking, Central America is the portion of North America embraced between the Isthmus of Tehuantepec and Panama, and of this vast territory Mexico holds about one-third. In a paper published in the *Bulletin of the American Geographical Society of New York*, of March 31, 1894, I dealt especially with this subject.[2]

The broken surface of Mexico formerly made travelling there very difficult, for which reason the country was but little known, even by Mexicans themselves, as its configuration did not allow of the building of good roads, and to travel any considerable distance it was necessary to go by mule paths, without comfortable inns, and running great risks, owing to the disturbed condition of the country. It required, therefore, time, expense, endurance, and an object in view to travel widely there. I was always desirous of knowing as much as possible of the country, and I have made long trips, many of them on horseback, solely for the purpose of studying certain regions, and I think that before the railway era, I was perhaps one of the Mexicans who knew

---

[1] In his *Notes on Mexico*, Lempriere, a distinguished traveller and historian, says: "The merciful hand of Providence has bestowed on the Mexicans a magnificent land, abounding in resources of all kinds—a land where none ought to be poor, and where misery ought to be unknown—a land whose products and riches of every kind are abundant and as varied as they are rich. It is a country endowed to profusion with every gift that man can desire or envy; all the metals from gold to lead; every sort of climate, from perpetual snow to tropical heat, and of inconceivable fertility."

[2] A copy of that paper is appended to this article.

most of the country and who could, therefore, most clearly realize the difficulty of knowing it thoroughly. From this it can be readily understood how difficult it would be for a foreigner, without any previous knowledge of the country and ignorant of its language, to know it by a few days' sojourn there. Yet many travellers who have been in Mexico only a few days write about it on their return home, just as if they knew it perfectly, making necessarily many serious and sometimes laughable mistakes.

The natural beauties of Switzerland are well known ; but to me that country is hardly to be compared with Mexico, as everything in Mexico is on a much grander scale. In the latitude in which Switzerland is situated the snow line is quite low, and, therefore, most of the peaks of the Swiss mountains, while not so high as the Mexican mountains, are covered with perpetual snow, which embellishes the country, and which, melting in summer, supplies the beautiful lakes of that country with fresh water. Therefore, only in the beauty of many snow peaks, beautiful fresh-water lakes, good roads, and fine hotels has Switzerland the superiority over Mexico.

Historians, travellers, and writers of the present day compare Mexico with Egypt. There is no doubt that between the legends and romance with which the history of each of these countries abounds there is a striking resemblance. The pyramids and ancient relics in the form of buildings, images, and undeciphered hieroglyphics on stones, coins, etc., found in both countries, all contribute to the general belief that, centuries ago, the people of Mexico and Egypt were connected by some tie, were in some way of the same race and had the same ideas. To-day in Mexico, the manner of living, of cultivating the soil, and many other peculiarities in the manners and customs of the Mexican people forcibly remind the traveller of Upper and Lower Egypt.[1]

[1] In a very bright article about Mexico by Mr. Charles Dudley Warner, published in *Harper's Illustrated Monthly Magazine* for June, 1897, I find the following sentence supporting my assertion :

" In the cities he is reminded of Spain, and often of Italy (since the Catholic Church prevails), but in the country and in small towns the appearance is Oriental, or rather Egyptian. This resemblance to Egypt is due to the color or colors of the inhabitants, to the universal use of the donkey as a beast of burden, to the brown adobe walls and mud huts covered with cane, to the dust on the foliage, the clouds of dust raised in all the highways, and to a certain similarity of dress, so far as color and rags can give it, and the ability of men and women to squat all day on the ground and be happy."

Mr. Theodore W. Noyes, of Washington, in a descriptive article on Mexico, published in December, 1895, makes the following parallel between Mexico and Egypt :

" . . . The Egyptian shaduf finds its counterpart in the well sweep of Irapuato where strawberries are grown and sold every day in the year, and where irrigation is resorted to, systematized, and on a grand scale. In the absence of trees and rocks

I, myself, although I have only visited Lower Egypt, and that as a tourist in a very hasty manner and for a very few days, was greatly struck by the great similarity that I found between the two countries and between the habits of the native Egyptian and the Mexican Indians. The Egyptian plows are used by the Mexican Indians, and they are drawn in Mexico as in Egypt by oxen whose yokes are fastened to their horns, while in other countries they are fastened on their necks. Several of the agricultural products of Egypt and Mexico are exactly the same, and the way in which foods are prepared in both countries is, too, very similar; and I also found similar traits and race characteristics between the Egyptian Copts and some tribes of the Mexican Indians.

The great difference between Egypt and Mexico is that Mexico lacks "irrigation," which has made Egypt—that small corner of the earth—the most remarkable and productive country in the world. Owing to the great stretch of latitude from the Rio Grande to the Guatemala boundary, everything that grows in Egypt, and in fact in any other part of the world, can be produced in Mexico by the aid of irrigation.

the Egyptian shaduf is small, is composed of prepared timbers, and the counterpoise to the well bucket is an immense chunk of dried, hardened Nile mud. The Mexican shaduf utilizes a forked tree and swings across it a long tapering tree trunk or branch, and the counterpoise consists of a large sink stone or mass of stones fastened together. Although Mexico stretches farther south than Egypt, the two countries lie, generally speaking, between the same parallels of latitude, but the altitude of Irapuato is 5000 feet above the sea-level of the Nile, so that the same degree of undress is not expected or found in the Mexicans as in the Egyptian shaduf workers. I saw, however, in the neighborhood of Irapuato two Indians at well sweeps working side by side who were dressed only in white cotton loin cloths, who looked like the twin brothers of shaduf workers whom I have seen photographed on the Nile. . . . The water-carrier of Cairo is much like his brother of Guanajuato, where a long earthen jar is used. The groups about the fountains with jars of water bodily borne on the women's heads or on a protecting turban-like ring, or balanced on the men's shoulders, are also Oriental. Corn is ground between two stones in Asiatic fashion.

"Egyptian sand spouts are common. Also Egyptian types of domestic utensils of pottery. The Mexican woman with a baby at her back securely fastened in the reboso, which throws the infant's weight on the mother's shoulders, is to be compared with the Egyptian woman whose reboso covers her face while the child straddles her shoulders, holding to her head and leaving her hands unfettered as in the Mexican fashion. There are no Egyptian camels, but even more numerous donkeys, the patient burros. The Indian villages, either of adobe or bamboo, the thatched roofs and organ cactus fences, and alive with goats, donkeys, or snarling curs, are African in effect. There Aztecs picture writings resemble the Egyptian, the paper being made from the maguey instead of the papyrus. The Aztecs employed captives on great public works as in Egypt. Mexico thus has pyramids with much broader base than those of Egypt, though not nearly so high, and idols quite as ugly. Gold ornaments, beads, and other highly prized antiquities are found in the tombs as in Egypt."

GEOLOGY.

The geology of Mexico has been but imperfectly studied. In the higher ranges the prevailing formations are granite, which seem also to form the foundations of the plateaus, above which rise the traps, basalts, mineral-bearing porphyries, and more recent lavas. Hence, Lyell's theory that Mexico consisted originally of granite ranges with intervening valleys subsequently filled up to the level of the plateaus by subterranean eruptions. Igneous rocks of every geologic epoch certainly form to a large extent the superstructure of the central plateau. But the Mexican table-land seems to consist mainly of metamorphic formations which have been partly upheaved, partly interpenetrated, and overlaid by igneous masses of all epochs, and which are chiefly represented by shales, greywacke, greenstones, silicious schists, and especially unfossiliferous limestones. All these formations are alike remarkable for the abundance and variety of their metalliferous ores, such as silver, silver glance, copper, and gold. Gneiss and micaceous schists prevail in Oaxaca and on all the southern slopes facing both oceans. But the highest ranges are formed mainly of plutonic and volcanic rocks, such as granites, syenites, diorites, mineral-bearing trachytes, basalts, porphyries, obsidian, pearlstone, sulphur, pumice, lavas, tufa, and other recent volcanic discharges. Obsidian (itzli) was the chief material formerly used by the natives in the manufacture of their cutting implements, as shown by the quarries of the Cerro de las Navajas (Knife Cliff), near Real del Monte and Pachuca in the State of Hidalgo. Vast deposits of pumice and the purest sulphur are found at Huichapam and in many of the craters. But immeasurably the most valuable rocks are the argentiferous porphyries and schists of the central plateau and of Sinaloa, unless they are destined to be rivalled by the auriferous deposits of Sonora. Horizontal and stratified rocks, of extremely limited extent in the south, are largely developed in the northern states, and chalk becomes very prevalent towards the Rio Grande and Rio Gila valleys. To this chalk and to the sandstones are probably due the sandy plains which cover vast tracts in North Mexico, stretching thence far into New Mexico and Texas. Here the Bolson de Mapimi, a vast rocky wilderness inhabited until recently by wild tribes, occupies a space of perhaps 50,000 square miles in Coahuila and parts of the surrounding States.

None of the horizontal layers seem to be very rich in ores, which are mainly found in the metamorphic, palæozoic, and hypogene rocks of Durango, Chihuahua, and the south. Apart from Sinaloa and Sonora, which are now known to contain vast stores of the precious metals, nearly all the historical mines lie on the south central plateau at elevations of from 5500 to 9500 feet. A line drawn from the capital to Guanajuato, and thence northwards to the mining town of Guadalupe y Calvo of Chihuahua, and southwards to Oaxaca, thus cutting the main axis of upheaval at an angle of 45°, will intersect probably the richest known argentiferous region in the whole world.

Of other minerals the most important are copper, found in a pure state near the city of Guanajuato, and associated with gold in Chihuahua, Sonora, Guerrero, Jalisco, Michoacan, and elsewhere; iron in immense masses in Michoacan and Jalisco, and in Durango, where the Cerro del Mercado is a solid mountain of magnetic iron ore; lead associated with silver, chiefly in Oaxaca; tin in Michoacan and Jalisco; sulphur in many craters; platinum, recently found in Hidalgo; cinnabar, also recently found in Morelos and Guerrero; "steppe salt" in the sandy districts of the north; "bitter salt" at Tepeyac and many other places; coal at various points; bismuth in many parts; marble, alabaster, gypsum, and rock-salt in great abundance throughout the plateaus and the sierras.

MINING.

Mexico is, perhaps, the richest mining country in the world, and the production of silver—notwithstanding the imperfect methods and other drawbacks with which it has contended—represents over one-third of the product of the world, according to official statistics. Almost all the mountains of Mexico are of the metalliferous character, but those which seem richest in mining deposits are the western cordillera, extending from the State of Oaxaca to Sonora, a distance of about 1600 miles from northwest to southeast.

Humboldt gave as his opinion that Mexico would be "the treasure house of the world." Subsequent history has, in a great measure, confirmed the opinion of the great savant of his time. Still a more conservative authority has quite lately asserted that only one-tenth of the mining resources of Mexico is known. This last estimate, I am sure, is inside rather than outside of the facts. Mexico has always been considered the great silver producer, and, considering her area, and taking the century as a measure, she is the greatest silver producer of the world.

Silver.—The central group of mines in the three mining districts of Guanajuato, Zacatecas, and Catorce, in the States of Guanajuato, Zacatecas and San Luis Potosi, which have yielded more than half of all the silver heretofore found in Mexico, lies between 21° and 24° 30' N., within an area of about 13,000 square miles. Here the Veta Madre lode of Guanajuato alone produced $252,000,000 between 1556 and 1803.

In the beginning of this century Humboldt found two Guanajuato mines—the famous "Conde de Valenciana" and the "Marques de Rayas"—producing annually 550,000 marks, 4,400,000 ounces, of silver, one-seventh or one-eighth of the entire American output. From January 1, 1787, to June 11, 1791, the Valenciana yielded 13,896,416 ounces of silver, its ore averaging a little over 100 ounces to the ton. Though flooded, this fine old mine is still far from exhausted.

Gold occurs chiefly, not on the plateau in association with silver, but on the slopes facing the Pacific, and apparently in greatest abundance in Sonora, near the auriferous region of Lower California. The production would have been larger if an improved process of reducing the metals had been used, but during the whole colonial period and up to the present time, we have used the patio system, which consists in grinding the ore, stirring it until it is reduced to a fine dust and mixing it then with salt and copper amalgam ; after the paste dries somewhat, salt is added in proportion to the amount of silver supposed to be in the ore ; the material is then mixed with shovels and trodden by mules, and, after a day or two, another mixture of copper, vitriol, and salt is added ; after that it is mixed and trodden again ; then quicksilver is finally added, and then more mixing and treading. This process is repeated from five to fifteen times until the silver and quicksilver unite to form an amalgam, which is gathered into bags, and that requires about forty days. Most of the quicksilver is squeezed out and the rest is evaporated and run off into tubs. This method saves 50 or 60 per cent. of rich ore and, besides being very long, is rather imperfect, as it leaves a great deal of silver in the ore, and only rich ores could be treated by it ; but it was on the whole the easiest and cheapest.

Some of the old mines were worked until finally they became so deep that, with the methods then used, as buckets were employed instead of pumps, and steam had not been employed as power, it was impossible to drain them. Naturally in a deep mine the water flows in from springs, and the deeper a mine becomes the more water it has. These mines were worked until it was seen that it was impossible to drain them, and then they were abandoned, even though they were rich in metals. During our war of independence almost all the mines were abandoned for the want of guarantee to life and property, and the mining industry, therefore, declined considerably ; but recently the old mines have been worked again and the production of silver has increased very considerably.[1]

[1] Mr. J. A. R. Waters of the firm of Waters Bros., Mining Engineers of the City of Mexico, said of his visit to the Jesus Maria District of the State of Chihuahu, where he went to examine the mine worked by the Pinos Altos Co., as follows :

"The district is very thoroughly mineralized and is pierced by veins more frequently than any district I ever saw. The general formation is very similar to that of Cripple Creek, with the exception that it is not traversed by the great porphyry dikes that occur there and in other parts of Colorado. The country formation is largely braccia. The ore is generally free milling, and is treated with stamps and pan amalgamation, the finer ores being treated with Huntington mills. There is little waste of values."

Real del Monte Company.—It would be interesting to refer briefly to the ups and downs of one of the mining enterprises of Mexico—the Real del Monte—as a typical case which exemplifies what has happened with many other of our mines, namely, that sometimes they yield large profits, and soon afterwards they cause tremendous losses. The Real del Monte is located about three miles from Pachuca, a large mining centre and the capital of the State of Hidalgo, distant about sixty miles southeast of the City of Mexico.

In 1739, a Biscayan, by the name of Don Pedro Jose Romero de Terreros, came from Santander and settled in Queretaro. He acquired a fortune of $60,000 in a small store in 1749, closed up his affairs, and started to return to his native land. On reaching Pachuca he met an old mining friend, Don Jose Alejandro Bustamante, who called his attention to the Real del Monte. In company with Bustamante he staked out the Biscaina, Santa Brigida, and Guadalupe mines and began to get the water out, but they soon exhausted their united funds. However, they succeeded in raising money in the City of Mexico on hard terms and drained their properties by a tunnel, which started at Moran, on the northern slope of the mountains, and, running 9000 feet through hard porphyry rock, struck the vein at a depth of 600 feet. This was accomplished a few years later in 1759. Bustamante by this time had died, but Terreros continued the work. On striking the vein he drained it, and in 1760 began the erection of the Hacienda de Regla, to work the rich ore he was taking out. He took out $15,000,000 at a small cost, repaid his advances, built and presented to the King of Spain a man-of-war and 4700 bars of silver, for which he was created Conde de Regla. He lived in grand style in the City of Mexico, and built a palatial residence on Cadena Street.

He died in 1781, and was succeeded by his son, the second Conde, who from 1774 to 1783 struggled with the water, which, as depth was attained, was very severe ; according to Ward, twenty-eight horse-whims were employed in the drainage at great expense and unsuccessfully. However, they had gotten down to 324 feet below the Moran adit on the Biscaina vein in the Guadalupe and Santa Teresa shafts. The production was $400,000 per year, drainage costing $250,000 per year, and sinking was abandoned, and the work was confined to drifting above water level.

From 1801 to 1809, $300,000 per year was taken out, but the cost of extraction was severe. Humboldt visited the property, and in 1810 the war of independence broke out, and all operations were suspended. Meanwhile the water rose and the Moran tunnel caved in, and so allowed the water to rise to an enormous height, and the district went to rack and ruin.

In 1822 the Conde's administrator, Don Ignacio Castelazo, made a report, and by his Italian mining friend, Rivafinoli, sent it to the Conde, who was living in England.

That country was only too anxious to reap for themselves some of the spoils that Spain had gleaned from Mexican mines. Here was their opportunity, many became interested, and the celebrated mining expert of that day, Mr. John Taylor, the founder of the present London firm now so heavily interested in South Africa, Taylor Bros., was sent to make an examination, and in 1824 the English Real del Monte Company was formed on the following terms :—The company leased the mines and haciendas for twenty-one years : 1st. The capital invested was to be returned from the products of the mines with interest ; 2d. The Conde was then to have one-half of the remaining proceeds yearly ; 3d. Meanwhile he was to receive $16,000 per year as an advance against his portion or anticipated profits. In case of failure of this third clause the lease would be cancelled and everything revert to the Conde. As the outlay amounted to over $5,000,000 and no profit ensued, it amounted to a rent of $16,000 per year.

In 1824 Captain Vetch, of the Royal Engineers, was sent out as manager. He brought three ships filled with one thousand tons of machinery, pumps, etc., and after untold trials in transportation and erection, finally got them to their destination. All this was done by English engineers, machinists, miners, and workmen, nearly all Cornishmen, under the direction of Colonel Colquhoun, a Peninsular veteran, who finally died of yellow fever with over fifty of his men. After unheard-of troubles they got everything by 1826 safely landed in the Real del Monte. The magnitude of the task may be understood when the almost roadless condition of the country is considered, and the bringing up of the machinery from the coast was a splendid example of British tenacity and pluck.

Captain Vetch had now cleaned out the Moran adit and the Dolores shaft, and the machinery was at once erected. The stock now rose from $500 to $8000 per share. The Conde had, in the meanwhile, borrowed money from the company and made the twenty-one-year lease perpetual, the annual rent of $16,000 remaining in force.

By 1829 Captain Vetch had grappled with the water question, and with an annual cost of $30,000 had accomplished what the first Count had paid $250,000 for, and extracted metal 324 feet below the Moran adit.

Captain Tindall, R.N., succeeded Captain Vetch, and a new shaft (1830) was commenced on the Santa Teresa and called the Terreros shaft. It was 1140 feet to the vein and was started at four points, and was connected in 1834 by drifts run from several levels, and then raised and sunk on. The work came out as true as if it had been done from the surface, thanks to the correctness of the plans of the English mine surveyors.

A 54-inch engine was erected, and with it they sank to 720 feet below the Moran adit. At this point water overpowered them. This was in 1838, and Captain John Rule, who had succeeded Captain Tindall, put in a 75-inch engine at Dolores, and removed the 54-inch one to Acosta. Captain Rule enjoyed a salary of £10,000 per year, and all other payments were in proportion. He struck two bunches of rich ore, one on the Santa Brigida, near Acosta, and the other on La Biscains, near Dolores. From these two and one at Torreros they had produced $10,481,475 at a cost of $15,381,633 or nearly $5,000,000 loss in twenty-three years. By 1846 the stock had fallen to $12.50 from $8000 a share.

In 1848, Mr. J. H. Buchan arrived, representing the English stockholders. He found water in the mines and increasing; a heavy debt of $5,000,000, bearing a tremendous interest; no money on hand and no ore. So in October, 1848, by order of the bondholders he turned over the business to a Mexican company—the present one—composed of Manuel Escandon, Antonio and Nicanor Beistegui, Mr. Mackintosh, and others for the paltry sum of $130,000. The haciendas, stock, and ores on hand were worth millions, but the English company could not dispose of them.

This was the end of the famous English Real del Monte Company. Their Mexican successors reduced expenses, completed the adit from Omotitlan commenced by the first Conde, which, running 13,500 feet, cut the mines 1110 deeper and struck immediately the *bonanza* in the Rosario, which tradition says had previously been discovered and covered up by Captain Rule.

New Mines, Topia.—We have now a great many districts that were not known by the Spaniards and have recently been discovered. Notable among them is the Sierra Mojada district in the State of Coahuila. The State of Durango has, on the west slope of the Sierra Madre mountains, the mining camps of Topia, Sianori, Birimoa, Gusanillas, Canelas, Ventanos, El Pando, Rodeo, and San Fernando; and with the exception of San Fernando they are close together, a square, one of whose sides is forty miles, would almost cover them all. This section has all the elements to form the basis of a great mining and smelting centre, as is evident by the great deposits of galena in the Topia district; in fact, this is the only place on the coast where lead ore is found in abundance; and smelting, if done at all, must rely on Topia for its supply of lead ores. In no other part of Mexico are lead ores so cheap, because of the fact that to realize on them at all they must be transported on mule-back to Culiacan in the State of Sinaloa, a distance of 106 miles, at a rate of $26.40 silver per ton, and from there by rail to Altata, a distance of thirty-nine miles; and from Altata by steamer to San Francisco, or to Guaymas, and thence by rail to the smelters in the United States, very much at the same cost. La Liona mine of this district is a very rich mine, its vein being almost vertical, and is tapped from both sides of the mountain, with tunnels at right angles to the vein. Where the tunnels intersect the vein, the vein is driven on in both directions from the tunnels; stopes are opened, and chutes for ore are put in every seventy-five feet. The vertical distance between the tunnels is 125 metres. This mine can easily produce one thousand tons per month of clean galena, and would produce that much metal if there was a market for it.

There are other mines as large and perhaps better than La Liona, as, for instance, La Madrugada mine, formerly owned by Santa Fé Railroad employees, but now controlled by Mr. Charles Miller, of Franklin, Pa., connected with the Standard Oil Company. Topia is a great dry-ore camp as well. One thousand tons of dry ores can easily be mined there per month, were there a market for them, such as a commercial smelter located centrally to treat the ores of this and adjoining districts. Such smelter would have the advantage of an inexhaustible supply of good water the year round, fine iron ore, and limestone for fluxes.

At Topia there are four mills for the treatment of zincy ores, and dry ores assaying below one hundred ounces silver per ton. The lixiviation process by hyposulphite of soda is employed in the four mills or haciendas, two of them employ occasionally the patio process as well. Two of the mills and two mines are lighted by electricity; the dynamo that furnishes light for one of the mills and both of the mines is driven by water power. Below the mills operated by water power, there is sufficient fall and sufficient water to furnish the power to operate compressed-air drills in all the large mines.

The other mining camps of this district, although not so well developed as Topia, are also in process of development and in a very good condition. Velardeña is also in the State of Durango, but on the other or eastern side of the mountains, and is located in a comparatively new district, where the previous owners had failed. Mr. James F. Mathews purchased the Velardeña property, erected a smelter after the International Railroad Company had extended their main line from Torreon to the city of Durango, passing near the mine, and from the beginning has run five of the six furnaces almost continuously. During 1896 the Velardeña smelter smelted on an average 175 tons of ore per day.

Li Hung Chang and the Mexican Silver Mines.—When Li Hung Chang, the Chinese Viceroy, was in Washington, in August, 1896, he inquired of me about the production of the Mexican mines, and I, trying to be conservative, informed him that they produced about $50,000,-000 a year. He then inquired how long they would continue yielding that amount. I answered that it was uncertain, but that, judging from present appearances, it could safely be said that it might be for one hundred years. This seemed incredible to him, and he said that I had been so long absent from Mexico—for he had previously asked me how long I had been in this country—I could not know the real wealth and abundance of our mines, and he was very positive that I had made a mistake. He assured me that the silver mines in China yielded occasionally something, but soon were exhausted, and it was impossible to get any silver out of them, and judging the Mexican silver mines from those he had seen at home, he was, of course, incredulous as to their yield.

Some years ago, and when the Mexican mines only yielded about $20,000,000 a year, I predicted that their annual yield would reach $100,000,000, and that prediction is about being verified, as the present product exceeds $60,000,000.

Gold.—Gold was used freely in Mexico before the Spanish conquest, and history teaches us how Cortez induced Montezuma to deliver to him his gold treasury.

As soon as Mexico was conquered, Bernal Diaz del Castillo, one of the cotemporary historians, tells us that Cortez inquired very carefully about the place where the Indians obtained their gold, whether there were placers, mines, or washings, and his agents were taken to some localities in the State of Oaxaca, where they were told was the gold supply, but, whether the Indians concealed the real location of the gold deposits, or for other reasons, the Spaniards did not obtain much gold. I have known recently of unavailing efforts having been made of persons from the United States who have tried to ascertain the localities where the Indians obtained their gold, that is—the places which were shown to Cortex in Oaxaca as gold deposits.

There is a river in the State of Guerrero which flows over a country with hills abundant in gold formation, which carries nuggets that the natives find without any difficulty, and it is called for that reason the Gold River. That river passes over some mountains where gold is found, and then comes to a place where a natural dam is formed, and the gold carried by the washings in the rainy season sinks when reaching that place, and every indication shows that there must be a very large deposit of gold there. A military engineer suggested, the last time I was Secretary of the Treasury in Mexico, that the bed of the river be changed by the Mexican Government, a work which did not present serious obstacles, and thus allow excavations to be made and the gold deposits found. It was thought advisable to make some preliminary examinations in the way of boring, and for that purpose the necessary orders were issued to send soldiers there, but I understand the project was given up and nothing was accomplished. I have no doubt that at some future time that matter will be taken up, and a great deal of gold will be found there.

Our production of gold has so far been comparatively small, because the mining and reduction of gold are more difficult and expensive than the same operations in silver, and our gold production has really been the amount of gold which has been found in our silver. For many years, when the amount was small, it was not separated, and for that reason old Mexican dollars have in China greater value than newly coined ones; but recent improvements have made it easy and cheap to make the separation of the two metals. Now that gold has risen so much in value, its mining is beginning to be developed in Mexico on a comparatively large scale, and I have no doubt that before long Mexico will be one of the largest gold producers of the world.

Mexico is an undeveloped country, in fact there are parts of Mexico as unknown as was Central Africa a few years back. From the Sonora gold district, south, on the west side of the Sierra Madre, to the State of Oaxaca, there is a gold belt as rich as California, Alaska, and South Africa combined. It is known that in the State of Sinaloa there are gold placers and gold washings, and that they are also found in every State from there south on the line of this belt.[1]

The gold output of Sonora, now beginning to attract attention, is only the first contribution of Mexico to the world's stock of the yellow metal. The west side of the Sierra Madre has a belt rich in gold, and when the world discovers this fact capital will flock to Mexico to dig it out, and Mexico will become one of the first gold producers of the world, as she has been in silver.

Specimens of " float " rich in gold have been brought from the State of Guerrero. These indications of gold have not been followed up, because no one has been progressive enough to advance the means necessary to prospect this belt. To prospect in a country where often water fit to drink must be carried, where food for man and beast must be carried, and where in many places roads must be cut with machete and axe, cannot be done without the spending of money in outfit and expenses.

The principal gold-producing States will be Sonora, Sinaloa, Guerrero, and Oaxaca, but in all of them gold-mining is yet in its beginning.

[1] I take from a report of Mr. Cramer, a mining engineer sent to Mexico by the Geological Society of Washington, D. C., as Commissioner to explore the gold fields of that Republic, the following, which refers to only one of the many new gold fields that are being found there :

" There exists an extensive ' gold placer ' situated about thirty miles from Durango in the mountain devoid of vegetation ; the rock that is found in greater quantities is porphyry. I estimate that one ton of ore will yield at least $50 of gold.

" Gold is found all over the mountain, though in such imperceptible filaments that it is hard to recognize it with the naked eye ; however, every piece of stone contains the same proportion of gold."

Coinage of the Precious Metals.—Mexico has produced about one-half of the silver supply of the world. In the statistical portion of this paper I shall give full details of the production of gold and silver in Mexico, coinage, etc., and here I will only append the total coinage of gold and silver according to official statistics of the Mexican Government, which is the following:

COINAGE OF MEXICO FROM THE ESTABLISHMENT OF THE MINTS IN 1537 TO THE END OF THE FISCAL YEAR OF 1896.

COLONIAL EPOCH.	GOLD.	SILVER.	COPPER.	TOTAL.
Unmilled coin from 1537 to 1731...................	$ 8,497,950	$ 752,067,456	$ 200,000	$ 760,765,406
Pillar coin 1732 to 1771...........................	19,889,014	441,629,211	....	461,518,225
Bust coin 1772 to 1821............................	40,391,447	888,563,989	342,893	929,298,329
INDEPENDENCE.	$68,778,411	$2,082,260,656	$ 542,893	$2,151,581,960
Iturbide's Imperial Bust, from 1822 to 1823........	$ 557,392	18,575,569	....	$ 19,132,961
Republic Eagle—1824 to 30 June, 1873..............	45,040,628	740,246,485	$5,235,177	790,522,290
REPUBLIC.	$45,598,020	758,822,054	$5,235,177	$ 809,655,251
Eagle coin, from 1 July, 1873, to 30 June, 1896.....	$11,561,080	$ 557,581,690	$ 203,296	$ 569,346,066

SUMMARY.

Colonial Epoch............1537 to 1821.............$2,151,581,960
Independence.............1822 to 1873............. 809,655,251
Republic.................1873 to 1896............. 569,346,066

Total.............$3,530,583,277

Iron.—Iron, the most useful of all the metals, is found in such vast abundance in Mexico that, could it be even partially utilized, that Republic would become one of the wealthiest of modern communities. One of the largest mines was discovered by Gines Vazquez del Mercado, in Durango, in 1562, and its appellation of "*Cerro del Mercado*" still preserves his name. The hill, which is 4800 feet long by 1100 feet in width and 640 feet in height, is almost a solid mass of mineral, averaging about seventy per cent. of metal and from which could be extracted more than 300,000,000 tons of solid ore ; this only to the level of the plain, beneath which it probably extends to an unknown depth.

The iron is also magnetic to a high degree and its power is greater when the grain is fine. This may delay fusion, but the result is an excellent wrought iron, with none of the inconveniences caused by earthy substances mixed with the iron. I have no doubt that when the coal mines are developed the iron industry will make great strides and that we will be able to manufacture most of at least the low grades of the iron goods required for our comsumption. In several other places besides our Iron Mountain we have iron with very little phosphorus, which makes first-class steel and is as good as the best produced in Cuba or Spain.

The deposits of iron in Mexico are sufficient to supply the universe for centuries to come. There is but one thing lacking, and that thing is—cheap fuel. Nature never works by halves ; those immense deposits of iron never were put where they are without the means near at hand for their utilization. Coal exists, but it has not been mined yet on a large scale, as it will be hereafter.

But even at the present time the principal supply of pig-iron comes from native ore, the output being consumed by the producers in the manufacture of iron goods. The main iron mines now being worked are located at Durango, Zimapán, Zacualtipán, Tulancingo, and Leon. For the most part these mines are found in the midst of great forests, in consequence of which cheap fuel is found in the form of charcoal, the iron made from which being of very superior quality, free from phosphorous, and, price and other things being equal, is always preferred to the imported pig. It is manufactured in charcoal furnaces exclusively.

There is, however, quite a considerable amount of pig imported, principally from Alabama, and Scotch pig from England. The great drawback to importations heretofore has been the immense quantity of scrap iron, which, during the lapse of centuries, had accumulated, unused, throughout the Republic. This, however, is becoming well-nigh exhausted ; and for that reason the demand for imported pig is increasing, the native output not keeping pace with the need for it. Much scrap iron also has come from railroads, another source of supply which is not increasing with the demand.

Imported pig ranges in price in the City of Mexico from $50 to $60 silver per ton, the native producers aiming to keep their price just about the same.

Iron Foundries.—There are in the City of Mexico, in addition to several small ones, seven large foundries, as follows : the Mexican Central Railroad foundry, the Mexican National Railroad foundry, the Artistic, the Delicias, Charreton Bros., V. Elcoro & Co., and Hipolito David. There are also large foundries at Pachuca, Puebla, Chihuahua, Durango, and Monterey, as well as smaller ones at Irapuato, Guanajuato, Zacatecas, Veracruz, Guadalajara, Mazatlán, Oaxaca, and Morelia.

Copper.—Copper is now quite an important product of Mexico, and is used to a certain extent in the country, but as the supply far exceeds the home demand, it is exported to the United States and Europe. That which finds its way to this country enters chiefly in the form of matte, and is refined into casting or electrolytic copper. What goes to Europe is blister copper, or approximately so, from the Boleo mine in Lower California, where a French company is working a large group of copper mines. The point of most activity is Santa Rosalia, on the

Gulf of California, where the company treats the ore in its own smelting plant adjoining. The matte, or black copper, is sent to Europe in the same vessels that bring out coke. The company gives employment to thousands of hands directly and indirectly, owns its own steamers, and solicits workmen all along the coast. But this enterprise, large as it is, shows the progress that has been made and the difficulties overcome by individuals. The country itself is arid and sterile, and there is little encouragement for others to prospect, or even develop, when found, apparently good prospects, owing to the natural difficulties to be overcome and the vast capital necessary to successfully carry on mining operations ; as success is hardly to be obtained except by treating the ores on the ground, as the Boleo Company has done.

At the same time the enterprising firm of Guggenheim has established its works at Aguas Calientes, adding very considerably to the copper product, and the increase of matte shipments from San Luis Potosi and Monterey makes a large difference from former returns. To judge from the official figures, the amount of copper produced in 1896 was not less than 22,000 metric tons, the greater production being from the Boleo mines.

Quicksilver.—The production of quicksilver can only be approximated from imports, as the native production is far short of the requirements of the country. In 1895 the amount imported was 818,704 kilos, with a value of $541,664, while during the past year the amount imported was 854,526 kilos, with a value of $574,153. The only inference to be drawn from these figures is that the production in Mexico in the past year as compared with 1895 has not increased, and the figures of production given in the *Engineering and Mining Journal* of 1895 may be accepted as correct for 1896.

Coal.—Fuel is perhaps the greatest and most pressing need of Mexico. For centuries the population of the whole country has used wood for fuel, until the most thickly inhabited portions of the country are completely destitute of trees. This condition of things is a very serious objection to the increase of manufacturing, as it is impossible to manufacture cheaply when fuel commands a very high figure. Coal, which has to be transported sometimes for thousands of miles before it reaches the centre of the country, becomes very expensive. At present rates the cost of wood in the City of Mexico is equal to $14 a cord, while coal ranges from $16 to $22 per ton according to grade, and one source of supply is the artificial fuel of compressed coal dust brought from England, and in use not alone on the Veracruz Railway, but in various local industries, while coal also comes from West Virginia, Alabama, etc. The distances of the sources of coal supply and its consequent cost led to the attempt of utilizing the peat deposits which

are of great extent and practically inexhaustible within ten miles of
the City of Mexico.

In the Tlahualilo district of the State of Coahuila, for instance,
owing to the distance from the nearest coal mines, the question of fuel
is very important, as there are at present more than three hundred
horse-power in constant use, and the amount is steadily increasing.
The main supply is from the mesquite brush, which is cleared from the
new lands as the work of ditching and preparation advances. The
hulls of the cotton seed also make a hot but quick fuel for some of
the larger stationary engines. The wheat, straw and cotton bushes are
utilized for brick-burning and for the domestic purposes of the labor-
ing population.

Those acquainted with industrial conditions in Mexico and making
investigations with a view to the establishment of new industries in
that Republic, are consequently impressed with the fact that, in spite
of the cheap labor, favorable climatic conditions, and good home
markets, the lack of cheap fuel is exceedingly detrimental to a large
proportion of the industries of this country ; but fortunately large deposits of coal are now being discovered in the Republic. At Salinas,
in the State of Coahuila, a large bed of coal is being worked by the
International Railroad Company, which furnishes fuel for that road
and even for a portion of the Southern Pacific Railroad and for some
of the manufactories in Monterey. In the district of Tlaxiaco, in the
State of Oaxaca, a very rich coal-field has been discovered, but for the
present it is inaccessible and before a railroad can be built to tap it
it cannot be used, as the expense of transportation would be exceedingly high. Sonora contains a carboniferous area, several miles in extent, with innumerable veins from five to sixteen feet in thickness, of
hard, clean, anthracite coal, carrying as high a percentage in fixed carbon as the best coal mined in Wales. The ledge is thirty miles in
length and averages sixteen feet in width, showing a quantity sufficient
to supply the entire Pacific coast with anthracite coal of the first quality
for years to come. The configuration of that State and the proximity
of the sea make it comparatively easy to work it.

At Jiquilpan, State of Michoacan, almost immediately south from
Negrete station on the Guadalajara branch of the Mexican Central
Railroad, a large coal-field has been discovered. While it is not probable that either anthracite or first-class bituminous coal will be found
in these fields, still the great value of even an ordinary class of coal
will be appreciated by those acquainted with industrial conditions in
Mexico. The coal measures of the Chapala district probably belong
to the tertiary period, and lie in stratified rock overlaid by an outflow
of basalt or lava, at an elevation of 250 or 300 feet above Lake Chapala. The general series of rocks has been examined and pronounced

as coal-bearing by an eminent geologist. The measures are quite extensive, being easily traced from Yurecuaro to near Ameca with occasional interruptions through volcanic intrusion. The developments already made, show that the coal or lignite veins extend over perhaps thirty square miles. How much beyond these limits, it would be impossible to state. It exists in considerable quantities. There are a number of veins overlying each other, and varying from two inches to fifty inches in width ; but, as the explorations have not yet found the veins in place, it is impossible to say exactly what their condition will be. A feature which adds considerably to the value of these deposits is an extensive deposit of bog iron in the immediate vicinity. If further exploration discovers considerable quantities of commercially valuable coal, it is easy to estimate the results to the industries. Other beds of coal have been discovered but of less consequence, and in several of the northern states of Mexico there are known to exist large deposits.

Mexican industries will be completely revolutionized when they can use cheap coal instead of wood for all purposes, thus cheapening the cost of manufacturing by using cheaper fuel, which is so important an item of expense in manufacturing.

Mexican Miners.—While the laborers employed in Mexico will not compare in efficiency with the labor of the miner in the United States, it must be borne in mind that the American miner works eight hours and receives $3 per day, or $6 in Mexican money, and $6 in Mexican money will employ from eight to twelve Mexicans, wages varying from 50c. to 75c. per day. As for the climatic conditions, it is only necessary to say that in all the mining districts of Mexico a miner can work 365 days in the year. There is never any snow or cold weather in winter, and the heat in the summer is not so extreme as in St. Louis, Chicago, or New York, and never enervating. A pair of blankets at night are indispensable every night in the year.

Mining Laws. — The mining laws of Mexico issued during the Spanish rule, which were kept in force until 1884, were both liberal and wise, and were intended to encourage mining. The domain of the mines remained in the Government and it gave temporary titles to anybody who discovered one, and who was willing to work it, but only as long as work was done in the mine. When the discoverer or owner could not for any reason continue to work it, and allowed a certain time to elapse without doing any work, the mine reverted to the Government and anybody else willing to work it could obtain a temporary title over it. This system was changed, by our Mining Code of 1884, to the effect of giving the mines in fee simple to the discoverers of the same, whether they were worked or not by those who denounced them, and the only cause for forfeiting the title is the failure to pay a tax of $10 per pertenencia, a "pertenencia" being our unit of a mining property and consisting of a hectare or a square 100 metres on each side, equivalent to 2.47 acres. The rights of the owner of the land are not interfered with, and in case anybody discovers a mine upon another man's property, the landlord continues to own the surface, and all the discoverer is entitled to is the mineral underground and so much of the surface as is necessary to work it, for buildings and other mining requirements, and for that the owner of the ground is compensated by agreement, or, if no amicable agreement can be reached, by arbitration.

Mining litigation is quite rare in Mexico, and it does not take long to get a final decision, as mining cases are tried before a single judge, and appeals lie to the Supreme Courts of the different states, and to the Federal Supreme Court in Mexico. To the honor of the courts in Mexico be it said, as may also be said of the judiciary in the States and the United States Federal Courts, they are above reproach.

A concise statement of the provisions of the present mining laws of Mexico will not be out of place here.

The law grants to all inhabitants of the country the right to acquire and work mines. He has to denounce a new mine. A denouncement means making a location. When the location of a claim has been determined upon, all possible data are obtained concerning it before the denouncement is made. It may be a rich old mine, and yet if the law has not been complied with it is subject to relocation. The law grants to any inhabitant of the Republic the right to explore for mineral. All districts have their mining agents and all the prospector has to do is to have the regular form of petition used in making out a denouncement, as it is called, made out and submitted to the mining agent of the district. If there does not happen to be a mining agent in the district, the petition is presented to the local postmaster. The expense of registering the petition is $1. After registering the petition, the mining agent has thirty days in which to appoint an expert to examine the property, who has eight days in which to reply to the summons, and if he accepts the service, the mining agent issues in duplicate a document stating that the claim has been denounced and directing objecting parties to make known their prior claims within a period of four months from the date of the denouncement, or forfeit any right to the property.

The charge of the expert for making a report upon the claim, together with the plans, is about $15 per claim and travelling expenses. The expert has sixty days in which to send in his plans and report. The notification that the property has been denounced is published in the official journal of the district, the cost of which varies in the different states, from $2 to $4 being the usual fee.

The cost of making up a mining title is from $10 to $12. Titles, when once granted, unless fraud is shown, are irrevocable so long as the taxes are paid, which are ten dollars per year on each "pertenencia," and no work or manual labor is necessary to hold the same. The taxes may be paid quarterly or annually, at the discretion of the holder, to the mining agent of the district in which the property is denounced, or by special arrangement they may be paid at the office of the Federal Treasury in the City of Mexico. After the title is granted, it must be registered in the district where the denouncement is made, and also entered upon the books of the stamp office, for which no fees are charged.

MINTS AND DUTIES ON SILVER.

Under the Spanish laws all silver paid a duty ; and as most of it was coined, that duty was levied on coinage, and the exportation of bullion was prohibited ; but of course a great deal was smuggled, both during the Spanish rule and still more when Mexico was opened to foreign trade after our Independence. When I occupied for the first time the Treasury Department of Mexico in 1868, it seemed to me an outrage against the mining industry of the country to require the miners—especially those who were far removed from the mints—to take their bullion from the mints, at a heavy expense and risk, coin it there and take it back to the mines, and from there to the ports to be exported to London, where it was often again turned into bullion ; and as the contracts made with the lessees of the mints did not allow the free exportation of bullion, I proposed and succeeded in having enacted a law for the purpose of allowing bullion to be exported, provided that it paid the coinage duty at the respective custom-houses for the benefit of the mint's lessees ; and this condition of things, extraordinary as it may seem, was a great relief to the silver producers, and continued until the Mexican Government could recover all the mints and be free to legislate on the subject, which it was able to do partially during my last incumbency of the Treasury Department ; they all since having been recovered.

We had thirteen mints in the country to coin the silver extracted from our mines, which, in the precarious condition of the Mexican Treasury, were sometimes rented to private parties who advanced a sum that seemed large at that time, although it was a trifle in comparison to their profits, as they collected a duty of nearly $4\frac{1}{2}$ per cent. upon the amount of bullion coined, and they credited to the Government only $1\frac{1}{2}$ per cent. of the same, the laws requiring that only coined silver could be exported. But now that silver can be transported easily from the mine to the mint, since a railway system has been built, the mints have been reduced to four,—one in the City of Mexico, which is the principal one ; one at each of the cities of Guanajuato, Zacatecas, and Culiacan, the last being the capital of Sinaloa.

Besides the mint or coinage duties, silver was taxed in Mexico with an export duty which sometimes was as high as twelve per cent. on the value of the silver, which, together with the mint duty, amounted to seventeen per cent., not taking into account other taxes and local duties. Only the rich character of the Mexican mines could stand that burden.

The duties on silver have been readjusted and reduced considerably, until now they only amount, as established by the law of March 27, 1897, to a coinage duty of two per cent. and a stamp duty of three per cent., which are paid at the Assay Office of the Mint when coined, or at the custom-house when exported in bullion, ores, or other compounds. When exported in ores in their crude condition, the duty has a rebate of ten per cent. A small duty representing the cost of the operation is also charged for assaying, refining, smelting, and separating the metals.

SMELTING PLANTS.

The Tariff Act of October 1, 1890, having levied a duty upon lead ore, which prevented that Mexican product from coming into the , United States in the shape it had come before, the American companies, who had been developing the lead ore in Mexico, established smelting plants in the country for the purpose of treating there the lead ore, and sending it as pig-lead to the United States.

The smelting plants that have been established in Mexico, and their capacity and output, taken from official data received from the Mexican Government, up to December 31, 1896, are the following :

Mexican Metallurgical Company.—This company, of which Mr. Robert S. Towne is president, obtained a charter from the Mexican Government on March 20, 1890, to establish five smelting plants in Mexico, two with the minimum capacity of 200 tons a day, two of 150 tons, and one of 100 tons. The first one is located at Morales, five kilometres west of the city of San Luis Potosi. During the fiscal year 1895 to 1896, this plant received 62,370 and 020/1000 metric tons of ore from the States of Chihuahua, Coahuila, Durango, Guanajuato, Jalisco, Mexico, Michoacan, Nuevo Leon, Queretaro, San Luis Potosi, and Zacatecas. This plant yielded during the same year 16,019 and 070/1000 metric tons of base lead bullion, with 3,198,924.14 troy ounces of silver, valued at $4,882,177.50 ; and 8268 and 37/100 troy ounces of gold, valued at $161,338.63.

National Mexican Smelter at Monterey.—This company, whose president is Mr. Daniel Guggenheim, obtained a charter from the Mexican Government on October 9, 1890, to establish three smelting plants in Mexico, two with a minimum capacity of 300 tons per day, and one with 100 tons. The first plant is located in the outskirts of the city of Monterey, has ten furnaces of the water-jacket system, and seven smelting furnaces for lead ore. From July, 1892, to June, 1896, this plant has smelted 521,809 and 769/1000 metric tons of ore, yielding 78,067 and 141/1000 tons of lead, with 515,382 kilograms of silver, with a value of $21,824,597.93, having used foreign coke to the value of $1,474,385.81, and Mexican coke to the value of $73,268.08.

Central Mexican Smelter.—The second smelter of the Guggenheim Company is located at Aguascalientes. It has a department for concentrating copper ores, one for smelting the same ores, consisting of three furnaces, and another with four furnaces for smelting lead ores. This plant smelted from the 26th of December, 1895, 606 and 190/1000 tons of lead, containing 6502 kilograms of silver and 28 and 71/100 kilograms of gold, with a value of $341,091.

Velardeña Mining Company.—This company, whose president is Mr. Edward W. Nash, obtained a charter from the Mexican Government on May 15, 1893, for the construction of two smelting plants in Mexico, with a capacity of 200 tons a day each. From November 30, 1893, to June 30, 1896, this plant smelted 110,000 tons of ore, yielding 9069 and 680/1000 tons of lead containing 1,850,685 troy ounces of silver and 6192 ounces of gold.

The Chihuahua Mining Company.—This company, whose president is Mr. John B. Shaw, obtained a charter from the Mexican Government May 26, 1893, and is located near the city of Chihuahua. Up to July 28, 1896, it had smelted 28,555 tons of lead ore, yielding 3761 tons of lead and 529,450 troy ounces of silver.

The Mazapil Copper Company, Limited.—This company established a plant at Concepcion del Oro, Zacatecas, and has smelted 5000 tons of lead ore containing silver.

Sabinal Mining and Smelting Company, Chihuahua.—This company owns the mines of Santa Juliana and Santa Inez, which yield 30 per cent. of lead, with a mixture of silver, and smelts their ore, notwithstanding that the cost of a ton of coke amounts to $37.50.

La Preciosa.—A smelter under that name has been established at Tepeyahualco, State of Puebla, but I do not have any data about the company owning it, and the date of its contract with the Mexican Government, nor the amount of ore smelted there.

The Boleo Smelter.—I have already spoken of this plant, which smelts copper ores at Santa Rosalia, Lower California.

OROGRAPHY.

Mexico is traversed by two cordilleras or high ranges of mountains running almost parallel to the coast, one along the Gulf of Mexico and the other along the Pacific Ocean. The former runs from ten to one hundred miles from the coast, leaving an imperceptibly inclined plane from the sea to the foot of the mountains ; while the cordillera on the Pacific side runs, on the whole, very near the coast, leaving a very narrow strip of land between the same and the sea, and from this run several branches in different directions. The most continuous range is the Sierra Madre of the Pacific, which may be traced, at a mean elevation of over 10,000 feet, from Oaxaca to Arizona. Parallel to this is the Lower Californian range (Sierra de la Giganta) 3000 feet, which, however, falls abruptly eastwards, like the Atlantic escarpments. The California peninsula seems to have been detached from the mainland when the general upheaval took place which produced the vast chasm now flooded by the Gulf of California. Corresponding with the Sierra Madre on the west are the more interrupted eastern scarps of the central plateau, which sweep around the Gulf of Mexico as the Sierra Madres of Nuevo Leon and Tamaulipas at an elevation of about 6000 feet. These are crossed by the routes from Tula to Tampico, the highest pass being 4820 feet ; from Saltillo to Monterey 3400, and at several other places.

Of the central cross ridges the most important orographically and historically is the Cordillera de Anahuac, which surrounds the Mexican (Tenochtitlan) and Puebla valleys, and which is supposed to culminate with Popocatepetl and Ixtacihuatl. But these giants belong to a different or rather more recent system of igneous upheaval, running from sea to sea between 18° 59' and 19° 12' N. in almost a straight line east and west, consequently nearly at right angles to the main axis of the central plateau. The line is clearly marked by several extinct cones and by five active or quiescent volcanoes, of which the highest is Popocatepetl, lying south of the capital, nearly midway between the Pacific and the Atlantic. East of the central point of the system are Citlaltepetl, better known as the peak of Orizaba, on the coast south of Veracruz, to which correspond on the west the recently upheaved Jorullo in Michoacan, Colima (12,800) near the coast in Jalisco, and the volcanic Revillagigedo group in the Pacific. South of this line and nearly parallel, are the sierras of Guerrero, and southeast of the Tehuantepec Isthmus those of Oaxaca and Chiapas towards the Guatemala frontier. In the same direction run the islands of Cuba and Hayti, which probably belong to the same Central American system.

In the course of centuries these high mountains have become disintegrated by the rains and other natural elements, and a great many spaces between them filled up, forming a series of valleys and other spots quite delightful in climate and very rich in agricultural resources. This series of valleys, which we call the central plateau, runs from about one hundred and fifty miles east of the City of Mexico, traversing all of Mexico in a northwesterly direction. So level is the plateau that even when there were no wagon roads in Mexico one could travel in a carriage from the City of Mexico to Santa Fé. Baron Humboldt and other geologists considered the cordilleras of Mexico as a portion of the Andes of South America, which originate in Patagonia, extending over the whole of that continent ; but researches were made specially by a corps of engineers, who surveyed Mexico during the French Intervention, arrived at a different conclusion, and consider that the Andes proper end in Panama, and that the Mexican cordilleras are entirely independent from that lofty chain of mountains.

In contrast with the plains and at times barren districts of the central plateau, it is occasionally broken by depressions of the soil, known as barrancas, descending sometimes one thousand feet and measuring several miles across, which are covered with a luxuriant vegetation of trees and shrubs, and watered by small streams running through the middle of the valley. Among the most remarkable ones are the barranca de Beltran descending the western slope from Guadalajara to Colima, and the barranca de Mochitilte from Guadalajara to Tepic.

One of the pre-eminently interesting features of Mexico is the mountain of Jerullo, in this section, which has been born within recent times. The natives described to Alexander von Humboldt the convulsions of the earth during its birth, and the frightful spectacle of the huge mass thrusting its giant shoulders among its neighbors, making room for itself in their ranks.

The best way to illustrate the broken surface of Mexico is to give the altitudes of some of the principal localities, both from the coast to the interior and from the interior back to the coast, taken from the measurements made by the railroad companies and by the engineers of the Mexican Government in the national wagon roads where railroads are not yet running. I append to this paper a list of such altitudes, with their distances, whenever I have been able to find them, which I consider the best illustration that could be presented on this subject.

MOUNTAINS.	STATES.	ELEVATION IN FEET.
Popocatepetl	Mexico	17,540
Orizaba	Veracruz and Puebla	17,362
Toluca	Mexico	15,019
Ixtacihuatl	Mexico and Puebla	16,076
Colima	Jalisco	14,363
Zapotlan	Jalisco	12,743
San Martin or Tuxtla	Veracruz	4,921
Tancitaro	Michoacan	12,467
Jorullo	Michoacan	4,265
Tacana or Soconusco	Chiapas	7,436
Guarda	Federal District	9,731
Ajusco	Federal District	13,628
Cofre de Perote	Veracruz	13,415
Zempoaltepec	Oaxaca	11,141
Pico de Quinceo	Michoacan	10,905
Veta Grande	Zacatecas	9,140

The above are the principal mountain peaks of Mexico, the first ten being volcanoes, with their heights according to the most recent measurements :

HYDROGRAPHY.

The eastern Mexican coast, washed by the Caribbean Sea and the Gulf of Mexico, is low, flat, and sandy, except near the mouth of the Tabasco River, where at some distance from the coast appear the heights of San Gabriel, extending northeast and southwest for several miles ; but the majestic mountains of Veracruz, especially the volcano of Orizaba, visible for many leagues to seaward, form a picturesque background which relieves the monotony of the shore region of that State. On the Pacific side the coast, although generally low, is here and there roughened by spurs extending from the cordillera to the ocean.

The principal gulfs are those of Mexico, California, and Tehuantepec, the first of which ranks among the largest in the world.

We are not blessed with good harbors on the Gulf coast. Veracruz is an open roadstead, and we are now spending large sums of money in trying to make it a good port. Our best harbors are on the Pacific coast, as Acapulco, which is a large one ; Manzanillo, a very fine although a very small one ; and La Paz, on the Gulf of California. By artificial means we expect to improve our harbors considerably.

The development of the harbor of Tampico is remarkable. A short time ago the depth of the bar roadstead was only eight or nine feet. Now steamships drawing twenty-four feet of water enter the port. The deepening of the entrance to the harbor has been accomplished by means of jetties, just as the mouth of the Mississippi was deepened by the Eads jetties. A very large part of the imports of Mexico enter now by the port of Tampico.

The more noteworthy bays are those of Guaymas, Santa Barbara, Topolobampo and Navachiste, in the Gulf of California ; Concepción, La Paz, and Mulejé, on the west coast of the same gulf ; San Quentin, Magdalena, and Amejas, on the Pacific coast of Lower California ; and San Blas and Valle de Banderas, on the coast of Tepic.

We have no lakes as large as those with which the United States is favored, and the Lake of Chapala, a beautiful spot where country houses are now being built, is the largest lacustrine basin in Mexican territory. The Valley of Mexico has six lakes, two of fresh and six of salt water. The other lakes in Mexico are Catemaco, in the State of Veracruz ; Cairel and Carpintero, in the State of Tamaulipas ; Encantada, in Tabasco ; Bacalar, in Yucatan ; Alcuzague, in Colima ; Cuitzeo, Tacascuaro, and Patzcuaro, in Michoacan ; Yuriria, in Guanajuato ; and Meztitlan, in Hidalgo.

Mexico has a great many islands, situated near the coast, although not any of very great area, the greater number being uninhabited, although some of them are very fertile, and could be the seat of a large population. Among the most important are: El Carmen, the largest in the Gulf of Mexico; San Juan de Ulua and Sacrificios, opposite the port of Veracruz; Mujeres, in the Caribbean Sea; Guadalupe, about seventy-five miles from the west coast of Lower California; the Tres Marias group, about thirty miles from the same coast; the Revillagigedo group, not far from the coast of Colima; and adjoining the coast of the State of Michoacan, the Alcatraz Island.

As I have already stated, Mexico has a very broken surface, with high mountains, causing streams to run down a very inclined plane, forming torrents with rapid cascades, which contribute to embellish the natural features of the country. These conditions, however, prevent us from having large navigable rivers, and furnishing a cheap way of transportation, which is one of the greatest advantages the United States enjoys, and which so largely contributed in its early days to the development of the country, making transportation to long distances both easy and cheap. While the torrents descending from the mountains afford an immense water-power—which, in the course of time, may be used as a motor for industrial purposes—they meet when they reach a valley and run smoothly there through a ravine until finally they reach the coast, and it is therefore only at a comparatively small distance from the sea that they can be made navigable.

Our principal rivers, measuring their positions from north to south, are the Rio Grande—which from El Paso, Texas, to the sea, is the boundary line between the two countries, and which used to be a large river; but as it rises in Colorado and passes through New Mexico, and the inhabitants of both have taken for irrigation purposes most of the water that it carries, it becomes entirely dry during the dry season after the freshets, very much to the distress of the inhabitants of its borders from El Paso to Ojinaga, especially on the Mexican side, which has been inhabited for three hundred years, the people using the water for irrigation—on the other side there being hardly any population,— and now they find that their farms are entirely worthless for want of water. After passing Presidio del Norte, now called Ojinaga, the Conchos River and other tributaries of the Rio Grande River supply it with water, although not to the extent it had before the water was taken in Colorado and New Mexico. The Mescala, or Balsas River, rises in the central plateau near the Valley of Mexico, passes by the State of Puebla to the southwest, by Mixteca of Oaxaca, and finally empties into the Pacific at Zacatula. As indicated by its name, it is, to a limited extent, navigable along its lower reaches; above the bar it is accessible to small craft, which, higher up, are arrested by rapids, whirlpools, and a high cascade. The Pánuco River rises north of the Valley of Mexico. Under the names of Tula and Montezuma it describes a vast semicircular bend towards the west across the Hidalgo uplands and collects the waters of the Huasteca of Veracruz and Tamaulipas, beyond which it is joined by the various streams flowing from Queretaro, and finally empties into the Gulf of Mexico at the port of Tampico. The Tampico bar, improved by jetties, is now the best harbor on our Gulf coast. The Rio Lerma or Santiago, the Tololotlan of the Indians, is also a considerable stream. By the riverain populations it is, in fact, known as the Rio Grande, while the inhabitants of Michoacan call it also Cuitzeo, from the large lake situated in their State. It rises in the State of Mexico in the very centre of the Anahuac plateau, and its farthest sources, issuing from underground galleries, descend from the Nevado de Toluca down to the twin lake of Lerma, the remains of an inland sea which formerly filled the Upper Toluca valley north of the Nevado volcano. At its issue from the lake, or rather marshy lagoon, the Lerma stands at the great altitude of 8600 feet, and during its winding northwesterly course across the plateau, the incline is very slight. In this upland region it is swollen by several affluents, some of which, like the main stream itself, flow from lakes dotted over the table-land. After completing half of its course at La Barca, the Lerma is still 5600 feet above sea-level. Here, some 280 miles from its source, it enters the large Lake Chapala, near its eastern extremity ; but about twelve miles below the entrance it again emerges through a fissure on the north side of the lake, and still continues to flow throughout its lower course in the same northwesterly direction.

The Grijalva and Usumacinta rivers, rising in the State of Chiapas, after being joined by many others, some of them coming from Guatemala, empty into the Gulf of Mexico by one of its mouths at the city of Frontera in the State of Tabasco. The Papaloapam River rises in the State of Oaxaca, passes through the State of Veracruz, and empties into the Gulf of Mexico at the town of Alvarado, a few miles south of Veracruz.

The rains increase considerably the amount of water in the rivers, but as their duration is not very long this soon subsides. When the streams rise near the sea, as is the case on the coast of Chiapas on the Pacific, they become so swollen immediately after the rains that it is impossible to ford them, and as there are no bridges, it is necessary to wait until early the next day when the freshet has subsided.

Springs are rare, and some of the rivers run in deep mountain beds, without receiving smaller tributaries, while the rapid evaporation on a light soil, covering porous rocks, leaves the surface dry and hot and unable to support much vegetation beyond the cactus and low grasses.

We are blessed with quite a number of mineral springs, although very few of them are used, most of them being at places not easily accessible; but in this regard I do not think we have any cause to envy any other country.

CLIMATE.

By looking at the map it will be perceived that Mexico, being intersected by the Tropic of Cancer and stretching across eighteen parallels of latitude, must, from its position alone, necessarily enjoy a great diversity of climate. But from its peculiar configuration this feature is affected far more by the altitude of the land than by its distance from the pole or the equator. This is especially true of the more fertile and populous section lying within the torrid zone, where three distinct climatic regions are distinguished, not according to their horizontal, but according to their vertical position. The warm climate has the heat of the torrid zone and prevails on the sea-coast in the sandy and marshy tracts fringing the Gulf of Mexico and the Pacific Ocean, in other low places below 3000 feet above the level of the sea, and in some of the valleys higher than that, but protected entirely from the winds. But the night breezes refresh the temperature in the evening and make it bearable during the day, the heat never being so oppressive as it is in summer in the more northern latitudes. This region is also much refreshed in summer by the rains, which are abundant and fall regularly during that season. The heat of the sun increases considerably the evaporation from the sea, and when the evaporation reaches the cool atmosphere of the sky, it is naturally condensed into water and falls in this region. The rains begin generally in June, increase considerably in July, and end in November, although this varies in different regions, the rains lasting longer in those near the sea than in the inland districts. They are so abundant that they form the main reliance of the agricultural industry, and there are few regions which use water for irrigation, depending entirely upon the rainfall; therefore, when in a year by some atmospheric phenomena, the rains are late or very scarce, we had a famine in Mexico, which can now be averted by importing cereals through our railroads, as was the case in 1893. The rains fall regularly and at fixed intervals, that is, about from one to three hours every day, and after the rain is over, the atmosphere is clear and pleasant, and in well drained places the ground becomes dry, so that it causes no inconvenience to the inhabitants.

The rains have such a decided effect on the atmosphere that in most of the country the seasons are divided into the rainy and dry season, and very few realize what spring and fall mean. As our climate is so even, the trees do not lose their leaves at any given time, but one

by one as they grow old and die; and as the leaves die they are replaced gradually and imperceptibly by new ones, so that the phenomenon familiar to northern latitudes, of trees losing all their leaves in the
autumn and regaining them in the spring, is quite new to anybody
going to a temperature that has both extremes.

The differences of climate depending upon the different degrees of
altitude are so great in Mexico that the vegetable products of this vast
country include almost all that are to be found between the equator
and the polar circle.

The mean temperature in the hot region varies from 77 to 82 degrees, Fahrenheit, seldom falling below 60, but often rising to 100
degrees, and in the sultry districts of Veracruz and Acapulco occasionally to 104 degrees, although the heat is not oppressive as is the
summer heat of the eastern portions of the United States. The vegetation is, of course, in consequence entirely tropical. In the southern
region the climate on both seaboards may be described as humid, hot,
and rather unhealthy, and in places where stagnant water and marshes
exist—which are often found on the coast on account of the sea water
flowing in and remaining there—intermittent and remittent fevers prevail, and in some localities during the summer yellow fever and black
vomit are endemic. These conditions could easily be remedied by
proper drainage of the swamps and marshy districts.

The heat of the Gulf of Mexico when the atmosphere begins to cool
in the polar regions causes a depression in the barometer, and consequently very strong north winds, which sweep over the coast with terrible force, causing great havoc. They generally begin in September
and last until the winter season sets in about December. As the
country is narrow, the effect of the north wind is felt all over it and
that is the prevailing wind. In the City of Mexico, for instance, notwithstanding its altitude and that it is protected by high mountains
from the northern winds, the temperature falls when the northerns
prevail on the Gulf coast, and it becomes cloudy and drizzly, and the
same effect is felt, more or less, in other portions of the country. As
the country narrows towards the southeast, especially at Tehuantepec,
the northern wind blows with but small obstacles, and its force and
effects are felt all over it. The districts in the mountains bordering
the Pacific are affected in the same way as the City of Mexico.

From 3000 to 5000 feet above the level of the sea is located our
temperate zone, which succeeds the hot zone in a verticle position,
and embraces all the higher terraces, and portions of the central
plateaus themselves. The mean temperature is from 62 to 70 degrees,
Fahrenheit, varying not more than 4 to 5 degrees during the season,
thus making one of the very finest climates on the face of the earth.
In this privileged region both extremes of heat and cold are unknown,

and it has several cities—Jalapa and Huatusco in the State of Vera-cruz, Chilpancingo in Guerrero, Ameca in Jalisco, and many others too numerous to mention here. As these places are generally located on the slopes of mountains and not far removed from the ocean, the evaporations from the sea form clouds which are detained in their course by the high peaks and are precipitated into rain. In this region the semi-tropical productions are abundant, and with them are often combined the products of tropical and cold regions. I have seen in my own native place, the city of Oaxaca, located in the temperate region, a farm where wheat and sugar-cane were growing on the same piece of ground.

The cold region is located from 7000 feet above the sea-level up-wards, and has a mean temperature of from 59 to 63 degrees, Fahrenheit. Most of the grand central plateau is located in this region, except in such places as are in a great depression of ground and in deep ravines, where a warm temperature and tropical products are found. The rainfall is about five times less than in the temperate zone. This region, of course, produces all the growths of the cold latitudes, as wheat, oats, apples, etc., etc.

The portion of the country that is most thickly inhabited lies in the central plateau, and is quite high above the level of the sea, and so sheltered from the winds and storms by the mountains as to make the climate even, temperate, and delightful. The impression pre-vails in the United States that Mexico, lying to the south and run-ning towards the equator, must be much warmer than this country; but this is not so. Even in warm places, like the lowlands on the coast, we do not have the extreme hot weather that is experienced in summer in the United States. The sea breezes refresh the atmos-phere at night and cool it considerably, making, therefore, a very great contrast with the summer heat in this country. The medium climate of the Valley of Mexico, for instance, which is the one that has been best observed and understood, varies comparatively little between summer and winter, its greatest variations being between day and night on the same day.

The climatic conditions of Mexico are undergoing great changes on account of the destruction of the forests. The country had formerly a great deal of rain and much humidity in the atmosphere, being covered with thick forests; but with the difficulty of transporting the coal already found, the population has had to depend entirely for their supply of fuel upon charcoal, and this has in the course of time denuded the mountains, changing very materially the climatic con-ditions of some regions in the country. But in the lowlands, being thinly inhabited, the case is different, and the country is still so thickly wooded that it is impossible to pass through it, unless an open path is made with a great deal of difficulty, by felling very high trees and low brush and weeds. In this region abound forests of mahogany, cedar, rosewood, etc. I will later state more in detail the conditions of the fuel question in Mexico.

As a whole, the Mexican climate, if not of the most invigorating nature, is certainly one of the most delightful in the world. The zone of temperate lands, oceanic slopes, enjoy an everlasting spring, being exposed neither to severe winter, nor to intolerable summer heats; in every glen flows a rippling stream; every human abode is embowered in leafy vegetation; and here the native plants are intermingled with those of Europe and Africa. Each traveller in his turn describes the valley in which he has tarried longest as the loveliest in the world; nowhere else do the snowy crests or smoking volcanic cones rise in more imposing grandeur above the surrounding sea of verdure, all carpeted with the brightest flowers. In these enchanting regions there is still room for millions and millions of human beings.

The following table prepared by the Meteorological Observatory of the City of Mexico shows the meteorological conditions of the principal Mexican cities during several years, their elevation upon the sea-level being marked in metres and the temperature under the Centigrade scale.

SUMMARY OF THE METEOROLOGICAL OBSERVATIONS TAKEN IN SEVERAL CITIES OF MEXICO DURING SEVERAL YEARS.

LOCALITIES.	N. Lat.	Height above sea-level.	Number of years of observation.	Mean barometrical pressure.	TEMPERATURES IN THE SHADE.			Relative humidity.	CLOUDS.		WIND.			Rainfall. Average for a year.
					Max.	Min.	Mean.		Average.	Prevailing direction.	Prevailing direction.	Mean velocity.		
	° ′	m.		mm.	°	°	°							mm.
Monterey, N. L.	25 40	495.6	1	709.1	33.2	11.7	21.0				S.E.			3413.5
Saltillo, Coah.	25 25	1633.0	4	632.1	34.0	—2.8	16.8	61	4.4	N.	N.	1.4		527.3
Culiacan, Sin.	24 48	34.2	1	754.9	35.9	12.5	25.6	62						125.2
Mazatlan, Sin.	24 11	4.0	4	759.3	34.1	10.3	25.2	77	3.4	N.W.	N.W.	1.7		519.2
Zacatecas, Zac.	22 46	2496.0	10	573.4	21.8	6.1	13.2	48	3.2	S.E.	S.E.	2.6		819.1
San Luis Potosi, S. L. P.	22 9	1890.0	9	613.4	33.9	—1.8	17.4	60	4.4	W.	E.	1.3		389.0
Pabellon, Ag.	22 4	1924.0	10	607.8	24.0	12.2	18.2	57	4.0	S.S.E.	W.S.W.	1.2		537.0
Aguascalientes, Ag.	21 53	1861.0	1	605.1	29.5	2.8	18.6				N.			542.2
Huejutla, Hid.	21 41	376.0	1	765.1	34.0	10.0	23.0	81						2019.3
Leon, Gto.	21 7	1798.0	14	617.4	35.6	—1.1	18.9	66	4.9	S.W.	N.N.W.	0.6		729.8
Guanajuato, Gto.	21 1	2060.0	5	601.3	30.7	1.3	17.6	58	5.3		W.			964.5
Tuxpam, Ver.	20 59		2	763.0			24.5	82	4.3	N.W.	W.			1654.3
Guadalajara, Jal.	20 41	1567.0	7	636.2	35.5	—4.5	19.7	53						861.9
Queretaro, Que.	20 35	1850.0	3	613.8	33.1	1	18.1	59	4.1		E.	0.6		602.2
Pachuca, Hid	20 7	2460.0	1	574.8	27.2	0.6	13.7	59	4.2	S.W.	N.E.	2.4		436.8
San Juan del Rio, Que.	19 49	1976.0	1				18.3	60	3.5	E.	N.E.			567.1
Patzcuaro, Mich.	19 31	2138.0	1				16.1		4.3	E.	W.			1110.4
Mexico, D. F.	19 26	2282.5	15	586.4	31.6	—1.7	15.6	60	5.0	S.W.	N.W.	0.8		614.8
Tacubaya, D. F.	19 12	2322.6	9	583.6	28.6	0.8	15.5	62			N.W.			668.1
Puebla, Pue.	19 03	2172.0	14	593.2	31.9	—1.1	15.7	63	4.7	E.N.E.	N.E.	1.9		907.0
Tlacotalpam, Ver.	18 36	3.5	1	760.4			25.3	80	4.8	N.	N.E.			2264.0
Oaxaca, Oax.	17 04	1541.0	1	636.6	32.9	6.2	20.6	80			W.			649.3

SUMMARY OF THE METEOROLOGICAL OBSERVATIONS TAKEN IN SEVERAL LOCALITIES OF MEXICO, DURING THE YEAR 1869.

LOCALITIES.	N. Lat.	Altitude above the sea.	BAROMETRICAL PRESSURE REDUCED TO 0°. mean	max.	min.	TEMPERATURE IN THE SHADE. m'n mx.	m'n	mx.	min.	Humidity.	RAIN. Days of Rain.	Total Rains.	Rainiest Month.	Highest rainfall in 24 hrs.	Mean annual am'nt of rain.	CLOUDS. Dominant direction.	Average velocity per second.	WINDS. Prevailing direction.	Maximum velocity per second.	EVAPORATION. Shade.	Open Air.
		m.	mm.	mm.	mm.	°	°	°	°			mm.	mm.	mm.			m.		m.	mm.	mm.
Aguascalientes	21° 40'	1939.0	610.2	610.3	602.1			34.4	-0.8	53	107	82.9	July, 17.6	13 Oct., 8.6	5.1	W.		E. & N. W.	16.7		7.7
Colima (Seminario)	19° 11'	487.7	718.3					37.2	9.4	69	71	749.2	Oct., 206.7		5.2	S. W.	2.6	S. W.	6.7	4.2	7.9
Colima	19° 3'		634.7	639.7	632.1	24.8		36.1	-1.2	82	112	597.8	Aug., 379.0	2 April, 125.0	4.8	E. & N.E.	0.8	N. E.	10.5	4.6	
Guadalajara	21° 1'	1580.8	651.6	606.5	596.1	18.4		34.1	2.9	48	107	594.2	June, 100.3	14 Aug., 88.7	4.0	S. E.	1.8	E. N. E.		4.0	
Guanajuato	22° 1'	2060.8	649.3	618.6	667.9	18.5		33.5	5.6		202	779.4	June, 396.4	5 July, 88.8	6.2		1.5	N.	20.0	3.2	
Jalapa	19° 31'	1450.0	613.5	628.8	611.2	19.1		34.0	-3.6	58	109	395.1	Oct., 87.8	5 June, 35.8	3.9	S. W.	2.1	N. E.	36.0	2.3	4.3
Lagos	21° 21'	1912.5	617.2			19.1		34.7	2.4	47	117	314.0	July, 113.4	25 Sept., 33.1	4.9	S. W.		S. S. W.	15.6	3.9	8.2
Leon	30° 38'	1798.6				22.0		40.0	1.1				Aug., 417.0	11 Sept., 100.0		N.					
Magdalena	33° 13'	1508.0	759.8	794.0	749.3	35.8		43.5	11.7	75	70	594.2	July, 180.9	18 Sept., 85.9	3.2	E.	1.7	W.	22.0	2.3	6.9
Mazatlan	33° 55'	7.5	760.5	760.9	749.4	40.5		40.5	12.1	72	118	914.7	June, 294.0	21 June, 63.8	4.9	N. E.	1.9	N. E.	6.2	2.0	7.8
Merida (Central Observat.)	19° 26'	15.3	586.2	591.9	580.5	16.8		31.8	1.5	57	143	459.0	Oct., 105.0	8 Oct., 30.0	5.1	N. E.	1.2	N. & N. W.	15.0	2.3	6.0
Mexico (National School of Young Ladies)	25° 30'	2277.5	586.2	591.5	580.5	16.3		31.0	1.0	59	142	624.0	July, 106.0	8 Oct., 31.1	5.0	N. W.		N. W.		4.8	6.0
Monterey	25° 41'	495.6	714.9	728.7	703.4	22.9		43.8	-3.5	94	94	628.0	July, 131.9	4 Oct., 37.4	4.6	N. E.	1.4	N. W.	18.3	6.9	9.6
Morelia	17° 2'	1951.0	608.8	613.3	604.1	26.8		36.6	1.5	63	159	619.9	July, 112.4	5 June, 47.6	5.5	N. E.	1.5	S. S. W.		6.1	
Oaxaca	17° 2'	1574.1	696.9	642.2	632.5	21.2		36.0	3.1	65	128	226.5	Sept., 89.7	7 April, 36.6	3.8	N. E.	3.3	N. E.	18.0	3.3	9.7
Pachuca	20° 7'	2435.0	573.5	578.9	560.1	14.1		30.7	0.2	73	57	68.3	June, 50.4	8 Aug., 50.4	3.7	N. E. & S. W.	0.5	E.	20.0		
Puebla (Catholic College)	19° 2'	2167.7	594.0	598.0	609.6	17.5		31.5	1.8	58	88	689.7	Sept., 68.3	8 Aug., 24.8	4.1		1.4	N. N. E.			
Queretaro	20° 36'	1850.0	616.0	621.4	624.4	18.4		34.5	1.0	54	92	435.0	Oct., 216.0	6 Oct., 47.0				N. & S.	12.2	4.1	
Real del Monte	20° 8'	2772.2	548.6	553.3	543.0	13.1		26.5	0.1	63	86	773.0	Oct., 618.8	23 June, 93.0	3.7			W.	11.7	1.7	3.3
Saltillo	25° 25'	1645.5	632.3	636.5	644.1	18.5		28.2	-4.2	53	146	618.8	Sept., 41.4	23 June, 40.5	4.6	N. E.	1.4	S. E.	10.0	2.4	
San Luis Potosi	22° 9'	1890.3	616.3	621.9	609.3	19.5		32.4	4.0	53	99	347.5	July, 86.4	18 July, 33.2	3.5	N. E.	0.7	W. & W. S. W.	26.7	1.7	3.0
Silao	19° 17'	1848.0	556.6	950.5	551.9	13.8		35.9	6.0	58	146	647.8	Sept., 184.1	2 April, 75.8	4.6	N. E.	2.2	N. E.			
Trejo (estate of)	20° 56'	2625.0						31.1	15.9	76		1539.1	July, 359.1								
Veracruz	19° 11'	14.6	762.5	766.1	760.4	25.0		32.0	-5.2	59	52	473.4	Nov., 177.5	7 Oct., 34.0	5.2	E.	2.9	S. W.	17.1	4.0	
Zacatecas	22° 46'	2443.0	572.9	577.4	568.0	16.1		32.0													
Zapotlan	19° 36'	1562.0	636.8	640.4	633.6	20.5		35.9		59	151	610.0	July, 260.5	10 Aug., 78.6	5.6	N. E.	2.6	S. E.	18.0	2.1	10.0

The table on page 39 shows the results of the meteorological observations taken in the principal cities of Mexico during the year 1896.

Professor Mariano Barcena, director of our National Meteorological
Observatory or Weather Bureau, furnished me the following data about
the maximum and minimum of temperature and greatest oscillation
both in summer and winter of several cities in Mexico, located both at
the sea-level like Merida and Mazatlan, at different altitudes like Jalapa,
San Luis Potosi, Oaxaca, and at the highest level like the cities of
Mexico, Pachuca, and Zacatecas, showing the mildness of the Mexican climate.

CITY OF MEXICO.

Maximum temperature in the shade in summer......... 84.9, May 5th.
Maximum temperature in winter.................... 72.0, December.
Minimum temperature in winter.................... 32.9, January and February.
Greatest oscillation in one day in winter............ 13.7
Greatest oscillation in one day in summer........... 32.9

PUEBLA (STATE OF PUEBLA).

Maximum temperature in the shade in summer .... 83.8, April.
Maximum temperature in winter.................... 74.7, February.
Minimum temperature in winter.................... 32.9, January.
Greatest oscillation in one day in winter............ 36.3
Greatest oscillation in one day in summer........... 34.4

OAXACA (STATE OF OAXACA).

Maximum temperature in the shade in summer........ 93.7, May.
Maximum temperature in winter.................... 83.1, February.
Minimum temperature in winter.................... 39.2, January and December.
Greatest oscillation in one day in winter............. 39.1
Greatest oscillation in one day in summer........... 37.8

JALAPA (STATE OF VERACRUZ).

Maximum temperature in shade in summer.......... 89.6, April.
Maximum temperature in winter.................... 87.1, December.
Minimum temperature in winter.................... 33.8, February.
Greatest oscillation in one day in winter............. 35.3
Greatest oscillation in one day in summer........... 32.0

QUERETARO (STATE OF QUERETARO).

Maximum temperature in the shade in summer........ 90.1, April and June.
Maximum temperature in winter .... 80.4, December.
Minimum temperature in winter.................... 32.9, January.
Greatest oscillation in one day in winter............. 39.4
Greatest oscillation in one day in summer........... 34.7

GUANAJUATO (STATE OF GUANAJUATO).

Maximum temperature in the shade in summer....... 91.9, April.
Maximum temperature in winter.................... 82.0, February.
Minimum temperature in winter .... 36.0, January.
Greatest oscillation in one day in winter........... 36.7
Greatest oscillation in one day in summer........... 36.7

LEON (STATE OF GUANAJUATO).

Maximum temperature in the shade in summer. ...... 91.6, May and June.
Maximum temperature in winter.................... 77.0, February.

PACHUCA (STATE OF HIDALGO).

Maximum temperature in the shade in summer....... 80.2, May.
Maximum temperature in winter.................... 77.0, December.
Minimum temperature in winter.................... 32.4, December.
Greatest oscillation in one day in winter 33.3
Greatest oscillation in one day in summer........... 28.6

REAL DEL MONTE (STATE OF HIDALGO).

Maximum temperature in the shade in summer....... 80.2, March.
Maximum temperature in winter.................... 74.1, January.
Minimum temperature in winter.................... 31.6, January.

SALTILLO (STATE OF COAHUILA).

Maximum temperature in the shade in summer....... 89.6, April.
Maximum temperature in winter.................... 75.7, January.
Minimum temperature in winter.................... 12.2, February.
Greatest oscillation in one day in winter............ 32.8
Greatest oscillation in one day in summer........... 25.6

MERIDA (STATE OF YUCATAN).

Maximum temperature in the shade in summer........103.6, April and June.
Maximum temperature in winter.................... 92.8, January.
Minimum temperature in winter.................... 47.8, February.
Greatest oscillation in one day in winter............. 37.1
Greatest oscillation in one day in summer........... 38.7

MAZATLAN (STATE OF SINALOA).

Maximum temperature in the shade in summer....... 91.0, September.
Maximum temperature in winter.................... 84.0, December.
Minimum temperature in winter.................... 15.8, February.
Greatest oscillation in one day in winter............ 16.9
Greatest oscillation in one day in summer........... 17.5

MEXICO AS A SANITARIUM.

Although the City of Mexico, on account of its present unsatisfactory sanitary conditions, of which I will treat in speaking of that city and which I am sure will be remedied before long, cannot be considered now as the best place for invalids, there are many other localities in the country presenting great advantages as sanitariums.

The mild nature and evenness of most of our climate is very favorable to certain diseases—especially pulmonary ones—and when that advantage becomes well known the central plateau of Mexico will be the best sanitarium for lung diseases, and especially for tuberculosis. Other lung diseases requiring a warmer climate could find desirable places in certain valleys in the temperate zone like Cuantla, Cuernavaca, Tasco, Iguala, and others. These very conditions, namely, the even and mild climate both in summer and winter, will make it a country visited by thousands of pleasure or health seekers who wish to escape both extremes of the northern climate. Even now we would have a much larger travel from this country if we had convenient accommodations for travellers, but our hotels are not yet as comfortable as those in the United States.

FLORA.

The short and imperfect description of the climate of Mexico, made above, will show that we can raise all the products of the three different zones into which the earth is divided, and the most remarkable thing is that we can raise them almost on the same ground. By going only a few miles, for instance, travelling on horseback four or five hours from a low to a higher locality, we change from the torrid to the temperate zone, and therefore we can have the products of both with comparatively little trouble ; and by going four or five hours higher still, we change from the temperate to the frigid zone, and these are advantages of our geographical position which can be appreciated only by those who have experienced them.[1]

[1] Mr. Charles Dudley Warner, editor of *Harper's Monthly Magazine*, in a brilliant article published in the July, 1897, number of that periodical, gives the following description of the rapid descent from the cold to the temperate and hot regions of Mexico, which may be considered as a specimen of the scenery in many other localities of that country. In many other places, where there are no wagon-roads, but only a footpath, the descent is a great deal more rapid, often 5000 feet in four or five miles, and then the contrast is still greater. At Maltrata for instance, an Indian town about 5000 feet above the level of the sea, the natives offer their tropical fruits to the passengers of the Mexican Railway going from Veracruz to the City of Mexico, and they leave with what they have left after the train starts to climb the mountains to the Central Plateau to an altitude of about 9000 feet, and they reach Esperanza, the first station on the Central Plateau far ahead of the train, which has to describe a long, zigzag course before getting there. I have selected the following extract from Mr. Warner's article because it relates to one of the historical places of Mexico :

"Cuernavaca is distinguished as the actual meeting-place of the pine and the palm. It lies only a little more than fifty miles south of the City of Mexico ; but in order to reach it there is a mountain to be crossed which is at an elevation of over ten thousand feet. A railway climbs up this mountain, over the summit, to a wind-swept plain, in the midst of pine forests, called Tres Marias—marked by the sightly peaks of the Three Marys. By long loops and zigzags it is crawling down the mountain on

The Mexican Southern Railway, from Puebla to Oaxaca, descends in a few hours, by a series of fertile terraces, from an elevation of seven thousand feet to one of about seventeen hundred and fifty feet, when ths wonderful Cañon de los Cues is reached, a region of cocoa-nuts and bananas. But all the valleys and terraces in March are green or yellow with wheat and corn and sugar-cane. It confuses one's ideas to pass a field of wheat, the green blades just springing from the ground, and then a field ripe for harvest, and then a threshing-floor where the grain is being trodden out by mules. This means that you can plant and reap every day in the year, if you can obtain water in the dry season, and do not wait for the regular and copious summer rains.

The magnificent arboreal vegetation embraces one hundred and fourteen different species of building timber and cabinet woods, including oaks, pines, firs, cedars, mahogany, and rosewood ; twelve species of dyewoods ; eight of gum trees : the cacao and india-rubber, copal, liquid-ambar, camphor, turpentine, pine, mezquite yielding a substance

the other side to Cuernavaca. Mexico City has an elevation of seven thousand five hundred feet, Tres Marias of about ten thousand, and Cuernavaca of five thousand. The descent by the wagon-road is in length only twelve miles, but the drop in that distance is five thousand feet, so that the traveller passes very quickly from temperate to tropical conditions. . . .

" From the heights Cuernavaca seems to lie in a plain, but it is really on a promontory between two barrancas, and the whole country beyond is broken, till the terraces fall off into more tropical places, where the view is bordered by purple mountains. Indeed, the little city in the midst of this tumultuous plain is surrounded by lofty mountains. The country around, and especially below to the south, is irrigated, and presents a dozen contrasts of color in the evergreen foliage, the ripening yellow crops of sugar-cane and grain, the clusters of big trees here and there about a village or a hacienda, and the frequent church-towers. All this is loveliness, a mixture of temperate and tropical grace, but there is grandeur besides. Looking to the east, say from the Palace of Cortez, over the fields of purple and green and yellow and brown, where the graceful palms place themselves just as an artist would have them in the foreground of his picture, the view is certainly one of the finest in the world. There is in the left the long mountain range with the peaks of Tres Marias, and along the foot of it haciendas and towers, cones of extinct volcanoes and noble rocky promontories. To form the middle-distance mountains come into the picture, sloping together to lead the eye along from one "value" to another, violet, purple, dark or shining as the sun strikes them, while on the left is a noble range of naked precipices of red rock, always startling in color. It is some two thousand feet up the side of one of these red cliffs that there is the remains of an ancient city of Cliff-dwellers— almost inaccessible now, but once the home of a race that understood architecture and knew how to carve. The lines of this natural picture, the fields, the intervening ledges, the lofty mountains, all converge to the spot the artist would choose for the eye to rest, and there, up in the heavens, are the snow-clad peaks of Popocatepetl and Iztaccihuatl, about seventeen thousand five hundred feet above the sea, volcanic creators of the region, and now undisputed lords of the landscape. In the evening these peaks are rosy in the sun ; in the morning their white immobility is defined against the rosy sunshine."

similar to gum-arabic, dragon trees, and the almacigo or *Callitris quadvalvis*, from which sandarac is extracted. Among the oil-bearing trees and plants, of which there are seventeen varieties, are the olive, cocoa palm, almond, sesame, flax, the tree yielding the balsam of Peru, and others. There are fifty-nine classified species of medicinal plants, and many more are mentioned by botanists as still unclassified by science.

Of the many delicious fruits which grow in the tropical regions, only a few—the pineapple, the banana, and the cocoa-nut—are known in this country, the orange being rather a semi-tropical fruit. The others require, as all fruits do, cultivated taste, and, therefore, if imported here would not find a market. Even those which do come here are of very inferior flavor, owing to the fact that they are cut green so as to prevent their decay during transportation, and they, of course, have a less agreeable taste than in the place where they grow. Of the banana, for instance, we have about twenty varieties, some of which— the richest in my opinion—grow to a size from twelve to fifteen inches in length and from two to three inches in diameter.

We can raise in Mexico all the products of the world because we have all climates, from the perpetual snow to the burning sun of the equator ; but it would take a great deal more space than I can dispose of in this paper, to mention all the agricultural products we can raise, and I will, therefore, confine myself to only such as I think are now of more importance.

Coffee.—Mexico has many localities well suited for the raising of coffee, and the production of that berry can in the future be very largely increased. In the proper locality, namely, zone, ground, and climate, coffee can be raised on a large scale at comparatively small cost, affording always a large profit, whatever may be in the future its price in foreign markets.

I have had personal experience in coffee-raising, having made a coffee plantation in the district of Soconusco, in the State of Chiapas ; and I took especial interest in visiting other plantations, both in Mexico and Guatemala, where coffee had attained a large development. My experience has shown me that the best zone for coffee is located between one and five thousand feet above the level of the sea, as coffee is not a product of the hot but of the temperate zone. On the highlands, as a rule, the quality of the coffee is better and the yield large, while the lowlands give an earlier but smaller yield. There are coffee plantations in Mexico, almost down to the level of the sea, which are yielding coffee, and from that to the elevation of six thousand feet, producing also a very good quality of coffee. For further information on this subject, I refer the reader to a treatise on coffee-raising on the southern coast of the State of Chiapas, which I published in the City of

Mexico in 1874, and which contains detailed information on the several factors affecting that industry.

It is interesting to know the production of coffee in Mexico, taken from some statistics for 1896 :

Cordoba produces..............................	10,000,000 lbs.
Huatusco and Coatepec	10,000,000 "
Oaxaca...	6,000,000 "
Tabasco..	5,000,000 "
Chiapas	3,000,000 "
Other districts................................	26,000,000 "
	60,000,000 lbs.

Sugar-Cane.—Mexico has many localities where sugar-cane can be raised at a very small cost, and where that industry can be made very lucrative, although we hardly produce enough sugar for our home consumption. From the sea-level to the frost line, which ranges, in different localities, from three to five thousand feet above the sea-level, sugar-cane can be raised in Mexico to great advantage. I have seen the cane in some places, especially in Soconusco, attain a height of twelve feet and a diameter of about five inches ; and in some localities it lasts from ten to eighteen years without need of replanting, and can be cut for grinding twice a year. When it is considered that in some places, like Louisiana, sugar has to be planted, as I believe, every two years, and that it is liable to be destroyed by frosts, the advantages of Mexico for that industry are apparent.

The favorable conditions of Mexico for raising sugar-cane are so great that I have seen the natives in the Indian town of Loxicha, in the State of Oaxaca, plant a small plot of sugar-cane, grind it with primitive wooden mills moved by hand power, using very primitive earthen pans, to evaporate the juice and make brown sugar—losing of course a great part of the saccharine matter in the cane,—transport the sugar, sometimes a distance of thirty miles on mule-back, and sell it at one cent per pound, and still make a profit.

For sugar-cane the lowlands are the best, and the plant is essentially a tropical one. It will grow, however, at very considerable altitudes, but when planted in the mountains it takes a longer time to ripen, and soon ceases to give remunerative crops. There was in southern Veracruz a sugar-cane only six months old which had a circumference of $7\frac{1}{2}$ inches. Where that cane grew the yield of cane per acre was about 80 tons when twelve months old. The elevation was something like 1000 feet. It is true, however, that the bulk of the cane grown in Mexico is to be found above 2000 feet, but I am convinced that a lower altitude would produce even better results.

Tobacco.—Among the tropical products of superior quality that we

raise in the hot zone, I should mention tobacco, the Mexican tobacco
being, in General Grant's estimation, superior to the Havana article.
The natural conditions of soil and temperature are the same in Cuba
and Mexico, but we had not the superior experience of the Cubans in
curing the leaf until the late insurrection broke out in Cuba, in 1868,
when a great many Cubans went to Mexico to plant tobacco. As the
land has been planted in Cuba with tobacco for nearly four hundred
years, and as tobacco is a very exhausting crop, it has become indispensable to manure the land with guano, while in Mexico we have
virgin land, and tobacco being a comparatively new industry, no guano
needs to be used. General Grant, whom I consider a competent
judge, detected the taste of guano in the Havana cigars, of which ours
is free, and he, therefore, preferred to smoke the Mexican cigars.

In Cuba the exhausted soil cannot produce all the leaves that are
required for the world's supply of Havana cigars, and the want can
only be filled through the use of Mexico leaf tobacco, the weed
produced in other countries having similar conditions. The Marquis
de Cabañas sent to Sumatra a quantity of seed when it became obvious that the soil of the tobacco region of Cuba was fast being worn out.
He sent seed also to Java and to the United States, but it was found
that it was impossible to raise tobacco of the quality of that raised in
Havana anywhere but in Mexico. That raised in Java from Havana
seed was very coarse and rank, replete with nicotine and meconic
acid, and devoid of those delicate essential oils that give the Havana
and Mexican tobacco their fine aroma.

The tobacco plant is a native of the tropics, and thrives best in the
hot lands. It is a hardy plant, however, and will grow well in northern
latitudes in the summer time. It often happens that the land in the
tropics is actually too rich for the successful cultivation of tobacco.

India-Rubber.—The lowlands of Mexico, especially those adjoining
the Pacific Ocean and which have a very warm and moist climate, are
very well adapted for the india-rubber tree, which attains a large size
and yields a considerable amount of india-rubber. We used to have
whole forests of them, which fact shows that they were in their proper
conditions of soil and climate, as they could outgrow the rank vegetation of the tropics, and prevent the growth of most of the other large
trees in the forests ; but india-rubber gatherers have destroyed most of
them, and I imagine that there is a comparatively small number left.

I have always thought that the production of india-rubber would
before long cease to be sufficient to supply the demand, and that,
therefore, the value of that article would increase with the lapse of
time. Now it is to be expected that the enormous expansion during
the last few years of the cycle-tire, electrical motor-car, cab, and
kindred industries will lead to the bestowal of increased attention on

the world's rubber supply, which is so intimately associated with the existence of these industries.

Thinking that a plantation of india-rubber trees would be very re-munerative, I devoted considerable attention to that subject, and in 1872 started one of 100,000 trees in a place admirably located for the purpose, bordering on the Pacific Ocean and between two large rivers, in the same district of Soconusco. In an article published in 1872, under the title "India-Rubber Culture in Mexico," I compiled all the information on the subject that I could obtain, supplementing it with the experience that I had acquired. Unfortunately, for reasons of a political nature, I had to abandon that plantation, and when the trees that I had planted grew large enough to yield rubber, they were tapped by the natives and entirely destroyed, but my work gave me an experi-ence which I considered of great value. For further information on this subject I refer the reader to the above mentioned article.

The india-rubber trees that grow in Mexico are not the *Haevea guianensis* that grows in Brazil, but the *Castilloa elastica*, and if we have any of the *Haevea guianensis* I have not seen them.

Enough has been written lately on rubber cultivation to show that the profits, in Mexico at least, would be very great ; indeed, 300 per cent. on the capital invested is a possible return, after five years, from cultivating *Castilloa elastica* in that Republic. This is a return which provides plenty of margin for contingencies. Rubber-growing is no longer in the experimental stage, as witness the plantation of La Esme-ralda, in Oaxaca, to which further reference is made below. Culti-vated india-rubber plantations are few, for the reason that, in some degree like the coffee plant, the india-rubber tree requires a long period of continuous cultivation before making any return to the cultivator. Mexico affords excellent opportunities for the development of this admittedly profitable industry. On this point the authority of Sir Henry Nevil Dering, the British Minister to Mexico, who, in a recent report to the Foreign Office on the cultivation of india-rubber, says : "The regions most favorable for the growth of this important, yet rarely cultivated, india-rubber tree are the plains of Pochutla, Oaxaca, and also along the banks of the Copalita River where the tree is found in astonishing numbers. Few are the plantations of india-rubber trees existing in the Republic of Mexico. The principal one is La Esmeralda, in Juquila, Oaxaca, which has over 200,000 trees, eight years old." According to the same report the total ex-pense for five years' cultivation of a "rubber plantation of 100,000 trees will not exceed $25,000 in silver and the yield of 100,000 trees at the first year's harvest will bring the planter $120,000, besides the product obtained from the corn, vanilla beans, cacao, and bananas raised from side planting. The net profit on the investment, after deducting the entire cost of the land and all expenses up to the first year of harvesting, will be $95,000, and each of the succeeding harvests, for twenty-five or thirty years, will bring a steady income of over $100,000." This is 400 per cent. per annum net profit on the investment. These calculations are based upon the production of a five-year-old tree, but the report adds that "this product will be gradually increased every year for the next four or five years."

Cotton.—We have many regions in Mexico very favorably located for the cultivation of cotton. I am aware that the cotton-growers of the United States hold that what they call their cotton belt has peculiar conditions for the production of their staple, which, in their opinion, do not exist in any other portion of the globe, and they believe, therefore, that nobody can compete with them in this regard. Without any intention of depreciating the advantages of the cotton belt of this country, I am of the opinion that there are in Mexico lands as well adapted for the production of cotton as the best in this country, and in some regions perhaps better ; yet, notwithstanding these advantages, and although our wages are low, cotton is produced cheaper in the United States, and is sold with profit by the planters for one-half the price that it commands in Mexico. So great is the difference in the price of this staple in the two countries that, notwithstanding an import duty on cotton of eight cents per kilogram, or almost five cents per pound, which is equivalent to fifty cents ad valorem, we import from this country a very large portion of the cotton we manufacture. I do not overlook the fact that cotton is raised here by negro labor, which is considerably cheaper than white labor, but, even assuming that wages in this case be the same in both countries, the difference in cost is so great that some other factor besides labor must enter into the expense of production.

As our cotton manufactories are increasing, more especially because of the protection afforded to home products by the depreciation of silver, we now produce only about one half of the cotton we manufacture, and have to import the other half from the United States ; but I am sure that before long we shall not only produce enough for our own consumption but also for export.

Agave.—The whole central plateau abounds in many species of agave, which are used for several purposes. In the eastern portion of the plateau, that is, from the City of Mexico towards Veracruz, in the region called the Plains of Apam, the agave yields a large quantity of a white juice, similar in appearance to milk, which when fermented is used as a tonic, and is an intoxicating beverage. The amount of alcohol it contains is small—about 7 per cent., I believe—but imbibed in large quantities it is quite intoxicating. The use of this beverage, called pulque, has become very extensive in Mexico, and it must have very superior qualities both as a tonic and nutritive, when many live on nothing but corn and pulque. In the mining districts, where a great deal of nervous force is expended working in a high temperature and under very unhealthy atmospheric conditions, this drink is almost indispensable, and I imagine that when a way is discovered to keep it for some time, and its medicinal qualities become better known, it will be exported in considerable quantities and used by foreign countries. From the agave of other districts a drink is made called mescal, which has some remarkable therapeutic properties, the most celebrated being made in a district of the State of Jalisco called Tequila, from which it takes its name; and in the very dry and stony regions of Yucatan another species of agave grows, which seems to derive its food wholly from the atmosphere, yielding a very good fibre, much like manilla, which we now export in large quantities, particularly to New York. All the agave yields a first-class fibre as raw material, either for paper or cordage—some of it being rather coarse, like the Yucatan henequen, and some of it almost as fine and glossy as silk, like pita.

Henequen.—By far the most important of our fibre industries is the cultivation and preparation of the fibre known as "Sisal hemp," so called from the name of the port from which it used to be principally exported, and in the United States as "henequen hemp." The plant which produces it is a species of agave which flourishes to best advantage in stony and arid land at the level of the sea. The present prosperity of the state of Yucatan, a large proportion of which is too sterile to yield any other crop, is due almost entirely to the development of this industry. The plant requires very little cultivation, and the separation and cleaning of the fibre is effected very cheaply. The yield of fibre is estimated at the rate of 1000 to 1200 pounds per acre.

Pulque.—The pulque plant is indigenous to Mexico, often growing wild on the uplands, where for months and years at a time no rain falls; and it is also largely cultivated on the Plains of Apam, a large tract of land lying in the States of Mexico, Puebla, and Hidalgo, about sixty miles east of the City of Mexico. The plants are transplanted when two or three years old with much care, then cultivated in fields especially prepared for the purpose, each acre containing from 360 to 680 plants.

Nature requires the plant to be milked, when the liquor is ready to flow, for the use of man, else the superfluity of juices will cause the growth of a thick stem from the centre of the plant, which shoots up some ten or fifteen feet, putting out branches at the top, with clusters of yellowish flowers. These branches are symmetrical, and the effect is like a lofty, branched candlestick.

When the pulque is first extracted, before the process of fermentation sets in, it is sweet and scentless, and in this state is preferred by those unaccustomed to the drink. The fermentation takes place in tubs constructed for the purpose, and to aid or expedite the process a little "madre pulque," or pulque mother, is added, which hastens the chemical change. At times fermentation is retarded by a cold spell at the vats. When the laborer draws the sweet sap with his rude siphon, made either of a gourd or a calabash and a hollow horn tip, he discharges the contents into a pig- or goat-skin swinging at his back. The "agua miel" in this stage is like a green water in appearance and taste. Soon carbonic acid is formed, and it becomes milky, and resembles in taste very good cider. The amount of carbonic acid contained is so great, and the decomposition so incredibly rapid, that in a few hours it would become vinegar if not closely watched. To prevent this the pulque dulce, or sweet pulque, is poured into a tinacal—an oxhide strapped to a square wooden frame, and capable of holding a considerable amount of the liquid. These tinacals are of various sizes, to meet the emergencies of the situation.

To the sweet pulque is added an equal proportion of milk, and then a slight dose of infusion of rennet. This is not enough to coagulate it, but sufficient to induce a slight amount of putrescence, as in cheese. The putrid odor and flavor of pulque as sold in the pulque shops is due to the rennet alone, for the belief that this is caused by the flavor of the pigskin, in which it is brought to market, is without foundation.

From the tinacal it is poured into a hogshead by means of pigskins, and it is transferred to the barrels of venders from the hogsheads of the "haciendado" by means of the same skins.

The plants are wholly independent of rain and storm, and are of a beautiful deep-green color. The pulque is carried every day to the City of Mexico, by special trains, in "barricas," or large tierces, and by "cueros de pulque," or pigskins filled with the liquid.

The plant does not arrive at maturity or yield its sap before its eighth year. During the growth of the plant a central bulb is formed for its coming juices. This is scooped out, leaving a cavity or hole large enough to hold a few quarts. This cavity is made in the bottom and middle of the plant. The juice exudes into this cavity and is taken out daily by being sucked into a long-necked gourd on the siphon principle, by the Indian laborers, and then poured into the tubs taken to the fields and then removed to the vats.

The outlay on each plant up to maturity is calculated generally at about $2, and the return is from $7 to $10, according to the size of the plant. Its period of production is about five months, and each plant supposed to yield from 125 to 160 gallons of liquid during that time.

The principal regions for the cultivation of the maguey are the arid limestone chains of hills, and here, in many places, the hole for the reception of the young plant is made with a sort of crowbar with a sharp point, used principally in the quarrying of tepatate, the chief building material of the Mexican capital. It is usual to aid the young plant by putting some good soil into the hole. These young plants are suckers which the mature maguey throws out on all sides, and which have to be removed before the heart is tapped for the sweet sap, which is the "agua miel," or honey water, of the pulque.

The leaves of the pulque plant are long and pointed, with prickles along the edges. Sometimes these leaves are very large, and the bunches of them springing from the common stalk are enormous. The bruised leaves are made into a kind of paper—a rather tough, stiff, and hard paper—and they are also used in their natural state as a thatch for the roofs of the common huts or houses occupied by the peons. A kind of thread is also made from the fibrous texture of the leaves. A rough needle and pin are made from the thorn, and from the root a cheap and palatable food is made.

Cactus.—Mexico is often called "the land of the cactus," and the multitudinous development of cactus forms in that country cannot be appreciated by any one who has not seen them in their home in the hot land. There is a species known as the giant or candelabra cactus, which has a single stem, from which spring innumerable branches, the whole plant resembling an immense candelabrum. I have seen in Oaxaca, some candelabra cacti about twenty feet in height by thirty in diameter. Some cacti shoot in single, column-like stems, others run like leafless vines, and others resemble needle cushions stuck full of needles.

Cocoa.—Cocoa is produced in several localities. That of Soconusco, in the State of Chiapas, is of so excellent a quality that when Mexico was a colony of Spain it was the only kind used by the Spanish royal family. On account of the expense and difficulty of transportation, and the cultivation of cheaper quality in other localities, the production has dwindled down to an insignificant amount, and now hardly enough is grown to supply the demand in that district; but it is universally acknowledged that the Soconusco cocoa is the best in the world.

The best elevation for cocoa is from 300 to 1000 feet, and the tree seldom thrives well at an altitude exceeding 3000 feet. Warmth and moisture are necessary for the successful cultivation of this plant.

The State of Tabasco produces a very good quality of cocoa, although it cannot be compared with that of Soconusco. In other places it grows very well also, but for various reasons the production, instead of being developed, has dwindled down until it is not enough for home consumption, and we have to import some, especially from Venezuela and Ecuador. One disadvantage of the cocoa industry is that the tree requires several years to reach maturity and to bear fruit, and few investors can afford to wait the necessary time.

Vanilla.—The vanilla bean grows very luxuriantly on the Gulf coast of Mexico, and it has been for some time a very profitable production, especially in the counties of Papamtla and Misantla, in the State of Veracruz, on account of the excellent quality of the bean and the high price which it brings. It grows in a region which is subject to intermittent and remittent fevers, and sometimes yellow fever, and where labor is very scarce; for these reasons it has not attained a greater development. I hardly think there is any locality where the vanilla vine grows better than in Mexico.

Vanilla requires a hot, moist climate, and, therefore, the lowlands are best suited for its culture. Very little of the vanilla produced in Mexico is at present grown at an elevation exceeding 1000 feet. At the same time it is claimed that in some places it thrives up to 3000 feet.

The vines will usually produce considerable vanilla in the third year, and they will yield considerably more during the fourth, fifth, sixth, and seventh years, and the production then begins to decrease. But before this time new rootlets have been dropped from the old plants, which form new vines that take the place of the old ones; thus the plantation is kept in a state of continued production. The central portion of the Isthmus of Tehuantepec is one of the most suitable regions for its cultivation, as much wild vanilla is found growing in the forests there.

The Mexican vanilla dealers have established five grades, namely: First, vanilla "fina," or legal, the beans and pods of six and a half inches long, or upwards, short in the neck, sound and black, and the beans which become split or open, provided they have the foregoing qualities and the split does not extend more than a third of the pod. This class is again divided into "terciada," which is composed of the shortest pods; "primera chica," "primera grande," "marca menor," and "marca mayor," the largest of all. Second, "vanilla chica," those pods which differ from the "terciada" only in being shorter, two of them counting as one of the first class. Third, vanilla "zacate," the pods of all sizes, which are off color through being gathered before becoming properly ripe, or being over-cured; "pescozuda," "vana," "cueruda," and "aposcoyonada," names for pods in a more or less damaged condition. Fourth, vanilla "cimarrona," the wild vanilla in good or fair condition, three pods counting as one of the first class. Fifth, the "rezacate," composed of the very short pods; of those split all the way up to the stalk, of the badly damaged, of the very immature, and of the greatly over-cured; of this, six pods count as one of the first class.

After the sizing and classification are finished, the pods are tied up in bunches of 100–150, so as to weigh one pound, and wrapped in filtering paper and tin foil.

Silk Culture.—The mulberry-tree and silkworm industries have a very great future in Mexico, and are destined to produce a veritable revolution in the industries of the central plateau of that country. The mulberry tree can be grown in Mexico almost to an unlimited extent, especially in the central plateau, and, as wages are low, the raw silk can be manufactured at a great profit. Several experiments have been made on a small scale, more particularly in the Valley of Mexico, by Mr. Hipolito Chabon, a gentleman of French descent, and he has obtained most satisfactory results. I have no doubt that the time is not far distant when the silk industry will assume great proportions in Mexico, and we will be able to stand among the foremost silk-producing countries of the world.

Cochineal.—The cochineal is a bug which feeds on the cactus ; and which, when fully developed, is brushed off the cactus leaves and roasted to prevent decomposition, being then ready for market. It is raised to great advantage in Mexico, and especially in the valleys of the State of Oaxaca. When it was the only article used to dye red it was very valuable, commanding sometimes between four and five dollars per pound, and it made the wealth of that State. But recent discoveries in chemistry have supplied other substances for dyeing which are very cheap, especially aniline, and the price of cochineal has fallen considerably, so that now it is hardly raised at all. When it had a high price, it was raised in Guatemala, and it was the beginning of the wealth of that State. It is now raised, I understand, in several other countries.

Rice.—Rice grows very well in Mexico, and I have not seen any district where it is necessary to inundate the fields to favor its production, although I understand it is also raised in that way in some localities. It is generally planted just as wheat and barley are in the United States, needing no irrigation and depending entirely on the rainfall. I imagine that raising rice by inundation would be more expensive, and also be dangerous, because it could not fail to affect the salubrity of the country.

Chicle, or Chewing-Gum.—This article, like many others, grows wild in Mexico, where the demand that has arisen for it in the United States has begun to develop its production. For some time past the shipments from Mexico have been on an increasing scale, owing, no doubt, to the comparatively high prices which ruled early in 1896.

Every year a larger extent of forests is worked for chicle, resulting in a steady growth of the production since the gum first became an important commercial article, about ten years ago. Prior to that

time 7 or 8 cents a pound was considered a good price, and in 1896
it was sold at 36 cents. The importation into the United States constitutes almost the entire production, and the amounts and values are
thus officially reported by the Statistical Bureau of the United States
for the fiscal years ending June 30 :

	1894.	1895–96.
Chicle	1,903,655 lib.	3,618,483 lib.
Value	$490,438	$1,167,101
Average	25¼ cents per lib.	32 cents per lib.

The following statement has been compiled from official data collected by the Mexican Government, the value of the chewing-gum
being in silver :

Year.	Pounds.	Value.
1885–86	929,959	$ 156,402
1886–87	1,254,853	353,641
1887–88	1,542,794	371,673
1888–89	2,037,783	592,810
1889–90	1,827,131	714,242
1890–91	2,457,653	1,284,682
1891–92	2,494,177	703,572
1892–93	1,757,813	705,167
1893–94	2,645,722	803,019
1894–95	1,668,636	679,367
1895–96	3,297,371	1,527,838
Total	21,913,932	$7,892,413

Yuca.—Yuca, or starch-plant, called manioc in South America, is
a bush from four to six feet high, having tubers, like horse-radish, six
to ten to every plant, and weighing from one to twelve pounds each.
It is an important product of Chiapas and may be sown at any time,
but it is better to do so from the stems when the rains begin, say in the
month of May, by opening ditches five feet apart, and planting the
cuttings, eight inches long, in them consecutively, leaving one foot between. Vegetable and sandy soil is best adapted for it, although it
can be planted and will thrive in any kind of land. In arid and hard
soil it needs plowing. If the land has been thoroughly cleared before
planting it requires but little weeding during cultivation. A year after
being sown, if the soil is rich, it will begin to yield tubers which must
be dug up at the time the tree begins to flower. In replanting after
digging the tubers, a slip is left standing and this will bear in twelve
months. Besides extracting the starch from the tubers, the leaves are
used as fodder for stock.

Sir Henry Dering, the British Minister to Mexico, sent recently to
the Foreign Office some practical notes on the cultivation in Mexico of
the "Yuca" or cassava plant, pineapple, ginger, "chicle" or chewing-

gum, sarsaparilla, jalap, licorice, canaigre, and ramie, and I shall quote here from his notes on some of those products.

The yuca is to the peon, in the tropical section of the Republic, what potatoes are to the poor and working people of Ireland. Yuca is a native of the country, and its rise dates back before the conquest of Hernan Cortez, and it has always formed a portion of the food of the ancient and present Mexicans, especially those living in Veracruz, Oaxaca, Chiapas, Tabasco, and Yucatan. It has been estimated that the returns of yuca cultivation are immense ; the yield of an acre contains more nutritive matter than six times the same area of wheat.

Ginger.—Ginger is found growing wild in various parts of Mexico. The returns from an acre of land vary considerably, but when culti-vated under favorable conditions, the crops ought to be 4000 pounds and upward. A ten-acre patch would yield annually from $5000 to $7000.

Canaigre.—Though for years canaigre has been used in Mexico, both for medicinal and tanning purposes, it has but recently attracted the attention of the outside commercial world as a valuable source of tannic acid. The result of investigations has been to create a great demand for canaigre in the tanning business of European countries, and more recently in the leather-making centres of the United States. The only supply now to be obtained of this plant is from the wild growth along the rivers and valleys of Western Texas, New Mexico, and Mexico, and a fear has been felt for some time that with the con-stantly increasing demand the present sources of supply must become exhausted.

Peppermint.—Water mint (*mentha vulgaris*) thrives very well on the central plateau of Mexico and in some sections of the warm zone, especially along the rivulets and small lakes. There is no reason why the peppermint (*mentha piperita*), as well as spearmint and tansy, should not grow in abundance in Mexico, as they belong to the same family and require the same climatic conditions. As the oil of pep-permint is very extensively employed in medicines and the arts, the cultivation of this plant will be profitable to Mexico.

Cabinet and Dye Woods.—In the low, hot countries we have all the cabinet woods growing wild and a great many dye woods, some of which are indigenous to Mexico, like the Campechy wood, not being found in other countries. It would take too long to enumerate the different kinds of cabinet woods we have, and I will only say that it happens with them as with our fruits, that only such of them as have been introduced here, like mahogany, cedar, rosewood, ebony, and a few others, are known in this country and in Europe, while hundreds of other kinds as hard as those and of as fine, if not a finer grain, are found in the wild woods of Mexico.

Grasses.—In the lower regions of Mexico, especially at the sea-level, we have various grasses which can be grown at very little expense and which make very good food for cattle, fattening them very much, and in comparatively short time. While I lived in Soconusco, I used to buy lean cattle, three years old, at $10 per head ; and letting them pasture on the grass, the expense being little more than that of a few men to take care of the cattle, without providing them with any shelter, pens, or anything of that kind, only giving them about once a month some salt, at the end of four or five months they became very fat and could be sold on the spot at $25 a head. The fattening grasses can be very easily cultivated, because they are of such rank growth that they do not allow any other vegetation to spring up on the same spot, and so save the expense of cleaning the ground of weeds ; which, in the hot regions is very great, as vegetation is there very rank.

Alfalfa.—The alfalfa grows very luxuriantly in almost every place in Mexico, and it is so abundant there, that it has very little commercial value. It is nowhere dried and kept for fodder, but of course such use can be made of it. Land good for alfalfa has a very low price, and we are greatly surprised when we hear that in California the alfalfa land is worth $100 an acre.

Cattle Raising.—Mexico has special advantages for the raising of cattle, not only because of its mild climate, which renders unnecessary the many expenses required in the northern section of this continent, but also on account of the grasses that grow in several localities and that constitute very good food for cattle, as I have just stated.

Mexico will be, before long, a very large producer of cattle and other animals, and they will form a large share of her exports. Mexico has sent within two years about 400,000 small undeveloped cattle to the United States at about $15, Mexican silver, per head, and has also sent nearly her entire output of cotton-seed meal to the United States and Europe at about $16, silver, per ton. The meal sent to the United States is fed to cattle. The Mexican cattle sent there take the place of the better stock which is sent to Europe, causing virtually a five-thousand-kilometre railway haul against the short haul in Mexico to reach the coast. In addition we have to pay import duties in the United States. This is a sufficient evidence that a large profit could be made by fattening cattle with the cotton-seed meal in Mexico, and shipping the fattened cattle direct to Europe, even using the best cattle of the country. But rapid improvement should be made in the class of cattle for beef purposes. Cotton-seed meal is the feed to be relied on chiefly. The quantity of it produced already is sufficient to fatten a large number of stock. The cattle should also be fed with a small amount of corn along with the meal during the last month of feeding to harden and whiten the meat, as feeding only with cotton-seed meal makes the meat dark, and militates against its selling value to some extent, and the corn can be easily and profitably supplied. The total cost of fattening a steer should not reach $15 silver. There is an unlimited demand in Europe for choice meats at about 12c., gold, per pound, and no import duties have to be paid. Poor classes of meat are a drug in all markets of the world. With these great advantages placed within easy reach, the producers in Mexico of grain and stock have a guarantee of ready sale at good prices for all they can produce.

Inquiry was made in Liverpool about the possibilities of the Mexican live-animal trade with England, and it was found that the initial difficulty is the small size of the Mexican cattle, as cattle weighing 1200 pounds are considered small by the trade there, and from 900 to 1000 pounds is therefore extremely small. The smallest Texan cattle ever imported in Liverpool averaged 1226 pounds.

The best Mexican steers can be made to weigh 1200 pounds if well fattened. The difference in cost of transportation on account of lighter weight is but small in proportion to the cheapness of Mexican cattle. Cattle breeders in Mexico, on the whole, have not advanced much in developing good breeds of cattle. They do not appreciate their value, nor would they pay one-half their actual cost, though they can be had from the United States at half of what they would cost from Europe. Herefords are the best breed. I am sure that the railroads will do all they can to encourage that industry by charging as low rates as possible, as they would thus develop an industry which in the course of time would become very profitable to them.

A great need of Mexico is a reliable supply of good and healthy water through artificial means, well distributed over the stock ranges to prevent the great loss by death through lack of water, as well as the heavy shrinkage of meat and tallow, by so much unnecessary travelling of stock to water. They cannot grow fairly, much less fatten, and over one-half the annual increase die of exhaustion, while the value of the stock lost in one year would supply permanent water at convenient distances and prevent three-fourths of the loss and shrinkage now sustained. It has been amply proved that stock water can be secured under the most unfavorable conditions.

It would be to the advantage of the breeder to import some English short-horn bulls, with the object of breeding larger cattle, so as to make profitable the export of cattle to England, as animals should weigh from 1200 to 1300 pounds. This has been done in Texas and in the Argentine with beneficial results, and the improvement in the cattle from the latter place has been most marked during the last five years. With the proper attention, the same good results could be achieved in Mexico.

The English steamers that bring a large quantity of merchandise to Mexican ports have trouble in even securing ballast to get out of those ports, and have to traverse the Gulf and United States coasts to secure loads for the return trip. Their owners are willing and ready to supply facilities for the exportation of live stock and frozen meats if assured of a sufficient traffic to justify them in the expense, for they prefer reloading direct for Europe to going elsewhere for freight. The time required to return direct from Mexican ports is but little more than from New York and Baltimore, and is sufficiently short to warrant good service in transportation of live stock, and the cost would practically be the same as from United States ports. The United States is beginning to export beef and stock from Galveston to Europe, which is practically the same distance as from the Gulf ports of Mexico.

Mexico could export annually and easily after the next ten years 400,000 of fattened cattle, which would increase considerably the amount of our exports, and this trade would greatly assist the development of many other industries.

The desired result in question could be hastened by mixing good foreign labor with the native labor. The latter would be better fed, clothed, and educated, as well as encouraged, taught, and compelled to do better work, and thus the country's physical and mental welfare would be greatly promoted.

Sheep.—The same conditions apply to the sheep and wool industry. It is a great mistake for the Mexican sheep-owners to raise a class of sheep that yield each only from one to two and one-half pounds of very coarse and inferior wool, annually, while they themselves wear goods manufactured from foreign wools, and the domestic-cloth manufacturers are also under the necessity of importing largely of fine wools. Mexico possesses natural resources for producing all the wools of every grade that she needs, with a large quantity over for export, not to speak of choice grain-fed mutton for domestic and foreign consumption.

The custom of killing so much poor stock is a terrible waste of resources, as one well-fattened animal will render twice as much as a thin or poor one.

Products of Cold and Temperate Regions.—I will not speak of the products of the cold and temperate regions of Mexico, such as Indian corn, wheat, oats, barley, and others, because their cultivation is well understood in the United States, and I could say here nothing new to the American reader, but will only state that they all grow very well in the proper regions of Mexico.

FRUITS.

We produce in Mexico a great many tropical fruits that are not sent to the United States because there is no market for them for the reason that they are not known here. Some of them are delicious, and with the facilities of communication, I have no doubt that they will become known and a taste will be developed for them in this country. I will speak here only of such of our tropical fruits as come to the United States.

The advantage of tropical fruits growing in their proper zone and climate is immense, as the expense of planting and cultivating them outside of their proper limits is very great and there is always danger of their destruction.

Oranges.—Orange trees, like any other fruit trees, depend in Mexico on the rain, and, except in a private garden or private grounds, are not irrigated. While the orange tree is a hardy plant, it thrives best and yields the most luscious fruit in the tropics. Elevation exceeding 2500 feet is not, as a rule, desirable for orange culture.

The advantages of irrigation in orange culture are great in the subtropical regions of Mexico. The fruit of the irrigated orange tree is of a very superior quality, while the tree itself has a longer lease of life and is less subject to attacks from insects and diseases of a fungoid nature. One of the conditions primarily requisite to the growing of a marketable orange is that the trees be watered at judiciously regulated intervals during and for a short time after the blossoming season. Attacks from insect and fungoidal pests, which are most disastrous, and to which the trees are peculiarly subject during the blossoming period, are rendered even more dangerous by the prevalence of a considerable amount of humidity in the atmosphere which is always conducive to the development of parasitic germs or fungoidal spores. An abundance of moisture in the ground but a comparatively small amount in the air is the condition most to be desired during and just after the blossoming season. This is to be had by irrigation, but, generally speaking, not without it. Under irrigation, the soil is also much less subject to deterioration, owing to the superior fertilizing properties of water taken from wells and streams. Rain water, aside from containing a small percentage of ammonia, which it receives from the air, only acts as a medium to transmit the nutriment from the soil to the tree, while water taken from wells or streams holds in solution the renewing materials which are directly communicated to the plant proper.

In the more elevated orange districts of Mexico, the trees should be watered about once every twenty days during the dry season.

In some places our oranges are as sweet as if they had been preserved in sugar, and this, notwithstanding the fact that no attention is paid to their cultivation, that they grow almost wild, and without irrigation.

I think that the distillation of orange blossoms would prove very profitable. The production of flowers per tree is given at from 22 to 55 pounds in the case of sweet oranges, and from 60 to 100 pounds per tree from the bitter variety.

In flavor and productiveness the Mexican orange is unsurpassed. In the majority of the districts but little care or attention is given to the cultivation of the trees. Scientific orange culture in Mexico is practically unknown. The introduction from other countries of different varieties of the plant for experimental purposes is just being commenced.

The price of oranges in Mexico at the present time, in districts reasonably near lines of transportation, is about $11 per thousand, Mexican money, on the tree. It is the practice of the producer to sell the fruit on the trees, the buyer picking, packing, and shipping it at his own expense.

About one hundred trees are usually set out to the acre, the average yield being from 800 to 1000 oranges to the tree. I know of trees in Mexico which have a record of having produced 10,000 oranges. This, however, is very exceptional.

A properly cultivated and prudently managed grove at the end of five years' growth should prove as profitably as a coffee plantation of the same size, at the end of five years.

The production of the orange trees begins in the third or fourth year and increases up to the twelfth, and, in some cases, to the fifteenth or sixteenth year. It is considered best to cut the fruit up to the fifth year, not permitting it to mature.

A book prepared by Frederico Atristain, entitled *Cultivo y explotacion de Naranja*, and published by the Department of Fomento of the Mexican Government, contains a great deal of reliable information on the subject of orange culture in Mexico.

After an orange tree has been yielding sweet oranges for many years, it very likely exhausts the substances of the earth which give the sweet taste to the fruit, and it begins to lose its sweetness, until finally, if the land is not manured, as is almost always the case in Mexico, the oranges become bitter.

A recent cyclone, which lowered considerably the temperature in Florida, destroyed in one day, I understand, about 12,000,000 orange trees, thus causing ruin or serious loss to thousands of men engaged in that large industry, while the orange region in Mexico is entirely free from frosts and consequently from such dangers.

Lemons.—In the hot and temperate regions of Mexico lemons grow very well. There are some districts of the country, like Soconusco, where the natives plant the lemon trees very close together, for the purpose of making a hedge or fence, and, notwithstanding that the trees have not the necessary conditions of sunlight and air for their proper development, they grow very well. I do not know of any place in Mexico where lemons have been cultivated for commercial purposes ; but I am sure they could be made a very lucrative industry.

Limes and Shaddocks.—Lime trees prosper very well in Mexico, bearing large amounts of delicious fruit. I have not seen in the United States any of our limes, at least such as are imported here are not like ours, and I have no doubt that if known our limes would find a good market in this country. The lime should not be planted at an altitude exceeding 1000 feet. We grow also a very large kind of shaddock, which we call "toronja," and which is not imported in this country, but which if known here would find a good demand. It grows very luxuriantly and attains at times a very large size, even eight inches in diameter, having a very thick peel.

Bananas.—The banana thrives anywhere from the sea-level to an elevation of 5000 feet, and is one of the many Mexican fruits which yield to the planter an immense profit. The whole Mexican coast produces the banana spontaneously and in very great abundance. On the lands near the sea, at an elevation of 600 to 700 feet, large plantations of bananas can be started at a cost of five cents per plant, including all expenses. At the end of the first year, the plants begin to bear, and 1000 plants, which have cost $50, will produce $1000 as a minimum. The following year the yield is double that amount, and almost without expense. At the end of one year, the plant produces one bunch which is worth in the United States from 75 cents to $1 gold, the cost to the farmer being not more than 25 cents per bunch in Mexican currency. After the first year, the sprouts from the old plant grow up and give double the first year's yield.

There is perhaps no tropical plant easier of cultivation than the banana. The suckers having been planted out at the commencement of the rainy season, they will grow vigorously, and produce fruit in about a year. The land must be kept free from weeds, and an occasional turning up of the soil will prove beneficial. Before the plant throws out its flowering stem, suckers will make their appearance above the ground, and these will require careful attention. While the plant is young, all the suckers except one should be cut away, the best plan being to sever them with a sharp spade. Thus all the vigor of the plant is thrown into the fruiting of the first stem, and the growth of the one to supplant it, and, in this way, fine large bunches can be reckoned on. The second stem usually produces a finer bunch of fruit than the first, but, as the land becomes exhausted, the bunches of course decrease in size, and this shows the necessity for manure in some form or other.

Bananas are used extensively as shade for young coffee and cocoa trees, and in places where an export banana trade has been established, the formation of a cocoa plantation is a very inexpensive matter, as the return in fruit from the bananas will pay for the cultivation of the cocoa until the trees are able to give a small crop.

The important feature, and the one upon which the success and profit of the industry depend largely, is that of cheap and certain transportation facilities. That requisite is easily obtainable ; for instance, there are extensive and cheap lands for sale along the Tampico branch of the Mexican Central Railroad, from which the fruit can be shipped either all by rail, or by rail to Tampico, and thence by boat.

We have many kinds of bananas in Mexico, of different sizes, colors, and flavors, ranging in length from two to eighteen inches, and from one-half of an inch to three inches in diameter. The largest, which in some places are thought unfit for food, are in others, like Soconusco, considered the best ; very likely on account of their different quality. When roasted the latter are very juicy, and taste exactly as if they had been preserved in sugar. Some people on the coast live almost entirely on bananas, this fruit forming their principal food. The banana is likewise a tropical plant, and thrives best on the lowlands.

Pineapple.—The Toltecs and Aztecs knew how to cultivate the pineapple, and when the Spaniards conquered Mexico, they found the fruit in the markets of the towns on their way from Veracruz to the great Tenochtitlan. "From time immemorial," Sir Henry Dering says, "the pineapple has been cultivated in Amatlan, a town five miles south of Cordoba, from where the ancient Mexicans used to get their main supply." Now it is grown in tropical Hidalgo, Puebla, Veracruz, Tabasco, Chiapas, Oaxaca, Morelos, Guerrero, Michoacan, Colima, Jalisco, and Tepic. "Besides the fruit being very delicious and wholesome," Sir Henry Dering says, "a fine wine and vinegar are made of the juice. The leaf furnishes a fibre of extraordinary strength and fineness, making it even more valuable than the fruit. The fibre is made into ropes, cables, binding twine, thread, mats, bagging, hammocks, and paper. A pineapple rope three and a half inches thick can support nearly three tons. A textile fabric as fine and beautiful as silk is made of this fibre too. It is believed that the fine cloth of various colors used by the upper classes among the Aztecs was made of the pineapple fibre. The modern Mexicans do not manufacture it much now, except in the Isthmus, where the Zapotec Indians still make a cloth from it and from wild silk. One cause for its disuse is the slow and wasteful manner in which it is separated." Pineapples will grow at elevations of from 2000 to 3000 feet above the level of the sea, but the best and most delicate fruit is produced on the lowlands.

Cocoa-Nut.—We have in our lowlands near the sea many kinds of palms called corozo, bearing different kinds of fruit, growing in large bunches and the fruit very abundant, being in the shape of a small egg, very rich in oils, and making also a very good food, although it is hardly used now for any purpose. The palm tree bearing the cocoa-nut grows, of course, very luxuriantly, and does not require any care after it is once planted. The cocoa-nut prefers the sea-coast and high temperature. The saline breezes from the sea are very beneficial to it. I have not seen in Mexico the species of palm bearing the date, perhaps because it has not been planted there ; but I am sure that we could raise it, as we have several sections with a climate similar to that of Egypt and Asia Minor, where the date palm grows so well.

Mangos.—The mango is a very fine fruit, but requires a cultivated taste, and is generally disliked the first time it is eaten. It has a very large bone, although that is not the case in fine qualities, called Manilla mango, which has a very thin one and a great deal of pulp. The mango occasionally comes to the United States, but being a very frail fruit, has to be taken from the tree when very green. It does not ripen well, and, if taken when beginning to ripen, it reaches its destination in a decayed condition.

Alligator Pear.—The alligator pear is one of the most delicious fruits that we raise in Mexico, and is properly called vegetable butter, being a good substitute for butter. It is not eaten by itself ; the most usual way to eat it is in salad. We have several kinds and sizes of this fruit. The seed of the alligator pear is oval-shaped and quite large, about 4 inches in length by $1\frac{1}{2}$ in diameter, and of some oily substance, which, I have no doubt, has some good medicinal properties.

Mamey.—The same is the case with the seed of the mamey, a fruit unknown in the United States, having a red pulp, and a very large seed covered with a thin shell. The Indian women extract an oil from that seed and use it for their hair, and I think it must have many more useful medicinal properties.

A great many other of our fruits have seeds containing substances which I have no doubt will be found, when analyzed, to be very valuable to therapeutics.

Zapote.—The zapote is one of our tropical fruits which does not come to this country. I have just heard that the seeds of the zapote have recently been found by a Mexican doctor to be a very good narcotic, which does not produce the ill effects of the drugs now in use.

Papaya.—This fruit, which grows in our hot lands resembles the melon in shape, pulp, and seeds, but its color is of a yellowish-red. It was considered a very common fruit, but recently it was found to be a powerful digestive, and it is already used in Europe as a medicine under the name of Papaine.

Flowers.

Mexico is a favored country for flowers. They grow wild in a great many places, and they can be raised at very little cost, as there is no need of hot-houses or any other expensive appliance to cultivate them. The Indians in the small towns around the City of Mexico make a business of raising flowers, and they sell handsome bouquets, as artistically made as any in this country, for a mere trifle. A bouquet which, for instance, in New York would cost $5 in winter, could be had in the City of Mexico all the year round for 25 cents ; and I look forward to the time when flowers will be exported in large quantities from Mexico to the United States if the protective policy of the country does not interfere.

IRRIGATION.

At the time of the Spanish invasion of Mexico, the Indians in those parts of the country where the population was greatest were dependent upon irrigation for a large part of their cereals, and for cotton, which played so important a part in their economy. As the same method had been employed from time immemorial in Spain, it followed that on the partition of the soil among the Spanish conquerors, irrigation became an important factor in their agriculture ; but with expansion of population large tracts of land have come to depend entirely upon the rain.

In recent years Mexican agriculture has depended almost altogether on the rainfall, except in a few places well supplied with water, and where irrigation is both cheap and easy ; but the inhabited portions of the country have been depleted of their timber by the natives for the purpose of using the wood for fuel or lumber. In more recent years, the building of railroads has increased considerably the demand for wood both for sleepers and for fuel for locomotives, and the consequence is that a great change is taking place in the climatic conditions of the country and that fuel is exceedingly high. In no other country is there so much timber—a good deal of it not yet full grown—consumed annually as in Mexico. The consumption of timber for railroad purposes alone, not to mention that used in mines, smelters, and as fuel in cities and towns, is incalculable.

Competent authority in Mexico, among whom is the Inspector of Manufactories, created for the purpose of insuring the collection of the internal-revenue tax, considers that only in the Federal District of Mexico the consumption of wood exceeds 4000 English cords daily, used as fuel in the factories, railroads, and other plants of that city.

The consumption of charcoal by private families in the old-style open cooking grates is at least 500,000 pounds in the Federal District of Mexico, which is equivalent to 2,500,000 pounds of wood taken from the scanty forests of the central plateau, and that consumption would be very much reduced if, instead of those old-fashioned grates, iron cooking stoves should be used ; and to encourage their use, when I was last in the Treasury Department of Mexico, I was instrumental in reducing considerably the duties on the same.

Another cause of the destruction of the forest in Mexico consists in the primitive way in which the Indians raise their crops. They own in common a large tract of land, and they begin to till near their towns, commencing by destroying the forests and planting every year in a different locality, because, more especially in the lowlands, the vegetation springs up so rank after the first year's crop that it is very difficult to keep the ground clear of weeds. In this way they clear new land every year, going farther and farther from their town, until sometimes their crops are raised at a distance of as much as thirty or forty miles from their homes. The natural result is the destruction of the forests around the towns and at some considerable distance from the same, and consequently the diminution of the rainfall. I was greatly struck, on my last visit to Mexico, in 1896, by the scantiness of water at an Indian town called San Bernardino, in the sierra district, about five miles north of Teotitlan, the county seat of the district, which I had visited in November, 1855, and found then exceedingly abundant in rainfall and consequently in water, as well as all the mountains north of that place, which extend for about eighty miles to the lowlands on the Gulf of Mexico. On my recent visit, however, I found a great scarcity of water : a small stream of probably not more than one-half an inch in diameter, carried in very primitive wooden troughs, was all the water the town had, and that only during the rainy season, the people being obliged to go a considerable distance for water in the dry season ; this being only one illustration of what the destruction of the woods is doing in Mexico.

The city of Oaxaca, at the foot of the Sierra, used to be, in my young days, very well supplied with water, using for that purpose several streams coming from the mountains ; but during the last dry season the scarcity of water has been such as to cause a real water famine.

The diminution of the rains, together with other atmospheric phenomena, which takes place from time to time, produces in some years drought that prevents the crops from being raised ; as the country produces at present only the corn necessary for its consumption, which cannot be kept from year to year on account of its being eaten by insects. This diminution was very disastrous before the railroad era, causing serious famines. Since the railways were built, we import in such years corn from the United States, spending several millions of dollars in providing ourselves with that staple. All that will be changed, and we shall be able to produce cereals enough not only for home consumption, but even for export, when we begin to use irrigation. The configuration of the country allows dams that will retain sufficient water both for irrigation and manufacturing purposes, to be built at comparatively little expense.

Large tracts of land in Western Asia, Northern Africa, and Southern Europe—countries which, according to historians, were once densely populated and gardens of the world—are now uninhabited and barren wildernesses ; and this has been brought about by the wholesale destruction of the forests and the absence of any law to protect them and provide for their replanting.   In the United States it has been seen that not only does the decrease of the forest area lessen the rainfall, but also the fall of snow in the winter months, the consequence being a marked decrease in the supply of water for irrigation purposes from the streams and rivers dependent for their supply on the snowy mountain tops.

Along the Mississippi River it is a common observation of the river pilots and old steamship hands that the summers are becoming more and more dry and the streams smaller, and that the big river itself has shown a marked decrease of " navigability " every year during the past twenty years.   All this is caused by the indiscriminate chopping down of the forests at the head of the principal tributaries of the big river. Statistics from Russia, Germany, Spain, Italy, Palestine, Australia, and India all prove beyond a doubt that the protection of the forests is a matter of vital importance.

Mexico is not only suffering from an annual decrease in rainfall, owing to the continual decrease in the timber-bearing area, the rainfall being more and more unequal every year during the past twenty years but the winters are becoming more and more severe, and the frosts are reaching farther and farther south each year.   This is undoubtedly due to the wholesale destruction of timber now going on throughout that Republic.

The Government can cope with this matter only by legislation, and having before it the example of the rest of the world, the Mexican Government should act without delay and in a manner that would benefit, not only the present, but also future generations ; and I understand it has been studying the advisability of prohibiting the use of wood for the locomotives and sleepers.   Experience has shown that in tropical countries iron sleepers last much longer, and are, on the whole, cheaper than wooden ones, and our supply of coal will soon be ample enough to furnish all the fuel necessary for the railway and mining industries.

One of the most profitable investments for capital in the near future will undoubtedly be the construction of reservoirs in the mountains, dams in the rivers, artesian-well boring, the erection of pumping machinery on a large scale, together with the introduction of modern devices and appliances that will facilitate the successful cultivation of the soil and assure crops of all descriptions in all parts of the country where it has been proved that irrigation must be resorted to.   Not only are these requirements essential for the conservation of water for irrigation purposes, but many large cities throughout the Republic are without any certain water supply ; and many that have a sufficient supply show by their death-rates that that supply is bad, and during the greater part of the year is the cause of wide-spread disease.

Again, much is to be gained by the use of these waters for the generating of power for the use of factories, mines, electric lighting, railways, and street cars, even should one hundred miles or more intervene between the generating plant and the machinery it is proposed to apply to it.

It seems marvellous that the Mexico of to-day—presenting, as it does, more natural resources, a greater variety of climate, cheaper labor, and better facilities for the construction of dams, reservoirs, canals, etc., than almost any other country—should be so far behind the times in a matter that has become an absolute necessity before the greater portion of its area can be thoroughly populated. The great increase in value of a piece of land after it is irrigated ought to be inducement enough for capital to be invested in such works. Competent engineers contend that Mexico, owing to its topographical and geological features, will be found to present most favorable conditions for the construction of reservoirs, dams, gravitation canals, the erection of pumping plants driven by wind, steam, gasoline, electricity, or even water power, and also for the cutting off and bringing to the surface of the underflowing waters, which are known to exist in greater abundance there than elsewhere on the face of the globe, as nature has been very prodigal to it in these respects.

Irrigation in arid countries is the corner-stone of civilization, and, to make a country self-sustaining, agriculture should be the first aim of its inhabitants. Agriculture must come first ; manufacturing and mining cannot thrive until the food supply is forthcoming.

With the extension of railway lines and the notable impulse given to agricultural enterprise within the last twenty years, Mexican landowners have improved more and more upon the earlier methods, and have, to an increasing extent, applied the principles of engineering science to the methodical cultivation of the large tracts into which their holdings are usually divided.

The Nazas Irrigation.—Some notice of an irrigation enterprise in Mexico will show how much we are now doing in this line.

The great plan of northern Mexico embraces nearly the whole of the States of Chihuahua and Coahuila, being bounded east and west by the sierras of the Pacific and Gulf coasts respectively. It consists of two watersheds,—that of the Rio Grande to the north, and the the so-called desert of the Bolson of Mapimi in the south. It is about four hundred miles wide by six hundred long, and maintains a general level of about four thousand feet above the sea, although much broken by local mountain ranges. The Bolson of Mapimi has much the same formation as the basin of the Great Salt Lake.

It receives the drainage of all the eastern slopes of the Durango sierras and the western slopes of the Coahuila ranges, but possesses no outlet. As a consequence, throughout its whole area, the rivers run into broad, shallow lakes, whence the waters are gradually lost by evaporation during the dry season. Of these rivers, the largest is the Nazas, which has a course of nearly three hundred miles from its source to where it is dispersed over the shallows, called on modern maps Lake Mayran. Sixty or seventy years ago the Nazas discharged its waters into a series of extensive lagoons, occupying what is now the fertile Laguna district of Durango and Coahuila.

At that time a phenomenal and long-continued rainfall so over-charged the, then, bed of the Nazas as to cause it to open a new course, and leave the Cayman lagoons thirty miles on one side. In the course of years these lagoons were converted into a mesquite wilderness, almost dead level, and composed of a deposit of the finest detritus, of unknown depth. The central depression of this lake-bed filled a broad valley running north and south, and surrounded by a parallelogram of mountains. The area thus comprised was about two hundred and ten square miles of pure vegetable loam, locally known as the Lake of Tlahualilo. This cuenca, or bowl, was the spot chosen about six years ago for the establishment of the great irrigation enterprise.

The problems involved called for courage and high administrative qualities, as well as technical engineering knowledge. It had early developed that the lands left dry by the changed course of the river were of extraordinary fertility, and half a century ago these tracts, immediately adjacent to the river, had been taken up and brought under irrigation after the rough methods then practised. The result was that, by 1890, about 250,000 acres of this land were under ditch, and the region was producing the greatest part of the cotton grown in Mexico, as well as heavy crops of corn and wheat. The Tlahualilo basin was known to be the richest portion of this district, but the thirty miles of sun-baked desert separating it from the present course of the river presented an obstacle to utilization which proved too formidable for the cultivators of the Laguna country. In 1889 a project was formulated for carrying a ditch across the intervening desert to the head of the Tlahualilo cuenca, and converting the whole of the latter area into a huge hacienda.

Preliminary survey showed that the lowest level of the basin to be irrigated was about 100 feet below the point on the river Nazas which it was proposed to dam; that the main canal, on account of topographical conditions, would require a development of 39 miles; and that the slope of the lands within the basin was such that about 175 square miles out of the 210 composing the basin could be advantageously irrigated. A company was formed to undertake the work.

A dam of piles and riprap was thrown across the river at a point where it is about 1500 feet wide at flood. From this dam the line of the main canal was traced to the entrance of the Tlahualilo,—a distance of 39 miles. The canal terminated in a distributing tank at the entrance to the irrigable area, whence it bifurcated, one arm being carried along the western side of the basin.

The rainfall in the Bolson of Mapimi is confined to a few days of heavy showers about the beginning of June and the beginning of December. But up in the mountains of Durango, where the Nazas takes its rise, the rainfall at the same season is very heavy and protracted, resulting in high water in the river, which lasts for several weeks at a time. It is during these freshets that the cultivated lands in the Nazas district are irrigated. For the rest of the year they receive no water, except from occasional brief showers. In the Tlahualilo basin, a week or ten days of irrigation is all that is needed in the course of a year, the water soaking easily and quickly through the almost impalpable silt, and the hot sun forming a protecting crust which checks evaporation, and retains the moisture in the subsoil for a surprisingly long time. In fact, owing to their long roots, the cotton plants strictly require irrigation only once every other year, but corn and wheat, of course, must receive it at each planting. The distribution of the waters is regulated by government schedule, each property on the river being allotted its proportion of water, according to priority of settlement. Each canal on the river is permitted to take as many irrigations as it desires during the season of high waters, but in strict rotation. That is, after a property has taken one quota, it cannot repeat the process until all the others have taken theirs, when its second quota is available. Where another property, as often happens, does not care to use all the water to which it is entitled, its further allotments may be used by its neighbor. The waters, on leaving the river, are heavily charged with sediment largely volcanic in its origin, and this is deposited on the lands at each flooding in the shape of extremely fine mud.

Six years of experience with this property demonstrates the fact that irrigation, when applied to fertile land under a carefully planned and thoroughly executed system, where the water supply is owned by the user, puts agriculture among the least dubious of industries. The system adopted by the Tlahualilo Company is especially worthy of attention, because of the notable unity of plan pursued from the inception of the enterprise to its fullest development, and of its resultant economies. It was on this property that a disastrous experiment of colonization from Alabama took place in the year 1896, when hundreds of negroes were taken from Alabama and other points of the southern portion of the United States under the supposition that they could withstand the down-pour of the tropical sun of Mexico, and by their knowledge of the cultivation of cotton succeed in carrying out the purpose of the men who undertook the enterprise. Unused to food conditions in Mexico, especially for want of bacon and corn bread, they were infested with sickness, which caused great mortality among them, and frightened and demoralized they fled from Tlahualilo, this experiment showing very plainly that Mexican planters cannot rely for labor on the colored people of the United States.

The production of cotton and corn in the vicinity of Torreon can be increased eightfold by building reservoirs in the Nazas River and its tributary cañons, to hold the water back for the irrigation of the vast area of fine cotton and corn lands that are yet unproductive, simply through the non-retention of the great amount of water flowing to the sea, unused, annually, and the same result could be obtained by doing the same thing with many other rivers in Mexico. With one-fourth of the water now needed to produce a good crop, the same amount of grain can be produced by good cultivation. The reason is that by the methods now in vogue in most parts of the country, so little soil is loosened by the plow that nearly all the water runs off, where rain is relied on, and only with a great amount of rain can a crop be raised. When irrigation is used, the water required to keep the hard ground moist is entirely in excess of the reservoir, rain, and river supplies. This is the reason of the short grain supply and of the necessity for importing during years of drought large quantities of corn. If the ground were plowed deep and well, it would absorb most of the rainfall and create sufficient surface moisture to meet the moisture from below, which would counteract the dry action of the atmosphere on the soil and roots of the grain, which, by its luxuriant growth, would soon shade the ground, and thus contribute still further to the retention of moisture.

The fact is, taking Mexico as a whole, that there is not a year so dry but that with good cultivation, sufficient grain can be raised to supply domestic demands, while all the excess above that quantity in favorable seasons should be used as feed for stock, which would supply the large quantities of lard, tallow, hard-oil, etc., now being imported, and would leave a large amount for export, together with a consider-able quantity of meat for the same purpose, thus helping to cover the balance of foreign trade and keeping our silver dollars in the hands of the farmers and stockmen, to improve and increase their lands, herds, and flocks.   .

FAUNA.

The present Mexican fauna belongs, like its flora, to the North American zone, so far as regards the plateau regions, and to the An-tilles in respect to the coast lands round the Gulf, while that of the

Pacific seaboard is intermediate between the Californian and South American. In the general aspect of its terrestrial animals, Mexico is connected more with the United States, whereas in its marine forms the reverse movement has taken place. Thus the prevailing species in the Gulf of Mexico as far as Tamaulipas and Texas, and the Pacific coast northwards to Sonora and Lower California, have migrated from South America. The species in the two oceanic basins differ almost completely; and, despite the proximity of the Pacific and Atlantic shores, their shells are quite distinct.

The fauna includes three species of large felidæ, the puma or American lion, jaguar, and ocelot; among the smaller is the wildcat. Wolves are common in the northern States, and also the coyote; besides which there are bears, wild boars, and bisons. A species of sloth is found in the southern forests, with five varieties of monkeys. Of the other wild animals the principal are hares, rabbits, squirrels, two or three kinds of deer, beavers, moles, martens, and otters.

All the domestic animals introduced by the early Spanish settlers have multiplied prodigiously. The horses, though small, retain the spirit and graceful form of the Andalusian or Arabian stock, from which they mainly sprang.

The waters of the estuaries and coast streams teem with fishes, all the numerous varieties of which differ on the two oceanic slopes, but still present a certain analogy in their general distribution. Turtles are taken in considerable numbers on the coast, and the *carey*, or turtle-shell, of Yucatan and Guerrero is the object of a trade valued at $20,000 yearly.

The ophidians are represented by a few boas in the southern forests, and several species of snakes, some extremely venomous, as the rattle and coral snakes. The largest lizard is the iguana, whose flesh is by some of the natives used as food. Noxious insects infest the hot regions in myriads; alacranes, or scorpions, in two different varieties, are everywhere feared, and many children were every year killed by their sting in the city of Durango before the proper antidote was found and used. Scolopendras, gigantic spiders, tarantulas, and mosquitoes abound.

Bees are numerous and their wax is an article of export, and the silkworm, though comparatively neglected, yields an annual profit of some importance. The birds of prey are eagles, hawks, and zopilotes, or turkey-buzzards, the scavengers of the coast towns, with three or four species of owls. Domestic fowl are extremely abundant. The parrots, humming-birds, trogons, and so forth, vie in richness of plumage with those of Brazil, and the Mexican songsters, the prince of which is the zenzontle, or mocking-bird, are unequalled by those of any other country.

Of all the Mexican fauna, two only have been domesticated : the huahulotl (*Meleagris Mexicana*), which is a species of duck, and the turkey, introduced into Europe by the Spaniards from the West Indies, hence by the French called "coq d'Inde." The techichi, an edible dumb dog, was soon exterminated when taxed by the Spanish authorities. The other farmyard animals have all been introduced into Mexico by the conquerors.

In the Gulf of California, and especially near La Paz, and the neighboring archipelagoes, extensive beds of pearl oysters are fished. Some other islands in the same gulf are frequented by myriads of various species of aquatic birds, and have already yielded many hundred cargoes of guano.

It is noteworthy that the Pacific islands, lying at some distance from the coast, have all a fauna different from that of the mainland. Thus the little Tres Marias group, about sixty miles off the coast of Jalisco, has a special species of humming-bird. The Revillagigedo Archipelago also forms a separate zoölogical zone, and the island of Guadalupe, over one hundred and fifty miles distant from Lower California, has eleven species of land birds, every one of which differs from the corresponding species on the adjacent continent.

ETHNOLOGY.

Mexico is inhabited by native Indians found there during the Spanish conquest, by descendants of the conquerors of Mexico and other European races, and by a mixture of the two. There are so few inhabitants of African descent that it is hardly worth while speaking of them. The proportion of this population is about as follows : Of European descent, 19 per cent. ; native Indians, 43 per cent. ; mixed races, 38 per cent.

Mexican Indians.—The native Indians found by the Spaniards belong to several nations and tribes, having different features and entirely distinct languages. The principal of these tribes are the following, some of which are now extinct :

Otomi,	Apache,	Tarahumara,
Chichimec,	Irritilas,	Tepehuan,
Huaxtec,	Tamaulioecs,	Sabaibos,
Totonac,	Zacotec,	Acaxee,
Mixtec,	Huastec,	Xixime,
Zapotec,	Zoqué,	Concho,
Mahuas,	Opata,	Manosprietas,
Toltec,	Guaicuri,	Comanche,
Olmecs,	Yaqui,	Cuachichils,
Xicalancs,	Mayo,	Tarascos,
Tula,	Seri,	Mixé.

These tribes have been classified in the following families :

Mexican Family ;	Totonaca Family ;
Sonorense Opata-Pima Family ;	Mixteco-Zapoteca Family ;
Guaicura y Cochimi Laimon Family ;	Matlalzinga ó Pirinda Family ;
	Maya-Quiche Family ;
Seri Family ;	Chontal Family :
Tarasco Family ;	Huave Family ;
Zoque-Mixé Family ;	Apache Family ;

Otomi Family.

There is a great deal of similarity between the Mexican Indians and the Malay Asiatic races—especially the Japanese branch—which gives foundation to the idea that the aborigines of Mexico originally came from Asia, or *vice versa.*[1] Their intensely black hair and eyes, their brown or yellow color, their small stature and the slight obliquity

[1] The following extracts from the San Francisco, Cal., *Bulletin* of June 7, 1897, confirm my views on the subject :

" Information is received from Australia concerning the reports of F. W. Christian of the Polynesian Society, who has returned to Sydney after an extended tour of the islands of the South Seas, the Caroline group especially, where he has been on a successful search for ethnological specimens. These reports are of great importance to the scientific world and are said to let much light on a vexed question which has puzzled the most learned savants for years. Mr. Christian has discovered extensive traces of the Chinese and Japanese in the islands of the Pacific, and claims to have discovered evidence pointing to the existence of a civilization of nearly two thousand years ago, which is linked with the ancient civilization in Central America, and will probably explain the origin of the Aztec races.

" Under the auspices of the Polynesian Society, according to advices from Sydney, *via* Honolulu, received per *Coptic* yesterday, Mr. Christian worked. The gentleman spent nearly two years looking for traces of the Chinese in the islands, and was lucky enough to find ancient records, specimens of handiwork and weapons which proved that Asiatic races were extensive traders among the South Sea group thousands of years ago. Evidence of a very decisive nature was secured which shows that a large trade was carried on *via* the islands of the Caroline group, between China and Central America, and that the ancient Chinese were more inclined to emigrate than their latter-day brethren and colonized extensively.

" Extensive inquiries were made as to the traditions of the islanders, and many discoveries were made concerning the early history of the Malays with regard to navigation, all proving that the Torres strait's route to the Pacific was not taken, but that voyages were made to many of the Caroline islands.

" The coincidence is a strange one that a despatch from Hermosillo, Mexico, dated June 6th, reports that a rock recently discovered in the mountains of Magdalena district, State of Sonora, which is covered with Chinese inscriptions, has just been visited by Sen Yup, a well-educated Chinese of Guaymas. He says the inscriptions are Chinese, but are somewhat indistinct. He made a copy of them, and has translated enough of the lines to show that the writing was probably inscribed on the rock at least two thousand years ago."

of their eyes, are features common to the Mexican Indians and the Japanese. When I first came to Washington, at the end of 1859, not having been out of Mexico before, I retained very vivid recollections of the Mexican Indians, with whom I had been somewhat closely associated ; and shortly afterwards the first Japanese Embassy came to this country and was received in a very solemn manner by Mr. Buchanan, then President of the United States. The Embassy consisted of about forty persons altogether, comprising ministers, secretaries, interpreters, servants, etc., and were dressed in their national gala costumes, not having yet adopted the European one. The Diplomatic Corps having been invited to the reception, I attended as a member of the same, and was greatly struck by the remarkable similarity which I found between the Japanese members of the Embassy and the Mexican Indians, whom I had just left. It seemed to me that had I collected at random forty Mexican Indians and dressed them in the same gorgeous costumes that the Japanese wore, nobody could have detected the difference.

Some of the Indian languages seem to me to resemble strongly the Oriental ones, though of course I cannot speak with authority, as I do not know any of those languages and have heard only the Chinese, Japanese, and Korean spoken ; but I am sure that if any educated and intelligent Chinese should go to Mexico and spend some time among the Indians, he would find traces in the language which would contribute greatly to clear up this problem. Mr. Tateno, a former Japanese Minister, who visited Mexico, found, during his short stay in that country, several words that are used in Japan and that have the same meaning in both countries. I am aware that Señor Pimentel, a very learned philologist, who made a special study of the languages of the Mexican Indians, finds no similarity at all between them and the Chinese or other Oriental languages ; and that even the Otomi language, which is monosyllabic, he finds to have no similarity to the Chinese. But, notwithstanding that great authority, I believe that the aborigines of both continents, that is, Asiatic and American, were originally of the same race, and that there must be some relationship between their respective languages.

The Indians of the different tribes do not generally mix with one another, but intermarry among themselves, and this fact contributes largely to their physical decay, and makes very difficult, at least for some time to come, the complete assimilation of all the Mexican population.

The Mexican Indians are on the whole a hard-working, sober, moral, and enduring race, and when educated they produce very distinguished men. Some of our most prominent public men in Mexico, like Juarez as a statesman, and Morelos as a soldier, were pure-blooded

Indians,[1] and fortunately there is no prejudice against their race in Mexico, and so when they are educated they are accepted in marriage among the highest families of pure Spanish blood.[2]

I have been a great deal among them, and my knowledge of their characteristics only increases my sympathy and admiration for them. In the State of Oaxaca, for instance, where I spent the early years of my life, I have seen Indians from the mountain districts, who, when they had to go to the capital, especially to carry money, would form parties of eight or ten to make a ten days' round trip, carrying with them their food, which consists of roasted ground corn, which they take three times a day ; stopping at a brook to mix it with water, and

[1] Sir William Hingston, President of the Surgery Section in the Second Pan-American Medical Congress, held at the City of Mexico in October, 1896, in an interview which was published by *The Gazette* of Montreal, Canada, of December 2, 1896, said, concerning his visit to Mexico, among other things :

" The pure-blooded Indian was seen on all sides. . . .

" The Spaniards would seem to have pursued the same course as was followed by the original French settlers, *they did not shove aside the native Indians as useless lumber, to be gotten out of the way*, as a distinguished Harvard professor puts it, but they treated them as people in possession of the soil, with whom it was not only right but proper to ally in marriage. I have always regarded our North American Indian as the best type of the aborigines in stature. I still believe he is, but not so in intellect. The broad, massive forehead of the native of Mexico, and his soft but prominent and intelligent eye, are evidences of mental power. . . ."

[2] I take from a spicy article published by Mr. Charles Dudley Warner, in *Harper's Magazine* for June, 1896, the following description of the dress of the poorer classes in Mexico :

" Herbert Spencer might extend here his comments on the relation of color to sex. It is the theory that all the males of birds have gay plumage in order to make them attractive to the other sex, while the females go in sober colors. This is also supposed to hold true of barbarous nations. The men who dress at all, or use paint as a substitute, wear bright colors and more ornaments than the women, while the gentle sex is content to be inconspicuous. Needless to say that in what we call civilization, this rule is reversed. The men affect plain raiment, while the women vie with the tropical birds of the male gender. Tried by this test Mexico has not reached the civilization of the United States. The women of the lower orders are uniformly sober in apparel, and commonly wear drawn over the head a reboso in plain colors. The scant dress is usually brown or pale blue. It is the men who are resplendent, even the poorest and the beggars. The tall conical hats give to all of them an " operatic " distinction ; the lower integuments may be white (originally) as also the shirt and the jacket ; or the man may have marvellous trousers, slit down the sides and flapping about so as to show his drawers, or sometimes, in the better class, fastened down with silver buttons ; but every man of them slings over his left shoulder or wraps about him, drawing it about his mouth on the least chill in the air, a brilliantly colored sarape, or blanket, frequently of bright red. Even if he appears in white cotton, he is apt to wear a red scarf round his waist; and if he is of a higher grade, he has the taste of a New York alderman for a cravat. This variety and intensity of color in the dress of the men gives great animation and picturesqueness to any crowd in the streets, and lights up all the dusty highways."

sleeping on the bare ground, preferring always the open air; getting up before daylight and starting on their journey at daybreak immediately after their early meal, speaking no Spanish and travelling about forty miles a day. When they reached the city of Oaxaca, they would remain there one or two days, and go back to their homes without taking part in any dissipation. They prefer to live in the high, cool localities, and they have their patch of ground to raise corn and a few vegetables in the hot lowlands, sometimes thirty miles away from their homes, and carry their crops on their backs for all that distance. They make very good soldiers, and military leaders have used them to great advantage during our revolutions.

Professor Starr's theory that we are all on this Continent assuming the type of the Indian, is, in a measure, true. It is nothing new, for it was already indicated by an English physician travelling in the British colonies before the United States were thought of.

The great task of the Mexican Government is to educate our Indians and make them active citizens, consumers, and producers, elevating their condition. Before we think of spending money to encourage European immigration to Mexico, we ought to promote the education of our Indians, which I consider the principal public need of the country.

Increase of Mexican Population.—In the beginning of the century Baron Humboldt, who visited Mexico and studied very carefully the conditions of the country, thought that the Indian race, which was then very numerous, would continue to increase and would be the preponderant race of Mexico, as far as numbers were concerned, as it showed a large proportion in a census made in 1810 by Don Fernando Navarro y Noriega, and which appears in Baron Humboldt's *Political Essay of New Spain.* According to that census the population of Mexico was then divided as follows :

```
European and American Spaniards..........1,097,928
Indians....................................3,676,281
Mixed races or castes......................1,338,706
Secular ecclesiastics......................    4,229
Regular ecclesiastics......................    3,112
Nuns.......................................    2,098
                                           _____
              Total..............6,122,354
```

Including among the Europeans the ecclesiastics and nuns, the population was, according to that census :—

```
Europeans...................1,107,367 or 18 per cent.
Indians.....................3,676,281  "  60  "   "
Mixed races.................1,338,706  "  22  "   "
                          _____
       Total........6,122,354  " 100  "   "
```

In the census of 1875 the following results appear :—

European race and descen-
dants of the Spaniards......1,899,031 or 20 per cent.
Mixed race..................4,082,918 " 43 " "
Native Indian race..........3,513,208 " 37 " "

Total.........9,495,157 " 100 " "

The increase of population in the 65 years which elapsed between the two censuses mentioned, deducting from the census of 1810 the inhabitants of Texas, New Mexico, and Upper California, who had passed to the United States, numbering 58,338, was

Population of 1810........................6,064,016
Census of 1875...........................9,495,157

Increase of the population in the 65 years.....3,431,141

From the preceding data it appears that the European race nearly doubled its population in the space of 65 years, and at the rate of 1.1 per cent. of increase per year ; that the mixed race trebled it at the rate of 3.25 ; and that the native race diminished it at the rate of 0.058 per cent. per annum.

Families in Mexico are generally very large, often having ten or fifteen children. I remember how much surprise it caused in Washington, my stating in the presence of Señor Don Jacobo Blanco, the Mexican Commissioner in the late International Boundary Commission, who was recently here for a year finishing his office work and maps and preparing his report, that he was the twenty-fourth child in his family, his father having been twice married.

Decrease of the Indian Population.—It further appears that the Indian population has been decreasing since the beginning of the present century, notwithstanding the fact that the Indian race on the whole is very prolific.

The causes of the decrease of the Indian population in Mexico are various ; bad nourishment, insufficient shelter from the inclemency of the weather, wretched attendance in sickness, and many others, some of which I shall mention here, having contributed toward the degeneration and decline of the race.

The small-pox, owing to the carelessness or indolence of the parents in regard to vaccination, or their repugnance to it, causes deplorable ravages in this race, more especially among the individuals that live at any considerable distance from the cities.

Indian women, even when far advanced in pregnancy, do not abstain from hard labor, and, without any care for their coming offspring, continue grinding their corn until the moment of parturition. Then, before the proper time for taking the child from the breast, it is fed with food unsuitable for its age and difficult of digestion, which occasions diarrhœa or other maladies that either cause its death or at least contribute to its imperfect development.

Another circumstance which causes the degeneration of the Indians is their premature marriages. In Mexico the marriageable age for women has been fixed by law at eighteen years, and in the tierra caliente, or hot country, at fourteen ; but in some places Indian girls are married at twelve. Every Indian father considers it his duty to marry his children, whether boys or girls, as soon as they are of age, the parents of course making the match to suit themselves.

This used to be the case not only with the Indians, but even with persons of Spanish descent. I once heard General Degollado, a very good and prominent man in Mexico, say, that the day he married he took, immediately after the ceremony was over, his bean-shooter and went to shoot birds, because he had no conception of what he had done, his parents having arranged the match for him ; but he added that he could not possibly have made a better choice of a wife.

The Indians are strong by nature ; and in this is to be found the fact that so many of them reach an advanced age, in spite of their scant and poor food, their unhealthy mode of living, and their damp and unwholesome habitations, consisting of miserable huts where whole families are huddled together.

The Spaniards in Mexico.—The Spaniards are a money-making, wonderfully frugal race, since they have been battling with hard conditions at home for centuries. The Spaniard in Mexico is—as Richard Ford who spent thirty years in the peninsula, and who was a close observer, depicts him—a hardy, temperate man, well fitted, under favorable conditions, to become a dominant influence.

In Mexico, the energy of the Spaniard is remarkable. He is forceful of word and phrase, energetic in his movements, immensely vital, tremendously persistent, and wonderfully enduring. After thirty years behind a counter selling groceries, he retires, a man of fortune ; not always large, but sufficient, and is still a man of force and ready for undertakings demanding good brain power and courage. They come over mere lads, from ten to fifteen, toil and moil, feed frugally, and sleep hardly, and they become millionaires, bank directors, great mill owners, farmers on a grand scale, hot-country planters and monopolists, for the Spaniard is born with the " trust " idea ; while his sons are too often dudes and spendthrifts.

The thrifty Spaniard toils and saves, and his ambition is to marry a rich girl, frequently the daughter of a Mexican landowner, and so he lays the foundation for permanent wealth ; for everywhere, the world over, the man who gets the lands and holds on to them is the wealthy man. Speculators and financiers come and go like bubbles on a river, but the landed proprietor keeps a permanent clinch on humanity.

There is one check to the growth of Spanish influence in Mexico, and that is the climate. All Europeans, no matter what their nationality, become physically modified by residence in the new world ; and nowhere is the effect of climate more noticeable than in the tropics. The children of the Spanish residents are less energetic than the parents, and the third generation are altogether Creoles. Just as the Mexican of Spanish descent is, as a rule, less energetic, not so vascular, and less · vigorous than the Spaniard, so is the American less full-blooded and leaner than the Englishman. The change that takes place in the human organization, transplanted from the old world to the new, is a profound one.

English and Germans in Mexico.—The present century has seen many changes in the commercial world of Mexico ; the great English houses have almost all disappeared ; especially has this been marked in the dry-goods, or draper's business. The Germans, with superior economy, if with no more of enterprise, drove the English out of that profitable business, and in time themselves succumbed to the still closer methods of the Barcelonettes who gained a foothold in the business which they have successfully maintained. The dry-goods business in the Republic is largely in the hands of men who speak the French language. From the great houses of the capital go forth bright young men, trained to business habits who are established over branch concerns in the interior and coast towns. Their employers become their backers, and a close intimacy is maintained, to the mutual advantage of older and younger merchants.

Very few of the foreigners who settle in Mexico, and especially Spaniards, are educated, as most of them hardly know how to read and write. They very seldom become naturalized Mexicans, and almost always keep their allegiance to the country of their origin. That seemed natural when Mexico was in constant turmoil, and many of the foreigners going there expected to make large fortunes by means of diplomatic claims ; but that reason can hardly hold good now, when the country is at peace, and perfect security is extended to every inhabitant. If the foreigners continue keeping their old nationality when they become permanent settlers of Mexico, some changes may be necessary in the legislation of the country affecting their condition.

Americans in Mexico.—It will be very difficult for the fun-loving, self-indulgent, Anglo-Saxon Englishman of America to compete with these self-denying Spaniards, capable of living with the nose to the grindstone twenty, twenty-five, or thirty years, eating always sparingly, drinking wine, but in moderation, spending no money, dressing poorly, and ever with a fortune accumulating. The American wants to cut a dash and so does the Englishman, else the English would have maintained their commercial supremacy in Mexico. They lost it to the more frugal and economical Germans.

The American is a speculator, a dreamer of golden dreams ; he lives for the eyes of other people ; he is not capable of the patience that keeps a man tied to a desk or shop for half a lifetime, making a savings bank of himself.

Some Mexicans are afraid that a free influx of citizens from this country may Americanize it. This is true as to the means of transportation, the introduction of electric lights, improved hotel accomodations, and where similar improvements are concerned. But there is no doubt of the persistence of traditions and habits, and the influence of climate. It is difficult to introduce the American push and restlessness in business, and to overcome the habits formed in many centuries of letting the morrow take care of itself. There must be the mid-day siesta, and the number of working days is reduced by several feast days, saints' days, and holidays, besides the Sundays. There is no doubt that the productiveness of nature is an inducement to very leisurely labor, and the lack of any sharp division of seasons is a sort of moral discipline, as well as a stimulus to extra exertion in summer to prepare for winter. What must be the effect upon character when this stimulus is wanting? It is possible, of course, that industry will be stimulated by the inflow of settlers from the north, and that Mexico will take on new enterprise and productive vigor ; but I think it is easier for Americans in Mexico to fall into Mexican ways and Mexican moral views than it is to convert the Mexicans to the American view of life. I do not doubt that Mexico has a great industrial, agricultural, and manufacturing future, but I fancy that its power of absorption, like that of Egypt, is greater than its facility of adaptation.

Ruins.—We have in Mexico some of the most ancient and remarkable ruins, and although there are different surmises about the time at which they were built and the people who built them, nothing is known positively about them.

The principal ones are in Uxmaland and Chichen Itza in Yucatan Comalcalco in Tabasco, Teotihuacan and Cholula in Puebla and Tlaxcala, and Mitla in Oaxaca.

Uxmal.—Uxmal is not far from the city of Merida, the capital of the State of Yucatan, supposed to have been built by the Mayas, and different books have been written about them, especially one by Dr. Augustus Le Plongeon, a French savant, who passed many years in Yucatan, studying its magnificent ruins, and published in New York, in 1896, a book entitled *Queen Mod and the Egyptian Sphinx,* in which he contends that the empire of the Mayas, which had its seat at Yucatan, was the cradle of civilization, and that from there it went to India, Egypt, and finally to Greece and Western Europe.

Palenque.—Very likely the same Mayas built the large ruins which still exist in the district of Palenque in the State of Chiapas, and in some places in Guatemala.

Cholula.—The great pyramid of Cholula, made known to the scientific world by Humboldt, which is eight miles from Puebla, has been pictured and described. Its base is 1000 feet on each side, and it is built in two great terraces, the first being 71 feet, and the second 66 feet, in height. The top is 203 by 144 feet. So far as investigations have revealed, the great pyramid is artificial and is constructed of sun-dried brick.

Teotihuacan.—Teotihuacan, an ancient city lying twenty-five miles northeast of the City of Mexico, and occupying an area of about one and a half or two miles, contains some of the most remarkable series of ruins. To the north of the ruins is a truncated pyramid, rectangular in form, squared to the points of the compass, and known as the Pyramid of the Moon. South of it, at a distance of about 1300 yards, is another pyramid of similar form, known as the Pyramid of the Sun. Its perpendicular height is 223 feet, and its base measures about 735 feet from east to west. Both pyramids are united by a straight street, which starts from a circular plaza at the south side of the Pyramid of the Moon, and loses itself in the barranca south of the Pyramid of the Sun.

These colossal pyramids are regarded as among the most ancient monuments of Mexico, far antedating the civilization found by the Spaniards. They are wonderful illustrations of what perseverance and time will accomplish. Now even the means which the builders used for handling the immense blocks of volcanic stone with which they constructed is unknown. Other ruins, in the character of little mounds, are found scattered over the extensive plain in which the two pyramids are situated. The street or avenue which united the latter is called the "Road of the Dead." Along its entire length, parallel to it on both sides, there is a terrace constructed of cement, clay, and broken lava, faced with a coating of mortar or plaster, highly polished, and painted red and white. Desire Charnay removed the rubbish from one of the mounds on the side facing this road, and discovered what he calls a "palace," with two large halls and various small rooms. In 1886, Señor Don Leopoldo Batres made an excavation in one of the mounds, and found two polychrome frescos painted on the wall of the building which was laid bare. The question is naturally asked, how these monuments came to be covered? Was it by an earthquake, or by the hands of the builders themselves? Señor Batres inclines to the latter view, as he found the roofs of the houses perfectly preserved, while the interior of the rooms was in every case filled with stones neatly fitted into the spaces, and joined with a clayish cement to form a compact mass. His conclusion as to the pyramids is, that they are two great temples erected to two old Mexican divinities. Each pyramid consists of five terraces, which diminished in size until the height of 223 feet was reached. Each has on one of its sides a stairway six and one-half feet in width, which makes five zigzag turns, and leads to the sanctuary or shrine on the summit. The outer surface of the pyramids, and perhaps the interior as well, was plastered over with a mortar of lime, hard and smooth, and decorated with frescoes, representing quasi-historical events and scenes.

The small mounds scattered over the area occupied by the ruins were, according to Batres, dwellings and small shrines. Each contained from six to twelve rooms, quadrangular and rectangular in form. The cornices as well as the walls were beautifully ornamented in colors. On some as many as twenty tints had been used. The doors were rectangular, never trapezoidal in form, although the latter style has been erroneously attributed to ancient American architecture. They measure eight feet in height by about three feet in width. The houses had neither windows nor balconies. The city was crossed by subterranean aqueducts constructed of stone, the walls of which were plastered with firm and smooth mortar. Near the Pyramid of the Moon, among the rubbish, there was a monolithic statue of colossal dimensions. It represents a woman with a characteristic head-dress, and wearing a necklace of four strings of beads. Travellers in Teotihuacan can find countless miniature heads modelled in clay anywhere on the freshly-plowed stretches of level land that lies across the broad, straight Micoatl, or " Path of the Dead." They vary in length from one to two inches, and invariably have nothing more than a neck attached to them. They may be distinguished by this peculiarity from those that are applied as ornaments to terra cotta vases, and from fragments of "idols." The features and peculiar head-dresses that adorn these little heads of Teotihuacan vary greatly, and this diversity has given rise to, and been quoted in proof of, the migration of tribes, of the mixtures of widely differing races, or of their succession to each other in the occupation of the Valley of Mexico. Owing to the unfamiliar aspect of some of these head-dresses, it has been asserted that they could not be even "Toltec," but must be relics of still more remote and unknown races of men. Various uses have been assigned to them, the commonest supposition being that they were in some way associated with ceremonies relating to the dead. There is probably no subject connected with Mexican archæology, except the calendar, that has given rise to more discussion. Dr. E. B. Tylor regarded them as a puzzle, and Professor F. W. Putnam has spoken of them as the "riddle of the many heads." Desire Charnay saw in some of them Chinese and Japanese masks, and even types of the white race, proving in his opinion how many races must have been mingled or succeeded each other on this old continent.

Mitla.—About twenty miles east of the city of Oaxaca is an Indian town called Mitla, near which still remain the ruins of great edifices and palaces. The temples were built, it is supposed, by the ancient Zapotecas, and are the most interesting relics of the earlier civilizations of Mexico. The first description of these ruins was given by the Spanish priest, Burgoa, who accompanied the conquerors of Montezuma. The interior of the principal hall or room of the main palace is supposed to be the teocali of the high priest. The peculiar architecture and elaborate and grotesque decoration can easily be observed. It is astonishing to see the enormous size of the stones used in the walls of these temples. Professor Bickmore said that he had seen nothing to equal them except at Baalbec, in Syria. At Mitla are found some clay images, mostly miniature, doubtless of gods, but some of them no doubt portraits, and some of these bore a striking resemblance to the little heads found at the pyramids of the Sun and Moon in the Valley of Mexico ; that is, some of them had the slant Oriental eyes, and others Ethiopian features, very different from any races we now know in these regions. The ruined temples of Mitla are covered with stucco, which was painted Pompeiian red. There is a pyramid also at Mitla, and there are some elaborately wrought sepulchral chambers.

I borrow from Mr. Vivien Cory the following extracts of his description of the ruins of Mitla.

"There are four of these places ; the first is almost entirely destroyed, only some huge monolithic slabs supported horizontally upon tottering piles of broken stones remaining ; while everywhere amongst the ruins have sprung up the grass huts of the Mexican Indians, and of the fourth or one farthest from the hamlet nothing but indication of the site is left, upon which the Spaniards have reared a modern church. It is in the two palaces that lie between, each slightly raised above the surrounding country on a separate eminence, that the interest centres.

"One of these is in the form of a double Greek cross, its stem running north and south, and its arms extended east and west. In the centre is the large court, surrounded on all sides by rising ground and ruined mounds of stones : there are traces still remaining of the foundations, that speak of four apartments built upon these mounds to face the court, but of these those on the west and south sides have disappeared ; on the east side, only two colossal pillars and a portion of the walls remain, while to the north side the whole apartment forming the head of the cross has been spared and stands almost unharmed in its original beauty and richness. The façade of this apartment extends the whole length of the court, one hundred and forty-one feet, and its height is a little over fifteen feet : the material is freestone, the color a faint, dull, amber tint, soft as the light seen in the sky at evening. In the centre are three square portals and above these forming the head-piece to them all extends one long and narrow panel of carving, a high relief of the natural stone on a crimson ground. The whole façade is composed of a series of these panels, from the straight line of the foundation-stone to the straight line of the summit, nine panels being on each side of the entrance, arranged in three tiers, divided by horizontal bands of the natural stone. In some of the panels, the ground retains still a faint tint of its former rich vermillion, in others, all color has subsided into the soft neutral shade of the freestone. The designs are wonderfully rich and varied, thirteen different patterns being represented on this façade alone ; all these designs are remarkable for the straight lines in which they are executed and the absence of all curves. Throughout all the ruins, upon the walls of which appear twenty-three different models of carving, only two of these represent any curve in their design. In one of these two there is visible the form of the Arabic letter ' L ' placed horizontally, and in the other a double curve ' S,' possibly intended to represent or suggest the snake. With these exceptions the designs are of the Greek key pattern, variations on this, or parallelograms.

" Behind this façade is a narrow court, roofless as all the courts are, and empty, save for six colossal pillars standing at even distances down the centre, and giving to this chamber the name of Hall of the Monoliths. Each pillar is one solid stone, eleven feet high and eleven feet in circumference. A low stone passage leads from this chamber northward to the smallest and richest court of all, entering it at the southeast corner. There is comparatively little trace of the destructiveness of the elements or the iconoclasm of man here. The court and all the four chambers opening from it are perfect and singularly rich in carving. The court is perfectly square and the chambers are entered from it, each through one square doorway, the roof of which is formed by a huge monolith, thirteen feet long and with a richly carved face. Of these four lintels each has a separate design. Each of the four walls has six panels, the uppermost extending the whole length of the wall, two smaller panels being on either side of the entrance, and one long narrow one above it. Between the panels stand out in high relief the horizontal and vertical edges of the freestone, forming a symmetrical frame to each panel.

" Within the four chambers the walls are designed differently, the carving running simply and evenly round the entire room in three straight horizontal bands, each band possessing a separate pattern and being about three feet in width. Beneath these bands of carving was originally, evidently, a dado of vermillion stucco, of such fine and delicate quality that the smooth and polished surface resembles marble. Portions of this delicate stucco still adhere to the crumbling walls in places and are of various colors, scarlet, black and white. In some instances this stucco seems to have been plain, simply bearing a brilliant polish, in others, there remains distinctly traced in white upon a crimson ground, a wierd, fantastic, yet handsome design, the head ; half horse, half dragon, repeated in four inch squares. This latter ornamented stucco, however, does not appear except in the fourth palace, containing the Spanish church, where it is visible on the walls of one of the courts, now used as a stable for the padre's horse. Leaving the richest of the centre palaces, passing through a gap in the ruined wall on the south side, descending the elevation on which it is placed and ascending the opposite eminence, the patio of the second palace is reached. This is almost wholly in ruins ; three of the façades that face the court remain indeed, but the great smooth slabs with which the walls were faced have been torn away at the base, and most of the beautiful panels of carving stripped from the front. Yet it is in this ruined palace that one lingers longest and to which one's feet return, drawn by an irrisistible fascination ; for this palace contains the tomb and the pillar of death.

" This subterranean vault is called by general consent a sepulchre, but there is no line of history, no record, no tradition even, left to explain to us its origin and use. It may have been a torture-chamber, sacrificial hall, or tomb. The excavation is but a little below the surface of the court, now carried down so deeply that the light is wholly excluded. From the entrance there is enough to fill the interior with a sad, gray twilight. The vault is in the form of a simple cross lying north and south ; its walls are massive and heavily decorated with panels of carving let into their sides, while it is roofed by enormous monolithic slabs that reach from wall to wall. In the centre of the cross, just where by descending a few steps one enters the tomb, stands the pillar of death, round which, the Indians say, should a man clasp his arms he must shortly afterwards die. Does not this very tradition, handed down perhaps through the long file of countless years, seem to indicate that this pillar was some ancient stone of sacrifice to which human victims were bound or chained, and from which death alone released them ? As one gazes at the massive column, that one man's arms alone could not entirely encircle, the eye notices an indentation round the base where the column sinks into the floor. The stone is corroded and worn away as by the long friction of ropes or chains.

" Most of the panels do not consist of actual carving, though they produce that effect at a few yards' distance ; they are formed in reality by small slabs of the freestone cut perfectly square and inserted edgeways into the wall, the remaining edges standing out at various distances from it and thus forming the different designs. This, although a work of infinite patience, does not necessarily presuppose a high stage of civilization, no instrument sharper than hard stone being required to cut the slabs of soft freestone ; and that only a stone instrument was employed by the workers seems indicated by the fact that, in the large panels where the stone is actually carved, the edges are not sharp, but rounded, as if made with a blunt tool. The effect of the panels of inserted squares of stone, however simply produced, is that of the most finished and clear-cut carving and the designs themselves are rich and elaborate. There is no crudity, no harshness in them, no suggestion of the primitive savage's scratching on his native rock ; but rather that of Greek work on some Athenian temple. The patterns have a complicated elegance and distinction of line that can only be produced by a people of cultivated mind and eye.

" Evidence, too, of what high grade of civilization in some ways at least they must have arrived at, lies in the gigantic stones that they have placed as lintels over their doorways and which in their immense weight and bulk have defied the greed or rage of all the succeeding races to remove or destroy. The mystery here is the Egyptian mystery of the Pyramids ; that these enormous blocks of stone are resting here in positions and elevations where it would require all the modern knowledge of mechanics, engineering skill, and mechanical appliances to place them ; and, as in Egypt, so here the mystery will never be solved, as the builders have passed hence and left no clue. The solid stone rests there upon its supporting pillars before the eye as it has rested for a thousand years, but how the perished hands lifted and placed it there remains its own inviolable secret.

" Leaving the palace court by the south side and following the road to the dry and stony bed of a wide river, if one turns aside here a little to the eastward he finds himself facing a Zapotecan mound, a solid base composed of earth and stones, in which are visible at intervals large slabs of cement, portions of terraces and tiers that originally formed its sides. Ascending this, from the summit one can overlook the whole valley."

LANGUAGES.

About one hundred and fifty different Indian languages are known to have been spoken by the Mexican Indians. The Spanish monks accompanying the conquerors and who went to the country soon afterwards compiled grammars and even dictionaries of some of these languages; but the Indians falling into a semi-barbarous state after the conquest, having lost their civilization and literature, their languages have either disappeared completely or become very primitive. and it is ascertained that some of them have become entirely extinct.

The Spanish is, of course, the language of the country and most of the Indians speak it, although very imperfectly and incorrectly; only a small portion of them speaking no language but their own.

The chief languages spoken in Mexico proper, excluding Chiapas and Yucatan, are as follows :

Nahuatl or Mexican (Aztec) with Acaxee, Sabaibo, Xixime, Cochimi, Concho and other members of the same family.

Seri, Upanguaima, and Guaima.

Papago, Opata, Yaqui, Mayo, Tarahumara, Tepehuan, Cora, etc.

Apache or Yavipai, Navajo, Mescalero, Llanero Lipan, etc.

Otomi or Hia-hiu, Pame, Mazahua, etc.

Huaxtec, Totonac.

Tarascan, Matlaltzincan.

Mixtec, Zopotec, Mixé, Zoqué, Chinantec.

Señor Don Manuel Orosco y Berra wrote a treatise on the language of the Indian tribes in Mexico entitled " Geography of Languages," which describes the languages of the races who inhabited Mexico, and Señor Don Francisco Pimentel enlarged upon that work, making philological comparisons, and from the data collected by both authors Señor Don Antonio Garcia Cubas a distinguished Mexican geographer made the following synopsis of the Indian languages spoken in Mexico.

SYNOPSIS OF THE INDIAN LANGUAGES OF MEXICO, FORMED ACCORD-
ING TO THE CLASSIFICATION OF DON FRANCISCO PIMENTEL.

NOTE.—The sign * indicates that the classification is doubtful.

GROUPS.	FAMILIES.	LANGUAGES.	DIALECTS.
		1st Order.—Languages polysyllabic, polysynthetic of sub-flexion.	
MEXICAN-OPATA.	I. MEXICAN.	1. Mexican, Nahuatl or Azteca................. *2. Cuitlateco..	Conchos, Sinaloense, * Mazapil, Jalisciense, Ahualulco, Pipil, Niquiran.
		3. Opata, Teguima or Teguima Sonorense........ 4. Eudebe, heve or hegue, dohme or dohema-batuco .... 5. Joba, joval ova.............................. 6. Pima, nevome, ohotama or Otama............ 7. Pepehuan................................... 8. Papago or Papabicotan....................... 9 to 12. El Yuma comprising Cuchan, Coco-maricopa or Opa, Mojave or Mahao, Die-gueño, or Cuñeil, Yavipai, Yampai, and yampaio............................... 13.* Cajuenche, Cucapa or Jallicuamay.......... 14. Sobaipure .... 15. Julime..	Tecoripa. Sabaqui. Various.

GROUPS.	FAMILIES.	LANGUAGES.	DIALECTS.
		1st Order.—Languages polysyllabic, polysynthetic of sub-flexion.	
MEXICAN-OPATA.	II. SONORENSE OR OPATA-PIMA.	16. Tarahumar..............................	Varogio or Chinipa, Guazapare, Pachera, and others.
		17. Cahita or Sinaloa......................	Yaqui, Mayo, Tehueco or Zuaque.
		18. Guarave or Vacoregue..................	
		19. Chora, Chota, Cora del Nayarit..........	Muutzicat, Teacucitzin, Ateanaca.
		20. Colotlan .... 21. Tubar................................. 22. Huichola.............................. 23. Zacateco.............................. 24. Acaxee or Topia, comprising Sabaibo, Tebaca, and Xixime, the last of doubtful classification.....................	Various.
	III. COMANCHE SO-SHONE.	25. Comanche, Nauni, Paduca, Hietan or Getan. 26. Caigua or Kioway. 27. Shoshone or Chochone. 28. Wihinasht. 29. Utah, Yutah or Yuta. 30. Pah-Utah or Payuta. 31. Chemegue or Cheme-huevi. 32. Cahuillo or Cawio. 33. Kechi. 34. Netela. 35. Kizh or Kij. 36. Fernandeño. 37. Moqui and some others spoken in the United States...............................	Various.
	IV. TEXANA OR COA-HUILTECA.	38. Texano or Coahuilteco....................	Various.
	V. *KERES ZUÑI.	39. Keres or Quera..........................	Kiwomi or Kivome, Cochiteumi or Quime, Acoma and Acuco.
		40. Tesuque or Tegua...................... 41. Taos, Piro, Suma, Picori.................. 42. Jemez, Tano, Peco...................... 43. Zuñi or Cibola..........................	Various.
	VI. MUTSUN.	44. Mutsun. 45. Rumsen. 46. Achastli. 47. Soledad. 48. Costeño or Costanos and other languages of California.............................	
	VII. GUAICURA.	49. Guaicura, Vaicura or Monqui. 50. Aripa. 51. Uchita. 52. Cora. 53. Concho or Lauretano....................	
	VIII. COCHIMI-LAIMON.	54 to 57. Cochimi, divided into four sister languages, viz.: Cadegomo and the languages used in the missions of San Javier, San Joaquin, and Santa Maria................ 58. Laimon or Layamon......................	
	IX. SERI.	59. Seri or Ceri........................... 60. Guaima or Gayama...................... 61. Upanguaima............................	
	X. TARASCA.	62. Tarasco .... 63. Chorotega de Nicaragua....................	
	XI. ZOQUE-MIXE.	64. Mixe................................. 65. Zoque................................ 66. Tapijulapa	Various.

GROUPS.	FAMILIES.	LANGUAGES.	DIALECTS.
	XII. TOTONACA.	67. Totonaco (mixed language).................	Four.
		2d Order. Languages polysyllabic polysynthetic of juxtaposition.	
	XIII. MIXTECO-ZAPO- TECA.	68. Mixteco................................. 69. Zapoteco............................... 70. Chuchon .... 71. Popoloco .... 72. Cuicateco............................... 73. Chatino .... 74. Papabuco............................... 75. Amusgo .... 76. Mazateco .... *77. Solteco .... *78. Chinanteco	Eleven. Twelve. Two. Two. Two.
	XIV. PIRINDA OR MA- TLALZINCA.	79. Pirinda or Matlalzinca.;....................	Various.
		3d Order.—Languages Polosyllabic Synthetic.	
	XV. MAYA.	80. Yucateco or Maya......................... 81. Punctunc............................... 82. Lacandon or Xochinel .... 83. Peten or Itzae........................... 84. Chañabal, Comiteco, Jocolobal............ 85. Chol or Mopan .... 86. Chorti or Chorte......................... 87. Cakchi, Caichi, Cachi or Cakgi............ 88. Izil, Izil................................ 89. Coxoh.................................. 90. Quiché, Utlateco......................... 91. Zutuhil, Zutugil, Atiteca, Zacapula.......... 92. Cachiquel, Cachiquil .... 93. Tzotzil, Zotzil, Tzinanteco, Cinanteco....... 94. Tzendal, Zendal......................... 95. Mame, Mem, Zaklohpakap................. 96. Poconchi, Pocoman...................... 97. Atche, Atchi............................ 98. Huaxteco .... *99. Haitiano, Quizqueja or Itis, with their af- finities, Cubano, Borigua and Jamaica......	Various.
	XVI. CHONTAL.	*100. Chontal doubtful in its morphologic char- acter...................................	
	XVII. DERIVATIVES OF NICARAGUA.	*101. Huave, Huazonteca....................... *102. Chiapaneco	
	XVIII. APACHE.	103. Apache	North American Apache, Mexi- can Apache, Mimbreño, Pinaleño, Nava- jo, Xicarilla or Faraon, Lipan Mescalero.
		4th Order.—Languages cuasi-mo- nosyllabic.	
	XIX. OTOMI.	104. Otomi or Hiahiu........................... 105. Serrano .... 106. Mazahua .... 107. Pame................................... 108. Jonaz or Meco. (Perhaps the rest of the ancient Chichimeco)....................	Various.

FAMILIES INDEPENDENT AMONG THEMSELVES AND OF THE MEXICAN-OPATA GROUP.

POPULATION.

We have until recently taken a regularly correct census of our population. The first reliable census was made in 1795, under Revillagigedo's viceroyalty, the second in 1810 by Don Fernando Navarro y Noriega, the third one was estimated by Mr. Poinsett, United States Minister in Mexico, in 1824, and the others have been taken by the Mexican Government.

The following is a statement of the general results of our various censuses :

Years.	Inhabitants.
1795	5,200,000
1810	6,122,354
1824	6,500,000
1839	7,044,140
1854	7,853,395
1869	8,743,614
1878	9,384,193
1879	9,908,011
1886	10,791,685
1895	12,570,195

The population of Mexico appears to be, from our last census, taken in 1895, 12,570,195, which would give 16.38 for each square mile ; but from my personal knowledge of the country, I am quite sure that it is not less than 15,000,000. It is very difficult to take a correct census in Mexico, because there is not the proper machinery in operation for that purpose, and especially because a great many districts are inhabited by Indians, who are impressed with the fear that if they inscribe themselves in the census they will be taxed or drafted into the military service, and they try to avoid registration.

A great many of our people live in such remote districts that they are practically cut off from communication with other portions of the country, and in fact are almost isolated ; and this constitutes still another difficulty in the way of taking a correct census. These people generally raise everything they need for their living, as well as for their clothing. They also raise their domestic animals, and wear either cotton or woollen clothes, manufactured by the women. The configuration of the country, which makes transportation very expensive, together with the very sparse population, has caused their isolation, and this explains why some agricultural products which are very cheap in other countries are very dear in certain districts of Mexico, as prices can be easily controlled, there being no possibility of competition. While sugar, for instance, costs 25 cents per pound in some districts, it can be had in others for one cent. This fact shows also that a year of good crops was often a real misfortune to these districts.

The upper lands being the healthiest, most of the population in Mexico is settled in the central plateau ; a relatively small portion lives in the temperate zone, while the torrid zone is very thinly populated. I imagine, at a rough calculation, that about 75 per cent. of the population make their abode in the cold zone, from 15 to 18 per cent. in the temperate zone, and from 7 to 10 per cent. in the torrid zone.

From the synopsis of our censuses, inserted above, it appears that the population in Mexico has duplicated during the last century, and although that increase does not keep pace with the increase in the United States, because this has been really wonderful, it compares favorably with the increase in other countries. Mexico also, as a new country and one full of possibilities, ought to have increased its population more rapidly, but its slow progress can be accounted for in several ways.

Under the head of Ethnology I enumerated the different races inhabiting Mexico and stated the number of inhabitants belonging to each, and I gave at length the reasons for the slow increase of the Indian population, which is the largest in Mexico. I will only add here that while the Indians lead a very abstemious and simple life, marry while very young and generally have a family of several children, they are at the same time subject to epidemics. Notwithstanding that the race on the whole is sturdy and little subject to disease, the mortality is very large among the children for want of proper nutrition and care. The losses caused by our civil wars could not at all explain the slow increase of our population, and the only way in which I can account for it is that they are not so well prepared as the people of the United States and other more advanced countries, to bear the discomforts of life and climate, and that, therefore, they cannot bring up all the children born in the family, among whom there is annually a great mortality.

Classification of Mexican States. Under the Spanish rule Mexico was divided into several provinces, the Spaniards trying to divide the provinces in accordance with the different nationalities of the aborigines found there, and each province possessing a very large extent of territory. After our independence and when we established a Federal government, each province was made a state, and since then some of the largest states have been divided into two or even three smaller ones. In the chapter on Political Organizations I shall give further information on this subject.

The Mexican states are classified in several ways, and generally as Northern, Southern, Central, Pacific, and Gulf States ; but it is difficult to make a proper division of them, because there are several included in two denominations. I will, therefore, divide them into Northern States, calling so those bordering on the United States ; Southern States, those bordering on Gautemala and Belize ; Gulf, Caribbean Sea, and Pacific States, those bordering on their respective waters ; and Central States those which do not belong to any of the above denominations, although I do not consider this a proper classification, because the State of Tamaulias included among the Northern States, and the States of Tabasco, Campeche, and Yucatan among the Southern States, are all on the Gulf of Mexico, and are, therefore, Gulf States, the latter being also washed on their southern side by the Caribbean Sea, and the State of Sonora, classified as a Northern State, borders on the Pacific ; the State of Chiapas, included among the Southern States, also borders on the Pacific, and, therefore, is, like Sonora, also a Pacific State.

Our last official census, taken in 1895, gives the following results by States, which I compared with the census of 1879.

AREA AND POPULATION OF THE UNITED MEXICAN STATES.

STATES.	AREA IN SQUARE MILES.	POPULATION in 1879.	POPULATION in 1895.	POPULATION PER SQUARE MILE.	CAPITAL.	POPULATION.
Northern States bordering on the U.S.						
Tamaulipas	32,585	140,137	204,206	6.3	Ciudad Victoria	14,575
Nuevo Leon	24,324	203,284	309,607	13.1	Monterey	56,855
Coahuila	62,376	130,026	235,638	3.7	Saltillo	19,654
Chihuahua	87,820	225,541	266,831	3.0	Chihuahua	18,521
Sonora	76,922	115,424	191,281	2.4	Hermosillo	8,376
Southern States bordering on Guatemala.						
Yucatan	35,214	302,315	297,507	8.4	Mérida	36,720
Campeche	18,091	90,413	90,458	5.0	Campeche	16,631
Tabasco	10,075	104,747	134,794	13.3	S. Juan Bautista	27,036
Chiapas	27,230	205,362	313,678	11.5	Tuxtla Gutierrez	7,882
Atlantic.						
Veracruz	29,210	542,918	855,975	29.3	Jalapa	18,173
Pacific.						
Oaxaca	35,392	744,000	882,529	24.9	Oaxaca	32,641
Guerrero	25,003	295,590	417,621	16.7	Chilpancingo	6,904
Michoacan	22,881	661,534	889,795	38.8	Morelia	32,287
Colima	2,273	65,827	55,677	24.5	Colima	19,305
Jalisco	31,855	983,484	1,107,863	34.8	Guadalajara	83,870
Sinaloa	33,681	186,491	256,414	7.6	Culiacan	14,205
Central						
Aguascalientes	2,951	140,430	103,645	35.1	Aguas Calientes	31,619
Durango	38,020	190,846	294,366	7.7	Durango	42,165
Guanajuato	11,374	834,845	1,047,238	92.1	Guanajuato	39,337
Hidalgo	8,920	427,350	548,039	61.6	Pachuca	52,189
Morelos	2,774	159,160	159,800	57.6	Cuernavaca	8,554
Mexico	9,250	710,579	838,737	90.7	Toluca	23,648
Puebla	12,207	784,466	970,723	80.2	Puebla	91,917
Querétaro	3,558	203,250	227,233	63.9	Querétaro	32,790
Tlaxcala	1,595	138,988	166,803	104.6	Tlaxcala	2,874
San Luis Potosi	25,323	516,486	570,814	22.5	San Luis Potosi	69,676
Zacatecas	24,764	422,506	452,720	18.2	Zacatecas	40,026
Territories.						
Tepic	11,279	....	144,308	12.8	Tepic	16,266
Lower California	58,345	30,208	42,287	0.7	La Paz and Ensenada de Todos Santos	4,737 / 1,259
Federal District	463	351,804	484,608	1046.7	City of Mexico	339,935
Islands	1,471	....				
Totals	767,226	9,908,011	12,570,195			

RELIGION.

All Mexicans are born in the Catholic Church, that being the prevailing religion of the country ; but there is no connection between
Church and State, and the Constitution guarantees the free exercise of
all religions.

While Mexico was a colony of Spain and for many years afterwards,
the catholic religion was the only one allowed in the country, and
anybody professing any other would expose himself to great hardships
if he avowed that he was a dissenter, especially while the Inquisition
was in existence.

The clergy became one of the principal pillars of the Spanish domination in Mexico. In the early part of the present century the Church
was flourishing, and it was the high-water mark of clerical prosperity. The humble Mexican priests did the hard laborious work,
while the Spanish-born ecclesiastics filled the great bishoprics and
other great posts and lived at their ease, and the great convents in
their most lucrative positions of control were practically in Spanish
hands.

Huge convents occupied a considerable part of the site of the
City of Mexico, Puebla, Morelia, Guadalajara, Querétaro, and other
cities. The incomes of the convents were derived from endowments,
amounting to a large sum. To support the high ecclesiastics, great
sums were derived from tithes. The archbishop of Mexico had an
income of $130,000 a year ; the bishops of Puebla, $110,000 ; of
Michoacan, $100,000 ; and of Guadalajara, $90,000. Meantime, the
parish priests, who bore the brunt of Christian work among the masses,
were living on very moderate sums. The Church erected in Mexico
buildings which are remarkable for their dimensions and taste.[1]

---

[1] Mr. Charles Dudley Warner in the Editor's Study of *Harper's Illustrated
Monthly Magazine* for July, 1897, speaks in the following way of the church edifices
in Mexico :

"Somebody of authority, by the way, ought to explain why Mexico has so many
church edifices that go to the heart of the lover of beauty, and why the United States
has so few that are interesting. Aside from the great Gothic monuments in Spain,
Mexico surpasses Spain in interesting ecclesiastical architecture. It has more variety,
more quaint beauty, more originality in towers and façades. The interiors are generally monotonous, and repetitions of each other. The Spaniards, in an age of faith,
built churches, convents, monasteries, all over the county, in remote and unimportant
Indian villages, and as far north as their patient ministers of religion wandered, even
to the bay of San Francisco. In these edifices the Spanish ingenuity and enthusiasm
prevailed, but they were largely executed by Indian builders and artists ; and if there
is Sarasenic feeling shown, there are also, especially in ornamentation, traces of that
aboriginal artistic spirit which, long before the Spanish conquest, executed both in stone
and in pottery singularly attractive work. Even within a hundred years of our own time
Indian genius has been distinguished. Those who think that this genius is only exhib-

Not all the great dignitaries of the Church exhibited an unchristian selfishness, for many often spent their income in pious and charitable works, and in prosecuting missionary undertakings among the Indians of the remote distances.

The wealth of the Church was loaned out at a moderate rate of interest to landed proprietors, who formed the moral support of the Church among the laity and whose influence was prodigiously strong. The wealth of the Church was mostly in mortgages, while it held a large amount of real estate. In the City of Mexico and other places, the clergy owned a large portion of the real estate and held a great many mortages, and, to its credit be it said, was not at all usurious, exacting only a fair rate of interest and being hardly ever oppressive in dealing with delinquent debtors.

After the Revolution which effected the independence of the country, the ecclesiastical life began to cease having many of the attractions it had before. While many men became friars from genuine inclination and vocation, not a few went into the religious life because it gave them support without hard labor, and because it was one of the best careers opened to young men at the time.

The nunneries sheltered a great many pious women, who effected some good as educators of the young, as almoners for the wealthy, and as nurses of the sick. There were abuses, of course, but on the whole the religious life afforded a refuge for many thousands of good women who felt drawn to works of charity and usefulness. Rich young girls were often over-persuaded to enter the convents, by avaricious and scheming priests, but such abuses are common to all religions. The Liberal party thought that the best way to destroy the Church influence in Mexico was to suppress convents, both of friars and nuns, because they

ited in bizarre forms, and in such small details of design and color as the potter can attain, should see at Querétaro the work of Tresguerras, architect, sculptor, and painter. Any modern architect, who is led away by straining after effect in a grotesque combination of distinct Greek styles with mediæval and early English, having no note of originality anywhere, could study with profit the simple elegance—as simple as the Old Louvre—of the Bishop's Palace in Querétaro, or the wood-carving in the church of the sequestered Convent of Santa Rosa. In my remembrance there is not, on such a great scale, any wood-carving in the world equal to it in freshness and largeness of execution and in beauty of design. It could not have been all done by the hand of Tresguerras, but it was all from his designs and under his superintendence. Of course, as to civic and ecclesiastic architecture, climate and lack of popular taste for the beautiful put limits upon our architectural work, but it is worth the while of the American architect to consider whether he cannot learn more from our sister republic below the Tropic of Cancer than he is likely to get from the well-studied structures of Europe. In many petty and poverty-stricken Indian villages are charming towers and curious façades which would be a most valuable education in the principles of taste to any American community."

were considered a nest of superstition, and they thought that the best interest of the country required to close them.

During our civil wars the clergy contributed large amounts to the support of the conservative governments, which it often established. It is thought that in 1853, General Santa Anna abandoned the Conservative Government, which he then presided over, because the Archbishop of Mexico did not give him all the money he required to carry on the war waged against him by the Liberal party.

The wealth accumulated by the Church of Mexico was used for the purpose of supporting the conservative governments, whose policy was to keep the statu quo, and was therefore opposed to progress of any kind. The Church became a very prominent factor in politics, and could upset and establish governments at its pleasure, fomenting the many revolutions which were constantly breaking out. It was thought necessary, therefore, to destroy the political power of the Church before we could establish and maintain peace, and that work was done by what we call our Laws of Reform, issued in 1859, which established a complete independence between the Church and the State, and were intended to completely end the domination of the Catholic Church in civil affairs in Mexico : the Church property was confiscated, so that even the houses of worship are now the property of the government ; all convents of friars and nuns were closed, all religious ceremonies—such as processions and wearing a distinctive dress,—were ordered to be confined to the interior of the edifices ; the cemeteries were secularized, and marriage made exclusively a civil contract. No religious instruction or ceremony is allowed in the public schools, and never is a prayer offered as a part of the program of a national celebration. In an article, which I published in the *North American Review*, of January, 1895, entitled " The Philosophy of the Mexican Revolutions," I dwelt especially on this subject, and to that article I refer the reader who may desire more detailed information.

The Liberals were not the first to dispose of the Church property and revenues, as the Spanish Government, under the rule of Godoy, in 1805 and 1806, to secure funds to form a redemption provision for the royal *vales* or credit notes, pounced on the property of the Church in Mexico, and that, later on, when the Mexicans rose in their war for independence, the royal authorities took another part of the Church's wealth to fight the patriots.

The bigoted Catholic element which used to be decidely opposed to any liberal government and was always conspiring to overthrow it, has since the downfall of Maximilian, become satisfied that the condition of things has changed having accordingly changed their course, and now there are thousands of progressive catholics in Mexico sincerely devoted to their Church, who see only danger and eventual disastrous defeat in the adoption of a program of reaction. They go with the times and support the administration of Gen. Diaz because, on the whole, it suits them, and manifests no hostility to their conscientiously held convictions. The pope's influence seems to be directed to assuaging ancient rancors, and to the calming of passionate resentments, which is a great deal better for the Church.

Protestantism in Mexico.—The Liberal party proclaimed as an inherent right of man, freedom of conscience and the free exercise of one's religion ; but the question was really only a theoretical one, since excepting a few foreigners, no one in Mexico had any other religion than the Catholic. The clergy, the Church party, and all strict Mexican catholics were greatly opposed to the introduction of Protestantism, because protestants were looked upon as heretics whose purpose was to divide the Mexican people into different sects, disturbing their religious unity, which they considered a source of national strength, and ultimately aiding in what some Mexicans fear is the aim of this country, that is : the final absorption of Mexico. When the struggles between the Liberal and the Church party terminated in favor of the former in 1867, with the withdrawl of the French army from Mexico and the downfall of Maximilian, the time came to put into practice the principles of the Liberal creed, and protestant organizations in the United States sent missionaries to Mexico for the purpose of establishing and propagating the protestant religion there. The Mexican Government could not refuse to allow the missionaries the free exercise of the Protestant or any other faith, because that right was guaranteed to all men in our constitution, and also because it has been a principle for which the Liberal party had been contending during many years.

But we went, then, further than allowing the Protestants the free exercise and preaching of their religion, and as I am in a measure responsible for that step, I think it proper to give my reasons for the same. My opinion has never been favorable to missionary work, because although I recognize that some religions have higher moral principles than others, I think that on the whole they are all intended to accomplish the same purpose, that all are good, when practised in good faith. It has always seemed to me that Christian missionaries sent to heathen countries would be looked upon in the same manner as would be heathen missionaries sent to Christian countries. But even supposing that it should be proper and desirable for the Christian religion, on account of its high morals and principles, to send missionaries to heathen countries for the purpose of converting them to Christianity, that principle would scaracely hold good in Christian countries of different denominations, and Catholicism is a Christian religion—whatever abuses it may have committed,—and I think the natural tendency of all religions when they are predominant is to absorb and misuse power ; but that Protestants should send missionaries to a Catholic country seems to me inconsistent. In principle, therefore, Mexico is hardly the proper field for Protestant missionaries, notwithstanding that there is a great deal of room for improvement there, in so far as religious matters are concerned.

After having witnessed the terrible consequences of religious intolerance and political domination of the Catholic Church in Mexico, I was of course greatly impressed with the condition of things existing in the United States, where all religions are tolerated and none attempts to control the political destinies of the country. I thought that one of the best ways to diminish the evils of the political domination and abuses of the clergy in Mexico was to favor the establishment of other sects, which would come in some measure into competition with the Catholic clergy and thus serve to cause it to refrain from excesses of which it had been guilty before. When, after having lived for ten years in the United States, from 1859 to 1868, I returned to Mexico and took charge of the Treasury Department there, just at the time when the religious question was being solved, I, therefore, favored the establishment of a Protestant community as planned by Mr. Henry C. Riley, since made a Bishop, a gentleman of English parentage, born in Chili, who had been educated in London and New York and was graduated with high honors at Columbia College, New York, who spoke equally well English and Spanish, and eagerly desired to establish a Mexican National Church in competition with the Roman Catholic, in which undertaking, I understand, he used his own funds. He proposed to buy one of the finest churches, the main church of the Franciscan convent, which had been built by the Spaniards, located in the best section of the City of Mexico, and which could not now be duplicated but for a very large amount of money ; and with the hearty support of President Juarez, who shared my views and who was perhaps a great deal more radical than I was myself on such subjects, I sold the building which had become national property after the confiscation of the Church property, for a mere trifle, if I remember rightly about $4000, most of that amount being paid in Government bonds which were then at a nominal price.

The magnificent building sold to Dr. Riley's community was bought recently by the Catholic Church to restore it as a Catholic temple, for the sum of $100,000, as I understand. My assistance was rendered to the Protestant cause for the reasons that I have stated, and not because I had adopted the Protestant faith ; therefore the action of the Mexican Government in the matter at the time I speak of, was all the more praiseworthy. Dr. Butler bought about the same time another part of the same convent of San Francisco, where he established a Methodist Church in a very creditable building.

It is true that a great many Mexicans, namely the Indians, do not know much about religion and keep to their old idolatry, having changed only their idols, that is, replaced their old deities with the images of the Saints of the Catholic Church, but it would be difficult for the Protestant missionaries to reach them. The Spaniards labored zealously to make the natives adopt the Catholic religion, and although they succeeded wonderfully, it was a task too difficult to fully accomplish in the three centuries of the Spanish domination in Mexico.

I do not think that the American Protestant missionaries in Mexico have made much progress, and I doubt very much whether Mexico is a good field for them ; but they are satisfied with their work, and they think that under the circumstances, they have made very good progress.

The number of Catholic churches and chapels in the country was, in 1889, 10,112, while the number of Protestant places of worship was 119. On August 12, 1890, there were in the municipality of Mexico 320,143 Catholics and 2623 Protestants.

The American missionaries, and especially Dr. Riley, whom I consider a very benevolent and unselfish man, have established Protestant schools and asylums for children, spending considerable money in maintaining such institutions. Of course poor parents were glad to send their children to the Protestant schools and asylums when they could not afford to keep them at home or send them to more desirable places, and these Protestant institutions were of a very benevolent character and worthy, therefore, to be encouraged. Parents in such cases declared themselves to be partial to Protestantism, but only for the sake of having their children accepted in the Protestant schools and asylums, and this made the Protestants think they were making a great many converts.

Now and then a Catholic priest would renounce Catholicism and accept Protestantism, and such occurrences were always considered as great triumphs for the Protestant cause, but although in some instances such changes have been made in good faith, in others they were made for selfish purposes, and they never had any great weight with the community.

I have no prejudice against Protestantism ; on the contrary, I admire greatly many of its principles, and in speaking on this subject I consider myself perfectly impartial and unbiassed.

In February, 1888, the Evangelical Assembly, representing the various Protestant denominations and Evangelical Societies conducting missionary operations in the Republic of Mexico, was held in the City of Mexico. They claimed that, notwithstanding the difficulties of language and climate and the other obstacles with which they had to contend, they found that they had over 600 congregations, 192 foreign and 585 native workers, over 7000 in the day schools, and about 10,000

7

in the Sunday-schools, 18,000 communicants and a Protestant community of over 60,000 souls.   Ten small publishing-houses are turning out
millions of pages each year, and their church property is valued at
nearly a million and a quarter dollars in silver.

POLITICAL ORGANIZATION.

Mexico was the largest and richest American colony of Spain, and
for this reason it was called New Spain.   The City of Mexico grew
during the Spanish rule to be larger than Madrid, the capital of the
Spanish Kingdom, the population of the country being estimated in
1810, just before the independence movement began, at 6,122,354 ;
while the public revenue of the whole colony amounted to the very
large sum of $20,000,000 yearly, the only exports of the country
being silver and gold, and commodities of great value in small volume
and weight, such as cochineal, vanilla, indigo, and a few others.

Mexico, accomplished her independence in 1821, and since then
has had two Federal Constitutions, both modelled after the Constitution of the United States ; two Central Constitutions, which organized
the country into a centralized republic, and two ephemeral empires,
one under Iturbide, lasting ten months, from 1822 to 1823, and the
other under Maximilian, established by French intervention, lasting
from 1864 to 1867.

Mexico is now organized, under the Constitution of the 5th of
February, 1857, with its several amendments, into a Federal Republic,
composed of twenty-seven states, two territories, and a federal district,
and the political organization is almost identical with that of this
country.   The powers of the Federal Government are divided into
three branches—Legislative, Executive, and Judicial.   The Legislative
is composed of a House of Representatives and a Senate ; the members of the House are elected for two years and the senators for four,
the Senate being renewed by half every two years.   Representatives
are elected by the suffrage of all male adults, at the rate of one member for every 40,000 inhabitants.   The qualifications requisite are to
be at least twenty-five years of age and a resident of the State ; and for
senators thirty years.

The Executive is exercised by a President elected by the electors
popularly chosen, who holds his office for four years, without any
provision forbidding his re-election.   He has a cabinet of seven members, namely : Secretary of Foreign Affairs, of the Interior, of Justice
and Public Instruction, of Fomento, which means promotion of Public Improvements, and includes public lands, patents, and colonization ; of Communications and Public Works, of the Treasury, and
of War and Navy.   No Vice-President is elected, but by an amend-
ment to our Constitution, promulgated April 24, 1896, in the per-

manent or temporary disability of the President, not caused by resignation or by leave, the Secretary of State, and after him the Secretary of the Interior, shall exercise that office until Congress elects a President *pro tempore.* In case of resignation, Congress, accepting it, elects a President *pro tempore,* and in case of leave the President recommends to Congress the person to fill that office.

The Federal Judiciary is composed of a Supreme Court, consisting of eleven Judges, four substitutes, one Attorney-General, and one Fiscal, chosen for six years; three Circuit and thirty-two District Courts. The States are independent in their domestic affairs, and their governments are similarly divided into three branches : the Governor, the Legislature, and the State Judiciary.

As we adopted the federal system rather to follow the example of the United States than to suit the conditions of Mexico, that system did not work with us so easily or so satisfactorily as it works here ; and the tendency is rather to centralization and to the increasing of the powers given by the Constitution to the Federal Government.. In the article above mentioned published in the *North American Review,* for January, 1896, entitled, "The Philosophy of the Mexican Revolutions," [1] I dwelt particularly on the results of our having copied almost literally the political institutions of the United States, and gave a general idea of our political condition.

Political Division.—When the federal system was established in Mexico, in 1824, each of the old provinces under the Spanish rule was organized as a State, and our Constitution of October 4, 1824, enumerated nineteen States. After the war with the United States we lost Texas, New Mexico, and California ; but since then as I stated in the chapter on population some of the larger States have been divided into two, or even three States, as was the case with the old State of Mexico, out of which were formed the three present States of Mexico, Hidalgo, and Morelos. Our present Constitution, of February 5, 1857, enumerates twenty-four States ; but we now have twenty-seven.

The tabular statement published above, under the head of "Population," shows the number of States which form the Mexican Confederation, their area, population, and capital cities.

Army and Navy.—During our civil wars, and for some time later, we had to keep a very large standing army, and our army acquired recently a very high degree of discipline and efficiency. The Liberal party always favored the reduction of the army, while the Church party favored a large army, as our old regular army, on the whole, took sides with the Church. Soon after the restoration of the Republic, in 1867, the Mexican army consisted of : Infantry, 22,964 ; engineers, 766 ; ar-

[1] This article will appear in this volume under the head of "Historical Notes on Mexico."

tillery, 2304 ; cavalry, 8454 ; rural guards of police, 2365 ; gendarmerie, 250 ; total, 37,103 ; and was commanded by 11 Major-Generals, 73 Brigadier-Generals, 1041 Colonels, Lieutenant-Colonels, and Majors, and 2335 Commissioned Officers. The total fighting strength, including reserves, is stated to be 132,000 infantry, 25,000 cavalry, and 8000 artillery. Every Mexican capable of carrying arms is liable for military service from his twentieth to his fiftieth year.

Notwithstanding that General Diaz is himself a soldier, he has followed the policy of the Liberal party of reducing the army as much as possible, and in his report of November 30, 1896, in which he informs his fellow citizens of his results of his sixteen years administration, he gives the following figures, showing the reduction he has been able to accomplish in the army since 1888 :

The army had, in 1888, according to President Diaz's report, the following personnel :

Major-Generals	16
Brigadier-Generals	84
Commissioned Officers	1,205
Non-Commissioned Officers	2,566
Soldiers	29,367
Total	33,238

In 1896 the personnel had been reduced in the following numbers :

Generals	24
Commissioned Officers	166
Non-Commissioned Officers	299
Soldiers	8,170
Total	8,659

The Mexican navy is now in its inception, as it consists of a fleet of two dispatch vessels, launched 1874, each of 425 tons and 425 horsepower, and severally armed with a four-ton muzzle-loading gun, and four small breech-loaders. A steel training ship, the *Zaragoza*, of 1200 tons, was built at Havre, in 1891 ; four gun-boats are building, and a battle-ship and cruiser are projected ; five first-class torpedo-boats have been ordered in England. The fleet is manned by ninety officers and five hundred men.

EDUCATION.

In 1521, the City of Mexico fell into the hands of the conquering Spaniards, and exactly eight years after that event there was established in the City of Mexico the College of San Juan de Letran, for giving secondary education to intelligent Indians as well as to the sons of the invading race. Thus, ninety years before the landing of the Pilgrims, the City of Mexico had its "Harvard."

Universities Established by the Spanish Government.—The first vice-roy of New Spain, as Mexico was called then, fourteen years after the conquest, petitioned the King of Spain to permit him to found a university in Mexico, and, anticipating from his knowledge of the good-will of the Spanish-rulers that the desired permission would be given, the viceroy took the responsibility of establishing certain classes in the higher learning, a fact which does not support the commonly held theory that Spain has always been the enemy of education and of popular enlightenment. Owing to the slow means of communication in those days, and the legal steps necessary to be taken in the mother country, the university was not formally established until 1553, or eighty-three years before Harvard College was opened. The great event of setting on foot the university came under the enlightened rule of the second viceroy, Don Luis de Velasco, who did so many great things for Spain's new dependency.

Later on, in 1573, there were founded in Mexico the colleges of San Gregorio and San Ildefonso, the latter still open, but modernized into the national preparatory school, a really great institution in that city of many schools. A few years later, long before the 17th century had dawned, came the founding of two more colleges and a divinity school, so that in the first sixty-five years of Spain's control in Mexico no less than seven seats of the higher learning had been established on secure foundations.

No wonder that Mexico's capital became known as the Athens of the new world, producing men of great learning, such as Don Juan Ruiz de Alarcon and such notably erudite women as Juana Inez de la Cruz. The extensive library of "Americana," belonging to Don Jose de Agreda, of that city, containing over 4000 books, many of them invaluable, attests the literary, antiquarian, scientific and artistic activity of the Spaniards who planted there in a short space of time so much of learning and such vast institutions dedicated to the instruction in all the higher branches of knowledge.

At the outset the University of Mexico gave instruction only in mathematics, Latin and the arts. Medicine and surgery were not esteemed highly during the middle ages, and it was not until long after the revival of learning in the Renaissance that the physician came to be considered as a true man of science. So it is not to be marvelled at that the University of Mexico waited until 1578 to establish a chair of medicine—the first in the new world discovered by Columbus. The first chair of medicine was a morning class, and a single professor carried his students through a four years' course unaided. In 1599, a second medical professorship was added ; in 1661, anatomy and surgery were added, and, consequently dissection was authorized. At the outset the viceroys appointed the professors, but after a time the candidates for chairs had to win the coveted prizes through competitive examinations.

The early students were not railroaded through. They had to study four years to obtain the diploma of a bachelor of medicine; then went out into active life, and, on gaining practical knowledge, received, passing a fresh examination, the diploma of licentiate of medicine, and, later, that of doctor of medicine.

School of Medicine.—In 1768 a decree was issued for the establishment in the City of Mexico of a royal college for surgeons, similar to institutions in Cadiz and Barcelona. This college was a very complete one, instruction being given in anatomy and dissection, in physiology, operations, clinical surgery, and medical jurisprudence. There were graduated also from the college all the dentists, bonesetters, phlebotomists, and midwives. A knowledge of Latin was not essential to receive a medical degree until 1803.

In 1821, Mexico having achieved her independence, the same careful watch over education continued, and in 1833 a general revision of educational institutions was ordered under the administration of Don Valentin Gomez Farias a leader of the Liberal party and the university was closed, because it was considered to have conservative tendencies, and a general board of education organized, which, among other things established what was called the School of Medical Science, with ten professors, giving a remarkably complete and modern course. On account of a revolution which occurred in 1834 which overthrew the Gomez Farias Government, the new school of medicine was closed, and the old university reopened; but, as the officials of the university, on making a careful study of the conditons of the new school of medicine rendered an impartial report, setting forth its manifold advantages it was decided to keep open the institution.

The incessant revolutions and consequent changes of government brought many evil things to pass, and the medical professors at times found themselves without salaries, and nobly devoted themselves to their classes without remuneration. They at one time were deprived of their building and literally thrown into the street. Better times came, however, the successive governments began to give substantial aid to the school, and in 1845 it took the name it still bears, the National School of Medicine. After more vicissitudes, many movings and trials which bore hard on the enthusiastic professors, the National School of Medicine finally was located where it now remains, in a part of the enormous edifice belonging formerly to the Inquisition.

In the chaos of succeeding revolutions the salaries of the professors were often unpaid, but the devoted men of science struggled on, assisted by wealthier students and contributing often out of their own slender means to keep the school alive ; but, in 1857, a better era commenced, and not since then, with rare exceptions, have there been any interruptions in financial aid from the various governments. All the other institutions of learning suffered the same fate and were exposed to similar ups and downs.

School of Engineering.—Our mining college is the best in Spanish America, and it was established when engineering was hardly taught, and endowed by a portion of the taxes levied by the Spanish Government on mines. Its edifice is one of the best built by the Spaniards in their colonies, and still stands as a great monument, embellishing the City of Mexico.

The above given facts will show how early did Mexico open great schools for the higher education, and how solicitous was the Spanish government to maintain them. But, three centuries of devotion to learning, antedating the war for independence, planted there firmly a love of knowledge which is now exhibited in the great government schools, in a city full of students, in innumerable private schools, in the well-filled public primary institutions, in night schools for adults, and in the thirty-five bookstores of that city.

Mexican Technical Schools in the Present Time.—The edifice of the first University in America, founded by the Spanish crown in 1551, is to-day occupied by the National Conservatory of Music. The National Academy of Art, ancient Academy of San Carlos, stands where Fray Pedro de Gante founded, in 1524, the first school of the New World—a school for Indians. The Normal School for males, with its six hundred pupils and its first-class German equipment, occupies the old convent of Santa Teresa, (1678). The Normal School for females has fourteen hundred pupils, an expensive building of 1648. The fine old Jesuit College of San Ildefonso, erected in 1749 at a cost of $400,000 is now filled with a thousand pupils of the National Preparatory School. The National College of Medicine is housed in the old home of the Inquisition (1732), an edifice whose four hanging arches at each corner of the lower corridor are famous. The building was taken for its present purpose in this century, the Holy Office dying in America with the Independence, but the medical college was established by royal decree of 1768. It has now several hundred pupils. San Lorenzo (1598) is now the manual training-school where poor boys are gratuitously taught lithography, engraving, printing, carpentry, and many other trades. The similar institution for girls is of course modern, dating only from 1874. The National Library, with its 200,000 volumes, dwells in the splendid sequestered Church of San Agustin. The National Museum occupies part of the million-dollar building erected in 1731 for the royal mint. And so on through a list that would rival that of any other country. The School of Mines and Engineering, however, stands as one of the first. Its magnificent building of Chiluca, the nearest to granite the valley affords, was built for it by Tolsa in 1793, and cost three millions. The institution named the Colegio de la Paz, better known as the Vizcainas is one of the principal establishments for the education of young women, founded in 1734, at a cost for construction alone of about $2,000,000, subscribed by three Spanish merchants, who also provided funds for its support. These funds, when insufficient to meet expenses, are supplemented by the Federal Government. We have also a very high grade Military School located at the historical grounds of Chapultepec, which educates fine soldiers.

As late as 1824 Humboldt declared, "No city of the New Continent, not excepting those of the United States, presents scientific establishments so great and solid as those of the capital of Mexico." Except as to the buildings, of course, so much could not be said today, as wealth and numbers have made other countries take more rapid strides in higher education. Some of the universities of the United States pay even $10,000 a year to professors and they therefore can secure the best talent.

From the time of the Spanish domination in Mexico to but a few years ago, the Mexican Government considered itself bound to give to the people free secondary education, and for this purpose colleges for all literary and scientific professions were established in the City of Mexico, and each State did the same in its respective capital, in so far as its means allowed it, so that anybody who intended to follow a scientific career could do so without any expense to himself.

The result of the free technical schools has been that most of the young men of well-to-do families in Mexico follow a literary career and that does not cost them anything, and we have more lawyers, doctors, engineers than we really need for the country.

Reorganization of the Technical Colleges.—We had before 1868 several higher colleges and in each of them the same careers were taught, as law, medicine, engineering, etc., but in the reorganization of our national colleges which took place in that year, it was thought proper to establish a special college for each career, and a preparatory college for such elementary studies as would be required for all careers, such as elementary mathematics, physics, chemistry, etc., etc., so that we now have in the City of Mexico, supported by the Federal Government a special school for engineering, one for law, one for medicine, another for agriculture, etc., etc., but each State generally supports one technical college where all literary careers are taught.

Primary Education.—Comparatively little attention was paid to the primary education, and the public schools were so deficient that parents of some means did not send their children to them, but to private schools where they were better attended to. The fact that the elevation of the people depends on their primary education has caused common schools to be established in the country, and now the States vie with each other for the purpose of establishing the best system of common schools and increasing their number.

The Mexican Government has been too much disturbed since its independence to earnestly promote the education of the Indians. I consider that one of the first duties of Mexico is to educate the large number of Indians which we have, and when that is accomplished the whole condition of the country will change, as it will be able in a few years to increase by several millions its productive and consuming population.

In 1896 the Federal Congress of Mexico passed a law which was promulgated on June 3d of that year, making primary education obligatory on all the inhabitants of the Federal District and Territories, and placing public education under the control of the Federal Government, having been before under the respective municipalities.

In almost all the States education is free and compulsory, but the law has not been strictly enforced. Primary instruction is mostly at the expense of the municipalities, but the Federal Government makes frequent grants, and many schools are under the care of the beneficent societies.

School Statistics.—Statistical reports on public instruction for 1876 showed an aggregate of 8165 primary schools, with an attendance of 368,754 children of both sexes throughout the Republic. Reports for 1895 show a total number of public schools for both sexes throughout the Republic amounting to 10,915, in which are instructed 722,435 scholars, at an aggregate cost of $5,455,549.60. The proportion of children of both sexes attending the school is, with respect to the general population, nearly five per cent., and that of the children of school age, actually attending school about 27 per cent. with an average yearly outlay per capita of $7.55. The entire number of private schools for both sexes, including those supported by religious and civil associations, is 2585, with a total attendance of 81,221. Adding these to the preceding figures we have an aggregate of 13,500 schools with an attendance of 803,656 scholars. The number of schools in the country for professional technical education is 136, attended by 16,809 pupils of both sexes.

In the Federal District there are 454 public primary schools with an attendance of 44,776 pupils, and 247 private schools with an attendance of 19,334 pupils. In the matter of education Mexico now stands upon a plane as high, if not higher, than any of the Spanish American Republics, out-ranking even Chili and the Argentine Republic, both of which greatly surpassed her in former years.

The statistical part of this paper will contain detailed information about the number of schools established in each State, their cost, etc., during the year 1895, which complements the information embraced in this chapter.

Libraries.—Many great and noteworthy public and private libraries attest the ineradicable love of learning characteristic of the Mexican people. In 1894 there were in the Republic the National Library, with 200,000 volumes, and 102 other public libraries. There were in that year 22 museums for scientific and educational purposes, and 3 meteorological observatories. Our National Library at the City of Mexico collected all the books possessed by the libraries of the different convents when they were suppressed by the National Government, and has therefore a very large number of rare and valuable books.

Newspapers.—The number of newspapers published was 363, of which 94 are published in the capital : 4 in English, 2 in French, and 1 in German, showing that the Press has not attained there the great development that it has in this country.

THE VALLEY OF MEXICO.

The Valley of Mexico is one of the finest spots in the world. Surrounded by high mountains—almost at the foot of the two highest in the country, Popocatepetl and Ixtaccihuatl—with a very rare and clear atmosphere and a beautiful blue sky, especially after a rain ; it is really a centre of magnificent scenery. The rareness of the atmosphere makes distant objects appear to be very near, and when looking from the City of Mexico at the mountains which surround the Valley, one imagines that they are at the end of the City, while some of them are at a distance of forty miles. The view of the Valley from Chapultepec Hill, which is about one hundred and fifty feet high and distant about three miles from the City, towards its western extremity, where our military school now is and where the President has made his summer residence, is one of the most beautiful with which the earth is endowed. I have seen the Bosphorus, Constantinople, the Bay of Naples and other spots in the world which are considered to be most remarkable for their natural beauty, but I think the view of the Valley of Mexico from Chapultepec can be advantageously compared with any of them, if it does not excel them all.

Six lakes are within the limits of the Valley,—Chalco, Zochimilco, Texcoco, Xaltocan, San Cristobal, and Zupango, the two former being of fresh water and the others of salt water—and, as they have no natural outlet the City of Mexico has been deprived for some time of a proper drainage and its health has been affected very materially thereby. But the colossal undertaking of making an artificial outlet is now practically finished. In an article which I published in the *Engineering Magazine* in January, 1895, I dwelt especially on the work done during four centuries to accomplish that great end.[1]

The prevailing wind in the Valley of Mexico is northwest and north-northwest, which blew 250 times during the year 1883 ; while the southern winds, which are very dry, are rare, as they only blew 51 times in that year ; but at the same time they have greater velocity than the others, and the greatest relative velocity of the winds is 3.0. The west and northwest winds are very damp.

At the present stage of industrial development, speaking especially of the Valley of Mexico, the question of a cheaper combustible is the one of supreme importance. In the absence of water-power of importance and permanence of volume, the only solution of the problem so vital to the growth of manufactures there lies in procuring abundant and cheap fuel.

THE CITY OF MEXICO.

The City of Mexico, located in the western end of the valley, on the Anahuac plateau, at an altitude of 7350 feet above the sea level in 19° 26' north latitude and 99° 07' 53" .4 longitude west of Greenwich, covering about twenty square miles, is one of the most ancient cities of this continent, was the capital of the Aztec Empire, of the Spanish Colony of New Spain and now of the Mexican Republic, and of the Federal District of Mexico.

Mexico dates either from the year 1325 or 1327, when the Aztecs, after long wanderings over the plateau were directed by the oracle to settle at this spot. For here had been witnessed the auspicious omen of an eagle perched on a nopal (cactus) and devouring a snake. Hence the original name of the city, Tenochtitlan (cactus on a stone), changed afterwards to Mexico in honor of the war god Mexitli. The eagle holding a snake in her beak and standing on a cactus upon a stone, is the coat-of-arms of the Mexican Republic. With the progress of the Aztec culture the place rapidly improved, and about 1450 the old mud and rush houses were replaced by solid stone structures, erected partly on piles amid the islets of Lake Texcoco, and grouped around the central enclosure of the great teocalli. The city had reached its highest splendor on the arrival of the Spaniards in 1519, when it comprised from 50,000 to 60,000 houses, with perhaps 500,000 inhabitants, and seemed to Cortes, according to Prescott's, " like a thing of fairy creation rather than the work of mortal hands." It was at that time about 12 miles in circumference, everywhere intersected by canals, and connected with the mainland by six long and solidly constructed causeways, as is clearly shown by the plan given in the edition of

[1] That article is appended to this paper.

Cortes's letters published at Nuremberg in 1524.[1] After its almost
destruction in November, 1521, Cortes employed some 400,000 natives
in rebuilding it on the same site ; but since then the lake seems to
have considerably subsided, for although still 50 square miles in extent,
it is very shallow and has retired two and a half miles from the city.

During the Spanish rule the chief event was the revolt in 1692,
when the municipal buildings were destroyed.   Since then Mexico has
been the scene of many revolutions, was captured by the United States
Army after the battle of Chapultepec, on September 13, 1847, and by
the French Army under Marshall Forey in 1863.   But since the overthrow of Maximilian, and the French Intervention in 1867, peace has
been established and it has become a great centre of civilizing in-
fluences for the surrounding peoples.

The City of Mexico is 263 miles by rail from Veracruz on the
Atlantic, 290 from Acapulco on the Pacific, 285 from Oaxaca, 863
from Matamoros on the frontier with the United States, and 1224 miles
from El Paso.   Mexico is the largest and finest city in Spanish America,
and at one time larger than Madrid, the capital of Spain, forming a
square of nearly 3 miles both ways, and laid out with perfect regu-
larity, all its six hundred streets and lanes running at right angles
north to south and east to west, and covering within the walls an area
of about ten square miles, with a population now of 539,935.

The present City of Mexico is almost twice as large as the old one, it
having increased towards the northwest, and, strange to say, the new
portion is not laid out as regularly as the old one.   All the main
thoroughfares converge on the central Plaza de Armas, or Main
Square, which covers 14 acres, and is tastefully laid out with shady
trees, garden plots, marble fountains, and seats.   Here also are grouped
most of the public buildings, towering above which is the Cathedral,
the largest and most sumptuous church in America, which stands on
the north side of the plaza on the site of the great pyramidal teocalli
or temple of Huitzilopochtli, titular god of the Aztecs.   This church,
which was founded in 1573 and finished in 1657, at a cost of $2,000,-
000, for the walls alone, forms a Greek cross, 426 feet long and 203 feet
wide, with two great naves and three aisles, twenty side chapels, and a
magnificent high altar supported by marble columns, and surrounded
by a tumbago balustrade with sixty-two statues of the same rich gold,
silver, and copper alloy serving as candelabra.   The elaborately carved
choir was also enclosed by tumbago railings made in Macao, weighing
twenty-six tons, and valued at about $1,500,000.   In the interior, the
Doric style prevails, and Renaissance in the exterior, which is adorned
by five domes and two open towers 218 feet high.   At the foot of the

[1] Reproduced in vol. iv. of H. H. Bancroft's *History of the Pacific States*, San
Francisco, 1833, p. 280.

left tower was placed the famous calendar stone, the most interesting relic of Aztec culture, which is now at the National Museum.

The east side of the plaza is occupied by the old vice-regal residence, now the National Palace, with 675 feet frontage, containing most of the Government offices, ministerial, cabinet, treasury, military headquarters, archives, meteorological department with observatory, and the spacious halls of ambassadors, with some remarkable paintings by Miranda and native artists. North of the National Palace, and forming portions of it, are the post-office and the national museum of natural history and antiquities, with a priceless collection of Mexican relics.

Close to the cathedral stands the Monte de Piedad, or national pawnshop, a useful institution, endowed in 1744 by Don Manuel Romero de Terreros with $375,000, and now possessing nearly $10,-000,000 of accumulated funds. Facing the cathedral is the Palacio Municipal, or City Hall, 252 feet by 122, rebuilt in 1792 at a cost of $150,000, and containing the city and district offices, and the merchant's exchange.

Around the Plaza San Domingo were grouped the convent of that name, which contained vast treasures buried within its walls, the old inquisition, now the school of medicine, and for some time the Custom House, which has now been removed to the city boundary. In the same neighborhood are the Church of the Jesuits and the School of Arts, which is, in the language of Brocklehurst, " an immense workshop, including iron and brass foundries, carriage and cart mending, building and masonry, various branches of joinery and upholstery work, and silk and cotton hand-weaving."

Other noteworthy buildings are the national picture gallery of San Carlos, the finest in America, in which the Florentine and Flemish schools are well represented, and which contains the famous *Las Casas*, by Felix Parra ; the national library of St. Augustine, with over 200,-000 volumes, numerous MSS., and many rare old Spanish books ; the mint,[1] which since 1690 has issued coinage, chiefly silver, to the amount of nearly $3,000,000,000 ; the Iturbide Hotel, formerly the residence of the Emperor Iturbide ; the Mineria, or schools of mines, with lecture-rooms, laboratories, rich mineralogical and geological specimens, and a fossil horse, three feet high, of the Pleistocene period.

[1] The Spanish Government intended during last century to build a spacious, costly, and magnificent mint in the City of Mexico, and its plans and specifications were approved by the king, but by a mistake of the clerks in Madrid, they were forwarded to Santiago, Chili, instead of being sent to the City of Mexico, and it was in consequence built there. The building was so fine that, not having any mint at Santiago, it was used as the Government House, and it is now the Executive Mansion and Departments, and it is called " La Moneda," an abbreviation of " La Casa de Moneda," which is the Spanish name for mint.

Among the twenty scientific institutes, mention should be made of the Geographical and Statistical Society, whose meteorological department issues charts and maps of unsurpassed excellence.

Owing to the spongy nature of the soil, the Mineria and many other structures have settled out of the perpendicular, thus often presenting irregular lines and a rickety appearance.

Before 1860 half of the city consisted of churches, convents, and other ecclesiastical structures, most of which have been sequestrated and converted into libraries, stores, warehouses, hotels, and even stables, or pulled down for civic improvements. Nevertheless there still remain fourteen parish and thirty other churches, some of large size, with towers and domes. San Francisco Street is the leading thoroughfare, and is rivalled in splendor only by the new Cinco de Mayo Street, running from the National Theatre to the cathedral.

It would take a great deal more space than it is convenient to give in this paper, should I attempt to make a longer description of the City of Mexico which, being one of the oldest on this continent and the largest and principal one during the three centuries of the Spanish rule, it has quite a number of remarkable buildings and monuments and a very important history, a great deal of romance being connected with it.

The City of Mexico is not only the capital of the country, but the real head of the Republic ; and the aim of all other Mexican cities is to follow in its footsteps and imitate as much as possible the City of Mexico, which to them is a beau ideal and a real paradise.

The City of Mexico is now literally encircled with a belt of factories—cotton, paper, linen, etc., packing houses, brick works, cork factories, soap works, etc., and cheaper fuel will add largely to their number. They have been able to show profits under the load of a dear combustible, and they will welcome the introduction of any fuel, which will enable them to work even more successfully.

Climate.—From the official reports of Professor Mariano Barcena, Director of the National Meteorological Observatory of the City of Mexico, of the weather conditions in 1895, it appears that there were 121 cloudy days. But the rains were mostly at night or late in the afternoon, of short duration, and immediately succeeded by sunshine showers. Long periods of rainy weather are unknown there. The total rainfall for the year, less than twenty inches, will convey a fair idea of the dryness of the climate. The mean temperature in the shade for 1895 was 60 degrees, the highest being 65, reached in April, and the lowest 53, in January, a temperature rather which avoids both extremities. The mean temperature for the summer months were : June, 64 degrees ; July, 62 ; August, 62 ; September, 61.

The table on page 112, prepared by the Weather Bureau of the City of Mexico, contains the average annual climatological data of that city from the years 1877 to 1895.

More detailed data about the climatological conditions of the City of Mexico during the year 1896, prepared also by our Weather Bureau, is appended on page 113.

Mortality in the City of Mexico.—During the year 1896 the total mortality in the City of Mexico, under a recorded population of 330,698, was 15,567, not including 1275 still-births, equivalent to 4.70 per cent. The principal diseases which caused that mortality were those affecting

---

[1] A BRIEF HISTORICAL SKETCH OF THE METEOROLOGY IN THE MEXICAN REPUBLIC.

Priest José Antonio Alzate stands in the first place among those who have cultivated the meteorological science in our country, being he who first devoted himself to its study, and made regular observations during more than eight years, as he himself says in his *Descripcion topográfica de México* (1738 to 1799). Of these observations, he, unfortunately, only published those belonging to the last nine months of the year 1769, in his famous *Gaceta de Literatura de México*, 1788 to 1795. He also published many articles describing some phenomena and instruments, climates of towns, value and usefulness of observations, as he had done in others of his publications : *Diario Literario de México*, 1768 ; *Asuntos varios sobre Ciencias y Artes*, 1772 to 1773 ; and *Observaciones sobre la Física Historia Natural y Artes útiles*, 1787. He was the first in determining the height of the City of Mexico.

After these labors of Father Alzate, we find in the journal *El Sol* regular series of observations published, daily, from the 14th of June, 1824, to the 14th of January, 1828. Dr. John Burkart in 1826 ; Sr. Francisco Gerolt from 1833 to 1834, at the School of Mines ; Sr. José Gómez de la Cortina, Conde de la Cortina, from 1841 to 1845 ; the members of the Geographical Section of the Army Staff from 1842 to 1843 ; the Astronomer Sr. Francisco Jiménez in 1858 ; the School of Mines in the years 1850, 1856, 1857, and 1858 ; Sr. Ignacio Cornejo, M.E., at the same school from 1865 to 1866 ; and Sr. Juan de Mier y Terán at the " Escuela Preparatoria " from 1868 to 1875, respectively, made some meteorological observations.

A series of observations from 1855 to 1875 were made at the Hacienda de San Nicolás Buenavista, and another one at the city of Córdoba from 1859 to 1863, by Dr. José Apolinario Nieto ; Sr. Carlos Sartorius at the Hacienda del Mirador (State of Veracruz) ; Sr. Miguel Velázquez de León, and his sons, Joaquín and Luis, engineers, from 1869 up to the present, at the Hacienda del Pabellón ; Sr. Gregorio Barreto from 1869 to 1880, at the city of Colima ; General Mariano Reyes, Sr. José María Romero, engineer, and Sr. Pascual Alcocer, from 1870 to the present date, at the city of Querétaro ; Sr. Lázaro Pérez from 1874 to 1885, at the city of Guadalajara ; Sr. Isidoro Epstein at the City of Monterrey, 1855 ; Sr. Vicente Reyes, a civil engineer and architect, at the city of Cuernavaca, 1873, 1874, and 1876 ; Sr. Joaquín de Mendízabal Tamborrel, an engineer, at the city of Puebla, 1872 to 1873 ; Sr. Augustin Galindo at the same city, 1875 ; Professor Manuel M. Cházaro at San Juan Michapa (State of Veracruz), 1872 to 1873 ; Priest Pedro Spina, S. J., at the city of Puebla, 1876, and perhaps many others from whom we have no notice, have devoted themselves to making meteorological observations.

The " Sociedad de Geografía y Estadística " the most ancient scientific society in Mexico, distributed, in 1862, some instruments and instructions to observers.

Finally, on the 6th of March, 1877, being President of the Republic, General

CLIMATOLOGICAL DATA OF THE CITY OF MEXICO.

ANNUAL SUMMARIES AND GENERAL SYNOPSIS, 1877–1895.

(ENGLISH MEASURES.)

Lat. N. 19° 26'.   Long. W., Greenwich 6 h, 36 m, 31 s., 56 or 99° 87' 53" 4.   Height, 7472 (Eng. feet).

METEOROLOGICAL DATUM.	1877.	1878.	1879.	1880.	1881.	1882.	1883.	1884.	1885.	1886.	1887.	1888.	1889.	1890.	1891.	1892.	1893.	1894.	1895.	Average, 1877–1895.
Mean barometrical height reduced to the freezing point	23.10	23.09	23.11	23.10	23.10	23.11	23.09	23.08	23.07	23.07	23.07	23.07	23.08	23.08	23.08	23.07	23.07	23.08	23.09	23.08
Maximum barometrical height	23.31	23.28	23.40	23.38	23.34	23.38	23.32	23.38	23.38	23.40	23.30	23.27	23.27	23.28	23.27	23.28	23.28	23.30	23.33	23.33
Minimum barometrical height	22.80	22.87	22.80	22.89	22.84	22.89	22.84	22.88	22.88	22.83	22.85	22.87	22.87	22.89	22.89	22.84	22.89	22.87	22.86	22.83
Mean temperature in open air	61.2	61.2	59.5	59.5	59.9	59.7	59.4	59.4	59.7	59.7	59.0	59.0	60.7	59.8	59.5	59.9	59.5	60.6	59.9	59.7
Mean temperature in shade	85.1	88.0	84.2	86.0	85.1	89.9	89.5	89.5	60.1	84.4	59.2	59.0	85.1	84.0	59.5	59.9	60.4	60.6	84.9	60.3
Maximum temperature in open air	106.5	120.5	105.5	112.8	100.6	101.8	100.0	93.5	84.0	93.0	59.1	100.9	85.1	95.0	59.5	93.0	91.0	95.9	98.6	88.0
Maximum temperature in shade	35.2	30.2	30.9	33.1	28.9	28.9	103.1	26.0	36.9	33.8	97.7	36.4	99.0	84.0	31.8	35.6	31.8	31.9	31.9	30.5
Minimum temperature in open air	28.2	19.0	21.9	26.4	27.0	27.5	26.0	27.9	36.5	30.7	32.0	30.2	36.5	33.8	36.5	33.8	35.5	34.3	31.9	28.9
Minimum temperature in shade							25.8	27.2	25.8	26.7	36.3	32.1	31.5	31.8	56.7	28.9	25.2	22.6	22.6	19.0
Mean temperature of water in shade, per cent, in shade							55.8	56.8	56.8	56.7	56.3	56.8	57.0	55.9	56.7	58.5	58.5	56.5	56.5	56.7
Mean humidity of the air, per cent, in shade	59	57	58	59	61	60	62	59	62	60	63	64	60	61	61	58	59	59	57	60
Mean humidity of the air, per cent, in open air							67	62	63	68	65	64	58	62		58	59	58	58	61
Mean vapor tension in shade	0.397	0.330	0.326	0.322	0.355	0.319	0.337	0.311	0.399	0.333	0.335	0.347	0.320	0.315	0.330	0.315	0.315	0.315	0.315	0.320
Mean vapor tension in open air						0.319	0.320	0.320	0.345	0.310	0.339	0.348	0.303	0.320	0.312	0.312	0.320	0.315	0.315	0.332
Mean evaporation of water in shade	0.083	0.099	0.118	0.103	0.091	0.095	0.087	0.103	0.095	0.103	0.091	0.091	0.111	0.095	0.103	0.107	0.095	0.083	0.099	0.099
Mean evaporation of water in open air	0.268	0.264	0.339	0.323	0.371	0.233	0.209	0.256	0.244	0.244	0.229	0.224	0.286	0.252	0.276	0.276	0.271	0.292	0.277	0.260
Days of rain, total amount	104	120	135	132	162	135	157	123	108	112	166	130	143	155	138	134	136	112	145	138
Rainfall, total amount	15.006	18.987	22.740	21.740	23.433	26.602	23.995	16.085	26.602	20.013	29.130	29.130	19.610	23.017	22.386	17.288	22.369	23.069	22.073	22.015
Greatest precipitation in 24 hours	1.032	2.442	1.288	1.517	1.457	1.575	1.221	1.071	1.686	1.231	2.064	2.501	1.138	1.398	1.595	1.013	1.158	1.639	1.260	2.502
Average cloudiness	4.6	4.4	4.8	4.9	5.3	4.8	5.5	4.7	5.7	4.9	5.3	5.6	5.2	4.9	4.7	4.4	4.6	4.7	5.0	4.9
Prevailing direction of clouds	S.W.	S.W.	W.	W.	S.W.	S.W.&N.E.	S.W.&E.	N.E.	S.W.&N.E.	S.W.	N.	S.W.	N.W.	N.E.	S.W.	S.W.	N.E.	N.E.	N.E.	S.W.
Amount of cloudy days	69	108	121	123	116	118	145	107	146	114	142	158	141	112	105	87	109	103	131	118
Amount of clear days	88	142	135	120	99	110	83	83	75	121	110	81	99	108	137	136	135	119	107	114
Prevailing wind	N.W.	N.W.	N.	N.E.&N.W.	N.W.	W.	N.W.	N.W.&N.E.	N.W.	N.E.	N.E.	N.W.	N.W.	N.W.	S.W.	N.W.&N.	N.W.	N.W.	N.W.	N.W.
Mean velocity of wind, per hour (miles)	2.68	2.45	2.23	2.01	2.23	1.56	2.01	1.70	1.79	1.79	0.89	0.89	0.89	1.34	2.23	2.68	2.23	1.68	2.33	2.01
Maximum velocity of wind, per hour (miles)	28.16	40.23	35.76	40.23	39.41	28.61	31.29	27.94	30.96	46.93	40.23	35.76	34.64	33.08	34.64	45.15	35.55	34.41	32.41	46.93
Direction of the wind of maximum velocity	N.W.	N.E.	N.W.	N.E.	N.W.	N.E.	N.&N.W.	N.E.	N.E.&N.E.	N.E.	S.E.	S.W.	N.&E.	N.&N.W.	S.W.	N.&N.	N.W.	N.L.	N.E.	N.W.
Ozone (mean) (0–10)	4.9	3.4	3.8	4.3	4.6	4.7	4.6	4.5	5.0	4.8	4.6	4.2	3.2	1.5	4.5	3.7	3.5	4.2	3.5	4.6
Amount of lightning days	77	118	111	146	160	164	149	161	189	101	138	146	133	150	119	119	142	157	155	138

MARIANO BÁRCENA, *Director.*   JOSÉ ZENDEJAS, *Vice-Director.*

GENERAL SUMMARY OF THE METEOROLOGICAL OBSERVATIONS TAKEN IN THE CENTRAL OBSERVATORY OF THE CITY OF MEXICO DURING THE YEAR 1896.

Lat. N. 19° 26'. Long. W. of Greenwich, 6 h. 36 m. 31 s. 56 or 99° 07' 53' 4. Height of the barometer above sea level, 7472.25 (Eng. feet).

	Jan.	Feb.	March.	April.	May.	June.	July.	August.	Sept.	Oct.	Nov.	Dec.	YEAR. 1896.
Mean barometrical height, reduced to freezing (inches)	23.083	23.039	23.051	23.075	23.071	23.079	23.106	23.122	23.071	23.071	23.091	23.071	23.079
Maximum barometrical height (inches)	23.276	23.181	23.193	23.209	23.177	23.248	23.240	23.240	23.150	23.173	23.240	23.307	23.307
Minimum barometrical height (inches)	22.878	22.854	22.890	22.906	22.941	22.902	22.902	22.992	22.957	22.957	22.957	22.953	22.854
Mean temperature in shade (Fahrenheit)	55.04	55.94	61.52	65.48	67.04	65.48	63.50	62.96	62.42	61.34	58.46	51.98	60.98
Maximum temperature in shade (Fahrenheit)	72.50	75.20	83.48	86.90	86.24	83.48	81.50	78.44	77.36	75.38	71.06	71.60	89.24
Minimum temperature in shade (Fahrenheit)	36.50	37.40	40.10	43.70	50.00	42.80	51.80	50.00	50.00	49.10	47.30	34.70	34.70
Mean temperature in open air (Fahrenheit)	55.94	56.84	62.42	65.84	67.82	66.02	63.86	63.14	62.78	61.88	59.00	52.70	61.52
Maximum temperature in open air (Fahrenheit)	81.14	87.80	94.10	97.16	98.06	95.00	94.10	91.40	89.06	86.90	84.20	78.80	98.06
Minimum temperature in open air (Fahrenheit)	30.20	29.84	31.28	36.68	42.80	36.50	45.68	44.06	42.98	41.72	38.30	33.00	29.84
Maximum daily range in shade	29.70	35.20	37.80	32.04	33.94	34.20	27.00	25.92	33.30	24.84	33.30	30.00	37.80
Maximum daily range in open air	45.90	53.28	54.36	48.60	52.02	48.60	44.28	35.92	42.48	42.30	42.30	38.30	54.36
Mean temperature of soil (31.5 inches deep)	56.30	55.94	56.66	57.56	61.16	62.78	62.60	62.24	62.24	62.24	61.34	58.64	59.90
Mean temperature of water in shade	52.16	52.52	57.38	60.80	62.60	60.98	60.26	59.54	59.00	57.92	55.04	52.70	57.56
Mean humidity of the air, per cent., in shade	54	48	42	46	47	54	65	65	65	71	68	61	57
Mean humidity of the air, per cent., in open air	54	46	41	46	47	54	65	65	69	70	70	64	58
Mean vapor tension in shade (inches)	0.244	0.221	0.236	0.284	0.311	0.343	0.380	0.382	0.410	0.406	0.354	0.259	0.319
Mean vapor tension in open air (inches)	0.244	0.207	0.239	0.288	0.311	0.347	0.380	0.386	0.410	0.406	0.384	0.271	0.323
Mean evaporation of water in shade (inches)	0.083	0.048	0.107	0.111	0.142	0.139	0.095	0.079	0.079	0.071	0.071	0.055	0.091
Mean evaporation of water in open air (inches)	0.199	0.197	0.264	0.311	0.358	0.331	0.295	0.229	0.232	0.217	0.162	0.118	0.236
Days of rain, total amount	1	6	6	7	7	13	22	25	22	17	13	4	143
Rainfall, total amount (inches)	0.016	0.039	0.099	0.721	0.473	1.170	3.019	2.555	3.324	4.135	0.795	0.615	17.800
Greatest fall in 24 hours (inches)	0.016	0.035	0.024	0.296	0.197	0.433	0.787	0.394	0.914	1.181	0.300	0.538	1.181
Mean amount of clouds (0–10)	4.1	2.8	2.3	4.1	4.5	5.5	7.1	6.3	7.0	6.4	5.9	5.4	5.1
Prevailing direction of clouds	S.W.	S.W.	S.W.	S.W.	N.E. a N.W.	N.E.	N.E.	N.E.	N.E.	N.E.	N.E.	S.W.	N.E.
Amount of cloudy days	6	3	2	6	7	13	13	13	17	15	9	4	111
Amount of clear days	12	19	21	8	9	3	8	1	0	2	3	13	84
Prevailing wind	N.W.	S.W.	N.	N.	N.	N.	N.	N.W.	N.	N.W.	N.W.	N.W.	N. a N.W.
Mean velocity of wind per hour (miles)	1.79	2.68	2.68	2.90	3.35	4.69	3.79	3.35	2.68	1.79	1.12	0.67	2.68
Maximum velocity of wind per hour (miles)	30.96	25.25	29.05	25.25	27.94	27.27	33.52	20.37	30.17	20.33	16.76	11.78	33.52
Direction of the wind of maximum velocity	S.	S. a S.E.	N.E.	S.W.	N.W.	N.W.	N.E.	N.E.	N.E.	N.E.	N.E.	N.W.	N.E.
Ozone [mean] (0–10)	3.4	3.5	3.7	3.7	3.8	3.7	3.5	3.7	3.5	3.3	3.1	2.7	3.5
Amount of lightning days	0	1	4	13	17	19	26	26	24	21	10	0	101

MARIANO BÁRCENA, Director.   JOSÉ ZENDEJAS, Vice-Director.

the digestive and respiratory organs, the former amounting to 4472 or 1.35 per cent. of the population and the latter to 3904 or 1.18 per cent. of the population, and both causing 8376 deaths or 53.81 per cent. of the total number of deaths. Deaths by typhus and typhoid fevers and small-pox, which are supposed to make such great ravages in the City of Mexico, were in reality insignificant, the deaths by the former amounting in that year to 480 or 0.14 per cent. of the population, and the deaths by small-pox were, in the Federal District, embracing the City of Mexico and twenty-three suburban towns, 217 or 0.047 per cent. of the population of the District which is 473,820. Small-pox only attacks the very poor people, and, strange to say, also foreigners, even in case they have been vaccinated in their country, and to be free from small-pox they must be vaccinated in Mexico.

The months of the greatest mortality during the same year were from February to May, and of the smallest the month of August, showing that the unhealthy months are the dry months, that is before the rains set in.

The mortality in the City of Mexico is indeed very large, and it is due principally to two causes, first, the want of proper drainage and sewerage for the refuse of the city, a trouble which is now almost com-

Porfirio Díaz, and by the suggestion of General Vicente Riva Palacio, then Secretary of Public Works, the Central Meteorological Observatory was established. From that date up to the present, an uninterrupted hourly observation is regularly taken during the day and the night in the Central Meteorological Observatory. Some magnetical observations have also been made, and the Observatory is now thought of being removed to a more suitable spot.

After the establishment of the Central Meteorological Observatory, some official or private meteorological stations have also been established as follows : Aguascalientes (Instituto del Estado) ; Guadalajara (Escuela de Ingenieros), observer, Augustín V. Pascal ; Guanajuato (Colegio del Estado), observer, Genaro Montes de Oca ; León (Escuela Secundaria), observer, Mariano Leal ; Mazatlán (Observatorio Astronómico y Meteorológico), observer, N. González ; Oaxaca (Colegio del Estado), observer, Dr. A. Domínguez ; Pachuca (Instituto del Estado), observer, Dr. N. Andrade ; Puebla (Colegio Católico and Colegio del Estado), observers, Priest P. Spina and B. G. González respectively ; Querétaro (Colegio Civil), observer, J. B. Alcocer ; San Luis Potosí (Instituto del Estado), observer, Dr. G. Barroeta ; Toluca (Instituto del Estado), observer, S. Enríquez ; Veracruz, observer, G. Baturoni ; Zacatecas (Instituto), J. A. Bonilla. Dr. Manuel Andrade, of Huejutla ; Dr. Matienzo, of Tampico ; Father Pérez, of Morelia ; Father Arreola, of Colima ; Father Castellanos, of Zapotlán ; Sr. Pascual Borbón, of Tacámbaro, are enlightened observers to whom the Central Meteorological Observatory is indebted for their valuable co-operation, and also to the telegraph operators of the " Telegraph system," who send, daily, some weather observations to this office.

The staff of the Central Meteorological Observatory is now as follows : Director, Mariano Bárcena ; Vice-Director, José Zendejas, C.E. ; Second Observer, Francisco Toro ; Assistants, Rafael Aguilar, Francisco Quiroga, Angel Robelo, José Torres, and J. I. Vázquez.

pletely remedied, and the second, the unhygienic way of living of the poor classes, among whom takes place the largest mortality.

The very large number of still-births which occurred in the City of Mexico in 1896, almost exclusively among the poor classes, shows the little care that the poor women take of themselves, and is enough to explain the present large mortality.

RAILWAYS.

For many years the government earnestly endeavored to further the construction of railroads in Mexico, but the broken surface of the country made the building of these roads very expensive. Until 1873 the means of internal locomotion were mainly limited to a few wagon roads, over which travelled twenty-four regular lines of diligences, under one management; and bridle-paths from the central plateau over the sierras and terrace lands down to a few points on both coasts.

In 1854 the first railroad was finished, connecting the City of Mexico with Guadalupe, about three miles in length, and another from Veracruz to Tejeria towards the City of Mexico about twelve miles in length; these being the only railroads that were built, up to 1861. During the French Intervention the French army extended the Tejeria road to Paso del Macho, about thirty-five miles further, to the foot of the mountain, so as to be able to transport their army, with the shortest delay possible, out of the yellow-fever zone, toward the central plateau ; and an English Company, which had a grant for a road from the City of Mexico to Veracruz, which was supposed at the time to be the only one that could be built in Mexico, extended the Guadalupe road to Apizaco in the direction of Veracruz and not far from Puebla.

No construction of consequence was done immediately after the French Intervention, because the country was generally in a disturbed condition, although several efforts were made in that direction by President Juarez, under whose administration a new and very liberal grant was given to the Veracruz railway company. The Veracruz road was finished in 1873, during Señor Lerdo de Tejada's Presidency, and when General Diaz became President in 1876 he earnestly promoted railroad building ; and we now have two trunk lines connecting the City of Mexico with the United States—the Mexican Central to El Paso, Texas, with a branch from San Luis Potosi to the port of Tampico, and another from Irapuato to Guadalajara, which has recently been extended to Ameca, towards the Pacific ; and the Mexican National to Laredo, Texas, with several branches. Another trunk line from Eagle Pass to Torreon and Durango, which it is intended shall finally reach the Pacific, has also been built by Mr. C. P. Huntington and his associates. There is besides a line from Nogales to Guaymas, built and owned by the Atchison, Topeka, and Santa Fé

Company; and these four lines connect us with the main systems of the United States, our lines being in fact extensions of the United States railway system.

We have now two lines from the City of Mexico to Veracruz, the old Veracruz road passing by Orizaba, and the Interoceanic, which runs from Veracruz by Jalapa and the City of Mexico and is intended to reach the Pacific. All of our roads, excepting the one built by Mr. Huntington, have had large subsidies paid by the Mexican Government, and in one case, that of the Veracruz railroad, the subsidy paid was $560,000 per year, for twenty-eight years, or about $57,471 per English mile, although the average subsidy per mile, according to President Diaz's report, dated November 30, 1896, is $14,380.

The Tehuantepec railway, running from Coatzacoalcos on the Gulf of Mexico to Salina Cruz on the Pacific, about one hundred and thirty miles in length, has been built at great expense and at a great sacrifice by the Mexican Government. I published in the *Engineering Maga-zine* for March, 1894,[1] an article stating the different efforts made by the Mexican Government to have that road built, and the advantages that we expected from it as a highway of trade between the Atlantic and the Pacific. The Mexican Government has recently made a con-tract with Messrs. E. Weetman, Pearson & Son, of London, for the building of good harbors at both ends of the road, and when that is accomplished we expect that a great deal of eastern trade will pass through Tehuantepec.

With the exception of the Tehuantepec road, we have not yet any road running from the Atlantic to the Pacific, although several are in process of construction. The descent of the mountains is on the Pa-cific slope a great deal more difficult than on the Gulf coast, where the large centres of population are located near the Gulf, and this explains why none of the roads have so far been able to reach the Pacific Ocean.

Our railway system extends now, in the direction of Guatemala, as far as the city of Oaxaca, where we are only about five hundred miles away from our frontier with Guatemala. In other directions, our sys-tem reaches the principal cities and commercial and mining centres of the country.

The total mileage of railway in 1895 was 6989½ English miles. President Diaz, in his above mentioned report gives, the total mileage of railways in Mexico as 11,469 kilometres or 7126 miles; and in his message to Congress on April 1, 1897, he stated that the railway mile-age had been increased by 238 kilometres 550 metres, finished and received by the Government, and 248 kilometres built, but not yet re-ceived officially, making a total mileage of 11,955 kilometres 550 metres, or 7.429 miles.

[1] This paper will appear in this volume.

President Diaz's Railway Policy.—President Diaz deserves a great deal of credit for his efforts to promote in Mexico, material improvements, and especially in railroad building. When he came into power, in 1877, public opinion was very much divided as to the policy of allowing citizens of the United States to develop the resources of the country by building railroads, working mines, etc. Our experience of what took place in consequence of the liberal grants given by Mexico to Texan colonists made many fear that a repetition of that liberal policy might endanger the future of the country by giving a foothold in it to citizens of the United States who might afterward, if circumstances favored them, attempt to repeat the case of Texas. President Lerdo de Tejada seemed to share such fears judging by his policy in this regard. But President Diaz, as a broad-minded and patriotic statesman, believed that the best interest of the country required its material development, and that it would not be advisable to discriminate against citizens of the United States, as that country was more interested than any other, on account of its contiguity to Mexico, in developing the resources of our country by building an extensive system of railways, and would, therefore, be more ready than any other to assist in building them. He trusted, at the same time, that when the resources of the country should be more fully developed, it would become so strong as to be beyond reach of the temptation by foreign states or individuals. The results of the work done in Mexico so far show that General Diaz acted wisely, and proved himself equal to the task before him.

Many in Mexico, and myself among the number, thought that, as the railroads were such lucrative enterprises, especially in a country endowed with so many natural elements of wealth as Mexico, it would not be judicious to give their promoters any pecuniary assistance, in the shape of subsidies or otherwise, the more so as the finances of the country were then in a critical condition, and it would not be wise to increase its burdens by large pecuniary subsidies in aid of private enterprises. My opinion in this case was based mainly on what I had seen in the United States, namely : that long lines of railways are built in this country without any pecuniary assistance from the Government, and that when the Government subsidized any one line it became a source of great dissatisfaction and very unpleasant questions, which are yet unsettled. We feared also that such large subsidies as were asked by the railway promoters would amount in the end to so large a sum as to make it impossible for Mexico to pay it, discrediting the country. But in this case General Diaz's view seems to have been the right one, in so far as that it afforded a great inducement for the immediate building of large trunk lines of railways, which, without subsidy, might have been delayed for several years. He thought it worth while to spend large sums of money for the purpose of having railways built without delay, rather than trust to the fluctuations of confidence and credit in the foreign exchanges, that would enable the prospective companies to obtain the funds necessary to build their roads, trusting, at the same time, that the material development of the country promoted by the railroads would yield revenue enough to pay all the subsidies granted. Fortunately all railroad subsidies contracted by Mexico have been punctually paid, and their amount forms now a large item of our national debt. To pay some of them the mistake was made of negotiating a sterling loan on Europe, to pay a silver debt ; but even in that way the transaction is not altogether a bad one.

General Diaz's policy was to give a railway subsidy to anybody asking for it without investigating the responsibility of the concern, with the idea that if the road was built the country would get the benefit of the same, and if it was not built nothing would be lost, as there was in all grants, a clause to the effect that if no building was done within a given time, the grant should by that mere fact be forfeited, the forfeiture to be declared by the Administration.

The system of subsidizing railways has a great many drawbacks, but at the same time commands some decided advantages, like giving the government the strict supervision over the roads who have to submit to it for its approval, tariffs for freights and passengers, the free carrying of the mails, the duty of the company to present to the government a yearly statement of its traffic, receipts, etc., and other similar advantages. In all grants to subsidized railroads there is a stipulation that at the end of ninety-nine years the road-bed would revert to the Mexican government.

President Diaz's Statistics on Mexican Railways.—Before I close this chapter I think it will not be out of place to quote some remarks of President Diaz concerning our Mexican railroads, which occur in his above-mentioned report.

.   .   .   .

"In 1875 we had 578 kilometres 285 metres of railway, in 1885 we had 5915 kilometres, in 1886, 6018 kilometres, in November, 1888, 7940 kilometres, in June, 1892, 10,233, and including the tramways and other local and private lines, the amount was 11,067 kilometres ; in September, 1894, we had 11,100 kilometres ; in April, 1896, 11,165 kilometres, and now we have 11,469 kilometres. . . .

"We stand first in railroad building of all the Latin-American countries. During the years 1877 to 1892 Mexico built more railroads than any other Latin-American State, being 11,165 kilometres ; the Argentine Republic takes the second place, with 8108 kilometres, and Brazil the third, with 6193 kilometres, built during the years mentioned. The average number of kilometres built per annum in Mexico during this period was 689, the maximum having been reached in

1881–82.....................................	1938 kilometres
1882–83...............................,......	1727 "
1887–88.....................................	1217 "
1889	1263 "

The number of passengers carried in

1876.....................................	4,281,327
1890.....................................	19,531,395
1893.....................................	22,781,343
1895.....................................	24,269,895

The freight handled in

1876.....................................	132,915 tons
1890.....................................	2,734,430 "
1893.....................................	3,798,360 "
1895.....................................	4,117,511 "

The gross receipts in

1876.....................................	$2,564,870
1890.....................................	21,019,960
1893.....................................	26,121,624
1897.....................................	28,758,450

" The subsidies paid for railroads up to December, 1892, averaged $8935 per kilometre of road built and in operation at that date. This average is much less than that of the subsidies paid by other Latin-American countries, the Republic of Chili having averaged $17,635 per kilometre, and the Argentine Republic $31,396.

" The railroad system of the Republic has given the capital direct and rapid connection with our principal states. Throughout the length of the central plateau to the frontier, Mexico City is connected with the capitals of the states of Querétaro, Guanajuato, Jalisco, Aguascalientes, Zacatecas, Chihuahua, and San Luis Potosi by the Mexican Central Railway, and with Durango by the Mexican International; with the states of Mexico, Guanajuato, Michoacan, San Luis Potosi, Coahuila and Nuevo Leon by the Mexican National; with the cities of Puebla, Orizaba, Cordoba, Veracruz, and Jalapa by the Mexican Railway and by the Interoceanic, and with Tehuacan and Oaxaca by the Mexican Southern from Puebla. Three lines connect the capital with the northern frontier; the Central, which terminates in Ciudad Juarez; the National, which runs to Nuevo Laredo; and the International, which, from its junction with the Central at Torreon, runs to Piedras Negras. And as to our various ports Guaymas is connected with Nogale on the northern frontier; Manzanillo with Colima; Matamoros with Reynosa and San Miguel; Tampico with San Luis Potosi and Monterrey; Veracruz with Jalapa and Mexico; and the first really Interoceanic railway of the Republic across the Isthmus of the Tehuantepec, united the Atlantic and Pacific oceans by connecting the port of Coatzacoalcos, on the gulf, with the port of Salina Cruz on the Pacific coast. Southward from the capital of the Republic the Interoceanic traverses the State of Morelos, and the Mexico, Cuernavaca and Pacific Railway has its line located to the City of Cuernavaca and is pushing on through the state of Guerrero to the port of Acapulco. In the peninsula of Yucatan, the lines connecting Campeche and Merida are nearly finished; while the port of Progreso has rail communication with Merida."

Financial Condition of Mexican Railways.—Our railroads are doing remarkably well, and their traffic, especially domestic, is daily increasing and grows in much larger proportion than the foreign, or international traffic ; and they are paying the interest on their debt, which is due and paid in gold, notwithstanding that they collect their freights in silver, which has been for several years at a great discount, losing at the present rate of exchange about one hundred per cent. in the operation ; but their business is such that they can afford to suffer that loss.

In the statistical section of this paper will be found a list of our railroads, their mileage, earnings, and several other data, showing that they are in a prosperous condition, all of which will be of interest to those who desire to have a more intimate acquaintance with the railway system of Mexico. I will only insert here the following statement of the annual building and earnings of the Mexican railways, supplementing it with a comparative statement showing the tonnage moved by the principal railway lines, for the ten years ending December 31, 1896, which shows a great increase in their business, and consequently in their earnings.

ANNUAL BUILDINGS AND EARNINGS OF MEXICAN RAILWAYS.

YEAR.	MILES OF ROADS BUILT.		ANNUAL EARNINGS.
	Each year.	Total.	
1873...............	— —	359,306	$2,097,104.55
1874...............	5,393	364,699	2,665,496.18
1875...............	47,087	418,001	2,799,696.13
1876...............	2,265	414,052	2,563,241.00
1877...............	3,739	417,791	3,213,434.17
1878...............	40,748	458,539	3,400,799.89
1879...............	91,950	550,488	3,828,718.65
1880...............	120,328	670,817	4,504,135.39
1881...............	429,858	1,100,675	5,679,193.37
1882...............	1,204,118	2,304,792	9,883,719.51
1883...............	1,073,404	3,378,196	12,102,583.34
1884...............	282,523	3,660,719	11,089,136.39
1885...............	73,614	3,734,332	10,656,551.42
1886...............	49,099	3,783,432	11,373,667.63
1887...............	323,084	4,106,516	13,310,218.79
1888...............	756,522	4,863,060	16,121,267.79
1889...............	390,650	5,253,096	18,788,142.29
1890...............	784,744	6,037,752	20,919,287.14
1891....	495,015	6,532,711	23,762,172.87
1892...............	352,171	6,884,842	25,363,922.29
1893...............	14,829	6,870,015	25,359,244.06
1894...............	118,810	6,888,811	— —

COMPARATIVE STATEMENT, SHOWING APPROXIMATE TONNAGE MOVED
BY THE UNDERMENTIONED RAILWAYS FOR THE TEN YEARS
ENDED DECEMBER 31, 1896.

(*Compiled from published reports and information furnished by the respective railway companies.*)

YEAR.	CENTRAL RAILWAY.	NATIONAL RAILWAY.	INTEROCEANIC RAILWAY.	MEXICAN RAILWAY.	TOTAL.
	Tons.	Tons.	Tons.	Tons.	Tons.
1887........	346,898	77,935	141,090	273,194	839,117
1888........	477,530 Inc. 34.4	372,800 Inc. 378.3	197,231 Inc. 39.7	318,893 Inc. 16.7	1,366,454 Inc. 62.7
1889........	540,479 Inc. 13.1	428,314 Inc. 14.8	186,222 Dec. 5.5	354,321 Inc. 11.1	1,509,336 Inc. 10.4
1890........	609,382 Inc. 12.7	472,045 Inc. 10.2	281,769 Inc. 51.3	384,584 Inc. 8.2	1,747,780 Inc. 15.7
1891........	867,657 Inc. 42.3	502,856 Inc. 7.3	277,866 Dec. 1.3	409,185 Inc. .6	2,057,564 Inc. 17.7
1892........	1,091,785 Inc. 25.8	588,505 Inc. 17.	365,191 Inc. 31.4	367,980 Dec. 10.	2,413,461 Inc. 17.3
1893........	860,187 Dec. 21.2	552,123 Dec. 6.5	380,805 Inc. 4.3	385,923 Inc. 4.8	2,179,038 Dec. 9.7
1894........	898,484 Inc. 4.4	558,382 Inc. 1.1	444,191 Inc. 16.6	433,637 Inc. 12.3	2,334,694 Inc. 7.1
1895........	1,047,038 Inc. 16.5	636,193 Inc. 13.9	464,976 Inc. 4.4	453,289 Inc. 4.5	2,601,496 Inc. 11.4
1896........	1,231,025 Inc. 17.5	782,106 Inc. 22.9	479,744 Inc. 3.1	756,330 Inc. 66.8	3,249,205 Inc. 24.8
	7,970,465	4,971,259	3,219,085	4,137,336	20,298,145

(S.)   A. BLAKE.

CITY OF MEXICO, May 19, 1897.

TELEGRAPHS.

We have quite a number of miles of telegraph lines in Mexico, and our service is now as good as that of any other country.   The first telegraph line built and owned in Mexico by a private company, liberally assisted by the government, extended from Veracruz to the City of Mexico.   On November 5, 1851, the first section was inaugurated from the City of Mexico to Nopalucan, and on May 19, 1852, to Veracruz.

In 1853 another company established a line from the City of Mexico towards the north to Leon in the State of Guanajuato, and in 1865 a line was finished to San Luis Potosi.

In 1868 and 1869 a private company, called the " Jalisco Company " established the line between the City of Mexico and Guadalajara, which was soon afterwards extended to Manzanillo and San Blas.   After the restoration of the Republic in 1867, the Mexican government began to build lines to the principal centres of population of the country, and in 1890 it bought the Jalisco line, and in 1894 the Veracruz.

From 1869 to 1876 the States of Michoacan, Oaxaca, and Zacatecas established several lines in their respective jurisdictions. When General Diaz became President in 1876, the National Telegraphic Lines only had 7927 kilometres.

In 1885 the Federal Goverment transferred to the States, without any cost, all the telegraphic lines which were considered of local interest, keeping only such as could be called trunk lines.

In 1893 we had 37,880 English miles of telegraph lines, of which 24,840 belonged to the Federal Government, the remainder belonging in about equal parts to the States, private companies and railways.

The following statement, which I take from the *Anuario Estadistico de la Republica Mexicano, 1895*, shows the telegraphic lines belonging to the Federal Government, to the States, to private companies and to railroads :

```
Federal Lines...........................43,416 k 780 m
State Lines.............................. 5,544    068 "
Private Company Lines.................. 4,730    980 "
Railroad Lines......................... 9,761    611 "
                                        ─────────────
General Total.....................63,453 k 439 "
```

On November 30, 1896, the total mileage of our telegraph lines was, according to the President's report of that date, 45,000 kilometres, 27,962 English miles, and that amount was increased, according to the President's message of April 1, 1897, to 45,259 kilometres, 28,123 miles.

In 1891 the operations of the various lines throughout the Republic involved the transmission of 1,050,000 messages, of which about 800,-000 were private, and the remainder official. The receipts from this branch of the public service amounted to $469,305 collected at 767 offices ; the expenditure included for repairs an average of $3 per kilometre, and for salaries a total of $671,431.

The proceeds of the Federal telegraphic lines were, according to President Diaz's report of November 30, 1896, as follows :

```
Fiscal Year, 1883–1884.....................$239,051
    "      "    1890–1891..................... 462,076
    "      "    1893–1894..................... 524,634
    "      "    1895–1896..................... 537,308
```

In the statistical portion of this paper will be found a detail statement of the earnings and expenses of the national telegraphic lines of

Mexico for the 27 fiscal years which elapsed from July 1, 1869, to June 30, 1896, and such data as it is possible to obtain for the ten years which elapsed from July 1, 1869, to June 30, 1879.

Cables.—Up to 1887 there was no communication between Mexico and foreign countries. In 1880 the Mexican Cable Co. built their cables from Galveston to Tampico, Veracruz and Coatzacoalcos, on the Gulf of Mexico, and a telegraphic line from Coatzacoalcos to Salina Cruz, on the Pacific, which was extended to Central and South America. Cables had been laid between Jicalango and El Carmen and between the rivers Grijalva and Coatzacoalcos, and now through those cables we are in direct communication with the United States and Europe.

POSTAL SERVICE.

Our postal service has improved considerably of late. It was until recently quite imperfect on account of the difficult and expensive ways of communication. It used to be slow and so expensive that it was almost prohibitory, and up to 1870 the single postage of a letter, weighing one quarter an ounce was 25 cents, and double for any distance exceeding sixty miles. After Mexico entered into the Universal Postal Union, in 1870, the postage of letters for foreign countries was reduced to 5 cents, and that reduction made it necessary to reduce the home postage from 25 to 10 cents. Recently it has been reduced again from 10 to 5 cents.

There were in the whole country, in 1883, one head post-office at the national capital, 53 first-class post-offices, 265 second class, for the most part inefficient, and 518 postal agencies, little better than useless. The entire service as it was being rendered at 837 stations. The evils resulting from the very high postage were further aggravated by the insecurity of the mails. The revenue of the postal department in that year amounted to $817,244.

The total number of post-offices and postal agencies in 1893 was 1448, and the mail pouches are now transported on railways over a total distance of 10,000 kilometres, or more than 6000 miles. Over the remaining distances in the interior the mails are conveyed either by stages or by foot or mounted carriers.

President Diaz gives in his report of November 30, 1896, the following statistics about our postal services :

	Post Offices.	Postal Agencies.
1877	53	269
1888	356	719
1892	356	1430
1895	469	1471
1896	471	1500

President Diaz states in his same report that the total number of pieces distributed by our mails in the year 1878 was 5,169,892, while in the year 1896 the number increased to 24,000,000.

For the purpose of communicating with foreign countries, especially before railroads were finished, the Mexican government granted large subsidies to steamship companies, running especially between Mexican and United States ports, and their amount increased considerably the expenses of our post-office department.

In the statistical part of this paper I shall insert the statement of the earnings and expenses of the postal service in Mexico, in the twenty-seven years elapsed from July 1, 1869, to June 30, 1896.

PUBLIC LANDS.

The Spanish government considered itself the owner of lands in Mexico, and it granted them to private parties under certain very liberal regulations. The Indians having been the original owners, and needing the lands to raise their food, and textiles for their clothing, could not be entirely deprived of them, and a large portion of the land was left to each municipality to be held generally in common by the inhabitants of the same. Large tracts of land remain, however, which had not been granted either to the Indians nor to the Spanish settlers, and these we called vacant lands—Terrenos Baldios. The Mexican government succeeded Spain in the ownership of public lands, and with a view to make them available for colonization an easy system to dispose of them at a comparatively low price was established.

The greatest difficulty was to find the public lands, as they had never before been surveyed, and a great many were occupied without title by private parties. As such survey would be very expensive, the Mexican government devised a plan of contracting that work with private companies, paying them with one-third of the land measured, and in that way large portions of the public lands have been surveyed.

It appears from President Diaz's report to his fellow-citizens, dated November 30, 1896, that up to 1888 private companies had surveyed 33,811,524, hectares of public lands, for which they received in payment for their work one-third or 11,036,407 hectares. In the four years from 1889 to 1892, 16,820,141 hectares of public lands were surveyed by private companies, of which 11,213,427 hectares belonged to the government, and in that way in less than ten years it was possible to survey 50,631,665 hectares. Out of this amount the government sold to private parties and to colonization companies 1,607,493 hectares, and to private companies who were in possession of public lands held by them without any title, which we call *demacias*, 4,222,991 hectares. At the same time the government has been trying to divide the lands held in common by the Indian towns between the inhabitants of the same, and up to 1888 it had distributed in that manner 67,368 hectares among 2936 titles, and from 1889 to 1892 180,169 hectares among 4560 titles. In accordance with the provisions of our public land laws we sold to private parties, who pre-empted the lands for purchase, which we call *"denuncio,"* 3,635,388 hectares among 1504 titles, and from 1889 to 1892 1,353,137 hectares among 1218 titles. From July 1, 1891, to August 18, 1896, 9,677,689 hectares of land were surveyed, of which 6,504,912 hectares belong to the government, and the balance, 3,172,777 hectares, belong to private companies.

Every year the Department of Fomento publishes under authority of law a price-list of public lands, which have different prices in each state and are sometimes divided into three classes ; the first, second, and third having each a different price. The following is the official price of public lands fixed by the Department of Fomento for the fiscal year 1895–1896 :

STATES	PRICE PER HECTARE	STATES	PRICE PER HECTARE
Aguascalientes..........	$2.25	Oaxaca.................	$1.10
Campeche..............	1.80	Puebla.................	3.35
Coahuila	1.00	Queretaro	3.35
Colima.................	2.25	San Luis Potosi........	2.25
Chiapas................	2.00	Sinaloa	1.10
Chihuahua.............	1.00	Sonora................	1.00
Durango	1.00	Tabasco...............	2.50
Guanajuato............	3.35	Tamaulipas............	1.00
Guerrero..............	1.10	Tlaxcala..............	2.25
Hidalgo...............	2.25	Veracruz..............	2.75
Jalisco.................	2.25	Yucatan...............	1.80
Mexico................	3.35	Zacatecas.............	2.25
Michoacan	2.25	District federal........	5.60
Morelos...............	4.50	Territore de Tepic	2.00
New Leon.............	1.00	Territory of Lower Cal...	0.65

In the statistical part of this paper I shall insert some data about the sales of public lands by the Mexican government from 1867 to 1895, and a statement of the titles issued from the years 1877 to 1895.

IMMIGRATION.

It has always been the aim of the Mexican government from the time of the independence of the country, to encourage the immigration of foreigners, because Mexico being so large and the population so scanty, it was considered a necessity to promote the development of the country, to increase the population by inducing the settlement of foreigners, and different laws have been issued for that purpose.

Since the restoration of the Republic new laws have been sanctioned to encourage colonization, which allow colonists and the companies bringing them free importation of their personal goods and such articles as they may need for their subsistence and welfare for a reasonable term of years, exempting them at the same time from all kinds of taxes—federal, state, and municipal,—excepting only the stamp tax, and also exempting them from military and other personal service, and sometimes even going so far as to give a bounty for each colonist brought to the country.　Under such laws several contracts were made with different companies, and 32 colonies have been planted in different sections of Mexico, of which 13 have been established by the government and 19 by private parties.　In 1892 there were only 1266 families with a total number of 10,985 colonists.　On the whole, the efforts made and the expenses incurred by the Mexican government in the establishment of those settlements of colonists, have had but unsatisfactory results, but they have paved the way for future experiments on a larger scale, especially if undertaken by private parties, and with only such assistance from the government as can be rendered by liberal legislation.

The principle obstacle which has prevented us from having a large immigration is our low wages.　Those who immigrate are generally poor wage earners, who want to better their condition, and they could not go to a country where wages are a great deal lower than in the United States, or even in Europe, as they could never compete with the native labor of our Indians.　We have now a surplus of labor and a deficit of capital, and cannot have a large immigration until such conditions are changed.

What Mexico needs is capital to develop her resources and give employment to labor, and then immigration will flow in as naturally as water seeks its level.　Mexican credit will be established, so far as immigration is concerned, when her natural resources are developed, this being the only safe and reliable basis of such credit, and this will never be developed until those who have capital to invest are acquainted with the unparalleled opportunities for safe and profitable investment in Mexico.　This will only be accomplished by plain, blunt, matter-of-fact and well-informed press agents, who lay before people who have money to invest the plain facts of the case.

Immigration from the United States.—I have often been asked for my opinion of the chances of Americans going to settle in Mexico, and have always answered that while Mexico is desirous of attracting good settlers, and while that country undoubtedly offers great inducements to foreign settlers, especially to those having some means, there are serious drawbacks which ought to be pointed out to the prospective immigrant from the United States, as a warning against a possible failure and disappointment.

The comforts of life in the rural districts of Mexico, where a settler from this country has the best chances, are scanty compared with similar districts in the United States. The difference of race, language, religion, and education between a young man brought up in this country and the small Mexican farmers, are enough to create difficulties at first sight insuperable to any young man from the United States who settles there. If he establishes himself in a district inhabited only by Indians these difficulties are considerably increased. If the settler prefers the hot lands, which are the most fertile and productive, the severity of the climate is such as to challenge the courage of the bravest. The mosquitoes of several varieties, the flies, and many other insects are very annoying, besides the sickness inherent to such climate.

The question of labor is another great difficulty in the way, because, while it is cheap and abundant in the cold regions, it is generally scarce and unreliable in the hot lands.

The conditions of the two countries are so very different that the change experienced by one brought up in this country who goes into Mexico, is very apt to discourage the strongest and most sanguine, at least in the beginning, as the lapse of time makes anybody adapt himself to existing conditions and to appreciate the advantages of his new home.

The land question is also a serious objection. A large portion of the public lands have already been disposed of, and comparatively little of the public and private lands have been surveyed, and cannot easily be had in small lots. The large land-holders are unwilling to divide their estates, and the Indians holding large tracts of land are very reluctant to part with them at any price.

Coffee raising is undoubtedly one of the most profitable undertakings in Mexico, but at the same time it has serious drawbacks. It takes from three to four years before the trees begin to yield, and the planter must be provided with sufficient means to defray not only his personal expenses, but also those of the plantation, like houses, machinery, cultivation, etc., without receiving any proceeds until the third or fourth year. Besides, if he makes any mistake in the selection of his land, his profits will be considerably reduced. The general impression prevailing in Mexico is that coffee is the product of the hot lands, where the coffee trees need shade ; but a plantation in such lands would cost a great deal more money to make and to keep, and would yield smaller profits than one located in the temperate zone, that is, just below the frost line.[1]

[1] The same views were expressed in Mexico to the State Department by the United States Consuls, and even published in the *Consular Reports* for August, 1894, vol. xlv., No. 167, pp. 628, 629.

"Consular advices received at the Department of State warn Americans about emigrating to Mexico, with a view to permanent settlement, with insufficient means or without informing themselves in a reliable way as to the prospects for earning liveli-

For the American common laborer who looks to his day's pay for his living, Mexico is unquestionably not the proper place to go. He cannot compete with the Mexican laborer, whose usual pay is from 38 to 50 cents a day in silver, and he boards himself. For the man who has no means, unless he is especially qualified in some particular branch, and knows something of the language, and will work harder and longer hours, it is no place. There is room for the steady, sober, industrious mechanic or miner or tradesman who will adapt himself to new conditions and surroundings, leave all social, political, and other ambitions behind him, and who will attend strictly to his own business.

Those who are safest in going to Mexico are those who have a little capital, say from $2000 in gold and upward, which will give them about twice that amount there; who can look around and decide what they propose to do, and where they want to settle. There is an excellent field for the small general farmer of the New England or Middle States type, who will raise a little of everything. Butter, potatoes, hogs, poultry, corn, vegetables, and small grain find a ready sale at good prices. I have seen the common article of corn, which is nearly always a sure crop, sell at from $1 to $1.25 per bushel, Mexican money.

It is always best for the mechanic or miner to first secure a job before going to Mexico, and work for wages several months, and in the meantime study the situation, get acquainted with the language, the customs, and the people before going it alone.

The manner of living there and the customs of the people are totally different from those of the United States. Those going there will have to work harder and longer hours than in the United States, but they can save money. Ten years ago Americans went to Mexico to make money and return to the United States ; to-day they go to find homes. I know several Americans who would not live in the United States again.

The climate of Mexico permits a man to work every day in the year. The cost of living and clothing is cheap, and a dollar in Mexican money can be made to go as far there as a dollar in American money in the United States, and a dollar there is easier to get.

In mining, Mexico offers inducements superior to any other coun-

hoods. While there are undoubtedly good opportunities in Mexico for enterprise, frugality, and thrift, it is like other countries, a land of varying conditions, and it often happens that disappointment is the result of emigration undertaken upon insufficient or misleading information, or without resources, which are always necessary for success in a new country. Many Americans have been induced by alluring statements as to the cheapness of coffee raising, etc., to emigrate to Mexico within the past year, and some have lost their. all by so doing. For these reasons Consuls desire to caution Americans against the representations of speculators, who are always on the watch for the unwary."

try ; and whether a man has a thousand dollars or a million he can go there and make money if he exercises ordinary precaution and judgment, and if he makes up his mind to stand the discomforts of the country. It is a good country for the prospector, too, because there are no seasons against him, and there are many new fields entirely untouched; but he needs money enough to get there with and enable him to obtain the proper kind of outfit, and time to familiarize himself with the requirements of the law and select some district in which he wants to operate.

For the small capitalist, or for a small syndicate, there is no finer field for the organizing of small legitimate companies for the purposes of opening and working old abandoned mines, which are filled with débris or water, and which it will pay to clean out and work, and of which there are still many to be had. In times gone by they were abandoned because of the refractory condition of the ores, or lack of machinery, or want of transportation, all of which conditions have been removed. There is also a fine opening for capital for the exploration of the new gold-fields in the vicinity of Guadalupe y Calvo, in the range between Sonora and Chihuahua, in the State of Guerrero, and in many other localities.

There are in various parts of Mexico educated, experienced, and thoroughly reliable Americans to be found, who have lived a long while in the country, and know the language, the laws, and the people, and would be willing to give reliable information to young Americans wishing to go there.

PUBLIC DEBT.

The public debt of Mexico is represented by bonds drawing different rates of interest, some payable in gold and others in silver. In 1825, very soon after our independence, we contracted two loans in London, both for 10,000,000 pounds sterling, which we mainly used for buying war-ships and war material. On account of the disturbed condition of the country, the interest on that debt could not be paid punctually, and the bonds naturally fell to a very low nominal price. In 1851, after the war with the United States, we refunded that debt in new bonds, the interest of which was reduced from 5 to 3 per cent., which we expected to pay punctually, but the disturbed condition of the country made it impossible for us to do it. Finally, in 1888, the debt was readjusted and gold bonds bearing 6 per cent. interest issued, and as we have paid since punctually the interest, they have reached par.

We had issued bonds from 1849 to 1856 to pay claims of English, French, and Spanish subjects under certain conventions signed with those countries, and such bonds were exchanged at different rates for the 6 per cent. gold bonds of our foreign debt.

To build the Tehuantepec Railway we negotiated in London, in 1888, another gold loan for 3,000,000 pounds sterling at 5 per cent. interest.

The subsidies granted to railway companies were payable in silver, with a percentage of our import duties, but as they amounted to a considerable sum their payment reduced the revenue considerably, and the Mexican Government contracted in London in 1890 a gold loan at 6 per cent. interest, with which it paid the subsidies due up to that date to most of the railway companies.

We had to issue besides in 1850 what we call domestic or interior bonds, at 3 and 5 per cent. interest in silver, and we had other indebtedness of several kinds, caused by loans and other sources when the revenue of the Government was not enough to pay its expenses. All such debts have been consolidated into new bonds of 3 and 5 per cent. interest, payable in silver. Such railway subsidies as were not paid out of the proceeds of the loan of 1890 have been paid with bonds drawing 5 per cent. interest, paying both capital and interest in silver.

It is very onerous for Mexico when it is on a silver basis to pay in gold the interest of its foreign debt, because we have to buy gold at current prices, and it costs us now more than double its current price. When silver was about 50 cents on the dollar, as compared with gold, 6 per cent. interest of our foreign debt, cost us 12 per cent., and of course the further silver is depreciated the greater will be the cost of paying the interest of our gold debts.

President Diaz gives in his report of November 30, 1896, the following data about the cost to the Mexican Treasury of buying exchange to place in London the funds to pay us the gold interest on our foreign debt :

Fiscal year 1888–1889...................$ 729,178.17
    "   "   1890–1891................... 2,314,477.77
    "   "   1891–1892................... 3,225,246.77
    "   "   1892–1893................... 5,101,223.57

In the second part of this paper I will give a detailed statement showing the different kinds of bonds and obligations which constitute the Mexican debt, and here will only give the figures of the total amount, which are the following :

Sterling Mexican debt.................$114,675,895.49
Debt payable in silver...............   88,549,111.80
                                        ─────────────
            Total....................$203,225,007.29

It is not possible to fix the exact amount of the debt of Mexico, either in silver or gold, because of the daily changes in the price of silver ; but as silver is the currency of the country, when the Mexican dollar is worth 24 pence in London, the amount of our debt in silver would be equal to our sterling debt, that is : $114,675,895.40 added to our debt will make a grand total in Mexican silver of $317,900,902.78.

BANKING.

Banking in Mexico is in its incipient state. The National Bank of Mexico, established in the City of Mexico in 1882, with its branches in the principal cities of the country, has a monopoly for the issuing of notes in the capital which is only shared by such banks as were in existence before the National Bank of Mexico was chartered, like the Bank of London, Mexico, and South America, established during the French intervention in Mexico and recently remodelled under the name of the Bank of London and Mexico. The Mortgage Bank of Mexico enjoys that privilege also.

On June 3, 1896, a general banking law was issued by the Mexican Congress, which establishes the conditions under which banking institutions can be organized ; but, of course, that does not affect the rights of the National Bank and other banks in the City of Mexico which had been chartered before the date of that law.

Formerly, owing to the expense and dangers of transportation, it was difficult to transport money from one place to another, and therefore exchange between cities in Mexico was very high, sometimes even ten per cent. from one city to another in the country. The rate has been reduced considerably since the railroads were built, but it is still quite high. To draw money from the City of Mexico to the City of Oaxaca, for instance, and vice versa, costs now one per cent. each way ; when money is required to be sent to smaller places the expenses are much higher, as it is necessary to send a man to the nearest town where the money can be placed by the banks, and pay to him a large commission—the expenses sometimes reaching ten per cent. To keep up this rate of exchange the National Bank makes its bills payable at a certain place so that they cannot be paid at any other.

Banking is very profitable in Mexico. The following is a statement of the earnings and dividends of the National Bank of Mexico, which began with a capital of $3,000,000, increased since to $6,000,000, having now a reserve fund of $5,500,000, and is owned almost exclusively by Mexicans, being the fiscal agent of the Government :

	NET PROFITS.	DIVIDENDS.
1891	$1,813,623	23 per cent.
1892	1,839,418	23 " "
1893	2,355,464	29 " "
1894	1,961,801	24 " "
1895	2,200,626	27 " "

The following is a statement, from official sources, of the earnings and dividends of the Bank of London and Mexico. Up to 1891 it had a capital of $1,500,000, which was then increased to $3,000,000 :

	NET PROFITS.	DIVIDENDS EARNED, PER CENT.	DIVIDENDS DECLARED, PER CENT.
1889............	$243,246	16	10
1890............ .	569,351	36	20
1891...............	703,522	46	20
1892........	789,967	26	16
1893.....	618,653	20½	16
1894........	603,178	20	14
1895....	557,710	18½	14

Recently the capital stock of this bank was further increased to $10,000,000, without any expense to the stockholders, as the reserve fund, which amounted to about $2,000,000, was used to complete the new capital, and was issued to the regular stockholders as a stock dividend. The balance to complete the $5,000,000 of new stock was offered to the public, the subscriptions amounting to $22,000,000, or $17,000,000 more than was wanted.

From this statement it will be seen that the existing banks are prosperous and in a flourishing condition, but the demand for increased banking facilities is such that new banks are being formed, and the operations of the old banks increased and extended in various directions.

PATENTS AND TRADE-MARKS.

Patents.—On June 7, 1890, the present patent law of Mexico was issued, and its provisions are very similar to the respective laws existing in this country.

Since the date of that law the following patents have been issued by our Department of Fomento :

YEARS.	PATENTS.	INCREASE.	DIMINUTION.
1890........................	63	....	....
1891........................	153	90	....
1892........................	168	15	....
1893........................	122	....	46
1894........................	125	3	....
1895........................	154	29	....
	785		

Trade-Marks.—On November 28, 1889, our present law regulating trade-marks was promulgated, and since then the following trade-marks have been issued by the Department of Fomento :

YEARS.	TRADE-MARKS.	INCREASE.	DIMINUTION.
1890........................	97	....	....
1891........................	112	15	....
1892........................	161	49	....
1893........................	108	....	53
1894........................	79	....	29
1895........................	91	12	....
	648		

SHIPPING.

The mercantile marine of Mexico in 1895 comprised 52 steamers and 222 sailing vessels. The shipping included also many small vessels engaged in the coasting trade.

In 1893–94, in the foreign trade, 1237 vessels of 1,314,625 tons entered, and 1211 vessels of 1,296,834 tons cleared the ports of Mexico. In the coasting trade 7721 of 1,623,371 tons entered and 7708 of 1,592,754 tons cleared. In 1894–95, in the foreign and coasting trade, there entered 9575 vessels of 3,428,973 tons, and cleared 9557 of 3,359,684 tons.

In the statistical portion of this chapter I will give official information about the number of vessels and their tonnage, which have entered and cleared from Mexican ports in recent years, the nations from which they came, and other valuable data.

MONEY, WEIGHTS, AND MEASURES.

The standard of value is silver. There is no paper currency except ordinary bank notes.

The silver peso or dollar of 100 centavos is the unit of coin in Mexico.

The silver peso weighs 27.073 grammes, .902 fine, and thus contains 24.419 grammes of fine silver.

The 10-pesos gold-piece weighs 27.0643 grammes, .875 fine, and thus contains 23.6813 grammes of fine gold.

The weights and measures of the metric system were introduced in 1856 ; but the Indians and other ignorant people use the old Spanish measures. The principal ones are these :

Weight.—1 libra=0.46 kilogramme, 1.014 lbs. avoirdupois.
1 arroba=25 libras, 25.357 lbs. avoirdupois.
For Gold and Silver.—1 marco=½ libra, 4,608 granos.
1 ochava=62 tomines.
1 tomin=12 granos.
20 granos=1 French gramme.
Length.—1 vara—0.837 metre = 2 ft. 8$\frac{8}{10}$ English inches.
1 legua comun (1 common league) = 5,000 yards.
1 legua marina (1 marine league) = 6,666⅔ yards.

NON-OFFICIAL PUBLICATIONS.

The following is a partial and rather incomplete list of (principally English) books about Mexico :

ABBOTT, GORHAM D., *Mexico and the United States.* New York, 1869.

BANCROFT, H. H., *A Popular History of the Mexican People.* 8. London. *Resources and Development of Mexico.* San Francisco, 1894.

BROCKLEHURST, T. U., *Mexico To-day.* London, 1883.

BURKE, U. R., *Life of Benito Juarez.* 8. London, 1894.

CASTRO, LORENZO, *The Republic of Mexico in 1882.* New York, 1882.

CHARNAY, D., *Ancient Cities of the New World.* Tr. 8. London.

CHEVALIER, MICHEL, *Le Mexique ancien et moderne.* 18. Paris, 1886.

CONKLING, HOWARD, *Mexico and the Mexicans.* New York, 1883.

CONKLING, A. R. *Appleton's Guide to Mexico.* New York, 1890.

CRAWFORD, CORA HAYWARD, *The Land of the Montezumas.* New York, 1889.

CUBAS, ANTONIO GARCIA, *Mexico, its Trade, Industries, and Resources.* Mexico, 1893.

FLINT, H. M., *Mexico under Maximilian.* 12. Philadelphia, 1867.

GLONER, PROSPER, *Les Finances des Etats Unis Mexicains.* Bruxelles, 1895.

GOOCH, F. C., *Face to Face with the Mexicans.* London, 1890.

GRIFFIN, S. B., *Mexico of To-day.* New York, 1886.

HAMILTON, LEONIDAS, *Border States of Mexico.* Chicago, 1882.

HAMILTON, L. L. C., *Hamilton's Mexican Handbook.* London, 1884.

JANVIER, THOMAS A., *The Mexican Guide.* New York, 1886.

KOZHEVAR, E., *Report on the Republic of Mexico.* London, 1886.

LA BEDOLLIERE, EMILE G. DE, *Histoire de la guerre du Mexique.* 4. Paris, 1866.

LESTER, C. EDWARDS, *The Mexican Republic.* New York, 1878.

NOLL, ARTHUR HOWARD, *A Short History of Mexico.* Chicago, 1890.

OBER, F. A., *Travels in Mexico.* Boston, U. S., 1884.

PRESCOTT, W. H., *History of the Conquest of Mexico.* 8. London.

RATZEL, FRIED., *Aus Mexico, Reiseskizzen aus den Jahren 1874-75.* Breslau, 1878.

RICE, JOHN N., *Mexico, Our Neighbor.* New York. (No date.)

ROUTIER, G., *Le Mexique de nos Jours.* Paris, 1895.

SCHROEDER, SEATON, *The Fall of Maximilian's Empire as seen from a United States Gunboat.* New York, 1887.

SCOBEL, A., "Die Verkehrswege Mexicos und ihre wirtschaftliche Bedeutung." In *Deutsche Geographische Blätter.* Band X, Heft 1. Bremen, 1887.

Through the Land of the Aztecs ; or, Life and Travel in Mexico. By a " Gringo." London, 1892.

WELLS, DAVID A., *A Study of Mexico.* New York, 1887.

PART II.

STATISTICS

II. STATISTICS.

I do not know of any publication in which the latest statistical information about Mexico is compiled in a concise and complete form. One which perhaps is the fullest, published in Berlin by Messrs. Puttkammer & Muhlbrecht, entitled *Les Finances des Etats-Unis Mexicains*, written by Mr. Prosper Gloner, contains a great deal more statistical information than others, and is of later date.

It has required a great deal of work, energy, and time on my part to collect the data contained in this paper, most of which is of an official character, and I am sure it is the most complete ever published, I having tried to make it very concise, so as to take the smallest space possible.

REVENUES AND EXPENSES.

The financial question was for many years the leading and the most difficult one in Mexico, because the urgent needs of the Treasury, especially on account of the disturbed condition of the country, made public expenses considerably exceed the revenue, and this condition did not allow of a thorough overhauling and settlement of the finances, nor did it contribute to establish the credit of the Government ; but peace having prevailed since 1877, a great improvement has taken place in the financial condition of Mexico ; the revenue has increased considerably, and it has finally reached an amount amply sufficient to pay all our expenses. In fact, at the end of the fiscal year, ended June 30, 1896, we had for the first time in the history of Mexico since its independence, a surplus which amounted to $6,000,000. The obnoxious tax which we inherited from the Spanish, called *alcabalas*, or interstate duties on domestic and foreign commerce, was a great drawback to internal trade, was finally abolished on July 1, 1896 ; and the country being now in a condition when radical reforms can be introduced without serious disturbances.

Our expenses as an independent nation are necessarily large, and as a comparatively small portion of our population are really producers

137

of wealth, upon them lies the whole burden of such expenses ; that is, we are a nation of from twelve to fifteen millions of inhabitants, with a very large territory and a large coast on both oceans, requiring army, revenue, light-house, and police service, and other expensive institutions proportionate to such extent and population, when the portion which contribute to such expenses is only about one-fourth or one-third of the same.

It is a very difficult task to give a complete and correct statement of the revenues and expenses of the Mexican Government prior to the year 1867. The disturbed condition of the country made it often quite impossible to keep any account at all : such was the case especially from 1858 to 1860, as during that period the City of Mexico and a large part of the country was occupied by the Church party under Miramon, and from 1863 to 1867 by the French Intervention. Besides that cause it was a very difficult matter for us to keep a correct account of public receipts and expenses, in some way for lack of a good system of book-keeping. To make a statement of the revenues and expenses of the Mexican Government since the independence of the country from Spain, I had to rely upon the reports made by Secretaries of the Treasury, which are, however, lacking for many years, and which contain rather an estimate than an account of the revenues and expenses, and I have made in that way the statement which I append under No. 1, which embraces the revenues and expenses from the year 1808, the last of the Spanish rule in Mexico, to the year 1867.

The forming of accounts was under the charge of the Federal Treasury of Mexico, and the Treasury kept its accounts with a very defective system of book-keeping, which prevented them from being correct. To remedy that difficulty, after the restoration of the Republic in 1867, a bureau of accounts was established in the Treasury Department, but its accounts were seldom correct, because it did not have the necessary detailed data to make a complete account, and, as could be expected, the results in the accounts of both bureaus differ widely.

In 1880 the Federal Treasury was reorganized with a large number of clerks with a view to keep a full and correct account of public moneys, and from that year until 1888 their accounts began to be better than before. In 1888 the system was still remodelled and improved, and since then that office has been able to keep correct and complete accounts of our public revenues and expenses.

I also append a statement No. 2 of the revenues and expenses of the Mexican Treasury from July 1, 1867, to June 30, 1888. The first thirteen years in that statement are taken from the data furnished by the Bureau of Accounts of our Treasury Department. The account of the year 1879–1880 was taken from the account of the Federal

Treasury, and the data for the year 1880–1881 from the accounts published by the Liquidating Bureau established by the Mexican Government to close the old accounts and open the new ones under the new system. The accounts of the year 1888–1889, which appear in statement No. 3, are all taken from the Federal Treasury of Mexico, and are complete and correct.

I also append a statement of the appropriations approved by the Federal Congress during the fiscal years from 1868 to 1895. The actual expenses never exceeded the appropriations and the revenue was generally below them.

NO. I.—REVENUE AND EXPENSES OF THE FEDERAL GOVERNMENT OF MEXICO IN 1808 AND FROM 1822 TO JUNE 30, 1867.

	REVENUE.	EXPENSES.
1808, Colonial period................	$20,075,362 25	....
1822, Independence period..........	9,328,740 00	$13,455,377 00
1823...............................	5,249,858 96	3,030,878 50
1824...............................	15,254,601 03	15,165,876 05
1825 to Sept. 1st....................	7,903,163 42	13,110,187 24
Sept. 1, 1825, to June 30, 1826...... ..	14,770,733 30	13,112,200 65
1826–27............................	17,017,016 59	16,364,218 36
1827–28............................	13,644,974 69	12,982,092 86
1828–29............................	14,593,307 69	14,016,978 27
1829–30............................	14,103,773 28	13,728,491 39
1830–31............................	18,392,134 96	17,601,289 67
1831–32............................	17,582,929 15	16,937,384 67
1832–33............................	20,563,360 77	22,392,607 90
1833–34............................	21,124,216 81	19,934,490 42
1834–35............................	18,353,283 00	12,724,686 62
1835–36............................	26,382,303 90	17,766,262 81
1836–37............................	17,327,706 15	19,181,138 95
1837–38............................	25,018,121 77	26,588,305 03
1839...............................	29,136,536 64	27,318,729 73
1840...............................	21,227,263 43	21,235,097 67
1841...............................	23,995,766 52	22,997,220 18
1842...............................	30,682,369 40	30,639,711 00
1843...............................	34,138,581 72	34,035,277 13
1844...............................	31,873,019 47	31,260,225 87
1845...............................	24,159,050 04	19,584,812 91
1846...............................	24,026,938 36	27,845,487 28
1847...............................	26,154,222 84	31,251,467 91
1848 to June 30, 1849................	25,726,737 23	19,742,876 48
1849–50............................	18,281,835 38	17,291,233 25
1850–51............................	14,955,535 73	14,477,369 06
1851–52............................	11,022,291 17	10,475,686 10
1852–53............................	10,044,298 40	16,287,532 90
1853–54............................	19,028,975 00	18,726,088 00
1854–55............................	26,259,970 45	23,396,074 75
1855–56..	15,855,597 47	12,920,257 65
1856–57............................	16,035,609 81	12,977,265 90
1857–58.	15,529,887 47	15,927,102 01
1858–59............................	14,737,763 76	16,005,536 45
1859–60............................	14,306,675 28	16,589,034 47
1860–61............................	12,863,500 00	12,750,500 00
1861–62............................	15,500,000 00	15,300,600 00
1862–63............................	17,600,000 00	17,595,690 00
1863–64............................	7,000,000 00	6,990,000 00
1864–65............................	5,950,000 00	5,945,000 00
1865–66............................	5,057,500 00	5,053,250 00
1866–67............................	8,092,000 00	8,085,200 00

NO 2.—REVENUE AND EXPENSES OF THE MEXICAN GOVERNMENT FROM JULY 1, 1867, TO JUNE 30, 1888.

FISCAL YEARS	RECEIPTS				EXPENSES		
	Revenue.	Extraordinary and Incidental.	Loans.	TOTAL.	Expenses authorized by law.	Other expenses.	TOTAL.
1867–1868.	......			$ 17,736,538 19	......	......	$ 14,786,128 51
1868–1869.	$ 2,355,322 95	$ 14,109,931 96		16,465,254 91			16,862,024 12
1869–1870.	2,720,494 53	13,678,241 59		16,398,736 12	$ 13,867,208 59	$ 2,647,820 15	16,515,028 74
1870–1871.	2,674,676 17	16,033,649 71		18,708,325 88	15,080,349 52	2,541,938 90	17,622,288 42
1871–1872.	3,798,734 56	15,285,044 18		19,083,778 74	15,321,071 33	3,657,406 94	18,978,478 27
1872–1873.	4,402,386 91	15,739,239 94		20,141,626 85	15,558,623 89	4,827,965 64	20,386,589 53
1873–1874.	3,327,674 88	17,900,156 10		21,227,850 98	16,369,509 34	4,837,241 82	21,206,751 16
1874–1875.	4,181,077 58	17,597,916 26		21,778,993 84	17,286,167 44	4,081,712 51	21,367,879 95
1875–1876.	3,818,501 22	17,266,228 93		21,084,730 15	18,074,771 02	3,248,089 40	21,322,860 42
1876–1877.	4,741,742 59	18,408,803 80		23,150,546 39	18,183,958 78	5,041,925 03	23,225,884 41
1877–1878.	9,686,555 30	19,772,638 13		29,459,193 43	19,420,113 15	10,125,161 38	29,545,274 53
1878–1879.	11,403,237 47	17,811,124 96		29,274,302 43	17,698,255 20	11,418,550 37	29,316,805 57
1879–1880.	235,097 93	21,936,165 39		22,171,263 32	20,431,896 15	......	20,431,896 15
1880–1881.	1,789,614 11	24,089,698 07		25,879,312 18	24,092,198 16	160,663 13	24,252,861 29
1881–1882.	30,466,093 74	6,138,642 39	$ 10,283,731 74	46,888,407 87	30,595,891 81	15,600,899 37	46,196,791 18
1882–1883.	32,850,951 25	7,226,397 49	3,438,867 68	43,516,216 42	37,582,604 18	4,459,444 84	42,042,049 02
1883–1884.	37,621,065 29	18,435,299 84	2,697,900 42	58,754,265 55	42,714,229 29	13,606,247 74	56,410,477 03
1884–1885.	30,660,434 24	33,275,909 03	2,636,263 91	66,572,607 18	44,407,386 22	21,535,422 04	65,942,808 26
1885–1886.	28,980,895 76	31,925,011 61	2,332,033 51	63,237,940 88	26,164,198 18	40,526,366 85	66,690,565 03
1886–1887.	32,126,509 07	72,702,037 63	6,949,374 87	111,777,921 57	36,262,962 48	75,085,077 50	111,348,039 98
1887–1888.	40,962,045 23	85,488,474 33	24,039,637 72	150,490,157 28	54,956,554 45	89,552,905 48	144,509,519 93

NO. 3.—REVENUE AND EXPENSES OF THE MEXICAN GOVERNMENT FROM JULY 1, 1888, TO JUNE 30, 1896.

FISCAL YEARS.	REVENUE.				EXPENSES.			
	Cash.	Bonds.	Nominal.	Total.	Cash.	Bonds.	Nominal.	Total.
1888–1889.—Revenue receipts	$34,374,783 32	$20,427,141 26		$54,801,924 58	$49,325,109 50	$20,103,595 45	$4,493,624 48	$73,922,329 43
Loans	22,478,738 14			22,478,738 14	13,764,470 07		54,272,265 53	68,036,736 50
Nominal	11,934,096 11		$50,147,312 08	62,081,408 19				
	$68,787,617 57	$20,427,141 26	$50,147,312 08	$139,362,070 91	$63,089,580 47	$20,103,595 45	$58,765,890 01	$141,959,065 93
1889–1890.—Revenue receipts	$38,386,601 69	$22,716,725 61		$61,908,681 53	$51,641,115 34	$22,167,362 65	$4,350,475 75	$78,158,753 74
Loans	15,849,706 41		$665,354 23	45,849,706 41	4,163,849 84		45,016,373 95	49,180,223 79
Nominal	19,668,525 81		29,775,715 65	49,384,241 46				
	$74,044,833 91	$22,716,725 61	$30,361,069 88	$127,142,629 40	$55,804,965 18	$22,167,362 65	$49,366,649 70	$127,138,977 53
1890–1891.—Revenue receipts	$37,391,804 99	$932,799 50	$5,688,852 12	$44,142,856 61	$56,098,276 11	$932,799 50	$5,144,053 07	$63,005,128 68
Loans	26,645,962 80		3,614,283 04	30,260,246 74	10,360,442 26		65,086,034 91	75,446,377 17
Nominal	3,328,985 36		60,797,551 02	64,196,537 28				
	$67,366,753 15	$932,799 50	$70,230,087 98	$138,599,640 63	$67,288,518 37	$932,799 50	$70,230,087 98	$138,451,405 85
1891–1892.—Revenue receipts	$37,474,879 20	$1,868,171 91	650,692 83	$39,993,743 94	$40,053,990 03	$624,665 92	$4,671,491 67	$43,350,149 62
Loans	5,485,005 10		19,174,886 70	24,059,887 60	2,896,346 04	1,243,503 99	17,154,083 86	21,373,934 79
Nominal								
	$42,959,884 30	$1,868,171 91	$19,825,575 53	$64,053,631 74	$43,950,336 97	$1,868,171 91	$21,825,575 53	$64,624,084 41
1892–1893.—Revenue receipts	$37,602,293 31	$847,113 46	$115,363 54	$38,654,770 31	$42,813,455 71	$860,887 31	$5,271,699 41	$48,954,972 43
Loans	4,526,983 82			4,526,983 82	5,161,790 45	773,626 26	12,541,022 83	18,476,419 54
Nominal	5,484,854 56	795,400 11	17,697,268 70	23,978,523 37				
	$47,704,131 69	$1,643,513 57	$17,812,632 24	$67,160,277 50	$47,975,246 16	$1,643,513 57	$17,812,632 24	$67,431,391 97
1893–1894.—Revenue receipts	$40,211,747 13	$852,365 02	$152,581 36	$41,216,893 51	$41,554,162 16	$361,887 64	$3,799,741 67	$45,773,791 47
Loans	6,053,794 09		3,300,000 00	9,353,794 09	7,092,362 90	560,477 97	16,074,636 92	23,727,477 79
Nominal	2,054,285 12	69,800 59	16,421,797 23	18,545,822 94				
	$48,319,766 34	$922,365 61	$19,874,378 59	$69,116,510 54	$48,644,525 06	$922,365 61	$19,874,378 59	$69,441,269 26
1894–1895.—Revenue receipts	$43,945,699 05	$2,530,518 70	$430,905 41	$46,907,123 16	$41,372,264 63	$1,892,058 19	$2,389,803 96	$45,655,026 78
Loans	4,577,500 00		2,172,000 00	6,750,000 00	9,368,711 42	1,107,560 51	30,104,662 36	40,580,934 29
Nominal	2,468,360 68	470,000 00	30,891,060 91	32,829,421 59				
	$50,991,559 73	$3,000,518 70	$34,494,066 32	$86,486,544 75	$50,740,976 05	$3,000,518 70	$32,494,466 32	$86,235,961 07
1895–1896.—Revenue receipts	$50,341,470 48	$477,033 98	$441,552 55	$51,240,056 95	$45,070,123 13	$34,727 54	$6,482,189 96	$45,102,850 67
Nominal	708,277 60	5,121,667 46	6,240,637 41	12,070,582 53	5,399,533 73	5,563,973 90		17,447,697 59
	$51,249,748 08	$5,598,701 44	$6,482,189 96	$63,310,639 48	$50,469,656 86	$5,598,701 44	$6,482,189 96	$62,550,548 26

FEDERAL APPROPRIATIONS DURING THE FISCAL YEARS FROM 1868 TO 1895.

FISCAL YEARS.	POWERS.			Foreign Affairs.	Interior.	DEPARTMENTS.					TOTALS.
	Legislative.	Executive.	Judicial.			Justice and Education.	Fomento and Colonization.	Communications and Public Works.	Treasury and Public Credit.	War and Navy.	
1868–1869.	$735,360 00	$52,880 00	$188,290 00	$124,540 00	$1,025,080 00	$30,640 75	$2,292,932 00	....	$5,143,726 24	$8,450,939 86	$18,604,188 85
1869–1870.	754,300 00	56,395 20	265,290 00	148,540 00	1,437,609 84	737,643 18	3,096,186 00	....	4,870,732 08	6,067,931 49	18,324,431 22
1870–1871.	760,619 99	48,172 40	280,560 00	150,160 00	1,447,512 24	844,397 99	4,341,777 11	....	4,562,392 80	8,443,206 49	20,857,383 01
1871–1872.	811,920 00	48,172 40	280,560 00	150,160 00	1,656,146 50	879,127 99	4,353,411 55	....	4,643,922 80	10,144,601 59	22,938,412 76
1872–1873.	811,920 00	48,172 40	280,560 00	150,160 00	1,656,146 50	879,127 99	4,353,411 55	....	4,643,922 80	10,144,601 59	23,956,420 36
1873–1874.	877,200 00	48,172 40	291,680 00	260,360 00	1,773,886 50	873,127 00	4,557,863 00	....	5,021,688 75	10,633,869 59	24,144,331 36
1874–1875.	842,610 00	48,172 40	313,490 00	246,360 00	1,954,451 50	890,998 80	5,637,373 00	....	4,056,317 00	10,357,373 00	24,891,530 18
1875–1876.	1,074,160 00	48,172 40	318,228 00	209,860 00	1,063,475 55	910,533 20	5,063,353 00	....	4,179,070 70	10,554,747 00	25,290,755 93
1876–1877.	1,044,270 00	48,172 40	318,928 00	195,160 00	2,492,951 12	906,933 00	6,070,581 41	....	4,453,976 12	10,848,286 68	29,081,158 92
1877–1878.	957,319 12	48,572 40	318,228 00	189,160 00	2,262,165 60	991,513 20	2,777,000 00	....	4,715,054 60	6,618,045 43	19,715,902 78
1878–1879.	1,051,322 00	48,832 40	331,028 00	193,660 00	2,511,195 40	1,210,935 60	2,272,330 00	....	4,891,016 56	8,788,742 80	21,748,902 78
1879–1880.	980,241 00	48,832 40	347,878 00	176,660 00	2,488,496 30	1,103,865 20	1,849,722 00	....	3,895,116 57	8,004,569 18	18,905,965 31
1880–1881.	1,022,841 00	48,832 40	355,878 00	228,460 00	2,574,609 70	1,474,345 20	3,570,077 00	....	4,366,609 35	9,786,964 95	23,128,218 60
1881–1882.	990,402 00	48,832 40	370,976 00	317,660 00	3,152,607 55	1,352,820 00	6,166,627 00	....	4,173,385 75	8,646,033 12	25,217,633 82
1882–1883.	1,071,712 00	48,832 40	389,554 00	336,280 00	3,235,118 00	1,215,473 00	7,551,663 00	....	4,648,377 67	8,514,478 13	27,011,509 08
1883–1884.	1,015,633 00	48,832 40	406,652 00	391,580 00	3,285,577 75	1,243,510 00	11,127,600 00	....	4,066,161 81	8,252,352 18	30,713,999 14
1884–1885.	1,087,232 00	48,832 40	420,674 00	377,680 00	3,339,223 77	1,234,718 00	6,351,870 00	....	4,903,438 78	8,252,764 88	25,825,423 83
1885–1886.	1,007,144 15	49,251 50	432,392 90	418,762 50	3,441,616 10	1,252,376 85	8,330,728 35	....	11,832,644 95	12,138,435 86	38,973,353 16
1886–1887.	1,052,071 45	49,251 50	436,387 80	417,726 00	3,237,529 20	1,431,080 24	2,668,116 30	....	10,663,285 78	11,559,714 00	31,536,205 27
1887–1888.	1,002,028 75	49,846 45	430,994 00	434,030 60	3,466,888 30	1,398,850 00	4,426,132 17	....	11,664,391 97	13,386,495 24	36,270,451 46
1888–1889.	1,053,839 40	49,848 19	404,095 45	434,783 20	3,996,329 00	1,421,204 75	5,065,450 54	....	12,059,535 94	13,482,152 47	38,577,439 84
1889–1890.	1,009,036 50	49,849 40	405,095 55	432,695 70	3,553,128 80	1,350,471 10	6,145,555 69	....	11,310,386 29	12,449,603 37	36,705,906 54
1890–1891.	1,054,030 50	49,849 45	468,884 25	462,517 25	3,678,679 70	1,393,072 40	7,310,316 50	....	11,365,207 09	12,056,021 07	38,439,488 21
1891–1892.	1,009,036 50	49,977 20	476,784 50	558,483 25	2,480,896 76	1,639,696 25	677,106 95	$4,399,345 97	14,432,995 81	12,658,101 37	38,377,364 85
1892–1893.	1,050,638 06	49,977 20	1,478,083 90	990,379 84	2,564,151 00	1,557,215 60	951,054 51	4,483,569 25	15,857,392 61	12,684,685 67	41,367,047 64
1893–1894.	1,095,638 00	49,977 20	478,083 90	553,550 80	2,459,391 20	1,614,652 45	822,414 16	3,922,141 60	22,390,495 20	11,329,618 82	45,614,793 33
1894–1895.	1,095,638 00	50,977 30	478,171 30	510,965 50	2,560,741 70	1,547,824 54	615,610 06	4,455,597 15	24,000,570 85	10,378,683 34	45,610,279 92
Totals..	$26,139,803 42	$1,324,936 64	$11,437,427 75	$8,645,445 03	$68,824,781 15	$31,536,283 47	$119,667,222 75	$17,260,153 97	$223,521,911 01	$276,279,966 34	$784,657,936 53

Sources of Revenue.—The Federal revenue of Mexico consists mainly of three sources : import duties, internal revenue, and direct taxes in the Federal District. Under the head of import duties we collect duties on imports, extra import duties which we call additional duties, and duties on exports.

The sources of revenue of the Mexican Federal Treasury during the fiscal year 1895–1896, were :

```
Imposts on foreign trade...............$23,658,692 61
Internal revenue....  .................  20,447,096 42
Direct taxes in the Federal District and
    Territories .....................   3,357,611 81
Public services........................   1,811,045 30
Nominal..............................   1,955,301 94
                                      ──────────────
    Total......................$51,229,748 08
```

Import Duties.—Our tariff is a highly protective one, as we have always maintained a very high rate of import duties, almost prohibitory for a large portion of our population, which under such a system are practically excluded from the use of foreign commodities, to the material detriment of the fiscal revenue, the public wealth at large, and the advancement of the masses of our people. The causes which have induced such a high tariff are twofold : first, that, in a great measure, protective ideas have prevailed ; secondly, and especially, the need of revenue, and the idea that the higher the rate of duties the larger would be the revenue collected. A new source of protection has been created by the depreciation of our currency, which acts as a powerful protection to our home commodities, in favor of our manufacturers to the disadvantage of the great body of consumers.

The protective policy in Mexico has been so deeply rooted that notwithstanding that I lean to freer trade, and that I have been three times at the head of the Treasury Department, and once for five years, I never was able to modify substantially that policy, because the condition of the Treasury was so precarious, that it would have been very rash to attempt any radical change on the face of a great reduction of an insufficient revenue which would have brought about disastrous results. For the same reason I was unable to do away with the obnoxious alcabala tax.

Our present tariff is divided into the following sections : 1st, animal industry ; 2d, agricultural products ; 3d, metals and its manufactures ; 4th, fabrics ; 5th, chemicals, oils, and paints ; 6th, wines, liquors, and fermented drinks ; 7th, paper ; 8th, machinery ; 9th, carriages ; 10th, arms and explosives, and 11th, sundries.

Additional Import Duties.—The additional duties collected by the Custom-houses are 1½ per cent. of the amount of the import duties, which is levied for the respective municipality ; 2 per cent. of the same duties, for harbor improvements ; and 2 per cent. in revenue stamps, making in all 5½ per cent. of the import duties. The custom-houses collect besides the import duties, tonnage and light-house duties, and pilot fees.

Export Duty.—Our export duties are levied upon cabinet and dye-woods, india rubber, cochineal, coffee, henequen, ixtle, indigo, fequila, jalap, tamarind, tobacco, mother-of-pearl, orchilla, vanilla, zacaton, and onyx.

The following statement shows the amount of export duties collected in Mexico from the fiscal year 1881–1882 to 1894–1895, expressing the commodities in which they were collected :

STATEMENT OF THE RECEIPTS FROM EXPORT DUTIES IN MEXICO FROM JULY 1, 1881, TO JUNE 30, 1895.

FISCAL YEAR.	RECEIPTS.	COMMODITIES TAXED.
1881–1882	$122,462 24	Orchilla, wood.
1882–1883	144,597 93	" "
1883–1884	179,439 97	" "
1884–1885	161,811 47	" "
1885–1886	107,484 80	" "
1886–1887	106,859 63	" "
1887–1888	114,869 04	" "
1888–1889	81,849 25	" "
1889–1890	98,386 12	" "
1890–1891	86,859 86	" "
1891–1892	96,560 48	" "
1892–1893	91,475 54	" "
1893–1894	1,045,105 44	Orchilla, wood, henequen, coffee.
1894–1895	1,227,719 24	Orchilla, wood, henequen, coffee, skins, zacaton, chewing gum, ixtle, vanilla.

Amount of Import Duties.—It is very difficult to give a correct statement of the receipts of the Mexican custom-houses before the year 1875. I append, however, one made from the reports of the Secretaries of the Treasury of Mexico, especially those of July 25, 1839, and September 16, 1870, and completed from the years 1839–1851, with data obtained from the *Comercio exterior de Mexico,* by D. Miguel Lerdo de Tejada. From the fiscal year 1875–1876, the Statistical Bureau of our Treasury Department began to publish detailed and correct statements of the custom receipts, and I append one embracing the fiscal years from 1875 to 1896 which shows how largely our import duties have increased. In the ten years elapsed from 1878 to 1888 the increase was over 67 per cent. as compared with the corresponding period from 1869-1879, and the increase in the last seven years, 1889-1896, was 16 per cent. as compared with the previous ten years, both periods making an increase of nearly 100 per cent. over the first ten years of said statement :

CUSTOMS RECEIPTS FROM 1823 TO THE FISCAL YEAR ENDING
JUNE 20, 1875.

1823. From April 1st to September 30 the receipts were
$971,345 77, which for a year of 12 months
would be..................................... $1,942,691 54

1825. From the 1st of January to the 1st of August,
1825, the receipts were $4,472,069 37, which for
a year of 12 months would be................ 7,666,404 63

1825-1826 From the 1st of September, 1825, to June,
1826, $6,414,383 26, which for a year of 12
months would be............................ 9,621,574 89

1826-1827.......... .... 7,828,208 44
1827-1828..................................·............ 5,692,026 70
1828-1829.............................·.............. 6,497,288 93
1829-1830................................. 4,815,418 25
1830-1831..................................... 8,287,082 92
1831-1832..................................... 7,335,637 76
1832-1833.......................... 7,538,525 47
1833-1834..................................... 8,786,396 94
1834-1835.................................. 8,920,408 28
1835-1836.. .... 5,835,068 51
1836-1837.................................. 4,377,579 52

From July 1, 1837, to December 31, 1838, $4,258,411 10.
Corresponding to one year of 12 months....... 2,838,940 73

1839... 5,577,890 67
1840... 8,309,918 65
1841... 6,597,912 32
1842... 6,034,342 29
1843... 8,507,478 79
1844.. 8,254,141 96
1845... 5,814,048 69
1846... 6,747,932 35
1847... 1,394,609 52

From January 1, 1848, to June 30, 1849, 18 months... 6,660,037 96
From July, 1849, to June, 1850..................... 6,338,437 50
1850-1851.........................·.................. 5,337,068 62
From July 1, 1851, to June 30, 1852............... 6,108,835 26

1852-1853, according to the calculations of M. Haro y
Tamariz average from the preceding five years. 4,906,533 17

1853–1854, according to the report of M. Olazagarre
  (1855)... 8,399,208 93
1854–1855, according to the report of M. Lerdo de
  Tejada (1857)....................................... 8,096,208 85
1855–1856, according to the report makes the receipts
  for the first six months amount to $3,379,761 35,
  which for the year is............................... 6,759,522 70
1856–1857, average for the six years previous........ 6,854,061 78
1857–1858   "   "   "   " 6,854,061 78
1858–1859   "   "   "   " 6,854,061 78
1859–1860   "   "   "   " 6,854,061 78
1860–1861   "   "   "   " 6,854,061 78
1861–1862   "   "   "   " 6,854,061 78
1862–1863   "   "   "   " 6,854,061 78
1863–1864   "   "   "   " 6,854,061 78
1864–1865   "   "   "   " 6,854,061 78
1865–1866   "   "   "   " 6,851,061 78
1866–1867   "   "   "   " 6,851,061 78
1867–1868, according to the amount of the receipts.... 9,566,360 99
1868–1869   "   "   " 9,606,491 73
1869–1870... 7,824,525 57
1870–1871... 10,014,277 60
1871–1872... 8,430,211 00
1872–1873... 11,833,117 52
1873–1874... 13,981,795 42
1874–1875... 11,821,533 49

                Total.............................$367,725,836 01
        Average in one year........................$7,071,650 69

Internal Revenue.—The Federal Treasury of Mexico depended
up to 1867 mainly upon import duties, and as it was not safe to have
only that source of revenue, when I occupied for the first time the
Treasury Department, I introduced a system of internal revenue
through the use of stamps, which met with a great deal of opposition
at the time, but which has finally been developed very largely, yielding
now almost as much as the import duties. The receipts during the
six months from January 1st to June 30th, 1875, amounted to $1,097,-
668 28, which in a whole year would make, duplicating it, $2,195,-
336 56, while in the fiscal year ended June 30, 1896, the receipts
amounted to $18,078,952 54, or nearly eight times as much.

We have had since 1861 a comparative large source of revenue
called Federal Tax, which up to 1892 was 25 per cent. of all the revenues collected by the States and Municipalities in Mexico. That rate

RECEIPTS OF THE CUSTOM-HOUSES DURING THE TWENTY-SEVEN FISCAL YEARS ENDING JUNE 30, 1896.

FISCAL YEARS.	IMPORT DUTIES — Tariff.	Additional.	Total.	EXPORT DUTIES — Precious metals.	Commodities.	Total.	TOTAL GROSS RECEIPTS.	COST OF COLLECTION — Annual expenditures.	Per-centage.	NET RECEIPTS.
1869-1870	$4,036,046 61	$3,203,833 78	$7,239,880 39	$1,270,501 27	......	$1,270,501 27	$8,510,531 66	$493,346 90	5.796	$8,017,184 76
1870-1871	5,094,768 00	4,316,886 59	9,411,654 59	1,473,299 13	......	1,473,299 13	10,884,953 72	566,228 51	5.202	10,318,725 21
1871-1872	4,466,410 78	3,681,849 73	8,148,260 51	914,510 72	......	914,510 72	9,062,771 23	471,690 42	5.205	8,591,080 81
1872-1873	8,048,293 29	132,211 08	8,180,504 37	1,063,700 30	......	1,063,700 30	9,244,204 67	553,049 99	5.983	8,691,154 68
1873-1874	10,354,158 85	74,347 38	10,428,506 23	881,042 30	......	881,042 30	11,309,548 53	575,591 80	5.090	10,733,956 73
1874-1875	9,200,033 06	71,236 49	9,271,269 55	854,873 99	......	854,873 99	10,126,143 54	718,036 74	7.090	9,408,106 80
1875-1876	8,390,636 05	60,306 05	8,450,942 10	726,843 55	......	726,843 55	9,177,786 30	697,458 27	7.598	8,480,328 03
1876-1877	8,308,293 94	51,555 14	8,359,849 08	957,087 47	$ 2,736 75	959,824 22	9,319,673 30	632,041 27	6.781	8,687,632 03
1877-1878	9,518,567 31	65,772 31	9,584,339 62	1,009,806 96	6,839 47	1,016,646 43	13,449,850 35	811,493 28	6.642	9,648,689 01
1878-1879	13,768,410 33	60,335 31	13,850,260 79	886,340 75	78,287 32	964,628 07	12,753,128 40	849,584 25	2.796	12,638,357 07
1879-1880	17,002,961 23	69,645 66	13,850,260 79	871,047 37	14,426 70	885,474 07	14,666,522 82	993,055 14	6.662	13,673,467 68
1880-1881	18,173,720 89	81,853 46	18,595,708 90	738,531 00	77,722 03	816,253 03	18,447,431 04	1,141,442 69	6.775	17,395,988 35
1881-1882	15,279,586 37	556,944 34	17,547,793 10	588,637 95	199,907 52	788,545 47	17,058,179 67	1,327,620 19	6.133	15,730,559 48
1882-1883	14,852,980 16	355,825 91	15,445,571 27	317,873 54	144,597 93	462,471 47	17,727,233 16	1,364,472 09	7.757	16,364,761 07
1883-1884	17,268,650 10	165,681 37	17,441,758 03	......	179,439 97	179,439 97	15,607,382 74	1,501,149 17	7.685	14,106,233 57
1884-1885	18,038,415 17	148,048 67	15,007,029 00	......	161,811 47	161,811 47	15,108,513 82	1,847,009 10	9.631	13,461,504 72
1885-1886	20,725,839 17	173,108 20	17,441,758 03	......	107,484 80	107,484 80	17,548,617 99	1,827,313 96	12.224	15,651,304 03
1886-1887	20,178,744 17	215,530 83	18,174,746 10	......	106,859 63	106,859 63	19,289,615 14	1,928,129 93	10.811	17,361,486 11
1887-1888	20,031,365 52	369,495 36	21,094,667 86	......	114,869 04	114,869 04	19,374,717 11	1,994,737 23	10.291	17,379,979 88
1888-1889	20,178,744 17	728,315 56	20,863,454 73	......	81,849 35	81,849 35	23,553,540 85	2,017,166 85	9.070	22,535,372 30
1889-1890	20,031,365 52	685,077 76	20,715,815 66	......	98,386 15	98,386 15	20,950,181 77	2,077,439 86	9.916	18,720,159 94
1890-1891	30,175,744 17	636,644 46	17,445,921 43	......	86,359 86	86,359 86	30,812,476 14	2,002,217 10	10.953	28,873,241 93
1891-1892	15,531,926 66	546,243 58	15,860,170 57	......	95,556 48	95,556 48	17,537,396 07	2,008,707 95	11.397	15,148,999 00
1892-1893	17,738,129 66	716,009 40	18,454,139 08	......	91,475 54	91,475 54	16,897,281 84	1,097,912 43	11.499	14,069,368 84
1893-1894	15,531,926 66	546,243 58	15,860,170 57	......	1,037,110 05	1,037,110 05	19,681,499 51	1,811,243 63	9.208	21,870,755 88
1894-1895	17,738,129 66	716,009 40	18,454,139 08	......	1,227,360 45	1,227,360 45	19,681,499 51	1,811,243 63	9.208	21,870,755 88
1895-1896	21,492,211 91	853,482 25	22,345,694 16	......	1,078,861 48	1,078,861 48	23,444,555 64	1,825,178 73	7.705	21,599,376 91
Total in 27 years	$376,341,901 33	$19,097,570 30	$395,439,471 53	$12,554,066 33	$4,992,927 03	$17,546,993 36	$415,086,614 89	$35,026,276 78	8.048	$379,961,338 11
Average per annum	$13,938,588 93	$707,317 41	$14,645,906 35	$464,965 42	$184,923 22	$649,888 64	$15,395,857 58	$1,297,269 51	8.482	$14,072,642 15

Abstract of sums and annual averages of the two periods of ten years and the last of seven years.

Totals and averages.	Tariff	Additional	Import Total	Precious metals	Commodities	Export Total	Gross receipts	Annual expenditures	Per-centage	Net receipts
1869-79.—Totals...	$79,784,770 27	$11,778,574 33	$91,973,344 60	......	......	$10,046,705 98	$101,550,040 58	$6,334,825 43	6.338	$95,215,215 15
Average...	7,978,477 03	1,171,857 43	9,150,334 46			1,004,670 60	10,155,004 06	633,482 54		9,521,521 52
1879-89.—Totals...	$163,237,737 17	$4,558,822 22	$165,796,559 39	$1,252,809 53	131,360 95	$3,784,118 80	$169,580,742 19	$14,841,893 15	8.752	$154,738,849 04
Average...	16,323,773 72	355,882 22	16,579,655 94			378,411 88	16,958,074 22	1,484,189 32		15,473,884 90
1889-96.—Totals...	$133,319,493 79	$4,820,223 75	$138,139,717 54	$3,717,114 88	531,016 41	$4,248,131 29	$141,856,832 12	$13,849,558 20	9.763	$128,007,273 92
Average...	19,045,641 97	688,603 39	19,734,445 30			607,161 61	20,265,261 73	1,978,508 31		18,286,753 42

was increased in 1893 from 25 to 33⅓ per cent. on account of the deficit caused to the Federal Treasury by the depreciation of silver, and that tax which is paid in Federal stamps, constitutes a very large portion of our internal revenue receipts.

I append a statement of our internal revenue taxes with full details.

INTERNAL REVENUE RECEIPTS FROM JANUARY 1, 1875, TO JUNE 30, 1896.

FISCAL YEARS.	GROSS RECEIPTS.	GROSS RECEIPTS OF THE FEDERAL TAX.	TOTAL RECEIPTS.	COLLECTION EXPENSES.		NET RECEIPTS.
From January 1 to June 30, 1875...	$328,631 26	$769,037 02	$1,097,668 28		Percentage.	
1875–1876.........	$668,930 14	$1,145,624 37	$1,814,554 51	$167,937 42	9.255	$2,247,617 09
1876–1877.........	728,192 71	1,905,806 66	2,633,999 37	120,334 94	4.567	2,513,664 43
1877–1878.........	920,901 29	2,154,249 51	3,075,150 80	302,612 65	9.840	2,772,538 15
1878–1879.........	763,879 23	2,239,267 37	3,003,146 60	300,490 02	10.006	2,702,656 58
1879–1880.........	1,311,463 95	2,336,431 73	3,647,895 68	484,215 36	13.274	3,164,180 32
Average per annum in five years	$878,673 46	$1,956,275 93	$2,834,949 39	$275,118 08	9.705	$2,680,131 31
1880–1881.........	$1,037,730 93	$2,371,369 31	$3,409,100 24	$351,980 01	10.325	$3,057,120 23
1881–1882.........	1,429,655 61	2,775,149 84	4,204,805 45	376,005 30	8.943	3,828,710 15
1882–1883.........	1,591,189 33	3,099,170 93	4,690,369 26	420,132 04	9.000	4,270,237 22
1883–1884.........	1,919,461 99	2,912,967 08	4,832,429 07	441,080 10	9.126	4,391,348 87
1884–1885.........	3,231,872 75	3,127,481 85	6,359,354 60	489,043 89	7.690	5,870,310 71
Average per annum in five years	$1,841,982 12	$2,857,229 60	$4,699,211 72	$415,666 27	8.845	$4,283,545 44
1885–1886.........	$2,761,886 56	$3,115,759 85	$5,877,646 41	$428,390 78	7.288	$5,449,255 63
1886–1887.........	3,930,429 16	3,587,339 96	7,517,769 12	638,011 29	8.486	6,879,757 83
1887–1888.........	4,654,190 93	3,324,937 53	7,979,128 46	728,431 31	9.000	7,250,697 15
1888–1889.........	5,108,911 59	3,679,493 52	8,788,405 11	771,601 95	8.777	8,016,803 16
1889–1890.........	5,575,067 62	3,791,695 27	9,366,762 89	799,721 78	8.538	9,567,041 11
Average per annum in five years	$4,406,097 17	$3,499,845 23	$7,905,942 40	$673,237 42	8.516	$7,432,710 98
1890–1891.........	$5,624,340 94	$3,865,650 49	$9,489,991 43	$853,834 28	8.955	$8,636,157 15
1891–1892.........	5,402,495 76	3,969,987 88	9,372,483 64	868,161 60	9.263	8,504,322 04
1892–1893.........	6,625,265 53	4,431,022 65	11,056,288 18	945,076 71	8.548	10,111,211 47
1893–1894.........	9,164,063 10	5,216,547 31	14,380,610 41	1,120,760 85	7.190	13,259,849 56
1894–1895.........	10,098,795 63	5,471,173 92	15,569,969 55	1,146,419 41	7.363	14,423,550 14
1895–1896.........	12,519,676 93	5,559,255 61	18,078,932 54	1,196,053 14	6.616	16,882,879 40
Average in six years	$8,239,106 31	$4,752,272 98	$12,991,379 29	$1,021,717 67	7.865	$11,969,661 63
Total in 21½ years.	$85,397,032 94	$70,849,428 66	$156,246,461 60	$12,950,384 83	8.288	$143,799,908 39

Direct Taxes.—The third source of revenue of the Mexican Government are direct taxes collected in the Federal District, which includes the City of Mexico. They are levied on real-estate, scientific professions, commercial and industrial establishments, and work-shops. The real-estate for the purpose of this tax is divided into rural and urban, the former paying a tax of 12 per cent. on its rent when occupied, and 3 per cent. when not occupied, and the latter paying 8 per thousand of its registered value.

Taxes on professions vary from 50 cents to $20.00 a month. The tax on commercial and industrial establishments is regulated by law. The commercial establishments, which pay license taxes are commission agencies of all kinds : banking firms ; dry goods, groceries, wines, furniture, and jewelry stores ; insurance companies ; restaurants, hotels, and boarding-houses. Among the industrial establishments are embraced especially railway, telegraph and telephone companies ; cotton, woollen, and silk mills ; factories of all kinds ; iron smelters ; printing, engraving, and photographic establishments ; coffee, corn, and flour mills, etc., etc.

When the alcabalas were abolished a direct tax was established upon some of the articles which paid the largest sums, namely : pulque, wheat flour, and domestic brandy distilled from molasses.

I annex a statement showing the proceeds of Direct Taxes in the Federal District during the last twenty-seven fiscal years.

RECEIPTS FROM DIRECT TAXES IN THE FEDERAL DISTRICT DURING THE TWENTY-SEVEN FISCAL YEARS ENDING JUNE 30, 1896.

FISCAL YEARS.	GROSS RECEIPTS.	COLLECTION EXPENSES.	PERCENTAGE EXPENSES.	NET RECEIPTS.
1869–1870	$485,451 73	$55,481 65	11.42	$429,970 08
1870–1871	502,146 64	53,924 28	10.74	448,222 36
1871–1872	471,228 78	50,034 37	10.62	421,194 41
1872–1873	477,654 75	51,939 05	9.90	425,715 70
1873–1874	524,494 76	57,205 69	10.90	467,289 07
1874–1875	531,149 09	56,663 64	10.67	474,485 45
1875–1876	1,350,705 56	69,957 24	5.18	1,280,748 32
1876–1877	516,510 80	47,685 23	9.23	468,825 57
1877–1878	538,300 09	37,970 00	7.05	500,330 09
1878–1879	559,217 21	51,160 08	9.15	508,057 13
1879–1880	592,688 44	52,126 21	8.79	540,562 23
1880–1881	634,498 92	52,260 50	8.23	582,238 42
1881–1882	674,973 66	53,161 23	7.87	621,812 43
1882–1883	753,579 80	98,264 24	13.08	655,315 56
1883–1884	830,010 26	100,937 90	12.16	729,072 36
1884–1885	1,092,656 37	89,892 38	8.23	1,002,763 99
1885–1886	1,023,349 52	91,464 07	8.97	931,885 45
1886–1887	1,040,143 16	84,861 27	8.16	955,281 89
1887–1888	1,074,489 54	121,011 50	11.26	953,478 04
1888–1889	1,125,202 97	97,635 14	8.68	1,027,567 83
1889–1890	1,213,458 49	100,134 87	8.25	1,113,323 62
1890–1891	1,306,746 37	103,740 02	7.35	1,203,006 35
1891–1892	1,369,225 30	104,320 34	7.62	1,264,904 96
1892–1893	1,436,875 70	115,817 86	8.06	1,321,057 84
1893–1894	1,445,270 81	110,290 73	7.63	1,334,980 08
1894–1895	1,497,251 90	108,255 57	7.36	1,388,996 33
1895–1896	1,620,480 35	110,347 13	6.81	1,510,133 22
Totals in the 27 years	$24,687,760 97	$2,126,542 19	....	$22,561,218 78
Average per annum	912,028 18	78,760 82	8.65	835,600 69
Totals and Annual averages of the first five years	$2,460,976 66	$268,585 04	....	$2,192,391 62
Annual average	492,195 33	53,717 01	11.14	438,478 32
Total of the second five years	$3,495,882 75	$263,436 19	....	$3,232,446 56
Annual average	699,176 55	52,687 24	7.54	646,489 31
Total of the third five years	$3,485,751 08	$356,750 08	....	$3,129,001 00
Annual average	684,550 38	71,350 02	10.42	625,800 20
Total of the fourth five years	$5,355,841 56	$484,864 36	....	$4,870,977 20
Annual average	1,071,168 31	96,972 87	9.05	974,195 44
Total of the fifth period of five years	$6,771,576 67	$534,303 82	....	$6,237,272 85
Annual average	1,354,315 33	106,860 76	7.89	1,247,454 57
Total of the sixth period of two years	$3,117,732 25	$218,602 70	....	$2,899,129 55
Annual average	1,558,866 13	109,301 35	7.01	1,449,564 78

REVENUES OF THE MEXICAN STATES FROM 1884 TO 1895.

STATES.	1884.	1885.	1886.	1887.	1888.	1889.	1890.	1891.	1892.	1893.	1894.	1895.	TOTAL.
Aguascalientes	$117,672	$103,043	$82,656	$80,400	$81,206	$89,656	$90,095	$144,507	$171,899	$136,615	$101,865	$90,885	$1,290,499
Campeche	130,841	132,038	177,045	190,516	176,553	233,024	239,869	265,419	247,951	252,495	283,777	279,210	2,601,538
Coahuila	222,586	168,211	195,283	185,679	262,725	220,937	431,412	273,318	393,606	333,843	341,093	380,757	3,339,450
Colima	118,337	126,420	126,490	95,870	103,871	116,186	130,237	171,951	158,370	175,383	170,534	263,681	1,657,160
Chiapas	136,025	154,550	125,218	143,322	135,126	183,279	204,332	229,608	274,749	441,520	350,184	421,428	2,268,291
Chihuahua	210,476	317,153	338,087	287,634	335,647	466,415	486,916	697,602	638,422	643,139	857,047		4,421,401
Durango	270,398	225,887	238,181	260,354	272,643	288,780	363,660	532,761	539,089	549,007	1,433,687	800,080	5,207,787
Guanajuato	839,890	967,610	952,017	1,028,064	998,006	1,038,109	1,143,221	1,174,248	1,136,123	1,289,202	1,433,687	1,339,662	13,318,819
Guerrero	221,055	935,578	393,291	286,038	499,785	426,205	443,149	495,556	519,550	530,980	952,072		4,423,359
Hidalgo	433,267	440,445	644,671	668,584	702,188	855,588	1,004,083	1,761,868	1,806,339	2,059,377	1,330,602	2,053,207	13,720,459
Jalisco	1,021,227	1,398,273	1,093,331	1,170,394	1,061,453	1,010,814	1,631,039	1,586,213	1,806,491	1,491,858	1,824,448	1,495,784	15,140,634
México	419,440	440,973	686,124	750,999	739,712	764,863	839,547	1,033,135	1,029,499	1,094,697	903,308	1,182,340	9,065,437
Michoacan	649,107	666,138	663,313	686,995	732,853	705,540	673,548	986,848	1,011,260	1,138,669	822,975	1,131,065	9,980,558
Morelos	328,066	359,653	338,982	338,769	347,233	336,256	359,811	437,187	428,697	436,433	497,824	360,956	4,460,273
New Leon	113,218	113,754	112,964	146,777	334,228	137,861	147,777	162,400	177,087	182,870	206,476	321,589	1,057,001
Oaxaca	680,207	714,471	889,463	988,163	1,126,034	1,019,703	1,063,274	898,355	1,049,477	1,933,587	982,350	905,504	6,243,555
Puebla	809,834	919,533	448,377	333,526	345,415	356,602	206,875	1,564,890	1,284,228	1,102,544	1,431,327	1,144,099	3,328,432
Querétaro	210,810	216,115	1,313,462	1,140,522	1,444,334	2,045,298	1,638,341	374,189	337,363	397,539	424,871	353,344	3,521,951
San Luis Potosí								1,350,031	1,396,375	1,187,854	1,955,791	1,602,899	14,895,008
Sinaloa	355,604	429,792	391,883	407,793	412,857	491,095	499,334	618,284	623,574	704,032	573,994	577,744	6,086,316
Sonora	302,052	293,136	390,959	404,179	347,456	353,258	367,307	561,511	571,298	493,239	374,365	471,753	4,884,455
Tabasco	170,149	185,307	176,831	184,934	353,488	356,832	391,149	298,668	571,298	493,239	336,365	331,537	3,050,141
Tamaulipas			160,931	160,231	114,866	130,299	391,833	199,497	178,458	189,557	135,137		1,533,835
Tlaxcala	131,331	153,362	111,724	116,868	114,224	107,345	166,710	173,066	203,361	189,036	187,379	199,166	1,973,420
Veracruz	722,448	773,516	814,285	730,231	686,838	779,413	865,383	1,239,184	985,395	867,044	57,441		8,535,339
Yucatan	374,466	441,485	457,435	591,453	683,796	511,634	498,366	397,186	611,657	637,149	680,900	66,695	6,485,788
Zacatecas	538,695	756,831	668,968	730,770	744,144	737,477	735,672	1,951,160	1,207,758	1,216,803	1,186,183	736,819	10,497,914
Total	$9,614,461	$10,735,534	$11,718,726	$11,993,413	$12,166,196	$14,186,465	$14,491,158	$19,038,682	$18,892,411	$18,962,976	$16,824,736	$11,131,917	$175,386,467
Federal Treasury	37,442,625	30,359,637	28,797,729	32,126,509	40,952,045	54,801,924	61,908,681	44,142,856	39,993,743	38,654,770	41,216,803	46,907,123	497,314,535
Total	$47,056,886	$41,095,171	$40,516,455	$44,049,922	$53,118,243	$68,988,389	$76,099,839	$63,181,538	$58,886,164	$57,617,746	$58,041,629	$64,039,040	$672,700,022

EXPENSES OF THE MEXICAN STATES FROM 1884 TO 1895.

STATES.	1884.	1885.	1886.	1887.	1888.	1889.	1890.	1891.	1892.	1893.	1894.	1895.	TOTAL.
Aguascalientes	$ 85,564	$ 86,626	$ 81,356	$ 78,400	$ 80,603	$ 89,186	$ 93,475	$ 144,487	$ 166,306	$ 135,384	$ 101,865	$ 90,395	$ 1,233,647
Campeche	134,901	133,426	177,159	189,492	168,558	217,778	244,180	250,866	244,872	244,742	265,180	267,288	2,547,433
Coahuila	234,835	183,489	190,436	176,418	226,093	210,031	232,162	260,094	317,445	392,074	341,093	304,873	3,006,043
Colima	115,030	124,474	124,474	100,348	109,535	114,487	131,770	171,240	162,105	168,548	163,611	152,590	1,638,202
Chiapas	135,370	155,231	135,052	142,815	135,197	181,885	195,972	174,740	268,293	430,949	359,918	423,103	2,728,535
Chihuahua	228,219	282,275						639,574	614,605	611,159			2,356,832
Durango	264,619	217,555	235,065	243,311	263,616	282,654	357,368	392,353	516,407	539,315	836,912	799,997	5,064,982
Guanajuato						1,049,015	1,102,697	1,132,089	1,168,058	1,299,855	1,204,964	1,338,106	9,294,784
Guerrero	216,627	242,532	209,870	220,598	223,819	238,936	335,840	273,100	280,527	340,450	260,603		2,742,982
Hidalgo	426,442	455,832	599,701	594,192	642,885	727,283	1,017,497	1,740,351	1,792,792	2,051,609	1,316,479	2,059,213	13,417,207
Jalisco	1,012,999	1,415,211	972,846	1,052,887	1,283,412	994,439	962,737	1,386,213	1,306,491	1,457,104	1,459,535	1,495,928	15,089,703
México	639,011	665,599	625,497	703,364	785,983	772,495	801,930	1,026,974	1,019,427	1,057,316	883,264	1,142,016	9,557,557
Michoacan	397,057	356,038	641,389	647,467	719,988	699,490	703,478	930,735	988,860	1,109,066	802,459	1,149,031	9,788,313
Morelos	99,785	103,199	344,412	326,511	351,415	336,390	355,109	433,738	418,861	430,427	394,229	335,742	4,413,793
New Leon	748,927	681,918		153,664	131,559	134,578	130,034	140,428	143,861	157,603	151,955	355,649	1,175,180
Oaxaca								749,105	884,411	953,636	973,723	895,436	5,868,156
Puebla	894,686	945,462	889,011	987,925	1,112,660	987,460	1,055,360	1,518,955	1,361,464	1,284,620	1,212,622	1,128,949	13,179,104
Queretaro	212,759	215,702	248,136	228,023	351,004	357,158	294,797	374,185	337,368	307,343	419,501	350,840	3,496,816
San Luis Potosi			1,399,827	1,156,149	1,150,279	3,580,051	1,699,971	1,544,776	1,561,652	1,162,662	1,046,668	834,265	14,131,133
Sinaloa	353,950	498,201	394,986	401,999	417,446	492,448	495,781	614,419	617,355	467,997	543,784	581,051	6,033,696
Sonora	289,598	326,331	169,781	493,056	336,140	368,416	315,977	535,870	541,439	354,155	354,155	387,153	4,535,693
Tabasco	166,771	188,948	175,993	192,154	229,854	272,042	286,706	393,998	281,405	290,187	335,022	338,306	3,051,398
Tamaulipas			166,790	158,851	118,357	133,094	191,134	192,977	177,693	180,984	213,019		1,526,838
Tlaxcala	135,101	148,311	116,720	118,826	118,723	164,773	272,780	174,599	198,199	189,411	185,960	184,484	1,904,597
Veracruz	708,606	760,873	750,070	730,393	772,218	777,607	742,065	871,266	954,055	799,019	542,615		8,417,671
Yucatan	371,562	430,712	449,005	444,200	438,347	487,658	480,315	580,304	620,784	630,099	672,738	670,994	6,297,609
Zacatecas	573,031	701,686	603,394	671,625	784,641	701,332	754,860	1,226,535	1,201,780	1,179,868	1,174,420	750,387	10,983,630
Total	$8,760,700	$9,759,904	$9,701,181	$10,136,566	$10,697,922	$13,149,777	$13,061,925	$18,089,393	$18,236,394	$18,301,264	$17,314,175	$16,311,699	$163,339,900
Federal Treasury	43,714,229	44,407,386	26,184,198	36,262,962	54,956,554	73,922,329	78,158,753	63,005,128	43,350,149	48,954,972	45,773,791	45,078,551	604,709,000
Total	$51,483,929	$54,167,290	$35,885,379	$46,399,528	$65,654,476	$87,072,106	$91,220,678	$81,094,521	$61,586,543	$67,256,236	$62,927,966	$61,390,250	$766,038,900

REVENUES OF THE MUNICIPALITIES OF MEXICO FROM 1884 TO 1895.

REVENUES.

STATES.	1884.	1885.	1886.	1887.	1888.	1889.	1890.	1891.	1892.	1893.	1894.	1895.	TOTAL.
Aguascalientes	60,147	55,176	58,989	59,106	62,053	68,260	71,735	75,434	78,138	64,179	71,587	73,140	797,044
Campeche	71,336	68,774	80,332	96,395	98,871	83,359	99,145	101,294	96,481	127,008	170,921	142,479	1,237,186
Coahuila	174,285	206,569	174,837	194,790	239,837	255,036	226,780	393,193	372,664	396,414	446,611	692,730	3,773,575
Colima	52,972	54,596	53,337	49,821	47,938	54,861	54,185	67,216	97,460	96,385	62,534	73,447	713,452
Chiapas	......	......	......	......	......	......	......	61,096	82,393	103,250	120,103	143,204	510,051
Chihuahua	......	......	......	......	306,604	322,363	384,340	544,369	532,015	540,740	......	......	3,168,393
Durango	......	......	......	......	......	......	......	......	......	......	......	......	......
Guanajuato	591,581	594,347	586,575	556,340	564,235	599,086	630,516	656,913	584,232	558,204	662,419	751,636	7,328,044
Guerrero	82,943	99,064	105,868	111,781	123,548	129,431	117,065	103,117	115,839	99,792	112,877	......	1,201,955
Hidalgo	331,726	334,462	307,109	315,772	318,556	310,061	318,057	521,426	533,224	537,085	385,954	586,695	4,999,319
Jalisco	498,723	675,100	233,671	445,392	246,687	266,793	252,090	354,934	266,086	276,042	390,680	291,911	3,586,809
México	178,996	210,900	226,264	235,349	229,174	245,197	256,335	395,700	306,877	348,066	379,043	401,070	3,026,776
Michoacan	......	68,965	......	108,092	104,215	111,405	114,459	335,598	330,989	348,066	156,506	184,371	2,923,069
Morelos	83,012	68,965	98,459	108,092	104,215	111,405	114,459	35,598	34,989	30,488	156,506	184,371	1,138,259
New Leon	156,773	155,761	160,614	180,819	195,739	240,438	253,524	343,994	330,758	377,011	418,719	433,566	3,247,846
Oaxaca	98,804	126,496	103,077	102,108	......	104,610	109,473	184,235	216,689	219,065	355,109	248,326	1,870,850
Puebla	894,686	945,469	......	......	......	593,061	609,957	656,129	669,291	795,359	754,985	804,682	6,653,512
Querétaro	55,529	52,475	......	......	......	......	......	77,041	70,918	65,351	70,397	80,736	472,437
San Luis Potosí	......	......	319,240	285,009	285,432	283,793	288,699	141,527	145,306	272,070	334,164	394,647	2,749,687
Sinaloa	190,144	159,832	397,067	410,575	481,194	495,429	516,366	478,714	470,688	447,745	437,543	473,958	4,599,279
Sonora	102,376	87,850	290,316	216,782	212,855	248,316	241,986	220,400	269,858	277,479	254,609	357,089	2,703,957
Tabasco	......	......	94,351	114,291	113,024	124,226	145,322	131,110	144,931	155,985	171,938	167,397	1,556,601
Tamaulipas	......	......	......	......	......	......	......	233,524	265,587	248,395	254,609	......	1,335,064
Tlaxcala	27,437	30,615	40,013	37,302	47,756	43,568	35,470	47,662	50,684	46,565	51,118	48,208	505,998
Veracruz	906,016	800,442	1,828,202	2,367,848	3,422,601	2,348,206	2,183,087	2,628,734	2,704,451	2,728,368	3,571,242	......	24,439,857
Yucatan	140,388	176,854	196,277	209,040	198,411	233,390	159,842	248,678	249,020	261,214	302,015	293,551	2,628,680
Zacatecas	438,890	443,054	238,557	306,443	409,053	459,393	427,019	454,396	412,377	431,511	438,904	512,204	5,011,801
Territory of Lower California	28,449	30,681	34,443	38,870	40,680	49,726	57,220	18,491	20,392	17,772	108,410	19,054	464,488
Territory of Tepic	127,445	119,717	65,002	82,989	83,795	85,771	85,195	136,501	142,043	158,846	185,491	210,947	1,484,622
Total	$5,294,108	$5,386,792	$5,857,057	$6,702,049	$6,728,675	$7,591,787	$7,881,082	$9,508,881	$9,760,610	$10,108,656	$10,883,094	$7,993,600	$93,907,291
Federal District	1,332,403	1,486,645	1,928,324	2,049,063	2,380,238	2,668,081	3,345,267	2,455,435	2,745,401	3,175,992	3,461,919	3,395,698	30,444,406
Total	$6,626,511	$7,073,437	$7,786,281	$8,751,112	$9,108,913	$10,379,868	$11,226,349	$11,964,316	$12,506,011	$13,284,648	$14,345,013	$11,399,238	$124,351,697

EXPENSES OF THE MUNICIPALITIES OF MEXICO FROM 1884 TO 1895.

STATES.	1884.	1885.	1886.	1887.	1888.	1889.	1890.	1891.	1892.	1893.	1894.	1895.	TOTAL.
Aguascalientes	$60,837	55,992	38,089	59,106	62,053	68,260	71,375	$75,677	$79,232	$64,734	$71,769	73,272	$781,226
Campeche	71,162	68,382	77,447	92,147	92,550	81,299	87,160	94,416	89,009	109,245	121,139	110,548	1,094,454
Coahuila	182,873	205,148	182,938	195,158	180,358	258,424	222,351	392,554	372,199	380,368	436,244	678,247	3,705,792
Colima	53,287	54,763	53,712	50,035	48,378	54,317	57,775	60,199	69,744	75,027	62,405	72,823	719,946
Chiapas	....	....	....	....	....	....	....	....	81,712	105,882	115,551	139,798	503,070
Chihuahua	....	....	....	....	306,604	324,363	384,340	502,605	511,012	534,422	....	....	3,137,368
Durango	....	....	....	....	....	....	....	....	....	....	....	....	
Guanajuato	594,345	595,480	390,727	287,435	553,036	553,036	639,547	662,072	614,853	571,115	654,363	734,697	5,577,468
Guerrero	82,462	87,432	103,031	108,757	114,481	120,605	125,929	101,936	120,768	99,654	112,314	234,499	1,176,991
Hidalgo	327,716	333,898	307,051	310,798	348,290	397,885	318,056	506,200	514,130	517,537	574,836	564,334	4,868,766
Jalisco	498,773	675,100	182,231	188,453	191,771	203,925	205,866	487,661	476,297	519,867	451,261	503,624	3,552,533
México	178,996	210,500	224,998	232,164	232,055	243,785	350,208	247,166	460,215	275,047	278,323	286,008	2,709,101
Michoacan	....	....	....	....	....	....	116,379	271,600	387,495	317,662	359,712	360,371	2,782,140
Morelos	84,985	68,586	97,205	107,096	104,301	109,110	116,379	35,374	34,506	35,759	155,823	150,791	1,029,984
New Leon	160,904	160,949	164,310	175,533	190,876	322,480	232,497	339,169	329,495	352,568	419,594	434,222	3,186,597
Oaxaca	114,073	113,632	96,998	94,852	93,239	94,570	160,597	170,293	202,516	227,028	236,286	234,499	1,769,423
Puebla	585,684	585,809				594,726	611,019	642,015	647,543	682,645	722,863	757,050	5,828,703
Queretaro	55,230	50,807						76,954	65,348	68,317	79,300	79,300	465,871
San Luis Potosi			293,697	285,867	248,330	241,214	303,632	298,779	370,032	299,003	327,704	387,372	2,096,750
Sinaloa			387,590	399,388	482,874	491,130	535,973	474,659	470,131	440,146	440,146	475,837	4,585,438
Sonora	188,730	159,728	208,880	217,683	211,318	248,516	240,422	217,209	268,690	277,227	432,110	349,544	2,587,947
Tabasco	82,125	85,537	96,674	112,404	133,573	123,573	138,024	123,713	135,453	144,473	164,777	166,859	1,485,631
Tamaulipas							235,398	223,713	261,507	243,649	255,419		1,219,686
Tlaxcala	27,379	29,071	39,654	47,756	47,756	41,199	34,518	45,609	48,880	46,333	50,390	46,999	494,860
Veracruz	847,470	878,432	1,783,602	2,078,831	2,217,032	3,332,273	2,200,568	2,581,042	2,770,385	2,596,628	5,515,127		23,841,311
Yucatan	136,046	179,005	185,119	233,057	166,712	267,635	230,021	242,913	248,949	257,654	428,707	299,116	2,746,406
Zacatecas	438,368	436,458	247,085	571,750	415,190	439,992	400,048	454,395	412,377	431,511	428,707	495,688	5,171,640
Territory of Lower California	29,437	30,783	31,710	37,494	41,422	45,783	60,088	18,362	20,260	77,638	104,323	18,358	455,158
Territory of Tepic	112,602	110,731	67,364	82,471	94,937	105,002	97,301	129,796	143,193	145,495	168,893	195,869	1,453,643
Total	$4,913,354	$5,169,953	$5,161,014	$5,866,886	$5,981,741	$7,570,001	$7,804,792	$9,443,363	$9,851,328	$9,028,338	$10,287,578	$7,657,055	$90,026,393
Federal District	1,337,451	1,491,055	1,882,825	2,082,396	2,391,464	2,638,093	3,239,286	2,580,074	3,210,371	3,040,865	3,460,845	3,378,595	30,728,320
Total	$6,245,805	$6,661,008	$7,043,839	$7,970,182	$8,373,205	$10,208,094	$11,134,078	$12,023,437	$13,061,699	$12,069,203	$14,048,423	$10,996,650	$120,744,623

STATE AND MUNICIPAL FINANCES.

The best way in which I can give the state and municipal revenues and expenses in Mexico, is by inserting the detail amounts of the last twelve years of the revenues and expenses of each of the Mexican States, and a similar statement of the revenues and expenses of the municipalities of each State. That statement gives also the revenues and expenses of the City of Mexico, which have increased very considerably of late. In the year 1867, after the restoration of the Republic, they only amounted to about $800,000, while in the year 1895, they had increased to $3,395,638. (These statements are on pp. 150–153.)

FOREIGN TRADE.

The foreign trade of Mexico was necessarily very small before the railway era, because transportation was exceedingly high on account of the broken condition of the country, and only articles of great value and comparatively small weight could be profitably exported, while the price of foreign commodities became very high, both on account of transportation charges and high import duties. Therefore, only rich people could afford to consume foreign commodities, and the exports of Mexico were practically reduced to silver and gold, and to a few commodities having small bulk and great value.

The normal cost of transportation on merchandise from the City of Mexico to Veracruz, a distance of one hundred Mexican leagues or 263¼ English miles, used to be, before the railroad connecting both places was built, $68.75 per ton of 2200 pounds, or more than 26 cents per mile and ton ; and in extraordinary circumstances, as during the French Intervention in Mexico from 1861 to 1867, the freight was as high as $330 per ton, or over $1.25 per mile and ton. Therefore, no article could be transported unless it was very much needed and it commanded a very high price. The result was that not only the foreign but also the domestic trade was reduced to its smallest proportions, and that the people raised just enough to provide for the wants of themselves and their immediate neighbors. A fact that may seem incredible is, that for the same reasons, among the farmers, a good crop was considered a great misfortune.

Since the railways have revolutionized transportation, our products, especially agricultural commodities, have begun to be sent to foreign markets, and their exportation is increasing considerably. As yet the precious metals, especially silver, are the main exports from Mexico, representing during the fiscal year ended June 30, 1896, 61 per cent. of our total annual exports ; but other commodities are now exported, and they are in a fair way to exceed, before long, the value of our silver exports. I have no doubt that with the opening of our railroads, if our exports continue to increase in the same proportion as they have recently done, Mexico will be able to supply the United States with most of the tropical products now consumed and not yet produced here, and even with others, that would find a market if they could be cheaply transported.

The same difficulties which prevented us from having correct accounts of our public revenues and expenses, and which I have stated in speaking on that subject, made it very difficult for many years to have correct statistics of our imports and exports.

Imports.—I could not give even a tentative statement, which I could vouchsafe, of our total imports and exports from 1821 to 1867, but the statement of the receipts of our custom-houses from 1823 to 1875, which appears on page 145 gives an approximate idea of our imports, considering that the receipts amount to about from 50 to 60 per cent. of the value of the imports.

I append a detailed statement of the imports and exports in Mexico during the years 1826, 1827, and 1828, and the total imports and exports during the year 1825.

From the fiscal year 1872–1873 our Statistical Bureau began to make its reports, and I have concised them in the three annexed statements comprising most of those years, up to the fiscal year ended June 30, 1896. The commodities are divided in their respective classes in accordance with the different schedules of the tariffs then in force.

MEXICAN IMPORTS AND EXPORTS FROM 1826 TO 1828.

MERCHANDISE.	1826.	1827.	1828.
Imports.			
Linen...............................	$2,384,715	$2,180,191	$1,711,051
Wool	934,295	493,760	245,901
Silk	1,432,578	844,732	398,003
Cotton..............................	5,017,700	6,913,126	3,417,766
Mixed..............................	122,968	107,108	38,654
Wines, liquors, groceries..............	2,888,066	2,867,320	3,244,498
Haberdashery	728,236	489,402	306,614
Medicines, drugs, and perfumeries.......	90,779	55,100	20,260
Books, blank and printed, paper.........	1,430,039	495,743	130,638
China, fine and ordinary, crystal and glass.	264,424	311,074	332,819
Furniture, of wood and metal..........	91,910	103,047	57,187
Machines and instruments for mining, science, and the arts...............	63,499	22,816	44,123
Furs...............................	912	4,517	318
Gold and silver	444	1,080	....
Total imports....................	$15,450,565	$14,889,016	$9,947,832
Exports.	Total imports in 1825: $19,093,716.		
Gold and silver.......................	$5,847,795	$9,669,428	$12,387,288
Cochineal...........................	1,356,730	912,049	1,483,746
Indigo, vanilla, jalap, and sarsaparilla ...	76,440	1,076,528	448,747
Other articles of indigenous products.....	367,164	513,769	169,005
Total exports....................	$7,648,129	$12,171,774	$14,488,786
	Total exports in 1825: $5,085,235.		

IMPORTS IN MEXICO FROM JULY 1, 1872, TO JUNE 30, 1875, AND IN THE YEAR 1884-1885.

	1872-1873.		1873-1874.		1874-1875.		1884-1885.	
	Invoice Value.	Duties.	Invoice Value.	Duties.	Invoice Value.	Duties.	Invoice Value.	Duties.
1. Cottons........	$7,036,913 45	$4,992,003 53	$8,814,123 34	$6,002,759 46	$7,379,339 12	$5,826,530 86	$6,153,559 86	$5,234,420 08
2. Linens........	1,003,595 70	603,559 96	1,173,572 41	700,445 22	703,052 21	496,896 20	548,191 22	459,798 70
3. Woollens......	1,031,378 82	676,339 40	1,306,932 77	877,078 29	988,292 75	695,216 55	1,376,365 04	1,066,491 36
4. Silks.........	401,995 37	260,004 52	337,560 01	217,398 44	274,744 88	189,815 46	337,550 28	281,978 04
5. Mixtures......	1,052,553 37	624,126 96	1,174,004 66	715,661 44	796,762 17	539,745 16	1,281,247 44	1,070,162 56
6. Groceries.....	3,613,162 45	2,184,375 85	3,334,152 92	2,058,713 20	2,955,852 55	2,038,344 16	3,761,080 40	2,632,185 86
7. Crystal.......	279,216 43	172,154 00	356,770 88	248,030 11	240,825 10	185,952 29	398,154 72	305,172 42
8. Haberdashery .	1,180,194 88	687,282 98	1,376,719 31	828,395 54	1,160,921 85	768,267 32	1,741,956 70	1,278,237 60
9. Chemicals	178,258 75	141,181 29	226,681 92	198,761 67	174,618 02	143,569 70	479,734 38	348,709 22
10. Sundries	1,404,297 58	1,125,142 38	1,635,461 81	1,111,199 21	1,322,722 14	898,919 65	1,769,536 32	1,203,434 20
11. Commodities paying 55%..	555,027 91	366,946 65	36,400 00	23,352 84	58,444 09	38,276 14	296,166 38	194,302 24
Free Articles.....	2,429,508 14	....	3,509,918 53	....	2,737,918 73	....	5,643,142 16	....
Total........	$20,166,012 85	$11,833,117 52	$23,282,298 56	$12,981,795 42	$18,793,493 61	$11,821,533 49	$23,786,684 90	$14,084,892 28

IMPORTS IN MEXICO FROM JULY 1, 1885, TO JUNE 30, 1886, AND FROM JULY 1, 1888, TO JUNE 30, 1890.

	1885-1886. UNDER THE TARIFF OF JANUARY 24, 1885.		1888-1889. UNDER THE TARIFF OF MARCH 1, 1887.		1889-1890.	
	Invoice Value.	Duties.	Invoice Value.	Duties.	Invoice Value.	Duties.
1. Free of duties	$2,682,343 26	......	$13,506,230 23	......	$21,238,598 91	......
2. Cottons	5,520,538 32	$6,953,659 28	7,534,088 70	$7,447,394 70	7,677,131 31	$8,109,445 45
3. Linens	556,115 48	639,234 50	674,029 52	671,590 87	681,879 69	645,276 72
4. Woollens	1,227,327 42	1,737,314 34	1,613,186 22	1,986,020 61	1,995,890 56	2,353,441 00
5. Silks	305,936 48	351,903 84	394,691 60	378,614 57	540,845 12	505,490 35
6. Mixtures	366,755 04	430,279 26	304,889 86	410,419 80	548,298 13	550,578 80
7. Food articles	2,390,360 48	2,037,829 30	4,893,706 49	3,789,270 57	5,954,813 02	4,627,227 87
8. Stones and earths	97,579 84	66,873 18	81,815 68	41,244 81	133,694 20	61,249 16
9. Crystal and porcelain	309,411 14	326,712 90	607,727 18	686,884 84	667,593 16	743,388 64
10. Gold, silver, and platinum	145,551 66	17,690 40	320,843 60	27,967 36	286,680 35	28,792 54
11. Iron and steel	852,065 14	674,270 34	1,510,129 91	1,259,480 12	2,034,625 21	1,507,561 26
12. Leather	303,577 72	238,771 08	593,166 91	324,225 37	705,768 54	428,993 02
13. Tin, lead, and zinc	42,620 20	34,558 16	75,968 92	39,289 76	93,421 20	50,877 98
14. Haberdashery	423,549 42	304,950 50	658,853 68	505,497 81	715,068 53	551,554 20
15. Machines	1,457,236 48	81,014 42	539,582 35	128,205 84	587,478 34	155,459 53
16. Carriages and wagons	75,024 30	41,868 66	213,796 20	116,206 57	272,264 46	150,161 03
17. Arms, ammunition, and gunpowder	285,926 12	141,862 40	280,453 04	172,830 78	348,652 13	200,487 78
18. Wood and its manufactures	202,492 52	171,495 12	473,684 25	368,523 72	620,984 55	480,905 30
19. Paper and its manufactures	951,677 28	626,525 02	1,352,143 12	1,161,250 81	1,359,477 23	1,754,445 55
20. Furs	253,677 12	197,113 18	414,109 54	290,211 92	506,693 83	348,989 86
21. Chemicals	736,656 94	496,131 56	1,697,830 38	997,449 42	1,737,395 37	1,036,988 80
22. Sundries	1,925,372 88	1,534,435 38	2,193,966 94	1,675,382 70	3,311,465 05	2,091,334 04
Total	$21,171,795 24	$17,104,492 82	$40,024,894 32	$22,477,962 95	$52,018,658 89	$25,782,648 88

IMPORTS IN MEXICO FROM THE FISCAL YEAR 1892–1893 TO THE FISCAL YEAR 1895–1896.

	FREE. Invoice Value.				DUTIABLE. Invoice Value.				TOTAL. Invoice Value.			
	1892-1893.	1893-1894.	1894-1895.	1895-1896.	1892-1893.	1893-1894.	1894-1895.	1895-1896.	1892-1893.	1893-1894.	1894-1895.	1895-1896.
1. Animal Industry:												
Live animals	$9,042	$10,797	$3,640	$7,353	$745,321	$260,010	$169,673	$374,555	$754,363	$370,807	$173,313	$381,907
Animal remains	1,523	11,922	13,370	26,271	370,441	302,880	567,391	707,499	371,964	302,880	567,392	707,499
Animal products	12,290		13,366	471	1,243,263	817,868	780,406	1,052,730	1,255,553	829,790	802,866	1,079,001
Animal manufactures	1,865	119	3,366		733,029	628,993	674,686	648,993	724,894	629,112	678,059	629,464
Total	$24,720	$22,838	$20,376	$33,094	$3,082,054	$2,009,751	$2,201,246	$2,763,877	$3,106,774	$2,032,589	$2,221,622	$2,797,871
2. Agricultural Products:												
Textiles			$13,935		$2,355,756	$2,026,616	$2,341,747	$1,761,488	$2,395,756	$2,026,616	$2,355,672	$1,761,488
Fruits and grains	30,847	19,026	16,905	25,716	7,380,439	1,118,146	883,923	1,553,036	7,420,286	1,137,172	900,128	1,578,752
Sundry vegetable substances	109,496	65,710	94,772	98,375	234,350	192,310	211,556	266,237	343,846	258,020	306,338	364,612
Sundry vegetable products	3,583	3,437	9,578	3,137	1,208,458	1,019,057	974,778	1,104,787	1,212,041	1,023,494	984,356	1,197,924
Wood and its products	937,383	675,950	600,512	666,411	341,752	276,858	296,230	391,658	1,279,135	952,788	805,742	1,158,069
Manufactures of sundry vegetable substances	395,958	20	3,225	2,470	225,671	383,608	464,063	360,334	531,629	383,718	467,908	382,604
Furniture					292,011	187,027	216,899	319,602	292,011	187,027	216,899	319,602
Total	$1,387,267	$764,143	$738,217	$1,095,909	$12,057,437	$5,194,602	$5,389,816	$5,867,142	$13,444,704	$5,958,745	$6,128,043	$6,963,051
3. Metals and its Manufactures:												
Gold, silver, and platinum	$200,610	$117,369	$834,472	$59,336	$150,220	$163,655	$201,850	$173,268	$339,813	$281,024	$1,036,322	$332,604
Copper	31,183	24,479	24,670	55,683	497,992	438,903	600,916	676,098	529,175	462,982	635,586	734,781
Tin, lead, and zinc	4,228	3,148	6,115	4,495	69,042	73,377	102,514	128,930	73,270	76,525	108,629	133,425
Iron and metals	1,216,596	441,254	285,165	1,049,435	1,855,228	2,054,929	2,437,516	3,140,827	3,071,824	2,496,183	2,713,681	4,190,272
Other metals	603,595	506,643	541,664	574,153	984	12,131	3,281	4,470	604,509	518,774	544,945	578,643
Stone and earthenware	1,804,277	1,951,373	1,040,790	1,046,402	826,979	614,356	675,187	982,678	2,631,256	1,665,629	1,774,977	2,029,080
Crystal, glass, china, and porcelainware	6,472	6,939	2,851	6,853	545,207	594,073	548,230	867,162	551,769	511,012	551,081	874,015
Total	$3,866,891	$2,151,205	$2,735,727	$2,796,357	$3,954,795	$3,860,924	$4,559,494	$5,973,443	$7,821,616	$6,012,129	$7,295,221	$8,769,800
4. Fabrics:												
Cotton					$4,119,936	$4,108,266	$4,576,433	$5,767,483	$4,119,936	$4,108,266	$4,576,433	$5,767,483
Linen					531,938	480,827	480,690	673,109	531,938	489,827	480,690	673,109
Wool	$2,133	$4,530	$5,268	$6,053	1,368,129	1,459,060	1,734,418	1,848,491	1,370,262	1,459,060	1,734,418	1,848,491
Silk					428,372	933,334	456,681	554,382	434,401	397,864	401,949	554,435
Silk with a mixture of other substances	4,029											
Total	$6,162	$4,530	$5,268	$6,053	$6,854,207	$6,933,610	$7,783,945	$9,420,050	$6,860,459	$6,938,440	$7,783,213	$9,426,103
5. Chemicals, oils, and paints	$146,659				$897,587	$1,099,350	$1,376,620	$1,725,345	$1,044,246	$1,099,350	$1,376,620	$1,725,345
6. Wines, liquors, fermented and unfermented drinks												
7. Paper and its manufactures	156,953	143,557	172,258	217,359	2,734,164	1,913,161	2,174,460	2,530,249	2,734,164	1,913,161	2,174,460	2,530,249
8. Machinery	1,935,081	146,047	157,894	269,224	1,203,340	924,858	1,167,419	1,430,202	1,360,293	1,068,415	1,330,617	1,647,561
9. Carriages	625,324	162,312	141,977	582,050	2,317,822	3,399,331	3,574,597	4,942,920	4,252,993	3,545,378	3,734,399	5,212,744
10. Arms and Explosives	444,182	1,058	979	5,587	308,095	151,891	137,538	231,411	933,419	314,903	279,515	811,461
11. Sundries	8,062				532,684	605,114	605,114	1,018,461	986,866	605,114	853,691	1,018,461
					879,645	798,201	900,000	1,100,109	887,687	799,259	909,979	1,114,696
Grand Total	$8,601,301	$3,395,690	$3,972,604	$5,004,533	$34,811,830	$26,691,793	$30,097,736	$37,012,902	$43,413,131	$30,287,483	$34,000,440	$42,016,742

I append a statement which shows the imports and exports of Mexico during the two fiscal years 1894–1895 and 1895–1896, both by countries and by custom-houses, and the imports and duties by countries in the fiscal years 1888–1889 and 1889–1890.

Exports.—It would be difficult to make a correct statement of our exports previous to the fiscal year 1867–1868. Their amount was very small for reasons already given, and as they principally consisted in silver, and almost all the silver coined was exported the coinage of which we have exact records, can be taken as the amount of exports, with the addition of from 30 to 40 per cent., representing the silver both in coin and bullion smuggled. I give a correct statement of our exports of agricultural commodities from the fiscal year 1877–1878 to 1895–1896, and also a statement of our exports of other commodities from the fiscal year 1886–1887 to 1895–1896, which shows the rapid pace at which they are increasing.

The exports from Mexico are embraced in the following articles :

MINERALS.

Chapopote.
Coal.
Copper in bars.
Gold and silver coin.
Gold and silver bullion.
Lead in pigs.
Onyx.
Opals.
Ores of silver, copper, and lead.

AGRICULTURAL PRODUCTS.

Beans.
Bitter almonds and various fruits, kernels.
Chick-peas.
Cocoa.
Coffee.
Honey.
India-rubber.
Molasses.
Piloncillo (brown sugar).
Sugar, all grades.

FIBRES.

Henequen.
Ixtle.
Mallows fibre.
Pita.
Ramie.
Sotol.
Wool.

ANIMAL PRODUCTS.

Bones.
Cattle.
Chihuahua terriers.
Donkeys.
Goats.
Hair, horse.
Hair, rabbit.
Heron feathers.
Hides, raw and tanned.
Hoofs.
Horns.
Horses.
Mules.
Ox grease.
Sheep.
Skins of sheep and goat, dressed and undressed.

MANUFACTURES.

Cotton, linen, worsted and silk domestic shawls (rebozos).
Guadalajara earthenware.
Maguey, brandy (Tequila and mescal.
Preserved sweet meats.
Rag puppets and dolls.
Rags (all sorts).
Wax, artificial flowers and figures.
Woollen and worsted Mexican plaids or blankets (Zarapes).

FRUITS.

Bananas.
Cocoanuts.
Lemons.
Limes.
Oranges.
Pine apples.
Walnuts, Nuevo Leon.
Tamarind pulp.

FORESTRY.

Cabinet woods, mahogany, moral, lind-aloe, tepeguaje, cedar, sandal, ebony, and rosewood.
Dye woods, brasil, camphor, moral, and other varieties of logwood.
Orchilla.

SUNDRIES.

Copal, chick, and sundry resinous substances.
Jalap, and other medicinal herbs.
Mother of pearl shells.
Pearls.
Tortoise shell from the Gulf of Cortez.
Vanilla.
Zacaton brush and broom grasses.

IMPORTS IN MEXICO BY COUNTRIES IN THE FISCAL YEARS 1888-1889 AND 1889-1890 AND IMPORTS AND EXPORTS BY COUNTRIES AND CUSTOM HOUSES IN THE FISCAL YEARS 1894-1895 AND 1895-1896.

COUNTRIES	1888-1889 VALUE	DUTIES	1889-1890 VALUE	DUTIES	1894-95 IMPORTS	EXPORTS	1895-96 IMPORTS	EXPORTS
Arabia	$8	$24	$19		1,245		417	
Argelia	13,649	15,907	15,960	14,416	5,358		10,434	
Argentine Republic			600	203	177	300	189	300
Australia	485	32	3,895	77	38,331		4,572	
Austria	96,436	74,814	117,544	87,658	87,655		116,155	
Bavaria			400					
Belgium	242,263	232,287	553,370	261,198	329,580	380,205	420,035	1,000,393
Bolivia	600	277			1,949		2,909	
Brazil	309	230	912	602	342		4,358	
Canada	108	72	220		2,469	30	653	
Chili	39,351	26,346	59,001	45,682	5,448		1,734	70
China	78,178	80,830	38,666	12,773	71,702	545	76,804	51,188
Colombia	22,495	6,580	24,742	6,260	375	71,274	131	8,455
Costa Rica			2,802	2,928	4,058	6,837	1,966	
Cuba	1,112	729	1,868	588	2,062		4,605	
Denmark	89,445	38,429	118,477	55,156	73,009		2,870	
Ecuador			3,951		1,701		63,644	
Egypt								
England	6,337,680	5,083,870	8,535,370	6,359,363	6,668,311	15,261,169	7,995,016	16,467,149
France	4,956,568	3,846,452	6,933,018	4,802,032	5,576,750	2,129,816	6,099,183	2,080,802
Germany	2,824,932	2,310,015	3,678,684	2,588,077	3,361,643	3,173,235	4,363,220	2,968,792
Greece	1,289	3,636	683	468	1,557		899	
Guatemala	11,548	53,010	218,402	11,448	14,357	889,753	21,874	1,076,442
Holland	72,009		160,535	129,319	127,187	65,440	134,484	133,955
Honduras				9		3,502		
India	69,629	123,364	85,490	144,032	151,870		142,629	
Italy	269,826	121,818	161,505	58,119	121,398	26,814	150,360	44,443
Japan	95	64	1,515	1,139	9,018	5,850	12,793	2,999
Morocco					17			
Nicaragua						3,615		4,954
Norway	34,376	33,358	44,462	34,397	40,228		70,052	
Persia	102	373	360	444	671		668	
Peru	772	347	129		674	2,155	725	18,247
Portugal	9,233	2,650	13,393	4,738	19,460		32,049	
Russia	11,335	386	393	104	7,811	283,349	17,789	536,535
Salvador	80	4,464	3,405	890	19,012	376,028	7,861	122,237
San Domingo		60	150	94	1,110		45	
Senegambia					340		1,073	
Spain	1,920,949	1,171,177	2,576,289	1,599,561	1,918,661	974,160	2,174,298	813,162
Sweden	1,667	2,295	4,445	6,005	24,992		30,461	
Switzerland	157,444	80,830	238,163	125,579	115,108	150	158,210	
Turkey	2,327	761	1,905	458	2,136		1,841	
United States	22,665,420	9,169,787	29,080,276	9,564,446	15,130,367	67,322,986	20,145,703	79,651,695
Uruguay	73,738	10	37,819	14,207	728		45	
Venezuela	20	35,435			23,950		16,896	
Zanzibar		37	80	211	4,026		2,367	
Total	$40,024,885	$22,477,043	$52,018,648	$35,782,631	$34,000,440	$90,854,953	$42,353,938	$105,016,902

CUSTOM HOUSES	1894-95 IMPORTS	EXPORTS	1895-96 IMPORTS	EXPORTS
Acapulco	161,684	124,251	198,095	101,672
Altata			45,807	931,759
Camargo	6,046	32,437	6,678	14,360
Campeche	186,307	938,972	258,161	1,097,183
Ciudad Juárez	2,571,977	14,255,800	3,677,525	19,599,797
Ciudad Porfirio Díaz	2,386,451	2,850,662	4,228,658	3,065,014
Coatzacoalcos	40,348	135,670	315,249	328,924
Frontera	321,219	334,136	306,235	428,863
Guaymas	453,199	904,618	557,261	19,991
Guerrero		11,481	3,645	14,553
Isla del Carmen	67,430	1,273,788	80,277	1,844,431
La Morita	29,641	350,549	59,965	640,444
La Paz	59,433	691,001	129,334	763,044
Laredo	3,449,852	324,146	3,868,696	3,321,273
Las Palomas		322,111	21,259	376,594
Manzanillo	88,570		91,349	246,463
Matamoros	189,795	6,285,777	279,047	5,451,864
Mazatlán	1,458,693		1,566,081	148,007
Mier	16,525	73,604	19,493	4,037,624
Nogales	549,189	2,087,590	626,675	2,102,098
Progreso	1,092,070	7,865,933	1,696,774	354,169
Puerto Angel	9,959	388,611	9,794	50,571
Salina Cruz	40,016	56,709	33,627	679,066
San Blas	181,153	669,122	214,894	3,288,030
Santa Rosalia	331,370	2,235,189	377,335	1,888,936
Soconusco		825,575	182,600	23,990,494
Tampico	3,642,027	15,546,228	8,695,442	53,443
Tijuana	7,438	36,740	14,688	127,506
Todos Santos	133,040	113,241	154,776	1,369,360
Tonalá	163,651	372,076	184,536	
Tuxpam	50,735	27,413,009	70,331	22,351,098
Veracruz	16,123,505	198,241	15,496,544	306,063
Zapaluta	3,893		12,539	
Total	$34,000,440	$90,854,953	$42,353,938	$105,016,902

The following is a list of the value of metals and commodities exported from Mexico during the fiscal year 1895–1896, which shows that they are all either mineral or agricultural products, these being only raw materials : The commodities are placed in the order of their relative importance in value.

METALS.

Gold ore	$160,555
Gold coin	169,794
Gold bullion	20,377,663
Silver ore	10,885,479
Silver coin	5,246,418
Silver bullion	26,345,160
Sulphate of silver	1,030,156
Foreign gold and silver and silver in other combinations	623,371
Total	**$64,838,596**

COMMODITIES.

Coffee	$8,103,302
Henequen	6,763,821
Cabinet and dye woods	4,206,880
Copper	3,909,485
Lead	2,531,624
Live animals	3,546,770
Hides and skins	2,331,999
Chewing gum	1,527,838
Tobacco	1,461,090
Vanilla	1,428,675
Ixtle	690,862
Zacaton—broom root	616,492
Chick-peas	352,737
Coal	270,176
Marble	258,668
Fruits	246,150
Sugar	169,662
Horse hair, beans, and jalap	247,768
All others	1,514,307
Total	**40,178,306**
	$105,016,902

EXPORTS OF MEXICAN COMMODITIES DURING THE TEN FISCAL YEARS, FROM JULY 1, 1886, TO JUNE 30, 1896.

FISCAL YEARS.	LIVE STOCK.		COCOA.		HIDES AND SKINS.		FRUITS.		WOOL. (raw.)		TOTAL VALUE of exports of domestic produce (not metals).
	Heads.	Value.	Weight, Kilo-grams.	Value.	Weight, Kilo-grams.	Value.	Weight, Kilo-grams.	Value.	Weight, Kilo-grams.	Value.	
1886–1887	100,467	$ 470,097	663	$ 425	6,308,820	$4,211,439	1,699,072	$ 74,815	873,951	$169,334	$ 2,926,100
1887–1888	106,221	566,997	659	397	5,109,243	1,864,471	1,796,978	51,945	56,683	12,518	2,456,308
1888–1889	84,257	585,894	197	231	4,957,043	2,011,128	1,551,505	53,612	364,013	90,567	2,744,432
1889–1890	91,913	493,343	7,666	3,633	4,743,326	1,913,129	1,896,515	68,581	124,950	26,846	2,595,392
1890–1891	30,331	182,620	149	93	4,571,830	1,804,829	2,795,369	103,850	49	30	2,091,422
Totals in five years......	413,189	$2,298,831	9,334	$4,779	25,690,262	$9,804,996	9,948,739	$352,803	1,419,446	$299,265	$12,700,674
Averages per annum......	82,638	$447,766	1,867	$956	5,138,052	$1,960,999	1,980,748	$70,561	283,889	$59,853	$2,460,135
1891–1892	7,932	$ 56,580			5,335,971	$ 1,931,791	2,524,239	$105,395	126	$ 56	$ 2,093,831
1892–1893	168,164	1,741,161	639	$ 699	5,666,320	2,067,156	2,425,873	104,042	39,648	8,881	3,921,979
1893–1894	19,054	144,132	1,591	1,983	5,619,377	2,356,166	2,034,573	139,147	68	15	2,641,277
1894–1895	7,733	137,382	83,877	42,800	4,639,909	2,339,866	2,945,688	131,460	58,759	11,952	2,767,165
1895–1896	266,828	3,543,549	2,774	2,543	3,909,841	2,422,999	6,485,921	240,150	41,376	5,851	6,500,192
Totals in five years......	469,711	$5,622,803	88,791	$47,974	25,490,568	$11,027,768	17,247,244	$720,194	138,977	$26,955	$17,444,794
Averages per annum......	93,942	$1,124,560	17,758	$9,595	5,098,113	$2,205,554	3,449,448	$144,039	27,795	$5,211	$3,488,959
Totals in ten years......	882,900	$7,861,634	98,125	$52,753	51,180,830	$20,832,764	27,195,983	$1,072,997	1,558,423	$326,320	$30,145,468
Averages per annum......	88,290	$786,163	9,812	$5,275	5,118,063	$2,083,276	2,719,598	$107,300	155,842	$32,532	$3,014,547

EXPORTS OF MEXICAN COMMODITIES DURING THE TEN FISCAL YEARS, FROM JULY 1, 1886, TO JUNE 30, 1896—(Continued).

FISCAL YEARS.	CABINET WOODS.		DYE WOODS.		COAL.		OTHER ARTICLES (not metals) exported. Value.	TOTAL VALUE of exports of domestic produce (not metals).
	Weight, Kilograms.	Value,	Weight, Kilograms.	Value.	Weight, Kilograms.	Value.		
1886–1887............	66,720,699	$ 974,739	48,169,637	$ 856,802	....	....	$10,860,786	$12,705,337
1887–1888............	46,922,426	660,322	44,944,581	773,071	402,243	$ 2,477	13,698,323	15,443,393
1888–1889............	39,678,782	694,609	36,565,209	684,592	83,552,558	350,171	16,920,344	17,631,716
1889–1890............	45,090,609	805,000	44,934,537	921,728	45,149,968	188,507	19,457,403	21,372,706
1890–1891............	53,044,451	907,273	39,981,205	811,604	39,482,132	160,702	23,049,002	24,928,601
Totals in five years....	251,436,881	$4,350,953	214,595,169	$4,061,417	168,586,895	$701,557	$83,967,817	$93,081,743
Averages per annum...	50,287,376	$870,190	42,919,034	$812,283	33,717,379	$140,311	$16,793,563	$18,616,340
1891–1892............	53,536,153	$ 882,658	39,180,385	$ 767,217	55,960,921	$221,154	$ 22,365,551	$ 24,336,980
1892–1893............	46,209,557	746,717	44,133,399	916,512	8,279,968	33,060	26,093,447	28,680,636
1893–1894............	44,762,231	673,560	61,333,004	1,399,576	49,749,184	205,605	28,045,199	30,323,940
1894–1895............	118,667	631,143	81,694,951	2,056,030	53,192,261	232,429	31,128,063	34,048,355
1895–1896............	56,271	971,678	110,239,715	2,912,476	66,174,597	270,176	29,803,784	33,958,114
Totals in five years....	144,742,879	$3,905,756	336,482,464	$8,051,811	233,345,931	$963,814	$138,336,044	$151,247,425
Averages per annum...	28,948,576	$781,151	67,296,493	$1,610,362	46,669,186	$192,763	$27,665,209	$30,249,485
Totals in ten years....	396,179,760	$8,256,708	551,077,633	$14,113,228	401,932,826	$1,665,371	$222,293,861	$244,329,168
Averages per annum...	39,617,976	$835,671	55,107,763	$1,811,323	40,193,283	$166,537	$22,229,386	$24,432,917

STATEMENT OF EXPORTS OF SOME AGRICULTURAL PRODUCTS DURING THE FISCAL YEARS FROM JULY 1, 1877, TO JUNE 30, 1896.

FISCAL YEARS.	ORCHILLA. Weight in Kilograms.	ORCHILLA. Value in Mexican Currency.	HENEQUEN. Weight in Kilograms.	HENEQUEN. Value in Mex. Currency.	IXTLE. Weight in Kilograms.	IXTLE. Value in Mexican Currency.	COFFEE. Weight in Kilograms.	COFFEE. Value in Mex. Currency.	TOBACCO. Weight in Kilograms.	TOBACCO. Value in Mexican Currency.	TOTAL VALUE OF EXPORTS. Successive Annual Increase per ct.	TOTAL VALUE OF EXPORTS.
1877–1878	3,802,343	$ 228,146	11,380,180	$ 1,078,076	2,167,236	$ 357,768	4,861,779	$ 1,242,041	111,211	$ 86,713	....	$ 2,892,744
1878–1879	2,211,203	159,679	13,442,489	1,267,375	1,628,395	191,287	8,654,494	2,230,097	182,995	142,532	+37.723	3,983,970
1879–1880	909,647	54,581	20,574,513	1,945,307	2,454,600	291,976	7,656,267	1,984,473	396,192	310,146	+15.123	4,586,483
1880–1881	255,240	15,315	24,161,197	2,285,389	3,432,676	408,278	8,706,827	2,243,782	477,188	371,674	+16.089	5,324,438
1881–1882	1,582,600	115,618	28,182,071	2,672,107	4,748,979	620,199	10,447,805	2,414,538	351,486	351,253	+15.931	6,173,715
Av'ge in 5 years	1,752,206	$ 113,268	19,149,890	$ 1,849,651	2,882,359	$ 353,902	8,065,634	$ 2,022,086	304,214	$ 252,464	+21.216	$ 4,592,270
1882–1883	1,189,430	74,629	30,065,409	3,311,063	5,153,025	596,533	8,556,899	1,717,191	265,481	272,160	– 3.274	$ 5,071,576
1883–1884	899,480	75,053	45,538,272	4,165,020	3,523,389	434,431	6,917,720	1,579,021	402,190	397,970	+ 9.879	6,561,495
1884–1885	506,097	73,772	46,173,579	3,988,790	6,190,409	672,583	5,824,276	1,201,673	363,686	412,933	– 3.227	6,349,731
1885–1886	989,999	71,870	40,505,805	2,999,116	6,046,153	523,972	8,385,641	1,659,724	545,916	528,568	– 9.394	5,673,250
1886–1887	1,311,786	116,891	39,536,048	3,901,628	3,881,621	584,842	8,306,215	2,627,477	834,420	850,807	+34.368	7,845,645
Av'ge in 5 years	979,358	$ 82,443	40,364,841	$ 3,659,123	4,958,959	$ 575,272	7,602,150	$ 1,755,017	480,339	$ 474,484	+ 5.670	$ 6,496,339
1887–1888	1,149,999	106,401	26,754,947	6,229,460	3,570,628	361,687	6,503,086	2,431,025	764,131	830,362	+26.908	$ 9,956,825
1888–1889	149,662	12,536	38,390,970	6,872,593	5,454,944	394,118	9,243,607	3,386,034	969,960	971,886	+23.907	12,337,167
1889–1890	1,312,550	144,797	39,371,274	7,392,245	7,449,770	827,981	10,009,642	4,811,000	1,014,745	948,333	+14.243	14,094,355
1890–1891	17,937	1,351	53,731,769	2,048,557	7,676,976	829,350	14,656,777	6,150,359	1,041,962	1,105,442	+ 7.341	15,199,064
1891–1892	17,982	985	56,337,769	6,358,220	6,610,561	617,300	11,058,279	5,514,355	1,560,610	1,746,928	– 5.891	14,337,788
Av'ge in 5 years	529,566	$ 47,194	44,918,618	$ 6,780,215	6,148,576	$ 644,887	10,299,175	$ 4,558,554	1,070,282	$ 1,120,591	+13.300	$ 13,151,040
1892–1893	319,751	16,657	60,444,057	8,863,071	6,327,570	588,487	14,514,049	8,727,119	1,301,368	1,459,690	+38.258	$ 19,685,024
1893–1894	540,330	14,019	56,625,651	6,718,667	5,667,424	461,614	14,866,690	11,766,090	1,083,364	1,755,134	+ 5.235	20,715,794
1894–1895	410,454	11,300	67,157,018	7,724,092	4,342,621	349,537	16,512,648	12,670,783	1,310,902	1,660,133	+ 7.242	22,215,845
1895–1896	382,295	10,368	59,342,038	6,768,007	7,154,843	604,922	11,463,558	8,103,302	1,333,109	1,461,090	–23.308	17,037,689
Av'ge in 4 years	413,207	$ 13,086	60,887,191	$ 7,525,950	5,873,115	$ 523,640	15,339,436	$ 10,316,823	1,504,686	$ 1,534,057	+ 6.882	$ 19,913,565
Total for 19 years	17,958,485	$1,266,858	765,715,506	$91,548,783	93,441,931	$9,664,865	191,197,543	$93,000,084	15,292,916	$15,373,018	....	$200,852,508
Av'ge in 19 years	945,183	$ 66,677	40,300,816	$ 4,818,357	4,917,996	$ 508,677	10,063,028	$ 4,368,426	804,890	$ 809,153	....	$ 10,571,184

REMARKS.—The records regarding the Exports to which this statement refers, before the year 1877-1878 are not reliable.

The increase of the average yearly amount of exports, on the second period of five years of this statement was 41.462 per cent, as compared with the average of the first period.
" " " " " third " five " " " " " " 102.438 " " " " second "
" " " " " fourth " four " " " " " " 51.421 " " " " third "

The grand total amount of the Exports of the five articles of domestic production specified in this statement was seventy times as much as the amount of the first year 1877-1878.

The *average* yearly successive increase of the Exports herein specified, was 10.852 per cent.

In regard to the decrease of something more than 23 per cent, in the amount of exports registered in the fiscal year 1895-1896, it may be stated that while there was undoubtedly a shortness in the coffee-harvest, the increase of home consumption, and consequent raise of the price of the article was the main factor for the said decrease of export. In proportion to the total amount of Exports, herein specified, that of each of the five articles, was as follows: *Henequen,* 45.580 per cent. *Coffee,* 41.334 per cent. *Tobacco,* 7.654 per cent. *Ixtle,* 4.812 per cent, and *Orchilla,* 0.631 per cent.

VALUE OF IMPORTS FROM MEXICO FROM JULY 1, 1882, TO JUNE 30, 1892.

PRECIOUS AND OTHER METALS.

NOMENCLATURE.	1882–1883.	1883–1884.	1884–1885.	1885–1886.	1886–1887.	1887–1888.	1888–1889.	1889–1890.	1890–1891.	1891–1892.
Argentiferous copper		235 00	187 00							317,242 75
Argentiferous lead	13,025 40	5,200 00	8,656 40	25,527 00	3,044 24	51,772 00	19,788 77			1,457,878 33
Base silver		2,500 00	2,016 00	3,450 00	5,400 00	8,102 00	11,657 69	1,810 00	1,830 00	3,900 00
Gold foreign coin	146,055 96	22,047 00	14,457 00	55,674 38	35,800 87	21,598 85	25,426 00	23,804 00	20,594 00	33,684 00
Gold in lingots	548,039 43	666,652 97	490,489 45	290,589 60	284,506 09	347,547 24	349,507 53	457,610 59	612,619 12	731,468 18
Gold Mexican coin	331,708 00	200,816 25	391,097 23	316,938 57	194,758 75	238,104 00	353,455 00	96,592 00	134,219 00	175,584 00
Gold ore	99,832 99	500 00				54,833 83				31,889 00
Silver foreign coin	146,635 59	205,595 75	97,821 50	56,862 37	395,584 37		154,347 02	141,093 70	229,806 85	97,885 00
Silver in lingots	4,773,028 15	5,312,310 49	5,881,178 03	5,014,437 88	5,568,735 66	6,504,251 23	6,609,202 75	7,239,958 68	6,751,219 07	6,559,670 30
Silver Mexican coin	22,960,583 90	25,999,875 68	25,394,260 03	21,969,957 88	21,955,759 85	16,841,117 86	22,686,337 39	23,684,489 40	17,622,171 10	26,478,376 00
Silver mixed with gold		898,354 98	18,118 98	247,263 62	559,593 82	184,807 22	333,247 23	368,871 87	729,734 81	1,294,087 14
Silver ore	592,180 20	99,862 19	1,332,896 91	1,809,896 84	3,737,882 79	5,928,303 97	7,623,589 97	6,394,662 41	8,874,457 24	10,478,265 99
Sulphite of silver	105,512 26		142,430 37	116,092 70	815,506 68	827,766 51	798,556 64	803,058 53	1,280,708 97	1,458,095 37
Total	$29,628,657 69	$33,473,283 30	$33,774,059 92	$29,906,400 84	$33,560,502 56	$31,026,187 71	$38,785,274 99	$38,621,290 23	$36,356,372 16	$49,137,303 98

COMMODITIES.

NOMENCLATURE.	1882–1883.	1883–1884.	1884–1885.	1885–1886.	1886–1887.	1887–1888.	1888–1889.	1889–1890.	1890–1891.	1891–1892.
Ale	1,468 95	946 38	691 06	1,121 00	3,510 35	2,444 00	39,288 56	31,332 50	29,989 03	22,473 45
Brandy	3,050 00	760 00	70,436 03	247,348 82	24,434 65	2,777 00	4,117 00	9,316 37	14,333 99	5,097 59
Coal	1,717,190 85	1,579,020 83	1,601,073 38	1,690,793 82	2,697,477 11	2,431,004 96	352,170 60	188,597 00	160,972 35	221,154 22
Coffee							3,886,034 53	4,811,000 48	6,150,358 72	5,574,355 15
Cotton	1,430 00	395 25	5,744 00	4,008 00	4,419 00	6,330 00	5,333 00	12,275 00	3,333 00	7,633 00
Empty barrels	181 00	800 13	4,495 00	10,139 04	18,169 00	3,367 30	2,444 00	2,444 00	18,769 99	1,850 00
Fresh and salted meats	62,007 77	79,704 76	67,681 30	71,133 38	55,401 80	61,318 45	58,884 82	64,207 13	66 00	1,180 00
Horse hair	159,884 72	202,496 09	66,307 73	108,188 18	179,329 51	169,385 66	124,547 77	97,445 75	58,477 50	69,450 05
India-rubber	630 50	45,855 00	30,156 25	119,086 50	64,862 40	79,226 66	17,987 50	85,305 37	72,558 88	47,384 32
Indigo	7,650 00	4,809 85	3,955 00	6,129 00	9,799 00	161,093 00	20,913 00		93,143 00	7,979 00
Jewels and precious stones	634,376 18	620,956 05	406,456 94	622,906 52	471,470 80	508,713 35	587,063 00	500,217 35	184,482 00	37,514 26
Live animals		125 00					1,138 00		501 00	59,335 90
Oils	3 50	3 00	3,014 00			130 00	728 00	2,225 00	10,368 40	33,359 00
Rice		3,020 00	800 00				1,840 00	11,181 00		8,294 87
Starch		177,266 11	34,271 26			1,840 00	40,880 36	61,963 80	24,018 00	
Sugar	198,365 16			178,887 00	124,934 24	107,276 98				21,888 59
Carried forward	$2,786,836 63	$2,716,122 45	$1,685,632 85	$3,068,971 26	$3,568,997 76	$3,534,479 76	$5,126,349 64	$5,882,944 15	$6,838,364 62	$6,058,067 91

COMMODITIES—(Continued).

NOMENCLATURE.	1882–1883.	1883–1884.	1884–1885.	1885–1886.	1886–1887.	1887–1888.	1888–1889.	1889–1890.	1890–1891.	1891–1892.
Brought forward	$2,786,836 63	$2,716,122 45	$1,985,633 85	$3,068,971 26	$3,568,907 76	$3,532,479 76	$5,126,349 64	$3,884,944 15	$6,898,564 61	$6,098,667 91
Bones	3,430 75	4,650 04	5,039 00	22,507 72	6,384 00	2,400 00	6,740 00	3,874 35	6,982 00	2,877 00
Brown sugar	32,131 17	11,767 10	3,603 50	29,888 53	17,321 15	39,027 44	8,886 25	12,516 30	29,202 38	41,659 10
Chapapote	653 52	1,570 08	3,603 97	4,462 80	6,786 44	3,371 50	3,667 50	97,245 15	29,203 38	9,083 00
Chewing gum	82,205 38	134,537 65	66,809 68	158,757 56	357,413 22	375,656 26	505,656 26	716,746 33	1,986,997 10	793,571 95
Chic peas	28,855 44	79,715 00	4,673 00	11,617 75	34,556 69	33,182 59	27,797 00	98,141 40	98,251 28	283,251 73
Copper	65,996 00	39,297 00	16,960 67	2,339 72	37,560 13	615,666 00	817,969 18	735,183 00	940,920 00	860,378 94
Copper ore			35,800 00				818 00	13,775 03	8,108 00	8,937 55
Corn	63,684 11	5,488 82	2,353 00	7,655 54	28,609 99	25,880 07	13,775 03	597 00	8,108 00	26,028 31
Documents							818 00	597 00	6,464 00	9,654 00
Equipages	19,481 00	12,428 00	14,005 41	19,980 75	23,543 00	12,033 00	28,211 00	111,535 00	30,734 45	19,090 00
Essence of aloes				9,851 75	18,073 00	2,807 66	84,972 75	15,366 00	8,415 00	17,086 00
Fine pearls	18,500 00	40,870 00	38,750 00	7,700 00	59,200 00	58,300 00	35,000 00	88,750 00	77,500 00	19,500 00
Fruits	78,868 42	78,936 59	74,928 38	73,942 00	74,814 99	51,945 00	53,612 00	66,581 25	103,849 62	105,395 28
Guano		1,933 84		23,300 00	49,111 00	68,024 14	35,362 30	28,095 00		39,000 00
Henequen	3,321,062 64	4,165,020 35	3,988,790 97	2,999,116 50	3,007,628 19	6,229,592 62	6,872,592 87	7,390,244 69	7,048,556 76	6,338,220 15
Honey	115,817 56	106,262 29	133,547 70	59,455 84	44,649 00	59,455 42	61,789 10	193,266 49	91,874 49	172,722 08
Ixtle	596,533 73	434,430 94	672,581 34	533,972 47	348,841 60	361,687 22	594,118 55	827,980 61	823,349 84	617,300 22
Lard	520 00	1,705 00					320 00	141 00	31 00	10,575 90
Lemons	745 50	877 46	1,596 50	3,283 00	8,397 45	63,079 75	54,023 00	79,788 90	79,675 00	43,280 04
Lima beans	60,641 11	75,518 91	68,486 00	43,501 74	70,969 82	120,839 84	151,145 99	370,839 56	208,506 38	197,552 85
Manufactures	7,052 46	16,430 70	13,672 07	11,228 07	12,389 61	18,092 33	14,811 32	15,402 00	13,063 74	12,413 17
Manufactures returned	13,655 00	24,334 88	81,292 00	483,953 75	161,053 60	44,067 50	59,398 33	178,435 00	97,154 69	99,748 00
Marble		49,925 00	14,369 25	8,198 21	15,353 75	35,917 14	57,530 55	162,131 26	87,555 85	169,664 50
Orchilla	74,608 68	75,953 30	73,777 30	7,890 30	18,890 96	105,290 10	12,535 60	114,795 68	1,351 00	983 00
Paper	8,172 66	5,396 33	3,977 00	10,040 07	9,253 81	11,149 36	12,885 73	10,910 44	22,951 75	20,215 90
Printed books	1,569 88	3,391 00		3,899 00	5,827 81	7,207 78	11,710 80	19,757 00	3,965 00	5,178 00
Samples			929 68	3,000 00	1,731 36	4,734 28	98,259 85	25,733 90	9,623 00	17,253 00
Skins	1,653,165 92	1,747,254 96	1,779,957 14	2,133,359 79	2,211,438 34	1,864,469 98	2,011,128 85	1,973,129 05	1,804,828 65	1,931,792 18
Tanning wood	6 21				39,683 28	35,078 36	10,533 50	44,484 00	22,163 00	8,850 00
Tin								140 00		11,600 00
Tin ore										14,040 68
Tortoise shell	48,420 14	59,435 54	67,663 85	20,198 88	6,836 00	19,993 50	32,643 45	30,256 74	24,411 31	26,959 73
Vegetables	19,596 60	14,958 55	13,063 79	16,784 68	32,603 24	15,648 05	3,374 95	1,512 85	1,768 61	2,244 53
Wood	1,037,373 67	2,008,913 65	1,753,346 14	1,688,799 14	1,848,702 98	1,759,496 66	1,390,214 30	1,739,138 30	1,726,527 08	1,676,351 40
Wool	306 00	43,148 01	171,859 20	220,071 09	169,324 33	12,518 40	90,566 70	20,826 40	30 00	55 75
Carried forward	$11,047,995 98	$11,844,583 34	$11,074,808 02	$11,671,118 92	$13,477,011 89	$15,572,660 31	$18,305,440 00	$20,804,555 53	$21,449,520 65	$19,590,910 25

COMMODITIES—(continued).

NOMENCLATURE.	1882-1883.	1883-1884.	1884-1885.	1885-1886.	1886-1887.	1887-1888.	1888-1889.	1889-1890.	1890-1891.	1891-1892.
Brought forward.....	$11,047,905 98	$11,844,583 34	$11,071,808 05	$11,671,118 92	$13,272,011 89	$15,572,666 91	$18,305,440 09	$20,804,555 53	$21,449,520 65	$19,520,910 25
Bags.................			10,164 00	2,800 00	2,480 00	8,030 10	13,279 00	23,333 00	3,139 00	2,534 00
Cheese..............	207 50	18 00	10 00	74 00	87 00	1,604 00	13,073 75	12,682 00	790 00	268,939 00
Cotton seed........							3,575 00	11,781 40	3,138 40	7,449 00
Feathers...........	1,372 90	1,900 12	1,055 75	2,355 00	2,960 00	910 00	1,331 00	3,224 00	17,911 00	50,144 22
Gypsum.............	4,010 00	700 00	6,575 00					6,842 00	4,609 00	7,993 02
Hats................	2,251 12	5,086 02	2,266 25	4,223 25	4,777 65	5,297 47	6,608 82	8,070 75	12,680 77	6,666 50
Jalap...............	34,592 41	56,159 46	36,726 00	24,559 00	13,656 85	10,926 90	11,152 53	10,023 04	67,457 66	42,935 05
Lead................	47,554 83	188,460 73	329,239 96	485,948 14	323,205 27	382,236 33	467,737 59	607,329 70	1,125,468 64	2,363,521 05
Other articles......	120,979 84	146,427 99	202,459 79	135,638 50	74,312 13	105,706 95	100,911 13	10,731 50	73,883 44	75,511 82
Plants..............	2,200 00	3,273 26	9,103 50	8,636 48	10,235 35	16,692 75	13,635 40	11,665 00	151,151 00	18,326 70
Salt................	535 00	3,860 00	1,512 00	2,217 00	2,235 00	3,633 25	6,481 00	5,645 00	2,765 25	15,035 68
Sarsaparilla........	50,699 04	37,476 14	53,822 44	119,837 23	69,511 93	108,310 03	27,724 59	15,993 55	31,350 06	44,719 47
Tobacco.............	274,160 18	307,969 85	412,912 84	528,568 28	850,807 39	830,362 50	977,885 97	948,333 17	1,105,446 73	1,746,927 96
Value in paper......	27,191 00	19,076 00	159,593 00		16,494 00	1,964 00	31,379 00	43,286 90	2,073,706 59	290,626 00
Vanilla.............	443,850 75	497,502 75	471,611 59	463,395 25	693,891 05	451,372 53	926,903 25	917,409 66	519,741 04	969,611 58
Zacaton (broom root)......	123,438 01	139,710 46	125,014 00	292,052 51	294,761 98	386,013 55	472,050 07	426,889 26	513,254 04	898,630 67
Total..............	$12,178,938 98	$13,252,213 12	$12,896,794 08	$13,741,316 56	$15,631,427 10	$17,870,720 67	$21,373,148 03	$23,878,098 46	$27,020,023 18	$26,330,410 97

RESUMÉ OF THE TOTAL EXPORTS.

	1882-1883.	1883-1884.	1884-1885.	1885-1886.	1886-1887.	1887-1888.	1888-1889.	1889-1890.	1890-1891.	1891-1892.
Precious metals......	$29,628,657 69	$33,473,283 30	$33,774,050 92	$39,906,400 83	$33,560,302 56	$31,006,187 71	$38,785,274 99	$38,621,290 23	$36,256,372 16	$49,137,393 98
Other articles......	12,178,938 56	13,252,213 12	12,896,794 08	13,741,316 56	15,631,427 49	17,870,720 67	21,373,148 03	33,878,098 46	27,020,023 18	26,330,410 97
Total..............	$41,807,596 25	$46,725,496 42	$46,670,845 00	$43,647,777 39	$49,191,930 05	$48,885,908 38	$60,158,423 02	$64,499,388 69	$63,276,395 34	$75,467,774 95

DESTINATION AND VALUE OF EXPORTS FROM MEXICO IN THE FISCAL YEARS FROM 1882 TO 1892.

PRECIOUS METALS.

DESTINATION.	1882-1883.	1883-1884.	1884-1885.	1885-1886.	1886-1887.	1887-1888.	1888-1889.	1889-1890.	1890-1891.	1891-1892.
Belgium	$	920 00		1,500 00	1,000 00	225 00				$18,667 00
Colombia	298,937 35	153,791 00	$372,556 98	47,359 00	52,490 00	68,976 21	77,575 00	35,908 85	$53,813 40	10,776 00
Costa Rica				3,000 00						
France	3,561,987 13	2,335,310 78	1,624,728 38	3,447,116 60	4,401,222 74	3,626,489 74	2,729,232 44	2,477,499 29	1,793,395 33	3,830,444 32
Germany	392,955 93	398,591 14	628,028 95	832,628 91	1,289,010 82	1,326,542 75	1,281,805 76	954,722 26	1,764,446 75	2,284,013 02
Great Britain	15,201,600 36	17,265,462 28	13,784,962 91	9,477,465 53	11,122,019 69	7,935,735 71	10,450,405 10	10,865,366 47	8,045,062 89	12,165,795 93
Guatemala	92,875 00	130,915 00	64,400 00	2,000 00	2,300 00	33,881 25	253,096 07	114,385 65	168,691 15	83,573 00
Honduras								1,000 00		
Nicaragua					7,550 62	2,500 00	6,027 74	8,303 20	4,662 60	
Russia					3,545 00					
Salvador	8,515 40	2,940 00	5,498 00	4,780 33	104,343 60	490 00	450 00	2,412 30	2,333 00	399 00
Spain	1,635,013 00	273,112 90	889,099 30	654,387 28	97,131 85	335,763 08	335,763 08	63,750 90	52,104 10	90,671 00
United States	9,036,773 33	12,822,249 50	16,404,776 20	15,406,336 17	16,576,120 00	17,915,115 83	23,647,919 80	24,098,147 31	33,400,833 94	30,447,566 41
Total	$29,628,657 69	$33,473,283 20	$33,774,050 99	$29,926,400 83	$33,560,502 96	$31,006,187 74	$36,785,274 99	$38,621,290 33	$36,256,372 16	$49,137,393 98

COMMODITIES.

DESTINATION.	1882-1883.	1883-1884.	1884-1885.	1885-1886.	1886-1887.	1887-1888.	1888-1889.	1889-1890.	1890-1891.	1891-1892.
Austria										15 00
Belgium	$29,040 00	$69,399 00	$32,370 00		$67,326 42	25,583 16	59,544 00		$845 00	322,592 97
China				35 00						
Colombia	59,229 59	55,394 95	38,087 11	43,663 00	41,757 56	41,085 95	28,442 55	41,603 50	3,602 88	20,272 75
Costa Rica	759 00	759 00		11,439 00	1,242 00	1,882 80	3,000 00			1,050 00
Ecuador	200 00									112 00
France	642,918 42	595,088 27	619,728 27	484,166 18	711,428 40	848,433 57	766,805 80	681,960 80	809,396 00	807,041 77
Germany	731,763 90	719,684 89	792,575 65	734,170 38	885,599 37	850,563 37	773,757 33	739,630 80	1,021,728 11	1,865,219 56
Great Britain	2,956,644 25	2,064,689 87	1,588,317 10	2,181,804 21	2,240,366 88	2,605,229 52	2,096,129 50	2,856,789 05	2,836,765 44	3,102,160 45
Guatemala	686 00	1,773 00	400 00	25 00	2,766 90	946 00	2,287 60	3,385 00	75,000 32	60,167 17
Hayti		30 00								
Holland		14,944 60	22,187 44			100 00	134,947 35	150,588 08	187,931 65	49,907 65
Honduras		609 50		73,188 00	870 00		2,750 00	2,750 00		4,400 00
Spain	954,245 74	743,644 09	353,545 67	359,236 50	590,950 24	360,710 77	323,567 88	470,306 37	465,689 64	571,178 80
United States	7,702,334 37	9,002,160 05	9,448,384 84	9,933,258 39	11,159,594 70	13,444,510 83	17,305,442 94	18,924,993 36	11,582,853 43	19,485,096 47
Carried forward	$13,178,049 66	$13,229,658 12	$12,880,496 08	$13,731,000 56	$15,624,832 39	$17,879,643 67	$21,370,905 06	$33,870,549 61	$27,011,304 47	$26,285,094 08

COMMODITIES—(Continued).

DESTINATION.	1882-1883.	1883-1884.	1884-1885.	1885-1886.	1886-1887.	1887-1888.	1888-1889.	1889-1890.	1890-1891.	1891-1892.
Brought forward	$12,178,049 66	$13,229,698 12	$12,880,496 08	$13,731,000 36	$15,624,832 39	$17,879,643 67	$21,370,995 06	$23,870,549 61	$27,011,304 47	$26,385,004 08
Argentine Republic	300 00			10 00	570 00	53 00	520 00		920 00	100 00
Italy			70 00	600 00	670 00			4,555 00	1,106 71	4,732 89
Nicaragua			30 00			25 00	787 60	266 00		10,914 01
Peru										
Russia	288 00	10,140 00	300 00		280 00		685 00	390 00	4,000 00	26,200 00
Salvador		13,375 00							2,502 00	3,120 00
Switzerland			48 00							
Venezuela	300 00		15,850 00	9,706 00	5,975 00		200 00	2,346 00		250 00
Total	$12,178,037 66	$13,252,213 12	$12,896,794 08	$13,741,316 36	$15,631,427 39	$17,879,720 67	$21,373,147 66	$23,878,106 61	$27,020,093 18	$26,330,410 98

TOTAL EXPORTS.

	1882-1883.	1883-1884.	1884-1885.	1885-1886.	1886-1887.	1887-1888.	1888-1889.	1889-1890.	1890-1891.	1891-1892.
Argentine Republic	$ 20,040 00	$	$	$	$	$	$ 520 00	$	$	$ 100 00
Austria				25 00						15 00
Belgium		70,349 00	38,370 00	74,688 00	67,326 42	35,383 16	50,544 00		845 00	340,699 97
China	358,167 14									
Colombia		309,185 05	410,644 09	90,960 00	94,447 66	109,959 86	99,997 55	77,511 35	57,416 28	31,048 75
Costa Rica		750 00	14,130 00	14,130 00	2,242 00	2,107 80	3,000 00	212 00	213 00	1,050 00
Ecuador	200 00									
France	4,844,995 55	2,881,998 98	2,235,436 65	3,936,276 78	5,112,521 14	4,474,723 31	3,496,098 33	3,159,259 50	3,653,551 33	4,644,385 51
Germany	1,135,719 21	1,218,176 13	1,420,604 60	1,571,399 20	2,175,770 11	2,177,106 09	2,061,363 09	1,603,773 15	2,785,874 86	4,344,231 60
Great Britain	17,258,244 61	19,330,155 15	15,367,286 01	11,600,067 74	13,362,186 57	12,540,965 23	12,535,534 99	13,722,122 52	15,267,955 08	
Guatemala	93,561 07	134,688 87	64,800 00	2,025 00	5,666 90	34,827 35	255,383 67	177,670 65	193,711 47	143,740 17
Hayti		30 00	22,187 44			100 00				
Holland	14,944 60			870 00		134,947 35	150,586 08	187,931 65	49,997 63
Honduras	609 30						3,700 00		4,400 00
Italy	300 00		70 00	10 00	570 00	53 00	50 00		920 00	4,732 89
Nicaragua					8,220 63	2,500 00	6,815 34	8,589 50	6,289 31	10,914 01
Peru			30 00	600 00		35 00				26,200 00
Russia		10,140 00			3,545 00	490 00	1,135 00	2,802 30	4,000 00	3,519 00
Salvador	8,803 40	15,315 00	5,798 00	4,700 33	280 00				4,535 00	
Spain	1,989,258 74	1,016,756 59	1,242,645 17	913,593 78	625,993 84	457,842 02	659,330 96	534,057 27	515,193 74	661,849 86
Switzerland			48 00							
United States	16,739,097 70	21,834,490 55	25,853,061 04	25,429,594 59	27,728,714 79	31,059,626 66	40,853,362 74	43,022,440 67	44,983,086 37	49,932,564 88
Venezuela	300 00		15,850 00	9,706 00	5,975 00	200 00	300 00	2,346 00		350 00
Total	$41,807,595 35	$46,735,586 43	$46,670,845 00	$43,647,715 42	$49,191,930 05	$48,885,908 38	$60,158,423 02	$62,499,388 69	$65,376,395 34	$75,461,774 95

TRADE BETWEEN MEXICO AND THE UNITED STATES.

It is quite difficult to make a correct statement of the trade between Mexico and the United States, because the official data of both governments never used to agree, especially on account of the different currencies prevailing in the two countries. As we have the silver standard, all our public accounts are kept in silver, and that makes our exports appear twice as large in value as they really are, when stated in the money of the United States, while we give our imports in the value of the country from whence they come, that is their gold value. That fact, which has often been overlooked, has caused the prevailing idea that there is a very large balance of trade in favor of Mexico, because the exports of United States commodities in Mexico amount to a given figure a year, the imports to this country of Mexican commodities amount to over double that figure ; but it must be borne in mind that the former is in silver while the latter is in gold. For instance, according to the Mexican Bureau of Statistics the imports into Mexico of merchandise from the United States in the fiscal year ended June 30, 1896, amounted to $20,145,763, while the exports of metals and commodities from Mexico to the United States during the same year amounted to $79,651,695, the proportion being almost four to one ; but if the imports are doubled as they ought to be, because the Mexican currency is silver, they amount to $40,291,526, and if the exports of Mexico into the United States, calculated also in silver, are reduced to gold, they will amount to one half or $39,825,847.50.

In corroboration of this statement I will mention the fact that according to the data of the Statistical Bureau of the United States Treasury Department, the exports to Mexico of commodities and precious metals from the United States during the last fiscal year, ending June 30, 1897, amounted to $23,535,213 while the imports into the United States of commodities and precious metals amounted to $30,714,366. Since March 1893, however, the Statistical Bureau of the United States Treasury Department, has reduced to gold the silver value of the Mexican metals and commodities imported in this country, and its data come now nearer to the mark, as in the year 1896 it gives the total exports of merchandise from this country into Mexico as $19,450,256, while the total imports of merchandise from Mexico into this country are $17,456,177.

The figures of our exports appear very large in the Mexican returns, because our merchandise is sold in gold markets, and their gold price is reduced to silver, and increased in the same proportion in which silver depreciates. It is not therefore the amount of merchandise which has increased so much, as that the price has been swollen in reducing it from gold to silver. In that regard the returns from the United States Statistical Bureau are more in conformity with the facts.

Another cause of the discrepancy between the statistics of both countries is that the Statistical Bureau of the United States Treasury Department had not, prior to March 3, 1893, any data of commodities exported to Mexico by way of the frontier, as there was no law which provided for the collection of such data, and a very large portion of the trade between the two countries is carried on by the frontier, especially since the railroads connecting both countries were finished.[1] That deficiency was only in relation to the exports, as the imports were duly declared for the payment of duties, and therefore the statistics of the United States necessarily were deficient and incomplete about the exports to Mexico of United States commodities, and that accounts in a great measure for the discrepancy between the official data published by both governments, and for the great discrepancy between exports and imports which appear in the statistics of the United States for those years.

From the preceding remarks it will be understood why there is such a great discrepancy between the data of the respective Bureaus.

It is very difficult to make a correct statement of the trade between the two countries previous to the organization of the Bureau of Statistics of the United States ; but I found in a book published in Washington in 1860 by Mr. Carlos Butterfield, entitled "The United States and Mexican Mail Steamship Line and Statistics of Mexico," a statement of the imports and exports between Mexico and the United States from 1826 to 1858, taken as he states from official data of the United States Treasury Reports, which I will use.

That statement is complemented by two tables furnished to me by Hon. Worthington C. Ford, Chief of the Bureau of Statistics of the Treasury Department. The first contains a statement of the trade between the United States and Mexico, during the forty-six years from 1851 to 1897, and the second is a full statement of that trade, including gold and silver during the same period. (Pages 174 and 175.)

I have prepared besides from the official publications of the Bureau of Statistics of the United States Treasury Department, a detailed statement of the commodities imported into the United States from Mexico, and exported from the United States to Mexico during the

---

[1] For these reasons the statements of the Statistical Bureau of the United States, previous to the fiscal year ended June 30, 1892, contained the following foot-note :

"In the absence of law providing for the collection of statistics of exports to adjacent foreign territory over railways, the values of exports to Mexico, from 1883 to 1893 inclusive, have been considerably under-stated. Since March, 1893, there has been a law in force for the collection of exports by railways. According to official information from Mexican sources, the value of imports into that country from the United States during the year ending June 30, 1888, was $19,264,673, including precious metals valued at $38,362. Prior to 1866 the figures include gold and silver imported and exported. For 1866 and subsequent years, merchandise only."

years 1858 to 1897, which is complete so far as the records of this government go, and contains very valuable information.

I will give first a partial statement prepared by the Bureau of Statistics of the Mexican Government of the total imports to Mexico and the imports from the United States of America from the fiscal year 1872–1873 to 1895–1896, and then another detailed statement prepared by the same Bureau of the total exports from Mexico and the exports to the United States of America from the fiscal year 1877–1878 to 1895–1896.

From said data it will be seen that the trade of Mexico with the United States is increasing very rapidly, notwithstanding the difficulty thrown in the way by high protective tariffs. Only a few years ago, as will be seen by the appended statement, our largest trade was with Great Britain, the United States occupying the second place, while now the United States occupies the first place, both in amount of our exports and imports.[1]

Value of exports during the fiscal year 1872–1873 with their destination.

Great Britain	$12,479,547.75	Guatemala and Honduras.	80,999.52
United States	11,366,530.76	Italy	17,389.00
France	4,604,417.38	Belgium	4,784.00
Panama (New Grenada)	1,579,015.12	Ecuador	2,931.75
Germany	802,643.83		
Spain and the Island of Cuba	752,891.91	Total	$31,691,151.02

TOTAL IMPORTS TO MEXICO AND IMPORTS FROM THE UNITED STATES FOR THE FISCAL YEARS, 1872–1873 TO 1895–1896.

	IMPORTS FROM THE UNITED STATES.	TOTAL IMPORTS.
	Value.	Value.
1872–1873	$5,231,255	$20,166,013
1873–1874	5,946,614	23,282,299
1874–1875	5,028,636	18,793,494
1884–1885 First 6 months	5,045,531	11,893,342
1885–1886 First 6 months	5,145,736	10,585,898
1888–1889	22,669,421	40,024,894
1889–1890	29,080,276	52,018,659
1892–1893	26,235,963	43,413,131
1893–1894	14,351,785	30,287,489
1894–1895	15,130,367	34,000,440
1895–1896	20,145,763	42,253,938

MEXICO, November, 1896.

[1] This statement is corroborated by the following extract from an official report addressed to Lord Salisbury by Mr. Lionel Carden, British Consul-General at the City of Mexico, on the trade of Mexico during the year 1896 :

" The great increase in the imports of American goods this year must be regarded by British merchants and manufacturers as another warning that unless they soon make a serious effort, they will have to give up all hope of profiting by the increase in the Mexican import trade, and may even lose part of the very limited share of it they at present enjoy."

TABLE SHOWING THE TOTAL EXPORTS FROM MEXICO AND THE EXPORTS
TO THE UNITED STATES OF AMERICA FROM THE FISCAL YEAR 1877–
1878 TO THE YEAR 1895–1896.

	EXPORTS TO THE UNITED STATES.			TOTAL EXPORTS FROM MEXICO.		
	Precious Metals.	Commodities.	Total.	Precious Metals.	Commodities.	Total.
1877–1878...	$ 8,664,052	$ 3,676,937	$ 12,340,989	$ 22,663,438	$ 6,622,223	$ 29,285,661
1878–1879...	7,439,815	4,741,724	12,181,539	21,528,938	8,362,540	29,891,478
1879–1880...	6,848,231	6,568,375	13,416,606	22,086,418	10,577,136	32,663,554
1880–1881...	7,601,767	6,556,424	14,158,191	19,354,704	10,573,994	29,928,698
1881–1882...	5,451,731	8,309,131	13,760,862	17,063,767	12,019,526	29,083,293
1882–1883...	9,036,773	7,702,325	16,739,098	29,628,658	12,178,937	41,807,595
1883–1884...	12,822,241	9,002,160	21,824,401	33,473,283	13,252,213	46,725,496
1884–1885...	16,404,776	9,448,285	25,853,061	33,774,051	12,896,794	46,670,845
1885–1886...	15,496,336	9,933,259	25,429,595	29,906,401	13,741,316	43,647,717
1886–1887...	16,576,120	11,152,595	27,728,715	33,560,503	15,631,427	49,191,930
1887–1888...	17,915,116	13,144,511	31,059,627	31,006,188	17,879,720	48,885,908
1888–1889...	23,647,920	17,205,443	40,853,363	38,785,275	21,373,148	60,158,423
1889–1890...	24,098,147	18,924,294	43,022,441	38,621,290	23,878,009	62,499,389
1890–1891...	23,400,833	21,582,253	44,983,086	36,256,372	27,020,023	63,276,395
1891–1892...	30,447,566	19,485,099	49,932,665	49,137,304	26,330,411	75,467,715
1892–1893...	40,113,882	23,723,761	63,837,643	56,504,305	31,004,916	87,509,221
1893–1894...	36,681,273	23,978,970	60,660,243	46,484,360	32,858,927	79,343,287
1894–1895...	38,852,843	28,470,143	67,322,986	52,535,854	38,319,099	90,854,953
1895–1896...	51,071,661	28,580,034	79,651,695	64,838,596	40,178,306	105,016,902
Total....	$392,571,083	$272,185,723	$664,756,806	$677,209,705	$374,698,755	$1,051,908,460

STATEMENT TAKEN FROM THE UNITED STATES TREASURY REPORTS
OF THE COMMERCIAL TRANSACTIONS BETWEEN MEXICO AND THE
UNITED STATES FROM 1826 TO 1850.

YEARS.	EXPORTS FROM MEXICO INTO THE UNITED STATES.	EXPORTS FROM THE UNITED STATES INTO MEXICO.	TOTAL TRADE BETWEEN THE TWO COUNTRIES.
1826...................	$ 3,916,000	$ 6,281,000	$ 10,197,000
1827...................	5,232,000	4,163,000	9,395,000
1828...................	4,814,000	2,886,000	7,700,000
1829...................	5,026,761	2,331,151	7,357,912
1830...................	5,235,241	4,837,458	10,072,699
1831...................	5,167,000	6,178,000	11,345,000
1832...................	4,293,954	3,467,541	7,761,495
1833...................	5,459,818	5,408,091	10,867,909
1834...................	8,666,668	5,265,053	13,931,721
1835...................	9,490,446	9,029,221	18,519,667
1836...................	5,615,819	6,040,635	11,656,454
1837...................	5,654,002	3,880,323	9,534,325
1838...................	3,127,153	2,787,362	5,914,515
1839...................	5,500,707	2,164,097	7,664,804
1840...................	4,175,000	2,515,341	6,690,341
1841...................	3,484,957	2,036,620	5,521,577
1842...................	1,996,694	1,534,493	3,531,187
1843...................	2,782,406	1,471,937	4,254,343
1844...................	2,387,000	1,794,833	4,181,833
1845...................	1,702,936	1,152,331	2,855,267
1846...................	1,836,621	1,531,180	3,367,801
1847...................	746,818	692,428	1,439,246
1848...................	1,581,247	4,058,446	5,639,693
1849...................	2,216,719	2,090,869	4,307,588
1850...................	2,135,336	2,012,827	4,148,163
Total.................	$102,245,303	$85,610,237	$187,855,540
Average	$4,089,812	$3,424,409	$7,514,222

STATEMENT SHOWING THE COMMERCE IN MERCHANDISE BETWEEN THE UNITED STATES AND MEXICO, BY YEARS AND DECADES, FROM 1851 TO 1897.

YEAR ENDING JUNE 30.	EXPORTS FROM THE UNITED STATES.			IMPORTS INTO THE UNITED STATES.			EXCESS OF EXPORTS (−) OR IMPORTS (+).
	Domestic.	Foreign.	Total.	Free.	Dutiable.	Total.	
1851	$ 1,014,690	$ 567,093	$ 1,581,783	$ 27,666	$ 693,120	$ 720,786	$ −860,997
1852	1,406,372	878,557	2,284,929	20,564	534,700	555,264	−1,729,665
1853	2,529,770	1,029,054	3,558,824	4,148	751,952	756,100	−2,802,724
1854	2,091,870	1,043,616	3,135,486	111,405	826,451	937,856	−2,197,630
1855	2,253,368	668,236	2,921,604	17,508	887,242	904,750	−2,016,854
1856	2,464,692	1,237,097	3,701,789	79,966	773,792	853,758	−2,848,031
1857	3,017,640	597,566	3,615,206	62,307	964,566	1,026,873	−2,588,333
1858	2,782,852	529,973	3,312,825	246,894	861,607	1,108,501	−2,204,324
1959	2,252,162	667,580	2,919,742	234,112	1,009,972	1,244,084	−1,675,658
1860	3,309,379	2,015,334	5,324,713	586,016	1,317,415	1,903,431	−3,421,282
Total 10 years..	$ 23,122,795	$ 9,234,106	$ 32,356,901	$ 1,390,586	$ 8,620,817	$ 10,011,403	$ −22,345,498
1861	$ 1,559,062	$ 651,364	$ 2,210,426	$ 253,703	$ 632,409	$ 886,112	$ −1,324,314
1862	1,840,720	340,454	2,181,174	289,011	441,977	730,988	−1,450,186
1863	7,441,579	1,579,045	9,020,624	446,070	2,597,812	3,043,882	−5,976,742
1864	7,765,133	1,505,464	9,270,597	385,037	5,743,408	6,128,445	−3,142,152
1865	13,819,972	2,530,867	16,350,839	369,915	5,850,959	6,220,874	−10,129,965
1866	3,701,599	871,619	4,573,218	402,568	1,323,524	1,726,092	−2,847,126
1867	4,823,614	572,182	5,395,796	402,779	669,157	1,071,936	−4,323,860
1868	5,048,420	1,392,919	6,441,339	482,228	1,108,439	1,590,667	−4,850,672
1869	3,835,699	1,047,408	4,883,107	511,319	1,824,845	2,336,164	−2,546,943
1870	4,544,745	1,314,955	5,859,700	522,907	2,192,758	2,715,665	−3,144,035
Total 10 years..	$ 54,380,543	$ 11,806,277	$ 66,186,820	$ 4,065,537	$ 22,385,288	$ 26,450,825	$ −39,735,995
1871	$ 5,044,033	$ 2,568,080	$ 7,612,113	$ 976,117	$ 2,233,571	$ 3,209,688	$ −4,402,425
1872	3,420,658	2,122,931	5,543,589	1,156,257	2,846,663	4,002,920	−1,540,669
1873	3,941,019	2,323,882	6,264,901	3,065,140	1,211,025	4,276,165	−1,988,736
1874	4,016,148	1,930,691	5,946,839	3,026,661	1,379,703	4,346,364	−1,600,475
1875	3,872,004	1,865,278	5,737,282	3,863,302	1,311,292	5,174,594	−562,688
1876	4,700,978	1,499,594	6,200,572	3,920,633	1,229,939	5,150,572	−1,050,000
1877	4,503,802	1,389,692	5,893,494	3,756,191	1,448,073	5,204,264	−689,230
1878	5,811,429	1,649,275	7,460,704	3,723,281	1,528,221	5,251,502	−2,209,202
1879	5,400,380	1,351,864	6,752,244	3,981,402	1,511,819	5,493,221	−1,259,023
1880	6,065,974	1,800,519	7,866,493	4,852,659	2,356,934	7,209,593	−656,900
Total 10 years..	$ 46,776,425	$ 18,501,806	$ 65,278,231	$ 32,321,643	$ 16,997,240	$ 49,318,883	$ −15,959,348
1881	$ 9,198,077	$ 1,973,161	$ 11,171,238	$ 5,643,176	$ 2,674,626	$ 8,317,802	$ −2,853,436
1882	13,324,505	2,158,077	15,482,582	5,310,796	3,151,103	8,461,899	−7,020,683
1883	14,370,092	2,216,628	16,587,620	4,211,328	3,965,795	8,177,123	−8,410,497
1884	11,089,603	1,614,689	12,704,292	5,334,689	3,681,797	9,016,486	−3,687,806
1885	7,370,599	970,185	8,340,784	5,173,441	4,093,580	9,267,021	+926,237
1886	6,856,077	881,546	7,737,643	6,808,757	3,879,215	10,687,972	+2,950,349
1887	7,267,129	692,428	7,959,557	9,928,122	4,791,718	14,719,840	+6,760,283
1888	9,242,188	655,584	9,897,772	11,042,772	6,287,117	17,329,889	+7,432,117
1889	10,886,288	600,608	11,486,869	13,825,242	7,428,359	21,253,601	+9,766,705
1890	12,666,108	619,179	13,285,287	15,536,100	7,154,815	22,690,915	+9,405,628
Total 10 years..	$ 102,271,566	$ 12,382,085	$ 114,653,651	$ 82,814,423	$ 47,108,125	$ 129,922,548	$ +15,268,897
1891	$ 14,199,080	$ 770,540	$ 14,969,620	$ 23,364,519	$ 3,931,473	$ 27,295,992	$ +12,326,372
1892	13,696,531	597,468	14,293,999	23,702,496	4,405,029	28,107,525	+13,813,526
1893	18,891,714	676,920	19,568,634	27,145,469	6,409,630	33,555,099	+13,986,465
1894	12,441,805	400,344	12,842,149	21,560,011	7,166,995	28,727,000	+15,884,857
1895	14,582,484	423,422	15,005,906	12,903,789	2,731,999	15,635,788	+629,882
1896	18,686,797	763,459	19,450,256	13,819,698	3,636,479	17,456,177	−1,994,079
1897	22,726,596	694,468	23,421,064	13,990,017	4,521,555	18,511,572	−4,909,492
Total 7 years..	$ 115,225,007	$ 4,326,621	$ 119,551,628	$ 136,485,999	$ 32,803,160	$ 169,289,159	$ +49,737,531

Treasury Department, Bureau of Statistics,   WORTHINGTON C. FORD,

September 4, 1897.   *Chief of Bureau.*

STATEMENT SHOWING THE TOTAL COMMERCE BETWEEN THE UNITED STATES AND MEXICO, BY YEARS AND DECADES FROM 1851 TO 1897.

YEAR ENDING JUNE 30.	EXPORTS FROM THE UNITED STATES.			IMPORTS INTO THE UNITED STATES.			EXCESS OF EXPORTS (−) OR IMPORTS (+).
	Merchandise.	Gold and Silver.	Total.	Merchandise.	Gold and Silver.	Total.	
1851........	$ 1,581,783	2,652	$ 1,584,435	$ 720,786	$ 1,083,993	$ 1,804,779	$ +220,344
1852........	2,284,929	3,255	2,288,184	555,264	1,093,942	1,649,206	−638,978
1853........	3,558,824	1,734	3,560,558	756,100	1,411,885	2,167,985	−1,392,573
1854........	3,135,486	528	3,136,014	937,856	2,525,334	3,463,190	+327,176
1855........	2,921,604	1,200	2,922,804	904,750	1,978,080	2,882,830	−39,974
1856........	3,701,789	450	3,702,239	853,758	2,714,923	3,568,681	−133,558
1857........	3,615,206	....	3,615,206	1,026,873	4,958,984	5,985,857	+2,370,651
1858........	3,312,825	3,000	3,315,825	1,108,501	4,368,964	5,477,465	+2,161,640
1859........	2,919,742	72,804	2,992,546	1,244,084	4,095,890	5,339,974	+2,347,428
1860........	5,324,713	29,360	5,354,073	1,903,431	5,032,441	6,935,872	+1,581,799
Total 10 years..	$32,356,901	$114,983	$32,471,884	$10,011,403	$29,264,436	$39,275,839	$+6,803,955
1861........	$ 2,210,426	5,464	$ 2,215,890	$ 886,112	$ 2,803,101	$ 3,689,213	$ +1,473,323
1862........	2,181,174	....	2,181,174	730,988	1,953,864	2,684,852	+503,678
1863........	9,020,624	51,588	9,072,212	3,040,882	1,485,702	4,526,584	−4,545,628
1864........	9,270,597	3,410,957	12,681,554	6,128,445	1,755,946	7,884,391	−4,797,163
1865........	16,350,839	664,241	17,015,080	6,220,874	1,133,299	7,354,173	−9,660,907
1866........	4,573,218	15,000	4,588,218	1,726,092	2,429,511	4,155,603	−432,615
1867........	5,395,796	56,452	5,452,248	1,071,936	2,849,038	3,920,974	−1,531,274
1868........	6,441,339	12,924	6,454,263	1,590,667	4,525,255	6,115,922	−338,341
1869........	4,883,107	2,000	4,885,107	2,336,164	4,695,842	7,232,006	+2,346,899
1870........	5,859,700	15,696	5,875,396	2,715,665	10,383,366	13,099,031	+7,223,635
Total 10 years..	$66,186,820	$4,234,322	$70,421,142	$26,447,825	$34,214,924	$60,662,749	$−9,758,393
1871........	$ 7,612,113	38,500	$ 7,650,613	3,209,688	$14,301,475	17,511,163	$ +9,860,550
1872........	5,543,589	35,000	5,578,589	4,002,920	4,504,204	8,507,124	+2,928,535
1873........	6,264,901	165,262	6,430,163	4,276,165	12,154,060	16,430,225	+10,000,062
1874........	5,946,839	57,531	6,004,370	4,346,364	8,893,541	13,239,905	+7,235,535
1875........	5,737,282	33,501	5,770,783	5,174,594	6,460,389	11,634,983	+5,864,200
1876........	6,200,572	7,600	6,208,172	5,150,572	7,355,181	12,505,753	+6,297,581
1877........	5,803,494	5,239	5,808,733	5,204,264	10,240,319	15,444,583	+9,545,850
1878........	7,460,704	32,180	7,492,884	5,251,505	8,394,146	13,645,648	+6,152,676
1879........	6,752,244	9,040	6,761,284	5,493,221	8,554,598	14,047,819	+7,286,535
1880........	7,866,493	3,371	7,869,864	7,209,593	9,115,824	16,325,417	+8,455,553
Total 10 years..	$65,278,231	$387,224	$65,665,455	$49,318,883	$89,973,737	$139,292,620	$+73,627,165
1881........	$ 11,171,238	1,500	$ 11,172,738	8,317,802	9,136,324	17,454,126	$ +6,281,388
1882........	15,482,582	18,446	15,501,028	8,461,899	6,631,938	15,093,837	−407,191
1883........	16,587,620	96,964	16,684,584	8,177,123	9,782,986	17,960,109	+1,275,525
1884........	12,704,292	335,635	13,039,927	9,016,486	13,015,901	22,032,387	+8,992,460
1885........	8,340,784	79,406	8,420,190	9,267,021	14,919,611	24,186,632	+15,766,442
1886........	7,737,623	110,035	7,847,658	10,687,972	16,935,396	27,623,368	+19,775,710
1887........	7,959,557	279,812	8,239,369	14,719,840	14,855,765	29,575,605	+21,336,236
1888........	9,897,772	319,408	10,217,180	17,329,889	14,032,637	31,362,526	+21,145,346
1889........	11,486,896	176,616	11,663,512	21,253,501	17,557,248	38,810,849	+27,147,337
1890........	13,285,287	240,912	13,526,199	22,690,915	18,155,809	40,846,724	+27,320,525
Total 10 years..	$114,653,651	$1,658,734	$116,312,385	$129,922,548	$135,023,615	$264,946,163	$+148,633,778
1891........	$ 14,969,620	227,734	$ 15,197,354	27,295,992	14,297,431	41,593,423	$ +26,396,069
1892........	14,293,999	168,584	14,462,583	28,107,525	19,174,034	47,281,559	+32,818,976
1893........	19,568,634	473,942	20,042,576	33,555,099	22,951,604	56,506,703	+36,464,127
1894........	12,842,149	708,932	13,551,081	28,727,006	12,790,199	41,517,205	+27,966,124
1895........	15,005,906	551,064	15,556,970	15,635,788	9,644,160	25,279,948	+9,722,978
1896........	19,450,256	926,560	20,376,816	17,456,177	29,106,241	46,622,418	+26,245,602
1897........	23,421,064	114,149	23,535,213	18,511,572	12,202,794	30,714,366	+7,179,153
Total 7 years..	$119,551,628	$3,170,965	$122,722,593	$169,289,159	$120,226,463	$289,515,622	$+166,793,029

STATEMENT SHOWING THE QUANTITIES AND VALUES OF THE PRINCIPAL AND ALL OTHER ARTICLES OF IMPORTS INTO THE UNITED STATES FROM, AND OF EXPORTS FROM THE UNITED STATES TO, MEXICO, 1858–1883.

IMPORTS OF MERCHANDISE FROM MEXICO.

YEAR ENDING JUNE 30—	BREADSTUFFS AND OTHER FARINACEOUS FOOD.*		COFFEE.	COPPER, PIGS, BARS, INGOTS, OLD, AND OTHER UNMANUFACTURED.	CHEMICALS, DRUGS, DYES AND MEDICINES.			HIDES AND SKINS OTHER THAN FURS.	HAIR UNMANUFACTURED.	INDIA RUBBER AND GUTTA-PERCHA, CRUDE OR UNMANUFACTURED.	JUTE, AND OTHER GRASSES, RAW.	
	Indian corn.	All other.	POUNDS.	POUNDS.	Cochineal and indigo.	Dye-woods in sticks.	All other.†			POUNDS.	TONS.	
1858	$34,686	$28,108	29,687	1,437	‡ 37,793	$207,649	$1,039	$406,999	$11,261	143	406	$50,173
1859	45,390	15,794	45,518	3,638	144,137	46,208	1,336	437,397	485	.....	389	44,861
1860	28,940	5,124	549,265	10,542	49,651	161,115	411	535,591	2,264	107	351	55,114
1861	10,612	8,445	461,416	1,350	91,645	115,757	.....	497,397	2,264	.....	382	35,690
1862	.....	6,399	7,175	12,938	49,504	91,976	.....	17,905	11,535	1,586	286	23,337
1863	.....	15,048	935,594	85,796	91,151	48,004	10,839	383,530	912	.....	898	44,047
1864	.....	9,818	11,736	129,880	123,434	110,299	14,632	563,978	2,140	259	843	63,455
1865	.....	6,337	595	114,761	134,959	130,341	7,127	547,109	1,667	.....	133	30,496
1866	6,975	5,163	544,777	40,299	96,362	69,350	40,722	385,186	3,196	201	889	104,453
1867	34,659	20,599	138,005	20,497	130,154	268,754	39,024	368,817	2,868	20	862	116,455
1868	71,163	53,140	884,351	29,536	144,144	187,337	38,526	411,505	2,613	214	1,513	237,803
1869	79,331	48,551	203,048	57,700	144,974	207,859	64,510	745,350	2,728	228	2,906	460,235
1870	104,554	68,313	110,627	7,326	44,933	98,836	70,090	833,743	4,697	600	3,300	631,090
1871	74,207	43,114	526,495	24,397	177,745	39,666	53,306	714,489	6,442	2,554	3,328	626,044
1872	53,547	62,720	1,898,301	161,711	104,772	30,666	286,781	1,360,082	15,040	34,842	4,244	782,809
1873	61,081	37,720	2,035,540	218	55,439	27,752	163,745	1,093,387	55,420	98,656	3,590	534,980
1874	33,608	31,002	4,932,285	3,120	61,964	65,062	70,090	1,561,830	18,625	93,046	4,867	604,234
1875	45,090	49,022	4,691,880	2,161	54,510	63,958	158,279	3,077,156	28,784	106,417	6,185	613,338
1876	25,701	39,411	3,941,429	4,611	39,736	150,413	247,427	1,812,567	79,230	184,154	6,846	542,756
1877	12,321	34,339	6,789,693	620	52,726	72,402	219,193	1,529,702	39,317	72,963	7,078	656,746
1878	33,497	56,433	6,337,063	23,050	62,483	112,482	204,135	1,565,546	42,710	115,607	9,163	889,061
1879	65,230	65,192	8,307,040	2,490	68,345	96,877	159,017	1,675,777	34,474	39,835	10,197	939,396
1880	87,840	43,141	9,818,525	7,082	99,973	149,651	106,706	1,951,918	36,964	43,314	14,086	1,324,075
1881	58,648	41,353	13,911,910	68,556	5,813	160,070	265,642	2,111,750	39,201	17,500	17,153	1,634,215
1882	22,072	50,192	17,020,669	3,562	.....	128,734	108,030	1,595,107	38,810	315,059	19,933	2,061,939
1883	.....	.....	8,578,532	124	.....	211,714	119,681	1,568,645	52,985	241,478	25,065	2,712,088

* All other breadstuffs comprise barley, barley malt, bread and biscuit, oats, rice, rye, wheat, wheat flour, meal of all kinds, peas and beans; all other farinaceous food and preparations of breadstuffs.

† All other chemicals, drugs, dyes, and medicines include: Argols; medicinal barks; camphor, crude; madder; soda, nitrate of; gums; cutch and catechu; opium; soda and salts of; sulphur or brimstone; chloride of lime or bleaching powder; all chemicals, not elsewhere specified. ‡ Cochineal only; no indigo included.

MEXICO, 1858–1883—*Continued.*

IMPORTS OF MERCHANDISE FROM MEXICO—*Continued.*

(In the LEAD and WOOL columns two figures are given for each year: the quantity in pounds and, following the slash, the value in dollars.)

YEAR ENDING JUNE 30—	LEAD, PIGS, BARS, AND OLD. (pounds / value)	ANIMALS, LIVING.	PRECIOUS STONES.	SALT.	SPICES OF ALL KINDS.	SUGAR AND MOLASSES OF ALL KINDS.	WOOL, RAW AND FLEECE. (pounds / value)	WOOD, UNMANUFACTURED.	OTHER MERCHANDISE.	TOTAL IMPORTS OF MERCHANDISE.
1858	36,517 / $825	......	......	$6,285	$1,252	$9,560	$4,137	$43,674	$275,902	$1,108,901
1859	91,440 / 1,829	......	......	11,321	1,272	8,473	9,864	55,949	39,064	1,244,084
1860	320,141 / 6,203	......	......	22,555	642	55,399	15,151	101,392	819,195	1,993,431
1861	57,482 / 1,150	......	......	12,266	1,835	33,333	1,641	102,311	141,120	886,112
1862	......	......	......	16,138	1,551	10,886	3,660	51,415	*480,510	730,988
1863	205,136 / 13,988	......	......	49,871	3,959	45,576	31,209 / 155,430	65,014	†1,084,058	3,343,445
1864	4,659 / 997	......	......	36,247	2,873	12,019	1,226,820 / 96,593	62,342	‡4,087,889	6,128,445
1865	648 / 60	......	......	6,452	10,850	816	702,676 / 45,590	83,921	§5,188,600	6,322,841
1866	25,152 / 1,399	......	......	13,356	10,020	79,924	18,667	82,908	‖770,268	1,726,692
1867	......	......	......	13,345	10,041	1,693	163,397 / 377	106,921	127,399	1,071,936
1868	79,504 / 2,799	......	......	21,368	40,324	29,735	4,386	72,973	217,444	1,590,667
1869	523,043 / 22,211	......	......	13,716	33,641	65,197	62,493 / 51,838	126,345	225,631	2,336,164
1870	456,516 / 14,607	......	......	30,235	104,476	28,123	716,068 / 49,689	157,868	377,916	2,715,665
1871	725,211 / 33,261	......	......	29,600	124,403	39,877	650,459 / 68,907	176,724	908,208	3,009,088
1872	461,274 / 14,653	$188,558	$34,449	20,984	10,396	52,027	865,909 / 128,375	275,020	263,991	4,002,920
1873	392,440 / 19,304	147,512	330	6,963	2,100	11,818	1,182,481 / 129,475	171,554	550,070	4,475,165
1874	817,579 / 41,978	134,701	102,048	8,944	1,882	17,682	1,182,414 / 112,226	324,520	379,457	4,346,394
1875	335,648 / 16,686	81,439	156,690	8,201	1,520	104,547	1,173,099 / 119,534	340,923	756,226	5,174,594
1876	837,698 / 24,253	108,050	63,399	6,803	5,481	164,597	1,095,283 / 85,887	247,833	735,763	5,150,577
1877	1,336,641 / 68,218	129,697	6,355	7,190	1,650	227,543	836,798 / 119,708	133,690	533,176	5,144,204
1878	1,136,453 / 58,245	134,971	1,540	6,768	3,760	155,700	1,495,083 / 73,216	257,853	580,051	5,051,502
1879	407,276 / 12,839	132,873	3,097	6,138	9,040	76,992	835,467 / 66,300	224,925	520,001	5,493,221
1880	630,047 / 27,661	175,395	5,416	8,419	5,219	239,655	819,784 / 144,875	408,754	889,136	7,209,593
1881	1,132,004 / 44,365	314,272	21,657	7,178	8,428	124,535	1,331,874 / 99,479	390,395	974,452	8,317,802
1882	......	455,017	76,241	802	10,775	104,374	1,000,376 / 18,937	499,776	1,212,601	8,461,899
1883	1,191,425 / 26,919	661,245	56,176	973	......	64,587	191,666 / 957	441,083	1,244,542	8,177,123

* Of this amount $60,497 was the value of unmanufactured cotton.

† Of this amount $1,750,615 was the value of unmanufactured cotton.

‡ Of this amount $4,859,735 was the value of unmanufactured cotton.

§ Of this amount $5,108,875 was the value of unmanufactured cotton.

‖ Of this amount $417,197 was the value of unmanufactured cotton.

MEXICO, 1858–1883—Continued.

EXPORTS OF DOMESTIC MERCHANDISE TO MEXICO.

YEAR ENDED JUNE 30—	SHEEP. NO.	SHEEP (value)	BREAD AND BREADSTUFFS. Indian corn. BUSHELS.	BREAD AND BREADSTUFFS. Indian corn $	BREAD AND BREADSTUFFS. Wheat and wheat-flour.	BREAD AND BREADSTUFFS. All others.*	COTTON, RAW OR UNMANUFACTURED. POUNDS.	COTTON, RAW OR UNMANUFACTURED. (value)
1858	.....	.....	.....	.....	$130,673	$3,609	9,084,609	$1,074,818
1859	.....	.....	49,579	$37,676	181,283	4,137	5,093,635	883,337
1860	.....	.....	48,932	29,886	247,206	8,247	9,043,327	1,076,750
1861	.....	.....	80,339	78,063	129,033	10,030	1,410,859	153,995
1862	.....	.....	13,877	9,993	282,810	31,935	......	......
1863	.....	.....	18,354	14,077	777,122	379,797	......	......
1864	$80	.....	268,553	263,849	855,772	50,730	477,497	331,199
1865	740	.....	187,014	35,024	1,063,026	90,238	......	......
1866	590	.....	158,625	347,464	584,022	66,227	50,317	17,611
1867	2,800	.....	14,418	16,533	547,065	117,066	3,310,642	934,436
1868	(†)	.....	7,292	9,051	343,905	10,938	8,228,598	1,349,085
1869	2,253	.....	72,216	72,439	298,111	10,093	2,044,224	458,495
1870	18,189	27,461	62,859	65,292	209,371	11,911	6,609,707	1,412,363
1871	33,837	36,347	173,585	169,350	225,718	14,009	11,309,408	1,586,557
1872	35,843	27,228	21,039	27,233	218,479	35,166	957,209	128,186
1873	59,935	57,217	104,146	99,166	110,525	22,310	550,639	74,351
1874	110,290	111,445	55,881	40,049	96,666	25,449	2,286,561	322,507
1875	133,222	112,553	9,862	9,092	102,473	21,532	1,305,276	184,186
1876	104,865	95,215	93,487	75,945	108,952	26,380	6,277,575	890,574
1877	144,908	161,549	64,776	55,658	88,913	23,756	3,060,812	462,902
1878	158,217	153,065	288,109	267,623	171,450	51,885	3,422,162	357,210
1879	103,789	89,689	126,613	95,802	129,071	50,001	9,898,229	912,363
1880	120,817	115,565	85,702	68,743	69,072	44,126	9,881,543	1,176,067
1881	118,498	108,886	354,510	240,182	93,757	60,198	13,386,186	1,494,101
1882	112,421	81,338	419,263	333,642	103,528	91,475	12,537,650	1,447,522
1883	364,866	235,585	476,453	391,751	178,468	118,744	20,577,771	2,217,259

* Bread and breadstuffs, all other, comprise barley, bread and biscuit, Indian corn-meal, oats, rye, rye-flour, other small grain and pulse, maizena, farina, and all other breadstuffs, or preparations of, used as food.

† Classed under the general heading "Animals, living, all kinds," total, $316,773.

EXPORTS OF DOMESTIC MERCHANDISE TO MEXICO—*Continued.*

YEAR ENDED JUNE 30	COTTON, MANUFACTURES OF.			DRUGS, CHEMICALS, MEDICINES, ACIDS, ASHES, AND DYE-STUFFS.	GLASS AND GLASS-WARE.	IRON AND STEEL, AND MANUFACTURES OF *	LEATHER, AND MANUFACTURES OF.	
	Colored.	Uncolored.	All other.				Boots and Shoes.	All other.
	YARDS.	YARDS.						
1858	....	....	$281,594	$30,957	$8,011	$188,214	$1,066	$4,494
1859	....	....	312,203	34,486	7,637	91,472	9,345	5,873
1860	....	....	641,870	63,727	5,981	320,326	8,999	4,994
1861	....	....	312,695	48,710	5,703	355,337	4,552	6,395
1862	....	....	157,874	75,194	14,468	265,225	9,696	4,667
1863	....	....	1,784,531	118,604	43,224	704,944	280,543	112,334
1864	....	....	777,622	166,741	40,670	1,165,541	373,146	67,404
1865	....	....	2,222,410	326,675	126,447	1,423,571	1,119,848	160,203
1866	29,186	3,718	98,663	89,690	23,515	420,034	39,131	35,114
1867	141,780	1,049	356,165	68,137	16,813	770,150	21,533	21,639
1868	51,828	45,383	387,610	85,535	27,010	764,897	61,227	23,974
1869	397,472	407,619	341,593	73,572	27,076	811,384	95,590	18,430
1870	(†)	(†)	106,373	113,105	21,217	654,498	116,761	11,591
1871	1,049,621	601,927	94,366	96,248	18,905	698,296	91,070	16,970
1872	758,338	1,451,277	38,368	93,734	26,419	803,668	98,565	28,480
1873	550,411	1,355,636	73,244	107,436	26,752	1,043,071	104,377	13,613
1874	500,156	1,258,921	50,337	126,437	26,007	1,073,530	70,417	12,757
1875	277,032	1,086,883	64,189	112,897	20,007	954,061	84,129	26,026
1876	369,855	1,019,907	60,595	111,348	37,361	1,062,687	70,353	11,182
1877	1,210,286	2,143,975	64,450	79,799	20,743	786,365	53,383	14,433
1878	6,355,489	5,876,817	87,278	133,069	24,763	1,001,574	60,950	27,779
1879	10,401,048	5,726,156	99,852	127,726	56,808	996,080	38,500	21,124
1880	7,664,001	3,886,748	106,406	145,331	47,831	1,257,731	53,466	25,133
1881	6,874,372	2,808,228	193,650	213,477	54,381	2,582,346	48,207	45,053
1882	6,745,817	3,657,611	206,133	288,824	87,313	4,235,712	85,327	65,537
1883	6,114,541	3,838,660	185,399	265,320	111,542	3,772,267	86,788	63,102

* Including, also, printing presses and type, scales and balances, sewing machines and parts of, steam and other fire engines and apparatus.
† Included in "All other."

EXPORTS OF DOMESTIC MERCHANDISE TO MEXICO.—*Continued.*

YEAR ENDED JUNE 30—	REFINED ILLUMINATING MINERAL OIL.	ORDNANCE STORES.			PROVISIONS.*			QUICKSILVER.	SUGAR AND MOLASSES.	TOBACCO AND MANUFACTURES OF.	WOOD AND MANUFACTURES OF.	OTHER MERCHANDISE.	TOTAL EXPORTS OF DOMESTIC MERCHANDISE.	TOTAL EXPORTS OF FOREIGN MERCHANDISE.	TOTAL EXPORTS OF MERCHANDISE.
		Cartridges and Fuses.	Gunpowder.	All other.	Bacon and Hams.	Lard.	All other.*								
					POUNDS.	POUNDS.									
1858			$7,015		40,198	506,208	$67,922	$77,460	$3,047	$15,387	$64,763	$754,634	$2,784,852	$599,973	$3,378,825
1859			14,409		43,431	679,033	65,413		7,054	14,163	61,496	502,773	2,252,162	667,580	2,919,742
1860			66,593		60,551	906,106	103,120	103,128	21,259	9,536	84,372	485,643	3,390,379	2,075,334	5,324,713
1861			35,775		37,592	117,487	17,344	107,765	11,391	9,526	55,065	303,806	1,559,062	651,364	2,291,426
1862			4,006		69,170	636,851	56,692	16,712	22,700		78,000	343,218	1,840,720	340,454	2,281,174
1863	$15,601		6,115		487,092	1,357,512	150,279	31,093	5,723	222,334	306,014	1,536,634	7,441,579	1,579,945	9,022,804
1864	26,657		6,244		321,756	2,885,411	340,683	110,627	13,692	370,972	544,885	1,072,979	7,765,133	1,395,464	9,270,597
1865	97,689	$34,317			294,721	2,334,603	453,797	191,442	53,375	436,420	871,314	1,322,080	13,809,972	2,250,807	10,330,039
1866	60,889	146,390	1,750	$32,457	120,353	889,408	212,256	295,006	36,364	302,222	211,896	895,138	3,701,599	871,619	4,573,218
1867	92,099	57,578	16,057	26,213	93,418	893,794	137,262	134,121	34,593	207,090	137,319	865,571	4,823,614	572,188	5,395,796
1868	64,657	118,793	10,790		98,490	981,178	134,619	112,476	53,099	182,120	179,130	650,841	5,048,420	1,392,919	6,441,339
1869		80,113	20,958	6,978	68,111	630,541	108,798	64,739	44,025	27,354	141,477	796,039	3,935,699	1,047,408	4,883,107
1870	157,034	32,839	26,230	2,838	95,852	734,083	93,708	335,782	73,385	87,690	144,227	793,532	5,044,033	1,314,955	5,899,700
1871	99,073	26,756	24,274	771	210,770	764,704	124,107	328,117	33,868	129,597	178,689	714,095	3,420,658	2,556,080	7,014,113
1872	171,480	55,271	49,800	130	31,686	1,079,754	83,681	325,980	77,316	139,577	156,058	842,646	3,941,029	2,112,931	5,543,569
1873	143,140	70,139	26,834	314	277,536	808,445	33,648	263,370	198,577	140,750	251,931	674,898	4,025,148	2,323,388	6,204,901
1874	164,160	47,608	33,788	213	269,882	364,246	28,032	495,048	197,613	91,218	253,249	763,413	3,972,004	1,930,691	5,046,839
1875	108,368	68,432	88,807	9,746	110,799	388,420	32,243	471,808	59,328	300,499	229,506	620,332	4,593,800	1,865,278	5,737,262
1876	171,348	146,390	35,210		128,983	311,862	41,769	365,097	36,442	329,558	226,816	780,361	5,811,496	1,490,594	6,200,572
1877	221,804	57,578	36,672	302	64,360	550,718	63,401	352,606	98,485	447,347	161,073	551,574	5,402,380	1,380,692	7,460,724
1878	173,438	118,793	34,867		141,535	1,055,063	137,179	290,249	75,274	122,844	253,055	790,361	6,065,974	1,649,375	6,753,244
1879	157,436	73,014	43,749	1,141	75,645	1,294,722	102,952	81,543	38,800	160,516	240,289	753,535	9,098,077	1,351,864	7,886,493
1880	155,368	80,113	49,647	356	92,460	1,508,535	186,319	71,820	41,673	152,791	240,480	871,182		1,800,519	11,171,178
1881	173,355	95,397	145,397		160,312	1,333,086	133,397	377,825	62,750	135,174	544,201	1,397,434	13,324,905	1,973,161	15,484,682
1882	224,715	98,303	226,135		214,523	1,188,847	145,793	460,159	71,582	142,671	1,426,411	2,906,302		2,158,077	16,587,620
1883	240,404	159,491	393,783		243,581	1,394,134	145,797	394,572	73,298	141,185	1,385,420	2,821,760	14,337,992	2,216,628	

* Provisions, all other, comprise: Beef, salted or cured; beef, fresh; butter; cheese, condensed milk; eggs; fish, dried, smoked, fresh, pickled, other cured; meats, preserved mutton, fresh; oysters; pickles and sauces; pork; onions; potatoes; other vegetables; vegetables, prepared or preserved.

STATEMENT SHOWING THE QUANTITIES AND VALUES OF THE PRINCIPAL AND ALL OTHER ARTICLES OF IMPORTS INTO THE UNITED STATES FROM, AND OF EXPORTS FROM THE UNITED STATES TO, MEXICO, DURING EACH OF THE YEARS SPECIFIED BELOW.

MERCHANDISE.—MEXICO, 1889–1897.

IMPORTS OF MERCHANDISE.

YEAR ENDING JUNE 30—	Breadstuffs and other farinaceous food.		Coffee.		Copper: Pigs, bars, ingots, old, and other unmanufactured.		Chemicals, drugs, dyes, and medicines.			Hides and skins, other than fur skins.	Hair unmanufactured.	India rubber and gutta percha, crude.		Jute and other grasses unmanufactured.		Lead and Manufactures of.	
	Corn.	All other.					Cochineal and indigo.	Dye-woods in sticks.	All other.								
			POUNDS.		POUNDS.							POUNDS.		TONS.		POUNDS.	
1889..	$1,682	$1,837	18,243,317	$4,895,862	81,471	$4,893	$1,000	$187,862	$1,142,124	$1,526,915	$47,452	233,096	$81,800	41,369	$6,257,610	......	$549,257
1890..	871	3,025	20,666,975	3,542,851	39,607	2,048	12,571	194,531	1,455,350	1,579,250	57,066	177,801	59,826	42,787	5,851,682	......	657,658
1891..	1,163	22,046	28,489,653	5,094,839	283,744	23,560	10,935	165,445	1,888,813	1,646,360	61,098	169,343	56,666	56,360	6,047,593	......	1,847,969
1892..	8,102	3,165	21,921,540	4,037,592	1,106,222	84,175	3,745	119,457	1,396,667	1,704,872	60,557	130,328	41,802	52,021	5,549,985	......	3,596,728
1893..	1,093	2,279	25,417,159	4,497,880	1,521,762	134,997	38,411	145,725	1,340,088	1,653,775	61,711	140,096	44,367	60,550	6,687,947	......	5,646,681
1894..	924	1,848	38,160,641	6,964,034	1,821,165	213,377	681	88,390	1,245,595	1,438,277	57,064	130,415	33,750	54,473	3,949,401	......	6,463,346
1895..	6,920	10,383	35,262,229	5,997,439	2,213,101	155,645	345	102,160	953,285	1,433,045	43,846	160,868	54,868	59,706	3,375,998	......	1,493,150
1896..	1,465	12,202	23,975,477	4,040,443	5,544,429	454,712	318	125,774	2,049,715	1,519,391	43,261	124,343	41,489	65,441	4,259,531	......	1,350,713
1897..	1,046	10,310	28,733,370	4,591,929	7,971,378	580,241	......	124,066	1,537,371	1,778,225	58,228	106,871	31,675	70,692	4,335,624	......	1,435,891

IMPORTS INTO, AND EXPORTS FROM, THE UNITED STATES FROM AND TO MEXICO, ETC.—*Continued.*

MEXICO, 1889–1897—*Continued.*

YEAR ENDING JUNE 30—	IMPORTS OF MERCHANDISE.									
	Animals.	Precious stones.	Salt.	Spices of all kinds.	Sugar and molasses.	Wool, unmanufactured.		Wood, unmanufactured.	Other merchandise.	Total imports of merchandise.
						POUNDS.				
1889	$399,493	$11,956	$2,302	$9,278	$7,022	761,828	$67,711	$301,142	$7,757,003	$21,253,601
1890	417,025	57,614	3,546	16,413	27,129	322,166	30,614	441,620	8,579,184	22,690,915
1891	140,642	3,025	4,659	11,507	35,460	1,709	158	470,564	9,764,647	27,294,441
1892	20,257	911	2,369	12,575	40,790	263	41	699,033	10,731,702	28,107,525
1893	36,391	1,164	11,933	19,891	48,157	92,709	10,727	631,238	12,743,844	33,555,099
1894	24,415	3,672	387	19,595	69,618	5,708	632	360,490	7,791,600	28,727,006
1895	760,000	10,121	440	166	55,156	74,574	3,928	230,499	1,043,700	15,635,794
1896	1,520,044	3,840	2	14,066	63,622	95,834	3,964	595,523	1,378,193	17,456,177
1897	1,954,783	847	1,451	30,135	19,111	140,053	7,608	539,499	1,572,552	18,511,572

YEAR ENDING JUNE 30—	EXPORTS OF DOMESTIC MERCHANDISE.								
	ANIMALS.		BREADSTUFFS.				Chemicals, drugs, dyes, and medicines.	Cotton, unmanufactured.	
	Sheep.		Corn.		Wheat and wheat flour.	All other.			
	NUMBER.		BUSHELS.					POUNDS.	
1889	77,569	$122,193	434,997	$194,778	$185,746	$85,558	$329,487	16,901,267	$1,607,395
1890	26,814	47,947	961,458	481,052	166,769	100,997	362,328	13,047,474	1,217,805
1891	9,147	21,464	615,332	389,619	213,299	125,718	377,586	12,841,122	1,281,072
1892	2,827	5,068	754,548	489,702	184,299	127,443	440,297	22,117,381	1,844,500
1893	1,310	4,682	6,960,356	4,343,777	230,576	144,031	418,452	20,905,980	1,890,461
1894	5,443	9,085	431,516	220,362	197,192	100,568	341,989	17,582,418	1,391,836
1895	909	3,338	179,611	108,272	175,637	80,649	408,795	37,976,422	2,352,299
1896	2,182	9,693	1,676,758	672,093	167,680	85,542	469,193	19,408,420	1,643,183
1897	4,628	11,877	8,825,860	3,233,583	96,794	128,527	481,652	15,103,628	1,236,447

IMPORTS INTO, AND EXPORTS FROM, THE UNITED STATES FROM AND TO MEXICO, ETC.—*Continued.*

MEXICO, 1889-1897.—*Continued.*

EXPORTS OF DOMESTIC MERCHANDISE.

YEAR ENDING JUNE 30—	COTTON, MANUFACTURES OF.				Glass and Glassware.	GUNPOWDER AND OTHER EXPLOSIVES.		Iron and steel, and manufactures of.	LEATHER, AND MANUFACTURES OF.	
	Cloths, colored.		Cloths, uncolored.		All other.		Gunpowder.	All other explosives.		Boots and Shoes.	All other.
	YARDS.		YARDS.								
1889	7,735,000	$461,765	1,845,659	$138,904	$218,993	$76,833	$10,227	$283,794	$2,290,757	$39,081	$48,648
1890	5,434,882	314,889	2,048,130	153,875	179,402	94,697	15,723	348,845	2,700,979	38,959	54,794
1891	5,450,725	377,576	1,706,753	126,753	158,053	126,688	18,680	375,320	3,414,397	24,366	41,231
1892	6,381,499	347,667	1,037,489	144,392	155,362	123,546	28,589	339,685	3,834,343	21,084	38,702
1893	3,445,400	205,450	1,000,704	86,643	140,393	117,979	8,787	410,513	3,862,876	26,731	42,308
1894	3,184,903	197,855	1,368,663	111,236	151,575	112,972	6,265	454,775	3,198,597	24,843	58,245
1895	4,276,338	244,114	2,159,210	145,430	151,024	121,488	43,028	572,031	3,793,566	26,532	51,648
1896	5,348,862	311,532	2,540,396	182,833	324,729	162,628	74,805	597,706	5,239,397	45,115	66,943
1897	3,867,100	231,527	1,706,708	134,846	346,710	168,437	75,657	671,096	6,435,645	58,639	63,453

EXPORTS OF DOMESTIC MERCHANDISE.

YEAR ENDING JUNE 30—	Oils: Mineral, refined.	PROVISIONS, COMPRISING MEAT AND DAIRY PRODUCTS.					Quicksilver.	Sugar and molasses.	Tobacco, and manufactures of.	Wood, and manufactures of.	Other merchandise.	Total exports of domestic merchandise.	Total exports of foreign merchandise.
		Bacon and hams.		Lard.		All other.							
		POUNDS.		POUNDS.									
1889	$246,381	997,657	$41,289	1,363,539	128,169	$386,117	$144,734	$66,843	$133,727	$964,310	$2,678,444	$10,886,373	$600,608
1890	234,435	359,658	34,021	1,639,355	119,976	433,962	169,341	42,035	130,440	1,303,448	3,919,306	12,666,708	619,179
1891	301,899	341,135	38,999	1,611,313	109,816	228,245	68,112	36,493	73,535	1,483,903	5,839,026	15,199,080	770,540
1892	238,952	436,897	48,280	2,050,997	142,953	193,414	111,340	34,449	89,394	1,206,672	3,506,236	13,696,531	597,468
1893	198,740	422,369	53,008	3,863,457	368,449	233,417	143,381	73,545	126,745	1,200,486	4,671,554	18,801,714	676,920
1894	140,696	368,993	34,993	1,414,492	116,198	173,281	361,781	57,459	129,205	998,805	3,846,069	12,441,805	400,344
1895	181,092	997,599	33,754	1,908,076	128,779	164,853	381,681	37,402	167,665	1,048,844	4,349,733	14,582,484	493,422
1896	142,819	340,546	38,113	3,440,157	209,727	167,490	466,359	38,731	175,541	1,611,477	5,795,658	18,685,707	763,459
1897	174,695	305,784	38,195	7,195,747	334,335	160,769	368,463	29,395	123,387	2,163,446	5,972,207	22,726,591	604,468

Increase of trade during the year 1896–97.—The data given in the chapter on Foreign Trade contain detailed statements of the amount of commodities and precious metals exported from Mexico into the United States during the last ten years, and I refer, therefore, to the same, those desiring more detailed information on that subject.

I give, however, a statement of the leading merchandise imported from Mexico into the United States, during the last fiscal year, compared with the fiscal year ended June 30, 1896, embracing only such imports as are not specifically stated in the data taken from the official reports of the United States Statistical Bureau, and which appear on pages 176 and 177. The following data, also taken from the last official report of the same Bureau, shows a comparative increase of trade.

LEADING MERCHANDISE IMPORTS FROM MEXICO.

	FISCAL YEAR 1896–1897.	FISCAL YEAR 1895–1896.
Henequen, tons...................	62,839	51,167
Value....................	$3,809,415	$3,339,180
Ixtle fibre, tons...................	6,313	12,207
Value....................	$335,841	$717,585
Oranges, value...................	$258,340	$212,913
Tobacco, lbs.....................	749,560	93,197
Value....................	$297,262	$28,025
Mahogany, feet...................	8,791	10,654
Value....................	$321,800	$414,817
Coal, tons.......................	99,760	72,056
Value....................	$218,456	$146,813

I also append a similar statement of some of the articles exported from the United States into Mexico during the last fiscal year, compared with the previous one, ended June 30, 1896, embracing only such exports as are not specifically stated in the data taken from the official reports of the United States Statistical Bureau, appearing on pages 178 to 183, and which I also take from the last official report of the same Bureau. When it is taken into consideration that the Mexican imports from the United States during the last fiscal year were made on a falling silver market, the annexed statement shows a considerable financial strength.

EXPORTS FROM THE UNITED STATES TO MEXICO.

(Fiscal year 1896–97 and preceding year.)

	1896–97.	1895–96.
Cattle, no.......................	690	1,112
Value.....................	$29,186	$39,509
Hogs, no.......................	22,164	17,540
Value.....................	$263,083	$206,807

	1896–97.	1895–96.
Agricultural implements	$130,825	$119,838
Books, maps, etc.	$161,143	$107,384
Carriages and cars.	$615,468	$687,425
Coal and coke, tons.	219,111	121,269
Value	$643,715	$377,469
Bicycles	$73,117	$24,278
Fruits and nuts.	$72,654	$78,497
Hops.	$55,610	$8,289
Hardware.	$2,874,283	$2,455,400
Leather.	$16,456	$24,014
Crude petroleum, gals.	7,090,853	6,779,059
Value	$349,021	$392,510
Refined petroleum, gals.	836,628	631,147
Value	$174,107	$142,761
(Includes lubricating oil.)		
Cotton-seed oil, gals.	1,616,407	1,588,504
Value	$320,496	$337,892
Paraffin, lbs.	2,888,475	2,975,476
Value	$144,805	$163,644
Tallow, lbs.	997,216	1,783,788
Value	$36,561	$77,050
Hams	$28,976	$29,487
Butter	$40,089	$33,169
Wool, lbs.	1,698,952	2,605,150
Value	$140,609	$238,316

Tropical Products Supplied by Mexico to the United States.—It will be interesting to state in what proportion Mexican imports of tropical products figure in the total imports of said commodities into this country.

From 1892 to 1896 the annual average of importation of vanilla beans into the United States was 205,197 pounds, of which Mexico furnished 142,727 pounds, or 69¼ per cent. Mexico receives for her vanilla crop, annually, $640,000 gold.

Mexico's average annual exportation of coffee to the United States for the past five years was 28,927,410 pounds, or 4.8 per cent., of the total American purchase of coffee, Brazil furnishing 70 per cent., Central America 7.6 per cent., Venezuela 6.4 per cent., and the British West Indies 1.1 per cent. There is plenty of room for the Mexican coffee-growing industry to expand. Mexico's fine flavored, mild coffees are steadily gaining in favor in the United States.

In henequen, or sisal grass, Mexico takes the leading place in the import trade of the United States, selling, of the total received there, 98.1 per cent. The average annual importation for the past five years was 50,129 tons, of which Mexico furnished 49,195, Cuba 277, British Australia 386, and all other countries 271. Mexico received a yearly average, during the five years, for her henequen, of $4,218,267, gold. All of which went to the State of Yucatan.

In sugar, Mexico holds but an insignificant place in the American importation, which showed an annual average, during the past five years, of 3,827,799,481 pounds, Cuba furnishing 46.5 per cent. and Hawaii 7.9 per cent.

We could expand very largely our sugar production and supply this country with almost all of that product, but as sugar is produced in Louisiana and as Hawaii is likely to belong to the United States the protective policy of this country will not allow us to supply the United States with that commodity on a large scale.

Mexico is sending on an average every year, 1,400,000 pounds of wool to the United States. In 1892 she exported but 190 pounds.

The United States takes, annually, an average of 50,493,000 pounds of goat skins, of which Mexico furnishes 3,007,000, or 5.9 per cent. Of other hides and skins the United States imports 167,993,000 pounds, Mexico's share being 4.3 per cent.

The cattle trade of Mexico with the United States increased considerably under the liberal provisions of the Wilson Bill, which taxed cattle with 20 per cent. ad valorem. The following statement shows how large the increase of that trade was under that bill :

CATTLE EXPORTED TO THE UNITED STATES.

Years.	Number.	Gold Value.
1892	1,438	$ 7,740
1893	2,597	16,376
1894	1,469	11,857
1895	148,431	720,864
1896	216,913	1,481,954

(Fiscal years ended June 30th.)

Mexico has been for at least two years the most important source of supply to the United States for cattle purchased abroad, Canada furnishing, in 1896, cattle to the value of but $18,902, and the United Kingdom $6,684. The cattle trade is one in which American, as well as Mexican capital is embarked, but it will be considerably diminished if not completely destroyed under the highly protective tariff.

COINAGE.

In the chapter on Mining I gave a concise statement of the silver and gold coined in Mexico from the time of its discovery by the Spaniards to the fiscal year ended June 30, 1896, and it appears from the same that the total coinage of silver amounted to $3,398,664,400.

According to the report of the Director of the Mint (page 347) on the "Production of Precious Metals in the United States during the Calendar Year 1895," the last one out as this paper goes to press, the total production of silver of the world from 1493 to 1895 is $10,-345,688,700, the Mexican coinage being over one-third of the whole.

It must be borne in mind that that statement embraces, so far as Mexico is concerned, only the silver coined, and it does not take into consideration the silver used in the arts, which used to be a considerable amount, as almost every well-to-do Mexican had forks, spoons, plates and other table ware and household articles of solid silver. It does not embrace either such silver as was smuggled in bullion, which, considering the large extent of the Mexican sea coast, its scanty population and the general demoralization during our civil wars represents a very large amount. It can, therefore, be safely stated that the production of silver in Mexico, not coined, represents at least from one-fourth to one-third of the amount coined. Therefore, the production of silver by Mexico may be safely estimated at from $5,000,000,000, to $6,000,000,000, which is about one-half of the total product of the world.

The following statement shows the amount of silver coined by the several mints of Mexico from their establishment to June 30, 1895, stating the years in which the coinage was made :

COINAGE BY THE MEXICAN MINTS FROM THEIR ESTABLISHMENT IN 1535 TO JUNE 30, 1895.

PERIOD OF COINAGE.	MINTS.	COINAGE.
1868–1895	Alamos	$ 22,828,869
1863–1866	Catorce	1,321,545
1811–1895	Chihuahua	62,465,756
1846–1895	Culiacan	46,438,169
1811–1895	Durango	67,128,366
1812–1895	Guadalajara	64,127,846
1844–1849	Guadalupe y Calvo	4,375,062
1812–1895	Guanajuato	307,364,150
1852–1895	Hermosilla	19,659,506
1535–1895	Mexico	2,453,110,110
1857–1893	Oaxaca	5,761,045
1827–1893	San Luis Potosi	113,143,358
1810–1812	Sombrerete	1,551,248
1827–1830	Tlalpam	1,162,660
1810–1895	Zacatecas	350,341,499
From 1535 to 1895	Total	$3,520,779,189

I give a statement of the production of gold and silver in Mexico in the fiscal years 1879–1880, 1889–1890 and 1894–1895, which shows a considerable increase in each of those years, and this statement only represents such amounts of the precious metals as were either exported in bullion or taken to the mints, and not the production that is otherwise disposed of.

PRODUCTION OF GOLD AND SILVER IN MEXICO IN THE FISCAL YEARS 1879–1880, 1889–1890 AND 1894–1895.

	1879–1880.			1889–1890.			1894–1895.		
	Kilograms.	Grams.	Value.	Kilograms.	Grams.	Value.	Kilograms.	Grams.	Value.
Gold coined........	772	598	$ 521,826	360	219	$ 243,298	807	260	$ 545,237
Gold exported.....	622	032	420,131	677	524	457,611	6,217	351	4,199,305
Total..........	1,394	630	941,957	1,037	743	700,909	7,024	611	4,744,542
Silver coined,......	587,034	804	24,018,529	594,606	526	24,328,326	675,277	551	27,628,981
Silver exported	74,302	310	3,040,079	362,418	697	14,828,361	747,283	490	30,575,104
Total..........	661,337	114	27,058,608	957,025	223	39,156,687	1,422,561	041	58,204,085
Total of gold and silver..........			$28,000,565			$39,857,596			$62,948,627

The following statement gives the exports of the precious metals from Mexico during the same years embraced in the preceding table.

EXPORT OF PRECIOUS METALS AND MINERALS FROM MEXICO IN THE FISCAL YEARS 1879–1880, 1889–1890 AND 1894–1895.

	VALUE IN MEXICAN DOLLARS.		
	1879–1880.	1889–1890.	1894–1895.
Argentiferous copper..............	....	....	....
Gold ore.........................	....	....	59,660
Silver ore.......................	....	6,394,662	10,935,353
Foreign gold coined	220,567	13,204	34,887
Mexican gold coined..............	760,683	96,592	164,113
Gold bullion.....................	420,132	457,611	4,139,645
Mixed gold......................	....	....	....
Foreign silver coined.............	314,537	141,033	485,326
Mexican silver coined.............	16,783,317	23,084,489	17,077,119
Base silver......................	....	1,810	50,866
Silver bullion....................	3,040,079	7,259,959	18,803,876
Manufactured silver..............	581	....	....
Mixed silver.....................	....	368,872	....
Sulphite of silver................	....	803,058	785,009
Argentiferous lead.......... ...	....	....	....
Argentiferous zinc...............	....	....	....
	21,539,896	38,621,290	52,535,854

It may be interesting to state the amount of silver exported and coined in Mexican mints from 1874 to 1896, which is the following:

	EXPORTED.	COINED.
1874-75	$ 16,038,215	$ 19,386,958
1875-76	....	19,454,054
1876-77	....	21,415,128
1877-78	20,853,074	22,084,203
1878-79	19,339,151	22,162,988
1879-80	20,307,563	24,018,529
1880-81	17,774,910	24,617,395
1881-82	15,700,704	25,146,260
1882-83	28,441,212	24,083,922
1883-84	32,242,770	25,377,379
1884-85	32,770,900	25,840,728
1885-86	29,160,835	26,991,805
1886-87	32,642,785	26,844,031
1887-88	30,286,247	25,862,977
1888-89	37,982,948	26,031,223
1889-90	37,912,848	24,328,326
1890-91	35,259,131	24,237,449
1891-92	46,272,391	25,527,018
1892-93	44,303,593	27,169,876
1893-94	36,012,950	30,185,612
1894-95	36,716,870	27,628,981
1895-96	46,722,823	22,634,788
	$616,741,920	$541,029,630

The preceding statement gives correct data of the exports of silver from the fiscal year 1874–1875 to the fiscal year 1895–1896, excepting the years 1875–1876 and 1876–1877, which are not included for want of data. The difference between the two amounts for these years is $75,712,290, showing the large proportion of silver which was not coined, and was exported in bullion.

The following statement shows that the export of Mexican silver reached almost its minimum in the year 1887–1888, and its maximum in the year 1892–1893, with the exception of the last one. The minimum coincided with the first sterling loan negotiated by Mexico; the second sterling loan negotiated in 1890 caused a decrease in the export of Mexican silver coin of 26 per cent., as compared with the previous fiscal year of 1889–1890.

The export of silver bullion has steadily increased since 1872–1873, until it was in 1895–1896 seventeen times as large as in the first named year. During the first fiscal year of those embraced in the above table, the export of silver bullion was 1.4 to 22.6 as compared with silver coin, and in the year 1895–1896 the proportion was 15.3 to 20.5. In the year 1872–1873 the export of silver bullion represented 6 per cent. of the total export of silver, while in the fiscal year 1895–1896 it represented 20 per cent.

The export of silver ore only began in the fiscal year 1886–1887.

EXPORTS OF SILVER FROM JULY 1ST, 1872, TO JUNE 30TH, 1896.

FISCAL YEARS.	COINS.	BULLION.	ORES.	OTHER FORMS.	TOTAL VALUE.
1872–1873..........................	$ 22,626,065	$ 1,459,426	$ 199,596	$ 8,716	$ 24,293,803
1873–1874..........................	17,021,405	1,217,853	240,769	1,359	18,481,386
1874–1875..........................	15,372,254	1,843,523	79,443	3,920	17,299,140
Average in three years.............	$ 18,339,908	$ 1,506,934	$ 173,269	$ 4,665	$ 20,024,776
1877–1878..........................	$ 18,120,297	$ 2,560,859	$ 19,920	$ 87	$ 20,701,163
1878–1879..........................	16,366,877	2,650,400	....	2,812	19,020,089
1879–1880..........................	16,783,317	3,040,079	....	581	19,823,977
1880–1881..........................	13,183,955	3,976,879	....	376	17,161,210
1881–1882..........................	11,607,888	3,540,994	10,129	5,079	15,163,990
Average in five years..............	$ 15,212,467	$ 3,153,842	$ 6,010	$ 1,787	$ 18,374,086
1882–1883..........................	$ 22,969,584	$ 4,773,928	$ 30,105	$ 113,537	$ 27,892,154
1883–1884..........................	25,999,876	5,311,310	67,815	111,112	31,490,113
1884–1885..........................	25,394,262	5,899,297	....	153,489	31,446,848
1885–1886..........................	21,060,958	5,261,502	1,800,873	145,070	29,186,403
1886–1887..........................	21,953,759	6,128,239	3,737,883	823,951	32,643,832
Average in five years..............	$ 23,657,488	$ 5,474,855	$ 1,129,135	$ 269,432	$ 30,531,870
1887–1888..........................	$ 7,794,245	$ 4,771,328	$ 4,547,250	$ 475,942	$ 27,588,765
1888–1889..........................	22,686,337	6,862,510	7,623,589	830,304	38,002,740
1889–1890..........................	23,084,489	7,628,831	6,394,662	804,869	37,912,851
1890–1891..........................	17,622,171	7,480,354	8,874,457	1,282,151	35,259,133
1891–1892..........................	26,478,376	7,853,757	10,478,264	3,237,116	48,047,513
Average in five years..............	$ 19,533,124	$ 6,919,356	$ 7,583,644	$ 1,326,076	$ 35,362,200
1892–1893..........................	$ 27,170,865	$ 8,126,593	$10,940,750	$ 9,008,215	55,246,423
1893–1894..........................	17,386,338	7,881,807	9,023,596	11,119,345	45,411,176
1894–1895..........................	17,077,119	18,803,876	10,935,353	835,875	47,652,223
1895–1896..........................	20,377,663	26,345,160	10,885,479	1,138,245	58,746,547
Average in four years..............	$ 20,502,996	$ 15,289,381	$10,446,294	$ 5,525,420	$ 51,764,092
Total in the twenty-two years.......	$429,047,100	$143,418,595	$85,898,933	$30,102,151	$688,471,479
Average for the twenty-two years...	$ 19,502,140	$ 6,519,027	$ 3,904,496	$ 1,368,279	$31,294,158

MEXICAN GOLD EXPORTS.

Our production of gold used to be very small for reasons already given, but the present high price of that metal is increasing considerably our output of the same.

The exports of gold from Mexico in the fiscal year ended June 30, 1896, amounted to $5,800,000, as declared by the Mexican Bureau of Statistics, but even this statement is not correct, as it needs the following additions, shown by experience and reliable authorities: about 15 per cent. for gold exports made without any return, 2 per cent. for undervaluation, 0.5 per cent. used in the arts in Mexico, 1 per cent., possibly more now, with the increasing prosperity of the country, retained in the banks, 2 per cent. in circulation, making a total of 20.5 per cent. to be added to the official return, which brings up the production of gold in Mexico to $6,989,000 for the year 1896 and even this figure is considered very low.

Mexican Gold Exported to the United States.—The United States is our principal market for the gold we produce.

The following statement furnished to me on February 6, 1897, by the Director of the Mint of the Treasury Department of the United States, contains the imports of gold bullion, ore and coin into the United States, as reported by the Collector of Customs, from 1891 to 1895, and from the fiscal years ending June 30, 1892, to June 30, 1896.

"IMPORTS OF GOLD BULLION, ORE AND COIN FROM MEXICO INTO THE UNITED STATES AS REPORTED BY COLLECTORS OF CUSTOMS.

YEARS.	ORE.	BULLION.	COIN.	TOTAL.
1891....................	$ 222,088	$1,192,183	$ 367,015	$ 1,781,286
1892....................	711,672	1,714,440	380,711	2,806,823
1893....................	507,647	1,566,728	265,315	2,339,690
1894....................	673,583	1,064,721	38,376	1,776,680
1895....................	997,221	2,435,296	34,217	3,466,734
Total................	$3,112,211	$7,973,368	$1,085,634	$12,171,213

" For additional information see *Report on Production of Precious Metals*, 1894, page 248, and the same report for 1895, page 289.

" Yours, R. D. Preston,

" Mint Bureau, February 6, 1897."

"IMPORTS OF GOLD ORE, BULLION AND COIN FROM MEXICO INTO THE UNITED STATES AS REPORTED BY COLLECTORS OF CUSTOMS.

FISCAL YEARS ENDING JUNE 30.	ORE.	BULLION.	COIN.	TOTAL.
1892....................	$ 246,849	$1,336,593	$ 542,499	$ 2,125,941
1893....................	886,284	1,923,565	300,012	3,109,861
1894....................	502,023	1,210,757	116,823	1,829,603
1895....................	810,066	1,635,852	36,835	2,482,753
1896....................	1,108,839	2,826,327	72,482	4,007,648
Total................	$3,554,061	$8,933,094	$1,068,651	$13,555,806

" Treasury Department, Mint Bureau, February 6, 1897."

Mr. Preston completed the above information with other data obtained from private parties in the following manner : communicated to me in a letter dated, February 6, 1897, enclosing the two preceding statements.

" I would add, for your information, that from returns received by this Bureau, from private refineries, and the deposits of foreign bullion at the Mints and Assay

Offices of the United States during the calendar years 1894 and 1895 the amount of gold credited to Mexico was reported to be as follows :

1894.

Reported by private refineries as extracted from Mexican ores and
bullion... $2,360,765
Gold bullion deposited at the United States Assay Office at New York...   735,787
Deposited at the Mint at San Francisco...............................   290,713

Total.. $3,387,265

1895.

Gold extracted from Mexican ores and bullion by private refineries....... $3,843,783
Gold deposited at the United States Assay Office at New York..........   560,775
Mexican gold bullion deposited at the United States Mint at San Francisco   504,745

Total.. $4,909,303

The preceding official data from the United States Treasury Department was not complete, as will appear from the following table prepared by the Bureau of Statistics of the Mexican Republic :

GOLD EXPORTED FROM MEXICO TO THE UNITED STATES.
CALENDAR YEARS.

	1891.	1892.	1893.	1894.	1895.	1896.
Gold ore...............	$ 16,700	$ 100,595	$ 113,548	$ 5,767	$ 87,695	$ 324,305
Coined..............	53,769	45,290	91,936	177,089	109,421	477,505
Bullion [1].............	497,400	279,699	99,415	1,606,152	4,368,898	6,851,564
Mixed [1]..............	....	126,184	257,761	144,515	....	528,460
Cyanide...............	....	....	....	....	31,231	31,231
Sulphite..............	....	....	....	....	3,026	3,026
According to information from Mexico.........	$ 567,869	$ 551,768	$ 562,660	$1,933,523	$4,600,271	$8,216,091
According to information from the United States	$1,781,286	2,806,823	2,339,690	1,776,680	3,466,734	12,171,213
Differences.............	+$1,213,417	+$2,255,055	+$1,777,030	− $ 156,843	−$1,133,537	+$3,955,122

FISCAL YEARS.

	1891–1892.	1892–1893.	1893–1894.	1894–1895.	1895–1896.	TOTAL.
Gold ore................	$ 31,289	$ 145,785	$ 55,799	$ 8,889	$ 160,555	$ 402,317
Coined..............	41,259	74,798	121,915	150,544	147,981	536,497
Bullion [1].	474,156	115,643	116,904	3,687,872	4,608,959	9,003,623
Mixed [1]..............	....	271,913	256,547	....	....	528,460
Cyanide...............	....	....	....	....	80,947	80,947
Sulphite..............	....	....	....	....	31,332	31,332
According to information from Mexico.........	$ 546,704	$ 608,138	$ 551,255	$3,847,305	$5,029,774	$10,583,176
According to information from the United States	2,125,941	3,109,861	1,829,603	2,482,753	4,007,648	13,555,806
Differences.............	+$1,579,237	+$2,501,723	+$1,278,348	−$1,364,552	−$1,022,126	+$2,972,630

[1] From the 1st of July, 1894, the " Bullion " includes the value of the gold contained in the mixed ore.

This instance shows how difficult it is for the commercial statistics of both countries to agree, even when the merchandise is entered with the same value in both as in the present case.

RAILWAYS.

The following table contains a list of all the railways, exclusive of the tramways, built in Mexico up to October 31, 1896, prepared by the Department of Communications of the United Mexican States :

OFFICIAL STATEMENT MADE BY THE DEPARTMENT OF COMMUNICATIONS OF THE MEXICAN GOVERNMENT OF THE RAILROAD MILEAGE IN OPERATION ON OCTOBER 31, 1896.

(1) The initials at the beginning of each line of this table stand for the guage of the railroads ; S. for standard, N. for narrow, and B. for both.

NAME.	DATE OF CONCESSION.	LENGTH.	FROM AND TO.
(1) S. Mexican.	Nov. 27, 1867	292.50	Mexico to Veracruz and Apizaco to Puebla.
S. Mérida to Progreso.	Jan. 17, 1874	22.65	Mérida to Progreso.
N. Hidalgo.	Feb. 2, 1878	92.43	Tepa to Sototlan, Tepa to Pachuca and San Augustin to Tepa.
B. Veracruz to Alvarado.	Mar. 26, 1878	43.75	Veracruz to Medellin and Medellin to Alvarado.
N. Mérida to Peto.	Mar. 27, 1878	68.97	Merida to Ingenio de Sta. Maria.
N. Interoceanic from Acapulco to Veracruz.	Apr. 16, 1878	489.74	Mexico to Veracruz, Mexico to Puente Ixtla by Morelos and branches of Virreyes to Libres and San Nicolas.
N. Puebla to Izucar de Matamoros.	May 6, 1878	52.39	Los Arcos to Cholula, Cholula to Atlixco and Atlixco to Matamoros.
S. Mexican Western.	Aug. 16, 1880	38.48	Culiacan to Altata.
S. Mexican Central.	Sept. 8, 1880	1,877.15	Mexico to Paso del Norte, Silao to Guanajuato, Irapuato to Guadalajara, Aguascalientes to Tampico, San Blas to Huaristemba and Guadalajara to Ameca.
N. Mexican National.	Sept. 13, 1880	1,056.16	Mexico to Laredo, Acambaro to Psatzcuaro, Matamoros to S. Miguel, Mexico to Salto, belt tramways from suburbs of Mexico called La Colonia extension to Salto.
N. Mexican National Construction Company.	Sept. 13, 1880	88.30	Manzanillo to Colima and Zacatecas to Ojo Caliente.
S. Sonora.	Sept. 14, 1880	262.40	Guaymas to Nogales.
N. Mérida to Valladolid.	Dec. 15, 1880	67.53	Merida to Valladolid and Progreso to Conkal.
N. Tlalmanalco.	Feb. 3, 1881	16.56	Tlalmanalco to Chalco and Amecameca.
N. Mérida to Campeche.	Feb. 23, 1881	97.80	Mérida to Campeche, Campeche to Calkini and connecting line with the railroad from Mérida to Progreso.

NAME.	DATE OF CONCESSION.	LENGTH.	FROM AND TO.
N. Campeche to Lerma.	Feb. 23, 1881	3.73	Campeche to Lerma.
S. Mexican International.	June 7, 1881	658.28	Porfirio Diaz City to Torreon and Durango, Sabinas to Hondo, Matamoros to Zaragoza, Hornos to San Pedro, branch from Velardeña and Monclova to Cuatro Cienegas.
N. Nautla to San Marcos.	June 25, 1881	47.22	San Marcos toward Nautla and branch to Libres.
N. San Juan Bautista to Paso del Carrizal.	Sept. 17, 1881	3.57	S. Juan Bautista to Tamulte.
S. Chalchicomula.	Sept. 20, 1881	6.43	San Andres Chalchicomula.
S. Orizaba to Ingenio.	Sept. 22, 1881	4.69	Orizaba to Ingenio.
S. Santa Ana to Tlaxcala.	Dec. 11, 1882	5.28	Santa Ana to Tlaxcala.
N. Cardenas to the River Grijalva.	May 12, 1883	4.66	Cardenas to the River Grijalva.
N. Toluca to San Juan de las Huertas.	May 25, 1883	9.77	Toluca to San Juan de las Huertas.
N. Vanegas, Cedral, Matehuala and Rio Verde.	June 11, 1883	40.39	Vanegas to Cedral and branch to Potrero.
S. Tehuacan to Esperanza.	Nov. 28, 1883	31.07	Esperanza to Tehuacan.
S. Mérida to Izamal.	May 15, 1884	40.91	Mérida to Izamal.
S. Chihuahua and Hidalgo to the Sierra Madre.	Nov. 13, 1884	6.83	Chihuahua to the Sierra Madre and Jimenez to Balleza.
N. Southern Mexican.	Apr. 21, 1886	228.00	Puebla to Oaxaca.
S. Tonala to Textla and Frontera.	Dec. 16, 1886	31.07	Tonala to Kilomete.
S. Lower California.	May 25, 1887	16.78	San Quintin to the Colorado River.
S. Monterey to the Gulf.	Nov. 10, 1887	388.12	Monterey to Treviño and Monterey to Tampico.
N. Tecolutla to Espinal.	Dec. 10, 1887	13.04	Tecolutla to Espinal.
S. Córdova to Tuxtepec.	May 19, 1888	31.69	Córdova to Motzorongo.
S. Pachuca to Tampico.	June 5, 1888	6.21	Isolated Branch.
N. Maravatío to Cuernavaca.	Aug. 16, 1888	40.84	Maravatío towards Cuernavaca and branches to Agangueo to Trojes.
N. Mexican Northeastern.	Aug. 28, 1888	31.12	Mexico to Tizayuca.
N. Salamanca to Jaral.	Aug. 30, 1888	21.75	Salamanca to Jaral.
N. Monte Alto.	Aug. 30, 1888	6.21	Tlalnepantla to Pedregal.
N. Veracruz to Boca del Rio.	Aug. 31, 1888	13.67	Veracruz to Boca del Rio.
S. National Tehuantepec.	Government Road.	192.38	Coatzacoalcas to Salina Cruz.
S. Ometusco to Pachuca.	May 25, 1889	28.40	Ometusco to Pachuca.
S. Puebla Industrial.	July 21, 1889	22.21	Puebla to Constancia, Cholula and Huejotzingo.
S. Tula to Pachuca.	Dec. 20, 1889	43.49	Tula to Pachuca.
S. Minero.	Mar. 20, 1890	80.94	Escalon to Sierra Mojada and branches.
S. Mexico to Cuernavaca and the Pacific.	May 30, 1890	58.65	Mexico to Tres Marias and Puente de Ixtla to Mexcala.
N. Mixcalco to Santa Cruz.	June 13, 1890	2.77	Mixcalco to Santa Cruz.

NAME.	DATE OF CONCESSION.	LENGTH.	FROM AND TO.
N. Izucar of Matamoros to Acapulco.	Nov. 21, 1890	24.85	Matamoros towards Acapulco.
N. Toluca to Tenango.	Nov. 24, 1891	4.35	Toluca to Tenango.
N. Hacienda of Xavaleta to the San Rafael Paper Factory.	Mar. 24, 1892	2.49	Hacienda of Xavaleta to San Rafael Paper Mill.
S. Esperanza to Xuchil.	Nov. 29, 1892	15.84	Esperanza to Xuchil Station.
N. Guanajuato to Dolores, Hidalgo and San Luis de la Paz.	May 24, 1893	6.21	Rincon on the National Railroad to San Luis de la Paz.
S. Villa Lerdo to San Pedro de la Colonia.	June 3, 1893	15.84	Villa Lerdo to Sacramento.
N. Celaya to the farms of Roque and Plancarte.	June 2, 1893	9.07	Celaya to the farms of Roque and Plancarte.
N. From La Compañia to the Zoquiapan farm.	June 13, 1893	5.17	La Compañia to the Zoquiapan farm.
S. Cazadero to Solis.	May 24, 1893	18.64	Cazadero to point between the stations of Solis and Tepetongo.
S. Industrial Railroads.	Dec. 18, 1895	1.86	Mexico to Xochimilco.
	Total.......	(1) 6,791.30	

(1) This amount does not include the tramways.

RESUME OF RAILWAYS IN MEXICO IN 1895.

	KILOMETERS.	MILES.
Railroads under Federal Grants............	10,723, k 113	6,663,022
Tramways	427, 583	265,687
Surburban Railways connecting towns.......	410, 164	254,863
Railroads belonging to private parties	87, 000	54,059
Portable Railroad, Decauville System.......	242, 252	150,527
Total.................	11,890,k 112	7,388,158

As I have already stated most of the roads built in Mexico have obtained large subsidies from the government, and that fact has contributed very materially to their present prosperous financial condition, as they have used the proceeds of the subsidy, not only to build the roads, but in some cases to pay the interest on their bonds. On the whole Mexican roads are very prosperous, and the following statements taken from the official reports of the principal roads shows their trade and earnings are increasing considerably.

The Mexican roads like the Mexican Government have been very much crippled by their obligation to pay in gold the interest on their bonds and dividends on their shares, and as they collect their freights in silver, they have to buy gold at current prices to pay their gold obligations, and the depreciation of silver causes them a very great loss, but notwithstanding that serious drawback, the increase in their business and earnings has been such as to place them in a position to meet their gold obligations.

I give below a statement of the traffic and receipts of the three principal railways in Mexico, namely : the Mexican Central, Mexican National, and Mexican International, which I have obtained directly from the respective companies. I also give similar statements from the other roads, which I have taken from statements published by the *Anuario Estadistico de la Republica Mexicana* of 1895.

Mexican Central.—The Mexican Central is the largest road so far built in Mexico. The whole of the main line was opened for traffic in 1884, and all figures for traffic previous to July 1, 1884, were thrown into Construction Accounts. The annexed statement of freights and earnings of this road begins therefore in 1885, and shows a decided increase every year. I also append a statement of the traffic and earnings of this road and its branch from Tula to Pachuca, from 1881 to 1895, taken from the *Anuario Estadistico de la Republica Mexicana* of 1895, which has been compiled from data furnished by the company to the Mexican Government. (See first table on page 197.)

EARNINGS OF THE MEXICAN CENTRAL RAILWAY FROM 1885 TO 1896.

MEXICAN CURRENCY.

CALENDAR YEAR.	MILEAGE OPERATED.	METRIC TONS FREIGHT.	FREIGHT EARNINGS.	NUMBER OF PASSENGERS.	PASSENGER EARNINGS.	ALL OTHER EARNINGS.	TOTAL GROSS EARNINGS.
1885.....	1,235.90	226,138	$ 2,287,410 14	512,272	$ 1,100,268 62	171,882 00	$ 3,559,560 76
1886.....	1,235.90	245,308	2,511,028 78	573,896	1,168,750 24	177,926 83	3,857,705 85
1887.....	1,235.90	346,808	3,458,006 46	601,393	1,235,284 05	193,288 16	4,886,578 67
1888.....	1,316.40	507,631	4,244,648 52	581,967	1,321,511 96	208,170 83	5,774,331 31
1889.....	1,461.85	540,546	4,683,290 74	675,144	1,420,375 76	233,558 88	6,337,225 38
1890.....	1,527.20	609,382	4,702,142 48	723,928	1,436,317 68	287,233 92	6,425,694 08
1891.....	1,665.11	867,657	5,625,668 51	742,993	1,470,940 51	277,929 00	7,374,538 02
1892.....	1,824.83	1,091,785	6,183,149 29	731,425	1,439,571 60	340,532 80	7,963,253 69
1893.....	1,846.64	860,187	6,130,347 06	792,025	1,443,793 73	407,627 52	7,981,768 31
1894.....	1,859.83	898,484	6,440,713 23	945,434	1,576,801 33	408,510 72	8,426,025 28
1895.....	1,859.83	1,047,038	7,145,041 44	1,030,911	1,828,072 61	522,751 63	9,495,865 68
1896.....	1,869.60	1,231,025	7,646,257 99	1,259,623	1,934,612 78	627,149 62	10,208,020 39
Total..	18,938.99	8,472,169	$61,057,704 64	9,171,011	$17,376,300 87	$3,856,561 91	$82,290,567 42

Mexican National.—The Mexican National obtained its first concession from the Mexican Government in 1877, but it was amended from time to time thereafter, until all the amended grants were grouped in the concession approved July 5, 1886, under which the road is now operated. The old companies did not print any reports, and there is no data running back further than the time when the bondholders took possession of the property at the foreclosure sale, which occurred in the City of Mexico on May 23, 1887. I give a statement of the traffic and earnings of the road from 1873 to 1895, taken from the *Anuario Estadistico de la Republica Mexicana* in 1895, which was compiled with data furnished to the Mexican Government by the company.

CENTRAL RAILWAY AND BRANCH FROM TULA TO PACHUCA.

YEARS.	PASSEN-GERS.	PASSENGER RECEIPTS.	FREIGHT.		MISCELLANEOUS RECEIPTS.	TOTAL RECEIPTS.
			Tons.	Kilos.		
1881.	303,543	$ 62,270 20	7,012	436	$ 33,413 44	$ 95,683 64
1882.	491,985	442,726 54	202,304	993	1,289,387 24	1,732,113 78
1883.	653,669	726,830 09	167,356	565	2,876,906 29	3,603,736 38
1884.	761,687	1,111,906 96	190,423	972	2,662,684 86	3,774,591 82
1885.	694,894	1,111,062 54	331,700	260	2,484,325 68	3,595,388 22
1886.	769,655	1,185,662 53	255,027	111	2,754,613 02	3,940,275 55
1887.	797,693	1,251,743 98	356,448	976	3,721,358 13	4,973,102 11
1888.	756,560	1,337,734 10	519,261	394	4,554,830 53	5,892,564 63
1889.	683,147	1,436,301 06	576,324	408	5,081,628 68	6,517,929 74
1890.	736,730	1,487,086 60	694,966	914	5,212,261 40	6,699,348 00
1891.	753,276	1,512,415 42	1,005,447	237	6,167,092 56	7,679,507 98
1892.	735,363	1,442,310 99	1,100,364	029	6,534,507 42	7,976,818 41
1893.	792,025	1,443,793 73	860,186	545	6,537,974 58	7,981,768 31
1894.	945,434	1,576,801 35	898,484	071	6,849,223 95	8,426,025 30
1895.	1,030,911	1,828,072 61	1,047,037	836	7,767,793 03	9,595,865 64
Total	10,906,572	$17,956,718 70	8,212,346	747	$64,528,000 81	$82,484,719 51

MEXICAN NATIONAL RAILROAD.

YEARS.	PAS-SENGERS.	PASSENGER RECEIPTS.	FREIGHT.		MISCEL-LANEOUS RECEIPTS.	TOTAL RECEIPTS.
			Tons.	Kilos.		
1873.	247,547	$ 17,425 65	....	....	....	$ 17,425 65
1874.	584,075	40,446 01	298	860	$ 298 86	40,744 87
1875.	486,788	43,027 18	221	140	221 14	43,248 32
1876.	486,000	43,437 24	698	245	709 41	44,146 65
1877.	565,572	52,759 84	346	499	275 75	53,035 59
1878.	529,333	71,193 68	3,209	097	3,845 61	75,039 29
1879.	535,806	74,277 07	8,102	920	15,329 07	89,606 14
1880.	466,897	91,505 23	18,191	400	41,983 90	133,489 13
1881.	903,049	124,452 13	26,234	150	47,320 00	171,772 13
1882.	900,855	225,267 21	105,549	146	229,586 51	454,853 72
1883.	1,071,835	341,614 87	140,185	779	366,320 26	707,935 13
1884.	878,878	517,316 80	254,804	000	743,423 74	1,260,740 54
1885.	839,573	492,822 92	177,179	000	803,291 20	1,296,114 12
1886.	891,711	538,359 97	132,661	000	1,018,018 51	1,556,378 48
1887.	884,541	537,520 17	307,435	000	1,120,950 34	1,658,470 51
1888.	907,113	691,915 03	370,300	527	1,880,684 24	2,572,599 27
1889.	929,685	864,309 90	430,166	055	2,640,418 14	3,504,728 04
1890.	937,527	887,437 19	487,598	563	2,684,550 59	3,561,987 78
1891.	998,617	994,951 69	515,164	143	3,057,891 00	4,052,842 69
1892.	1,012,786	973,768 72	605,545	610	3,643,784 47	4,617,553 19
1893.	935,167	972,488 57	571,524	780	3,191,146 37	4,163,634 94
1894.	576,574	865,698 53	527,440	000	3,246,375 07	4,112,073 60
1895.	926,516	1,005,515 55	642,535	071	3,426,841 93	4,432,357 48
Total	17,496,445	$10,467,511 15	5,325,390	985	$28,152,266 11	$38,609,777 26

STATEMENT OF EARNINGS AND EXPENSES OF THE MEXICAN NATIONAL RAILWAY, FROM 1889 TO 1896 INCLUSIVE.

ROAD OPENED FOR THROUGH TRAFFIC IN NOVEMBER, 1888.

MEXICAN CURRENCY.

EARNINGS FROM	1889.	1890.	1891.	1892.	1893.	1894.	1895.	1896.
Freight	$2,612,509 38	$2,654,208 04	$2,956,817 91	$3,474,405 42	$2,956,148 19	$3,087,466 29	$3,129,461 43	$3,871,117 08
Passenger and Mail	869,133 94	902,023 41	1,020,627 10	994,071 43	985,399 34	924,454 28	1,010,047 75	1,010,150 14
Express	127,822 31	129,151 00	156,670 31	179,623 45	199,730 71	227,939 76	262,014 13	278,138 62
Telegraph	17,715 31	20,509 92	23,358 12	24,738 14	22,305 98	25,834 93	34,775 78	58,318 06
Miscellaneous	32,943 30	49,073 99	48,949 30	83,191 50	61,219 89	63,383 39	76,906 82	81,301 87
Total	$3,660,124 24	$3,754,966 36	$4,206,422 74	$4,756,029 94	$4,224,804 11	$4,329,078 65	$4,513,205 91	$5,299,025 77
Operating Expenses	2,993,431 54	2,927,961 89	3,047,401 56	3,055,416 55	2,586,366 45	2,437,116 41	2,441,797 41	2,773,068 06
Net Earnings	666,692 70	827,004 47	1,159,021 18	1,700,613 39	1,638,437 66	1,891,962 24	2,071,408 50	2,525,957 71
Per cent. of Earnings for Operation	81 78	77 97	72 45	64 24	61 22	56 30	54 10	52 33
Expenditure for Extraordinary Repairs and Replacements		135,194 15	419,955 87	149,080 83	151,612 22	93,451 32	121,534 70	156,586 37
Gold Purchases taken up in Exchange Account	25,887 88	18,338 25 Gain.	64,745 18	310,777 59	542,802 54	885,149 80	861,681 42	991,760 43

I also append a statement of the freights, passengers, express, tele-
graphs, and miscellaneous receipts, as well as the expenses and earnings of the road from the year 1889 to 1896, taken from the last
official report of the companies. It will be noticed that the traffic and
receipts of this road, like the Central, have been steadily increasing
from the time at which it began to be operated. (See table on page 198.)

MEXICAN INTERNATIONAL RAILROAD COMPANY.
GROSS EARNINGS IN MEXICAN MONEY.

YEAR.	NO. OF PASS'G'RS.	PASSENGER RECEIPTS.	FREIGHT.		FREIGHT RECEIPTS.	TOTAL RECEIPTS.
			Tons.	Kilos.		
From Dec. 3d, 1883–1884.....	15,942	$ 32,408 45	15,129	723	$ 37,575 00	$ 69,983 45
1885.....	9,853	25,881 44	50,896	181	118,177 80	144,059 24
1886.....	10,411	29,242 61	55,877	079	144,311 09	173,553 70
1887.....	9,796	32,516 71	86,889	772	189,184 86	221,701 57
1888.....	41,170	125,848 48	116,561	273	459,906 57	585,755 05
1889.....	53,194	140,676 05	180,544	270	691,477 04	832,153 09
1890.....	59,327	149,258 43	222,856	211	894,944 35	1,044,202 78
1891.....	64,641	170,304 00	216,465	739	956,546 91	1,126,850 91
1892.....	60,967	181,378 14	390,802	838	1,836,958 51	2,018,336 65
1893.....	74,577	219,624 38	335,200	769	1,743,140 42	1,962,764 80
1894.....	77,456	208,551 86	376,734	430	1,873,974 91	2,082,526 77
1895.....	102,858	276,514 04	469,641	859	2,197,463 36	2,473,977 40
1896.....	111,480	313,904 13	525,951	874	2,453,223 54	2,767,127 67
Total..	691,672	$1,906,108 72	3,043,552	018	$13,596,884 36	$15,502,993 08

MEXICAN INTERNATIONAL RAILWAY.
(STATEMENT FURNISHED BY THE COMPANY.)

YEAR.	AVERAGE KILOMETRES OPERATED.	GROSS EARNINGS.	AVERAGE EARNINGS PER KILOMETRE.	AVERAGE EARNINGS PER MILE.
1884..................	245.20	$ 103,307 98	$ 421 49	$ 612 37
1885..................	273.58	153,916 18	562 59	905 39
1886..................	273.58	185,150 25	676 76	1,098 11
1887..................	273.58	237,394 13	867 73	1,396 43
1888..................	573.97	656,781 41	1,144 28	1,841 47
1889..................	636 34	911,698 51	1,432 73	2,305 64
1890..................	637.38	1,126,366 41	1,745 64	2,839 77
1891..................	658.30	1,197,856 55	1,819 69	2,924 02
1892..................	746.37	2,095,726 14	2,807 89	4,518 67
1893..................	922.19	2,050,934 01	2,226 15	3,579 04
1894..................	922.19	2,169,121 47	2,352 14	3,785 29
1895..................	947.23	2,664,126 08	2,812 54	4,526 28
1896..................	1,011.02	2,900,925 33	2,869 30	4,617 69
Total.........	8,120.93	$16,453,304 45	$21,738 93	$34,950 17

Mexican International. The Mexican International, which has been
built without any subsidy from the Mexican Government, was opened
for traffic in 1883, and its traffic and receipts, like the other two roads,
have steadily increased. I append two statements of this road; the

first, furnished me by the company, embraces its traffic and earnings from 1883 to 1896 ; and the second is another statement furnished me also by the company, showing the average kilometres operated, gross earnings, average earnings per kilometre, and average earnings per mile from the years 1884 to 1896. (See the two tables on page 199.)

Mexican Southern Railway.—I give below a statement of the number of passengers, amount of freight and earnings of the Mexican Southern Railway, furnished to me by the Company, embracing nine months of the year 1893 and the whole of 1894, as before the 1st of April, 1893, the road was run by the Contractors, and the Company has no data in their possession. I also append a statement taken from the *Anuario Estadistico de la Republica Mexicana* of 1895, embracing the traffic and

MEXICAN SOUTHERN RAILWAY.

MONTHS.	PASSEN-GERS.	PASSENGER RECEIPTS.	FREIGHT.		FREIGHT RECEIPTS.	TOTAL RECEIPTS.
			Tons.	Kilos.		
1893.						
January	....	....	......	.....	....	....
February	....	....	......	.....	....	....
March.......	....	....	......	.....	....	....
April........	12,099	$ 14,647 21	2,554	810	$ 20,243 01	$ 38,172 41
May	9,943	11,683 15	2,262	790	15,421 87	29,506 27
June	8,154	7,119 78	1,344	950	9,541 00	18,209 89
July.........	11,865	8,740 20	1,355	420	5,707 05	16,671 95
August	10,375	9,577 91	2,568	330	23,762 64	35,959 30
September...	10,405	9,751 47	2,019	000	17,322 40	30,947 32
October	10,897	10,317 54	2,145	150	16,941 41	29,945 71
November ...	11,893	12,661 99	3,296	070	16,276 89	31,839 26
December ...	14,452	17,096 43	2,943	420	15,702 01	38,308 76
Total	100,083	$101,595 68	20,489	940	$140,918 28	$269,560 87

Number of Passengers according to official Tables........ 142,919.
" Tons " " " .... 27,917,510 k.

MONTHS.	PASSEN-GERS.	PASSENGER RECEIPTS.	FREIGHT.		FREIGHT RECEIPTS.	TOTAL RECEIPTS.
			Tons.	Kilos.		
1894.						
January	15,255	$ 16,146 67	3,187	880	$ 20,083 75	$ 39,725 34
February	14,900	14,925 48	3,060	140	22,616 16	40,935 29
March.......	29,545	21,348 92	3,744	290	25,224 36	50,001 11
April........	16,527	17,195 89	4,010	380	25,184 73	45,742 46
May	18,229	14,864 75	4,322	880	21,406 14	39,720 18
June........	20,543	15,173 98	3,942	590	23,279 97	42,037 56
July	19,471	14,023 23	3,828	110	20,637 28	38,168 24
August......	18,218	14,602 85	3,515	420	17,531 15	35,709 56
September...	18,653	15,354 80	3,189	740	16,285 34	35,156 99
October	17,814	14,954 13	2,973	510	19,374 02	38,068 95
November ...	16,300	14,257 08	2,453	800	17,145 58	34,691 02
December ...	20,994	18,776 23	2,682	690	17,900 02	40,519 83
Total	226,449	$191,624 01	40,911	430	$246,668 50	$480,476 53

earnings of the Company during the years from 1890 to 1895, taken
from data furnished by the Company to the Department of Communications of Mexico.

MEXICAN SOUTHERN.

YEARS.	PASSEN-GERS.	PASSENGER RECEIPTS.	MERCHANDISE.		OTHER RECEIPTS.	TOTAL RECEIPTS.
			Tons.	Kilos.		
1890.........	......	......	......	....	....	....
1891.........	76,788	$74,259 78	11,506	820	$ 59,427 26	$ 133,687 04
1892.........	104,296	109,011 90	26,977	490	152,859 11	261,871 01
1893.........	143,037	153,233 01	27,921	510	246,862 75	400,095 76
1894.........	225,447	191,624 01	40,911	430	246,668 50	438,292 51
1895........	218,213	196,462 34	36,511	210	287,426 59	483,888 93
Total......	767,781	$724,591 04	143,828	460	$993,244 21	$1,717,835 25

Other Railroads. The following statement shows the traffic and
earnings of the Mexican, Interoceanic, Sonora, and minor railroads in
Mexico, taken from the *Anuario Estadistico de la Republica Mexicana*
of 1895, compiled from data furnished by the respective companies to
the Department of Communications of the Mexican Government.

MEXICAN RAILROAD.

YEARS.	PASSEN-GERS.	PASSENGER RECEIPTS.	MERCHANDISE.		OTHER RECEIPTS.	TOTAL RECEIPTS.
			Tons.	Kilos.		
1873...	476,287	$ 482,565 39	150,473	812	$ 1,348,344 49	$ 1,830,909 88
1874...	459,601	467,816 73	121,935	229	1,887,028 76	2,354,845 49
1875...	267,776	476,546 91	136,632	65	1,970,008 55	2,446,555 46
1876...	245,675	380,018 73	132,216	831	1,841,717 53	2,221,736 26
1877...	300,591	533,520 58	158,537	56	2,255,466 03	2,788,986 61
1878...	279,893	518,318 74	169,287	672	2,440,513 39	2,958,832 13
1879...	293,179	517,711 92	190,908	638	2,823,013 02	3,340,724 94
1880...	323,088	548,941 72	219,930	162	3,242,343 11	3,791,284 83
1881...	331,749	587,135 85	278,942	924	4,433,648 24	5,020,784 09
1882...	385,621	696,235 87	333,979	556	5,396,090 55	6,092,326 42
1883...	409,098	710,636 88	373,389	634	5,115,639 84	5,826,276 72
1884...	389,421	655,458 83	236,030	480	3,191,916 10	3,847,374 93
1885...	377,512	603,886 11	246,169	949	2,812,764 22	3,416,650 33
1886...	367,260	604,278 41	266,432	333	2,714,082 96	3,318,361 37
1887...	380,153	655,312 23	301,185	300	3,141,903 40	3,797,215 63
1888...	393,679	694,138 08	351,070	36	3,352,439 37	4,046,577 45
1889...	444,149	765,118 71	391,627	274	3,512,566 64	4,277,685 35
1890...	502,139	701,916 00	443,794	979	3,565,083 50	4,266,999 50
1891...	620,988	832,185 94	464,123	453	3,239,764 53	4,071,950 47
1892...	628,591	797,878 35	408,709	417	2,286,389 71	3,084,268 06
1893...	629,892	768,616 68	387,400	277	2,140,061 75	2,908,678 43
1894...	717,076	857,525 26	433,637	485	2,063,486 26	2,921,011 52
1895...	772,139	993,016 63	453,294	579	2,087,844 19	3,080,860 82
Total.	9,995,557	$14,848,780 55	6,649,709	141	$66,862,116 14	$81,710,896 69

INTEROCEANIC RAILWAY.

YEARS.	PASSENGERS.	PASSENGER RECEIPTS.	MERCHANDISE.		OTHER RECEIPTS.	TOTAL RECEIPTS.
			Tons.	Kilos.		
1880.....	228,053	$65,277 91	11,431	145	$ 36,515 46	$ 101,793 37
1881.....	367,116	105,083 31	49,942	548	159,535 64	264,618 95
1882.....	411,090	111,029 25	53,382	385	258,221 05	369,250 30
1883.....	406,016	223,049 58	56,822	222	356,906 46	579,956 04
1884.....	634,306	247,528 50	131,385	319	407,593 64	655,122 14
1885.....	606,510	240,233 70	167,970	265	436,345 10	676,578 80
1886.....	569,421	224,815 19	148,001	913	482,003 18	706,818 37
1887.....	621,295	239,812 48	174,194	156	570,033 20	809,845 68
1888....	673,169	254,809 77	200,386	400	658,063 22	912,872 99
1889.....	596,812	271,562 69	190,902	920	710,848 78	982,411 47
1890.....	657,616	383,107 10	288,836	358	1,153,999 13	1,537,106 23
1891.....	795,625	456,685 80	282,311	491	1,176,562 22	1,633,248 02
1892.....	799,487	466,799 31	367,762	660	1,376,488 38	1,843,287 69
1893.....	879,005	486,075 54	383,503	000	1,705,859 74	2,191,935 28
1894.....	881,810	491,914 20	440,648	000	1,912,192 58	2,404,106 78
1895.....	906,550	491,388 67	464,975	000	1,771,268 92	2,262,657 59
Total..	10,033,881	4,759,173 00	3,412,455	782	13,172,436 70	17,931,609 70

SONORA RAILWAY.

YEARS.	PASSENGERS.	PASSENGER RECEIPTS.	MERCHANDISE.		OTHER RECEIPTS.	TOTAL RECEIPTS.
1881.....	....	$ 11,303 29	....	.....	$ 17,254 95	$ 28,558 24
1882.....	....	68,410 83	....	.....	157,694 60	226,105 43
1883.....	33,464	99,461 33	24,202	791	119,347 56	218,808 89
1884.....	36,428	87,793 47	21,115	382	108,531 43	196,324 90
1885.....	47,271	101,918 90	29,927	682	193,189 89	295,108 79
1886.....	45,298	98,613 06	33,635	621	191,981 24	290,594 30
1887.....	38,189	87,098 20	34,660	670	193,981 40	281,079 60
1888.....	38,335	84,143 57	37,621	60	204,146 63	288,290 20
1889... .	44,691	104,367 85	43,321	710	239,697 67	344,065 52
1890.....	48,196	97,662 48	46,147	870	259,360 01	357,022 49
1891.....	56,565	112,919 18	53,947	663	332,938 65	445,857 83
1892.....	54,621	119,784 37	58,867	359	363,128 91	482,913 28
1893.....	52,678	126,657 56	63,687	055	393,319 17	519,976 73
1895.....	62,715	141,744 09	69,982	389	469,950 09	611,694 18
Total...	558,451	1,341,878 18	517,117	252	3,244,522 20	4,586,400 38

HIDALGO AND NORTHEASTERN RAILWAY.

YEARS.	PASSENGERS.	PASSENGER RECEIPTS.	MERCHANDISE.		OTHER RECEIPTS.	TOTAL RECEIPTS.
1881.....	39,759	$ 9,897 17	2,264	000	$ 1,659 36	$ 11,556 53
1882.. ...	30,940	12,270 02	7,624	000	10,442 30	22,712 32
1883.....	37,198	25,715 04	17,852	283	33,220 80	58,933 84
1884.....	35,209	32,648 22	34,958	222	54,955 16	87,603 38
1885.....	51,823	32,295 08	40,960	794	76,710 43	109,005 51
1886.....	44,666	36,692 27	51,760	395	117,603 55	154,295 82
1887.....	53,958	43,582 66	65,524	057	145,702 22	189,284 88
1888.....	55,055	45,805 05	77,203	173	161,773 18	207,578 23
1889.....	90,241	90,194 56	100,110	733	262,081 27	352,275 83
1890.....	113,605	106,397 87	137,467	201	328,124 49	434,522 36
1891.....	127,972	120,128 18	176,432	664	404,735 74	524,863 92
1892.....	148,540	141,360 09	186,041	471	422,052 91	563,413 00
1893.....	168,422	161,908 45	178,174	047	468,566 69	630,475 14
1894.....	214,837	178,477 10	200,685	687	643,700 93	822,178 03
1895.....	206,194	181,043 96	164,176	000	616,641 61	797,685 57
Total...	1,418,419	$1,218,415 72	1,441,234	727	$3,747,970 64	$4,966,384 36

MÉRIDA AND PROGRESO RAILWAY.

YEARS.	PASSEN-GERS.	PASSENGER RECEIPTS.	MERCHANDISE.		OTHER RECEIPTS.	TOTAL RECEIPTS.
			Tons.	Kilos.		
1881......	56,085	$ 28,639 50	....	......	$ 53,236 00	$ 81,875 50
1882......	84,016	37,642 38	41,934	297	75,242 88	112,885 26
1883......	83,231	36,239 83	59,859	715	108,248 80	144,488 63
1884......	87,159	37,940 54	95,962	902	139,299 59	177,240 13
1885......	64,173	29,078 41	79,611	737	120,389 13	149,467 54
1886......	77,139	33,353 16	58,239	254	78,168 66	111,521 82
1887......	85,044	22,844 42	46,055	714	52,995 68	75,840 10
1888......	109,997	29,812 76	30,872	512	64,291 88	94,104 64
1889......	158,534	56,763 81	44,619	200	97,017 37	153,781 18
1890......	162,701	55,566 97	53,949	818	89,139 81	144,706 78
1891......	129,989	46,155 85	34,486	000	67,460 18	113,616 03
1892......	108,119	36,528 45	28,656	499	83,593 75	120,132 20
1893......	91,291	39,276 08	34,406	476	96,230 47	135,506 55
1894......	79,653	33,387 18	38,659	401	68,513 05	101,900 23
1895......	....	38,228 81	....	......	97,850 38	136,079 19
Total...	1,377,131	$561,458 15	647,313	525	$1,291,677 63	$1,853,135 78

TEHUACAN AND ESPERANZA RAILWAY.

YEARS.	PASSEN-GERS.	PASSENGER RECEIPTS.	Tons.	Kilos.	OTHER RECEIPTS.	TOTAL RECEIPTS.
1884.....	18,343	$ 11,427 64	6,043	813	$ 32,921 87	$ 44,349 51
1885.....	15,049	10,077 20	5,857	257	31,905 66	41,982 86
1886.....	12,942	9,111 04	6,603	705	38,271 80	47,382 84
1887.....	14,848	10,080 15	7,669	730	47,437 77	57,517 92
1888.....	17,116	15,376 57	8,764	045	54,500 93	69,877 50
1889.....	19,385	20,673 00	9,858	360	61,564 09	82,237 09
1890.....	20,462	18,459 96	16,625	870	75,744 37	94,204 33
1891.....	17,426	11,087 06	14,381	340	68,684 08	79,771 14
1892.....	15,102	8,792 35	4,179	510	44,602 09	53,394 44
1893.....	16,096	9,411 51	5,663	530	37,997 45	47,408 96
1894.	....	....	....	......	....	....
1895.....	19,905	10,941 81	4,062	500	18,724 99	29,666 80
Total...	186,674	$135,438 29	89,709	660	$512,355 10	$647,793 39

MÉRIDA AND PETO RAILWAY.

YEARS.	PASSEN-GERS.	PASSENGER RECEIPTS.	Tons.	Kilos.	OTHER RECEIPTS.	TOTAL RECEIPTS.
1881.....	22,852	$ 3,913 69	....	......	$ 430 60	$ 4,344 29
1882.....	81,102	12,293 58	....	......	2,637 41	14,930 99
1883.....	88,920	14,422 31	5,654	115	4,833 23	19,255 54
1884.....	81,566	17,818 29	11,063	915	11,588 49	29,406 78
1885.....	64,118	16,795 70	16,919	464	20,222 10	37,017 80
1886.....	62,983	16,728 82	17,368	079	21,710 91	38,439 73
1887.....	62,763	15,943 55	15,827	969	26,619 71	42,563 26
1888.....	92,773	22,146 61	20,231	714	37,013 76	59,160 37
1889.....	99,761	25,351 70	25,397	822	52,553 95	77,905 65
1890.....	126,978	24,514 70	30,024	477	69,390 02	93,904 72
1891.....	134,438	55,007 97	27,106	666	85,602 24	140,610 21
1892.....	129,163	59,742 62	28,266	475	118,214 20	177,956 82
1893.....	163,852	71,970 64	36,202	439	128,115 61	200,086 25
1894.....	157,311	70,898 03	32,260	765	121,547 79	192,445 82
1895.....	140,193	67,134 69	37,853	723	118,179 11	185,313 80
Total...	1,508,773	$494,682 90	304,177	623	$818,659 13	$1,313,342 03

SINALOA AND DURANGO (ALTATA TO CULIACAN) RAILWAY.

YEARS.	PASSEN-GERS.	PASSENGER RECEIPTS.	FREIGHT.		MISCELLA-NEOUS RECEIPTS.	TOTAL RECEIPTS.
			Tons.	Kilos.		
1882.....	2,727	$ 3,712 04	1,864	589	$ 5,155 65	$ 8,867 69
1883.....	12,251	7,816 94	3,913	457	18,717 39	26,534 33
1884.....	21,776	8,584 57	5,962	325	25,019 62	33,604 19
1885.....	15,816	8,786 88	4,953	364	19,719 92	28,506 80
1886.....	23,171	10,681 46	4,316	116	20,880 39	31,561 85
1887.....	25,487	10,705 56	5,962	325	16,661 71	27,367 27
1888.....	27,904	11,459 15	6,736	532	23,650 34	35,109 49
1889.....	21,850	9,318 46	6,535	236	25,537 79	34,856 25
1890.....	42,987	14,871 77	4,722	749	18,911 41	33,783 18
1891.....	54,678	19,170 23	7,442	886	25,381 35	44,551 58
1892.....	39,494	14,837 39	10,371	701	28,131 17	42,968 56
1893.....	56,503	14,152 07	12,893	822	35,205 12	49,357 19
1894.....	38,451	14,040 41	12,093	568	38,393 29	52,433 70
1895.....	37,627	15,768 25	8,538	024	29,390 59	45,158 84
Total...	420,722	$163,905 18	96,306	694	$330,755 74	$494,660 92

MÉRIDA AND CAMPECHE RAILWAY.

1883.....	22,944	$ 3,586 10	462	169	$ 1,120 32	$ 4,706 42
1884.....	97,295	13,161 59	3,952	565	5,203 67	18,365 26
1885.....	76,135	12,535 94	7,794	570	9,306 31	21,842 25
1886.....	65,274	10,779 44	6,265	722	9,579 90	20,359 34
1887.....	68,883	11,793 63	8,106	813	13,263 22	25,056 85
1888.....	86,329	22,172 11	11,514	018	21,106 70	43,278 81
1889.....	58,383	17,017 46	12,534	035	28,300 44	45,317 90
1890.....	75,496	28,939 04	6,779	458	19,057 69	47,996 73
1891.....	96,994	35,303 04	17,328	478	36,035 70	71,338 74
1892.....	87,954	33,598 11	17,363	510	39,330 26	72,928 37
1893.....	124,983	56,034 03	21,775	101	53,390 97	109,425 00
1894.....	....	....	....	......	....	....
1895.....	139,349	66,174 14	24,699	277	72,923 31	139,097 45
Total...	1,000,019	$311,094 63	138,575	716	$308,618 49	$ 619,713 12

MÉRIDA AND VALLADOLID RAILWAY.

1883.....	18,123	$ 2,570 17	....	......	$ 609 18	$ 3,179 35
1884.....	75,541	12,595 63	4,248	788	5,287 96	17,883 59
1885.....	100,015	18,548 61	6,040	957	8,487 63	27,036 24
1886.....	132,210	25,798 73	25,181	498	33,276 45	59,075 18
1887.....	176,501	32,298 87	41,496	479	58,096 41	90,395 28
1888.....	183,973	37,957 45	35,975	207	65,864 26	103,821 71
1889.....	280,348	58,691 70	54,206	189	115,032 74	173,724 44
1890.....	295,034	63,485 18	50,781	662	96,611 23	160,096 41
1891.....	264,781	60,366 76	47,064	535	98,212 31	158,579 07
1892.....	254,344	61,573 70	46,124	159	134,209 85	195,783 55
1893.....	244,040	79,223 48	50,633	534	139,384 68	218,608 16
1894.....	....	....	....	......	....	....
1895.....	199,670	72,828 22	62,342	134	165,983 26	238,811 48
Total...	2,224,580	$525,938 50	424,095	142	$921,055 96	$1,446,994 46

TLALMANALCO RAILWAY.

YEARS.	PASSEN-GERS.	PASSENGER RECEIPTS.	FREIGHT.		MISCELLA-NEOUS RECEIPTS.	TOTAL RECEIPTS.
			Tons.	Kilos.		
1883.....	39,688	$ 4,022 44	10,813	000	$ 5,564 91	$ 9,587 35
1884.....	40,211	4,596 80	9,641	000	7,276 95	11,873 75
1885.....	41,226	4,577 43	7,466	713	6,830 06	11,407 49
1886.....	41,905	4,621 28	6,845	349	6,360 51	10,981 79
1887.....	47,808	5,098 09	8,083	538	6,788 75	11,886 84
1888.....	46,150	5,076 07	10,722	122	9,164 56	14,241 53
1889.....	49,866	5,536 16	13,710	170	11,566 53	17,102 69
1890.....	55,345	6,654 20	24,988	131	12,019 62	18,673 82
1891.....	61,236	6,765 86	15,469	050	12,684 68	19,450 54
1892.....	62,618	7,225 65	12,303	020	9,853 83	17,079 48
1893.....	60,835	6,492 30	18,572	715	15,430 59	21,922 89
1894.....	....	....	....	....	....	....
1895.....	71,777	7,358 10	13,824	250	12,284 66	19,642 76
Total...	618,665	$68,025 28	152,439	058	$115,825 65	$183,850 93

SAN JUAN BAUTISTA AND CARRIZAL PASSENGER RAILWAY.

YEARS.	PASSEN-GERS.	PASSENGER RECEIPTS.	FREIGHT.		MISCELLA-NEOUS RECEIPTS.	TOTAL RECEIPTS.
			Tons.	Kilos.		
1888.....	99,504	$ 5,123 13	....	.....	....	$ 5,123 13
1889.....	56,880	4,406 10	....	.....	....	4,406 10
1890.....	110,731	6,733 92	1,022	000	$1,022 60	7,756 52
1891.....	105,251	7,923 34	922	000	922 79	8,846 13
1892.....	152,606	9,462 23	1,803	000	1,442 28	10,904 51
1893.....	150,243	9,965 56	2,052	000	1,842 70	11,808 26
1894.....	....	....	.....	....	....	....
1895.....	167,994	12,003 21	3,455	454	3,131 00	15,134 21
Total...	843,209	$55,617 49	9,254	454	$8,361 37	$63,978 86

SAN ANDRÉS AND CHALCHICOMULA RAILWAY.

YEARS.	PASSEN-GERS.	PASSENGER RECEIPTS.	FREIGHT.		MISCELLA-NEOUS RECEIPTS.	TOTAL RECEIPTS.
			Tons.	Kilos.		
1882.....	6,851	$ 1,905 53	1,658	614	$ 2,847 76	$ 4,753 29
1883.....	15,053	4,002 51	4,802	280	9,548 51	13,551 02
1884.....	14,218	3,683 23	4,485	960	11,681 15	15,364 38
1885.....	10,928	2,834 42	4,723	310	4,805 87	7,640 29
1886.....	9,994	2,595 58	4,079	294	4,980 84	7,576 42
1887.....	9,794	2,428 25	5,835	696	6,850 94	9,279 19
1888.....	10,173	2,489 80	8,324	735	9,592 88	12,082 68
1889. ...	12,727	3,137 07	5,832	417	7,100 57	10,237 64
1890.....	13,010	3,163 15	4,385	480	6,225 35	9,388 50
1891.....	12,711	3,079 10	6,258	307	8,140 76	11,219 86
1892.....	12,223	6,327 21	7,980	430	9,376 67	15,703 88
1893.....	12,239	3,061 75	10,011	250	11,474 05	14,535 80
1894.....	13,998	3,398 65	7,781	980	9,266 42	12,665 07
1895.....	13,454	3,444 35	....	....	10,383 00	13,827 35
Total..	167,373	$45,550 60	76,159	753	$112,274 77	$157,825 37

ORIZABA AND INGENIO RAILWAY.

YEARS.	PASSEN-GERS.	PASSENGER RECEIPTS.	FREIGHT.		MISCELLA-NEOUS RECEIPTS.	TOTAL RECEIPTS.
			Tons,	Kilos.		
1882.....	38,636	$ 4,473 30	....	....	$	$ 4,473 30
1883.....	91,949	10,645 94	237	168	197 64	10,843 58
1884.....	94,323	10,920 74	360	972	300 82	11,221 56
1885.....	34,921	4,365 12	435	720	363 10	4,728 22
1886.....	86,047	9,962 57	384	813	350 18	10,312 75
1887.....	40,364	4,673 38	121	344	101 12	4,774 50
1888.....	41,945	4,800 00	182	400	152 00	4,952 00
1889.....	46,640	5,400 00	168	000	140 00	5,540 00
1890.....	106,773	12,362 20	504	000	420 00	12,782 20
1891.....	103,011	12,532 10	612	000	510 00	13,042 10
1892.....	99,553	13,303 20	750	000	728 36	14,031 56
1893.....	104,030	13,900 50	....	....	400 00	14,300 50
1894.....	104,019	13,990 77	704	000	528 00	14,518 77
1895.....	132,650	17,438 04	748	000	561 00	17,999 04
Total..	1,124,861	$138,767 86	5,208	417	$4,752 22	$143,520 08

SANTA ANA AND TLAXCALA RAILWAY.

YEARS.	PASSEN-GERS.	PASSENGER RECEIPTS.	FREIGHT.		MISCELLA-NEOUS RECEIPTS.	TOTAL RECEIPTS.
			Tons,	Kilos.		
1883.....	58,068	$ 2,860 20	....	....	$ 494 38	$ 3,354 58
1884.....	117,560	8,580 60	....	....	1,494 14	10,074 74
1885.....	174,204	12,714 98	....	....	1,483 00	14,197 98
1886.....	156,676	6,733 14	....	....	1,482 37	8,215 51
1887.....	117,518	8,463 85	....	....	1,373 25	9,837 10
1888.....	120,910	9,179 28	....	....	1,651 02	10,830 30
1889.....	110,574	8,294 98	....	....	1,475 20	9,770 18
1890.....	145,263	8,398 00	....	....	1,469 82	9,867 82
1891.....	66,716	9,098 30	....	....	1,769 28	10,867 58
1892.....	55,768	7,011 74	750	000	1,280 03	8,291 77
1893.....	59,127	7,326 40	3,829	003	2,434 13	9,760 53
1894.....	....	....	....	....	....	....
1895.....	71,843	8,670 35	2,038	440	2,344 38	11,014 73
Total..	1,254,227	$ 97,331 82	6,617	443	$18,751 00	$116,082 82

CÁRDENAS AND RIO GRIJALVA RAILWAY.

YEARS.	PASSEN-GERS.	PASSENGER RECEIPTS.	FREIGHT.		MISCELLA-NEOUS RECEIPTS.	TOTAL RECEIPTS.
			Tons,	Kilos.		
1886.....	....	$ 263 01	....	....	$ 526 00	$ 789 01
1887.....	....	401 43	....	....	722 57	1,124 00
1888.....	....	309 07	....	....	781 13	1,090 20
1889.....	....	216 72	....	....	839 69	1,056 41
1890.....	....	380 00	....	....	839 69	1,219 69
1891.....	.... ..	480 00	....	....	939 69	1,419 69
1892.....	....	....	....	....	....	....
1893.....	....	....	....	....	....	....
1884.....	....	....	....	....	....	....
1895.....	....	....	....	....	....	....
Total..	....	2,050 23	....	....	$4,648 77	$6,699 00

TOLUCA AND SAN JUAN DE LAS HUERTAS RAILWAY

YEARS.	PASSEN-GERS.	PASSENGER RECEIPTS.	FREIGHT.		MISCELLA-NEOUS RECEIPTS.	TOTAL RECEIPTS.
			Tons.	Kilos.		
1885.....	75,052	$ 7,016 39	....	....	$ 1,138 19	$ 8,154 58
1886.....	97,535	9,078 95	6,133	000	5,201 59	14,280 54
1887.....	94,874	8,788 61	9,361	000	6,755 49	15,544 10
1888.....	93,512	8,475 83	7,251	750	4,729 99	13,205 82
1889.....	134,193	12,677 97	13,483	088	8,087 03	20,765 00
1890.....	178,072	16,264 75	18,595	861	12,156 67	28,421 42
1891.....	156,917	15,293 69	13,998	185	11,082 76	26,376 45
1892.....	107,122	13,777 47	13,924	530	11,702 56	25,480 03
1893.....	176,241	16,340 90	14,128	510	11,690 24	28,031 14
1894.....	121,949	15,328 76	13,778	920	11,536 10	26,864 86
1895.....	204,591	18,210 13	13,860	796	10,136 78	28,346 91
Total..	1,440,058	$141,253 45	124,515	640	$94,217 40	$235,470 85

VANEGAS, CEDRAL, MATEHUALA, AND RIO VERDE RAILWAY.

YEARS.	PASSEN-GERS.	PASSENGER RECEIPTS.	FREIGHT.		MISCELLA-NEOUS RECEIPTS.	TOTAL RECEIPTS.
			Tons.	Kilos.		
1889.....	....	$ 449 69	28	540	$ 335 24	$ 784 93
1890.....	10,848	5,763 16	1,840	661	15,492 27	21,255 43
1891.....	36,742	12,783 05	5,939	568	61,513 43	74,296 48
1892.....	44,502	16,083 11	94,112	500	124,565 69	140,648 80
1893.....	46,083	16,030 02	83,115	000	114,505 49	130,535 51
1894.....	35,213	13,798 53	113,384	000	185,649 51	199,448 04
1895....	....	....	....	...	....	....
Total..	173,388	$64,907 56	298,420	269	$502,061 63	$566,969 19

MÉRIDA AND IZAMAL RAILWAY.

YEARS.	PASSEN-GERS.	PASSENGER RECEIPTS.	FREIGHT.		MISCELLA-NEOUS RECEIPTS.	TOTAL RECEIPTS.
			Tons.	Kilos.		
1887.....	42,812	$ 7,280 38	2,729	000	$ 3,954 64	$ 11,235 02
1888.....	78,102	18,981 70	7,871	541	17,656 81	36,638 51
1889.....	106 089	38,330 34	11,633	376	28,069 91	66,400 25
1890.....	106,883	54,462 10	10,146	374	29,995 33	84,457 43
1891.....	80,042	41,891 51	13,775	771	44,798 43	86,689 94
1892.....	94,634	49,729 03	18,094	768	65,565 47	115,294 50
1893.....	96,458	45,684 12	21,476	676	65,714 14	111,398 26
1894.....	....	52,564 78	....	....	61,335 45	113,900 23
1895.....	....	49,735 12	....	....	63,295 49	113,030 61
Total..	605,020	$358,659 08	85,727	506	$380,385 67	$739,044 75

SAN MÁRCOS AND NAUTLA RAILWAY.

YEARS.	PASSEN-GERS.	PASSENGER RECEIPTS.	FREIGHT.		MISCELLA-NEOUS RECEIPTS.	TOTAL RECEIPTS.
			Tons.	Kilos.		
1891	4,582	$ 3,181 70	5,307	750	$ 5,968 12	$ 9,149 82
1892	10,894	5,968 34	12,000	570	17,835 93	23,804 27
1893	14,136	7,339 14	19,576	000	27,008 47	34,347 61
1894	15,481	7,918 63	....	...	29,519 97	37,438 60
1895	17,309	8,195 77	24,452	440	27,603 55	35,799 32
Total...	62,402	$32,603 58	61,336	760	$107,936 04	$140,539 62

MONTEREY AND GULF RAILWAY.

YEARS.	PASSEN-GERS.	PASSENGER RECEIPTS.	FREIGHT.		MISCELLA-NEOUS RECEIPTS.	TOTAL RECEIPTS.
			Tons.	Kilos.		
1889.....	16,714	$ 17,144 65	4,197	432	$ 13,440 52	$ 30,585 17
1890.....	57,096	70,185 08	168,204	600	791,398 47	861,583 55
1891.....	94,052	112,910 64	174,829	706	876,563 75	989,474 39
1892.....	99,802	119,390 74	193,437	800	664,072 42	783,463 16
1893.....	107,378	141,093 86	238,442	000	820,433 06	961,526 92
1894.....	....	....	....	....	....	....
1895.....	127,900	150,005 75	329,059	008	1,162,009 39	1,312,015 14
Total..	502,942	$610,730 72	1,108,170	546	$4,327,917 61	$4,938,648 33

CÓRDOVA AND TUXTEPEC RAILWAY.

YEARS.	PASSEN-GERS.	PASSENGER RECEIPTS.	FREIGHT.		MISCELLA-NEOUS RECEIPTS.	TOTAL RECEIPTS.
			Tons.	Kilos.		
1889.....	26,537	$ 4,815 27	....	....	$ 1,285 13	$ 6,100 40
1890.....	49,142	8,917 06	....	....	2,379 97	11,297 03
1891.....	23,542	14,009 84	....	....	5,097 98	19,107 82
1892.....	39,885	12,767 51	2,235	571	5,111 19	17,878 70
1893.....	46,086	17,433 62	3,730	424	9,828 94	27,262 56
1894.....	....	....	....	....	....	....
1895.....	....	....	....	....	....	....
Total..	185,192	$57,943 30	5,965	995	$23,703 21	$81,646 51

MARAVATÍO AND CUERNAVACA RAILWAY.

YEARS.	PASSEN-GERS.	PASSENGER RECEIPTS.	FREIGHT.		MISCELLA-NEOUS RECEIPTS.	TOTAL RECEIPTS.
			Tons.	Kilos.		
1890.....	3,466	$ 3,389 66	....	....	$ 3,372 10	$ 6,761 76
1891.....	6,190	6,283 94	....	....	16,741 42	23,025 36
1892.....	9,081	8,047 76	....	....	30,160 42	38,208 18
1893.....	12,867	9,418 26	....	....	28,201 99	37,620 25
1894.....	15,138	11,235 58	....	....	32,238 33	43,473 91
1895.....	13,964	11,364 72	....	....	39,714 80	51,079 52
Total..	60,706	$49,739 92	....	....	$150,429 06	$200,168 98

SALAMANCA AND SANTIAGO VALLEY RAILWAY.

YEARS.	PASSEN-GERS.	PASSENGER RECEIPTS.	FREIGHT.		MISCELLA-NEOUS RECEIPTS.	TOTAL RECEIPTS.
			Tons.	Kilos.		
1889.....	4,709	$ 1,486 51	132	270	$ 304 26	$ 1,790 77
1890.....	18,836	5,946 04	529	080	1,217 04	7,163 08
1891.....	25,432	8,554 11	3,324	430	7,237 67	15,791 78
1892.....	21,923	8,020 59	2,815	940	5,325 03	13,345 62
1893.....	22,674	7,719 44	3,380	060	8,910 74	16,630 18
1894.....	27,496	8,740 90	4,142	690	9,584 17	18,325 07
1895.....	30,094	10,376 66	7,799	050	13,969 73	24,346 39
Total..	151,164	$50,844 25	22,123	520	$46,548 64	$97,392 89

MONTE ALTO RAILWAY.

YEARS.	PASSEN-GERS.	PASSENGER RECEIPTS.	FREIGHT		MISCELLA-NEOUS RECEIPTS.	TOTAL RECEIPTS.
			Tons.	Kilos.		
1892......	31,080	$ 2,652 89	4,006	000	$1,330 13	$ 3,983 02
1893......	30,888	3,260 28	6,135	000	1,965 72	5,226 00
1894......	31,913	3,318 14	6,221	000	2,002 79	5,320 93
1895......	39,041	4,005 14	5,430	000	1,410 85	5,415 99
Total..	132,922	$13,236 45	21,792	000	$6,709 49	$19,945 94

VALLEY OF MEXICO RAILWAY.

YEARS.	PASSEN-GERS.	PASSENGER RECEIPTS.	FREIGHT		MISCELLA-NEOUS RECEIPTS.	TOTAL RECEIPTS.
			Tons.	Kilos.		
1891......	1,423,652	$ 99,615 09	9,108	000	$ 5,912 38	$105,527 41
1892......	1,639,873	119,379 76	21,154	000	12,310 35	131,690 17
1893......	1,637,135	110,160 60	24,361	000	21,497 48	131,658 08
1894......	....	....	......	....	....	....
1895......	....	....	......	....	....	....
Total..	4,700,660	$329,155 45	54,623	000	$39,720 21	$368,875 66

PUEBLA INDUSTRIAL RAILWAY.

YEARS.	PASSEN-GERS.	PASSENGER RECEIPTS.	FREIGHT		MISCELLA-NEOUS RECEIPTS.	TOTAL RECEIPTS.
			Tons.	Kilos.		
1891......	151,380	$ 23,234 66	....	....	$ 1,398 00	$ 24,632 66
1892......	125,766	20,052 34	....	....	1,239 00	21,291 34
1893......	155,112	24,082 55	....	....	1,380 00	25,462 55
1894......	190,480	31,620 62	....	....	3,149 37	34,769 99
1895......	226,275	36,264 00	14,250	000	11,122 35	47,386 35
Total..	849,013	$135,254 17	14,250	000	$18,288 72	$153,542 89

MEXICAN NORTHERN RAILWAY.

YEARS.	PASSEN-GERS.	PASSENGER RECEIPTS.	FREIGHT		MISCELLA-NEOUS RECEIPTS.	TOTAL RECEIPTS.
			Tons.	Kilos.		
1891......	4,870	$14,802 61	94,726	000	$ 740,122 98	$ 754,925 59
1892......	4,369	14,802 61	177,781	825	1,337,853 47	1,352,656 08
1893......	4,088	13,087 90	176,801	913	1,334,524 47	1,347,612 37
1894......	....	....	....	....	....	....
1895......	4,274	13,420 18	151,744	929	1,149,069 15	1,162,489 33
Total..	17,601	$56,113 30	601,054	667	$4,561,570 07	$4,617,683 37

MEXICO CUERNAVACA AND PACÍFICO RAILWAY.

YEARS.	PASSEN-GERS.	PASSENGER RECEIPTS.	FREIGHT		MISCELLA-NEOUS RECEIPTS.	TOTAL RECEIPTS.
			Tons.	Kilos.		
1895......	17,209	$19,214 84	84,434	000	$130,662 86	$149,877 70

FEDERAL DISTRICT TRAMWAYS.

YEARS.	PASSENGERS.	PASSENGER RECEIPTS.	FREIGHT.		MISCELLA-NEOUS RECEIPTS.	TOTAL RECEIPTS.
			Tons.	Kilos.		
1873..	3,760,653	$ 232,347 92	......	....	$ 16,421 10	$ 248,769 02
1874..	3,088,808	240,277 12	......	....	29,628 70	269,905 82
1875..	3,597,197	286,248 25	......	....	23,644 10	309,892 35
1876..	3,545,589	278,068 94	......	....	19,289 15	297,358 09
1877..	4,455,595	357,262 43	......	....	14,179 54	371,441 97
1878..	4,605,223	360,175 98	......	....	6,752 49	366,928 47
1879..	5,084,669	390,298 10	......	....	8,089 47	398,387 57
1880..	6,165,461	458,547 60	......	....	19,020 46	477,568 06
1881..	7,675,829	586,167 20	......	....	52,547 54	638,714 74
1882..	9,851,614	703,422 06	......	....	87,584 95	791,007 01
1883..	10,101,302	775,550 34	......	....	90,644 72	866,195 06
1884..	9,926,621	717,264 90	......	....	114,307 69	831,572 59
1885..	9,407,751	690,457 87	......	....	63,423 48	753,881 35
1886..	10,841,928	746,107 46	......	....	134,133 77	880,241 23
1887..	11,121,575	810,974 85	......	....	155,972 22	966,947 07
1888..	12,185,031	881,646 36	......	....	171,418 11	1,053,064 47
1889..	13,533,217	981,922 98	......	....	203,011 13	1,184,934 11
1890..	14,457,203	1,028,871 57	......	....	247,868 09	1,276,739 66
1891..	15,585,919	1,002,224 50	......	....	206,601 54	1,208,826 04
1892..	16,164,644	1,023,617 85	......	....	194,358 01	1,217,975 86
1893..	15,622,879	990,265 03	......	....	217,905 64	1,208,170 67
1894..	15,844,425	1,028,430 01	......	....	230,935 43	1,259,365 44
1895..	18,281,729	1,194,335 17	......	....	229,571 08	1,423,906 25
Total.	224,904,862	$15,764,484 49	......	....	$2,537,308 41	$18,301,792 90

VERACRUZ AND ALVARADO RAILWAY.

1885......	39,078	$ 18,451 01	....	...	$	$ 18,451 01
1886......	37,772	18,673 04	882	500	4,942 00	23,615 04
1887......	29,971	16,677 46	......	...	14,316 16	30,993 62
1888......	58,127	33,174 25	....	...	26,549 26	59,723 51
1889......	63,328	36,779 93	8,500	412	31,779 57	68,559 50
1890......	72,292	42,128 89	11,500	892	34,829 14	76,958 03
1891......	74,317	39,304 87	16,845	178	44,831 36	84,136 23
1892......	73,249	47,831 14	14,498	000	51,025 73	98,856 87
1893......	73,705	47,298 50	22,976	000	49,955 98	97,254 48
1894......	32,964	44,294 74	20,197	000	56,927 90	101,222 64
1895......	87,291	53,050 84	22,764	103	69,450 61	122,501 45
Total..	642,094	$397,664 67	118,164	085	$384,607 71	$782,272 38

Total Traffic and Receipts of Mexican Railways.—Before concluding this chapter, I append a statement of the total traffic and receipts of the Mexican Railways from 1873 to 1895, taken from the *Anuario Estadístico de la Republica Mexicana of 1895*, compiled in the Department of Communication of the Mexican Government from data furnished the same by the respective companies, in compliance with the provisions of their grants.

RAILWAY SUBSIDIES PAID BY THE MEXICAN GOVERNMENT.

I append a statement of the railway subsidies paid by the Mexican Government from the beginning of railway construction to June 30, 1896, which is entirely correct, as it has been obtained from the accounts of the Federal Treasury of Mexico. I insert after that statement a detailed account of each of the railways to whom subsidies have

TRAFFIC AND RECEIPTS OF THE MEXICAN RAILWAYS.

RAILWAYS.	YEARS.	PASSENGERS.	PASSENGER RECEIPTS.	FREIGHT. Tons.	FREIGHT. Kilos.	OTHER RECEIPTS.	TOTAL RECEIPTS.
Mexican Railway	1873–1895	9,995,557	$14,848,480 55	6,640,709	141	$66,862,116 14	$81,710,896 69
District Tramway	1873–1895	225,104,862	15,764,484 49			2,537,308 41	18,301,792 90
Mexican National	1873–1895	17,496,445	10,457,531 15	4,783,356	914	28,152,266 11	38,609,777 26
Veracruz and Alvarado	1883–1895	64,294	307,664 67	118,164	085	384,607 77	692,272 38
Sonora Railway	1880–1895	568,451	1,341,878 18	577,117	353	3,244,522 20	4,586,407 38
Interoceanic Railway	1880–1895	10,023,881	4,759,173 00	3,472,455	978	13,172,436 70	17,931,609 70
Mexican Central and Branch from Tula to Pachuca	1881–1895	10,023,572	17,985,718 70	4,232,346	747	64,568,200 81	82,484,719 51
Hidalgo and Northeastern	1881–1895	1,418,419	128,413 72	1,441,234	727	3,147,970 64	4,666,384 36
Hidalgo and Progreso	1881–1895	1,377,131	961,468 15	647,313	555	1,293,677 63	1,853,145 78
Tehuacan and Esperanza (Tramway)	1881–1895	186,674	135,438 29	125,709	623	514,355 10	447,793 39
Mérida and Peto	1881–1895	1,508,674	504,682 90	304,177	694	818,659 13	1,323,341 03
Sinaloa and Durango (Altata and Culiacan)	1883–1895	420,722	163,905 18	96,306	716	331,755 74	495,660 92
Mérida and Campeche	1883–1895	1,000,019	311,094 63	138,575	143	368,618 49	619,713 12
Mérida and Valladolid	1883–1895	2,224,580	525,938 50	426,135	058	921,055 96	1,446,994 46
Tlalmanalco	1883–1895	68,095	68,095 28	252,439	744	115,825 95	183,850 93
Mexican International	1891–1895	580,192	1,590,654 34	2,517,600	766	11,143,660 82	12,734,315 16
San Márcos and Náutla	1888–1895	62,392	32,603 58	61,336	454	107,936 04	140,539 62
San Juan Baptista and Paso del Carrizal	1882–1895	843,209	55,617 49	9,254	753	8,361 37	63,978 86
San Andrés and Chalchicomula	1883–1895	167,373	45,550 60	76,539	417	112,274 77	157,825 37
Orizaba and Ingenio	1883–1895	1,122,861	138,767 86	5,208	443	4,752 22	143,520 08
Santa Ana and Tlaxcala	1883–1895	1,254,427	97,331 82	6,617		18,751 00	116,082 82
Cárdenas and Río Grijalva	1886–1894		2,050 23			4,648 77	6,699 00
Toluca and San Juan de las Huertas	1885–1895	1,440,058	141,253 43	124,515	640	94,217 40	235,470 85
Vanegas, Cedral, Matehuala, and Río Verde	1887–1894	173,388	64,907 36	208,420	269	502,061 63	566,069 10
Mérida and Izamal	1887–1894	605,020	358,659 08	85,727	508	380,385 67	739,044 75
Mexican Southern	1890–1895	761,781	724,591 04	143,828	460	993,244 21	4,938,648 33
Monterey and Gulf	1889–1895	500,942	610,730 72	1,108,170	546	4,327,917 61	81,646 51
Córdova and Tuxtepec	1889–1894	185,192	57,043 30	5,965	995	23,793 21	200,168 96
Maravatío and Cuernavaca	1890–1895	60,706	49,739 92			150,429 06	97,392 89
Salamanca and Valley of Santiago	1892–1895	151,164	50,844 25	12,123	520	46,548 64	19,045 94
Monte Alto	1892–1895	134,922	13,336 45	21,792	000	6,709 49	368,875 66
Valley of Mexico	1891–1893	4,700,660	329,155 45	54,623	000	39,720 21	153,542 89
Puebla Industrial	1891–1895	849,013	135,354 17	14,450	000	18,288 72	4,647,683 47
Mexican Northern	1891–1895	17,601	56,113 30	601,054	667	4,561,570 17	149,877 70
Mexican, Cuernavaca, and Pacific	1895....	17,209	19,214 82	84,434	008	130,662 86	
Total		296,570,955	$73,589,396 84	32,258,024	640	$209,605,020 29	$283,194,417 13

SUBSIDIES PAID BY THE MEXICAN GOVERNMENT TO RAILWAY COMPANIES UP TO JUNE 30, 1896.

#	NAME OF RAILWAY.	DATE OF CONTRACT.	LENGTH OF LINE IN KILOMETRES.	AMOUNT OF SUBSIDY DUE.	PAYMENTS IN Cash.	PAYMENTS IN Certificates.	PAYMENTS IN Bonds.
1	Mexican (Mexico City to Veracruz, via Orizaba and Cordova)	1867, Nov. 27.	614,460	$14,000,000	$13,685,104 59		
2	Progreso & Mérida, Yucatan	1874, Jan. 17.	36,453	218,718	218,718 37		
3	Hidalgo Ry. (Mexico City to Pachuca)	1878, Feb. 2.	154,011	1,231,688	931,296 37		
4	Veracruz & Alvarado (coast line)	1878, March 26.	55,000	440,000	394,000		
5	Mérida & Peto, Yucatan	1878, March 27.	108,000	648,000	577,445 85		
6	Interoceanic (from Veracruz to Acapulco)	1878, April 16.	743,467	5,570,511 12	2,896,938	$2,673,573 12	
7	Puebla and Matamoros Izucar Railway	1878, May 6.	84,312	674,496	674,496		
8	Tehuantepec Railway	1870, June 2.	300,617	19,181,172 72	5,681,172 72		$13,500,000
9	Sinaloa & Durango R. R. (from Durango City to Mazatlan)	1880, Aug. 16.	61,927	557,343	557,343		
10	Mexican Central (Trunk line and branches, Mexico City to El Paso)	1880, Sept. 8.	2,932,753	26,600,003 50	14,417,936 45	7,108,070 80	
11	Mexican National (Trunk line and branches, Mexico City to New Laredo)	1880, Sept. 13.	1,737,045	12,042,815		11,929,870	
12	Sonora Railway (from Nogales to Guaymas)	1880, Sept. 14.	422,312	2,956,184	2,171,310 60		
13	Mérida & Valladolid R. R. Yucatan	1880, Dec. 15.	108,668	622,008	597,608		
14	Tlalmanalco (Local line in the State of Puebla)	1881, Feb. 3.	26,650	159,900	159,900		
15	Mérida & Campeche Railway (via Calkini, Yucatan)	1881, Feb. 23.	135,153	810,915	766,915		
16	Náutla & San Márcos Railway (States of Puebla and Veracruz)	1881, June 25.	75,000	450,000	70,500		349,000
17	San Juan Bautista & Tamulté-Pass. Railway (State Tabasco)	1881, Sept. 17.	5,759	20,125	20,125		
18	Chalchicomula Branch Railway (State of Puebla)	1881, Sept. 20.	10,353	22,238 65	22,238 65		
19	Tlaxcala & Santa Ana Railway (State Tlaxcala)	1882, Dec. 11.	8,000	28,000	28,000		
20	Cárdenas & Grijalva River Railway (State Tabasco)	1883, May 12.	7,500	33,750	33,750		
21	Toluca & Las Huertas Railway (State of Mexico)	1883, May 25.	15,521	33,023 50	46,250		
22	Vanegas, Cedral, Matehuala & Rio-Verde (State S. Louis Potosi)	1883, June 11.	65,000	357,088	341,000		
23	Mérida & Soluta (State of Yucatan, via Izamal)	1884, May 15.	65,848	395,088	395,088		
24	Jimenez & Sierra Madre, via Hidalgo District (State Durango)	1884, Nov. 13.	5,000	40,000	40,000		
25	Mexican Southern (States of Puebla and Oaxaca)	1886, April 21.	367,000	11,248,865 10	880,805 10		10,368,000
26	Tonalá & Fontera (States of Chiapas and Tabasco)	1886, Dec. 16.	50,000	444,444			444,000
27	Monterey & Mexican Gulf (States of N. Leon and Tamaulipas)	1887, Nov. 10.	624,040	5,534,572 24			5,534,572 24
28	Tecolutla (Gulf of Mexico) & Espinal (State of Veracruz)	1887, Dec. 10.	19,000	100,500	40,500		60,000
29	Cordova (State Veracruz) & Tuxtepec Railway	1888, June 19.	51,000	408,000	408,000		
30	Pachuca (State Hidalgo) & Tampico Railway	1888, June 5.	10,000	80,000			80,000
31	Maravatío & Iguala (States Michoacan and Guerrero)	1888, Aug. 16.	50,000	316,666 50	112,000		166,000
32	Mexican Northeastern (State Tamaulipas)	1888, Aug. 28.	50,000	300,540	294,000		
33	Salamanca & Valley of Santiago Railway (State Guanajuato)	1888, Aug. 30.	35,000	280,000	280,000		
34	Veracruz & Boca del Rio Railway	1888, Aug. 31.	11,504	92,031	83,000		
35	Tula, Zacualtipan (State of Hidalgo) & Tampico Railway	1889, Dec. 20.	70,000	560,000			556,000
36	Matamoros Izucar (State of Puebla) & Acapulco (Pacific coast)	1892, March 5.	40,000	988,776 49	111,370 62		
37	Lower California Railway	1894, June 3.	20,000	177,777 77			
38	Monte-Alto branch Railway (State of Mexico)	1894, Sept. 14.	10,000	66,666 66			66,000
	Total, 38 subsidized Railway Concessions.		9,106,533	$107,743,660 25	$46,896,901 95	$21,711,513 92	$31,127,572 24

been paid, stating the number of kilometres built, the amount of subsidy due for the same, and the manner in which the subsidy was paid, that statement being the most complete that has so far been published :

RÉSUMÉ.—Amount paid in Cash.......................... $ 46,896,901 95
    "   " Certificates of Construction (convertible
          in five per cent. bonds)............ 21,711,513 92
    "   " Bonds............................. 31,127,000 00
    " of Balance due (payable either in cash or Bonds), 8,008,244 38

    Total amount of Subsidies, as per corresponding concessions, $107,743,660 25

The Tehuantepec Railway cost of construction is herein included, in order to give a complete statement of the Government's pecuniary outlay for the construction of railways in the country. As the $13,500,000 amount of the five per cent. Bonds paid on account of the construction of this line to the contractors, McMurdo & Co., represent a gold indebtedness, if reduced at the rate of 24 pence per dollar, the above total cost of railway construction should be increased by an equal amount, say $13,500,000 Mexican currency—or a grand total of $121,243,660.25.

DETAILED STATEMENT OF THE SUBSIDIES PAID BY THE MEXICAN GOVERNMENT TO THE RAILWAY COMPANIES.

1. MEXICAN RAILWAY.—(From Mexico City to Veracruz.)

Subsidy as per original concession, $560,000 per annum, during
    25 years, equal to.................................. $14,000,000 00
Paid previous to October 21, 1890........... 10,187,315 79
Balance in favor of the company, on October
    21, 1890, as per special agreement of the
    same date......................... $3,497,878 80
9% deduction, for cash payment, according to
    the second clause of said agreement....... 314,805 41
        Total payment................................. 14,000,000 00

2. HIDALGO RAILWAY.—(From Mexico City to Pachuca, Hid.)

Subsidy, $8000, per kilometre, as per concession $1,232,088 00
Paid on account thereof in cash.............. $931,296 37
In 3% and 5% Bonds........................ 300,791 63
        Total payment....................................... 1,232,088 00

3. VERACRUZ & ALVARADO RAILWAY.—(Coast Line between the said ports.)

Subsidy due the Company, $6000 per kilometre, as per concession... $440,000 00
Paid on account thereof, in cash............. $394,000 00
In 3% Bonds.............................. 46,000 00   440,000 00

4. MERIDA & PETO RAILWAY.—(Between the two named towns, State of Yucatan.)

Subsidy, due the Company, $6000 per kilometre, as per concession................................. .... $648,000 00
Paid in cash.............................. $577,445 85
In 3% Bonds.............................. 70,554 15
        Total payment....................................... 648,000 00

5. INTEROCEANIC RAILWAY.—(Narrow gauge, from Veracruz to Acapulco, Pacific Coast.)

Subsidy due the Company.................................		$5,570,511 12
483.₁₀/₁₀₀ Kilometres at $8000.............	$3,866,469 12	
81.₀₀₀ " " 6500.............	526,500 00	
140.₀₀₀ " " 6000.............	840,000 00	
38.₀₀₀ " unsubsidized........		
Construction bounty earned, as per concession on the Mexico & Cuautla division........	137,542 00	
Construction bounty earned, as per concession on the Jalapa & Veracruz division........	200,000 00	5,570,511 12
Paid in cash................. $2,896,938 00		
In certificates already paid for, out of the 3% of the Customs Receipts... .... 2,673,573 12		
Total payment....		5,570,511 12

6. OCCIDENTAL RAILWAY.—(Between points in the States of Sinaloa and Durango.)

Length of the road, according to the concession 1373 kilometres, subsidy at the rate of $8000, per kilometre, as follows:

From Altata, (Port on the Pacific Coast, Gulf of California), to Culiacan, capital of the State of Sinaloa...... 61.₉₂₇ kilometres constructed		
From Culiacan to Durango and Fresnillo cities 600		
A Branch to Guaymas 536		
" " " Mazatlan 237		
1,373		
Subsidy due for the first 61.₉₂₇ kilometres already built...........	$495,416 00	
Construction bounty according to concession $1000 per kilometre....................	61,927 00	
Total amount due and paid for to the Company..............		$557,343 00

7. MEXICAN CENTRAL, and sundry branches.—(Trunk-line, from Mexico City to El Paso del Norte, on the Rio Grande River.)

Subsidy due in accordance with the corresponding charter was $26,609,003 50		
As follows: for 1970.₀₀₀ kilometres of the trunk-line, of which 107 kilometres were subsidized at $1500 per kilometre.................... $	160,500 00	
And 1,863.₀₀₀ kilometres at $9500 per kilometre........	17,704,200 00	$17,864,700 00
For 258.₅₅₀ kilometres of the		

Gaudalajara branch, which reduced as per special contract of Feb. 25, 1887, to 218.⁸³⁰ kilometres at $9500 per kilometre..................... .... **$2,076,510 00**

For 653.⁸⁰⁰ kilometres of the Aguascalientes & T a m p i c o Branch, at $9500 per kilometre..................... 6,208,250 00

For 25 kilometres of the San Blas & Guaristemba at $9500 per kilometre.............. 237,500 00   8,522,260 00

For 23.⁸⁷⁸ kilometres of Silao & Guanajuato Branch at $9500 per kilometre.............. 222,043 50

Total payment.. $26,609,003 50

This total amount, was settled and paid for in accordance with special agreement entered into by and between the Department of Public Works and the Company, on August 23, 1890, as follows :

Lands, art-works, drafts and plans, etc., due by the Company as per settlement effected December 22, 1881...................... $ 34,204 39

Rebate off the subsidy corresponding to 6600 kilometres of parallel lines, between Zacatecas & Guadalajara, as per agreement therefor 52,800 00

Rebate off the subsidy on 50 kilometres of the line, between Tantoyuquita & Tampico, as per agreement......................... 75,000 00

Cash received by the Government of the State of San Luis Potosi, on account of the old branch line to Tampico................. 48,000 00

Certificates of construction paid at various Custom Houses out of the 8% of the receipts of the same, during the fiscal years 1881–1890   7,108,070 80

Paid with bills of exchange on London out of the proceeds of the loan negotiated in 1890................................. 14,335,732 06

25% discount on $19,820,793 01, amount of the balance acknowledged in favor of the Company, according to the above mentioned agreement, (August 23, 1890)........... 4,955,196 25

Total payment................................ .... $26,609,003 50

8. MEXICAN NATIONAL, and branches. — (Trunk-line from Mexico City to Laredo, Tamaulipas.)

The Company constructed 1737.⁰⁴⁸ kilometres for which the Government owed the following subsidies :—

On 1444.<u>045</u> kilometres of the trunk line, at the
rate of $7000 per kilometre............ . $10,108,315 00
On 273.<u>000</u> kilometres of the trunk line, at the
rate of $6500 per kilometre............. 1,774,500 00
On 20 kilometres of the Salto Branch at the rate
of $8000 per kilometre................. 160,000 00
Total amount of subsidy due............................... $12,042,815 00

The above amount was paid in certificates of construction for..$11,929,870 00 of which the sum of $8,746,722 60 was paid at several Custom-Houses during the fiscal years 1882-1895, and the balance of $3,183,147 40, was converted, by special agreement between the Treasury Department and Messrs. Lionel Carden and H. P. Webb, as representatives of the Company in 5% Bonds. The balance of $112,945 which in the preceding statement, appears as pending of payment, was accepted by the Company, as the value of the Government's shares in the Salto Branch.

9. "SONORA RAILWAY."—(From Guaymas, on the Gulf of California, to Nogales, on the boundary line.)

Subsidy on 422<u>012</u> kilometres at the rate of $7000 per kilometre, $ 2,956,184 00
Paid to the Company, cash.................. $ 2,071,310 60
Fine against the forfeiture of the concession... 100,000 00
3% Bonds in accordance with the provisions of
the law of September 6th, 1894.......... 784,873 40
Total payment,................................. $ 2,956,184 00

10. "MERIDA & VALLADOLID RAILWAY," with a branch.—(Between these two towns in the State of Yucatan.)

Subsidy due on 108.<u>668</u> kilometres at $6000 per kilometre..... $642,008 00
Paid for as follows, cash.................... $ 597,608 00
In 3% Bonds (law of September 6th, 1894).... 44,400 00
Total payment.. $642,008 00

11. "MERIDA & CAMPECHE RAILWAY," *via*. Kalkini.—(Between the capitals of the States of Yucatan and Campeche.)

Subsidy due on 135.<u>152</u> kilometres at $6000 per kilometre, $810,915 00
Paid to the Company in cash................ $766,915 00
In 3% Bonds.............................. 44,000 00
Total payment.. $810,915 00

12. "SAN MARCOS & NAUTLA RAILWAY."—Between San Marcos station on the Mexican Ry. and Nautla bar on the Gulf of Mexico.)

Subsidy due on 75 kilometres at $6000 per kilometre......... $450,000 00
Paid to the Company as follows : Cash....... $ 70,500 00
In special 5% subsidy Bonds................ 349,000 00
In 3% Bonds according to the provisions of the
law of September 6th, 1894............. 500 00
Rebatement of subsidy on 5 kilometres running
parallel with the "Interoceanic Ry....... 30,000 00
Total payment.. $450,000 00

13. "TOLUCA & SAN JUAN de las HUERTAS RAILWAY."—(Between the capital of the State of Mexico and the San Juan estate.)

Subsidy due on 15.<u>781</u> kilometres at $3500 per kilometre.......		$55,023 50
Paid to the Company, cash...................	$46,250 00	
In 3% Bonds (law of September 6th, 1894).....	8,773 50	
Total payment..		$55,023 50

14. "VANEGAS, CEDRAL, MATEHUALA & RIO VERDE RAILWAY."—(All townships within the State of San Luis Potosi.)

Subsidy due on 65.<u>000</u> kilometres at $5500 per kilometre.....		$357,500 00
Paid to the Company, cash.................	$341,000 00	
In 5% Bonds (September 6th, 1894)...........	16,500 00	
Total payment...................................		$357,500 00

15. "JIMENEZ and SIERRA MADRE RAILWAY."—(Through the Hidalgo District, State of Chihuahua.)

Subsidy due on 5.<u>000</u> kilometres at $8000 per kilometre....... $40,000 00
The whole paid to the Company in 3% Bonds (Law of September 6th, 1894.

16. "MEXICAN SOUTHERN RAILWAY."—(367 kilometres from the City of Puebla to Oaxaca.)

Subsidy due under agreement of May 4th, 1892.............		$11,248,805 10
First annuity of interest paid to the Company in conformity with the original concession of April 21st, 1886....................	$880,800 00	
Conversion of the remaining 14 annuities, as per the above named agreement, in special Bonds denominated of the "Oaxaca Trunk Line"..............................	8,558,888 55	
Bounty paid to the Company, as per original concession, in Bonds (special)...........	1,809,116 55	
Total payment....................		$11,248,805 10
Of the total amount of special Bonds issued, $10,368,000 00		
Cashed	1,108,000 00	
Outstanding.............................	9,260,000 00	

17. "TONALA" (State of Chiapas, Pacific Coast) and "FRONTERA RAILWAY."—(State of Tabasco, on the Gulf of Mexico.)

Subsidy on 50 kilometres at $8000 per kilometre......... ... $400,000 00
Paid to the Company with 6% Bonds, valued at 90% of their nominal.................. $444,444 00
The balance shown in the preceding statement in favor of the Company for $44,444.00 proceeds from the want of a Bond of less value than $1000 of the corresponding issue.

18. "MONTEREY" (Capital of the State of Nuevo Leon) and "MEXICAN GULF RAILWAY."—(Port of Tampico.)

Subsidy on 624.$\frac{840}{}$ kilometres at $8000 per kilometre........ $5,534,572 24[1]

Wholly paid for in 5% Bonds, issued under the law of September 6th, 1894, with the exception of a balance of $572.24, which, on account of the want of bonds of less value than $1000, is still pending of settlement. Of the original issue of special Bonds given to the Company in payment of the subsidy, $235,000 is still pending of conversion.

19. "TECOLUTLA" (a bar on the Mexican Gulf) and "ESPINAL RAILWAY."—(Both in the State of Veracruz.)

According to the original concession, the subsidy granted to this Company was on 19 kilometres at the rate of $4500 in cash per kilometre ; but under a new agreement, dated January, 20th, 1892, it was settled as follows :

9 kilometres at the rate of $4500 each in cash,	$40,500 00	
10 kilometres in Bonds at $6000 each.........	60,000 00	
Total payment..............................		$100,500 00

20. "PACHUCA" (Capital of the State of Hidalgo) and "TAMPICO RAILWAY."—(On the Mexican Gulf.)

Subsidy on 10.$\frac{000}{}$ kilometres at $8000.................... $80,000 00
Totally paid in Bonds, in accordance with the law of September 6th, 1894.

21. "MARAVATIO" & "IGUALA RAILWAY."—(Towns in the States of Michoacan and Guerrero, respectively.)

Subsidy on 50 kilometres at $3000 in cash and $3000 in special Bonds, under 10% discount off their nominal value, and paid for, cash,	$112,000 00	
Bonds..............................	166,000 00	
Total payment.................................		$316,666 50[1]

22. "MEXICAN NORTHEASTERN RAILWAY."—(An extension of the "Hidalgo" Ry. to Tizayuca, in the State of that name.)

Subsidy on 50.$\frac{000}{}$ kilometres at $6000......................		$300,540 00
Paid for, in cash..........................	$294,000 00	
In 3% Bonds..............................	6,540 00	
Total payment..		$300,540 00

[1] Some of the total payments in this table do not correspond to the amount of subsidy due, because in some of those cases other payments have been made, like bounty, of which no account appears in the respective statement. In some cases a bounty was offered provided the road was finished before the time fixed in the respective grant.

23. "Veracruz & Boca del Rio Railway."

Subsidy acknowledged on 11.⁵⁰⁴ kilometres at $8000 per kilo-
metre $92,032 00
Paid for, cash............................. $83,000 00
In 3% Bonds............................. 9,032 00
　　Total payment...................................... $92,032 00

24. "Tula, Zacualtipan" (State of Hidalgo), and Tampico Railway.

Subsidy on 70.⁰⁰⁰ kilometres at $8,000 per kilometre......... $560,000 00
The whole amount paid for in 5% Bonds, of which $285,000
were outstanding on the 30th of June, 1896.

25. "Matamoros Izucar" (State of Puebla) and "Acapulco Railway."—(On the Pacific coast.)

Subsidy under contract of March 22d, 1895, on 40 kilometres.. $988,776 49
Paid as follows : cash, for the amount of 2% in-
terest annuities paid to the Company in
conformity with the original concession... $111,370 62
In 5% Bonds, according to the above contract............................... 877,405 87
　　Total payment.................................. $988,776 49

26. "Lower California Railway."—(From the town of San Quintin to a point on the "Mexican Central," Chihuahua.)

Subsidy on 20 kilometres, payable in 6% Bonds at the rate of
$8000 per kilometre, the said Bonds, afterwards converted
in conformity with the corresponding law of conversion,
were taken by the Company under 10% discount off their
nominal value.... .... $177,777 77

27. "Monte Alto Railway."—(Starts from the town of Tlalne-pantla, on the Salto branch of the "Mexican National," towards Alizapan and Villa del Carbon.)

Subsidy on 10 kilometres at $6000 per kilometre, payable in
6% Bonds taken by the Company at the rate of 90% of their
face value................ .... $66,666 66

28. Tehuantepec R. R.—(Between Coatzacoalcos on the Gulf of Mexico, and Salina Cruz, on the Pacific coast.)

COSTS OF CONSTRUCTION TO THE MEXICAN GOVERNMENT.

1. Contractors, Edward Learned & Co.—(Contract of June 2d, 1879.)
35 kilometres, of which only 25 were paid
for, at $7500...................... $187,500 00
The Learned contract was rescinded by
the Mexican Government on August
16th, 1882 ; but by agreement ad-
justed with J. Tyng, as representative
of the contractors, who received the
following payments :

December 21st, 1882, $125,000 00
July 9th, 1883.......   403,618 44
July 19th, 1883......   101,068 48
July 12th, 1888......   1,075,726 90   1,705,413 82
Total amount paid to Learned & Co.................... $1,892,913 82
Of which amount the sum of $230,413.82 represents
interest accrued at the rate or 6% per annum ; so that
the 35 kilometers built by these contractors actually
cost $14,083.25 per kilometre.

2.   CONTRACTOR, MR. DELPIN SANCHEZ.—(Agreement of October 5th, 1882.)

This contractor received from the Government the sum of................... $1,079,135 40

For the purchase of material, which he only accounted for the amount of $908,-910.50 the balance of $170,224 90
Having been donated to the contractor according to special agreement of April 25th, 1888.
The same contractor received in 150 weekly installments of $1900 each during the fiscal years 1885, 1888 .... $285,000 00
Mr. Sanchez delivered as constructed 74 kilometers which were paid to him at the rate of $25,000 each............... $1,850,000 00 $2,305,224 90

3.   MAC-MURDO CONTRACT.—(Agreement approved by Decree of October 15th, 1888.)

For the completion of the construction and the furnishing of all the rolling material, etc., and for which the Contractors received in payment in 5% Bonds, special issue, principal and interests payable in sterling currency, £2,700,000,................................ ... $13,500,000 00
This contract was rescinded on the 13th of January, 1892, when the contractors, in settlement of accounts, surrendered to the Government the sum of about $2,000,-000 as surplus proceeding from the sale of the said bonds, and delivered, more or less, 250 kilometres of the lines as built or repaired within the stipulations of the said contract.

4.   STANHOPE, HAMPSON & CORTHEL CONTRACT.—(Made under Decree of December 6th, 1893.)

For the construction of 59 kilometres and the completion of all the necessary works for the preservation and working of the whole line, for the fixed sum of,...... $1,483,035 00

Total cost of the line................................ $19,181,173 72

PUBLIC DEBT.

In the first part of this paper I gave a brief statement of the different loans and liabilities which constitute the Mexican debt, and that statement will make it easy to understand the different issues and denominations of our bonds. Here I append a detailed statement of the National Debt of Mexico, up to June 30, 1896, submitted to Congress by the Secretary of the Treasury on the 14th of December, 1896, and a further statement containing the same data in a more concise form.

STATEMENT OF THE NATIONAL DEBT OF MEXICO TO JUNE 30, 1896.

Bonded Debt, Principal and Interest payable in Sterling currency.

Six per cent. interest bearing Bonds for the Loan of 1888, with .. ⅝ sinking fund, Capital and Interest........	$51,908,786 50
Six per cent. interest bearing Bonds for the Loan of 1890, with .. ⅝ sinking fund, Capital and Interest........	30,068,710 25
Six per cent. interest bearing Bonds for the Loan of 1893, with .. ⅝ sinking fund, Capital and Interest........	15,325,561 50
Five per cent. interest bearing Bonds for the Construction of the Tehuantepec Railway, 1889, Capital....	13,500,000 00
Six per cent. (non converted balance) Bonds of the Loan, contracted in London, 1851, Capital..............	134,153 12

Total amount of outstanding Bonds, payable in Sterling currency.................... **$110,937,211 37**

Bonded Debt, Principal and Interest payable in Mexican Silver currency.

Three per cent. interest bearing Bonds of the Interior Consolidated Debt, Capital and Interest...........	$52,464,927 60
Five per cent. interest bearing Bonds of the Interior Redeemable Debt, first series, Capital and Interest....	19,995,689 48
Five per cent. interest bearing Bonds of the Interior Redeemable Debt, second series, Capital and Interest.	987,127 15
Subsidy Bonds, non converted balances, for sundry works and railways, Capital......................	9,792,865 75

Total 83,240,609 98

Railway Construction Certificates, pending of conversion, Capital...................................	219 17
Balance-certificates corresponding to the fiscal years comprehended between 1882 and 1894, Capital pending of conversion........	329,221 91

Total amount of bonded debt, payable in Mexican Silver currency...................... 83,570,051 06

Grand Total of Bonded Liabilities............. **$194,507,262 43**

Liabilities from various sources, and in forms, other than Bonds, payable in Mexican Silver currency.

To Railway, Harbor Works and Drainage of the Valley of Mexico, Contractors...........................	$ 501,741 02
To Unpaid for Appropriations in the Budgets for the fiscal years between 1891 and 1896..	612,337 82
To other credits pending of settlement: on account of the same Budgets.........................	600,894 63
To Balances in Account-current due various Contractors with some of the Executive Departments..........	315,818 95
To sundry, cash or otherwise executed, Deposits, as guarantee for pending contracts	2,681,662 95
To provisional certificates issued on account of the 1888, 1890 and 1893, Sterling Loans...................	3,738,684 12
To cash or other values pending of classification in the corresponding accounts......................	74,434 57
To cash Receipts on account of credits, other than fiscal and pending of payment to the corresponding offices.	32,829 68
To Balance due to Mint-Lessees.......................	48,214 80
To outstanding Bills Payable..........................	111,186 28

Total Amount of Liabilities from various sources and in forms other than Bonds.... 8,717,804 91

Grand Total of the Mexican National Debt..... **$203,225,067 34**

STATEMENT OF THE FEDERAL PUBLIC DEBT ON JUNE 30, 1896.

	Interest bearing annual.	Sinking fund.	BONDED DEBT.		INDEBTEDNESS SETTLED IN SUNDRY FORMS OTHER THAN BONDS.	
			Principal and interest payable in sterling money.	Payable in Mexican silver currency.	Payable in sterling money.	Payable in Mexican silver currency.
Balance of the loan contracted in London in 1851, not presented to conversion.	6 %		$ 134,153 12			
Loan of 1888 in Berlin and London to refund the loan of 1885.	5 "	½	51,908,765 50			
Loan of 1889 for the Tehuantepec Railway.	5 "	⅓	13,500,000 00			
Loan of 1890 for the payment of railway subsidies.	6 "	1⅓	30,068,720 35			
Loan of 1893 to pay public indebtedness.	6 "	½	15,335,561 30			
Conversion of 1886 to 1896 of the interior debt.	3 "			$59,464,097 60		
Conversion of 1894 in settlement of railway and public works, claims, first series.		1 "		19,005,689 48		
Conversion of 1895 in settlement of railway and public works, claims, second series.	5 "	1 "		987,127 15		
Special subsidy bonds pending conversion under the law of September 6, 1894.	5 "	½		9,792,865 75		
Balances of certificates of railway construction.						219 27
Certificates of balances due for public service, pending of conversion.					$	329,221 91
Balances due to several railways, public works, and drainage of the Valley of Mexico contractors.						504,741 02
Unpaid appropriations of 1891 to 1896.						612,337 82
Sundry claims on said appropriations pending liquidation.						600,894 63
Balance, favor of sundry contracts with the various departments.						315,818 95
Sundry deposits to guarantee pending contracts.						2,681,662 95
Provisional certificates—not submitted to conversion—issued on the sterling loans of 1888, 1890, and 1893.					$3,738,684 12	
Cash receipts on account of municipal dues—pending of payment.						39,829 68
Cash receipts pending of classification for the corresponding accounts.						74,434 57
Balances due to mint leases.						48,214 89
Outstanding treasury bills.						111,186 28
Total.			$110,937,211 37	$83,249,609 98	$3,738,684 12	$5,308,561 87
Grand total.						$203,225,067 34

POST-OFFICE AND TELEGRAPH SERVICE.

I append a statement containing the number of post-offices, and postal agencies in each of the Mexican states in 1895, and the number of postal pieces transported by Mexican mails from the years 1878–1879 to 1894–1895. (See page 225.)

I have prepared a statement of the earnings and expenditures of the post-office and telegraph services in Mexico during the twenty-seven fiscal years elapsed from July 1, 1869, to June 30, 1896. It was not possible to obtain full data of the earnings of the telegraph lines during the first ten years of that period, on account of the defective way in which the books were kept by the Federal Treasury of Mexico. With that exception the data embraced in the following statement is correct, as it has been taken from the official accounts. (See p. 224.)

POST-OFFICES IN MEXICO IN 1895 BY STATES.

STATES.	POST-OFFICE.	POSTAL AGENCIES.		TOTAL.
Aguascalientes..........	5	5	..	10
Campeche.	8	3	..	11
Chiapas..............	7	24	..	31
Chihuahua............	24	58	..	82
Coahuila	25	26	1	52
Colima.	2	9	..	11
Durango	19	42	..	61
Federal District........	1	8	10	19
Guanajuato...........	27	38	..	65
Guerrero.............	13	31	..	44
Hidalgo.	19	43	..	62
Jalisco...............	35	83	..	118
Lower California.......	7	17	..	24
Mexico	14	21	..	35
Michoacan	22	59	..	81
Morelos.............	9	9	..	18
New Leon............	18	33	..	51
Oaxaca..............	22	39	..	61
Puebla..............	27	77	1	105
Querétaro...........	7	10	..	17
San Luis Potosí........	18	34	..	52
Sinaloa..............	16	28	..	44
Sonora..............	14	75	..	89
Tabasco..............	5	16	..	21
Tamaulipas...........	17	36	..	53
Tepic...............	7	13	..	20
Tlaxcala	9	7	..	16
Veracruz............	36	82	..	118
Yucatan.............	16	40	..	56
Zacatecas	20	23	1	44
Total..........	469	989	13	1471

EARNINGS AND EXPENDITURES OF THE POST-OFFICE AND TELEGRAPH
SERVICES DURING THE LAST TWENTY-SEVEN FISCAL YEARS, FROM
JULY 1, 1869, TO JUNE 30, 1896.

FISCAL YEARS.	POST-OFFICE.		TELEGRAPH.		BOTH SERVICES.—TOTAL.	
	Dr. Expenditure.	Cr. Earnings.	Dr. Expenditure.	Cr. Earnings.[1]	Dr. Expenditure.	Cr. Earnings.[1]
1869–1870...	$ 132,399 06	$ 120,120 24	$ 29,212 73	$ 1,809 53	$ 161,611 79	....
1870–1871...	154,574 90	167,348 85	84,150 00	....	238,724 90	....
1871–1872...	340,324 63	265,440 22	48,379 77	....	388,704 40	....
1872–1873...	457,153 19	474,819 11	72,418 96	....	529,572 15	....
1873–1874...	491,199 48	523,583 09	174,504 32	....	665,703 80	....
Total in five years..	$ 1,575,651 26	$ 1,551,311 51	$ 408,665 78	....	$ 1,984,317 04	....
Average per annum.	$ 315,130 25	$ 310,262 30	$ 81,733 16	....	$ 396,863 41	....
1874–1875...	$ 641,836 35	$ 549,820 14	$ 190,366 06	....	$ 832,202 41	....
1875–1876...	480,299 37	455,473 12	161,795 66	....	642,095 03	....
1876–1877...	530,032 95	441,329 10	134,830 02	....	664,862 97	....
1877–1878...	682,076 21	590,384 36	241,200 00	....	923,276 21	....
1878–1879...	867,789 75	679,392 06	259,095 86	$ 1,789 15	1,126,885 61	....
Total in five years..	$ 3,202,034 63	$ 2,716,398 78	$ 987,287 60	....	$ 4,189,322 23	....
Average per annum.	$ 640,406 93	$ 543,279 76	$ 197,457 52	....	$ 837,864 45	....
1879–1880...	$ 892,856 73	$ 708,080 39	$ 348,290 24	$ 101,064 69	$ 1,241,146 97	$ 803,145 08
1880–1881...	983,606 17	833,830 87	196,542 94	135,144 02	1,180,149 11	968,974 89
1881–1882...	873,201 78	704,766 47	570,155 25	174,301 24	1,443,357 03	879,067 71
1882–1883...	840,354 70	795,122 86	916,657 53	219,384 91	1,757,012 23	1,014,507 77
1883–1884...	878,519 75	698,019 36	677,729 50	239,051 45	1,556,249 25	937,070 81
Total in five years..	$ 4,468,539 13	$ 3,733,819 95	$ 2,709,375 46	$ 868,946 31	$ 7,177,914 59	$ 4,602,766 26
Average per annum.	$ 893,707 83	$ 746,763 99	$ 541,875 09	$ 173,789 26	$ 1,435,582 92	$ 920,553 25
1884–1885...	$ 1,411,183 03	$ 642,660 19	$ 618,829 54	$ 180,820 77	$ 2,030,012 57	$ 823,480 96
1885–1886...	751,227 37	672,329 80	622,858 67	155,442 82	1,374,086 04	827,772 62
1886–1887...	943,332 74	739,732 65	718,821 70	197,478 87	1,662,154 44	937,211 52
1887–1888...	956,701 47	793,873 74	799,074 24	275,856 95	1,755,775 71	1,069,730 69
1888–1889...	1,049,880 10	880,530 93	820,072 05	329,493 13	1,869,952 15	1,210,024 06
Total in five years..	$ 5,112,324 71	$ 3,729,127 31	$ 3,579,656 20	$ 1,139,092 54	$ 8,691,980 91	$ 4,868,219 85
Average per annum.	$ 1,022,464 94	$ 745,825 46	$ 715,931 24	$ 227,818 51	$ 1,738,396 18	$ 973,643 97
1889–1890...	$ 1,126,436 69	$ 994,112 87	$ 872,316 89	$ 388,926 07	$ 1,998,753 58	$ 1,383,038 94
1890–1891...	1,196,329 63	1,084,153 40	972,164 06	462,076 59	2,168,493 69	1,546,229 99
1891–1892...	1,342,437 11	1,127,563 18	1,045,726 44	501,802 33	2,388,163 55	1,629,365 51
1892–1893...	1,278,587 20	1,153,401 20	1,073,105 81	528,881 96	2,351,693 01	1,682,283 16
1893–1894...	1,250,855 82	1,213,309 46	954,864 48	524,634 33	2,205,720 30	1,737,943 79
Total in five years..	$ 6,194,646 45	$ 5,572,540 11	$ 4,918,177 68	$ 2,406,321 28	$11,112,824 13	$ 7,978,861 39
Average per annum.	$ 1,238,929 29	$ 1,114,508 02	$ 983,635 54	$ 481,264 26	$ 2,222,564 83	$ 1,595,772 28
1894–1895...	$ 633,201 36	$ 1,337,691 40	$ 531,949 48	$ 547,308 67	$ 1,165,150 84	$ 1,885,000 07
1895–1896...	1,228,784 30	1,062,415 99	1,025,347 29	622,340 69	2,254,131 59	1,684,756 68
Total in two years..	$ 1,861,985 66	$ 2,400,107 39	$ 1,557,296 77	$ 1,169,649 36	$ 3,419,282 43	$ 3,569,756 75
Average per annum.	$ 930,992 83	$ 1,200,053 70	$ 778,648 38	$ 584,824 68	$ 1,709,641 21	$ 1,784,878 38
Total in the 27 years ...	$22,415,181 84	$19,703,305 05	$14,160,459 49	$ 5,584,000 49	$36,575,641 33	$21,019,604 25
Average per annum.	$ 830,191 92	$ 729,752 04	$ 524,461 46	$ 328,471 14	$ 1,354,653 38	$ 1,236,447 30

[1] The totals and averages per annum in the colums marked "Earnings" and "Total Earnings" only embrace seventeen years, as the returns for the first ten years being very incomplete are not computed.

NUMBER OF PIECES TRANSPORTED BY MEXICAN MAILS FROM 1878–1879
TO 1894–1895.

FISCAL YEARS.	NUMBER OF PIECES.
1878–1879	5,992,611
1879–1880	5,786,790
1880–1881	6,141,790
1881–1882	6,732,504
1882–1883	10,640,516
1883–1884	10,488,518
1884–1885	11,905,209
1885–1886	13,289,591
1886–1887	16,504,034
1887–1888	27,429,018
1888–1889	43,052,800
1889–1890	95,852,939
1890–1891	111,406,893
1891–1892	116,778,853
1892–1893	122,821,359
1893–1894	35,818,148
1894–1895	24,773,636
Total	665,415,209

Printed matter, samples, and parcel post articles in the year 1894–1895, weighed in grammes, 1,107,755,679.

The notable reduction which appears in the last two years is due to the fact that in the preceding years all correspondence was counted, namely : such pieces as were received and sent, and such as came in transit, while in the last two years only are accounted such as were sent.

BANKS.

The following statement contains a list of all the banks existing in Mexico up to December 31, 1895, and their respective condition :

LIST OF MEXICAN BANKS.

STATE.	LOCATION.	NAME OF BANK.	DATE OF CHARTER.
Federal District.	Mexico City....	National Bank of Mexico.....	February, 1882.
" "	" "	International and Hypothecary Bank of Mexico..........	May, 1883.
" "	" "	Bank of London and Mexico..	October, 1886.
Chihuahua.. ...	Chihuahua City..	Mexican Chihuahua Bank....	September, 1888.
"	" " ..	Chihuahua Mining Bank.....	September, 1888.
"	" " ..	Chihuahua Bank............	December, 1889.
"	" " ..	Chihuahua Commercial Bank..	December, 1890.
Yucatan........	Merida.........	Yucateco Bank.............	February, 1890.
"	"	Yucatan Mercantile Bank.....	March, 1890.
Durango	Durango City...	Durango Bank	June 1, 1891.
Zacatecas.......	Zacatecas City..	Zacatecas Bank............	December, 1891.
New Leon......	Monterey	New Leon Bank............	February 18, 1892

SITUATION OF THE MEXICAN BANKS ON DECEMBER 31, 1894.

	NATIONAL BANK OF MEXICO.	BANK OF LONDON AND MEXICO.	INTERNATIONAL AND HYPOTHECARY BANK OF MEXICO.	CHIHUAHUA MINING BANK.	MEXICAN CHIHUAHUA BANK.	CHIHUAHUA COMMERCIAL BANK, ON FEBRUARY 15, 1895.
Social capital....	$20,000,000 00	$3,000,000 00	$5,000,000 00	$ 600,000 00	$610,000 00	$600,000 00
Unpaid capital.	12,000,000 00	....	1,500,000 00	....	....	300,000 00
Accumulated capital......					50,342 62	
Reserve funds..	1,796,100 51	1,100,000 00	34,500 00	105,000 00	108,600 00	5,000 00
Emergency funds........	2,500,000 00			22,729 55	6,928 00	....
Real estate.....	190,000 00	111,266 94	242,662 76	....	100,855 86	....
Cash..........	20,630,086 89	7,783,647 78	656,496 33	292,555 01	265,630 62	52,026 61
Cash in hand...	11,962,994 35	8,892,749 25	1,581,974 19	1,167,942 29	281,713 84	229,199 13
Guarantee advances.......	3,093,555 21	....	....		94,124 01	
Advances on mortgages....	....	....	2,788,527 85	....	94,124 01	....
Debtors' current accounts....	12,605,302 02	5,318,895 69	1,854,417 78	264,538 80	786,198 62	222,115 58
Bills in circulation.........	16,417,061 00	9,195,535 00	....	538,429 25	287,133 28	122,782 00
Mortgage bonds in circulation.	....	....	1,947,200 00	....	....	....
Deposits and creditors' current accounts.	21,768,776 96	8,811,024 66	1,642,378 91	458,877 30	465,519 05	75,559 32

	CHIHUAHUA BANK, ON JANUARY 15, 1895.	YUCATECO BANK.	YUCATAN MERCANTILE BANK.	DURANGO BANK.	ZACATECAS BANK.	NEW LEON BANK.
Social capital....	$500,000 00	$1,000,000 00	$ 750,000 00	$500,000 00	$600,000 00	$600,000 00
Unpaid capital.	200,000 00	....	....	....	240,000 00	....
Reserve funds..	5,666 25	22,654 71	17,716 89	3,396 88	6,500 00	8,278 82
Real estate, furniture, etc.....						175,619 63
Cash..........	40,174 41	475,519 43	508,805 68	178,282 55	250,376 35	240,066 38
Cash in hand...	109,113 11	1,346,715 63	1,001,457 81	603,039 90	565,032 52	600,323 71
Guarantee advances.......	....	....	....	71,894 13	98,196 13	231,094 10
Debtor's current accounts......	285,441 59	172,391 75	426,601 32	322,927 09	339,306 74	118,521 26
Bills in circulation.........	98,885 00	658,726 00	658,312 00	227,079 00	185,346 00	565,418 00
Deposits and creditors' current accounts.	30,277 86	313,246 10	510,835 92	445,667 79	701,065 74	191,928 26

PUBLIC LANDS.

I append four statements of the titles of public lands issued by the Mexican Government. The first one embraces a résumé of the titles issued without cost, and under the act of December 14, 1874, of the Indian town lands held in common, called in Spanish " Ejidos " to the respective inhabitants of the said towns, from 1877 to 1895 : the second embraces a résumé of the titles issued in 1894 and 1895 for public lands held by private parties as portions of public land bought from the government but which were in excess of the respective titles, which we call in Spanish " Demacias " : the third one embraces a résumé of the titles of public lands issued to private parties in the years 1894

and 1895 : and the fourth contains a résumé of the titles issued by the
Mexican Government to surveying companies for one-third of the land
respectively surveyed by them in 1894 and 1895, according to law and
the respective contracts.

FREE TITLES ISSUED UNDER THE ACT OF DECEMBER 14, 1874, OF
THE INDIAN TOWN LANDS TO THE RESPECTIVE
INHABITANTS FROM 1877 TO 1895.

YEARS.	TITLES.	AREA.		
		Hectares.	Ares.	Cts.
1877.............................	1	85	06	00
1878.............................	195	3,572	71	41
1879.............................	72	128,144	94	56
1880......	2	5,000	00	00
1882.............................	195	5,629	29	69
1883.............................	259	14,616	14	13
1884.............................	1,932	61,497	56	94
1885.............................	383	13,068	18	08
1896.............................	774	20,662	93	12
1887.............................	254	2,999	85	98
1868.............................	1,524	20,547	73	16
1889.............................	2,237	100,627	65	32
1890.............................	1,130	68,086	31	86
1891.............................	499	6,516	74	22
1892.............................	1,449	15,807	30	95
1893.............................	452	17,709	59	08
1894.............................	791	6,262	71	49
1895.............................	273	6,160	03	65
Total.....	12,422	496,994	79	64

TITLES ISSUED FOR UNWARRANTED POSSESSION BY PRIVATE PARTIES
OF PUBLIC LANDS IN 1894 AND 1895.

YEARS.	Number of Titles.	AREA.			VALUE.
		Hectares.	Ares.	Cts.	
1894..................	17	34,781	98	04	$21,554 91
1895..................	10	69,557	33	21	20,254 12
	27	104,339	31	25	$41,809 03

TITLES OF PUBLIC LANDS ISSUED TO PRIVATE PARTIES IN
1894 AND 1895.

YEARS.	Number of Titles.	AREA.			VALUE.
		Hectares.	Ares.	Cts.	
1894	21	86,385	63	26	$140,067 72
1895..................	19	59,265	24	84	81,883 95
	40	145,650	88	10	$221,951 67

TITLES ISSUED IN 1894 AND 1895 TO SURVEYING COMPANIES FOR
ONE-THIRD OF THE LAND SURVEYED BY THEM.

YEARS.	Number of Titles.	AREA.		
		Hectares.	Ares.	Cts.
1894...................................	32	484,257	30	70
1895...................................	29	243,576	11	81
	61	727,833	42	51

EDUCATION.

The following official data received by the Census Bureau of the
Mexican Government contains the number of schools in the different
States of Mexico, supported by the Federal, State, and municipal ad-
ministrations, and the number of students attending the same. That
statement does not include the States of Mexico and Veracruz, which
are among those having the largest number of schools and attendance.

I also append a statement of the number of schools supported by
private parties, with the number of pupils attending the same and
their cost ; and finally a detailed statement of the public libraries existing in Mexico, and newspapers published in the country, taken from
the publication of the Census Bureau in 1895.

NEWSPAPERS PUBLISHED IN MEXICO IN 1895.

Aguascalientes	10	New Leon........................	8
Campeche	4	Oaxaca...........................	5
Chiapas	4	Puebla	17
Chihuahua	19	Queretaro........................	1
Coahuila........................	6	San Luis Potosí..................	6
Colima..........................	13	Sinaloa...........................	14
Durango.........................	7	Sonora	12
Federal District, City of Mexico....	115	Tabasco..........................	14
Guanajuato	14	Tamaulipas	20
Guerrero	6	Territory of Tepic................	6
Hidalgo	3	Tlaxcala	2
Jalisco	43	Veracruz	24
Lower California (Territory).......	5	Yucatan.	18
Mexico..........................	11	Zacatecas.........................	12
Michoacan	30		
Morelos	5	Total....................	454

These are published in several languages, namely :

English.........................	12	German	1
French	2	Spanish..........................	439
		Total....................	454

Dailies...........................	44	Bi-monthly	3
Semi-weekly	33	Quarterly.........................	5
Tri-weekly.......................	5	Yearly	3
Weekly..........................	185	Unknown.........................	10
Semi-monthly	79		
Monthly	87	Total....................	454

EDUCATION.

PUBLIC SCHOOLS SUPPORTED BY THE FEDERAL, STATE, AND MUNICIPAL ADMINISTRATIONS OF MEXICO IN 1895.

STATES.	SCHOOLS SUPPORTED BY THE GOVERNMENT.				SCHOOLS SUPPORTED BY THE MUNICIPALITY.				GRADES.			Total.
	Males.	Females.	Both sexes.	Total.	Males.	Females.	Both sexes.	Total.	Primary.	Secondary.	Professional.	
Aguascalientes	1	1		2	90	14		43	43	2	1	45
Campeche	30	18		48	16	8		27	72			75
Coahuila	3			3	69	55	3	199	131	2		132
Colima	21	21	120	42	1		5	1	43			43
Chiapas	31	97		178					177	1	1	178
Chihuahua	71	31	16	118					116			118
Durango	70	38	8	116					112	1	2	116
Guerrero	266	57		323	55	47		102	339	2	2	333
Guanajuato	88	77	292	365	6	4			363	2	2	367
Hidalgo	122	104	92	518				10	515	2	2	518
Jalisco	194	189	92	475					499	2	4	495
Michoacan	194	94	115	288			11		285	1	2	288
Morelos	53	54		222			167	311	221	2		222
Nuevo Leon	4	1		5	210	90			311	1		316
Oaxaca	512	101	1	614	18	286	156	1,170	698	1	4	640
Puebla	11	3	4	18	777		186	156	1,182	3	1	1,088
Querétaro	89	30	19	119			6	252	117		3	119
San Luis Potosi	86	81	185	185	36	36		162	340		1	342
Sinaloa	1			1	107	49	4	119	352			353
Sonora					74	41		71	162	1		162
Tabasco	35	22	32	79	40	22	132	425	77		1	79
Tamaulipas	4	2		6	174	119	26	270	119	6		125
Tlaxcala	132	66	34	232	128	116		91	931	1	3	932
Yucatan	168	92	1	261	58	29	4	98	388	1	3	332
Zacatecas	2	2	8	4	7	8	13	1	445		1	449
Federal District	9	6		23			1		392			903
Territory of Tepic									91			91
Lower California Territory, Southern District	2	2		6					28			28
Lower California Territory, Northern District			6	10					11			11
Totals	2,180	1,119	748	4,056	1,754	932	708	3,394	7,380	34	36	7,459

EDUCATION.

PUBLIC SCHOOLS SUPPORTED BY THE FEDERAL, STATE, AND MUNICIPAL ADMINISTRATIONS OF MEXICO IN 1895—Continued.

STATES.	ALUMNI INSCRIBED IN THE YEAR.			MEDIUM ATTENDANCE DURING THE YEAR.			AGES.				ADVANCEMENT.		
	Males.	Females.	Total.	Males.	Females.	Total.	Over 5 years.	From 5 to 10 years.	From 10 to 15 years.	Over 15 years.	Alumni examined.	Alumni passing examination.	Graduated.
Aguascalientes	2,574	1,715	4,289	1,790	1,218	3,008	129	2,479	1,375	306	2,954	2,735	41
Campeche	2,320	1,462	3,782	1,725	1,121	2,846	375	2,540	611	256	3,070	1,074	32
Coahuila	6,472	5,656	12,128	5,199	4,919	10,118	1,046	6,082	4,436	564	7,780	7,206	75
Colima	1,741	1,723	3,464	1,119	1,214	2,333	35	1,817	1,348	264	2,495	1,608	135
Chiapas	1,510	1,284	2,794								30	30	14
Chihuahua	6,387	4,257	10,644	4,218	2,977	7,195	881			618	7,816	7,198	207
Durango	5,044	3,664	8,708	4,690	2,068	6,758	387			977	6,534	5,062	97
Guerrero	9,427	3,743	13,170	5,871	2,490	8,361	221			216	8,037	6,131	268
Guanajuato	17,837	13,867	31,704	11,397	8,920	20,377	866			349	12,777	11,824	58
Hidalgo	19,981	5,476	25,457	14,704	6,563	21,267	4,247			3,093	17,193	14,575	413
Jalisco	14,651	9,745	24,396	14,731	14,445	29,176	356			1,426	17,155	16,363	430
Michoacan	6,991	5,525	12,516	4,611	4,437	9,048	273			925	14,877	9,765	1
Morelos	13,159	7,309	20,468	9,492	5,251	14,743	6,209				13,899	7,795	815
Nuevo Leon							1,986						1,479
Oaxaca	54,713	12,181	66,894	19,288	3,719	23,007	4,966				19,171	13,751	584
Puebla	37,003	17,032	54,035	26,802	11,243	38,045					37,499	33,144	129
Querétaro	3,725	1,417	5,142	2,886	1,062	3,948	310				3,384	2,925	1,933
San Luis Potosi	13,936	11,359	25,295	10,882	8,777	19,659	148				18,590	14,724	367
Sinaloa	7,363	5,077	12,440	5,501	4,160	9,661	103				9,334	8,250	45
Sonora	5,052	4,598	9,650	4,600	4,200	8,800	2,132				6,800	3,100	125
Tabasco	3,165	1,630	4,795	4,921	861	5,782	842				67	58	129
Tamaulipas	5,746	3,388	9,134	3,766	2,078	5,844	1,045				5,961	4,942	133
Tlaxcala	7,096	3,720	11,716	7,209	3,002	10,211	798				9,226	8,825	1,306
Yucatan	9,106	4,998	14,104	9,652	4,491	14,143	90				12,846	12,572	434
Zacatecas	15,791	12,184	27,975	11,263	8,821	20,084					16,293	12,604	771
Federal District	17,218	12,610	29,828	12,302	9,559	21,861					14,880	13,299	50
Territory of Tepic	3,154	2,323	5,477	2,141	1,540	3,681	206				2,777	1,848	
Lower California Territory, Southern District	931	927	1,858	575	626	1,201					1,234	671	
Lower California Territory, Northern District	200	157	357	172	127	299					312	276	
Totals	310,496	181,484	491,980	208,717	129,349	338,066	27,403	235,887	167,513	42,722	295,705	226,560	10,271

EDUCATION.

SCHOOLS SUPPORTED BY PRIVATE PARTIES.

STATES.	SCHOOLS SUPPORTED BY PRIVATE PARTIES.				SCHOOLS SUPPORTED BY THE CLERGY.				SCHOOLS SUPPORTED BY SOCIETIES.				ALUMNI INSCRIBED DURING THE YEAR.		
	Males.	Females.	Both sexes.	Total.	Males.	Females.	Both sexes.	Total.	Males.	Females.	Both sexes.	Total.	Males.	Females.	Total.
Aguascalientes	6	2		8	1	1		1					185	80	265
Campeche	4	4		8	1	1		1					282	83	365
Coahuila	37	25	13	75	1	1		5					1,647	1,473	3,120
Colima			24	24	4	2	2	6		7		9	660	708	1,368
Chiapas					3	1		2	2	2		2			
Chihuahua	3	1	2	6	1			1					187	133	320
Durango	39	13	14	66	1	1	2	1	5	6		11	2,516	1,526	4,042
Guerrero	14	9	1	24	3			5					1,297	700	1,997
Guanajuato	63	47		110	4	1		5					3,591	2,351	5,942
Hidalgo	30	17	111	47	14	14		28	8	3	1	12	2,471	1,791	4,262
Jalisco	86	74		274	39	34	9	82	1	3		4	12,009	8,914	20,993
Michoacan	54	58	29	141	30	11	4	34	1		1	2	4,516	3,405	7,921
Morelos	10	5	8	23	2	1		3				1	804	570	1,473
Nuevo Leon	52	31	12	95	1			3					2,010	1,508	3,518
Oaxaca	11	13	80	40	1	5	21	27	14	12	2	26	5,972	8,339	14,521
Puebla	27	33	13	53	4	6		19	11	6		19	4,515	2,112	6,627
Queretaro	14	10	19	43	4	1		4					1,267	852	2,119
San Luis Potosí	49	39	336	424	1	1	2	2	10	9		19	2,127	1,905	4,032
Sinaloa	10	5		15											
Sonora	1		2	3									73	29	102
Tabasco	27	12	3	42	6	7		14	1	1		2	740	952	1,692
Tamaulipas	24	8	14	46					1	1		2	708	486	1,194
Tlaxcala	11	8	3	22	2			2					427	252	679
Yucatan	9	19	9	37	7			8	9	2		9	1,438	527	1,965
Zacatecas	58	46	35	139	6			9	3			5	3,802	3,324	7,026
Federal District	14	11	6	31	5			12	10	1		17	1,690	1,582	3,272
Territory of Tepic	2	3		16	5	2	2	12		1			1,504	1,166	2,670
Lower California Territory, Southern District	1	1	2	4	1			1		1	6		129	16	145
Totals	650	460	697	1,816	141	92	43	275	78	57	11	146	56,657	44,683	101,340

EDUCATION.

SCHOOLS SUPPORTED BY PRIVATE PARTIES—*Continued.*

STATES.	MEDIUM ATTENDANCE DURING THE YEAR.			GRADES.				AGES.				ADVANCEMENT.		
	Males.	Females.	Total.	Primary.	Secondary.	Professional.	Total.	Five years.	From 5 to 10 years.	From 10 to 15 years.	Over 15 years.	Examined.	Passed.	Graduated.
Aguascalientes	119	14	133	8	1		9	14	39	92	129	226	221	7
Campeche	244	78	322	9			9	14	333	113		350	205	3
Coahuila	1,492	1,271	2,763	88	1		89	252	1,407	1,300	161	2,356	2,377	101
Colima	570	397	957	32			32	120	707	508	33	992	962	15
Chiapas	132	112	244	4										
Chihuahua	2,004	1,094	3,098	80	5		9	7	103	133	77	353	333	390
Durango	798	284	1,082	27	1	1	82	539	2,073	1,205	325	2,690	2,571	44
Guerrero	3,109	2,225	5,334	110	1		89	407	691	537	362	1,500	1,145	
Guanajuato	1,855	1,233	3,088	74			110							
Hidalgo	9,256	7,295	16,551	396	1		75	493	2,112	1,304	393	177	169	3
Jalisco	3,429	2,721	6,150	179	7	3	368	3,224	8,907	6,503	2,289	12,305	9,041	311
Michoacan	638	507	1,145	26	7		179	626	855	2,777	1,244	5,141	4,190	268
Morelos					2		28	148		404	66	1,296	46	8
Nuevo Leon				93	5		99	2,256	4,358	4,581	3,106	1,807	1,107	61
Oaxaca	1,482	939	2,421	93		1	93	494	3,127	3,127	735	5,052	4,559	173
Puebla	3,592	1,530	5,122	85	5		91	307	887	700	225	1,186	1,089	149
Queretaro	1,076	743	1,819	45	1		47							
San Luis Potosi	2,079	1,896	3,975	445			445							
Sinaloa				15	3		15	17	48	37		651	538	6
Sonora	60	25	85	4		1		152	859	610	71	593	448	16
Tabasco	652	860	1,512	58		1	58	61	684	427	22	1,734	1,907	258
Tamaulipas	504	347	851	48			48	122	364	129	44	5,446	4,393	263
Tlaxcala	367	319	686	26			26	377	543	1,060	167	1,977	1,812	98
Yucatan	1,116	445	1,661	43			47	327	3,613	2,595	441	1,518	1,119	6
Zacatecas	3,018	2,393	5,411	150			152	250	1,880	959	97	115	69	
Federal District	1,229	1,246	2,475	42			42	11	1,454	872	85			
Territory of Tepic	1,111	867	1,978	45			45		112	22				
Lower California Territory, Southern District	103	13	116	5										
Totals	40,135	28,744	68,879	2,193	34	11	2,238	10,413	38,350	29,208	9,872	47,413	38,181	2,099

PUBLIC LIBRARIES IN MEXICO.

STATES.	NAME OF LIBRARY.	WHERE LOCATED.	NUMBER OF VOLUMES.	ANNUAL NUMBER OF STUDENTS.	HOW SUPPORTED.
Aguascalientes	Scientific Institute	Aguascalientes	3,668	1,037	State funds.
Campeche	Campeche Institute	Campeche	3,408	150	Institute funds.
"	Carmelita Lyceum	Cármen	1,194	.....	Carmelita Lyceum funds.
"	Melchor Ocampo	.....	.....	585	Miguel Hidalgo School funds.
Coahuila	State	Saltillo	2,102	4,400	State funds.
"	Commercial	.....	.....	.....	School funds.
Colima	Public	Colima	355	.....	Government funds.
"	Parochial "Christopher Columbus"	"	350	.....	Clergy funds.
"	Seminary	.....	3,322	.....	"
Chiapas	Preparatory School	San Cristóbal	3,450	.....	Federal Government funds.
"	Public	Tapachula	.....	.....	"
Chihuahua	Franklin Society	Chihuahua	2,563	775	Franklin Society funds.
"	Literary Institute	"	1,690	.....	Institute funds.
"	San Francisco College	.....	490	.....	College funds.
Durango	Juárez Institute	Durango	5,000	6,000	State funds.
Federal District	National	Mexico	159,000	.....	Federal Government funds.
"	Preparatory School	"	10,000	.....	"
"	Commercial "	.....	2,000	.....	"
"	Law	.....	14,000	.....	"
"	Fine Arts	.....	2,000	.....	"
"	Engineering	.....	7,000	.....	"
"	Agricultural	.....	4,000	.....	"
"	Medical	.....	3,000	.....	"
"	Museum of Natural History	.....	2,000	.....	"
"	Geographical and Statistical Society	.....	4,000	.....	"
"	Judicial Archives	.....	1,000	.....	"
"	General Archives	.....	8,000	.....	"
"	Normal School for Men	.....	400	.....	"
"	Normal School for Women	.....	400	.....	"
"	Conservatory of Music	.....	1,021	.....	"

PUBLIC LIBRARIES IN MEXICO—*Continued.*

State	Institution	Location			Funds
Federal District	Arts and Trades for Men	Mexico	2,117	...	Federal Government funds.
Guanajuato	State College	Guanajuato	12,500	10,900	State funds.
Guerrero	Literary Institute	Chilpancingo	2,346	8,400	"
Hidalgo	Scientific and Literary Institute	Pachuca	2,628	...	"
Jalisco	State	Guadalajara	...	16,000	"
Mexico	Municipal	Cuautitlan	300	15	Special donations.
"	"	Coyotepec	38	5	"
"	"	Ixtlahuaca	36	5	"
"	"	San Felipe del Progreso	27	15	"
"	"	Mineral del Oro	13	20	"
"	"	Jilotepec	25	15	"
"	"	Lerma	130	10	"
"	Benito Juárez	Otumba	77	20	"
"	Municipal	Saltepec	16	25	"
"	"	Sacualpan	16	9	"
"	"	Texcaltitlan	15	14	"
"	"	Temascaltepec	64	14	"
"	"	Tejupilco	56	12	"
"	"	San Simon de Guerrero	87	12	"
"	Scientific Institute	Toluca	13,700	12	"
"	Municipal	Bravo Valley	25	12	"
"	"	Asuncion Malacatepec	62	10	"
"	"	Tenango Valley	45	4	"
"	"	Guerrero Valley	10	4	"
Michoacan	Public	Morelia	13,922	8,864	$1 tax on the estate of deceased persons.
"	San Nicolás College	"	...	...	College funds.
"	Seminary	Pátzcuaro	30,000	3,000	Special donations.
"	Compañía College	"	1,000	200	"
"	Seminary	Uruápam	333	43	Municipal funds.
"	Seminary	Zamora	7,000	1,392	Special donations.
Morelos	Public	Cuernavaca	2,348	...	State funds.
"	Yautepec	Yautepec	30	...	"
"	Morelos	Cautla	522	...	"
"	Tetecala	Tetecala	225	...	"
"		Jojutla	352	...	"
Nuevo Leon	Public	Monterey	3,458	...	"
Oaxaca	Public	Oaxaca	15,000	...	"

PUBLIC LIBRARIES IN MEXICO—*Continued.*

State	Library	City	Volumes	Funds	Source
Puebla	Palafoxiana	Puebla	27,000	4,000	State funds.
"	Lafragua	"	21,000	15,012	"
"	Serrano	Atlixco	200	80	Special donations.
"	Benito Juárez	Zacatlan	400	2,408	"
"	Manuel M. Flores	Chalchicomila	350	100	Political Prefect donations.
"	"Porfirio Diaz" Municipal	Matamoros Izucar	500	50	Municipal funds.
Querétaro	Civil College	Querétaro	7,743	......	"
San Luis Potosí	State	San Luis Potosí	13,751	20,345	State funds.
Sinaloa		Culiacan	3,000	495	"
Sonora		Hermosillo	4,714	4,870	"
"	Sonora College	"	800	......	"
"	Board of Public Instruction	Guaymas	1,138	......	Junta
"	Education Society	Sahuaripa	800	......	State
Talasco	Juárez Institute	San Juan Bautista	165	......	"
"	José Eduardo Cárdenas		1,800	......	"
Tamaulipas	State	Ciudad Victoria	1,650	3,600	"
"	Juárez Society	Matamoros	500	......	Juárez Society funds.
Tlaxcala	General Archives	Tlaxcala	11,030	......	State funds.
Veracruz	Pueblo	Veracruz	13,995	3,000	"
"	Public	Tlacotálpan	333	1,100	Municipal funds.
"	Preparatory College	Orizaba	9,704	......	"
"	Preparatory "	Córdova	805	......	"
"	Normal School	Jalapa	697	......	State funds.
"	Preparatory College		1,377	......	"
"	Seminary		2,796	......	"
"	Gabino Barreda	Papantla	97	......	"
"		Tantoyuca	824	......	"
Yucatan	Benito Juárez		400	......	"
"	Cepeda	Mérida	2,317	7,300	Special funds.
"	Iturralde	Valladolid	200	720	"
"	Catholic College	Mérida	4,000	......	"
"	Eulogio Ancona	Progreso	445	340	"
"	Traconis	Ticul	300	......	"
Zacatecas	Public	Zacatecas	22,000	10,000	State donations.
"	"	Fresnillo	2,000	500	"
Lower California Territory	Municipal	La Paz	700	50	Municipal funds.

SUMMARY OF FACTORIES EXISTING IN MEXICO IN 1893.

STATES.	Cotton and woolen mills.	Brandy.	Mezcal.	Beer.	Chemical products.	Chocolate.	Paper.	Soap.	Tobacco.	Matches.	Powder.	Cake and crackers.	Pottery.	China.	Glass.	Starch.	Cotton gins.	Candles.	Artificial stone, bricks, tiles, etc.	Ice.	Grape wine.	Total.
Federal District	13			8	11	8	5	16	22	16		13		2	6	7		118	25	3		273
Aguascalientes	3							2													6	11
Campeche		37																				37
Chiapas		13																				13
Chihuahua	9	13	4					1														20
Coahuila	3							1														10
Colima	7	5																				8
Durango	8	24	11					8					2				5					48
Guanajuato	1	47	3	6		1	2		4	1		7										80
Guerrero	7	77		8								1										79
Hidalgo	4	191	1	1		2	1	40	4			3										263
Jalisco	2	111	9	3	1	2		21	4	4		5			1	1		1				207
Michoacan	15	178	50	2				24		2		3										285
Mexico	2	44	6					6						1								72
Morelos	2	49	4	2												1						57
Nuevo Leon	19	666	33	3			1	3								1	5		1	3		635
Oaxaca	4	88	3					1				2										128
Puebla	2	515		3																1		539
Querétaro	1	82	36							1	1	1										87
San Luis Potosí		213	14	3		3		2		1												256
Sinaloa	5	71	66																			166
Sonora	5	21	4					1														144
Tabasco		13																				35
Tamaulipas		17	12																			35
Tlaxcala	3	137	7				1	4														39
Veracruz	2	42						8	6										1	1		146
Yucatan		58						8		2								7				274
Zacatecas		31	3																		2	64
Territory of Tepic	3		6																		1	41
Territory of Lower California	1	69							1											1		73
Total	123	2,899	276	31	12	16	10	146	41	28	1	35	2	3	7	9	10	126	27	9	9	3,800

MANUFACTURING ESTABLISHMENTS IN MEXICO IN 1893.

I take from *Les Finances des Etats-Unis Mexicains* of Mr. Prosper Gloner the following table, which purports to give the number of some of the manufacturing establishments in Mexico during the year 1893. Mr. Gloner acknowledges that his table is very deficient, as he says in a note that appears at the foot of it that he failed to receive the data from 117 districts in different states of Mexico, and that besides the manufacturing establishments mentioned in his table there are in the City of Mexico the following : (See page 236.)

Carriages and wagons	11
Wax works	28
Agricultural implements	9
Wall paper	1
Coloring substances	2
Mineral and soda-waters	4
Carriage varnishes	2
Jewelry boxes, etc	9
Mucilage and paste	11
Card-board	6
Scientific instruments	1
Playing cards	1
Pianos, organs, and harmonicas	4
Passementeries	6
Type foundries	1
Gold and silver ribbons	2
Perfumeries	6
Hats	49
Musical instruments	6
Total	159

NAVIGATION.

The total number of vessels, both steamers and sailing vessels, which arrived at and departed from Mexican ports during the year 1895, appears in the following statement.

I also append a statement showing the number of passengers who arrived in and departed from Mexico by sea and rail during the year 1895, mentioning both their nationality and the port of their arrival. The number appears exceedingly small when compared with the very large number coming from Europe to the United States ; but I feel sure that before long we will have a large immigration.

VESSELS ARRIVED AT MEXICAN PORTS IN 1895.

COUNTRIES	TOTAL NUMBER			STEAMERS			SAILING VESSELS			LOADED			IN BALLAST		
	Vessels	Tons	Crew	Vessels	Tons	Crew	Vessels	Tons	Crew	Vessels	Tons	Crew	Vessels	Tons	Crew
Mexican ports	4,042	1,757,700 58	77,290	2,406	1,655,634 69	68,392	1,636	102,065 89	8,899	3,329	1,531,227 11	66,422	713	225,473 47	10,868
United States	466	397,059 07	12,393	317	396,480 20	11,214	149	36,569 87	1,089	408	382,935 97	11,526	58	14,134 10	787
Colombia	14	20,509 34	407	11	19,561 66	440	3	947 68	27	11	19,561 66	440	3	947 68	27
Venezuela	15	5,777 59	140	1	1,389 00	22	14	4,330 59	118	3	1,725 35	35	12	3,992 24	105
Brazil	31	11,121 90	289				31	11,121 90	289				31	11,121 90	289
Guatemala	35	53,720 25	2,284	32	53,064 35	2,249	3	655 90	35	28	46,304 99	1,919	7	7,415 26	365
Norway	16	7,482 81	199	1	1,024 00	24	15	6,458 81	175				16	7,482 81	199
Honduras	1	186 00	9				1	186 00	9				1	186 00	9
Costa Rica	10	9,641 95	207	8	9,086 00	191	2	555 95	16	8	9,086 00	191	2	555 95	16
Antilles	2	912 00	22				2	912 00	22	1	446 00	11	2	912 00	22
Chili	1	446 00	11				1	446 00	11						
Hayti	8	12,126 15	326	8	12,126 15	326				8	12,126 15	326			
Holland	5	1,810 56	49				5	1,810 56	49				5	1,810 56	49
Italy	7	8,804 00	184	7	8,804 00	184				7	8,801 00	184			
England	226	217,055 31	4,215	80	137,593 22	2,547	146	79,552 09	1,668	114	181,443 77	3,280	112	35,611 54	935
Germany	36	47,882 01	1,012	23	36,706 22	821	13	11,175 79	191	32	46,460 69	975	4	1,422 32	37
Belgium	6	7,030 00	138	5	7,577 00	127	1	358 00	11	6	7,030 00	138			
France	30	27,973 24	2,291	12	21,944 11	2,023	18	6,029 44	168	15	22,753 90	2,039	15	5,220 34	142
Spain	202	345,314 42	11,426	160	338,204 11	11,084	42	7,090 31	342	155	379,517 91	10,962	47	55,796 51	464
Australia	4	3,476 67	72				4	3,476 67	72	2	2,022 60	41	3	1,454 07	31
Africa	3	807 53	25				3	807 53	25				3	807 53	25
Argentine Republic	3	1,115 33	25				3	1,115 33	25				3	1,115 33	25
Portugal	2	687 30	10				2	687 30	10				2	687 30	10
Unknown	10	7,074 30	167	6	5,223 50	125	4	1,851 00	42	8	6,637 50	151	2	437 00	16
Totals	5,174	2,946,545 42	113,070	3,077	2,668,381 10	99,758	2,097	278,164 32	13,302	4,135	2,603,062 60	98,640	1,039	336,582 82	14,430

VESSELS DEPARTED FROM MEXICAN PORTS IN 1895.

COUNTRIES.	TOTAL NUMBER.			STEAMERS.			SAILING VESSELS.			LOADED.			IN BALLAST.		
	Vessels.	Tons.	Crew.	Vessels.	Tons.	Crew.	Vessels.	Tons.	Crew.	Vessels.	Tons.	Crew.	Vessels.	Tons.	Crew.
Mexican ports	4,109	1,807,230 18	77,942	2,454	1,705,994 55	69,243	1,655	101,955 63	8,699	2,880	1,394,899 85	58,770	1,229	412,330 33	19,172
United States	548	544,768 74	13,685	411	489,504 13	12,460	137	55,264 61	1,225	345	437,468 44	10,592	203	107,300 30	3,093
Colombia	4	4,167 80	196	4	4,167 80	196				1	1,081 75	62	3	3,086 05	134
Guatemala	31	57,619 30	2,085	30	57,332 30	2,075	1	287 00	10	15	26,599 51	1,184	16	31,026 79	901
Honduras	2	548 00	29	2	548 00	29							2	548 00	29
Costa Rica	1	752 60	15				1	752 60	15				1	752 60	15
Nicaragua	1	693 36	14				1	693 36	14				1	693 36	14
Italy	3	962 00	29				3	962 00	29	3	962 00	29			
England	169	85,583 45	2,114	16	29,970 00	556	153	55,613 45	1,558	150	80,515 45	1,050	19	5,068 00	164
Germany	34	39,768 02	985	21	34,783 00	859	13	4,995 02	126	34	39,768 02	985			
Belgium	1	1,565 00	29	1	1,565 00	29				1	1,565 00	29			
France	39	24,757 03	1,585	7	13,279 83	1,265	32	11,477 20	320	38	24,353 03	1,575	1	404 00	10
Spain	193	333,554 71	11,488	160	330,180 15	11,242	33	3,374 56	246	153	314,319 43	10,931	41	19,235 28	557
Russia	21	12,104 48	276				21	12,104 48	276	19	8,984 00	194	1	3,120 48	82
Ecuador	1	241 87	9				1	241 87	9	9			1	241 87	9
Unknown	2	954 00	13	13			2	954 00	13	13			2	954 00	13
Totals	5,159	2,915,230 54	110,494	3,106	2,666,624 76	97,054	2,053	248,665 78	12,540	3,638	2,330,449 48	86,301	1,521	584,781 06	24,193

RÉSUMÉ OF THE YEARS 1885 TO 1895.

ARRIVED.

Year.	Total number of vessels.	In-crease.	De-crease.
1885	4,456		
1886	4,741	285	
1887	5,123	382	
1888	5,448	325	
1889	5,220		228
1890	5,164		56
1891	5,170	6	
1892	5,675	505	
1893	5,618		57
1894	5,489		129
1895	5,174		315

DEPARTED.

Year.	Total number of vessels.	In-crease.	De-crease.
1885	4,396		
1886	4,687	291	
1887	5,076	389	
1888	5,293	217	
1889	5,055		238
1890	4,918		137
1891	5,083	165	
1892	5,640	557	
1893	5,582		58
1894	5,504		78
1895	5,159		345

FOREIGN PASSENGERS ARRIVED AT MEXICAN PORTS IN 1895.

GULF PORTS.

PORTS.	Total number of passengers.	Mexicans.	Americans.	Chilians.	English.	French.	Germans.	Chinese.	Italians.	Spanish.	Russians.	Swiss.	Austrians.	Turks.	Colombians.	Other nationalities.	Spain.	United States.	England.	France.	Guatemala.	Germany.	Italy.	Costa Rica.	Colombia.	Belgium.	Salvador.	Other nations.
Alvarado	2		1			1											1	2										
Campeche	1	1																										
Coatzacoalcos	2	2																										
Frontera	13		3		1	2						2						13	1									
Isla del Carmen	28				1		2			6		1					6		4									
Progreso	601	126	55		16	7	5	45	4	296			1	48		43	493	104	4			1		1			43	
Tampico	447	35	74		18	13	11	205	7	40							299	97	4	3								
Tuxpan	9		8							1								9										
Veracruz	4,072	170	456	5	214	445	164	21	170	2,285		33	10	62	3	34	2,472	732	191	597		52	1		20	7		
Total	**5,153**	**334**	**597**	**5**	**250**	**468**	**182**	**271**	**181**	**2,628**		**36**	**11**	**110**	**3**	**77**	**3,271**	**957**	**200**	**600**		**53**	**1**	**1**	**20**	**7**	**43**	

PACIFIC PORTS.

PORTS.	Total number of passengers.	Mexicans.	Americans.	Chilians.	English.	French.	Germans.	Chinese.	Italians.	Spanish.	Russians.	Swiss.	Austrians.	Turks.	Colombians.	Other nationalities.	Spain.	United States.	England.	France.	Guatemala.	Germany.	Italy.	Costa Rica.	Colombia.	Belgium.	Salvador.	Other nations.
Acapulco	59	22	10		3	2	12		3							9		37	1		21							
Guaymas	34		11		4	3	3	7										20	4		9							
La Paz	31	5	8	7	2	4	10											21			2							
Mazatlan	196	107	59		1	2	3	7		1						2		187										
Puerto Angel	1		1															1										
San Blas	15	2	5															13										
San José del Cabo	87	24	2		3			55										7			25							58
Salina Cruz	12	7	2															9			6	1						
Santa Rosalía								8										9	2									
Tonalá	7	1																1										
Todos Santos	603	179	357		39	9	1		10									603										
Total	**1,026**	**353**	**462**	**7**	**52**	**20**	**29**	**77**	**13**	**1**						**11**		**897**	**7**		**63**	**1**						**58**

FOREIGN PASSENGERS DEPARTED FROM MEXICAN PORTS IN 1895.

GULF PORTS.

PORTS	Total number of passengers	NATIONALITY															DESTINATION											
		Mexicans	Americans	Chilians	English	French	Germans	Chinese	Italians	Spanish	Russians	Swiss	Austrians	Turks	Colombians	Other nationalities	Spain	United States	England	France	Guatemala	Germany	Italy	Costa Rica	Colombia	Belgium	Salvador	Other nations
Alvarado	2		2																									
Campeche	24				2													2										
Coatzacoalcos		3																										
Frontera													9															
Isla del Cármen			5			1	2		1			1					11	13										
Progreso	453	96	32		9	7	1	35	18	208	1	10		29		7	308	115	30									
Tampico	161	19	97		9	4	11	3	6	12							48	110	2									1
Túxpan	139	132								2							3	136										
Veracruz	2,261	187	284		45	333	75	5	55	1,192	1	4	1	54	1	24	1,399	407	9	433		13						
Total	**3,040**	**437**	**435**		**65**	**345**	**89**	**43**	**80**	**1,414**	**2**	**15**	**10**	**83**	**1**	**31**	**1,769**	**783**	**41**	**433**		**13**						**1**

PACIFIC PORTS.

PORTS	Total number of passengers	NATIONALITY															DESTINATION											
		Mexicans	Americans	Chilians	English	French	Germans	Chinese	Italians	Spanish	Russians	Swiss	Austrians	Turks	Colombians	Other nationalities	Spain	United States	England	France	Guatemala	Germany	Italy	Costa Rica	Colombia	Belgium	Salvador	Other nations
Acapulco	33	4			3		4		2									27			6							
Guaymas	30	9	18		3	7				2								30										
La Paz	33	18	14			5	11	4										33										
Mazatlan	124	59	34				5	8	4	2								114			10							
Puerto Angel	7	1				1																						
San Blas	19	2			3													18			1							1
San José del Cabo	8	7							1									8										
Salina Cruz	44	40	6			6				2								44										
Santa Rosalia	61	34						10									35	17	9									
Tomatá	14	14																14										
Todos Santos	461	144	266		33													457	4									
Total	**834**	**332**	**361**		**63**	**19**	**23**	**22**	**7**	**6**						**1**	**35**	**767**	**13**		**17**							**1**

GENERAL RÉSUMÉ.

	Total number of passengers	NATIONALITY															DESTINATION											
		Mexicans.	Americans.	Chilians.	English.	French.	Germans.	Chinese.	Italians.	Spanish.	Russians.	Swiss.	Austrians.	Turks.	Colombians.	Other nationalities.	Spain.	United States.	England.	France.	Guatemala.	Germany.	Italy.	Costa Rica.	Colombia.	Belgium.	Salvador.	Other nations.
Arrived......	6,179	687	1,059	12	302	488	211	348	194	2,629		36	12	110	3	88	3,271	1,854	207	600	63	54	1	1	20	7	43	58
Departed.....	3,874	769	786		128	364	112	65	87	1,420	2	16	10	83	1	31	1,804	1,550	54	433	17	14						2
Total........	10,053	1,456	1,845	12	430	852	323	413	281	4,049	2	52	22	193	4	119	5,075	3,404	261	1,033	80	68	1	1	20	7	43	60
Difference...	2,305	82	273	12	174	124	99	283	107	1,209	2	20	2	27	2	57	1,467	304	253	167	46	40	1	1	20	7	43	56

Passengers arrived by the Central Railroad during 1895.......... 9,091
" "   National Railroad during 1895.......... 3,387
" "   International Railroad during 1895.......... 3,238
        16,616

Passengers departed by the Central Railroad during 1895.......... 9,589
" "   National Railroad during 1895.......... 3,126
" "   International Railroad during 1895.......... 2,691
        15,406

Total of passengers arrived and departed by rail in 1895.......... 32,022

Difference between passengers arrived and departed by railroads in 1895....... 1,210

Passengers arrived by the ports.......... 6,179
" "   railroads.......... 16,616
        22,795

Passengers departed by the ports.......... 3,874
" "   railroads.......... 15,406
        19,280

Total of passengers arrived and departed by ports and rail in 1895.......... 42,075

Difference between passengers arrived and departed by ports and railroads in 1895.. 3,515

VESSELS ARRIVED AT AND DEPARTED FROM MEXICAN PORTS DURING
THE FISCAL YEARS 1894–95 TO 1895–96.

	ARRIVED.				DEPARTED.			
	Steamers.		Sailing vessels.		Steamers.		Sailing vessels.	
	Vessels.	Tonnage.	Vessels.	Tonnage.	Vessels.	Tonnage.	Vessels.	Tonnage.
Total navigation in the fiscal year 1894–1895.............	4,078	3,083,050	5,497	345,923	3,399	3,026,964	5,566	332,720
Total navigation in the fiscal year 1895–1896.............	4,471	3,300,444	5,723	395,041	4,378	3,242,711	5,856	390,765
Difference....	393	217,394	226	49,118	979	215,747	290	58,045

AGRICULTURAL PRODUCTS.

I take from the *Anuario Estadistico de la Republica Mexicana* of 1895 the following table, which gives the total production of some of our agricultural staples, although I feel perfectly satisfied that they are very much under-rated in said table, because of the difficulty in obtaining complete data about our agricultural productions, both for want of a proper machinery to collect it, and because manufacturers conceal the extent of these products for the purpose of avoiding taxation. I think if the figures in said table are duplicated they will be nearer the true production.

RÉSUMÉ OF AGRICULTURAL PRODUCTS IN MEXICO.

ARTICLES.	BUSHELS.	POUNDS AND OTHER MEASURES.	VALUE.
Cereals :			
Rice................	....	27,174,320 59	$ 1,400,299 40
Barley.................	4,752,239	....	3,587,682 65
Indian corn..............	71,900,598	....	75,695,383 21
Wheat................	10,034,328	....	13,273,790 50
Leguminous:			
Chickling vetch (Arvejon)...	251,230	....	336,771 40
Beans.................	4,319,834	....	7,269,123 25
Chick-peas................	774,351	....	932,608 60
Lima beans...............	561,159	....	624,530 22
Lentils................	34,123	....	64,441 25
Root plants :			
Sweet potatoes...........	2,051,854	....	859,461 50
Huacamote...............	235,939	....	108,348 82
Potatoes................	....	29,472,894 45	879,430 15
Solanaceous :			
Dried pepper..............	....	9,724,443 98	1,731,857 67
Green pepper.............	1,007,049	....	758,199 90
Cane products :			
Sugar cane................	....	5,924,612,232 56	25,692,281 25
Sugar................	....	316,531,239 02	10,283,994 38
Brown sugar.............	....	152,300,903 95	7,942,787 60
Molasses	....	12,748,079 24	3,304,787 82

ARTICLES.	BUSHELS.	POUNDS AND OTHER MEASURES.	VALUE.
Oleaginous :			
Sesame seed.............	214,469	....	$ 144,773 00
Peanuts................	357,569	....	325,413 00
Coquito de Aceite.........	69,388	....	130,955 00
Cocoanuts...............	....	(310,953,000 cocoa-nuts)	3,522,789 00
Linseed................	303,425	....	373,115 00
Palma Christi...........	59,460	....	83,434 00
Turnip seed.............	20,708	....	34,806 00
Lime-leaf sago..........	9,968	....	20,168 00
Alcohol and Fermented Drinks:			
Rum...................	....	12,768,716 gals.	5,056,474 82
Pulque whiskey.........	....	270,876 gals.	199,935 00
Mezcal................	....	6,011,602 gals.	3,078,372 00
Pulque................	....	54,624,835 gals.	3,562,435 05
Tlachique or unfermented pulque.......	....	24,013,901 gals.	1,294,575 00
Textiles :			
Henequen..............	....	93,427,740 04	4,104,096 00
Ixtle..................	....	9,608,026 79	325,250 95
Cotton................	....	78,511,486 26	10,176,050 50
Grape Products :			
Grape.................	....	3,114,519 05	161,372 25
Wine.................	....	162,816 16 gals.	146,028 70
Brandy...............	....	91,656 69 gals.	83,724 80
Dyeing Plants :			
Indigo................	....	299,761 56	285,530 00
Brazil................	....	632,135 85	64,795 00
Campeachy............	....	171,604,086 41	2,110,098 50
Moral................	....	19,826,253 38	195,300 00
Tanning Plants :			
Cascalote.............	....	4,798,994 96	242,070 25
Tanning bark..........	....	33,036,812 04	457,167 26
Tropical Plants :			
Cocoa................	....	5,346,718 17	1,123,180 00
Coffee...............	....	42,019,015 76	11,565,519 28
Tobacco..............	....	124,852,597 69	6,464,733 50
Pepper...............	....	119,273 60	14,055 00
Vanilla..............	....	(10,714,000 vanilla beans)	667,145 50
Gums :			
Chewing gum..........	....	3,996,630 32	549,865 50
India rubber..........	....	1,354,851 48	410,290 00
Mesquite gum.........	....	139,896 97	7,292 75
Copal gum............	....	21,485 47	10,313 55
Medicinal Plants :			
Jalap.............	....	50,099 00	6,945 00
Sarsaparilla...........	....	1,514,331 90	100,730 00

CONCLUSION.

It has taken me a great deal of time and required a great deal of effort to obtain and prepare the data contained in this paper. I am sorry I have not been able to make it more complete than it is ; but I hope my article, by giving a general and superficial idea of Mexico, may promote the desire to read other papers and books treating on that subject in a fuller and more complete manner.

ADDENDA.

Since this paper has been printed the Federal Treasury of Mexico finished the accounts of the fiscal year ended June 30, 1897, and I give below the general results, showing the total amount of the Federal revenues and expenses during that year. I also give a statement, taken from the Statistical Bureau of the Treasury Department of Mexico, published since this paper has gone to press, of the imports and exports in the same year, both by countries and custom houses, these two statements completing the data contained in this paper, and finally some data of the trade of both countries during the first nine months of the present calendar year.

FEDERAL REVENUE AND EXPENSES OF MEXICO IN THE FISCAL YEAR 1896–1897.

RECEIPTS.

Duties on imports and exports...................	$23,639,580.91	
Internal revenue..............................	24,323,798.46	
Public services................................	2,057,409.92	
Extraordinary and incidental...................	2,084,496.30	
		$52,105,285.59
Extraordinary revenues proceeding from contracts and other sources		2,819.17
		$52,108,104.76

EXPENSES.

1.	Legislative power.........................	$ 989,758.38	
2.	Executive power..........................	62,100.26	
3.	Judicial power............................	428,687.46	
4.	Department of Foreign Affairs.............	470,122.37	
5.	Department of Interior....................	3,354,888.95	
6.	Department of Justice and Public Education.	2,184,556.52	
7.	Department of Fomento, Colonization, and Industry..............................	611,863.83	
8.	Department of Communications and Public Works..............................	5,494,593.34	
9.	Department of the Treasury and Public Credit...............................	24,218,207.75	
10.	Department of War and the Navy..........	10,550,955.18	
	Total...................		$48,365,734.04
	Surplus...........................		$3,742,370.72

IMPORTS AND EXPORTS OF MEXICO BY COUNTRIES AND CUSTOM
HOUSES IN THE FISCAL YEAR 1896–97.

COUNTRIES.	IMPORTS.	EXPORTS.	CUSTOM HOUSES.	IMPORTS.	EXPORTS.
Algiers......	$ 802	....	Acapulco	$ 206,275	$ 123,481
Arabia......	282	....	Altata	101,159	813,899
Argentine			Camargo....	6,897	8,735
Republic..	1,897	....	Campeche....	175,027	747,710
Australia....	24,833	....	City of Juarez.	2,910,359	17,929,521
Austria.....	128,367	....	City of Porfirio		
Belgium.....	479,850	$ 1,134,325	Diaz......	4,710,415	2,888,535
Bolivia	214	....	Coatzacoalcos.	105,148	285,195
Brazil	240	....	Frontera......	246,918	418,352
Canada	3,356	17	Guaymas.....	451,959	40,307
Chili........	6,203	20	Guerrero	6,863	15,754
China	51,357	5,396	Isle of Carmen	89,894	1,693,767
Colombia....	64,317	17,675	La Morita....	24,943	498,765
Costa Rica..	....	31,658	La Paz.......	62,937	430,144
Cuba	363	53,503	Laredo	4,693,818	3,701,086
Denmark....	3,614	....	Las Palomas..	18,794	420,011
Ecuador	53,249	....	Manzanillo ...	77,395	221,551
Egypt	10,271	....	Matamoros ...	185,370	312,987
England	6,881,701	14,280,527	Mazatlan	1,572,568	5,808,037
France	4,989,082	1,873,522	Mier.........	8,157	78,609
Germany....	4,003,263	4,416,744	Nogales......	944,312	5,776,575
Greece......	1,660	....	Progreso	1,463,515	8,443,130
Guatemala ..	46,323	1,197,247	Puerto Angel.	15,150	525,075
Hawaii	....	1,200	Salina Cruz...	11,676	68,114
Holland.....	132,728	57,906	San Blas.....	152,643	638,398
Honduras....	3	....	Sta. Rosalia..	547,726	3,279,390
India	210,845	....	Soconusco....	231,078	1,608,446
Italy........	184,186	10,765	Tampico......	8,773,275	29,952,441
Japan	23,673	1,660	Tijuana......	14,297	116,238
Nicaragua...	....	2,110	Todos Santos.	140,268	199,367
Norway.....	41,670	....	Tonala	106,494	255,582
Persia.......	784	....	Tuxpam	76,926	1,154,313
Peru........	108	19,690	Veracruz	14,036,136	22,484,633
Portugal	22,653	....	Zapaluta	35,703	408,346
Russia......	31,387	294,165			
Salvador	452	12,185			
San Domingo	1,071	....			
Senegambia .	902	....			
Spain........	1,983,794	1,192,328			
Sweden.....	29,078	180			
Switzerland..	163,293	720			
Turkey	3,267	....			
United States	22,593,860	86,742,951			
Uruguay	33	....			
Venezuela...	27,608	....			
Zanzibar	1,456	....			
Total....	$42,204,095	$111,346,494	Total......	$42,204,095	$111,346,494

A comparison between the foreign trade in the fiscal year 1896–97
with the year before, 1895–96, gives the following results: During
the year 1896–97 Mexico's exports increased $6,329,592, but the value
of the exports sent to the United States increased $7,091,256. The

total of Mexico's imports for the year 1896–97 shows a falling-off of $49,843, but, notwithstanding this fact, Mexico's imports from the United States increased $2,448,097. During the year England's exports to Mexico decreased $1,023,315, and her imports from Mexico show a loss of $2,186,622, a combined loss of over 12 per cent. in her commercial relations with the Republic. Imports to Mexico from France fell off $1,110,101, a loss of one-sixth of all France's exports to Mexico. In 1895–96 the United States imported 75.8 per cent. of the total exports from Mexico ; in 1896–97 American exporters furnished 53½ per cent. of all that Mexico bought abroad, and, more than this, the United States took 47.67 per cent. of all that was exported from Mexico. These figures sustain the prediction made, that any unsettlement or diminution of Mexico's importations either because of fluctuating silver or the increased production of home manufactories would affect American exporters less than those of any other country. The statistics given above show that these causes have affected them less than those of all the other countries combined ; in fact, their loss has been the gain of the United States.

TRADE BETWEEN MEXICO AND THE UNITED STATES DURING THE FIRST NINE MONTHS OF THE CALENDAR YEAR 1897.

The following data, taken from the publications of the Statistical Bureau of the United States Treasury Department, shows the results of the trade with Mexico in the nine months ended September 30, 1897, as compared with the similar period ended September 30, 1896.

Mexican Exports to the United States.—In the following items the first group of figures represents the amounts and values exported in the first nine months of this year, and the second those of the similar period in 1896 :

Coffee, 30,016,967 pounds, worth $4,574,252 gold, against 19,715,264 pounds, worth $3,333,385. The much lower price of coffee this year accounts for the disproportionate valuation.

The people of the United States, besides being Mexico's chief customers for coffee, are buying more and more of our tobacco, which they now know and appreciate on its merits. The amount exported to the United States was 600,987 pounds, worth in gold $294,536, against 191,303, worth $78,769.

Mexico exported, in the period under consideration, to the United States, hides and skins to the value of $1,534,306 gold, against $1,055,-299. The quantities, respectively, were 11,764,000 pounds, and 7,102,-465 pounds. No diminution of activity there.

It is worth noting that oranges were shipped out to the value of $22,444 gold against $19,359.

Mexico's great argentiferous lead business did not fall behind, the nine months' exportation being 108,776,560 pounds, worth in gold $1,226,525, against 97,818,833 pounds, worth $949,926. The bulk of the American purchase of lead is from Mexico.

Yucatan is Mexico's henequen-growing region, and the exportation has been heavy, standing at 48,410 tons, worth in gold $2,889,003, against 35,746 tons, worth $2,323,585, a noteworthy increase. The henequen or sisal-grass trade into the United States is overwhelmingly Mexican, " other countries " furnishing but 399 tons in the first nine months of this year!

Mexico both exports and imports coal, and shipped into the United States 85,890 tons, worth in gold $182,416, against 52,674 tons, worth $115,015.

Logwood exports were $44,028, against $15,250.

Mahogany fell off, being $290,044 gold, against $306,715, but this trade is always variable.

Mexican Imports from the United States.—It is worthy of note that, in spite of the extraordinarily heavy gold premium, Mexico should be increasing her buying abroad of electrical apparatus, the purchase from the United States alone, in the first nine months of this year, amounting to $228,000 gold, as against $200,000 in the same period last year. Sewing machines went in to the value of $164,000 gold in the nine-month period, against $154,000 last year. Builders' hardware fell off from $556,600 gold value, in the first nine months of last year, to $424,000 this year, but lumber for builders ran up to $1,079,000 gold, against only $544,000 last year, all coming from the United States. Furniture increased slightly, $141,000 gold, against $126,000.

Carriages, cars, and other vehicles, in the nine-months' period, came from the United States to the value of $664,000 gold, as compared with $463,000 last year. Bicycles amounted to $56,000 gold, as against $37,700.

Other importations were as follows :

	9 MOS., 1897.	9 MOS., 1896.
Cotton :		
Bales..........................	9,936	23,127
Value...................... ..	* $411,973	* $1,020,000
Crude petroleum imports :		
Gallons........................	6,260,164	5,486,667
Value........................	* $277,300	* $299,422
Refined petroleum :		
Gallons....	734,466	588,242
Value........................	$136,180	$122,447
Cotton seed oil :		
Gallons................	1,010,580	912,905
Value........................	* $199,000	* $195,000

* Gold.

APPENDIX.

In the preceding paper I stated that I would give as an appendix some data concerning several subjects treated in the same, and I now append the documents mentioned ; the first one being a paper published in the *Bulletin of the American Geographical Society of New York* for March 31, 1894, under the title of "Mexico a Central American State," the second, some itineraries of the principal roads in Mexico, which show the broken surface of that country, and the third and last, a paper on the "Drainage of the Valley of Mexico," published by the *Engineering Magazine* of New York, Vol. viii., No. 4, for January, 1895.

MEXICO A CENTRAL AMERICAN STATE.

In the chapter of this paper entitled "Location, Boundaries, and Area," I referred, (page 9) to an article under the above heading, which I published in the *Bulletin of the American Geographical Society of New York* of March 31, 1894, and offered to give it in the appendix. That paper is the following :

MEXICO A CENTRAL AMERICAN STATE.[1]

There is in this city a social gathering of ladies and gentlemen called "The Travellers' Club," meeting weekly during the winter of each year, for the purpose of studying a foreign country, on the supposition that its members are then travelling in that particular country, and with that view papers are read referring to the same, and they are illustrated with an exhibition of views and objects manufactured in the country under study, and of everything else that may contribute to impart more or less complete information regarding the place supposed to be visited.

During the winter of 1887–88 Mexico was chosen as the country under study by the club, and for that reason I received at the beginning of the year 1888 an invitation to attend some of its sessions, and to say something about the Republic. I accepted the invitation to attend some session, but stated to the invitation committee that, not having time to prepare a paper, I would only give some general notions on

---

[1] This article was published in the *Bulletin of the American Geographical Society of New York* of March 31, 1894, and it is inserted here without any changes. Although the data contained in this article was published in the years 1887 and 1893, as it refers to the area which has not changed, I have not thought it necessary to revise the same. So far as the Mexican States are concerned, I have later and more accurate data ; but the differences are insignificant, and it is not worth while to notice them. As regards the population, the increase has been proportionate ; in respect to all the countries mentioned in this article there is no marked change in the general proportions.

Mexico, in a conversational form, and would be glad to answer any question that might be put to me by those attending the meeting who felt the desire to have further information and more details.

Accordingly, the evening of the 16th of January, 1888, I attended the meeting of the club and spoke for about an hour on the geographical position of Mexico, its physical conditions, its natural resources, and other matters connected with the situation of the country, but carefully avoiding to touch any political question, especially of an international character.

With a view to leave a record of what I intended to say, I had with me a stenographer to take down what I would say, and although his notes were not complete, by using them, and those taken by reporters, some extracts of my conversation were prepared and published the next morning.

Speaking of the geographical position of Mexico, I naturally stated, what is a fact, although not generally realized, that while the main portion of the territory of Mexico is located in North America it occupies a considerable portion of Central America, although politically it is considered as wholly situated in North America. On this subject I made the following remarks, taken from the newspapers, but which were correct:

" The isthmus of Panama divides the New World into two continents, one situated on the northern and the other on the southern hemisphere, but as the position of that isthmus does not correspond with the line of the equator, and lies considerably north of that line, a large portion of South America proper lies in the boreal hemisphere. North America proper is divided by the isthmus of Tehauntepec in two subdivisions—Central America from Panama to Tehauntepec, and North America from Tehauntepec to the North Pole.

" Central America in its present political organization includes the following States: Guatemala, Salvador, Honduras, Nicaragua, and Costa Rica, but from a geographical standpoint it has a much larger area, since it begins at the isthmus of Panama and ends at the isthmus of Tehuantepec. Taking this view, Mexico exercises sovereignty over a large portion of Central America, larger still than any single State of the five which are generally considered as the only components of the same, and representing a third of the total territorial area of Central America.

" The Mexican State of Chiapas and a part of Oaxaca, on the Pacific ; of Yucatan, Campeche, and Tabasco, and a portion of the State of Vera Cruz on the Gulf of Mexico, are situated in geographical Central America.

" The following *résumé* of the territorial area and population of the several sections of Central America, taken from the *Statesman's Year Book*, London, 1887, shows that Mexico is a Central American as well as a North American power:

FIVE STATES OF CENTRAL AMERICA.

	Area in sq. miles.	Population.
Guatemala	46,800	1,224,602
Salvador	7,225	634,120
Honduras	46,400	458,000
Nicaragua	49,500	275,815
Costa Rica	23,200	213,785
Total	173,125	2,806,322

MEXICO.

State.	Area in sq. miles.	Population.
Chiapas..............................	16,048	242,029
Oaxaca (one-fifth).....................	6,718	152,255
Yucatan..............................	29,567	302,319
Campeche............................	25,832	90,413
Tabasco.............	11,815	140,747
Vera Cruz (one-fourth)......	6,558	145,610
Total...........................	96,538	1,073,373

This shows that 36 per cent. of the total area of Central America belongs to Mexico.

In the foregoing list I omitted to take into account that, besides the States referred to, there are in Central America proper the British Colony of Belize or British Honduras, and that part of the State of Panama, in Colombia, which lies north of the isthmus of Panama.

Taking the area and population of those places from the statistical and geographical data published by the *Almanach de Gotha* for 1893, and from some official information in possession of Señor Doctor Don Manuel M. de Peralta, Costa Rican Minister to Washington, a gentleman very well versed in Central American affairs, the following results are obtained :

	Area in square miles.	Area in square kilometers.	Population.
Chiapas	16,048	41,565	270,000
Oaxaca (one-fifth)	6,718	17,400	158,800
Yucatan	29,567	76,579	330,000
Campeche.............	25,832	66,905	94,000
Tabasco..............	11,815	30,600	140,747
Veracruz (one-fourth) ...	6,558	16,986	181,000
	96,538	250,035	1,174,547
Guatemala.............	48,300	125,100	1,520,000
Honduras.............	46,262	119,820	400,000
Salvador..	8,135	21,070	800,000
Nicaragua............	47,857	123,950	320,000
Costa Rica............	24,000	62,000	270,000
Panama (two-thirds).....	19,278	50,000	200,000
British Honduras.......	8,300	21,475	31,500
	202,132	523,415	3,541,500

GEOGRAPHICAL EXTENSION OF CENTRAL AMERICA.

	Square miles.	Square kilometers.
Mexican Central America.............	96,538	250,035
Five Republics of Central America.....	174,554	451,940
British Honduras....................	8,300	21,475
Panama (two-thirds)	19,278	50,000
	298,670	773,450

The foregoing table shows that a little more than 32 per cent. of the whole of Central America, geographically speaking, belongs to Mexico.

When those statements were translated into Spanish and published by *Las Novedades*, of New York, in its issue of the 18th of January, 1888, they were read by Señor Don Manuel Montufar, Secretary of the Guatemalan Legation in Washington, who, in the absence of the Minister, Señor Don Francisco Lainfiesta, was acting as Chargé d'Affaires, and he considered my statements in this connection as a geographical heresy, and as an evidence of the design of Mexico against the several States of Central America. His alarm was so great that he called the attention of the other representatives of the Central American States in Washington to this incident, in order to point out to them the serious dangers which he foresaw for their respective countries on account of my views, which he considered as more than extraordinary.

Fortunately, one of them, the representative of Costa Rica, Señor Doctor Don Manuel M. de Peralta, had attended the meeting of the Travellers' Club at which I spoke, and, I think, Doctor Don Horacio Guzman, the Nicaraguan Minister, was also present, although I am not sure of this, and both failed to see anything in what I stated in this connection that was not a geographical fact, and that, consequently, it could not be disputed; and therefore this incident, that threatened to assume certain proportions, died in its very cradle.

Señor Montufar showed himself over-sensitive at my remarks when there was not the slightest ground for such feeling. If I had made a geographical mistake in averring that a portion of the territory of Mexico was in Central America, geographically speaking, I would be the only sufferer by my mistake, because I would have been the laughing-stock of everybody, including the school-boy studying geography; and, on the contrary, if I had stated a fact, nobody had reason to complain, and much less to be alarmed.

My object in now mentioning this incident is to show the extreme sensitiveness of some Guatemalan gentlemen in regard to Mexico, which goes so far that they cannot listen sometimes to indisputable facts without umbrage, and without ascribing it to purposes and designs against their country. Fortunately this incident happened when the long-pending boundary dispute between Mexico and Guatemala had already been settled for several years, as, had it taken place before, when that question was opened, the situation would have been still more embarrassing and unpleasant.

M. ROMERO.

WASHINGTON, *December 29, 1893.*

MEXICAN PROFILES.

In the chapter on Orography of this paper (page 31) I stated that I would give some profiles of the Mexican surface, which would show in an exact manner the different altitudes from the sea-level to the high plateaus of the country. I have selected for that purpose the principal measurements by railroads built in Mexico, as they naturally followed the easiest ascent and descent, both from the coast to the interior and back to the coast. I will also supplement those measurements with others made for wagon roads to and from important places.

FROM VERACRUZ TO MEXICO BY ORIZABA, BY THE MEXICAN RAILWAY.

STATIONS.	Distance between each station.		Distances.		Altitudes.	
	Kilom's.	Miles.	Kilom's.	Miles.	Metres.	Feet.
Veracruz..................	15.500	9.63	0.000	0.00	1.89	6.20
Tejeria..................	15.250	9.48	15.500	9.63	32.34	106.10
Purga	11.250	6.99	30.750	19.11	44.77	146.89
Soledad.................	21.250	13.21	42.000	26.10	93.08	305.39
Camaron................	12.750	7.92	63.250	39.31	340.76	1116.47
Paso del Macho..........	10.000	6.22	76.000	47.23	475.55	1560.25
Atoyac	19.750	12.27	86.000	53.45	400.77	1314.91
Cordova	26.250	16.52	105.750	65.72	827.88	2713.61
Orizaba................	20.250	12.58	132.000	82.04	1227.63	4027.80
Maltrata...............	20.250	12.59	152.250	94.62	1601.79	5255.40
Boca del Monte..........	6.500	4.04	172.500	107.21	2415.36	7924.66
Esperanza	24.250	15.07	179.000	111.25	2451.79	8044.20
San Andres	20.500	12.74	203.250	126.32	2430.42	7974.08
Rinconada	18.000	11.19	223.750	139.06	2357.32	7734.24
San Marcos............	17.250	10.72	241.750	150.25	2373.21	7786.37
Huamantla..............	25.500	15.84	259.000	160.97	2488.06	8164.97
Apizaco................	27.000	16.79	284.500	176.81	2411.51	7912.03
Soltepec	19.500	12.12	311.500	193.60	2507.62	8227.37
Apam	15.500	9.63	331.000	205.72	2486.92	8159.45
Irolo	22.000	13.67	346.500	215.35	2452.58	8046.78
Otumba................	11.500	7.15	368.500	229.02	2349.41	7708.28
Teotihuacan.............	11.250	6.99	380.000	236.17	2281.57	7485.71
Tepexpam	32.500	20.20	380.000	236.17	2244.99	7365.69
Mexico	....	....	423.750	263.36	2239.83	7348.76

FROM APIZACO TO PUEBLA, A BRANCH OF THE SAME ROAD.

	Kilom's.	Miles.	Kilom's.	Miles.	Metres.	Feet.
Mexico..................	139.250	86.54	0.000	0.00	2239.83	7348.76
Apizaco................	16.750	10.41	139.250	86.54	2411.51	7912.03
Santa Ana..............	18.250	11.29	156.000	96.95	2288.31	7507.82
Panzacola..............	12.000	7.52	174.250	108.24	2192.01	7191.86
Puebla	....	....	186.250	115.76	2154.63	7069.22

FROM VERACRUZ TO MEXICO BY JALAPA, BY THE INTEROCEANIC RAILWAY.

STATIONS.	Distance between each station.		Distances.		Altitudes.	
	Kilom's.	Miles.	Kilom's.	Miles.	Metres.	Feet.
Veracruz................	20.234	12.58	0.000	0.00	2.00	6.56
Santa Fé................	15.200	9.46	20.234	12.58	28.60	93.84
La Antigua	9.820	6.09	35.434	22.04	5.50	18.04
San Francisco	21.644	13.45	45.254	28.13	24.44	80.18
Rinconada..............	16.312	10.14	66.898	41.58	254.00	833.36
Colorado...............	9.781	6.07	83.210	51.72	520.70	1708.39
El Palmar	15.603	9.70	92.991	57.79	690.08	2264.12
Chavarrillo..............	14.675	9.12	108.594	67.49	941.24	3088.16
Pacho	8.558	5.32	123.269	76.61	1170.44	3840.15
Jalapa..................	10.510	6.53	131.827	81.93	1336.18	4383.94
Banderilla..............	14.227	8.84	142.337	88.46	1490.00	4888.62
San Miguel	14.870	9.25	156.564	97.30	1780.22	5840.82
Cruz Verde	16.569	10.29	171.434	106.55	2073 09	6801.70
Las Vigas..............	20.827	12.95	188.003	116.84	2421.10	7943.50
Perote.................	29.476	18.31	208.830	129.79	2390.30	7842.44
Tepeyahualco	17.041	10.59	238.297	148.10	2321.50	7615.23
Virreyes...............	17.064	10.61	255.338	158.69	2346.40	7698.41
Ojo de Agua............	11.303	7.02	272.402	169.30	2348.33	7704.74
San Marcos	14.014	8.71	283.705	176.32	2412.60	7915.61
La Venta	10.357	6.44	297.719	185.03	2559.05	8396.10
Acajete................	11.344	7.05	308.076	191.47	2469.25	8101.48
Amozoc.................	19.391	12.05	319.420	198.52	2312.04	7585.67
Puebla.................	7.919	4.92	338.811	210.57	2155.60	7072.39
Los Arcos..............	15.586	9.69	346.730	215.49	2130.96	6991.56
Analco	15.231	9.47	362.316	225.18	2197.50	7209.88
San Martin Texmelucan...	12.721	7.91	377.547	234.65	2258.61	7410.38
Atotonilco	24.259	15.05	390.268	242.56	2472.10	8110.83
Nanacamilpa............	23.275	14.49	414.527	257.61	2740.16	8990.31
Calpulalpam............	9.302	5.78	437.802	272.10	2576.10	8990.31
San Lorenzo	9.648	5.99	447.104	277.88	2484.22	8150.60
Irolo	15.617	9.71	456.752	283.87	2447.25	8029.30
Soapayuca	4.724	2.94	472.369	293.58	2409.05	7903.96
Otumba................	31.209	19.39	477.093	296.52	2361.30	7747.29
Texcoco	11.452	7.92	508.302	315.91	2249.10	7379.13
San Vicente	9.353	5.19	519.754	323.03	2235.20	7333.52
Los Reyes	17.495	11.50	529.107	328.22	2240.10	7349.60
Mexico.................	....	....	546.602	339.72	2240.00	7349.27

FROM THE CITY OF MEXICO TO MORELOS, A BRANCH OF THE SAME ROAD.

	Kilom's.	Miles.	Kilom's.	Miles.	Metres.	Feet.
Mexico.................	17.495	11.50	0.000	0.00	2240.00	7349.27
Los Reyes	7.005	3.73	17.495	11.50	2240.10	7349.60
Ayotla.................	9.300	5.77	24.500	15.23	2243.30	7360.09
La Compañia............	12.900	8.02	33.800	21.00	2244.50	7364.03
Tenango................	10.800	6.71	46.700	29.02	2324.20	7625.53
Amecameca	12.200	7.59	57.500	35.73	2466.50	8092.42
Otumba................	22.900	14.23	69.700	43.32	2324.45	7626.33
Nepantla...............	26.800	16.66	92.600	57.55	1968.65	6459.04
Yecapixtla	16.500	10.25	119.400	74.21	1570.20	5151.75
Cuautla de Morelos	8.200	5.10	135.900	84.46	1216.48	3991.20
Calderon...............	14.000	8.70	144.100	89.56	1258.15	4127.92
Yautepec	18.000	11.19	158.100	98.26	1154.72	3788.59
Ticuman................	8.200	5.09	176.100	109.45	968.22	3176.69
Tlaltizapan	8.700	5.41	184.300	114.54	934.10	3064.73
Tlalquitenango..........	2.300	1.43	193.000	119.95	900.20	2953.51
Jojutla	12.100	7.52	195.300	121.38	890.64	2922.15
San Jose...............	7.600	4.73	207.400	128.90	992.35	3255.84
Puente de Ixtla..........	....	....	215.000	133.63	896.99	2942.99

FROM PUEBLA TO IZÚCAR DE MATAMOROS, A BRANCH OF THE SAME ROAD.

STATIONS.	Distance between each station.		Distances.		Altitudes.	
	Kilom's.	Miles.	Kilom's.	Miles.	Metres.	Feet.
Puebla................	7.919	4.92	0.000	0.00	2155.60	7072.36
Los Arcos.............	5.000	3.11	7.919	4.92	2130.96	6991.52
Cholula...............	8.900	5.53	12.919	8.03	2145.00	7037.58
Santa María...........	18.100	11.25	21.819	13.56	2120.10	6955.89
San Augustin..........	5.850	3.64	39.919	24.81	2030.20	6660.94
Atlixco...............	19.150	11.90	45.769	28.45	1196.60	3925.99
San José Teruel........	8.850	5.49	64.919	40.35	1685.18	5528.99
Tatetla...............	10.543	6.56	73.769	45.84	1584.94	5200.10
Matamoros.............	....	....	84.412	52.40	1443.80	4737.03

FROM MEXICO TO EL PASO DEL NORTE OR CIUDAD JUAREZ, BY THE CENTRAL MEXICAN RAILROAD.

	Kilom's.	Miles.	Kilom's.	Miles.	Metres.	Feet.
Mexico.................	11.700	7.27	0.000	0.00	2240.00	7349.32
Tlalnepantla...........	5.900	3.67	11.700	7.27	2250.10	7392.46
Barrientos.............	3.300	2.05	17.600	10.94	2298.50	7541.26
Lechería...............	6.800	4.23	20.900	12.99	2253.20	7392.63
Cuautitlan.............	8.300	5.15	27.700	17.22	2252.50	7390.33
Teoloyucan............	10.500	6.52	36.000	22.37	2253.20	7392.63
Huehuetoca............	6.000	3.74	46.500	28.89	2258.80	7411.00
Nochistongo...........	9.900	6.15	52.500	32.63	2248.00	7375.57
El Salto	17.600	10.96	62.400	38.78	2162.60	7095.37
Tula..................	13.500	8.39	80.000	49.72	2030.00	6660.32
San Antonio...........	24.300	15.10	93.500	58.11	2187.00	7175.43
Leña..................	3.800	2.37	117.800	73.21	2471.80	8109.84
Marquez..............	8.300	5.15	121.600	75.58	2426.50	7961.22
Nopala................	8.000	5.04	129.900	80.73	2341.40	7682.00
Dañú..................	14.000	8.63	137.900	85.77	2387.70	7833.92
Polotitlan.............	9.200	5.72	151.900	94.40	2292.30	7520.91
Cazadero..............	10.900	6.77	161.100	100.12	2249.50	7380.49
Palmillas.............	18.600	11.57	172.000	106.89	2162.00	7093.40
San Juan del Rio........	13.300	8.26	190.600	118.46	1905.50	6251.84
Chintepec	12.200	7.59	203.900	126.72	1894.90	6217.07
Ahorcado..............	24.400	15.16	216.100	134.31	1907.70	6259.07
Hércules...............	5.000	3.11	240.500	149.47	1843.90	6049.74
Querétaro	18.500	11.50	245.500	152.58	1813.20	5949.02
Mariscala..............	14.500	9.01	264.000	164.08	1788.20	5867.00
Apaseo................	13.000	8.08	278.500	173.09	1767.40	5798.75
Celaya................	18.200	11.31	291.500	181.17	1757.40	5765.94
Guaje.................	22.800	14.17	309.700	192.48	1740.00	5708.85
Salamanca	11.100	6.90	332.500	206.65	1721.50	5648.15
Chico.................	9.200	5.72	343.600	213.55	1720.80	5645.85
Irapuato..............	16.600	10.31	352.800	219.27	1723.70	5655.37
Villalobos.............	13.200	8.20	369.400	229.58	1746.10	5728.87
Silao.................	19.000	11.82	382.600	237.78	1776.50	5828.61
Trinidad..............	14.200	8.82	401.600	249.60	1818.00	5964.77
Leon..................	16.400	10.19	415.800	258.42	1785.80	5859.12
Francisco......	15.400	9.58	432.200	286.61	1765.00	5790.88
Pedrito...............	13.700	8.51	447.600	278.19	1795.00	5889.30
Loma.................	13.600	8.55	461.300	286.70	1890.40	6202.31
Lagos.................	10.600	6.59	474.900	295.15	1871.00	6138.66

FROM MEXICO TO EL PASO DEL NORTE OR CUIDAD JUAREZ, BY THE
CENTRAL MEXICAN RAILROAD.—*Continued.*

STATIONS.	Distance between each station.		Distances.		Altitudes.	
	Kilom's.	Miles.	Kilom's.	Miles.	Metres.	Feet.
Serrano (Altamira)........	10.300	6.77	485.500	301.74	2015.80	6613.68
Los Salas...............	24.700	15.35	495.800	308.14	2035.00	6676.68
Santa María............	16.700	10.38	520.500	323.49	1844.50	6051.71
Encarnacion............	26.400	16.41	537.200	333.87	1851.00	6073.04
Peñuelas...............	21.500	13.36	563.600	350.28	1878.60	6163.60
Aguascalientes..........	30.100	18.71	585.100	363.64	1884.00	6181.31
Pabellon...............	8.500	5.28	615.200	382.35	1908.50	6261.69
Rincon de Romos........	20.500	12.74	623.700	387.63	1296.60	6321.08
Soledad................	5.800	32.20	644.200	400.37	1979.00	6493.00
Guadalupe..............	9.900	6.15	696.000	432.57	2330.20	7645.22
Zacatecas..............	13.500	8.39	705.900	438.72	2442.00	8012.03
Pimienta...............	16.100	10.00	719.400	447.11	2306.50	7567.46
Calera................	28.000	17.41	735.500	457.11	2152.60	7062.52
Fresnillo...............	15.500	9.63	763.500	474.52	2091.50	6862.06
Mendoza...............	15.000	9.32	779.000	484.15	2103.20	6900.44
Gutierrez..............	22.100	13.74	794.000	493.47	2087.10	6847.63
Cañitas................	13.500	8.39	816.100	507.21	2006.60	6583.51
Cedro..................	20.700	12.86	829.600	515.60	1962.40	6438.53
La Colorada............	25.800	16.04	850.300	528.46	1957.20	6421.48
Pacheco...............	19.000	11.81	876.100	544.50	1889.00	6197.72
Guzman...............	19.700	12.24	895.100	556.31	1810.60	5940.49
Gonzalez..............	21.400	13.30	914.800	568.55	1757.30	5765.60
Camacho..............	21.900	13.61	936.200	581.85	1664.60	5461.47
San Isidro.............	23.200	14.42	958.100	595.46	1582.30	5191.44
Symon.................	24.000	14.92	981.300	609.88	1568.90	5147.48
La Mancha............	21.000	13.05	1005.300	624.80	1557.60	5110.41
Calvo.................	23.900	14.85	1026.300	637.85	1525.00	5003.44
Peralta...............	15.500	9.64	1050.200	652.70	1353.10	4439.45
Jimulco...............	14.400	8.95	1065.700	662.34	1267.20	4157.63
Jalisco................	14.300	8.88	1080.100	671.29	1232.10	4042.46
Picardias...............	25.200	15.67	1094.400	680.17	1205.10	3953.87
Matamoros............	16.400	10.01	1119.600	695.84	1145.30	3757.66
Toueon...............	5.200	3.16	1136.000	705.85	1140.30	3741.13
Lerdo.................	17.700	11.25	1141.200	709.01	1135.50	3725.51
Noé..................	20.000	12.43	1158.900	720.26	1116.90	3664.49
Mapimí...............	24.000	14.92	1178.900	732.69	1125.70	3693.36
Peronal...............	22.200	13.79	1202.900	747.61	1114.20	3657.63
Conejos...............	22.700	14.11	1225.100	761.40	1146.50	3761.61
Yermo................	18.900	11.75	1247.800	775.51	1158.70	3801.64
Cevallos..............	18.500	11.55	1266.700	787.26	1188.50	3899.41
Zavalza...............	14.600	9.07	1285.200	798.76	1201.60	3942.39
Escalon...............	18.000	10.57	1299.800	805.83	1263.20	4144.50
Rellano...............	21.400	13.30	1317.800	819.02	1330.00	4363.66
Corralitos.............	19.400	12.06	1339.200	832.32	1442.70	4733.43
Dolores...............	14.700	9.13	1358.600	844.38	1379.90	4527.38
Jimenez...............	19.100	11.87	1373.300	853.51	1381.20	4531.65
La Reforma............	18.800	11.69	1392.400	865.38	1347.60	4421.41
Diaz..................	19.200	11.93	1411.200	877.07	1298.90	4261.63
Bustamante............	15.700	9.76	1430.400	889.00	1257.70	4126.46
Santa Rosalia..........	16.000	9.94	1446.100	898.76	1226.00	4022.45
La Cruz...............	20.400	12.68	1462.100	908.70	1216.60	3991.61
Concho................	15.600	9.70	1482.500	921.38	1219.90	4002.43
Saucillo...............	16.100	10.00	1498.100	931.08	1210.20	3970.61
Las Delicias...........	7.300	4.54	1514.200	941.08	1170.30	3839.69
Ortiz.................	24.300	15.08	1521.500	945.62	1157.10	3796.39

FROM MEXICO TO EL PASO DEL NORTE OR CIUDAD JUAREZ, BY THE CENTRAL MEXICAN RAILROAD.—*Continued.*

STATIONS.	Distance between each station.		Distances.		Altitudes.	
	Kilom's.	Miles.	Kilom's.	Miles.	Metres.	Feet.
Bachimba	17.400	10.76	1545.800	960.70	1264.10	4147.45
Horcasitas	22.400	13.91	1563.200	971.54	1366.50	4483.42
Mápula................	22.900	14.24	1585.600	985.45	1514.40	4968.66
Chihuahua..............	23.100	14.36	1608.500	999.69	1412.30	4633.68
Sacramento	15.100	9.38	1631.600	1014.05	1519.90	4986.71
Ferragas................	11.600	7.21	1646.700	1023.43	1591.50	5221.63
Sauz....................	19.900	12.37	1658.300	1030.64	1564.40	5132.71
Encinillas	13.900	8.64	1678.200	1043.01	1533.60	5031.66
Agua Nueva.............	13.400	8.33	1692.100	1051.65	1527.50	5011.65
Laguna.................	20.400	12.67	1705.500	1059.98	1535.70	5038.55
Puerto..................	20.200	12.56	1725.900	1072.65	1618.90	5311.53
Gallego.................	29.000	18.02	1746.100	1085.21	1622.00	5321.71
Chivatito	15.400	9.57	1775.100	1103.23	1480.50	4857.45
Moctezuma..............	13.100	8.14	1790.500	1112.80	1382.80	4536.89
Las Minas	13.500	8.33	1803.600	1120.94	1318.10	4324.62
Ojo Caliente............	11.300	7.09	1817.100	1129.27	1233.30	4046.39
Cármen.................	22.800	14.17	1828.400	1136.36	1216.00	3989.64
San José...............	24.100	14.97	1851.200	1150.53	1194.60	3919.42
Ranchería....	28.700	17.84	1875.300	1165.50	1281.80	4205.52
Los Médanos.............	18.200	11.32	1904.000	1183.34	1298.30	4259.66
Samalayuca	16.100	10.00	1922.200	1194.66	1274.50	4181.57
Tierra Blanca	14.400	8.95	1938.300	1204.66	1263.50	4145.48
Mesa...................	17.600	10.94	1952.700	1213.61	1207.10	3960.40
Ciudad Juarez...........			1970.300	1224.55	1133.10	3717.64

FROM AGUASCALIENTES TO TAMPICO, A BRANCH OF THE SAME ROAD.

	Kilom's.	Miles.	Kilom's.	Miles.	Metres.	Feet.
Aguascalientes...........	14.300	8.90	0.000	0.00	1884.00	6181.31
Chicalote	6.200	3.84	14.300	8.90	1891.00	6204.28
Cañada.................	10.500	6.52	20.500	12.74	1921.50	6304.34
Gallardo................	4.600	2.86	31.000	19.26	1955.75	6416.71
El Tule.................	15.200	9.45	35.600	22.12	1962.75	6439.68
San Gil.................	8.200	5.10	50.800	31.57	2011.50	6599.62
San Marcos..............	11.000	6.84	59.000	36.67	2031.25	6664.42
Garcia	12.800	7.95	70.000	43.71	2117.40	6947.07
La Honda...............	11.000	6.84	82.800	51.46	2138.50	7016.30
Peñon Blanco............	16.200	10.07	93.800	58.30	2100.75	6892.44
Salinas.................	13.600	8.44	110.000	68.37	2075.63	6810.91
Zotol	13.500	8.39	123.600	76.81	2120.50	6957.24
Espíritu Santo...........	25.400	15.79	137.100	85.20	2038.25	6687.39
Solana	62.200	38.65	162.500	100.99	2234.80	7332.25
San Louis Potosi.........	17.300	10.96	224.700	139.64	1877.00	6158.35
Laguna Seca.............	27.100	16.84	242.000	150.40	1827.00	5994.30
Corcovada	15.100	9.37	269.100	167.24	1700.00	5577.62
Peotillos	7.500	4.69	284.200	176.61	1740.00	5708.86
Silos	6.450	4.00	291.700	181.30	1509.00	4950.95
Puerto de San Jose.......	15.650	9.72	298.150	185.30	1566.00	5137.97
San Isidro..............	13.400	8.33	313.800	195.02	1257.00	4124.16
Cerritos................	11.200	6.97	327.200	203.35	1136.00	3727.16
Santa Toribia (El Gato)....	17.300	10.76	338.400	210.32	1100.00	3609.04
San Bartolo.............	43.300	26.90	355.700	221.08	1030.00	3379.38
Tanque de la Tinajilla.....	14.200	8.82	399.000	247.98	1190.00	3904.33
Cárdenas...............	14.700	9.14	413.200	256.80	1200.00	3937.14
La Labor...............	8.200	5.10	427.900	265.94	1200.00	3937.14

FROM AGUASCALIENTES TO TAMPICO, A BRANCH OF THE SAME ROAD.—
Continued.

STATIONS.	Distance between each station.		Distances.		Altitudes.	
	Kilom's.	Miles.	Kilom's.	Miles.	Metres.	Feet.
Las Canoas	7.900	4.91	436.100	271.04	990.00	3248.14
Los Llanos (Zacate).......	18.800	11.68	444.000	275.95	825.00	2706.78
Tamazopo (La Garita)......	16.800	10.44	462.800	287.63	350.00	1148.33
Rascon..................	15.100	9.38	479.600	298.07	295.00	967.88
Las Crucitas..............	9.500	5.91	494.700	307.45	275.00	902.26
El Salto (Micos)..........	10.700	6.65	504.200	313.36	218.00	715.25
San Mateo................	13.800	8.58	514.900	320.01	175.00	574.16
Valles	11.900	7.39	528.700	328.59	75.00	246.07
San Felipe...............	2.300	1.43	540.600	335.98	160.00	524.95
El Abra..................	4.000	2.49	542.900	337.41	165.00	541.35
Taninul..................	8.000	4.98	546.900	339.90	125.00	410.11
Las Palmas...............	68.700	42.68	554.900	344.88	50.00	164.05
Chijol	13.700	8.52	623.600	387.56	65.00	213.25
Salinas (Chila)............	17.900	11.13	637.300	396.08	5.00	16.40
Tamos...................	13.100	8.14	655.200	407.21	20.00	6.56
Tampico.................	....	....	668.300	415.35	0.00	0.00

FROM IRAPUATO TO GUADALAJARA, A BRANCH OF THE SAME ROAD.

STATIONS.	Kilom's.	Miles.	Kilom's.	Miles.	Metres.	Feet.
Irapuato.................	5.100	3.17	0.000	0.00	1724.00	5656.36
San Miguel...............	11.300	7.02	5.100	3.17	1721.00	5646.52
Rivera...................	7.600	4.73	16.400	10.19	1712.00	5616.99
Cuitzeo	8.000	4.96	24.000	14.92	1700.00	5577.62
Abasolo (Rio Turbio)......	6.200	3.85	32.000	19.88	1695.00	5561.21
San Rafael...............	11.600	7.22	38.200	23.73	1690.00	5544.81
Pénjamo.................	14.300	8.89	49.800	30.95	1700.00	5577.62
Villaseñor...............	7.100	4.41	64.100	39.84	1690.00	5544.81
Palo Verde...............	13.500	8.40	71.200	44.25	1685.00	5528.40
Cortez...................	6.600	4.10	84.700	52.65	1675.00	5495.59
La Piedad................	20.100	12.49	91.300	56.75	1675.00	5495.59
Patti	14.300	8.89	111.400	69.24	1665.00	5472.78
Yurecuaro................	21.000	13.05	125.700	78.13	1540.00	5052.56
Negrete..................	6.400	3.97	146.700	91.18	1531.00	5023.13
La Barca.................	4.700	2.93	153.100	95.15	1537.00	5042.82
Feliciano.	8.300	5.15	157.800	98.08	1540.00	5052.66
Limon...................	13.200	8.21	166.100	103.23	1543.00	5062.50
Ocotlan	17.500	10.88	179.300	111.44	1525.00	5003.44
Poncitlan	21.600	13.41	196.800	122.32	1522.00	4993.60
Atequiza	8.300	5.17	218.400	135.73	1512.00	4960.79
La Capilla...............	7.600	4.73	226.700	140.90	1515.00	4970.63
El Castillo...............	24.800	15.40	234.300	145.63	1525.00	5003.44
Guadalajara..............	....	....	259.100	161.03	1543.00	5062.50

FROM MEXICO TO LAREDO TAMAULIPAS, BY THE MEXICAN NATIONAL RAILWAY.

STATIONS.	Kilom's.	Miles.	Kilom's.	Miles.	Metres.	Feet.
Mexico...................	4.600	2.86	0.000	0.00	2240.00	7349.32
Tacuba...................	4.800	2.98	4.600	2.86	2250.00	7382.13
Naucalpan...............	3.900	2.42	9.400	5.84	2280.00	7480.56
Rio Hondo...............	8.700	5.41	13.300	8.26	2300.00	7546.17
San Bartolito.............	5.500	3.42	22.000	13.67	2460.00	8071.13
Dos Rios.................	5.500	3.41	27.500	17.09	2680.00	8792.94
Laurel...................	5.900	3.68	33.000	20.50	2820.00	9252.27
Cumbre..................	2.500	1.55	38.900	24.18	3050.00	10006.89

FROM MEXICO TO LAREDO TAMAULIPAS.—*Continued.*

STATIONS.	Distance between each station.		Distances.		Altitudes.	
	Kilom's.	Miles.	Kilom's.	Miles.	Metres.	Feet.
Salazar..................	3.200	1.99	41.400	25.73	3000.00	9842.84
Carretera de Toluca.......	3.400	2.11	44.600	27.72	2900.00	9514.74
Fresno...................	2.500	1.56	48.000	29.83	2800.00	9186.75
Jajalpa..................	5.600	3.48	50.500	31.39	2720.00	8924.18
Ocoyoacac...............	3.000	1.86	56.100	34.87	2600.00	8530.46
Lerma...................	13.900	8.64	59.100	36.73	2540.00	8333.60
Toluca..................	7.400	4.60	73.000	45.37	2640.00	8601.70
Palmillas...............	16.700	10.38	80.400	49.97	2630.00	8628.89
Del Rio.................	14.700	9.14	97.100	60.35	2580.00	8464.84
Ixtlahuaca..............	12.300	7.64	111.800	69.49	2540.00	8333.60
Tepetitlan..............	9.800	6.09	124.100	77.13	2520.00	8267.98
Flor de María...........	20.200	12.56	133.900	83.22	2520.00	8267.98
Basoco..................	4.000	2.48	154.100	95.78	2580.00	8464.84
Venta del Aire..........	5.800	3.60	158.100	98.26	2560.00	8399.22
Tultenango.............	11.200	6.97	163.900	101.86	2540.00	8333.60
Solis...................	10.900	6.77	175.100	108.83	2430.00	7972.70
Tepetongo..............	7.100	4.41	186.000	115.60	2320.00	7611.79
Agua Buena (Buena Vista).	7.800	4.85	193.100	120.01	2240.00	7349.32
Mayor..................	4.800	2.99	200.900	124.86	2160.00	7086.84
Pateo..................	3.400	2.10	225.700	127.85	2100.00	6889.98
Pomoca................	14.100	8.76	209.100	129.95	2040.00	6693.13
Maravatío..............	12.000	7.47	223.200	138.71	2010.00	6594.70
San Antonio............	8.700	5.40	235.200	146.18	2080.00	6824.37
Zirizícuaro............	12.000	7.47	243.900	151.58	2010.00	6594.70
Tarandacuao...........	8.400	5.22	255.900	159.05	1920.00	6299.42
San José..............	8.500	5.28	264.300	164.27	1860.00	6102.57
Providencia............	12.900	8.02	272.800	169.55	1880.00	6168.19
Acámbaro..............	12.500	7.76	285.700	177.57	1860.00	6102.57
San Cristobal..........	17.500	10.88	298.200	185.33	1840.00	6036.95
Salvatierra............	15.500	9.63	315.700	196.21	1760.00	5774.48
Cascalote	8.900	5.53	331.200	205.84	1760.00	5774.48
Ojo Seno..............	14.200	8.84	340.100	211.37	1770.00	5807.29
Celaya.................	5.200	3.22	354.300	220.21	1740.00	5708.86
Santa Rita............	7.400	4.60	359.500	223.43	1760.00	5774.48
San Juan..............	3.800	2.37	366.900	228.03	1780.00	5840.10
Soria..................	7.200	4.47	370.700	230.40	1785.00	5856.50
Chamacuero	8.900	5.57	377.900	234.87	1790.00	5872.91
Rinconcillo............	13.000	8.08	386.800	240.40	1810.00	5938.52
Begoña................	9.100	5.65	399.800	248.48	1825.00	5987.73
San Miguel de Allende.....	11.600	7.21	408.900	254.13	1870.00	6135.38
Atotonilco.............	11.300	7.03	420.500	261.34	1860.00	6102.57
Tequizquiapan	12.800	7.95	431.800	268.37	1870.00	6135.38
Dolores Hidalgo..........	7.200	4.48	444.600	276.32	1890.00	6201.00
Rincon	11.300	7.02	451.800	280.80	1900.00	6233.88
Peña Prieta	9.100	5.65	463.100	287.82	1930.00	6332.23
Trancas...............	9.000	5.59	472.200	293.47	1950.00	6397.85
Obregon...............	18.700	11.63	481.200	299.06	1990.00	6529.09
Ciudad Gonzalez (San Felipe)	14.400	8.95	499.900	310.69	2050.00	6725.94
Chirimoya..............	13.200	8.20	514.300	319.64	1860.00	6102.57
Jaral..................	16.700	10.38	527.500	327.84	1840.00	6036.95
Villa de Reyes..........	10.000	6.22	544.200	338.22	1830.00	6004.14
Jesus María............	14.800	9.19	554.200	344.44	1810.00	5938.52
La Pila................	15.000	9.33	569.000	353.63	1900.00	6233.88
San Luis Potosí..........	13.400	8.33	584.000	362.96	1860.00	6102.57
Peñasco................	15.100	9.37	597.400	371.29	1840.00	6036.95
Pinto..................	12.500	7.78	612.500	380.66	1820.00	5971.33
Bocas..................	13.600	8.45	625.000	388.44	1700.00	5577.62
Enramada	15.200	9.45	638.600	396.89	1680.00	5512.00
Moctezuma.............	18.900	11.75	653.800	406.34	1660.00	5446.38

FROM MEXICO TO LAREDO TAMAULIPAS.—*Continuea.*

STATIONS.	Distance between each station.		Distances.		Altitudes.	
	Kilom's.	Miles.	Kilom's.	Miles.	Metres.	Feet.
El Venado...............	17.000	10.56	672.600	418.09	1740.00	5708.86
Los Charcos.............	16.300	10.13	689.700	428.65	1880.00	6168.19
Laguna Seca	11.600	7.20	706.000	438.78	2020.00	6627.51
Berrendo................	15.400	9.58	717.600	445.98	1990.00	6529.09
La Maroma..............	16.000	9.94	733.000	455.56	1880.00	6168.19
Wadley.................	8.600	5.35	749.000	465.50	1840.00	6036.95
Catorce................	6.800	4.23	757.600	470.85	1820.00	5971.33
Poblazon...............	15.200	9.44	764.400	475.08	1780.00	5840.10
Vanegas	16.400	10.20	779.600	484.52	1720.00	5643.24
La Trueba (La Parida)....	15.800	9.81	796.000	494.72	1720.00	5643.24
San Vicente....	15.700	9.76	811.800	504.53	1700.00	5577.62
El Salado...............	15.700	9.75	827.500	514.29	1720.00	5643.24
Lulu	20.200	12.56	843.200	524.04	1720.00	5643.24
La Ventura.............	20.000	12.43	863.400	536.60	1720.00	5643.24
Santa Elena.............	20.900	13.00	883.400	549.03	1760.00	5774.48
Gomes Farías............	13.200	8.20	904.300	562.03	1940.00	6365.04
El Oro.................	17.300	10.77	917.500	570.23	1980.00	6496.28
Carneros...............	9.600	5.94	934.800	580.99	2080.00	6824.37
Agua Nueva.............	13.200	8.21	944.400	586.93	1920.00	6299.42
Encantada......	6.300	3.92	957.600	595.14	1840.00	6036.95
Buena Vista.............	9.700	6.03	963.900	599.06	1750.00	5741.67
Saltillo................	1.500	7.15	973.600	605.09	1600.00	5249.52
Los Bosques............	3.500	2.17	985.100	612.24	1430.00	4691.76
Ramos Arizpe...........	7.300	4.55	988.600	614.41	1400.00	4593.33
Santa Maria.............	9.700	6.02	995.900	618.96	1320.00	4330.85
Ojo Caliente............	7.000	4.35	1005.600	624.98	1220.00	4002.76
Los Muertos............	2.300	1.40	1012.600	629.33	1160.00	3805.90
La Mariposa	10.400	6.46	1014.900	630.77	1120.00	3674.66
Rinconada..............	7.700	4.78	1025.300	637.23	1000.00	3280.95
Los Fierros.............	5.500	3.42	1033.000	642.01	930.00	3051.28
Soledad................	10.200	6.34	1038.500	645.43	820.00	2693.38
Garcia.................	21.100	13.11	1048.700	651.77	740.00	2427.91
Santa Catarina..........	2.800	1.74	1069.800	664.88	640.00	2099.81
Leona	4.700	2.87	1072.600	666.62	600.00	1968.57
San Gerónimo	2.900	1.79	1077.300	669.55	590.00	1935.76
Gonzalitos.............	2.500	1.56	1080.200	671.34	580.00	1902.95
Monterey...............	7.600	4.73	1082.700	672.90	560.00	1837.33
Ramon Treviño..........	6.100	3.79	1090.300	677.63	510.00	1673.28
Topo..................	20.900	12.99	1096.400	681.42	480.00	1574.86
Salinas	8.100	5.03	1117.300	694.41	430.00	1410.81
Morales................	16.300	10.13	1125.400	899.44	460.00	1509.24
Stevenson (Palmito)......	8.700	5.40	1141.700	709.57	580.00	1902.95
Palo Blanco............	13.200	8.20	1150.400	714.97	560.00	1837.33
Álamo.................	12.600	7.84	1163.600	723.17	490.00	1607.67
Villa Aldama...........	2.100	1.31	1176.200	731.01	420.00	1378.00
Guadalupe	3.400	2.11	1178.300	732.32	420.00	1378.00
Bustamante	9.800	6.09	1181.700	734.43	440.00	1443.62
Huizache	1.400	7.08	1191.500	740.52	470.00	1542.05
Golondrinas............	12.000	7.46	1202.900	747.60	410.00	1345.19
Salome, Botello..........	12.100	7.52	1214.900	755.06	380.00	1246.76
Brasil	8.900	5.53	1227.000	762.58	340.00	1115.52
Lampazos...............	23.300	14.48	1235.900	768.11	300.09	984.28
Mojina	21.200	13.18	1259.200	782.59	240.00	787.43
Rodriguez..............	12.400	7.71	1280.400	795.77	200.00	656.19
Camaron...............	11.500	7.15	1292.800	803.48	200.00	656.19
Huizachito.............	16.500	10.25	1304.300	810.63	210.00	689.00
Jarita	13.100	8.14	1320.800	820.88	200.00	656.19
Sanchez................	16.100	10.01	1333.900	829.02	160.00	524.95
Laredo de Tamaulipas.....	....	......	1350.000	839.03	130.00	426.52

FROM ACÁMBARO TO PÁTZCUARO, A BRANCH OF THE SAME ROAD.

STATIONS.	Distance between each station.		Distances.		Altitudes.	
	Kilom's.	Miles.	Kilom's.	Miles.	Metres.	Feet.
Acámbaro..............	13.250	8.23	0.000	0.00	1840.00	6036.95
La Cumbre..............	17.610	10.96	13.250	8.23	1960.00	6430.66
Andocutin...............	6.170	3.83	30.860	19.19	1840.00	6036.95
Huingo.................	12.360	7.68	37.030	23.02	1840.00	6036.95
Queréndaro.............	4.000	2.49	49.390	30.70	1840.00	6036.95
Zinzimeo...............	10.000	6.22	53.390	33.19	1840.00	6036.95
Quirio.,...............	7.610	4.73	63.390	39.41	1860.00	6102.57
Charo.................	5.920	3.67	71.000	44.14	1870.00	6135.38
La Goleta..............	3.150	1.95	76.920	47.81	1870.00	6135.38
Atapaneo,..............	11.200	6.96	80.070	49.76	1880.00	6168.19
Morelia................	19.900	12.37	91.270	56.72	1890.00	6201.00
Jacuaro,,..............	9.610	5.98	111.170	69.09	2000.00	6561.89
Coapa	6.800	4.22	120.780	75.07	2060.00	6758.75
Lagunillas	10.380	6.46	127.580	79.29	2100.00	6889.98
Ponce.................	2.910	1.80	137.960	85.75	2120.00	6955.60
Chapultepec.	12.530	7.79	140.870	87.55	2100.00	6889.98
Pátzcuaro.............	....	....	153.400	95.34	2040.00	6693.13

FROM PIEDRAS NEGRAS OR CIUDAD PORFIRIO DIAZ TO DURANGO, BY
THE MEXICAN INTERNATIONAL RAILWAY.

	Kilom's.	Miles.	Kilom's.	Miles.	Metres.	Feet.
Ciudad Porfirio Diaz.......	6.540	4.06	0.000	0.00	220.00	721.81
Fuente	7.060	4.39	6.540	4.06	232.00	761.17
Rosa	26.200	16.29	13.600	8.45	278.00	912.11
Nava....................	11.960	7.44	39.800	24.74	324.00	1063.02
Allende.................	14.940	9.28	51.760	32.18	375.00	1230.35
Leona	15.640	9.71	66.700	41.46	455.00	1492.83
Peyotes................	21.430	13.32	82.340	51.17	486.00	1594.55
Blanco..................	12.850	7.99	103.770	64.49	387.00	1269.73
Sabinas.................	15.850	9.85	116.620	72.48	340.00	1115.52
Soledad,,...............	10.650	6.61	132.470	82.33	371.00	121´.23
Baroterán...............	14.120	8.78	143.120	88.94	425.00	1394.40
Aura....................	15.090	9.39	157.240	97.72	453.00	1486.27
Obayos.................	15.330	9.52	172.330	107.11	396.00	1299.26
Baluarte	10.690	6.65	187.660	116.63	373.00	1223.79
Hermanas..............	21.230	13.18	198.350	123.28	396.00	1299.26
Adjuntas...............	13.570	8.44	219.580	136.46	465.00	1525.64
Estancia	4.770	2.97	233.150	144.90	547.00	1794.68
Monclova..............	18.560	11.54	237.920	147.87	587.00	1925.92
Castaño................	14.920	9.29	256.480	159.41	748.00	2454.16
Gloria	19.590	12.16	271.400	168.70	823.00	2700.22
Bajan..	12.420	7.71	290.990	180.86	843.00	2765.84
Joya	20.410	12.68	303.410	188.57	829.00	2719.91
Espinazo...............	12.080	7.52	323.820	201.25	817.00	2680.54
Reata	22.860	14.21	335.900	208.77	900.00	2952.85
Treviño (Venadito).......	26.040	16.16	358.760	222.98	890.00	2920.05
Sauceda................	24.760	15.40	384.800	239.14	997.00	3271.11
Jaral	23.020	14.31	409.560	254.54	1144.00	3753.40
Pastora	21.610	13.44	432.580	268.85	1157.00	3796.06
Cármen	23.970	14.89	454.190	282.29	1182.00	3878.08
Paila	19.670	12.23	478.160	297.18	1188.00	3897.77
Mimbre................	16.540	10.28	497.830	309.41	1132.00	3714.03
Rafael	12.970	8.05	514.370	319.69	1102.00	3615.60
Pozo	11.290	7.02	527.340	327.74	1105.00	3625.44

FROM PIEDRAS NEGRAS OR CIUDAD PORFIRIO DIAZ TO DURANGO, BY
THE MEXICAN INTERNATIONAL RAILWAY.—*Continued.*

STATIONS.	Distance between each station.		Distances.		Altitudes.	
	Kilom's.	Miles.	Kilom's.	Miles.	Metres.	Feet.
Bola....................	13.480	8.38	538.630	334.76	1089.00	3572.96
Mayran................	10.870	6.75	552.110	343.14	1094.00	3589.36
Hornos................	13.410	8.35	562.980	349.89	1096.00	3595.93
Colonia....	17.620	10.95	576.390	358.24	1105.00	3625.44
Matamoros............	22.540	14.00	594.010	369.19	1112.00	3648.41
Torreon	8.050	5.00	616.550	383.19	1134.00	3720.59
San Carlos............	15.740	9.18	624.600	388.19	1137.71	3732.77
Loma	19.280	11.98	640.340	397.97	1181.52	3876.51
Chocolate.............	20.870	12.98	659.620	409.95	1377.25	4518.69
Huarichic.............	15.200	9.45	680.490	422.93	1325.37	4348.45
Pedriceña.............	25.640	15.93	695.690	432.38	1318.85	4327.07
Pasaje................	24.540	15.25	721.330	448.31	1605.28	5266.84
Yerbanís....	21.580	13.41	745.870	463.56	1908.73	6262.53
Noria	12.760	7.93	767.450	476.97	1895.00	6217.40
Catalina..............	12.150	7.56	780.210	484.90	1969.47	6461.73
Tapona...............	22.040	13.70	792.360	492.46	1982.72	6505.21
Gabriel	16.930	10.52	814.400	506.16	1955.20	9414.91
Chorro................	26.420	16.42	831.330	516.68	1868.10	6129.15
Labor.................	11.760	7.30	857.750	533.10	1864.38	6116.93
Durango..............			869.510	540.40	1880.13	6168.62

FROM SABINAS TO HONDO, A BRANCH OF THE SAME ROAD.

	Kilom's.	Miles.	Kilom's.	Miles.	Metres.	Feet.
Sabinas................	17.530	10.83	0.000	0.00	340.00	1115.52
San Felipe............	2.380	1.48	17.430	10.83	313.00	1026.93
Hondo..			19.810	12.31	319.00	1046.62

FROM THE CITY OF MEXICO TO CUERNAVACA AND ACAPULCO.
LINE FINISHED.

	Kilom's.	Miles.	Kilom's.	Miles.	Metres.	Feet.
Mexico	28.060	17.44	0.000	0.00	2240.00	7349.27
Contreras.............	17.883	11.11	28.060	17.44	2480.00	8091.75
Ajusco................	15.191	9.44	45.943	28.55	2840.00	9272.89
La Cima..............	12.966	8.07	61.134	37.99	3040.00	9974.08
Xacapexco (Tres Marías)...	18.400	11.43	74.100	46.06	2800.00	9186.75

LINE IN CONSTRUCTION.

	Kilom's.	Miles.	Kilom's.	Miles.	Metres.	Feet.
San Juanico..............	31.250	19.42	92.500	57.49	2290.00	7513.37
Cuernavaca,.............	7.250	4.51	123.750	76.91	1520.00	4987.04
Jiutepec................	6.750	4.20	131.000	82.42	1300.00	4265.23
San Vicente.............	21.000	13.05	137.750	85.62	1260.00	4134.00
Xoxocotla..............	14.050	8.73	158.750	98.67	1030.00	3379.38
Puente de Ixtla.........	8.950	5.56	172.800	107.40	900.00	2952.85
Rio Amacusac..........	23.250	14.45	181.750	112.96	890.00	2920.05
Buena Vista............	21.000	13.05	205.000	127.41	1200.00	3937.14
Iguala.................	11.000	6.84	226.000	140.46	720.00	2362.29
Tepecoacuilco..........	34.750	21.13	237.000	147.30	800.00	2624.76
Xalitla................	12.050	7.91	271.750	168.47	620.00	2034.19
Mexcala...............	28.700	17.84	283.800	176.38	480.00	1574.86
Venta del Zopilote........	11.500	7.15	312.500	194.22	760.00	2493.53
Zumpango	13.000	8.08	324.000	201.37	1000.00	3280.95

FROM THE CITY OF MEXICO TO CUERNAVACA AND ACAPULCO.
LINE IN CONSTRUCTION. (*Continued.*)

STATIONS.	Distance between each station.		Distances.		Altitudes.	
	Kilom's.	Miles.	Kilom's.	Miles.	Metre	Feet.
Tierras Prietas............	4.800	2.98	337.000	209.45	1320.00	4330.85
Chilpancingo.......... ...	15.200	9.45	341.800	212.43	1200.00	3937.14
Cima de Valadez	8.250	5.12	357.000	221.88	1300.00	4265.23
La Imagen...............	11.750	7.31	365.250	227.00	1060.00	3477.81
Los Cajones..............	6.000	3.72	377.000	234.31	1000.00	3280.95
El Rincon................	12.000	7.46	383.000	238.03	670.00	2198.24
Dos Caminos.............	12.000	7.46	395.000	245.49	600.00	1968.57
Tierra Colorada...........	9.000	5.60	407.000	252.95	300.00	984.28
Rio Omitlan.............	4.000	2.48	416.000	258.55	180.00	590.57
Peregrino................	32.000	19.89	420.000	261.03	140.00	459.33
Cacahuatepec.............	24.500	15.23	452.000	280.92	60.00	196.86
Marquez.................	16.500	10.25	476.500	296.15	20.00	65.62
Acapulco.................			493.000	306.40	0.00	0.00

FROM PUEBLA TO OAXACA, BY THE MEXICAN SOUTHERN RAILWAY.

Puebla....................	18.400	11.43	0.000	0.00	2157.00	7077.00
Amozoc..................	7.600	4.73	18.400	11.43	2312.00	7585.54
Santa Rosa..............	11.200	6.95	26.000	16.16	2295.00	7529.77
Tepeaca	17.400	10.82	37.200	23.11	2244.60	7364.41
Rosendo Márquez.........	10.500	6.53	54.600	33.93	2055.00	6742.34
Tecamachalco	12.600	7.83	65.100	40.46	2014.10	6608.15
Las Animas..............	9.400	5.84	77.700	48.29	2000.00	6561.89
Tlacotepec..............	31.300	19.46	87.100	54.13	1988.25	6523.35
Carnero..................	8.900	5.53	118 400	73.59	1752.37	5749.43
Tehuacan................	14.700	9.13	127.300	79.12	1662.57	5454.81
La Huerta	6.300	3.92	142.000	88.25	1453.29	4768.18
Santa Cruz	10.900	6.76	148.300	92.17	1370.31	4495.91
Pantzingo...............	14.600	9.09	159.200	98.93	1246.00	4088.07
Nopala	6.400	3.97	173.800	108.02	1060.56	3479.65
Venta Salada.............	15.200	9.46	180.200	111.99	972.07	3189.31
San Antonio..............	8.700	5.40	195.400	121.45	787.92	2585.13
Mexía	20.300	12.62	204.100	126.85	695.00	2280.26
Tecomavaca..............	10.900	6.78	224.400	139.47	559.71	1836.38
Quiotepec................	17.000	10.56	235.300	146.25	540.00	1771.71
Cuicatlan................	4.800	2.98	252.300	156.81	592.00	1942.32
Tomellin................	19.200	11.93	257.100	159.79	672.00	2204.80
Almoloyas...............	16.500	10.26	276.300	171.72	1055.00	3461.40
Santa Catarina...........	16.200	10.06	292.800	181.98	1332.00	4370.22
El Parian	13.700	8.52	309.000	192.04	1495.00	4905.02
Las Sedas	12.800	7.96	322.700	200.56	1927.00	6322.39
San Pablo Huitzo.........	13.100	8.13	335.500	208.52	1695.00	5561.21
Villa de Etla	18.000	11.19	348.600	216.65	1642.00	5387.32
Oaxaca			366.600	227.84	1545.00	5069.06

FROM COATZACOALCOS TO SALINA CRUZ, BY THE NATIONAL TEHUANTEPEC RAILWAY.

Coatzacoalcos	21.749	13.51	0.000	0.00	2.00	6.56
Los Limones	15.140	9.42	21.749	13.51	16.00	52.50
Chinameca..............	5.407	3.35	36.889	22.93	6.00	19.69
Jaltipan................	20.547	12.77	42.296	26.28	40.00	131.24
Ojapa..................	12.568	7.83	62.843	39.05	32.00	104.99
Almagres....	11.589	7.19	75.411	46.88	48.00	157.49

STATIONS.	Distance between each station.		Distances.		Altitudes.	
	Kilom's.	Miles.	Kilom's.	Miles.	Metres.	Feet.
Juile...................	9.284	5.77	87.000	54.07	40.00	131.24
Medias Aguas...........	9.672	6.01	96.284	59.84	32.00	104.99
Tortugas................	21.044	13.08	105.956	65.85	44.00	144.36
Santa Lucrecia..........	7.000	4.36	127.000	78.93	30.00	98.43
Los Muertos.............	10.000	6.21	134.000	83.29	35.00	114.83
Ubero..................	14.801	9.20	141.000	89.50	25.00	82.02
Tolosa.................	7.199	4.47	158.801	98.70	52.00	170.61
Palomares..............	20.570	12.78	166.000	103.17	88.00	288.73
Mogoñé................	15.176	9.43	186.570	115.95	92.00	301.85
Rincon Antonio.........	13.254	8.25	201.746	125.38	176.00	577.45
Lagunas................	17.764	11.04	215.000	133.63	260.00	853.05
Chivela................	10.236	6.35	232.764	144.67	244.00	800.55
Rio Verde..............	17.186	10.68	243.000	151.02	115.00	377.30
San Gerónimo...........	28.218	17.54	260.186	161.70	56.00	183.74
Tehuantepec............	3.596	2.24	288.404	179.24	36.00	108.12
Santa Cruz.............	17.617	10.94	292.000	181.48	36.00	108.12
Salina Cruz............			309.617	192.42	2.00	6.56

FROM THE CITY OF MEXICO TO PACHUCA, BY THE HIDALGO AND NORTHEASTERN MEXICAN RAILWAY.

LINE FINISHED.

NORTHEASTERN RAILWAY FROM MEXICO TO TIZAYUCA.

Mexico..................	19.000	11.80	0.000	0.00	2264.76	7430.56
Canal..................	11.400	7.10	19.000	11.80	2266.01	7434.66
Ojo de Agua.............	5.200	3.23	30.400	18.90	2272.96	7457.46
Santa Ana..............	14.800	9.20	35.600	22.13	2271.36	7452.21
Tizayuca...............			50.400	31.33	2294.65	7528.62

HIDALGO RAILWAY TO TUXPAN.

Tizayuca................	16.100	10.00			2344.87	7693.38
Tezontepec.............	10.800	6.52	66.500	41.33	2390.00	7841.46
San Augustin...........	6.000	3.92	77.300	47.85	2438.08	7999.21
Tepa..................	8.400	5.23	83.300	51.77	2538.00	8327.04
Tecajete...............	11.900	7.38	91.700	57.00	2638.50	8656.78
Somo Riel..............	10.600	6.60	103.600	64.38	2504.80	8218.10
Las Lajas..............	7.000	4.34	114.200	70.98	2392.80	7850.64
Los Romeros........ ...	11.700	7.28	121.200	75.32	2221.72	7289.33
Santiago...............	5.700	3.54	132.900	82.60	2187.29	7176.39
Tulancingo......	7.200	4.48	138.600	86.14	2171.46	7124.44
Sototlan...............			145.800	90.62		

FROM TEPA TO PACHUCA, A BRANCH OF THE HIDALGO RAILROAD.

Tepa...................	8.700	5.41	0.000	0.00	2438.08	7999.21
Xochihuacan............	17.300	10.75	8.700	5.41	2380.06	7808.85
Pachuca................			26.000	16.16	2420.99	7493.15

FROM SAN AUGUSTIN TO IROLO, A BRANCH OF THE HIDALGO RAILWAY.

San Agustin.............	14.600	9.08	0.000	0.00	2390.00	7841.46
Tlanalapa......	13.700	8.51	14.600	9.08	2437.39	7996.95
Irolo..................			28.300	17.59	2452.58	8046.78

FROM DURANGO TO MAZATLAN BY BRIDLE-PATH.

PLACES.	Altitudes.		PLACES.	Altitudes.	
	Metres.	Feet.		Metres.	Feet.
Durango............	1880.13	6168.62	La Ramona..........	1220.00	4002.76
Salitre	1925.00	6315.82	El Chapote..........	950.00	3116.90
El Salto............	1900.00	6233.80	Rio del Baluarte......	630.00	2067.00
Arroyo Seco	1890.00	6201.00	La Ventanita........	770.00	2526.34
Camino del Jaral.....	1890.00	6201.00	Sotolito............	1550.00	5085.47
El Escalon..........	1980.00	6496.28	El Carrizo de Adentro.	1825.00	5987.73
Las Indias..........	2120.00	6955.60	El Carrizo de Afuera..	1860.00	6102.57
Calzon Roto	2180.00	7152.46	Las Loberas	1970.00	6463.47
El Pino	2260.00	7414.94	El Venteadero........	1930.00	6332.23
Rio Chico	2020.00	6627.51	Puerta de los Pilares..	1250.00	4101.19
La Palmita	2220.00	7283.70	Arroyo del Leon......	1120.00	3674.66
Los Cerritos	2260.00	7414.94	Palotillo............	1010.00	3313.76
Los Mimbres........	2180.00	7152.46	Platanito	940.00	3084.09
Buena Vista.	2330.00	7644.60	Santa Catarina......	210.00	689.00
Los Charcos........	2340.00	7674.41	El Limon............	130.00	426.52
Los Navíos	2350.00	7710.22	El Tecomate........	110.00	360.90
Navajas	2260.00	7414.94	Tagarete	85.00	278.88
Llano Grande.......	2160.00	7086.84	Rio del Presidio......	55.00	180.45
Cruz de Piedra......	2230.00	7316.51	Porras..............	65.00	213.26
Coyotes	2270.00	7447.75	Sigueros............	50.00	164.05
El Salto............	2280.00	7480.56	La Cofradia........	45.00	147.64
Piloncillos..........	2390.00	7841.46	Confite............	62.00	203.42
La Florida..........	2440.00	8005.51	La Escondida........	68.00	223.11
Junta de los Caminos..	2390.00	7841.46	Las Higueras........	30.00	98.43
El Tecomate........	2100.00	6889.98	Las Conchas........	22.30	73.16
Chavarria...........	1710.00	5610.43	Carboneras	15.50	50.85
La Cienega	2160.00	7086.84	Palos Prietos........	1.54	5.05
Las Botijas	2050.00	6725.94	Mazatlan	0.00	0.00
La Escondida........	2035.00	6676.72			

FROM MANZANILLO TO GUADALAJARA BY WAGON ROAD.

Manzanillo..........	0.00	0.00	Ciudad Guzman (Zapot-		
Cerro del Vigia.......	125.00	410.11	lan)..............	1412.00	4632.70
Cola de Iguana.......	50.00	164.05	Santa Catarina......	1412.00	4632.70
El Ciruelo..........	75.00	246.07	La Cuesta	1450.00	4767.38
Canoa Verde........	75.00	346.07	San Nicolás........	1300.00	4265.23
Las Trojes..........	100.00	328.09	Amatitlan	1325.00	4347.25
Valenzuela..........	125.00	410.11	Sayula............	1350.00	4429.28
Tecolapa............	175.00	574.16	Ojo de Agua........	1360.00	4462.09
La Noria	312.00	1023.65	Cofradia............	1375.00	4511.30
La Presa	362.00	1187.70	Techolula	1375.00	4511.30
Colima............	560.00	1837.33	Cuevitas..........	1360.00	4462.09
La Puerta	650.00	2132.62	El Cuemasate.......	1325.00	4347.25
San Joaquin	650.00	2132.62	El Crucero..........	1325.00	4347.25
Los Limones........	850.00	2788.81	Cebollas..........	1350.00	4429.28
San Gerónimo...	900.00	2952.85	Los Pozos	1325.00	4347.25
Los Alcaracos........	1100.00	3609.04	Chimaltitan........	1325.00	4347.25
La Quesería........	1162.00	3812.46	Ocotan............	1330.00	4363.66
Tonila	1175.00	3854.61	Santa Ana Acatlan....	1350.00	4429.28
Barranca Cachepehuate	975.00	3198.92	Puerta	1500.00	4921.42
San Márcos..........	985.00	3231.73	Cofradia............	1512.00	4960.79
Barranca de Beltran...	850.00	2788.81	Santa Cruz........	1475.00	4987.05
Playa	1025.00	3362.97	Arenal............	1600.00	5429.52
Barranca Platanar....	950.00	3116.90	San Agustin........	1575.00	5167.49
Loma...	1225.00	4019.16	La Calera..........	1575.00	5167.49
Barranca de Atenquique	1025.00	3362.97	Puente de Santa María.	1550.00	5085.47
Ocote Gacho........	1250.00	4101.19	Guadalajara..........	1500.00	4921.42
Pedregal............	1375.00	4511.30			

FROM TEHUACAN TO OAXACA AND PUERTO ANGEL BY WAGON ROAD.

PLACES.	Altitudes.		PLACES.	Altitudes.	
	Metres.	Feet.		Metres.	Feet.
Tehuacan............	1660.00	5446.38	Tierra Blanca........	2000.00	6561.89
La Huerta..........	1480.00	4855.81	Rio Atoyac..........	1660.00	5446.38
Arroyo de Buena Vista.	1320.00	4330.85	San Pablo Huitzo.....	1700.00	5577.62
San Sebastian........	1120.00	3674.66	Santiago Huitzo......	1680.00	5512.00
Camino de Calipán....	1060.00	3477.81	Villa de Etla........	1660.00	5446.38
Calaveras............	960.00	3149.71	Dolores	1640.00	5380.76
San Antonio...	900.00	2952.85	Panzacola	1540.00	5052.66
Hacienda de Ayotla...	860.00	2821.62	Oaxaca.............	1540.00	5052.66
Rio de Reyes	900.00	2952.85	San Agustin Juntas...	1530.00	5019.85
Tecomavaca	620.00	2034.19	Coyotepec..........	1600.00	5249.52
Rio Salado..........	600.00	1968.57	Cúspide	1900.00	6233.70
Campanario.........	730.00	2395.10	Santo Tomás Jaliera..	1830.00	6004.14
Organo.............	700.00	2296.67	Ocotlan	1720.00	5643.24
Pajarito	680.00	2231.05	Magdalena..........	1700.00	5577.62
Gavilan	600.00	1968.57	San Martin..........	1700.00	5577.62
Paraje Blanco.......	580.00	1902.95	Rio Coapa..........	1590.00	5216.71
Rio Seco	560.00	1837.33	Ejutla..............	1540.00	5052.66
Chonoslar...........	700.00	2296.67	Arrogante	1600.00	5249.52
Rancho de Urrutia....	620.00	2034.19	Chichovo........ ...	1840.00	6036.95
Rancho de Cuagulotal.	620.00	2034.19	Zopilote............	1810.00	5938.52
Rancho de los Obos...	620.00	2034.19	Cúspide	1930.00	6332.23
Hacienda de Güendu-			Tlacuache	1840.00	6036.95
lain...............	620.00	2034.19	Tepehuaje..........	1780.00	5840.33
Rio Apoala..........	540.00	1771.71	Miahuatlan..........	1800.00	5905.71
Rio Tomellin	540.00	1771.71	Chapaneco..........	2230.00	7316.51
Balconcillo..........	680.00	2231.05	Agua del Sol........	2400.00	7874.27
Rancho del Chilar....	660.00	2165.43	San José del Pacifico..	2600.00	8530.46
Infiernillo	660.00	2165.43	Garganta del Encino..	2800.00	9186.65
Don Dominguillo.....	750.00	2460.72	Tres Cruces..........	3160.00	10367.79
Arroyo Dominguillo ..	720.00	2362.29	Rancho de Canoas....	3000.00	9842.84
Arroyo de Nopala....	710.00	2329.48	San Miguel Xuchistepec	2780.00	9121.04
El Pochote	1240.00	4068.38	Rio de San José......	2340.00	7677.41
Canton de Buena Vista.	1360.00	4462.09	Cerro de Santa Ana...	2720.00	8858.56
Cúspide............	1500.00	4921.42	Cerro de San Pedro...	2500.00	8202.36
Puente de la Joya.....	1400.00	3412.19	El Porvenir..........	800.00	2624.76
Venta Vieja.........	1600.00	5249.52	Garganta del Cerro de		
Paredones	1840.00	6036.95	la Pluma..........	900.00	2952.85
Llano del Timbre....	1900.00	6233.70	La Providencia.......	830.00	2723.19
Cieneguilla	2020.00	6627.51	La Soledad	750.00	2460.72
Portezuelo..........	2220.00	7283.70	San José Totoltepec...	530.00	1738.90
Las Trancas	2080.00	6824.37	Rio Chacalapa	340.00	1115.52
Carbonera..........	2160.00	7086.84	Pochutla	160.00	524.95
Ojo de Agua........	2100.00	6889.98	Puerto Angel........	0.00	0.00

THE VALLEY OF MEXICO'S DRAINAGE.[1]

Mexico is finishing a great work, the drainage of the valley where the capital city is located, which has required for its completion nearly three hundred years and many millions of dollars, and has cost the lives of hundreds of thousands of men. The necessity, importance,

[1] This article was published in the *Engineering Magazine* of New York for January, 1895 (vol. viii., No 4), but has since been revised and considerably enlarged.

and magnitude of this work, which will be classed among the grandest achievements of men, and the nearness of its completion, induce me to write this paper, which I hope will give some idea of its scope and purpose. I do not pretend to originality, as my work to some extent has been one of compilation from different monographs, which have appeared from time to time, and from some official publications of the Mexican Government.

Topographical Conditions of the Valley of Mexico.—The Valley of Mexico is an immense basin, of approximately circular shape with one extreme diameter of about sixty miles, completely bounded by high mountains, and having only two or three quite high passes out of it. No water drains out of the basin. The surface of this valley has a mean altitude above the sea of 7413 feet and an area of about 2220 square miles.

Mountain ranges rise on every side, making a great corral of rock containing dozens of villages and hamlets, with the ancient capital in the centre. In times past the fires of volcanoes licked up the earth, and such fires still live in the mammoth Popocatapetl, from whose great crater sulphur fumes and smoke with jets of flame have poured through the centuries.

The valley thus hemmed in with solid walls of rock had been an inland sea for many cycles, and during the early existence of man here the salt waters spread over a large extent of the depression. The waters have been gradually lessening by seepage and evaporation, and the Aztec pilgrims coming from the north in the fourteenth century, having received a sign that they were to build their queen-of-the-world city on a small island of the sea, set about building dikes and combating the overflow of the waters.

Evaporation is so excessive at certain periods of the year that malaria, consequent on drought, was far more dreaded by the inhabitants than the periodical floods, and thousands perished annually, so that proper drainage was an absolute necessity for the preservation of health.

Work done by the Indians.—Nearly fifty years before the discovery of America, which took place in 1492, Netzahualcoyotl, saw the necessity for a drainage canal, and commenced the work in 1450. He constructed an immense dike to divide the fresh from the salt-water lakes of the valley. The City of Mexico was at this time the centre of the Aztec nation, and was built on floating structures, like rafts, on the water in the numerous islets on the margins of the lakes, so that in the event of the water rising or the city being subjected to a state of siege, the whole city would float. Mexico City now occupies the site of the old Aztec capital.

The waters of these lakes were liable to disturbances of all kinds;

thus it is recorded by Prescott in his *History of the Conquest of Mexico*: " In 1510 the great lake of Texcoco, without the occurrence of a tempest or earthquake, or any other visible cause, became violently agitated, overflowed its banks, and, pouring into the streets of Mexico, swept off many of the buildings by the fury of its water."

When Cortez arrived in Mexico from Spain in 1519 to take possession of the country in the name of the King of Spain, he found, to his great surprise, the defense of the city admirably arranged, and an almost enchanting view of flowering islets forming the floating capital. Little towns and villages lay half-concealed by the foliage, and from the distance these looked like companies of wild swans riding quietly on the waves.

A scene so new and wonderful filled the rude heart of the Spaniard with amazement. So astonished was he at the extent of the water of Lake Texcoco that he describes it as " a sea that embraces the whole valley," but upon hearing that it was a lake, with a mean depth of a few yards, he gave orders to cut a way through the dike and destroy the aqueduct of Chapultepec. The central dike dividing the fresh from the salt water lake was of such dimensions as to serve Cortez as a roadway for his army.

Prescott, in the work before alluded to, page 297, says: " Leaving the mainland, the Spaniards came on the great dike or causeway, which stretches some four or five miles in length, and divides Lake Chalco from Xochimilco on the west. It was a lance in breadth in the narrowest part, and in some places wide enough for eight horses to ride abreast. It was a solid structure of stone and lime, running directly through the lake, and struck the Spaniards as one of the most remarkable works they had seen in the country."

Having cut the dikes and drained the lake, the " floating city " was at once besieged, and where originally stood the great temple of the Aztecs a Christian temple was afterward raised. The Spaniards, finding themselves in complete possession, proceeded to erect the new City of Mexico, and building on the plan adopted by them at home, they cut down the points of the floating islands and by gradual extension soon placed the town below the mean average level of the lake. Hence arose the great difficulties of the drainage of the Valley of Mexico.

One of the immense dikes built by King Netzahualcoyotl was ten miles long. It divided Lake Texcoco into two parts. Of the two lakes thus formed one was allowed to remain salt, but the other was freshened by letting only fresh water enter by the streams flowing in, the water for the use of the city being taken from this latter. Little by little the waters have subsided since that period, and have been fought back, until now they are confined to six great lakes—Chalco, Xochimilco, Texcoco, Xaltocan, San Cristobal, and Zumpango. Each of these lakes is fed by streams which have little volume during the dry season, but which in the rainy season swell to considerable size, and at times overflow the valleys. The lake of Zumpango was the most dangerous of these, for it received the waters of the Cuautitlan River, —a river draining a large area of country, and having during the rainy season a great volume of water. This river has been turned into the cut of Nochistongo, and has ceased to threaten Mexico and its environs with its overflow.

From these topographical conditions frequent floodings of the old Aztec city and of the Spanish capital, situated almost at the lowest point of the valley, were sure to come in times of unusually heavy rains. In early days, when the Aztecs lived in the middle of Lake Mexico, when their temples and wigwams were built on piles and the streets were often only canals, the periodical overflows from the upper lakes were a matter of small concern, though even then the Nahua engineers were called upon to protect the city by dikes. But when by evaporation, by filling in at the site of the city, by lessened waters, due to the fissures caused by earthquakes, Lake Mexico had disappeared, and the city had come to be built on the spongy soil, above all, when the short-sighted choice of Cortez had been confirmed and the capital of New Spain had come to stand on the ruins of the Aztec town, increasing rapidly in population and wealth,—it became a serious matter that on an average of once in twenty-five years the streets should be from two to six feet under water for an indefinite time.

Work done by the Spaniards.—From 1519 to 1553 the Spaniards were busily engaged in building Mexico, and another grand dike, similar to that built by Netzahualcoyotl in 1450, was formed around the city; this protection proved insufficient, for in 1580 another inundation took place. The Viceroy of the day, Señor Don Martin Enriquez de Almanza, assisted by engineers, engaged to find an outlet for the waters north of the valley. During the time they were thus engaged, important facts were gleaned respecting the River Cuautitlan, and its curious behavior at the foot of Nochistongo, whence it doubled its course at a certain altitude and ran toward Lake Texcoco, instead of into its own lake of Xaltocan. The scheme formed by Enriquez de Almanza to remedy this evil was kept in abeyance, as his services were required in Peru.

In the year 1604 a serious inundation attacked Mexico City. The Marquis de Montes Claros did all in his power to carry out the plan of Señor Don Martin Enriquez to relieve the rivers of the north and of the valley of the excess of water from the central and south lakes, which are of higher altitudes. The *pros* and *cons* of this plan were beset with many great difficulties, and respecting one of the methods tried, mention must be made of a dike of great strength, constructed to prevent any excess or overflow of water from destroying the town of Zumpango and washing away its crops. This dike, which was to check the strong current of the river Pachuca, would also direct the river Cuautitlan to Mexico, direct the rivers north into Zumpango, and would inundate that verdant district, and probably submerge the town; whereas, to divert them into Lake Texcoco would submerge Mexico. To prevent this evil it was decided to make a tunnel; but here, as in all countries and in all ages, engineers, when engaged in any work of magnitude, and of a different character from that commonly known, always find theorists to offer objections, and thus stop the way to actual progress. This was the case in Mexico City.

In 1607 another inundation, spreading over the whole valley, occurred, and, as all the dikes and other defences were swept away, caused a panic of terror among the inhabitants. The Marquis de Salinas was then Viceroy at Mexico City, and determined to carry out the plan of Señor Don Martin Enriquez, being assisted by an engineer of great repute named Enrico Martinez, and also solicited and obtained the co-operation of Father Sanchez, of the Society of Jesus. These three men, after many consultations, formulated the plan of embracing the whole of the lakes of the plain into one main channel of detention, and an outlet as required to keep the same under such control as to have at all times an abundance of water for use. The plan, broadly speaking, was to draw off the water from the south lakes which are at higher levels to those of the north, and to make them serve, by the scour the velocity of the water would cause, to deepen the passage for their exit, and, at the same time, assist the making of the grand canal

Great opposition to this plan was offered on the score of economy, and many insisted that the inundations were solely due to the waters of Cuautitlan and the freshets of Pachuca, and if these were directed north no more was needed, while the people of Zumpango tried to show that no more was needed to inundate their town and submerge the district. The Viceroy then requested Enrico Martinez to induce Father Sanchez to submit some modifications of his former scheme.

The plan was modified, and on November 28, 1607, Enrico Martinez started operations on the modified plan, and in about eleven months 6600 metres (4 $\frac{1}{10}$ miles) of canal, with a transverse section of 3.50 metres (11$\frac{1}{2}$ feet) wide, and a depth of 4.20 metres (13$\frac{3}{4}$ feet), was completed. At the same time other important drainage works were being made; the passage was opened from Boca de San Gregorio to Salto de Tula; this was 8600 metres (5$\frac{1}{3}$ miles) long, as well as two canals as aqueducts 6$\frac{1}{2}$ miles long, one for Lake Zumpango and the other for the river Cuautitlan from Teoloyucan to Huehuetoca.

In December, 1608, in the presence of the Viceroy Don Luis de Velasco and the Archbishop of Mexico, Enrico Martinez inaugurated the outlet of the waters, the whole of the work just described being executed in one year. Humboldt tells us that fifteen thousand native Indians were employed on these works.

In spite of the great good these works brought to the people, there was an outcry for economy, but it is certain that other motives prompted the disturbance and the attempt to harass and hamper the Viceroy. The object was to prevent a grant of money from being made to pay for the lining of the canal with cement. This was found to be necessary, as the greater part of the work was excavated in marl, and the liberated waters ran with such velocity that the symmetry of the tunnel was soon destroyed, and its passage and usefulness lessened by the *debris* that obstructed the fairway. This state of things was brought so forcibly home to the objectors that a small sum of money was reluctantly granted, sufficient to patch up the tunnel in places where the rush of waters had made the most havoc, hydraulic cement or mortar being used, but the sum granted proved to be totally inadequate, and for want of more money the tunnel was rendered perfectly useless by falling obstructions. This occurred in the year 1609. Gossips and theorists then united to run down the scheme, although it was conceded that the work had averted a terrible inundation or submergence of Mexico City.

A few years elapsed before the question of continuing the works for the tunnel again caused excitement; but a general feeling grew up that the work of the tunnel should be continued. The opposition was strong enough to obtain the hearing of an appeal in Madrid, with the result that the Spanish Government in 1614 procured the services of a Dutch engineer, named Adrian van Boot, to proceed to Mexico City to examine and report on the canal works, and to submit a plan to remedy the evils. As the result of his labors he condemned the plan of Father Sanchez, and recommended that the old means of defence used by the Indians should again be adopted, and that dams and dikes should be thrown up at once. This report had the effect of annoying almost everybody, and was the means of much fruitless discussion. In this dilemma the Spanish Government, when appealed to, confessed they were unable to advise the Viceroy of Mexico what to do, but sent the Marquis of Gelves to Mexico to see into matters, and he, having unbounded faith in the ability of the Dutch engineer, Adrian van Boot, and hoping to keep money in the treasury, ordered Enrico Martinez to close up the tunnel completely, and to return the rivers to their natural courses; but before these orders were half executed the enormous rush of waters grew so alarming that he had to accept again Enrico Martinez's plan over that of Adrian van Boot. The marquis was soon after deposed, his place being taken by the Marquis de Cerralvo, whose first act was to set Martinez free at the request of the city council who provided him with means of continuing his work on the canal and tunnel. The Viceroy revoked his predecessor's order and issued another to open up the tunnel, and that with all speed, on his personal responsibility. Although Cerralvo gave these orders, he forgot to give Martinez the money to carry them out, and, as a consequence, the works remained in a deplorable condition.

The tunnel was blocked up by this cause, and Martinez was cruelly scored for not having done his work aright by the very ones who had refused to give him the necessary material for it. He bravely essayed to repair the damage, but the water-soaked condition of the ground gave no resistance for the building of the needed walls, while death mowed down the enslaved workers. They were crushed to death by the frequent cavings in of the loose soil, or were sent to the grave by the deadly damps. Finally, the charge being made that the builder was blocking up the tunnel in revenge, he was thrown into prison, where he languished for many months. As there was no one else available who could carry on the great work, he was afterwards released and again put in charge. It was then decided that, the tunnel being completely useless, the next thing to be done would be to make a great cut down to the tunnel and thus open it out. This entailed the making of an excavation fourteen miles in length with an average depth of one hundred and eighty feet and width of four hundred feet.

On June 20, 1629, the ever troublesome river Cuautitlan over flowed and inundated the north of the plain, and swept with it other streams into Lake Texcoco. In the September following the increase of the water was greater than ever had been known. The city was so suddenly and completely submerged that thirty thousand persons perished, the bodies floating about the streets for some time after. The destruction of property and life, consequent on the inundation, was so great generally, and affected the tunnel to such an extent, that during a period of five years there was scarcely any reduction in the height of the water, and the water in the city remained during all this time as high as the second story of the houses; the slight difference in the heighth of the water being caused by evaporation.

The Spanish Government at Madrid gave orders to change the capital to a better and more secure site. To this suggestion the citizens demurred, saying, in effect, that to insure complete security an outlay of only $3,000,000 was necessary, this being the estimated cost of completing the tunnel, whereas to build a new city would involve an outlay of $50,000,000, with a loss of another $50,000,000 in leaving the old one.

Several plans were now submitted in opposition to that of Enrico

Martinez, and one by Simon Mendez was accepted, his plan being to direct all the waters of the valley by one canal into the neck of the Tula, the spot selected by Martinez for his outlet. It was soon discovered that the plan of Simon Mendez was far too costly, and as the money that could be spared was practically melting away without perceptible progress being made, Enrico Martinez was again requested to carry out the work as arranged with Father Sanchez.

The next Viceroy, the Marquis of Cadereita, was most desirous to see the work of the tunnel pushed on; but however enthusiastic he may have been, lack of funds prevented him from giving effect to his desires. The work continued very slowly, Martinez being unable to do any work at the tunnel, and he contented himself with improving the canal by lining it in bad places with cement. Martinez struggled on for thirty-seven years with this work, and died unnoticed and uncared for. All trace of his place of final rest was lost.

In 1637 an earthquake made sad havoc with the tunnel works, and for lack of funds no repairs could take place; but when funds were obtainable workmen could not be procured, the earthquakes and inundations having carried off many thousands of these poor fellows. The survivors lacked heart to return to such an unfortunate and, as they thought, accursed work.

In the year 1640 the work was being pressed on by men from the prisons, under the direction of the Franciscan monks, and carried on, with varying results, in this way for thirty-five years, until Señor Don Martin Solis was made head of the municipal council. He being an avowed enemy to the Franciscans, sent them away, and undertook the superintendence of the work himself; but his method of treating the prisoners was so harsh and cruel that they broke out into open revolt, and the works were threatened. Therefore, to save the works and his own life, he consented to the return of the Franciscans. It is estimated that up to this time some two hundred thousand men lost their lives on this work. The Franciscans steadily, but slowly, worked on, always with a very limited exchequer, until 1767, when there remained some 1935 metres (1¼ miles) still to be completed. A contract was entered into to finish this work in five years for $800,000; but instead of five years it took twenty-two years, and, instead of 8 metres (25 feet wide), as contracted for, it was only 3 metres (9 feet 10 inches) wide.

The Spaniards continued the work in other hands for one hundred and fifty years before the task of opening the cut was completed. Spasmodic work for a century and a half led at last to the accomplishment of this project in 1789. The old tunnel of Martinez is now a gigantic trench from 30 to 160 feet in depth and some 300 feet broad in some places, and is known as the Tajo de Nochistongo. The immediate vicinity of the workings was depopulated of its native inhabit-

ants by the insatiable demands of the killing labor, and recruits were
then drawn from Puebla and other thickly populated Indian centres.
Great prison barracks were built on the bare hills, and here all the
criminals were sent to enter the work.   The ones in charge were in-
different with regard to the lives entrusted to their care, and the
slaughter, of which scant record remains in the parish burial books,
and which resulted from a combination of defects in appliances for
both the safety and the comfort of the workmen, was terrific.   As the
burial trenches were filled with new dead, the depths of the cut were
tenanted by new laborers.

The victims of three years of bondage numbered fully two hundred
thousand ere the work was done.   Yet the results were but slight, only
the excess of water from the highest lakes and streams being carried
off.   However, the danger from inundations of the city has been very
materially decreased by the Nochistongo opening, and no more deluges
have occurred since its completion.

Still the fact that the bottom of the cut was thirty feet higher than
the surface of Texcoco, the lowest lying of the lakes, left the city in
danger of inundation, as Lake Texcoco is constantly filling up at the
rate of one and one-half inches a year and is now but a few feet below
the level of the main plaza of the city.

The drainage works had long been a heavy burden upon the Mexican treasury.   Up to 1637 Bancroft estimates that $3,000,000 had been
expended.   Up to the year 1800 the outlay had reached $6,247,670.
Up to 1830 the total expenditure was $8,000,000.

Work done by the Mexican Government.—The problem which the
Mexican Government had to face was very different from that which
confronted Martinez in 1607.   The question of preventing submergence
is practically solved.   The work of Martinez, unsatisfactory as it was,
did a great deal to solve it.   Since his day the area of the lakes has
been gradually diminishing.   The rapid evaporation in the rarefied air
and under the direct sun of the valley partly accounts for this.   Twice
the water in Lake Texcoco has almost entirely disappeared, leaving
only a sea of mud and a small pool.   The great problem which the
Mexican Government has now solved is not how to prevent an inflow
of water, but how to provide an outlet for sewage.   The danger to
be averted was not that of drowning, but that of dying from the plague.

Lake Texcoco more than any other now menaces the security of the
capital.   The unwise cutting down of forests since the Spanish conquest permits the waters pouring down into the valley to bring with
them annually great quantities of alluvial matter, which have so much
raised the lake bottom and the water level that inundations have been
of frequent occurrence.   The general level of the City of Mexico is
only 6.56 feet above the surface of the lake.   The rainy season lasts

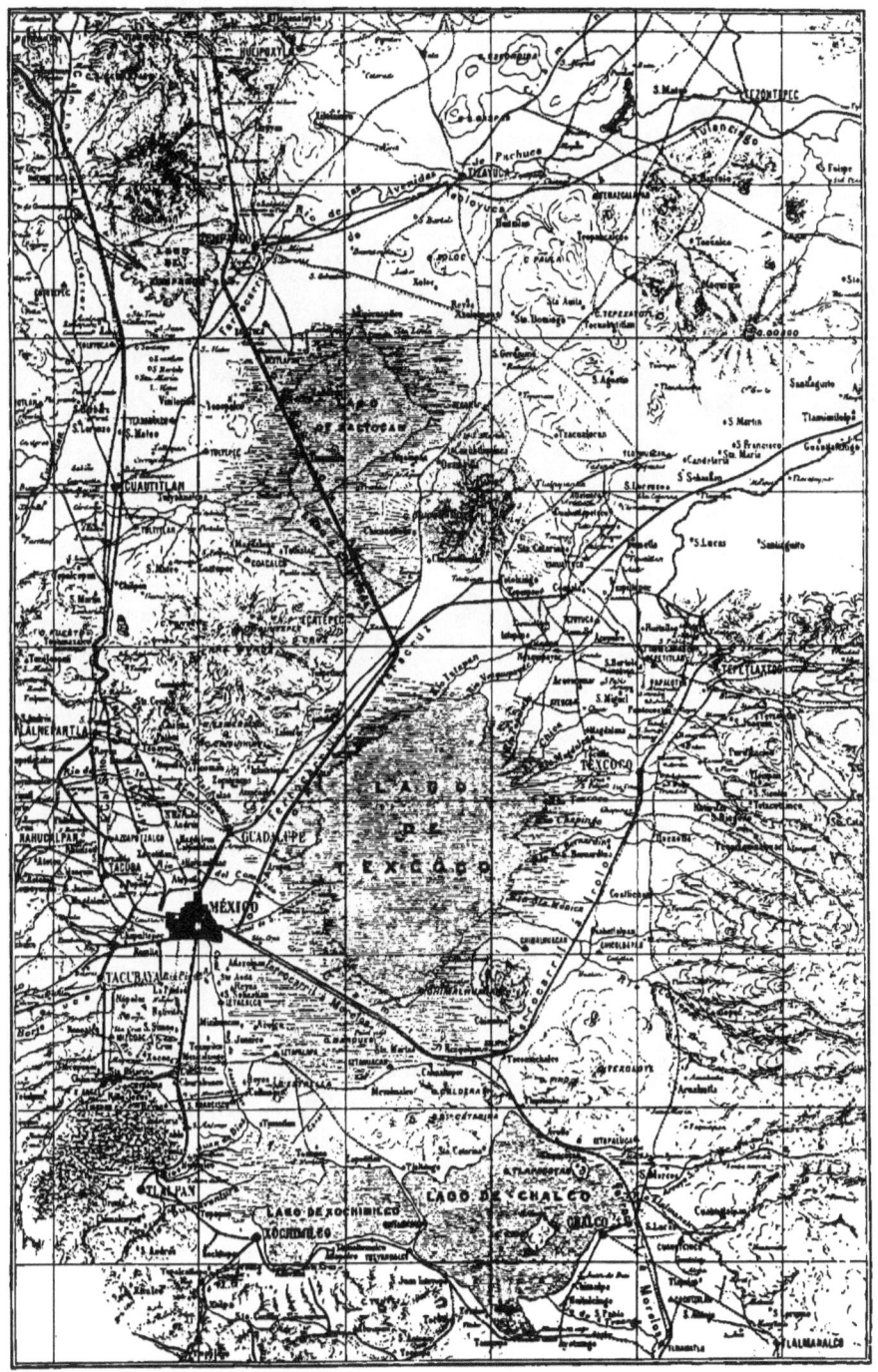

MAP OF THE VALLEY OF MEXICO, SHOWING THE CANAL AND TUNNEL.

from June to October inclusive. During this season five times as
much water falls as during the rest of the year, evaporation can no
longer compensate for rainfall, and the valley is more or less flooded.

Originally built in the midst of a lake, the city has been left on dry
ground by the receding waters. Lake Texcoco,—some three miles
distant,—Chalco, and Xochimilco have altitudes nearly four feet
greater than the pavement of the capital. Still more imperiously do
the lakes to the north dominate the city. San Cristobal and Xaltocan
are about five feet, while Zumpango is over thirteen feet, above it.

The project now almost completed is a modification of the scheme
projected by Simon Mendez in the time of the Spanish Government,
and which in 1849 was adopted by Captain Smith of the corps of
American engineers which accompanied General Scott's army. The
tunnel was ultimately located under the saddle and through the ravine
of Acatlan, its mouth being near the village of Tequixquiac. The
works have been begun several times, and then suspended without
effecting anything of importance. In 1866 the works now nearing
completion were commenced. A project proposed by Señor Don
Francisco de Garay, a well-known engineer of the City of Mexico,
was pronounced the most feasible. But the revolutionary struggle
succeeded, and for many years the work was relegated to the background.

In 1879 engineer Don Luis Espinosa, the present director of the
works, took charge of the undertaking. In the first period mentioned
the cutting of Tequixquiac was excavated, and the greater part of the
shafts were begun; but at that point the work was stopped by political
agitations.

The present gigantic work cannot have been considered to have
been seriously undertaken, with a view of completion at any cost, until
the year 1885, when the City Council of Mexico submitted a project to
the Government to which they offered to contribute largely in the
event of its being adopted.

A special commission, with ample authority to deal with the funds
set aside for the work, was appointed by President Porfirio Diaz.
The City Council set aside the sum of $400,000 per annum for the
canal works, which sum was materially increased by the Federal Government.

In 1887 the City Council raised a loan in London of £2,400,000 to
meet the cost of the work and guarantee its successful termination.
The entire responsibility of the work was now assumed by the City
Council, and the Government gave authority for the Council to make
and collect new taxes. Still, there was not sufficient money forthcoming, so another loan was raised in London for £3,000,000, a portion
of which was held for the work.

The drainage works, when carried out, will receive the surplus waters and sewage of the City of Mexico and carry them outside of the valley, and will also control the entire waters of the valley, affording an outlet, whenever found necessary, to those which might otherwise over-flow fields and towns, rendering the soil stagnant and marshy. The work consists of three parts—1st, the tunnel; 2d, a canal starting from the gates of San Lázaro, and having a length of 67½ kilometres, or 43 miles, its line following on the eastern side of the Guadalupe range of hills and between that range and Lake Texcoco, changing its direction after arriving at the 20th kilometre to a northeasterly one, so as to diagonally cross Lake San Cristobal, a part of Lake Xaltocan, and a part of Lake Zumpango, and arriving finally at the mouth of the tunnel near the town of Zumpango; and 3d, the sewage of the City of Mexico.

The tunnel.—The contract for completing the tunnel was let to Messrs. Read & Campbell, of Mexico, but for some reason they were unable to finish the work. It was therefore continued and satisfactorily completed by the City Council for a sum considerably less than the price contracted with Messrs. Read & Campbell under their superintendence as hereafter stated.

The tunnel has a length of 10,021.79 metres, or 32,869 feet (6¼ miles), with a curved section formed by four curves respectively of the following dimensions: The upper part has a span of 4.185 metres, or 13 feet 9 inches, and a rise of 1.570 metres, or 5 feet 1½ inches; the two lateral arches have a chord each of 2.36 metres, or 7 feet 9 inches, a radius with a chord of 2.429 metres, or 8 feet, and a rise of 0.521 metre, or 1 foot 8½ inches; the elevation is 4.286 metres, or 14 feet, and the greatest width is the span of the upper arch. The accompanying drawings show this section. The tunnel is lined with brick, having a thickness in the upper part of 0.45 metre, or 1 foot 6 inches, and in the lower part over which the water runs, of 0.04 metre, or 1 foot 4 inches in the side arches, and of 0.30 metre, or 1 foot in the radius, this latter lining being of artificial stone made of sand and Portland cement. The elevation of the invert at the beginning of the tunnel is 9.20 metres, or 30 feet 1½ inches below datum; at the end of the tunnel, 17.53 metres, or 57 feet 6 inches below datum. The gradient is 0.00069 for the first 2170.74 metres, or 1 in 1449 for 7120 feet; 0.00072 for the following 5831 metres, or 1 in 1389 for 19,125 feet 6 inches; 0.001 for 5100 metres, or 1 in 1389 for 16,728 feet; and 0.00135, 1 in 740, for the rest of the tunnel; these changes being in accordance with changes of details made from those of the original project, in some cases modifying the section and in other cases the lining. Twenty-five shafts, each 2 by 3 metres, or 16 feet 6¾ inches by 9 feet 10 inches, were opened at a distance of 400 metres, or 1312

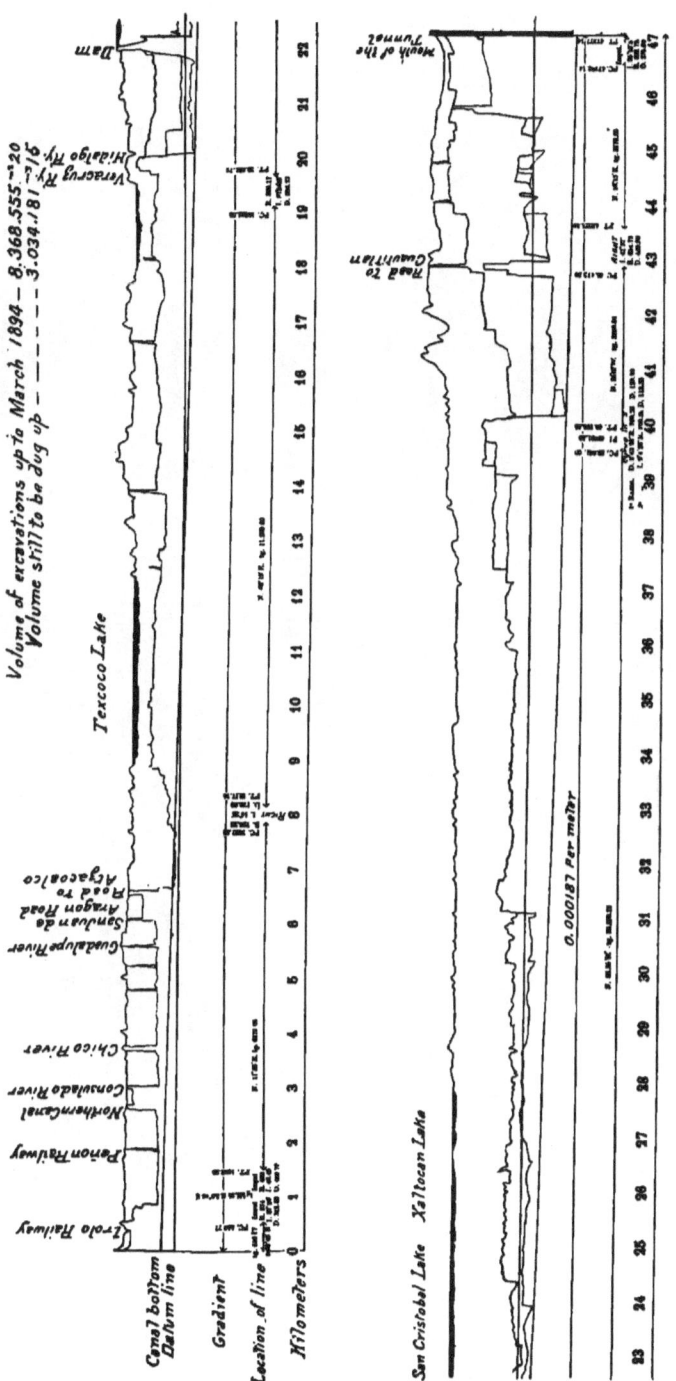

DRAINAGE OF THE VALLEY OF MEXICO
LONGITUDINAL SECTION OF THE
MAIN CANAL

(This Cut was made in March, 1894, before the Canal was finished.)

SCALE

Horizontal.......... $\frac{1}{50.000}$

Vertical.......... $\frac{1}{400}$

feet from each other. These served to ventilate the tunnel and to facilitate the work. The deepest of these shafts, situated on the saddle of Acatlan, has a depth of 92 metres, or 301 feet 9 inches; the shallowest is 21 metres, or 68 feet 10 inches.

To give an idea of the labor involved beyond the mere tunneling, it is as well to mention that the quantity of materials required per lineal yard of tunnel was 1800 bricks, 94 cement blocks, 3 cubic yards of mortar, and 70 cubic feet of volcanic stone.

Maximum discharge through the tunnel = 18 cubic metres, 635$\frac{4}{5}$ cubic feet.

When the drainage board took charge of the work, it was executed by day labor both in the canal and in the tunnel, the latter having the larger amounts expended on it. But, shortly afterwards, the contract for the tunnel was let to Messrs. Read & Campbell, of London, who, after having invested a considerable sum in the work, found themselves under the necessity of cancelling their contract at the beginning of the year 1892. These gentlemen continued to handle the work, but as managers, and under the direction of the board.

The canal.—In December, 1889, the Department of Public Works contracted with the Bucyrus Company of the United States, of which Colonel Ellis was the president, for the construction of the canal.

This company started with two spoon dredgers capable of raising a maximum of 1000 cubic metres, 1308 cubic yards, a day. They commenced operations at the twenty-second kilometre. In the opinion of the board of commissioners, the Bucyrus Company was not proceeding with the work at a suitable rate of speed, for at 1000 cubic metres, 1308 cubic yards, per day, the work of dredging alone, as there were some 16,000,000 of cubic metres, 20,928,000 cubic yards, of excavation to do, would take about forty-three years ; their contract was therefore cancelled.

In May, 1894, the Department of Public Works of Mexico contracted with Messrs. S. Pearson & Son of London for the completion of the canal, modifying former contracts of December 25, 1889, March 30, 1891, and April 18, 1893, under the following bases: the unfinished excavation in the first nine kilometres, and that between kilometre 47 and the entrance of the tunnel of Tequixquiac, are to be continued by the Board of Drainage Directors, who must have the latter portion completed to 10 metres below the surface of the soil by December 31, 1894, and to the required depth of the canal by May 31, 1895, in order that the water in the canal may settle to that level and permit the contractors to slope the walls as required by the contract. The contractors are to complete the canal between kilometres 9 and 47 for the sum of $3,506,000. For making the monthly estimates the canal will be divided into two sections—kilometres 9 to 22 and kilometres

22 to 47. In the first section the provisional estimate will be 40 cents per cubic metre; in the second a sum equal to the quotient obtained by dividing the remainder of the money by the number of cubic metres to be removed. The contractors may suspend the work of the dredgers when they fall below 40 cubic metres per hour, and can proceed with the excavation in any way they wish. The excavation had to be completed by May 1, 1896, except in the parts where the dredgers cannot work. Then for each day's delay the contractors must pay $500 fine, and after five months the contract will be rescinded.

These contractors carried out the work of the canal in two different ways—by hand work with centrifugal pumps to draw off the water which filtered into the work, and by means of enormously powerful Couloir dredgers which have a capacity for 3000 cubic metres of excavation per day, and which throw the excavated earth to a distance of more than 200 metres from the centre of the canal. They had five of these dredgers at work, and by means of them excavated to a depth of 20 metres or 65 feet, raising the earth to an elevation of more than 16 metres, 52½ feet, so as to empty it into the shoots, along which it was carried by a stream of water that delivered it at a considerable distance from the dredger. The dredgers have now done their work, and they have been taken to pieces, packed and transferred to the harbor works at Veracruz. The portion of the canal contracted for was completed to the satisfaction of all concerned in six years.

The level of the bottom of the canal above the datum line adopted is 2.25 metres, or 7 feet 4 inches, and the mouth of the tunnel is 9.20 metres, or 30 feet ⅓ inch below the same datum, supposed to pass 10 metres, or 33.80 feet below the bottom of the Aztec calendar stone, since transferred to the National Museum. The level of the ground at the beginning of the canal is 8.94 metres, or 29 feet 4 inches, and at the end 15.86 metres, or 52 feet above datum. The uniform slope of the canal is at the rate of 0.187 per kilometre.

The canal has a depth, at its commencement, of 5.50 metres, or 18 feet, which in the last few kilometres is increased to 20.50 metres, or 67 feet 3 inches. The side slopes were projected with a batter of 45 degrees, and the width of the bottom is 5.50 metres, or 18 feet for the first 20 kilometres, or 12½ miles, and 6.50 metres or 21 feet 2 inches in the rest of the canal. The first 20 kilometres, or 12½ miles, may be considered as a prolongation of the net of sewers in the city, and will receive only the water that passes through them. The flow is calculated for an average of 5 cubic metres, or 176½ cubic feet, although, when heavy rains require it, they can receive a greater volume; the rest of the canal communicates with Lake Texcoco, and will be utilized in controlling its waters,—the lowest in the valley,—which can be made to flow into the canal from all parts. Hence the canal has been built to

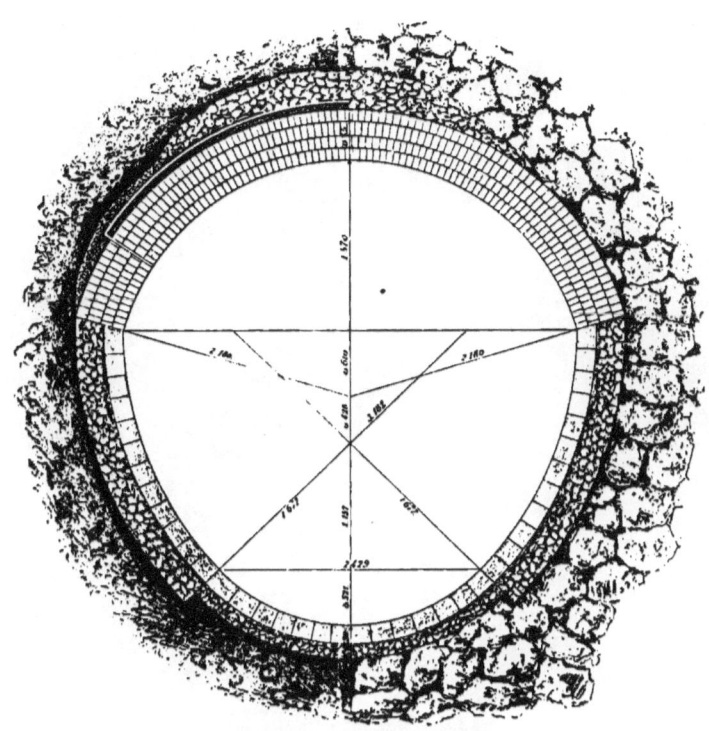

(Drainage of the Valley of Mexico.)

VERTICAL SECTION OF THE TUNNEL.

carry the largest flow that can pass through the tunnel, or 18 cubic
metres, 635⅔ cubic feet, per second.   The cutting is through a strictly
clay formation, comprising occasional thin strata of sand and sandstone.

For accommodation of railroads, wagon roads, and water-courses,
it was necessary to construct five aqueducts—four of masonry and one
of iron—to carry rivers, four iron bridges for the passage of railroads,
and fourteen bridges for vehicular traffic.

The sewage.—The sewers of the City of Mexico form a network
of covered channels, located sometimes in the middle and sometimes
on the sides of the streets, these being almost always gorges, communicating with a system of secondary sewers that empty into a collecting sewer discharging into the canal of San Lázaro, which transports
the sewage to Lake Texcoco.   If the water is high in the lake, water
backs up into the sewers and saturates the soil under the houses and
streets.   As this has been the condition for several centuries, the state
of the subsoil under the city can be better imagined than described.
The death-rate touches 40 per 1000—the highest in the civilized world.
Mexico's elevation of over 7000 feet is all that saves it from a pesti-
lence.   Malarial and gastric fevers are almost continually epidemic.

For a century the problem has been settling into one of pure sanita-
tion.   The plans which the Government has been working since about
1883, though called plans for draining the valley, really seek to get a fall
sufficient to dispose of the sewage.   In fact, in the original plan, from
considerations of economy, care was to be taken to keep out of the
projected canal all water both from the surface of the valley and from
the rivers.   The Consulado and the Guadalupe rivers were to be carried over the new canal in iron aqueducts.   The drainage system was
thus to be simply a part of the sewage system of the city.

The excavated materials have been tipped on each side of the canal
at their natural slopes, and a towpath near the canal level provided.
Sluice gates will direct the city drainage either to the canal or to Lake
Texcoco.   A sluice gate at the junction of the smaller with the larger
part of the canal will control the flow of Lake Texcoco, and another
sluice gate will be placed at the entrance of the tunnel.

Completion of the work.—As this paper goes to press, the drainage
works of the Valley of Mexico are practically finished, as the waters of
the valley have been for several years passing through the canal and
the tunnel to their outlet in the river which takes them to the Gulf of
Mexico, and the company with whom the canal was contracted is now
giving the finishing touches to the sides and bottom of the canal and
will deliver it to the Government Board of the Drainage Directors in
January, 1898.   It was agreed with the contractors that the portion of
the canal between the City of Mexico and the 20th kilometre, which is
comparatively easy, because the canal is not deep there, and the ex-

cavations do not exceed 200,000 cubic metres, will be made directly by the Board as soon as the other portion of the canal has been finished; this last section of the work is expected to be finished in June, 1898, when the waters of the City of Mexico will leave the valley by the drainage works here mentioned.

The canal and six-mile tunnel through the mountain range have a total length approaching fifty miles. The present works will take rank with the great achievements of modern times, just as the immense "cut" of Nochistongo, their unsuccessful predecessor, was the leader among ancient earthworks in all the world. The completed system will have cost $20,000,000.

I have dwelt on these works at some length, because their importance to the City of Mexico can hardly be overestimated. Instead of being one of the healthiest cities in the world, as it should be with its magnificent climate and situation, Mexico, unfortunately, has a terribly heavy death-rate, due principally to want of drainage and generally bad sanitary condition. When the existing danger of floods is removed, and the sanitary evils are remedied by a proper system of drainage, the increased security that will be enjoyed by life and property will certainly have its effect on the prosperity of the city. Property will rise in value, the population will grow with rapidity, not to mention the tide of tourists that will set in from the United States, and this will mean larger revenues for the municipality.

I could not well finish this paper without paying General Diaz, President of Mexico, a just tribute for the great interest he has taken in having this gigantic work brought to a close during his administration. To his exertions in this regard, and to his commanding position in Mexico, more than to anything else, this happy result, now in sight, is due. So after a weary search of centuries for relief, the beautiful Valley of Mexico will gain its deliverance not only from the engulfing floods, but from the sanitary evils which have long resulted from defective drainage.

COFFEE CULTURE ON THE SOUTHERN COAST OF CHIAPAS.

COFFEE CULTURE ON THE SOUTHERN
COAST OF CHIAPAS.

I.

INTRODUCTION.

The desire of contributing, in however slight a degree, to the development of the cultivation of coffee in the State of Chiapas, which, when undertaken on a large scale, will become the chief source of wealth of a considerable part of its territory, induces me now to take up my pen for the purpose of setting down the results of my own observations and of those of several experienced planters of Guatemala, giving them the form of practical instructions, which may also be of use to the people of the other States of the Mexican Confederation who may be favorably situated for this industry and who may desire to avail themselves of the advantages which it offers. I will note down, then, what I consider to be the fundamental principles of coffee culture; and I think I may say with certainty that the rules here given will produce good results in a soil and climate similar to those of Chiapas, if they be faithfully and judiciously followed. To give these rules is the purpose of the present work.

It is also my purpose to show how easy the cultivation of coffee is, and how large are the profits it yields, in order to encourage my countrymen to devote themselves to so profitable an industry. Those whose pecuniary resources will not allow them to undertake it on a large scale may do so on a small one, certain of good results, and of being able, with the profits which a small plantation will yield to form a larger one in the course of a few years, which will assure their future.

In order to appreciate the advantages to be derived by the Chiapas coast from coffee cultivation, it will be sufficient to compare the Guatemala of twenty years ago with the Guatemala of to-day. Lands entirely uninhabited have suddenly become transformed into well-cultivated fields; towns and cities that had fallen into decay have sprung into prosperity as if by magic, and are steadily increasing in wealth; new roads to facilitate transportation are being constantly constructed; commercial transactions have greatly multiplied ; the revenues are increasing; public credit is being re-established; and what, not long ago was a decadent, impoverished, and almost ruined country has become, thanks to the beneficent results of the cultivation of coffee, a rich and prosperous State. I see no reason why Chiapas, if it follows the same course, should not attain the same results.

The great agricultural progress made by Guatemala will be better understood if we consider how valuable land has become there. While the best land situated in the Valley of Mexico, in the vicinity of the capital, is estimated at an average value of $100,000 the square league, land situated in the vicinity of the city of Guatemala, for the reason that it is suitable for coffee, sells at $500 per lot of 10,000 square varas, at which rate the Mexican square league would be worth the fabulous sum of $1,250,000.

On the various occasions on which I have visited Guatemala I have made a special study of coffee culture, which is assuming such large proportions in the neighboring Republic. The greater number of the rules set down in this work, therefore, are based upon experience acquired in Guatemala, for, unfortunately, the cultivation of coffee in Soconusco has not yet attained the necessary proportions to base on it a body of rules. This will explain the frequent references which I shall make to Guatemala in the course of this work.

The best coffee-growing districts of Guatemala are those called there " Costa Grande " and " Costa Cuca," which are the prolongation of the chain of mountains which crosses the southern part of the State of Chiapas, and runs here, as in the neighboring Republic, very near the Pacific, and almost parallel with it. The land on that coast, therefore, is not inferior to the best in Guatemala; if there is any difference between them, it is that the Soconusco land is better watered.

I shall not give here the botanic classification of the coffee tree, a description of the plant, the chemical analysis of its fruit, nor an account of its discovery and use, for although all this is of undoubted interest, it would draw me aside from my main object, which is to lay down practical rules for the cultivation of coffee. I think it necessary, however, to say that science has done little hitherto, at least so far as I know, in favor of this industry. I have not been able to find any information regarding the chemical analysis of the soils suitable for the cultivation of coffee, nor of other scientific operations whose results would afford a sure basis for methods for its better cultivation. It is plain that if the component substances of the soil which nourishes the coffee tree and those which form its fruit were known with certainty, it might be determined with accuracy what kind of soil and what fertilizers are best adapted to it; and by using these not only might the plant be made to live longer but also to yield larger crops. Chemistry and geology have done much for certain plants; the cultivation of the cereals has attained to almost mathematical precision in Europe. Thanks to the advancement made in these sciences, the substances which each crop draws from the soil may now be determined with exactness, and, as a consequence, the substances which should be used as fertilizers, in order to supply the losses caused by the crops. When such data respecting coffee can be obtained, great advancement will have been made in its cultivation, which will not until then cease to be empirical.

II.

FUTURE OF COFFEE CULTURE IN MEXICO.

The use of coffee is becoming general everywhere. Whether it is that certain beverages at certain periods become fashionable, and that coffee is at the present time one of these, or that it really has properties which make it beneficial to the human constitution, certain it is that the sphere of its consumption is widening notably. Mexico is not exempt from this tendency; a few years ago coffee was hardly used in the Republic, while now it begins to compete with cocoa, and even with the national drink made of Indian corn.

Hardly five years ago coffee was sold in Soconusco at five dollars per quintal; low as this price was it yielded a profit, but did not make it worth while to extend its cultivation. Many still fear that the prices of the last two years were exceptional, that they will before long sink to their former level, and that coffee on the plantation will not sell for more than eight dollars per quintal. The crop of 1872 sold at from ten to twelve dollars per quintal on the plantation; and that of 1873 at eighteen dollars per quintal. Although it is true that this is an exceptional price, I think it probable that coffee will not fall lower than ten dollars on the plantation, which will still leave a good profit, as will be shown farther on.

Mexico is, besides, destined, from its proximity to the United States, to become the chief source of supply for that country, which is the country that consumes the largest quantity of coffee in proportion to the number of its inhabitants. Transportation will be easier when we are connected by rail with the United States, for the Central States of the Union would find it more to their advantage to import coffee from Mexico overland than by way of New York or San Francisco. That market would of itself suffice to consume all the crops that the country could raise for several years to come.

These considerations, which I touch upon briefly, lead me to believe that far from being attended by any risk, coffee-growing is, and will continue to be for some time to come, one of the most lucrative branches of agriculture to which the Mexican farmer could apply his labor and intelligence.

III.

ADVANTAGES AND DISADVANTAGES OF SOCONUSCO FOR COFFEE-GROWING.

Soconusco offers special advantages for the cultivation of coffee. It also has some disadvantages, which, although they may be regarded as transitory and easily remedied, it will be proper to mention here.

Each of these points, therefore, will now be considered separately.

1. THE ADVANTAGES WHICH SOCONUSCO OFFERS FOR THE CULTIVATION OF COFFEE.

Soconusco unites many conditions that render it suitable for the cultivation of coffee. The principal of these are the following:

A.—Advantages of the soil and climate of Soconusco.

B.—Cheapness of labor.

C.—Proximity of good coffee land to the sea.

D.—Facility with which the expenses of growing coffee may be defrayed by raising other crops at the same time on the same ground.

Each of these advantages will be considered separately.

A.—Advantages of the Soil and Climate of Soconusco.—The soil of Soconusco seems especially adapted for coffee-growing. In speaking further on of the conditions which make a locality suitable for coffee it will be seen that all of them are favorably combined in Soconusco. The character of the soil, the nature of the climate, a moist atmosphere, abundant rains, numerous streams and waterfalls, shelter from the prevailing winds, and all the other conditions which experience has shown to be favorable to coffee, are united in Soconusco.

The configuration of the land renders it very favorable to coffee. In an area of about fourteen leagues the required altitude (from one to five thousand feet above the level of the sea), with the corresponding temperature, is to be found. In the course of this paper the peculiar advantages which result from the favorable situation of the land will be pointed out.

Comparing the system of cultivating coffee in Soconusco with that followed in other parts of the Republic where highly esteemed coffee is produced, it will be seen that Soconusco has many advantages over these. While in Colima and Jalisco the coffee tree requires irrigation in order to grow and thrive, here it grows and flourishes without it. The rains, which continue in Soconusco for six months in the year, constitute a natural irrigation, and the soil retains during the dry season sufficient moisture to keep the plant from withering; the numerous rivers, streams, and waterfalls of the Cordillera contribute also to keep the ground moist, as do also the heavy dews, caused probably by the proximity of the sea. Shade trees, indispensable in the former localities, and which draw so much of its nutritive elements from the earth, to the detriment of the coffee-tree, are not necessary here. In other localities the soil must be manured, while in Soconusco manure is unnecessary. It is true that fertilizers contribute to make the crop more abundant and to prolong the life of the tree; but here no manure is used, nor is the necessity for it felt; and without its use the coffee plantations last a longer time and yield better crops than in other localities where manure is used.

The best proof of the advantages offered by Soconusco for the cultivation of coffee, is the cheapness with which it is raised. While in Colima coffee cannot be sold with profit to the planter at less than from thirty to thirty-five dollars per quintal, in Soconusco it will yield a profit at even eight dollars. This fact in itself is the plainest proof that could be adduced of the superior advantages of this locality, as compared with Colima, for the cultivation of coffee. In Colima, coffee is cultivated on a small scale only; the coffee crop up to the year 1871, notwithstanding the high price it brought, did not exceed two hundred quintals.

Farther on it will be seen wherein the excellence of the Colima coffee consists, and how coffee of approximately the same quality might be raised in Soconusco.

B. Cheapness of Labor in Soconusco.—Almost everywhere on the coast where there is a scarcity of hands—and this is the case along almost the whole of our coast line, where the population is so sparse—labor is much dearer than in the interior. Along the Southern coast of the State of Veracruz, for instance, the laborer is paid not less than fifty cents a day, and in many other localities he is paid even more. Soconusco may be considered, however, as an exception to this rule, for wages are here as low as in the interior of the Republic.

The price of labor in Soconusco is now regulated by the price paid in Guatemala. On coffee plantations it ranges from a real and a half to two reals and a half per day; the average wages being two reals a day, a sum which seems very moderate. In Costa Rica wages are now as high as a dollar a day.

The scarcity of labor in Soconusco is, however, the principal difficulty with which every agricultural enterprise has to contend, as will be seen farther on.

C. Proximity of good Coffee Land to the Sea.—The proximity to the sea, in Soconusco, of the land suitable for coffee cultivation is a very advantageous circumstance, not only because of the exposure of the land to the sea air, which contributes greatly to the excellence of the coffee and the abundance of the crop, but also because this proximity to the sea cheapens considerably the freight by land.

It may be considered that of the coffee plantations at present in this District, those farthest from the port are at a distance from it of twenty leagues, by the roads now in use, a distance which might be considerably shortened by building new roads.

D. Facility with which the Expenses of Coffee-Growing may be Defrayed by Raising other Crops at the same Time on the same Land.—One of the principal drawbacks to coffee-raising is that a plantation does not begin to yield until from three to five years after planting, according as it has been planted from seeds or from the nursery, and few persons can afford to make the outlay required during that time without obtaining meanwhile any return from the money invested.

Soconusco offers in this respect, also, advantages which are hardly to be met with elsewhere. The soil best adapted for coffee is also that which is best adapted for sugar-cane. In the cold, high lands adjacent to this District, which do not produce sugar-cane, there is a considerable population of Guatemalan Indians who are obliged to buy there the sugar they require, whether for food or to make brandy, which is largely consumed in that Republic. For this reason, there is generally a great demand in Soconusco for sugar, which consequently brings a good price. The buyers come down for the sugar to the ranches in which it is made, so that it is not even necessary to carry it to market.

As the sugar-cane requires much less time to come to maturity than the coffee plant, and its cultivation, by reason of the high price which sugar brings here now, and is likely to continue to bring, yields good profit, it is not only possible, but easy to derive from it the funds necessary to start a coffee plantation.

Those who may not have the necessary means to begin with coffee might begin by planting sugar-cane. This arrives at maturity at from eight to eighteen months, according to the altitude and the temperature of the locality in which it is planted. The cost of cultivation is very little, for it may be estimated that if the seed is near the plantation the cuerda (twenty-five yards square) will not cost more than $2.50, or $3.50 if the seed is at a distance. A plantation of fifty cuerdas, for instance, might be formed with from $125 to $175, including all expenses until the cane is ready to cut. A small iron sugar-mill, moved by oxen, with a boiler or evaporator, may be bought for $500 or $600. At a cost, therefore, of from $700 to $800, fifty cuerdas of sugar-cane may be planted and ground, the net profits of which may be estimated, at a minimum, at the present prices of sugar, at $20 a cuerda, which gives a gross profit of $1000. The total cost was estimated at $750;

there will remain, consequently, a net surplus of $250 the first year, which may be employed in starting the coffee plantation.   After the first year the yearly profit will be $1000, or even more, if the price of sugar should rise, or if the cane-field is enlarged.   If, instead of buying an iron mill with an evaporator, the planter begins with a wooden mill and an iron boiler, the expenses of the first year will not exceed $400.

With the sum of $1000 a year to employ in the cultivation of coffee it would be an easy matter to have, within a few years, a good coffee plantation which would yield the profits to be shown later.

2.   DISADVANTAGES OF COFFEE-RAISING IN SOCONUSCO.

Now that we have pointed out the natural and accidental advantages which Soconusco offers for the cultivation of coffee, it will be necessary to point out also the obstacles which are here encountered in every agricultural enterprise, and especially in the cultivation of coffee.   The principal of these obstacles is scarcity of hands, as will now be considered.

In the State of Chiapas, and more particularly in Soconusco, there is a system of labor which has serious disadvantages and which occasions heavy expenses and considerable losses.

All the laborers owe their employers various sums, which seldom fall below $20, and which frequently exceed $100.   To obtain laborers, therefore, it is necessary first to pay these debts, which may be estimated at an average of $50 for each laborer.   This expenditure is a dead loss, because the money employed in it brings no interest, and because the laborer, instead of applying part of his wages to the paying off of his debt, increases this by fresh loans, which he asks daily, and which represent a larger amount than he earns, so that the original debt, instead of diminishing, continues increasing daily.

If at any time the laborer is refused the money he asks because his debt is already very large, he considers this as sufficient cause for running away.   If he is given what he asks, his debt soon amounts to a large sum, and the laborer, thinking that it will now be difficult for him to pay it off, settles it by running away.   Without either of these reasons and on any frivolous pretext, he will escape, also, favored by the proximity of the frontier of Guatemala, where he cannot be pursued, and where, on the contrary, he is received with open arms, because the scarcity of hands is even greater there than in Soconusco.   Even without leaving Mexican territory the laborer can find employment where it will not be easy to discover him.   It may be said that there is hardly a workman who lets a year pass without running away.   This custom also gives rise to many abuses on the part of the employers toward the laborers.

With this labor system and depending only on the people of the place, it would not be possible to undertake planting on any considerable scale without having inexhaustible resources with which to pay the debts of laborers, who would shortly afterward run away; then to pay the debts of new hands, who before very long would do the same; and so on indefinitely. Fortunately, the Indians of the cold region of Guatemala, contiguous to this District, where poor people are numerous, have no reluctance to coming down to the temperate lands, which are the most suitable for coffee, and with them alone it would be possible to plant coffee plantations of considerable extent in Soconusco. Later on it will perhaps be easy to bring laborers from other parts of the Republic; but this will probably not be the case until some plantations have been already established; and meanwhile it will be necessary to depend on the laborers of Guatemala.

Nor is the work done by laborers from the cold lands of Guatemala exempt from expense and loss. To induce the laborers to leave their villages it is necessary to advance them for expenses a sum of money, generally five dollars a head, which sum is not always repaid. The demoralization has already extended to the cold lands of Guatemala, and the Indians of that region run away also; but, as the sums they owe are comparatively small, the losses suffered from this cause are inconsiderable. The evils of this system of labor make themselves felt in the large plantations of Guatemala, which have only a limited number of hands to depend upon for the most necessary labors, whose owners have large sums invested in advances to laborers, and who require to keep several clerks to visit the villages to engage new hands and to search for the runaways.

As the Indians of the cold region of Guatemala leave behind them their families, their occupations and their sheep, they cannot remain away from their villages very long at a time. As a general thing, they remain barely a month or two in the plantations, and return to their homes to take care of their cornfields. For this reason they cannot be considered permanent laborers, which is another serious drawback.

The only remedy for these evils would, in my opinion, be to bring laborers from other parts of the Republic, where the poor drag out a miserable existence, to these fertile districts. Coffee culture gives employment to the wives and children of the laborers, and the plantations are situated in temperate, healthy, and even agreeable climates. The difficulty lies in the first attempts. If, as is to be expected, these give good results, I think it certain that, notwithstanding the distance, many people would come from the interior of the Republic to settle in Soconusco, or at least to work for the season. If many laborers go, during the cotton harvest, from the valleys of Oaxaca, travelling considerable distances over rough roads, to the unhealthy coast of Veracruz I see no reason why they should not come to these mild and salubrious climates.

IV.

CONDITIONS OF LAND SUITABLE FOR COFFEE.

For the successful cultivation of coffee, various conditions must concur in the land selected to plant it, which will be briefly mentioned here, and the principal of which are the following:

1. Nature of the land and its configuration.
2. Temperature.
3. Altitude above the level of the sea.
4. Exposure to the sun.
5. Protection against prevailing winds.
6. Humidity.
7. Streams.
8. Sites for building purposes.

Each of these conditions will be briefly considered.

1. NATURE OF THE LAND AND ITS CONFIGURATION.

The following points concerning the nature of the land and its configuration will now be touched upon :

A.—Land suitable for coffee.
B.—Layer of vegetable soil.
C.—Depth of the layer of vegetable soil.
D.—Land of volcanic formation.
E.—Virgin forest soil and cultivated soil.
F.—Configuration of the land.

It will be necessary to consider separately each of these points also.

A. Land Suitable for Coffee.—As I do not know of any chemical analysis having been made of the soil most suitable for coffee, for the purpose of determining with exactness its component elements, I can give, on this subject, only very superficial ideas, entirely empirical, and many of them possibly erroneous, notwithstanding that they are based on experience.

It has been observed that land which has a clayey sub-soil is better adapted for coffee than that which has a sandy sub-soil. Among the clayey lands of Soconusco some, and these are the most abundant, are of a reddish hue, more or less vivid, and others of a yellowish color. These last are to be preferred for the cultivation of coffee. To this class belong those of " Union Juarez," in this District, and those of the " Cuca Coast " of Guatemala.

The soil of Cordova, a district which is also suitable for coffee, is in general of red clay.

Some consider pebbly ground favorable for coffee, as the pebbles give the soil greater consistency. Vertical thin strata of rock are also considered advantageous. The ground of the plantations in Guatemala called the plantations of St. Augustine, situated on the southern slope of the volcano of Atitlan, is somewhat stony, and this stony soil is considered very good for coffee.

Mr. William Sabonadière, in his *Coffee Planter in Ceylon*, published in London in 1870, says that the best ground for coffee in that favored island—whose coffee is of so excellent a quality that it is always quoted in the European markets higher than that of Central America—is of a dark chocolate color, pebbly, and with a substratum of rock. He considers a clayey soil unfavorable.

B. Layer of Vegetable Soil.—The land of Soconusco has generally, unless it has been washed away by the rains, a layer, more or less thick, of vegetable soil, formed principally of decayed vegetable matter which has accumulated in the course of time. This layer is of a black color when moist, and ashen when dry. The thicker this layer the better the ground containing it for the cultivation of coffee, provided always there be under it a layer of clayey soil of the depth specified below.

C. Depth of the Layer of Vegetable Soil.—As the top root of the coffee plant grows vertically and to a considerable depth, it requires a soil which it can penetrate without bending. If the root meets with any obstruction, whether stone or other substance, which it cannot penetrate, the plant sickens, turns yellow, ceases to produce fruit, and finally dies. It is therefore indispensable that there should be a layer of earth, of from three to six feet in thickness, which the root of the plant can penetrate without bending. It would be therefore well, before finally selecting a plot of ground to form a plantation, to make excavations in it at various points, for the purpose of ascertaining whether or not it possesses this requisite.

If a piece of land could be found which, to the conditions already mentioned, should unite that of being traversed by vertical strata of rock, it would be very suitable, as the soil would be, so to say, framed in between these strata, would not wash away with the rains, and would have greater consistency; but I have not seen in Soconusco any land that has these conditions.

D. Land of Volcanic Formation.—As observation shows that the soil in which coffee grows best is that on the slopes of volcanoes or in their immediate vicinity, it may be inferred that the best land for coffee is that of volcanic formation. It would be well, therefore, whenever possible, to select land situated on the slopes of volcanoes or in their immediate vicinity, if it should also have the other conditions enumerated.

E. Virgin Forest Soil and Cultivated Soil.—There is a notable difference, in fertile districts like Soconusco, between the soil of the virgin forest, which has never been cultivated or cleared by the hand of man, or which, if it was ever cultivated, has relapsed into a state of nature, and land recently cultivated or cleared. For the sake of clearness, it will be expedient to consider separately these three kinds of land. We will therefore now consider:

a.—Virgin forest land.

b.—Land recently cleared.

c.—Land best adapted for the cultivation of coffee.

Each of these kinds of soil will be considered with as much brevity as is consistent with clearness.

a. Virgin Forest Land.—On virgin forest land there are secular trees that cover with their shade the whole surface of the ground, for which reason only few plants, and those such as do not require for their growth the direct rays of the sun, can grow on it.

In the virgin forest, therefore, are seen colossal, medium and small sized trees, bushes, parasites, vines, and other productions of the vegetable kingdom; but the surface of the ground is not entirely covered with vegetation. If the seed of a thistle or other noxious plant should chance to fall on virgin forest land, it would either not germinate, or, if it germinated, it would not grow for want of sunlight.

b. Land Recently Cleared.—The aspect of land which has at any time been cleared is very different from that just described. The fertility of the soil which had been, so to say, dormant for years, awakens with extraordinary vigor as soon as it is once exposed to the vitalizing action of the sun's rays.

A year or two after it has been cleared the ground is so completely covered with vegetation—principally weeds and other plants whose use is not known, and which are therefore considered noxious—that not a single point of ground is visible, and it is not possible to advance a single step without previously opening a path. This prodigious fertility of the soil makes the chief expense of cultivation in those places. Weeds grow with such abundance and rapidity that it is necessary to keep cutting them down continually, and this operation, which is called "clearing the ground," must be repeated in some places as many as eight times a year, to keep the weeds from choking the young plants, and injuring them very seriously.

In the cleared lands of Soconusco, and especially in those situated at an altitude below two thousand feet above the level of the sea, a species of grass grows which attains a height of twenty-four inches, which, if not cut down in time, will choke the coffee plant completely, but which can hardly ever be entirely extirpated. Its seeds are probably carried by the wind, so that it grows everywhere. This grass is the chief foe of the coffee-tree. In order that it may not kill the plants the ground must be cleared as many as eight times a year, which constitutes, as has been already said, a heavy expense, and requires, besides, a great many hands in plantations of any extent.

c. Land Best Adapted for Coffee.—Experience shows that the coffee plant grows and thrives better in virgin soil than in soil that has been already cultivated. The reason of this is obvious. Virgin soil is richer, has its fertilizing elements almost intact, and produces fewer weeds. Because of this last advantage, virgin soil requires, during the years immediately following the planting of the coffee-trees, fewer clearings than that which has been already cultivated.

The only advantage of planting coffee in ground that has been already cultivated is that in that case the trifling expense of the felling is avoided; but, on the other hand, cultivated ground has, compared with virgin forest soil, the following disadvantages:

1. The soil is inferior.
2. It is more exposed to the sun and to the wind.
3. It is more easily washed away by the rains.
4. It produces a great many more weeds.

For these reasons, therefore, virgin soil is always, when possible, to be preferred.

In Ceylon also the superiority of virgin soil over that of ground that has been already cultivated, for planting coffee, is recognized.

F. Configuration of the Land.—It is a debatable question whether level or broken ground is preferable for the cultivation of coffee.

Regarding this point, we will consider here the following:

a.—Advantages of level ground.

b.—Advantages of hilly ground.

c.—Configuration of the ground best suited for coffee.

Each of these kinds of land and its advantages will be considered separately.

a. Advantages of Level Ground.—The advantages of level over broken ground are the following:

1. Greater facility for using implements and machinery which save time and labor, and consequently greater facility and cheapness of cultivation.

2. Greater duration of the layer of black or vegetable earth, which is not so readily washed away by the rains as in hilly ground, where the soil becomes loosened by the cultivation bestowed upon it.

Notwithstanding these advantages, the advantages presented by hilly ground are so great that, as a general rule, this is to be preferred to level ground for the cultivation of coffee, as will be shown farther on.

b. Advantages of Hilly Ground.—The advantages of hilly ground, as compared with level ground, are the following:

1. Impossibility of the ground, even when moist, becoming miry, as its inclination prevents the water from standing; while in level ground, without drainage and with a layer of impermeable clay near the surface, there is this danger, which is a serious one for the coffee-tree.

2. Greater facility for shielding the plant from the sun for a part of the day; as, when the hills run from north to south, which is their general direction in this Cordillera, the side facing the east receives the sun until mid-day, and that facing the west after mid-day.

3. Greater facility for obtaining water, whether for irrigating the plantation or moving the machinery.

4. Facility for obtaining laborers; for, the hilly land in the Cordillera being situated at a considerable altitude above the level of the sea, the Indians of Guatemala, who would not go to the plains, which are here low and hot, are willing to go there.

c. Configuration of the Ground best Suited for Coffee.—The advantages of hilly over level ground, especially the two last mentioned, are so notable in Soconusco that many think, and I share their opinion, that hilly ground, with the hills running from north to south, is that best adapted for the cultivation of coffee.

The coffee planters of Ceylon, pursuaded of the superior advantages of hilly over level ground, also prefer it for their plantations.

2. TEMPERATURE.[1]

The prevailing opinion regarding the climate most suitable for coffee is a very erroneous one. It is generally believed that the coffee-tree is a native of the tropics, and that, consequently, the hotter the temperature of a place the more suitable it will be for coffee, provided that the other conditions favorable to its cultivation exist there.

Experience has shown that the zone most suitable for the cultivation of coffee is bounded by isothermal[1] lines, the mean temperature of which is from $17° 50'$ to $20°$ centigrade; that is, a temperate climate, but where it never freezes, as frosts would ruin the plant.

The mean temperature of the localities in Soconusco which are considered best for coffee is, according to the observations of the able engineer, Don Miguel M. Ponce de Leon, as follows: Cacahuatan, $21° 15'$ and Union Juarez, $17° 57'$.

3. ALTITUDE ABOVE THE LEVEL OF THE SEA.

The temperature of a place has a direct relation to its altitude above the level of the sea, for, as a general rule, the greater the altitude the lower will be the temperature.

The following points relating to this subject will now be considered:

A.—Productiveness of the coffee-tree in relation to altitude.

B.—Advantages of high lands.

C.—Altitude most suitable for coffee-raising.

D.—Altitude of various places in Soconusco.

[1] I will insert in the Appendix to this paper, a brief statement of the causes affecting the climate of a locality, written since this book came out in Spanish.

Each of these points will be considered separately.

A. Productiveness of the Coffee-Tree in Relation to Altitude.—It has been observed that coffee planted in ground situated 500 feet above the level of the sea yields not more than half a pound of coffee per tree; from 500 to 1000 feet, one pound per tree; from 1000 to 2000 feet, two pounds per tree; from 2000 to 3000 feet, three pounds per tree; and from 3000 to 4000, it will yield as much as four pounds per tree.

But this yield is only obtained in the best soil and under the most thorough cultivation.

B. Advantages of High Lands.—The principal advantages offered for the cultivation of coffee by high lands, whose altitude does not exceed 4000 feet, may be summed up as follows:

1. Larger yield of fruit per tree.
2. Better quality of the coffee.
3. More time in which to gather the crop, as it ripens gradually and not all at once, as in the low lands.
4. The plant is not exposed to the heat of the sun during the whole of the day, as will be explained farther on.
5. The higher the land, the fewer weeds it will produce, and consequently fewer weedings in the year will be necessary.
6. The high lands enjoy a temperate, pleasant, and in general healthy climate, for which reason it is easier to obtain laborers for those lands than for the low lands, which are hot, less healthy, and always infested by mosquitoes. In Soconusco, especially, this advantage is very great, as the Indians of the cold regions of Guatemala will go down to the temperate lands to work, while they are not willing to go to the low lands.

C. Altitude most Suitable for Coffee-Growing.—Until very recently the low lands were preferred for coffee-raising. Experience has, however, demonstrated that the best lands for this purpose are those situated at from three to four thousand feet above the level of the sea.

The experience of other places proves the correctness of this statement. Mocha coffee grows in the mountainous regions of Arabia Felix. The best quality of Colima coffee is that which grows on the summit of the Platanarillo; and the districts of Cordova and Orizava, whose coffee is also highly esteemed, are situated, the former at an altitude of 2713, and the latter of 4028 feet above the level of the sea. The best coffee land in Ceylon is in Mr. William Sabonadière's opinion located on an average of 3000 feet above the level of the sea, although in some localities of that island the coffee tree grows well at an altitude of 5000 feet.

Anyone, not familiar with plantations, might be easily deceived by the appearance presented by the trees in the low lands; for sometimes, and especially when the plantations are new, their leaves are of a healthy green, and they have a thriving appearance; but very soon this appearance changes, the branches lose their leaves, and the quantity of fruit they produce is relatively small.

Nothing is more deceptive than to measure altitudes by the naked eye. To be able to calculate altitude with some degree of correctness one should provide oneself with an aneroid barometer, properly regulated, the price of which is within the reach of the most modest fortune; while from its small bulk—for it is about the size of a watch—it may be carried with perfect ease.

D. Altitude of Various Places in Soconusco.—Various observations which I have made with an aneroid barometer of localities in this District give approximately the following results: altitude of Cacahuatan, 1400 feet above the level of the sea; Paso del Rio Ixtal, 1000 feet; plantation of Mixcum, 1850 feet; plantation of Santo Domingo, 2300 feet; and Union Juarez, 3400 feet.

The approximate altitudes of some points in Guatemala where coffee grows well are as follows: El Rodeo, about 1500 feet; Las Mercedes, about 2500 feet; Las Nubes, from 3500 to 4000 feet; Guatemala City, a little more than 4000 feet.

4. EXPOSURE TO THE SUN.

Experience has shown that the coffee-tree thrives best and yields most fruit when the sun does not shine on it during the whole of the day. Four or five hours' exposure to the sun are sufficient to enable it to attain its best condition. The early morning sun is the least beneficial to it, for which reason it should, if possible, be shielded from it, either by planting shade trees to the east of the plantation, or by selecting ground on which the sun does not shine until one or two hours after it has risen.

The principal advantage of hilly ground when the hills run from north to south, is, as has been already stated, that the sun shines on them for only a part of the day—in the morning on the slopes which face the east, and in the afternoon on those which face the west.

The high lands of Soconusco have also the advantage that the sun does not shine on the trees during the whole of the day. On the slope of the Cordillera, that is, from 2500 feet above the level of the sea up, clouds prevail during the summer season—which is precisely when the sun is hottest—and frequently also, during the other seasons, from ten o'clock onward, which keep the trees from being exposed to the heat of the sun during the whole of the day. Perhaps it is to this circumstance that the superior excellence of the coffee grown at an altitude of 3000 or 4000 feet above the level of the sea is due.

5. PROTECTION AGAINST THE WINDS.

It is of the first importance that the plantation should be sheltered against the prevailing winds. If the plants were exposed to the north winds, which blow in Soconusco from the land and are very dry, they would wither, and if they were exposed to the southeasterly winds, which are here the prevailing sea winds, they would lose their blossoms and yield scanty crops, or none. But it is also necessary for the growth and good yield of the plant that it should be situated in a locality where the air circulates freely.

It is probable that the sea breezes, are highly beneficial to the coffee plant, for which reason it is expedient that the plantation should be made on land which faces the sea, although it should be sheltered from the prevailing winds. The principal plantations of Soconusco and Guatemala face the Pacific.

The violence of the north winds which blow from Tehuantepec to Tonalá, and which deprive the atmosphere of moisture, and wither vegetation, will be an obstacle to the planting of coffee on that part of the coast, except in such localities as may be sheltered from the north winds and have a moist atmosphere.

It has been observed in Ceylon that an eastern exposure is the most favorable. In Soconusco and Guatemala a southern exposure is the most favorable.

6. HUMIDITY.

The coffee plant requires moist but not miry ground. Water retained around its roots injures it greatly.

Even when the surface of the ground becomes dry, in the dry season, the land will still be suitable for coffee if, on digging down a little, the earth be found moist, but not wet.

A moist atmosphere should also be sought, as not only the roots of the coffee plant, but also its leaves require moisture. This is another of the reasons that render the vicinity of the sea desirable for a coffee plantation.

Shade trees also keep the ground moist, for which reason they may be required in certain localities.

7. STREAMS.

Although neither in Soconusco nor in Guatemala is it necessary to water the coffee plants—as the rains suffice to make them grow and thrive—it is always desirable to locate the coffee plantation near some river, brook, or spring, not only because water is an indispensable element of life for the laborers and the animals employed on the plantation, but also in order that the water may be used as motive power for the machinery that is to prepare the berry for the market. Plantations of any extent indispensably require considerable motive power, and water power is always to be preferred, as it is the cheapest.

In soil which is not as moist as that of Soconusco, it will probably be necessary to employ irrigation, in which case it would be still more necessary to locate the coffee plantation near some stream.

8. SITES FOR BUILDING PURPOSES.

It is desirable that the piece of ground selected for a coffee plantation should have a site suitable for the erection of the buildings required. If the ground be level there will be no difficulty in this respect. In hilly ground a level place should be selected for the drying-yard, in order to avoid the expense of levelling the ground to make a yard.

In a plantation situated on level ground the buildings should always be erected in the centre of the plantation, in order that no part of it may be far distant from the place where the coffee is to be prepared for the market. In sloping ground the buildings should be erected on the lowest part of it, in order that the carts or animals employed in the transportation of the fruit from the field to the place of preparation may go down laden and go up unladen, which will facilitate the labor, to the economizing of time and money.

The situation of the buildings will depend on the special conditions of each locality; but, as a general rule, it should be determined by the situation of the water, unless there be some means of conducting this to some other place which is more suitable.

V.

COFFEE CULTIVATION.

It is my purpose here to set forth with as much clearness and conciseness as may be possible the fundamental principles of modern coffee-culture, to the end that even those who have never seen a coffee-tree, may be able to undertake the raising of coffee with a good probability of success.

I will consider at greater length—because of the important bearing which they have on the success of the undertaking—the questions whether or not coffee-trees should be planted in the shade, and what distance apart they ought to be planted; discussing afterwards the other points directly connected with the cultivation of coffee and its preparation for the market.

I will make occasional references to the methods followed in the cultivation of coffee in Ceylon; for I have observed that there is a great similarity between them and the methods that have given the best results here. The excellence of Ceylon coffee is well known. In the year 1868, 913 plantations produced 1,007,214 English quintals of coffee. Trees planted in the last century still yield good crops. These facts show how far advanced coffee culture is there, and therefore the references that may be made to the system followed in Ceylon cannot but be useful to the Mexican planters.

The following points, then, will now be considered:

1. Shade.
2. Distance between the trees.
3. Nursery.
4. Perparation of the ground for planting.
5. Transplanting.
6. Cultivation of coffee.
7. Fertilizers.
8. Gathering the crops.
9. Preparation of the fruit for the market.

Each of these subjects will be considered separately.

I. SHADE.

The following points concerning the important question of shade will be now considered:

A.—General considerations regarding shade.
B.—Advantages of shade.
C.—Disadvantages of shade.
D.—Rules regarding shade.
E.—Trees to be preferred for shade.

Each of these various aspects of the question of shade will be considered separately.

A. General Considerations Regarding Shade.—The opinion has long prevailed that the coffee plant requires shade to attain its fullest development, and that a plantation which has no shade must necessarily give bad results. Up to a certain point this opinion may be considered to be well-founded, so far as regards plantations situated in the low lands. For the rest, it is evident that the heat and light of the sun being indispensable to vegetation, it cannot be absolutely affirmed that there are plants which thrive better in the shade than in the sun.

Shade may be made, however, a means of reducing the temperature, and thus acclimating in certain hotter zones plants which would not thrive in the sun in those localities. As the coffee-tree requires for its best development a temperature, for instance, of 18° centigrade, it is plain that if it be planted in a locality the temperature of which is from 23° to 24°, it will be out of its zone, and that if it then be given shade it will thrive better than when exposed to the sun : not because it absolutely requires shade, but because this reduces the temperature, and the coffee plant that is in the shade will enjoy a lower temperature, and consequently one that will agree better with it than a plant in the same locality that is exposed to the sun.

B. Advantages of Shade.—The advantages of shade are the following:

1. It reduces the temperature, which is, however, an advantage only when the coffee is planted out of its native zone, that is, in low lands.

2. It keeps the soil moist, sheltering it from the direct rays of the sun.

3. It tends to lessen the growth of weeds, which grow more vigorously and in greater abundance in ground exposed to the sun.

4. It affords some protection to the coffee-trees against the violence of the prevailing winds.

C. Disadvantages of Shade.—The disadvantages of shade are the following:

1. It lowers the temperature, which is a serious disadvantage when coffee is planted in its native zone, that is, from 3000 to 4000 feet above the level of the sea.

2. It keeps from the plant the light and heat of the sun, which causes it to thrive less and to yield smaller crops than if it enjoyed those advantages.

3. It interferes with the free circulation of the air, to the serious injury of the coffee plant.

4. It takes from the soil, through the roots of the trees which afford it, nutritious elements which should be reserved exclusively for the coffee-tree.

D. Rules regarding Shade.—From the preceding considerations the following conclusions may be drawn, which constitute the best rules that can be given regarding shade:

1. If the coffee be planted in its own zone, that is, at an altitude of from 3000 to 4000 feet above the level of the sea, in a temperature of 17° 50′, to 18° 50′ centigrade, it ought not to be given any shade.

2. Planted in lower lands, with a higher temperature, it would be advisable to give it shade, which should increase in density according as the altitude decreases and the temperature increases.

There are some localities, however, which, although at an altitude of from 3000 to 4000 feet above the level of the sea, and enjoying a temperature of from 17° to 18° centigrade, have yet so dry a soil that it becomes necessary to give the plant a little shade, at least for the first year after planting; taking away the shade the second year, when the plants have taken firm root. This is a peculiarity of the land of Union Juarez, which is undoubtedly among the best coffee-growing regions in Soconusco.

Perhaps this phenomenon is due to the fact that shade, in addition to its other advantages, has that of keeping the soil moist, as it protects it from the direct rays of the sun, which, in hot climates, produce a rapid evaporation. In localities where the soil is rather dry, shade may be avdantageous even when the temperature is temperate, as it preserves the moisture, which is so important for coffee, although in this case it is preferable to have recourse to irrigation.

These considerations show that it is necessary to proceed with caution in every instance, consulting the experience of men who are acquainted with the locality and making previously, in unfamiliar regions, investigations which will show what are the peculiarities of each locality.

The simplest rule which can be given regarding shade is not to plant coffee where shade is required.

In Ceylon, coffee-trees are never shaded, but, on the other hand, care is taken to plant them in their own zone.

E. Trees to be preferred for Shade.—In each locality some particular tree is preferred for shade, the plantain being used in many. Its shade is dense, and it has the advantage of generally keeping the ground moist; but, on the other hand, it has the disadvantage of absorbing many of the nutritious elements of the soil, some of which the coffee-tree probably requires for its better nutrition and greater fructification.

Should shade be absolutely required—a necessity to be regarded, however, as a serious evil—the best means of providing it is to leave standing the tallest and least umbrageous trees of the forest to give the shade which is indispensable, so as to obtain the best possible circulation of air in the plantation. The castor-oil plant may be used for shade in those nurseries and coffee plantations in high altitudes, in which shade should not be given for more than a year.

2. DISTANCE BETWEEN THE PLANTS.

To proceed with greater method in the discussion of this important subject, the following points will now be considered:

A.—General considerations regarding distance.

B.—Number of plants in each cuerda according to the distance between them.

C.—Yield of each cuerda.

D.—Space required by each plant.

E.—Advantages of long distances.

F.—Advantages of short distances.

G.—Rules regarding distance.

Each of these points will be considered separately.

A. General Considerations regarding Distance.—There is a great difference of opinion among planters with regard to the distance apart at which the trees should be planted, some preferring long and others short distances between them. The practice most generally followed is to plant them three varas apart, from tree to tree and from furrow to furrow. Some time ago this distance began to be regarded as too short, and plantations were laid out with the trees three and a half, four, and even four and a half varas apart. Afterwards a reaction set in, and there is now a tendency to shorten these distances.

I think that the distance apart at which trees should be planted depends on the zone, altitude, temperature, and kind of land selected for the plantation. In a climate and soil favorable to their fullest development, the trees should be planted farther apart than when they are planted where the conditions are less propitious.

The question of distance is also intimately connected with that of the pruning of the trees, as by means of this operation the trees may be considerably reduced in bulk, and may therefore be planted even a shorter distance apart than in localities more favorable for coffee, as will be seen farther on. This question, however, will be better understood and a correct decision more probably reached after a consideration of the data to be given farther on.

B. Number of Plants in each Cuerda.—A cuerda of land, which is the unit of agrarian measurement in Soconusco, and which contains twenty-five yards square, or six hundred and twenty-five square [1] varas, will contain, in round numbers, thirty-nine trees, planted four varas apart on all sides; planted three varas apart, from plant to plant, and four yards from furrow to furrow, the cord will contain fifty-two trees; planted three and a half varas apart on one side and three varas on the other, the cuerda will contain fifty-nine trees; planted three yards apart on each side, it will contain sixty-nine trees; and one hundred and four if planted two varas apart from plant to plant and three from furrow to furrow. Planted in this way there will be a square, or a rectangular parallelogram, between each four plants.

In some plantations the system is followed, when the trees are planted farther apart than three varas on each side, of planting an additional tree in the centre of each of the squares or parallelograms formed by the plants.

The results of that manner of planting are the following: When the trees are planted four yards apart on each side, each cuerda will contain, planting a tree in the centre of each square, twenty-seven additional trees; that is to say, a total of sixty-six trees instead of thirty-nine. If the same thing is done when the trees are planted four yards apart on one side and three on the other, the cuerda will contain thirty-eight additional trees, or a total of ninety, instead of fifty-two. If the trees are planted three yards and a half from furrow to furrow and three yards from plant to plant, the cuerda will contain forty-six additional trees, which gives a total of one hundred and five trees. In squares

[1] Yard is used here for a Mexican vara.

of three yards on each side, fifty-three additional trees may be planted, making a total, with the sixty-nine already counted, of one hundred and twenty-two; and when the trees are planted three yards apart on one side and two on the other, a cuerda will contain eighty-three additional trees, which, added to the original one hundred and five, give a total of one hundred and eighty-eight.

C. Yield of each Cuerda.—Considering the average crop per year of each plant to be two pounds of coffee, each cuerda, when the plants are four yards apart on each side, will yield seventy-eight pounds a year; one hundred and four pounds if the plants are three yards apart on one side and four on the other; one hundred and thirty-eight, if they are three yards apart on each side; and two hundred and eight pounds if they are two yards on one side and three on the other.

When the additional tree is planted in the middle of each square, or parallelogram, the yield of each cuerda will be one hundred and thirty-two pounds, if the trees are planted four yards apart on each side; one hundred and eighty pounds if they are planted four yards apart on one side and three on the other; two hundred and ten pounds, when they are three and a half yards apart on one side and three on the other; two hundred and forty-four pounds, when they are planted three yards apart on each side; and three hundred and seventy-six pounds when they are planted two yards apart on one side and three on the other.

It must be observed, however, that the yield of each tree depends also on the nature of the soil, on the climate, on the degree of moisture, and the other circumstances which have been already enumerated, including the distance apart at which the trees are planted, for if they are planted too close together, so that their roots interlace, the yield will be less.

D. Area Required by each Tree.—If the trees are planted two yards apart, from plant to plant, and three yards from furrow to furrow, each tree will have an area of six yards square; if planted three yards apart, from plant to plant and from furrow to furrow, each plant will have an area of nine yards square; if planted three and a half yards apart on each side, of twelve and a quarter yards; and of sixteen yards square, if planted four yards apart on each side.

When an additional tree is planted in the middle of each square, or parallelogram, each plant will have an area of ground nearly eight yards square; if the trees are planted four yards apart on each side, of a little more than six; when planted three yards apart on one side and four on the other, of nearly five yards square; when planted three and a half yards apart on one side and three on the other; of four and a quarter yards square, when planted three yards apart on each side; and of nearly one and three quarter yards when planted three yards apart on one side and two on the other.

E. Advantages of Long Distances.—The advantages of long distances are the following:

1. Unimpaired growth of the plant. This advantage is nullified when pruning is performed, as will be seen when this subject is spoken of.

2. Freer circulation of air and light.

3. Greater yield of fruit of each tree.

4. Greater facility for cultivating the soil and gathering the fruit without injuring the branches of the neighboring trees.

When the trees are planted far apart and by this I mean at a greater distance than three and a half yards, their branches will not interlace, and free circulation of air, light and heat among the branches and trunks of the plants will be secured. When there is a free circulation of air, and the branches of the trees are exposed to the light and heat of the sun, it is evident that the yield of each tree will be greater than if it did not enjoy these advantages. Besides which, there will be more space between the trees for the laborers to perform their several tasks and the gatherers of the fruit to perform theirs, without injury to the branches of the neighboring trees.

F. Advantages of Short Distances.—The advantages of short distances are the following:

1. A greater number of trees will be contained in the same space of ground.

2. Consequent economy of hands and money in the labors of the plantation.

3. Greater yield of fruit in a given extent of ground.

4. Greater facility for gathering the crop; for, the trees being nearer together, it will be easier to strip them of their fruit.

5. Fewer weeds will grow, as a smaller area of ground will be exposed to the direct rays of the sun.

These advantages are so important as to make short distances preferable, as will be shown farther on.

G. Rules regarding Distance.—The preceding data regarding the number of trees contained in each cuerda and their product, demonstrate the expediency of planting the trees as near together as possible, in order not to waste space, provided that this proximity does not injure the productiveness of the plants.

It is to be observed that in recommending, as of great advantage, the planting of the trees short distances apart, the question is not simply one of economizing ground on account of its cost, which would be a very trifling advantage, indeed, where ground costs as little as it does in Chiapas—but of economizing labor, time, and money, things worth considering everywhere, and more especially in Soconusco, where there is a great scarcity of hands.

Now, then, as the chief expense of a plantation is in keeping it clean of weeds, and as this is done by task work, the weeding of a cuerda being a day's task for a man, and costing on an average two reals, it is evident that the cost of keeping a cuerda free from weeds is the same whether it contains thirty-nine trees or one hundred and four trees, and whether each cuerda yields seventy-eight pounds or two hundred and eight pounds of coffee. Each weeding, for instance, of a plantation of 10,000 trees, covering an area of two hundred and fifty-six cuerdas, will cost $64, if the trees are four yards apart on each side; while, if they are two yards on one side and three on the other, the same number of trees would occupy an area of ninety-six cuerdas, and cost $24.

Besides which, where there is a scarcity of hands, it would be easy to keep a plantation of some extent free from weeds if there were one hundred and four trees in every cuerda; but, to keep the same number of trees free from weeds, if there were thirty-nine in each cuerda, almost three times the number of hands would be required.

The system of pruning which has been tried with so much success in various plantations of Guatemala, and which, it may be said, has been carried to perfection in Ceylon, has the advantage of diminishing the foliage and increasing the fruit, and of preventing the branches of the coffee-trees from interlacing. This system consequently allows of closer planting, without the objections above indicated.

Taking all these considerations into account, I am of opinion that, other circumstances permitting, the best system is to plant the trees at a distance apart not exceeding three yards between the furrows and two between the trees. An area of six yards square ought to be sufficient for each plant.

Planting an additional tree in the centre of every four trees, forming a quincunx, has the objection that the advantage of the straight furrows is thereby lost, and that the intermediate trees present an obstacle to the free circulation of the air. I think that this system should only be adopted in the case when, a plantation being already laid out at long distances, it is desired to shorten these.

The distance apart at which trees are usually planted in Ceylon is six English feet, or a little more than two yards on each side. Considering the size to which trees are allowed to grow there—which will be indicated when speaking of pruning—this distance does not seem unduly short. Mr. Sabonadière is of opinion, however, that it would be better to plant them at a distance of seven feet from furrow to furrow and six from tree to tree.

3. NURSERY.

The nursery is the bed where, for greater convenience in attending to them, owing to the limited space which they occupy, the young plants are grown, until they are of sufficient size to transplant to the plantation.

The nursery may be formed of seeds, young plants, or slips, as will be seen farther on.

The following points in relation to the nursery will now be considered:

A.—Advantages of a nursery.

B.—Land suitable for a nursery, and its location.

C.—Seed-plot.

D.—Nursery formed from seeds.

E.—Nursery formed from young plants.

F.—Nursery formed from slips.

G.—Nursery of plants that are for sale.

H.—Nursery in Ceylon.

Each of these points relating to the nursery will be considered separately.

A. Advantages of a Nursery.—It is advisable that the plants with which it is intended to stock the plantation should be grown in a nursery. The seed might, it is true, be at once sown in the plantation; but its cultivation would in this case be much more costly, and a considerable number of plants could not be so well cared for as when they are planted close together in a small space of ground.

A nursery of a cuerda will conveniently contain 4000 plants, set at a distance apart to be indicated below, and the weeding of the cuerda would cost fifty cents, supposing a man to employ two days in the work; or, at the most, a dollar, if four days be spent on it; while 4000 plants in a plantation, at a distance of three yards from furrow to furrow and two from plant to plant, would occupy at least thirty-eight cuerdas; and, fixing the weeding of each cuerda at twenty-five cents, the weeding of the 4000 plants would cost $9.50. As the weeding must be frequently repeated, especially while the plant is very young, the economy of the nursery system will be easily understood.

A nursery is, besides, indispensable to a plantation, not only to form it but also to maintain it, as plants which wither or die have constantly to be replaced, and a good supply of healthy plants must be kept on hand for this purpose.

B. Land Suitable for a Nursery and its Location.—To form the nursery, virgin soil should be selected. If there is level ground, this should be preferred. If undulating, ground should be chosen sloping from north to south, with lofty trees to the east, to shade the nursery from the heat of the sun in the early morning hours.

The ground is prepared beginning with what is here called stubbing; this consists in cutting down the young trees, bushes, and other vegetation which can be cut with the machete; the large trees are then felled. To dispose of the leaves, branches, and trunks which remain after these operations, it is customary to allow them to dry and then burn them.

In land intended for coffee it is not advisable to burn this waste matter; especially should burning be avoided on land intended for the nursery.

All the branches, twigs, and leaves left by the operation of stubbing and hewing should be gathered in heaps and placed above and below the nursery, at distances of from twenty-five to thirty yards apart. Trunks of trees which are very large are to be left where they have fallen, as it would take much time and labor to remove them. All the trunks and shoots that might sprout are to be destroyed by the machete and the axe, without using the spade. These operations being performed, the ground is ready for the sowing of the nursery.

Some planters dig up the ground for the nursery, with the object of making it more fertile, and, as will be seen farther on, this is done in Ceylon; but it seems to me that, while this system may be a good one in poor soil, it is not so good in the soil of this coast, as the nursery will thrive here without this requisite; and as, besides, if the ground were dug up, weeds would grow more luxuriantly, and the rains would soon wash away the richest part of the soil.

Nurseries are to be formed at various points on the land where the plantation is to be laid out, for convenience in transplanting the young trees. The seed-plot is to be placed beside the nursery.

C. Seed-Plot.—The seed-plot is a sort of nursery for the nursery. To form the seed-plot, the berries or seeds of the coffee, are planted, six inches apart, in holes half an inch deep, and lightly covered with earth. All the rules for choosing the land and for sowing the seed nursery, to be indicated farther on, are also to be observed in the care of the seed-plot.

When the seeds have germinated, and the young plants are sufficiently grown to bear transplanting, they are to be transferred to the nursery, where they are to be planted farther apart, and where they are to be kept until they have attained sufficient growth to be transplanted to the plantation.

For my own part, I consider the system of combining the seed-plot and the nursery preferable, as labor, time, and money are thus saved, and a transplantation, from which the young plant always suffers, is, besides, avoided. This is the system followed in Ceylon, as will be seen farther on, and this seems to me another proof of its superiority.

D. Nursery from Seeds.—It is preferable to form the nursery from seed. In regard to this subject the general rules for forming nurseries from young plants or slips will be given.

To take up the points in their order, the following will now be considered here:

a.—Preparation of the ground for the nursery.

b.—Time for planting.

c.—Seed.

d.—Planting.

e.—Replanting.

f.—Cultivation.

g.—Pruning.

h.—Time for transplanting.

Each of these points will be considered separately.

a. Preparation of the Ground for the Nursery.—The nursery must be laid out in ridges. Each ridge should be a yard and a quarter wide and as long as the ground will permit, if this is hilly, or as may be desired, if level. The ridges, in hilly ground and on slopes which run from north to south, should run from east to west. Between the ridges a space of a third of a yard must be left to serve as a path, and at the same time as a trench for draining the ridges.

The paths should be six inches deep; the earth, dug from the paths to give them this depth, is to be thrown on to the ridge lying to the north. All the paths are to be drained by means of a deep trench made on the east or the west of the land, according as this will allow, and which is to run from north to south, so that the rains may never flood the ridges. Care must be taken to keep the paths, as well as the ditches, open.

b. Time for Planting.—The rains must determine the time for planting the nursery. If planted from seed, the operation may take place a month before the rainy season begins, as the seed takes about six weeks to germinate, and when it appears above the ground the rainy season will have already set in The rainy season generally begins in April, in Soconusco; consequently the planting of the nursery may be done in March.

The seed should be sown on a cloudy day, and it will be better still to sow it when it is raining.

c. Seeds.—The seed of the coffee-tree proceeds from the fruit, which somewhat resembles a berry, each fruit containing two seeds of a semi-elliptical form.

It is generally supposed that the seeds of the coffee-tree will not germinate if they are dry when planted. If they are carefully dried, however, that is, if the mucilaginous part which covers the seed be not allowed to ferment, they will almost all germinate. It is better, however, to be on the safe side, and whenever it is possible to use fresh fruit. Of these the ripest and largest should be preferred.

It is better to separate the two seeds, which each berry generally contains, for, almost all of them will germinate without separation, germination will be more certain and the roots will grow straighter if they are separated.

Before sowing, the seeds should be put in water, and those that float should be rejected.

In an interesting article on coffee published in the *Mexican Agricultural Dictionary and Rural Economy*, various rules are given for improving the quality of the coffee-seed. Certain plants, called mother plants, are kept exclusively for seed; the best and largest fruits are selected; these are dried in the shade and otherwise carefully treated, so as to obtain seed of superior excellence. There is no doubt that the best seed will produce the best fruit, and that on this point, as on many others, coffee cultivation is susceptible of great improvement. All these rules may be found in the article referred to.

d. Sowing the Seed.—The ground being prepared in the manner already described, the seeds are to be sown, two by two, at intervals of a quarter of a yard. In each ridge four furrows are to be made, a quarter of a yard apart, and the plants in each furrow are to be set the same distance apart. The holes for sowing the seed may be made with the finger, half an inch deep; the seed being then covered lightly with earth. The whole ridge is then to be covered with grass or leaves, such as those of the wild plantain, or any other kind that may be suitable to prevent the seeds being washed away by the rains; but this should be done in such a way as not to exclude the moisture of the rain or the light and heat of the sun.

If any of this covering should still remain when the coffee begins to sprout, it is to be carefully removed; and if it should decay before the coffee appears above the ground, it is to be replaced by another covering.

e. Replanting.—Replanting is generally necessary, particularly when the nursery is formed from seeds, as some of the seeds do not germinate, and the young plants often wither shortly after appearing above ground. It will be necessary, therefore, to have near-by a seed-plot, from which the plants required to replace these may be taken without loss of time.

f. Cultivation.—When two plants spring up together in the nursery, the most robust is to be left and the other is to be transplanted to a place previously prepared for the purpose.

When the plants have appeared above the ground, the only care they require is that the nursery be kept free from weeds. Any other vegetation that appears must be pulled up by the hand, without employing a knife, machete, spade, or other instrument, as any of these might seriously injure the stalks and roots of the young plants.

It is not necessary to water the nursery in Soconusco, as the rains are sufficient for the purpose.

g. Pruning.—As soon as the young plant begins to send forth shoots, that is, about six months after planting, all shoots are to be cut off with the exception of one, care being taken that this be the most robust. In no case should the young plants be pruned in any other manner.

h. Time for Transplanting.—In Soconusco the nursery is long in attaining the growth necessary for transplanting—from eighteen months to two years. In Ceylon transplanting takes place a year after plant-ing. Perhaps this difference is because the young trees are transplanted there much younger than here.

In Soconusco and Guatemala, transplantation does not take place until the plants are of from three to four crosses, as they say here, that is, until they have six or eight branches, which, growing in opposite directions, take the form of a cross.

E. Nursery Formed from Young Plants.—In forming this nursery the same rules are to be observed as those given for the nursery formed from seeds, with the modifications to be indicated farther on.

Planting is done in Soconusco in the early part of May, that is, when the rainy season has well set in, the planter being always guided by the rains in this operation.

The holes for the plants are to be made a quarter of a yard apart, with a pointed stick, half an inch in thickness. Four inches from the point of this stick, a second and thinner stick, half a yard in length, is to be fastened crosswise. This rude implement has two objects: 1. That the holes may not be made too deep, for the tender roots of the plant would perish if they remained in a vacuum. 2. That, the point of the first being in the centre of the second stick, the two ends of the latter may mark off the distance of one quarter yard on either side of the first, a hole being thus made and the places marked for two other holes by the same operation.

To form the nursery from young plants the seed-plot is absolutely necessary, unless there should happen to be some neglected plantation in the neighborhood which might furnish those required. When the fruits are not all picked from the trees those that fall to the ground sprout, and, if the plantation is not weeded, become in due time trees which may be transplanted to the nursery. It is better, however, to make a seed-plot, as the plants grow better and with greater luxuriance in it than in the shade of the trees.

F. Nursery Formed from Slips.—In some localities that I have visited, the nurseries instead of being formed from seeds of very young plants, are formed from trees a year old or more, which generally have a slender trunk and little foliage; the trunk is cut off to about eight inches above the root; the main root and the lateral roots are also pruned; at the end of a year this plant will have put forth shoots, will have a thriving appearance, and will be in good condition for transplanting.

I think the system of forming the plantation from plants grown from seed the best, however.

G. Nursery of Plants for Selling.—When there is no nursery at hand, in the locality where a plantation is to be formed, it is necessary to make one; this will require in some localities as long as two years. To avoid this delay it will be better to buy the plants already old enough to be transplanted.

When these are scarce, as is generally the case here, a very high price must sometimes be paid for them. Thus it is that nurseries are sometimes formed for the purpose of raising plants for sale; and this is sometimes a very lucrative business. In Guatemala coffee plants in good condition for planting have brought as much as $40 per thousand. In Soconusco, plants in good condition have been sold as high as $15 per thousand. Plants that have grown up wild have been sold here at prices ranging from fifty cents to $5 per thousand.

As the total cost per thousand of raising plants from seed does not exceed $2.50, it will at once be seen that the business of keeping nurseries for the sale of young plants is a profitable one, and at the same time one by which coffee cultivation is favored and facilitated.

H. Nurseries in Ceylon.—In Ceylon a piece of virgin land of the best kind, level if possible, and near the water for convenience in irrigation, is chosen for the nursery. This is cleared; the trunks of all but the largest trees are removed. The ground is dug up to a depth of nine or ten inches, and then laid out in ridges, with narrow paths between them.

Coffee in the hull, generally taken from the tanks after it has been pulled, is used for seed; it is planted in furrows about six inches apart.

In planting the furrows a cord, stretched from end to end of the piece of ground intended for the nursery, is used for measurement. An opening an inch or two in depth is made the whole length of the furrow, and the seeds are deposited in it an inch apart, and covered lightly with earth of the best quality. This done, the cord is taken to the next furrow, where the same operation is repeated.

The necessary drains to prevent the rains from injuring the plants are then made.

The young plant soon appears above the ground, and at the end of a year it is ready to transplant.

When the plants spring up very close together, some of them are taken up and planted in the next ridge. In this operation care must be taken that the tap root of the young plant be not bent; to avoid this a stick is used to make the hole which is to receive the plant. Care must also be taken that no hollow space remain about the root, for if this should be the case, the water would settle in it and rot the root. To avoid these dangers, and when the main root is very long, that part of it which seems most flexible is cut off obliquely with a sharp knife.

A bushel of coffee in the hull will produce 30,000 plants.

4. PREPARATION OF THE GROUND FOR PLANTING COFFEE.

The preparation of the ground for planting coffee includes the following operations :

A.—Felling the trees.
B.—Simultaneous sowing.
C.—Forming of a plan for the plantation.
D.—Staking.
E.—Digging holes.

Each of these operations will receive due consideration.

A. Felling the Trees.—Virgin soil being preferable, as has been already said, for making the plantation, the first thing to be done is to clear it, an operation which is performed about the beginning of December, when the dry season begins in Soconusco. The trunks of the trees as well as their layer branches must be chopped in pieces as soon as they are felled. The cutting should begin as soon as the trees are felled, for, as has been already observed, they are much easier to put up when green than when dry. The clearing of the ground should be finished by the end of February, the three operations here called "stubbing," "hewing," and "chopping" having been performed in the manner already pointed out in speaking of the nature of the ground suitable for the nursery.

When the trees are planted in broken ground, the process of clearing the ground should be performed from below up, for otherwise the trees felled would present great obstacles to the work of clearing.

Dead trees should not be left standing, for if blown down by the wind they would seriously injure the plants on which they might fall.

The trunks and branches of trees that decay slowly should be piled between the furrows, in order that they may not interfere with the work of planting.

In many places the custom prevails of clearing the ground by felling and chopping the trees in the dry season and burning the fragments when they are dry, so that they may not be an impediment to the work of planting.

The advantages of this system are the following:

1. The staking and the other operations of planting are greatly facilitated, as the ground is left clear and free from obstacles.

2. The burned ground produces fewer weeds, as the outer crust

of the ground is calcined, and the cost of keeping it free from weeds is thereby lessened.

On the other hand, the objections to burning the ground are as follows:

1. The richest and best part of the soil, which is that of the surface, is burned out and is therefore lost, at least for some time.

2. The quantity of ashes that remains is injurious to the coffee, while, on the other hand, if the fragments of trees and bushes are left to decay they will in process of time be converted into a fertilizer, which will enrich the soil and prove highly beneficial to the coffee.

For this reason, therefore, it seems preferable not to burn the ground.

B. Simultaneous Sowing.—The custom prevails in Soconusco of sowing corn at the beginning of the rainy season, as soon as the ground is cleared and the waste matter burned, and shortly afterward laying out the plantation. It is true that in this way the slight advantage is gained of utilizing ground already prepared for the cultivation of the corn; but, in exchange, the corn draws from the earth some of the elements required by the coffee for its development, for which reason it is better not to plant corn in land intended for coffee, but to leave for the exclusive benefit of this all the elements which the ground contains.

C. Forming of a Plan for a Plantation.—The work of gathering the fruit will be greatly facilitated if the plantation be divided into squares of from twenty-five to thirty cuerdas each, making them, whenever possible, accessible on every side.

In some estates the plantation is divided into squares of smaller dimensions; but the size mentioned satisfies every requirement. Between the squares a path, five yards wide, available for carts, should, if possible, be left.

In level ground this operation is very simple, but even there it would be well to lay out a plan showing the situation of the various parts of the plantation, the roads, etc., but this will be of even greater utility when the ground is hilly.

Without such a plan there would be the danger of planting trees in places where the paths would have to pass, which would cause the useless expense of planting trees that would afterwards have to be uprooted, besides the loss of the time occupied in their growth.

D. Staking.—The following points relating to the staking of the ground will be now considered:

a.—Object, advantages, and time of staking.

b.—Staking in Soconusco.

c.—Staking in Ceylon.

Each of these points will be considered separately.

a. *Object, Advantages, and Time of Staking.*—The object of staking is to secure the planting of the trees in straight lines, each stake marking the place where a tree is to be planted.

It might at first sight appear an easy matter to mark straight furrows; but when this operation is performed in hilly ground and on a surface covered with obstructions, such as trunks and branches of trees, barrancas, rocks, etc., it is much more difficult than it seems.

It is of the greatest importance, however, that the furrows of the plantation should be straight, not only so that the air may circulate more freely among the plants but also in order to facilitate the future labors of the plantation. For this reason, therefore, no labor or expense should be spared to make the furrow straight. To obtain this result various methods are employed, which will be here briefly mentioned.

The staking of the ground should begin as soon as the burning has been done, or as soon as the branches and trunks of the trees that have been cut down, and other waste vegetation have been collected in heaps, if they have not been burned.

b. *Staking in Soconusco.*—To stake a piece of ground, two straight poles of a length equal to the distance apart at which the coffee-trees are to be planted, are cut of some strong wood, and given to two men Two lines, which are to serve as a basis for the others, are then drawn at right angles, and marked on the ground by means of two cords. When these two lines are marked, stakes are placed at regular intervals along the lines. Then one of the men will fix the end of his pole in the place marked by the second stake of one of the two lines which serve as base lines, and which have already been staked, and the second man will fix one end of his pole in the second stake of the other line which has been staked, so that the other ends of the two poles will meet, thus forming a rectangle. A third man will bring together these two ends of the two poles and will plant a stake at their point of intersection, taking care that the stake shall remain in a perpendicular position.

In this way the operation is to be continued, the end of one of the poles being placed at the third stake of the line, and the end of the other pole at the stake which has just been fixed on the ground, in order that the other stake may be placed in the vertex of the new angle thus formed, and so on successively.

When many hands are to be employed in staking, they are to be divided into parties of three, and the operation is to be conducted as described, two of each party being intrusted with the carrying of the poles and the third with the joining of the poles and the placing of the stakes.

Two of the men staking are also to see that the stakes are placed upright, and whenever they observe that a stake has been misplaced and requires to be replaced, they are to call the third man to do it. Without these precautions it would be difficult to trace straight lines.

The task for each of the stakers should be 750 stakes per day.

c. Staking in Ceylon.—Believing that rules for facilitating the operation of staking would be useful for planters, I give herewith a *résumé* of the systems followed in Ceylon. These are two, one recommended by Laborie and the other by Sabonadière.

Laborie System.—On a cord of the same length as the plantation, strips of cloth are fastened at regular intervals—as in the tail of a boy's kite—representing the places at which the coffee-trees are to be planted. Two men take the ends of the cord and stretch it tightly along the ground. If there should be any obstacles in the way, such as trunks of trees, the cord is not placed on one side of them but over them.

Other men plant stakes of from eighteen to twenty-four inches in length in the places marked by the pieces of cloth, taking care to fix them always on the same side of the cord. If the cord should be raised above the ground by any obstruction, the stake is let fall perpendicularly from the place marked by the piece of cloth, and driven in the spot where it falls. When this is done the cord is moved forward to mark another furrow, the distance between the furrows being marked at either end by poles of the required length; and so on with all the furrows.

Sabonadière System.—Eight or ten thick cords, of the length required, all being of the same length, are procured. Then a straight line, which is to serve as a base for the others, is traced, following, as far as possible, the direction of the slope or the undulations of the ground, so that the stones which become loosened may fall between the furrows and not injure the trees. The base line being marked, another line which shall intersect it is drawn at right angles to it, a carpenter's square being used for the purpose.

Then the distances at which the trees are to be planted are marked off with a pole on the lines which serve as base lines, and wherever a tree is to be planted a stake is set. To each of the transverse stakes the end of one of the cords is fastened, and the other end is carried over to the other side of the plantation. Three or four men, provided with poles of the same length as the distance apart at which the trees should be placed, which is the same distance as that at which the cords should be placed, are stationed there, for the purpose of seeing that the cords run parallel to one another, an operation which, as has been said, is difficult in broken ground where there are tree trunks, rocks, and ravines. In this case it will be necessary to fasten the cords to the ground at intervals with stakes.

After the cords have been fastened, bundles of stakes are placed at convenient points to be ready to be set in their respective positions.

Another thick cord is then taken by two men who stretch it across the ten parallel cords so that it will form right angles with them, at the distance apart at which the furrows are to be made, and which is to be measured off by poles. These two men place two stakes at the points at which the two extremities of the cord, stretched taut, are to be fastened. The stakers place the stakes at the points where the thick cord crosses the ten parallel cords.

In order to be certain that the cords cross at equal distances, it will be well to measure the distances before setting the stakes.

When all the stakes of one row are placed the cord is taken to the next furrow, and the operation is continued in the manner described, until the whole of the ground is staked.

When a row of stakes has been placed, it will be necessary to measure the distances with the poles only on the side on which there are no stakes, since the superadded cord is fastened to those already planted. Care should also be taken to use the carpenter's square every time the cords are placed anew, as only in this way can the furrows for the trees be made quite straight, and the trees form perfect squares.

When they cross at some distance above the surface of the ground, a stone is dropped from the point of their intersection to mark the place where the stake is to be set. When there is a rock, tree trunk, or other obstacle in the place where the stake should be set, this is not placed on one side of it, as the symmetry of the furrows would be thus destroyed, but the place is left vacant.

Ten boys and an overseer plant in Ceylon as many as 2400 stakes a day by this system.

Respective Advantages of the Two Systems.—The system of Laborie would be perfect, on account of its simplicity, in level land recently cleared, where the cord would rest upon the ground, but in hilly land with virgin soil, where there are insuperable obstacles to the regular placing of the stakes, the furrows could not be made straight, following this system; and for this kind of land the system described by Mr. Sabonadière is therefore preferable.

E. Digging the Holes.—In regard to this operation, which follows the staking of the ground, the following points are to be considered.

a.—Time for digging the holes.

b.—Manner of digging the holes.

c.—Size of the holes.

d.—Planting without holes.

Each of these points will be considered separately.

a. Time for Digging the Holes.—After planting all the stakes, a hole is made in the place marked by each stake, which operation is performed in Soconusco in April, at the beginning of the rainy season. The earlier it is done the better.

b. Manner of Digging the Holes.—In order that the holes may be made in the exact spot marked for them by the stake a circle should be traced around this before it is removed, care being taken that the hole be made in the centre of the circle, for if there should be the slightest deviation the furrows would not be straight.

The holes are generally dug with the machete. There is an American borer which works well and quickly in ground that has no stones.

The clay which is dug out is to be heaped up on the lower side of the hole, so that the rains may not wash it in again.

Exposing the earth dug out of the holes to the air, sun, light, and rain greatly improves its quality.

The task for small holes is 250 per day.

c. Size of the Holes.—The size of the holes depends upon the nature of the ground in which they are made; the more compact and the poorer this is the larger should be the hole, and *vice versa*, the richer and looser the soil, the smaller should be the hole. Its size also should be regulated by the size of the trees to be planted.

If the nursery be still small, or, as they say in Soconusco, of two or three crosses—that is, if each plant has only four or six branches, which, growing in opposite directions, take the form of a cross, as has been already explained, when speaking of the nursery—the holes should not be larger than a quarter of a yard in depth and a quarter of a yard in diameter.

When the soil of the nursery is black or when the young plants are of more than three crosses, the holes should be larger; for as black earth is very crumbly, the lump of earth attached to the roots of the plants will be larger than when the soil is clayey.

The general size of the holes in Ceylon is eighteen inches in diameter and eighteen inches in depth.

d. Planting without Holes.—In lands where the soil is loose, the young trees may be planted, introducing a long, thick stick in the hole left by the one which served as a mark, and moving it in every direction, to make a larger hole for the plant. The hole is filled up with earth, which must be pressed down with the foot to make it firm.

This mode of planting has the advantage of saving labor and money; but it has also some disadvantages, which will be mentioned when speaking of planting in slips.

5. TRANSPLANTING.

Transplanting coffee, or setting the trees in their places, which is the operation that follows the opening of the holes, is done in one of three ways, to be indicated further on.

A.—Time for transplanting.

B.—Transplanting with the earth adhering to the roots.

C.—Transplanting with the roots free from earth.

D.—Transplanting in slips.

E.—Transplanting in Ceylon.

Each of the methods of transplanting mentioned, and the time for performing it, will be considered separately.

A. Time for Transplanting.—Transplanting is to be begun as soon as the rainy season has set in. The trees which are transplanted at the beginning of the rainy season will have the advantage of the rains during the whole of the season, and will take firmer root and thrive better than those that are transplanted in the middle, or at the end of the season.

B. Transplanting with the Earth adhering to the Roots.—Taking up in their order the different points relating to this manner of transplanting, the following will now be considered:

a.—Advantages of transplanting with the earth adhering to the roots.

b.—Method of transplanting with the earth adhering to the roots.

c.—Quantity of earth adhering to the roots.

d.—Size of the plants at the time of transplanting.

e.—Pruning the root of the plant in transplanting.

Each of these points will be considered separately.

a. Advantages of Transplanting with the Earth adhering to the Roots. —Planting should be done in this manner whenever it is possible, as the plant then scarcely suffers any disturbance consequent to transplanting. It has been observed that when trees already bearing fruit have been transplanted with the earth adhering to the roots, the tree has suffered so little that it has not lost even its fruit.

To plant coffee with the earth adhering to the roots it will be necessary to have the nursery very near the plantation, as otherwise the transportation of the plants would be a slow and costly operation, and the earth would fall away in transporting the plants to a distance, leaving the roots bare. The safest way, therefore, is first to lay out the nursery, and when the plants are of a suitable size to transplant, which, in Soconusco, is generally at the end of a year and a half, or two years, to transplant them with the earth adhering to the roots. If this be done it is certain that a year after transplanting the plant will yield its first crop.

Transplanting with the earth adhering to the roots is more expensive, and requires more hands than when done with the roots bare. For these reasons, in Ceylon, coffee is transplanted in the former and not in the latter manner.

b. Manner of Transplanting with the Earth adhering to the Roots.— When the ground is hilly, transplanting should be begun in the lower part of the plantation, and from thence continued upward.

In transplanting in this manner, the root of the plant is placed in the hole made for it beforehand, the plant being held upright in one hand while the hole is filled in with earth with the other. When filling the hole, the earth is to be pressed with the hand around the root of the plant, care being taken not to detach the soil from it. After the hole has been filled in, the earth is to be pressed down with the foot.

Should the earth around the root be crumbly it should be enveloped with large leaves, which should be tied around it to prevent its falling apart.

Sometimes the leaves are removed before planting the tree, but, in my opinion, it is better not to remove them, as they will serve as a good vegetable manure.

The trees should be transported from the nursery to the plantation by hand, or on the shoulders of men, placing the trees in a species of barrow made of their branches, each barrow containing from ten to thirty plants, according to the quantity of earth adhering to the roots.

To fill in the hole, earth from the surface of the ground is to be preferred to that which was dug out of the hole, as the former is always better. Special care should be taken to observe this rule when the soil is poor.

The men who perform the transplanting must be closely watched, to make sure that the work is well done, for if badly transplanted the plants would wither, or at least would be a year later in bearing. In no case should transplanting be done by the job.

c. Quantity of Earth adhering to the Roots.—The quantity of earth adhering to the root, will depend on the size of the plant that is to be transplanted, and on the nature of the ground where the nursery is made.

When the plants that are to be transplanted are small—and farther on it will be shown that it is advisable to transplant them while small—about four inches of earth on either side may be left on the root.

When the plants are large, or when the soil of the nursery is very loose, sufficient earth should be left on the roots to avoid the danger of its falling away and leaving them bare. Seven inches on each side would be a suitable size.

d. Size of the Plants at the Time of Transplanting.—The plants at the time of transplanting should be small; that is, they should be of two or three crosses, as they then take root more readily, and grow better and quicker.

The plants should be transplanted very young, however, only when the plantation can be kept free from weeds and when the soil of the nursery is black, in which case it has little consistency. When these conditions do not occur, the plants should be transplanted when they are of four or five crosses.

e. Pruning the Root of the Plant in Transplanting.—The plants should not be pruned at the time of transplanting them.

The principal root of the plant, however, should be cut off level with the earth adhering to it, and in case this should fall away, leaving the roots bare, the main root should be shortened until it is of sufficient thickness not to bend; for, as has been already said, if this happens the tree will die, or will not produce fruit.

Some believe that when the tap root is pruned the plant will stop growing vertically, but will send out small roots on either side. I cannot speak with certainty on this point; but if such be the case it would be better not to prune the root, for the deeper this strikes into the ground the better able the plant will be to bear the dry season without requiring irrigation.

C. Transplanting with the Root free from Earth.—Trees are said in Soconusco to be set or transplanted with the roots bare when they are taken from the nursery or the place where they have grown up without any of the soil adhering to the roots, or when, on taking them out of the ground, the earth has fallen off, leaving the roots bare.

The following points with reference to this manner of planting will now be considered:

a.—Manner of planting coffee-trees with the roots bare.

b.—Disadvantage of transplanting coffee-trees with the roots bare.

c.—Case in which planting should be done with the roots bare.

Each of these points will be considered separately.

a. Manner of Planting Coffee-Trees with the Roots Bare.—In transplanting with the roots bare the same rules are to be observed as in transplanting with the earth adhering to the roots, it being observed that in the former case the earth must be pressed much more compactly around the root than in the latter, and if so the plant cannot be pulled up without great effort; this shows that it is well planted.

Care should be taken not to expose the young plants that are to be transplanted to the heat of the sun, which would wither them; they should be placed in the shade and their roots kept moist.

The operation of planting with the roots bare is sometimes simplified by omitting the digging of the holes. A long-pointed stick is driven into the ground in the place where the plant is to be set, this is placed in the hole thus made, the hole is filled with earth, and another hole is then made close beside the first with the same stick, so that the earth in the first hole shall be firmly compressed. In order to ascertain whether the plant has been successfully transplanted or not a slight effort should be made to pull it up, and if it offers some resistance it may be considered well planted. A man can plant in this manner from 80 to 150 plants a day. With this system several operations are shortened and the cost of planting is less. It has the disadvantage, however, that a vacant space almost always remains around the root, where the water gathers, sometimes causing the roots to decay. The roots are also more likely to deteriorate with this system than with the other.

b. Disadvantages of Transplanting with the Roots Bare.—When the planting is done with the roots bare, the plant suffers greatly from the disturbance caused by transplanting, and a year generally elapses before it returns to the condition in which it was when transplanted.

It is evident, therefore, that if the plant is put back a year by transplanting, this year might have been better spent in the nursery than in the plantation, for the reason that it would cost less to keep the ground free from weeds in the former case than in the latter, and that at the end of the year transplanting might be done with the earth attached to the roots.

Many planters, with the object of saving the year and a half or two years which the young plant would spend in the nursery, form their plantations with wild plants or plants taken from a nursery already formed, the planting being done with the roots bare, the distance of the place from which they are taken admitting of no other manner. This is a false economy of time, for in order to save a few months of care of the nursery, the whole year which the plants thus transplanted are put back is lost, and the heavy expense is incurred of from four to six weedings of the whole plantation.

c. Case in which Transplanting should be done with the Roots Bare.— The only case in which trees should be planted with the roots bare is when, from the distance between the place where they have been grown and the plantation, it would be difficult if not impossible to transport them to it with the earth attached to the roots.

D. Transplanting in Slips.—When the young plants for the plantation are taken neither from the nursery nor from an abandoned plantation, but from trees already grown, it is said that the plantation is formed from slips. The trunk is generally cut off eight or ten inches above the root, in order that it may grow more vigorously. This kind of planting is always done with the roots bare.

Transplanting in slips is the least advisable way of all, and should never be adopted except when there is no other way of forming the plantation. In some cases, however, it has given good results.

E. Transplanting in Ceylon.—Transplanting coffee plants in Ceylon is performed, according to Mr. Sabonadière, in the following manner: The young plants grown in the nursery are pulled up with the hand; those that have crooked roots are thrown away as useless; with a sharp knife the flexible part of the tap root is cut off; and the lateral roots are also shortened, as they are generally very long, and this trimming prevents them from becoming tangled in the transplanting, which would cause them to decay. The hole is then filled in with the earth that has been removed from it, care being taken to put no stones in with it and to keep the tap root from bending and the lateral roots from tangling. The plant should be set no deeper in the ground than it was in the nursery. When the hole is filled the earth must be pressed down with the hands and afterwards with the foot. To be sure that the plant has been firmly planted it is smartly pulled, and if it offers resistance it may be considered well planted. Care should be taken to leave no hollow spaces around the roots, as the water would settle in them and would rot the roots. Beside each plant a stake is to be set to support it and to prevent its being pulled up when the ground is being weeded; if the plant should die the stake will mark the place where the plant that is to replace it is to be set.

Stakes are indispensable in Ceylon, for without them the young plants would be unable to resist the violence of the winds. The stakes are four or five feet in length and last two years. They should be driven at least eighteen inches into the ground. The plant is fastened to the stake with a cord in such a manner as that the bark shall not be injured by the friction of the cord against it.

6. CULTIVATION OF COFFEE.

The various operations which coffee culture requires in Soconusco will be first considered, a description of the manner in which the same operation is performed in Ceylon being appended in each case. Then the operations that are not considered necessary here but are customary in Ceylon will be described. The following points, then, will now be considered:

A.—Clearing the ground.
B.—Replanting.
C.—Pruning.
D.—Cultivation of coffee in Ceylon.
Each of these operations will be considered separately.

A. Clearing the Ground.—Clearing the ground, or weeding, consists in destroying the weeds and other vegetation that may spring up in the plantation, in order that the coffee-trees may absorb all the nutritive elements of the soil.

The following points regarding weeding will now be considered :
a.—Necessity and advantages of weeding.
b.—Manner of weeding.
c.—Number of weedings to be made during the year.
d.—Weeding in Ceylon.
Each of these subjects will be separately considered.

a. Necessity and Advantages of Weeding.—The transplanting having been done in May and June, which are the best months in Soconusco for this operation, the trees will have the advantage of the whole of the rainy season, and will yield their first crop in September of the following year, unless the plants were very young at the time of transplanting and weeding was neglected. The time occupied in the cultivation of the coffee-trees, then, in the sense in which the word is used here, will be from sixteen to seventeen months, during which the chief work will be the weeding.

The chief labor in the cultivation of coffee will be the frequent weeding of the ground for the purpose of destroying all the vegetation that may spring up in it. The secret of success in coffee culture consists in allowing no other vegetation to remain in the ground where coffee is planted.

If the plantation is not weeded, the weeds will choke the coffee plants; and if the weedings are not performed with the required frequency, the crops will be very scanty.

b. Manner of Weeding.—Thus far no machine or implement to facilitate weeding has been used that has not injured the plant. In some of the plantations of Guatemala clutivators or ploughs are used for weeding, but aside from the fact that these implements can be used only on level ground, many are of opinion that they injure the tender roots which the coffee plant sends out near the surface of the ground, for which reason these implements are very little used. Besides which, three or four years after transplanting, the branches of the trees will have spread so much that it would be impossible for the mules or oxen drawing the plough to pass under them without injuring them greatly.

For the reasons above mentioned the hoe is little used in weeding, for, in addition to cutting the young roots of the coffee-tree, it loosens the soil, thus exposing it to be washed away by the rains—a very serious objection in hilly ground. For these reasons, as a general rule, only the machete is used in weeding. In Ceylon a means has been discovered of preventing the rains from washing the earth away in hilly ground, as will be seen farther on.

c. Number of Weedings to be Made during the Year.—In the first year after transplanting the ground must be frequently weeded, for, as from their diminutive size, the plants cast scarcely any shade, the ground is almost completely exposed to the sun, and this causes it to produce abundantly all sorts of weeds. As the plant grows it casts more and more shade, and the greater the shade the smaller the area of ground exposed to the fecundating action of the sun, and consequently, the fewer will be the weeds.

The number of weedings which the plantation is to receive during the first year and subsequent years will depend upon various circumstances, such as the altitude of the ground, its temperature, the nature of the soil, whether it has been virgin soil or soil that had been already cultivated, etc., and in each case will be determined according to the particular circumstances of the place. Generally, four weedings a year are made, although in some localities six, and even more, are given. It will be seen at once that this is the most costly operation on the plantation.

d. Weeding in Ceylon.—In Ceylon, as in Soconusco, weeding the ground constitutes the principal expense of coffee cultivation. Mr. Sabonadière advises weeding the plantations once a month, and this advice seems to me very judicious, as in this way the weeds are not given time to grow or produce seed. The cost of twelve weedings a year would thus be about the same as that of six, because, in the former case there being fewer weeds and the work of uprooting them being less, two cords might be given to each laborer as a task, while in the latter case only one cord could be given him.

There is the objection, however, that frequent weeding stirs up the soil and exposes it to being washed away by the rains. This difficulty might to a certain extent be obviated if, in new plantations, where there are as yet few weeds, the weeds were uprooted with a sharp stick and thrown into a bag which the laborer carried with him, gathered in a heap, and burned when dry. But in old plantations this system cannot be followed; the hoe is there used, and the earth is of necessity turned up.

Sometimes the weeding is done from the trunk of the tree out, and a sort of bank or ridge is thus formed between the furrows, causing the rain-water to run near the trunks of the trees and carry away the earth from their roots. To avoid this inconvenience, the weeding ought to be done from the middle of the furrows towards the trees, care being taken that their roots remain well covered with earth.

Weeding is generally done in Ceylon by contract, the weeding of each acre of ground, or a little more than niné cords, costing on an average thirty-six shillings, or nine dollars, or about a dollar per cord yearly. Women and children perform the weeding.

B. Replanting.—It frequently happens that some of the trees, from having been badly transplanted, or for some other reason, either die or become sickly. If many plants should suffer in this way, the cause should be ascertained in order to remedy it. The best means of doing this is to dig around the root of a tree to see if the tap root has become bent, if it has come in contact with a stone, or if some insect be not injuring it.

The necessity of constantly replacing the trees which die, or decline, makes it indispensable to have always on the estate nurseries from whence plants may be taken to replace those that have died or deteriorated.

C. Pruning.—Pruning having an important bearing on the success of a plantation, the following points connected with this subject will now be considered:

a.—General considerations on pruning.
b.—Principles of pruning.
c.—Advantages of pruning.
d.—Topping.
e.—Pruning.
f.—Rules for pruning.
g.—Manner of pruning.
h.—Time of pruning.

Each of these points will be considered separately.

a. General Considerations on Pruning.—At first sight it might seem that pruning would be prejudicial to the trees, since it may be said that this operation is contrary to nature, which has given the trees their branches and their appointed size, which should neither be reduced nor diminished by artificial means. Experience has demonstrated, however, that it is better to prune the trees, for if these are planted in their native zone, the force of their sap is so great that if it be not suitably directed, they become in a short time a tangle of branches which the sun cannot penetrate, and thus lose their fructifying power.

From the time of Laborie, that is, for about eighty years past, pruning has been employed, and with very good success, to increase the productiveness of trees. According to this writer, pruning consists in cutting from plants whatever in them deviates from natural symmetry, and preserving what is in accordance with it, directing in this way the vegetative principle to purposes of order, profit, and regeneration.

It is a well-known fact that fruit-trees are greatly improved by pruning, and there is no reason why the system applied to them should not produce equally satisfactory results as applied to coffee plants.

The rule to be followed with regard to pruning will depend on each particular locality, upon the nature of the soil, the temperature, altitude above the level of the sea, exposure, etc., but the principle is the same; that is, to remedy the deviations of the tree from natural laws caused by conditions of soil, climate, situation, etc., and to make it return to those laws; art in this way aiding nature. Regarded in this way, pruning is as necessary as weeding.

b. Principles of Pruning.—For a better understanding of the advantages to be obtained by pruning, it will be well to define some facts and to lay down some rules concerning it.

The branches growing from the trunk of the tree are called primaries; those that grow from the primaries are called secondaries; those that grow from the secondaries, tertiaries, and so on successively.

Each branch of the tree bears fruit only once, sending out in the following year other branches which in their turn bear fruit.

Nature has so placed the primary branches that they receive an equal amount of light. Each pair of branches grows in a direction, with regard to the branch next to them, which deviates a few degrees from a right angle, so that if there are twenty pairs of branches no two of them will be found to be in the same vertical plane. This arrangement gives each primary branch a sufficiently large space for its development and sufficient amount of light. But when the vertical growth of the plant is checked by pruning this space becomes reduced to a circle of not more than three feet deep and about six feet in diameter.

As each branch gives but one crop, there would soon be no room for new branches to grow, if the old ones were not removed, for the secondary branches, after yielding their crop, would produce tertiary branches, these quaternary branches, and so on, successively, until the tree would be converted into a thicket of branches and unproductive foliage. The production of branches which give fruit takes place only when there is room for them to grow and light to make them grow.

In pruning there are two distinct operations, tapping and pruning, properly so called. The former consists in removing from the plant the upper part of its main stem or leader; and the second in cutting off some of its branches.

The upper shoots being cut off, the power of the sap before long causes two or three supplementary shoots to grow beneath the highest branches, and renews them as often as they are removed. These shoots being prevented from growing, as care must be taken to cut them off whenever they appear, the sap flows to the primary branches and makes them grow about three feet from the trunk. When the sap ceases to nourish the primary branches, it goes to nourish the secondary branches, and in the management of these consists the art of pruning and the success of the plantation.

The only permanent parts of the tree are the trunk and the primary branches. The trunk should grow straight and thick, and the primary branches should be strong and straight, and should grow at right angles with the trunk. If a primary branch should die or grow sickly it cannot be replaced.

c. Advantages of Pruning.—The advantages of pruning, to sum up, are the following:

1. It gives the tree an artificial form which makes it suffer less in situations in which it is exposed to the winds.
2. It makes the gathering of the crop easier and cheaper.
3. It increases the yield of the tree.
4. It regularizes the crop.

The branches which are exposed to the sun and air are those which bear the best fruit. Consequently, the more closely the tree is pruned, ·

the larger the crops it will yield. This is seen better in the new trees, which bear more fruit in their second and third crops, because they then have fewer branches.

Generally, the trees give a bad and a good crop alternately. This evil may be remedied by pruning, as will be seen farther on.

Pruning is most required in high localities which are exposed to the cold winds.

d. Topping.—Topping consists in cutting off the top of the trunk or the leader of the plant.

This is the only kind of pruning practicable in Soconusco, and it is done arbitrarily and without following any rule. Farther on it will be seen that once the coffee plant has been thus cut, it will be indispensable to prune it.

When the trees have attained their ordinary height, that is, when they are about six feet high, their leader, or central branch, which is of little importance, is pruned, and also all the shoots that spring up near the roots. This stops the vertical growth of the plant, causing the branches to spread horizontally, sending out new branches which bear fruit, or strengthening the branches which it has already sent out.

Trees not thus pruned will grow as high as ten or eleven feet, and I have sometimes seen them as much as twelve feet high; but cutting stops the vertical growth of the tree, which then grows horizontally and through its branches.

The principal reasons in favor of cutting the leader are, according to Laborie, the following:

1. The fruit is brought by it within easy reach of the hand; it facilitates the gathering of the crops and prevents the branches from breaking when picking the fruit.

2. The tree acquires greater vigor as well under the ground as above it, and the trunk grows thicker.

3. The tree presents a smaller volume of resistance to the winds.

4. The tree loses none of its primary branches, but, on the contrary, these being nearer the source of vegetation, are better nourished and consequently more productive.

If the plant be pruned very near the highest primary branches, there is danger of the trunk splitting when the branches grow thick. This danger will disappear if the plant be pruned a little above the highest primary branches and these be removed.

The height at which the trees are to be left will depend in each case upon the distance apart at which they are planted, the nature of the ground, its altitude above the level of the sea, exposure, etc.

In Guatemala and Soconusco they are pruned to a height of six or eight feet.

In Ceylon plants are pruned to a height of two, three, three and a half, or at most four feet. Trees of more than four feet would not there be able to bear the violence of the wind. If the trunk is not topped they grow, in situations sheltered from the wind, to a height of ten or twelve feet.

e. Pruning.—The only kind of pruning that I have seen done in Soconusco is to cut all the shoots or branches which grow from the root of the tree, three months after transplanting, which operation is constantly repeated.

Cutting off the top of the tree causes the sap to produce numerous shoots which spring up in every direction. If these are allowed to grow, the tree will soon become a mass of tangled branches which the sun cannot penetrate, and will consequently have little capability of yielding fruit. The sap would produce numerous branches instead of being converted into fruit. Pruning is advantageous in every case, but it is still more so after the top of the tree has been cut off.

So many improvements have been made in pruning that there is now a complete system of pruning coffee-trees, which is, however, unfortunately unknown here. The best way of explaining this system is to give the rules which constitute it.

The difficulty of pruning lies in performing it so that the fruit will increase without exhausting the tree. It is the custom here to cure with clay the wounds caused by pruning.

f. Rules for Pruning.—The practical part of pruning is comprised in the rules which serve as a general guide for this operation. With the object of setting down all that I have found of value on this subject, I insert here, even at the risk of falling into repetitions, a *résumé* of the rules given by Laborie, Sabonadière, and a practical planter of Ceylon, and those published in the *Observer* of Colombo, the principal port of that island.

System of Laborie.—Laborie gives the following rules for pruning trees planted in good soil, in a hot climate, and which have been pruned before:

1. Every branch that looks sickly, that is broken, that has suffered any lesion, or that seems exhausted through over-production, is to be cut off.

2. Every branch that is decayed, withered, dry, or split, must also be cut off, following the principle of regeneration.

3. All vertical branches, branches that cross each other, or that do not grow in their natural direction, and all supernumerary branches which absorb the sap of the plant without producing fruit, are to be taken off, or, if very thick, sawed off.

4. The top and the middle part of the tree are to be pruned so as to give free access to the air and sun.

5. If, in spite of this, the tree should still be full of branches,

some of the secondary branches are to be cut off, choosing those that grow out of the natural direction, care being taken not to touch the primary branches.

This last rule should be followed, according to Laborie, only with trees in high lands and exposed to cold winds, these being generally full of branches and leaves. The twigs at the top, which run in every direction, are first to be taken off, then such of the larger branches as are crooked are cut off; and, finally, if the top or leader should be decayed, this decayed part is to be cut off.

All the primary branches that have kept their natural direction are to be left, for the reason mentioned above, that, once cut, they do not grow again. If they should be split or injured in any way, however, it would be better to cut them off. The same thing is to be done when they have taken a wrong direction, only the part being then cut that deviates from the natural direction.

In very cold localities, or when the trees produce very little fruit, because of their having too many branches, all the secondary branches are to be cut off, with the object of making new ones grow which shall bear fruit, and of giving a right direction to the sap.

When the primary branches have grown so long that they become interlaced with those of the neighboring trees, enough of them is to be cut off to prevent the branches from meeting.

After the tree has been pruned, any moss or parasites growing on its trunk are to be removed, using a wooden knife for the purpose.

System of Sabonadière.—The vertical shoots that first spring from the trunk of the tree should be taken off as they appear, without injuring the bark of the tree. Afterwards other shoots, as many as four in each bud, grow on the primary branches, in different directions. It will be advisable to remove these also, excepting one only in each branch, preferring that which is most vigorous and has the best direction. This operation is to be repeated every year, and will render pruning, properly speaking, or the removal of thick branches already formed which have some defects, unnecessary.

No secondary branch is to be left within six inches of the trunk, so that a vacant space, in the shape of a circle a foot in diameter, may be left around the trunk of the tree, in order that air and sunlight may circulate around it freely and prevent the growth on it of moss and parasites.

If the plantations are small the best system of pruning is to allow alternate secondary branches to fructify each year; that is, to cut those that have borne fruit one year, and leave those that have not borne fruit: but in large plantations it is difficult to follow this system, and in them the following rules should be observed:

1. To pull up all the shoots that are within a distance of six inches of the trunk of the tree.

2. To remove all the branches and shoots that grow toward the tree, or toward the other branches.

3. To reduce the number of shoots, leaving only one to each bud.

When the coffee-tree has not been pruned for some time, Mr. Sabonadière recommends that the primary branches nearest the ground be cut off, supporting his advice with these reasons:

1. They cause much humidity and shade, and prevent the free circulation of the air.

2. They rarely bear fruit, because of their superabundant leafage, and draw the nutritive sap from the tree unprofitably.

3. They interefere with the labors of cultivation, owing to their nearness to the ground, and they are injured by the laborers.

4. They cover the weeds and young coffee plants and serve as a hotbed for them.

No branch should be allowed to bear more than two, or at most three crops; when it has given these it should be removed, so that a new one may replace it which will bear fruit.

System of a Practical Cultivator of Ceylon.—This writer recommends that all the branches that are less than six inches from the trunk be cut off; that a vacant space of a foot in circumference be left around the trunk of the plant to permit a free circulation of light and air; and that one of every two secondary branches growing together be pruned, one on each side alternately of the primaries being left.

All the secondary branches that grow very near the trunk tend to debilitate the primaries, and the same is the case when they are allowed to grow in pairs.

Some set the rule that a primary branch should never be pruned; but this rule has its exceptions, as, for instance, when the branch splits or dies, or when it grows to such a length as to become intertwined with those of the neighboring trees. In this last case a part only of the branch should be pruned.

Some think also that when the primaries near the ground have grown to a great length and have become tangled they should be cut off up to the first good secondary branch, in order that this may receive all the sap that would otherwise go to nourish the branches that have been pruned.

System of the " Observer" of Colombo.—The natural consequences of the rules set forth, when speaking of the principles of pruning, which are in accordance with a notable article published in the *Observer* of Colombo, for June 17, 1861, are the following:

Being two different systems, they have some points in common.

All the secondary branches which are at a distance of less than nine or ten inches from the trunk of the tree, are to be removed. This will give the light access to the plant and will give the branches more room to grow.

Double or triple shoots shall be reduced to one, choosing that which grows at a right angle with the primary branch, and which lies in the same horizontal plane; the number of secondary branches on each side of the primaries will then be equalized, and, finally, the same number of secondaries will be left on each primary.

In deciding upon the number of secondary branches to be left on the tree, it must be borne in mind that if they be many the plant will become exhausted, and in the following year will produce fewer branches and less fruit. A number must be fixed upon, then, which, without exhausting the plant will cause it to yield good crops, and in this way the crops will be uniform, not as in plantations that are not pruned, which yield a fair crop one season and a bad one the next.

When the crop is gathered, all the secondary branches which have fructified to the extent of producing tertiary branches are to be cut off. Some advise that when there are enough branches to allow of it, all the secondaries that have produced fruit be cut off.

After the trees have been thus pruned, they send forth new shoots, which must also be pruned, as has been already indicated, as soon as they show the direction in which they are growing. If this pruning be deferred, it will be more difficult to perform, and the tree will be greatly injured by it, as it will then be deprived of its leaves when it most needs them.

The secondary branches must be cut off at their root, so that no part may be left that might send forth shoots in a direction other than the natural one, or cause the plant to sicken.

The number of branches to be left will depend upon the soil, climate, situation, etc.

When this system has been once established, it will be very easy to follow it, for the same thing that is done one year is repeated the succeeding years.

g. Manner of Pruning.—Laborie gives the following rules for the practical part of pruning:

1. To cut the trunk of a tree or any of its thick branches, a very sharp saw is to be used which can be managed with one hand, the trunk being firmly held with the other, to keep the tree from moving and to facilitate the work of sawing. The trunk must be cut obliquely from above downward, and the cut surface should face the north; the sun thus falls on it with less force and the rain will run off more easily, for, if the water should penetrate the wood, it would injure the tree greatly.

2. The large branches which cannot be easily pruned with a knife are to be sawed off in the manner above indicated. But the saw is to be used in no case in which a knife can be employed.

3. As the saw injures the bark around the cut surface, both the bark and the trunk of the tree should be trimmed off with the knife. When this is done, the wound heals more quickly and the bark grows better.

4. When the branches are pruned with the knife, the branch is to be held firmly with one hand, and with the other a sharp, quick blow is to be given it with the knife, from above downward. If the branch should not be severed at the first blow, this is to be repeated, bending the branch a little, but not so as to split it. If it should split, all the split part must be cut off.

5. The branch should always be cut close to its root.

6. When a secondary branch is pruned, this must be done very near its root, especially when it grows under another that has been already cut off.

7. To prevent many young shoots from growing in the place where a branch has been cut off, a piece of the bark is to be cut out at the top of the incision.

h. Time of Pruning.—Some planters prune the coffee-tree when it is two years old, or before it has borne fruit. It seems preferable, however, to prune it after it has reached maturity, that is, after it has given its first crop, for in this way it is not forced to produce a large crop, which would exhaust it.

Tapping should be done after the season of blossoming is over; for if it were done while the plant is in blossom the sap would go to produce blossoms and fruit, instead of strengthening and increasing the branches.

Pruning should begin immediately after the gathering of the crop and should be finished before the plant has begun to blossom.

Pruning is so essential to the success of a plantation that it should be suspended only for the four or five days during which the plant is flowering. It should then be performed with great care, so as not to destroy the flower, which contains the germ of the fruit; but it should not be altogether stopped.

After the flowering is over, the branches that have many blossoms should be left, and those that are exhausted and have few should be cut off.

The months of March, April, and May are the best months for pruning in Soconusco.

D. Cultivation of Coffee in Ceylon.—Coffee culture in Ceylon is much more complicated and costly than it is in Soconusco, as, in addition to the operations already described, with the modifications indicated when speaking of each of them, it is necessary to perform others also which are not customary in Soconusco, and the necessity for which has not yet been felt. These labors are the following:

a.—Making roads.

b.—Drainage.

c.—Making trenches.

d.—Loosening the earth.

e.—Making ridges.

f.—Irrigating.

g.—Destroying the insects which are enemies of the coffee-tree.

h.—Manuring the ground.

Each of these labors will be considered separately, that of manuring, which from its importance is deserving of special attention, being considered in a chapter by itself.

a. Making Roads.—It is desirable that the estate be traversed by cart roads, which shall place its different quarters in communication with the house in which the work of preparing the coffee for the market is performed. The transportation of the fruit, and of the fertilizers, when these are used, will be thus facilitated and rendered cheaper. The roads should not have a grade of more than ten per cent. The roads should be opened before the plantation is made, for, if they should be opened afterwards, many of the trees already planted and bearing fruit would have to be destroyed, and many of the neighboring plants would be injured by the work consequent on the opening of the road.

It is highly important that there should be easy means of communication between the various parts of the estate, so that the laborers may be able to get to their work without difficulty, and also that the superintendent or overseer may be able to go readily to the place where the workmen are employed, for if these know that they are not watched they will not be likely to work diligently.

It is an established fact that the trees near the roads are more vigorous and produce more fruit than those at some distance from them. The cause of this may be that the soil near the roads is looser than that of the rest of the plantation, and is renewed by means of the rains for which the roads form channels. This is another reason, therefore, which renders it advisable that there should be roads and paths in a plantation.

Mr. Sabonadière recommends that a road be made around the plantation with the object, among others, of separating it from the contiguous woods.

Although it may seem paradoxical to say so, it is really a saving to go to the expense of opening roads, for they lessen considerably the labor of cultivation.

The roads and paths should also be made to serve as channels to carry off the rains.

The ground in which coffee is planted in Ceylon is so hilly that frequently the roads can be made only in terraces. Mr. Sabonadière estimates the cost of making a path five feet wide, with a channel a foot wide, at £25 sterling, or $125 per mile, and that of a cart road, ten feet wide, with a channel eighteen inches wide, at $500 per mile.

b. Drainage.—It is advisable, in order to prevent the rains from washing away the richest soil of the plantation, to construct drains when making the roads, although this will require more capital and labor. The drains should be made before the plantation is laid out, for the reasons mentioned when speaking of roads.

Before enriching the soil with fertilizers means should be taken to preserve it—that is, to prevent the rains from washing away the richest part of it, and this is done by means of drains.

In Ceylon, and other places where coffee cultivation is most advanced, care is always taken to construct drains. Mr. Sabonadière recommends that these be fifteen inches in width and the same in depth; that they be distant from each other the space occupied by twenty trees, or about one hundred and twenty feet; that their grade be not more than one per cent., or even less, and that they run in the direction of the nearest ravine. Care should be taken to keep the drains always free from obstructions.

Mr. Sabonadière mentions an estate in Ceylon called Matelle, in which all the drains empty into a pit excavated in the lowest part of the ground, in which the soil washed away by the rains is deposited and afterwards carried to the plantation and scattered around the trunks of the trees.

c. Making Trenches.—In the estates of Ceylon where coffee culture is most advanced, a system is adopted which is entirely unknown in Soconusco, and which is at present considered unnecessary, but which I think it advisable to mention, as it might be adopted in some parts of Mexico with advantage.

It has for its object: 1st. To prevent the rains from washing away the soil. 2d. To prevent the water from standing around the roots of the trees. 3d. To augment the vegetable soil, which would be beneficial to the trees. The plan in question consists in making an excavation about three feet in length, a foot or a foot and a half in width, and the same in depth, between every four trees. The earth which is taken from these excavations is spread over the roots of the nearest trees.

These excavations serve not only to retain the rain-water and the soil which it carries with it, but also to receive the weeds cut down in weeding, the branches, twigs, and leaves that remain after pruning, and anything else at hand that will serve for manure. These excavations, therefore, will soon be filled; they should be cleaned twice a year, and the substances taken from them spread over the roots of the trees, making an excellent manure.

These excavations must be dug at right angles with the slope, so that they do not run down the slope but cross it horizontally. Mr. Sabonadière estimates the cost of these excavations, in ground that is not stony, at about $5.62½ per acre, or 61 cents per cord.

There is another system of making these trenches which is more costly. It consists in digging a trench two feet wide and two feet deep, the whole length of the furrows, the bottom of the trench being made as level as possible. This trench is filled with grass, dry leaves, branches of trees, or any other vegetable substance that may be at hand; it is then filled in with earth which is pressed down compactly. The result is that the roots of the trees spread out to the trench and penetrate the vegetable matter in it which is becoming converted into soil.

d. Loosening the Earth.—In places where the earth is very compact, and fertilizers are used, the ground is dug up in order that the roots of the trees may be able to reach out more easily in search of the manure. It has been observed in some places that manuring does not produce results as favorable to the coffee-tree as digging up the ground. This latter should be done, however, only in ground that has been manured and that is provided with drains, for otherwise the loosened soil would be easily washed away by the rains.

The cost of loosening the earth, according to this system, is in Ceylon $5 per acre, or a little more than 54 cents per cord.

There is another method of loosening the earth, which consists in moving it about gently in every direction with a species of iron pitchfork. In this case care must be taken not to turn up the soil, otherwise the rains would wash it away.

Loosening the earth contributes also to prevent the soil from being washed away, for, being loose, it readily absorbs the rain.

e. Making Ridges.—With the object also of preventing the rains from carrying away the richest part of the soil, ridges are formed in some of the estates in Ceylon, with the earth dug out of the trenches, which, directing the course of the rain-water, cause it to carry the earth which it washes out into the trenches.

This system has been used with success on several estates.

f. Irrigating.—In localities where the rains are not abundant, or where the ground does not retain sufficient moisture for the nutrition of the coffee-tree during the dry season, it is indispensable to establish a system of irrigation which, applied opportunely and with moderation, will make the tree thrive and will keep it in better condition than when it depends entirely on the rains.

g. Enemies of the Coffee-Tree.—The coffee-tree has in Ceylon many enemies which frequently destroy it, and which it is necessary to make war upon at a considerable expense of time and money. The chief of these are the following:

Grubs. When the tree is young it is attacked by a large grub which eats away the bark near the root, and thus kills the plant. This insect abounds in low ground. To protect the plant from its ravages it is recommended to apply turpentine to the stem.

Rats. When the trees are young they are attacked also, at certain seasons, by rats, which devour the primary branches of the young plants.

Coffee-bug. This insect, of which there are two varieties, the one white, the other black, is the most destructive of all the enemies of the coffee-tree. The white variety appears immediately after the flowering of the plant, during the heats of February, March, and April. It attaches itself to the branch, beside the fruit, and spreads around it a white glutinous substance which rots the stalk of the fruit and causes it to drop from the tree. The black bug attacks the leaves, fruit, and branches of the tree, and is covered with a sort of small thin shell, like a limpet in shape. This insect covers the leaves with a species of black filmy substance, and has the effect of diminishing very considerably the productiveness of the tree. The black bug attacks rather the plantations situated in the high lands than those which are in low ground. The time during which this insect infests the trees varies, but it generally remains for three years.

The most efficacious remedy for this plague is to manure the ground well, in order that the trees may be able to resist its ravages. Turpentine is also used, although not with as good results. The turpentine is sprinkled on the ground around the trunk of the tree, and the soil is then turned up, so that the turpentine may penetrate to the roots.

Ants. In low and dry localities, ants make their nests in the coffee-tree and greatly annoy the laborers, as their sting is very painful. The red ants are the worst.

In Soconusco and in Guatemala there is an ant, called with us *zompopo*, which loosens the soil greatly, and which is considered extremely injurious to the plantation in which it establishes itself. To exterminate these ants it is necessary to dig down until their nests are reached and then pour boiling water over them.

Fortunately, thus far none of the other plagues of Ceylon are known in Soconusco.

7. FERTILIZERS.

As fertilizers are hardly ever used in Soconusco, I shall have to make use of the terms and the rules employed in Ceylon, and used by Mr. Sabonadière in his *Coffee Planter*, when treating of them.

The following points, then, regarding fertilizers, will now be considered:

A.—Necessity for and advantages of fertilizers.

B.—Fertilizers used in Soconusco.

C.—Fertilizers used in Ceylon.

Each of these points will be considered separately.

A. Necessity for and Advantages of Fertilizers.—As I have already stated, fertilizers are not used either in Guatemala or in Soconusco, with the exceptions that I will presently state, nor has the necessity for using them yet been felt. But, as it is plain that, no matter how rich may be the soil, its nutritive properties will at last be exhausted if they are constantly drawn from it by the trees without being replaced in any way, it will be well to give some attention to this important branch of coffee culture. Besides, in other localities which are not so fertile as Soconusco, there may be greater need for fertilizers, and there they should be used from the time the plantation is laid out.

Without fertilizers a plantation might continue productive for ten years, let us say. With fertilizers, it may be made to last fifty or a hundred years in good condition, and the cost of fertilizers would in any case be much less than that of forming a new plantation.

The result of manuring, according to Mr. Sabonadière, is an increase in the production of each acre of from three to five English quintals in every crop, or, which is the same thing, of from 36 to 60 pounds per cord.

When fertilizers are used it is indispensable that the ground should have a complete system of draining.

B. Fertilizers Used in Soconusco.—The only way in which I have seen fertilizers used in Guatemala and Soconusco is to spread the waste matter of the sugar-cane around the trunk of the coffee-trees. The cane soon rots and forms a good fertilizer. It also contributes to prevent the rains from washing away the earth. As sugar-cane is generally cultivated in estates where coffee is grown, this fertilizer is cheap and easy of application.

The same use might be made of the pulp and the skins of the fruit of the coffee-tree, of which there is so great a quantity, instead of allowing it to go to waste as it now does in every plantation in Guatemala and Soconusco. Only common sense is needed, without any knowledge of chemistry, to know that in order to keep the ground from becoming impoverished it is necessary to restore to the soil the elements that have been taken from it. But I am sorry to say that I have never seen this fertilizer, which is at once excellent and cheap, used on any estate.

C. Fertilizers Used in Ceylon.—With regard to the system of manuring adopted in Ceylon the following points will now be considered:

a.—Substances which are used as manures.

b.—Manner of applying fertilizers to the soil.

c.—Period at which fertilizers should be used.

d.—Cost of fertilizers.

Each of these subjects will be considered separately.

a. Substances which are Used as Manure.—Various substances are used in Ceylon as manure. I will mention here only those that are generally known and easy to obtain, omitting such as are little known and difficult to procure, like poonac and sombreorum.

The fertilizers are these:

Cattle-dung, bones, super-phosphates, coffee-pulp, prunings, grass, salts, wood-ashes, burnt clay, lime, guano, and mixtures of these substances.

Cattle-dung. Cattle-dung is the best manure known for the coffee-tree. It may be used alone, or mixed with other fertilizers, as will be shown farther on.

Bones. It is well known that bones contain a large amount of phosphate of lime, and for this reason they make a good fertilizer for the coffee-tree, inferior only to cattle-dung. The principal effect of this fertilizer is to increase the productiveness of the tree. The bones can be used conveniently only in the form of powder, as in any other form they would dissolve very slowly and their effect would be proportionately slow. In Ceylon they are always used in the form of powder, this being imported from Australia.

Super-phosphates. Super-phosphates are now being largely used as fertilizers, and with good results, especially super-phosphate of lime. Half a pound is sufficient for each tree.

Pulp of the Fruit. As might be supposed, this excellent fertilizer, which goes to waste in Soconusco, is used extensively in Ceylon, and with very good results. Two medium-sized basketfuls are sufficient for each tree. This manure produces very good results mixed in equal parts with cow-dung. A basketful of the mixture should be applied to each plant, and it is to be used in the same way as unmixed dung. The pulp may be mixed with advantage with the other fertilizers, such as lime, bone-dust, etc.

Prunings. These make a very good vegetable manure. They are buried while green in pits, carefully covered over and pressed down; but they are now little used, owing to the great expense of making the excavations.

Mand Grass. This manure is used in the same manner as the former, and gives very good results. As this grass does not grow in Soconusco, I think it unnecessary to speak of it more in detail. I believe, however, that the grass of the country would give results similar to this fertilizer, more especially Guinea grass, and, in general, all vegetable substances that could be buried in the ground. Maná grass revives and rejuvenates plantations that have become exhausted.

In burying the grass care must be taken not to bury with it seeds or shoots that might grow, for should this be done the coffee plantation would be converted into a grass-field.

Mr. William King makes mention of a plantation in Ceylon in which the vegetation growing in swampy places is cut down every year before the gathering of the crop, piled in heaps and left to rot, and, when the coffee crop is gathered, spread as a fertilizer around the trunks of the coffee-trees.

Salts of Ammonia. These salts make an excellent manure; but owing to their great solubility and their affinity with water they are apt to be absorbed by the soil before they can reach the roots of the coffee-trees, or washed away by the rains, so failing in either case to benefit the plant.

Wood-ashes. This fertilizer has the advantage of being very cheap and very easy to obtain. It is also a good substitute for lime in localities where this is not found. The ashes must be buried in the earth, as, if left on the surface, the wind would blow it away.

Burnt Clay. This has been used in Ceylon with very good results. It has for us the additional advantage of being very cheap and very easily procured in Soconusco.

Lime. This is to be used, spreading it over the ground, once every five years. A good mixture would be half a pound of lime to an almud [1] of pulp for every tree.

Guano. This manure was at first used in Ceylon unmixed with any other substance ; but, being very active, it should never be used alone. Guano acts quickly and produces a very good crop, but its good effects pass quickly, and trees manured with guano soon lose their productiveness, which can be restored only by manuring them with cow-dung. This effect of guano is more noticeable in light soils; in compact soil and applied in small quantities its effects are permanent. It is more prudent, however, never to use guano alone, but mixed in small quantities with other fertilizers. Guano has almost entirely ceased to be used in Ceylon, and has been replaced by bone-dust.

Mixtures of these Substances.—Mixtures of the various substances mentioned have been used as fertilizers. A good mixture is a layer of cow-dung, another of maná grass, and another of the pulp of the fruit of the coffee-tree, and so on alternatively, leaving them to be assimilated. To render this mixture more active, each layer may be sprinkled with sal ammonia, lime, and bone-dust.

At present, however, such fertilizers as are considered most suitable to the soil, without any mixture, are preferred in Ceylon.

b. Manner of Applying Fertilizers to the Soil.—The best way of using fertilizers is to dig a hole in the earth at least eighteen inches from the plant and place the fertilizer in it. Care must be taken, in digging the hole, not to injure the tap roots of the tree; the small

[1] Almud, dry measure :—0.86 of a peck.

lateral roots may be cut without injury to the plant, this operation serving rather to benefit it, as it is a species of pruning which causes the roots to grow with renewed vigor. The size of the holes will vary according to the fertilizer used. If the fertilizer be cattle-dung or coffee-pulp the hole is made three feet long, eighteen inches wide, and one foot deep. As concentrated fertilizers are stronger they do not require holes as large.

When the ground is level and the trees are planted at short distances apart and in straight furrows, a quadrangular excavation may be made for the fertilizer between every four trees. In hilly ground it is preferable to dig the hole above each tree, so that the fertilizer, washed down by the rains, may be retained by the roots of the trees. This manner of making the holes has, besides, the advantage that the fertilizer remains in the shade and under shelter of the foliage of the tree, with the result that it evaporates less quickly and does not cause weeds to grow which would absorb all the fertilizing matter before it could benefit the coffee plant, as might easily happen if the fertilizer were put in a place exposed to the sun.

When mixed manures are used a hole is made on the ground above each tree, at the distance already mentioned; it should be semi-circular in shape, and nine inches wide and six inches deep.

All the holes made for fertilizers are to be filled with the prunings, and any other vegetable substance which may be at hand, and covered with loose earth taken from the surface of the ground. The earth taken from the hole is to be spread wherever there are any uncovered roots, and should be well pressed down, to prevent the rains from washing it away.

Fertilizers should be mixed with dry earth before using them.

c. Period at which the Fertilizers should be Used.—The best time to manure the ground is during the wet season. The only fertilizer that should be used in the dry season is cow-dung, which may be used at any time.

The beneficial effects of manure lasts for three years, and consequently it will be necessary to use the manure only once in three years.

It is advisable to manure the plantation before it begins to decline, not only because this increases its productiveness, but also because the cost will then be less than when, the vitality of the ground being almost exhausted, it will be necessary to restore it almost entirely.

d. Cost of Fertilizers.—Mr. Sabonadière calculates the cost per year of manuring an acre of ground at from $15 to $50, according to the price of the substance used as manure and the quantity employed, which gives an average of $32.50 per acre, or $3.52½ per cord.

The cost of fertilizers in Soconusco would probably be much greater.

Under this head the following will be considered:

A.—Gathering the crop in Soconusco.

B.—Gathering the crop in Ceylon.

Each of these points will be considered separately.

A. Gathering the Crop in Soconusco.—In regard to the gathering of the crop in Soconusco and Guatemala the following points will be considered:

a.—Time at which the coffee-tree begins to bear fruit.

b.—Time during which the coffee-tree continues bearing fruit.

c.—Blossoming and fructification of the coffee-tree.

d.—Gathering the crop.

Each of these subjects will be considered separately.

a. Time at which the Coffee-Tree Begins to Bear Fruit.—The second year after its removal to the plantation the plant, providing it was of three or four crosses at the time of transplanting, will bear its first crop, called in Soconusco its trial crop, or first trial. In ground best suited to it and with careful cultivation, each tree will yield on an average four ounces. The following year, after transplanting, it gives its second crop, which as it is still small, as compared to those which it yields afterwards, is called in Soconusco its second trial. It may be considered that on an average, and under the conditions already mentioned, the yield of each tree will be one pound in its second trial. In the fourth year after transplantation it gives its best crop, which averages double that of the second crop, and in the succeeding years it will continue yielding good crops.

b. Time during which the Coffee-Tree Continues Bearing Fruit.—As the coffee plantations of Soconusco and Guatemala are of comparatively recent planting, the duration of the life of the coffee plant cannot yet be determined with exactness. Trees planted twenty-five or thirty years ago still preserve much of their vigor and luxuriance and yield good crops, although they have never been manured and hardly ever pruned. It has also been observed that trees planted in the high lands last much longer than those planted in the low lands.

Some planters are of opinion that the duration of the life of the coffee-tree depends on the shade which is given to it, and that when it is exposed to the sun it will live a shorter time than when protected by shade. In this regard what I have already pointed out is the case; that is, that a coffee plantation in low land, with shade, gives about the same yield as a plantation without shade on higher land or on land which has a lower temperature; and it is natural that it should last longer than a plantation planted in low land and also exposed to the sun.

c. Blossoming and Fructification of the Coffee-Tree.—In the month of January, in the low, and in March in the high lands, green buds appear on the branches of the coffee-tree which afterwards become white flowers, and later on fruit. At first the fruit is small and of a dark green color; as time passes it grows larger, and when it begins to ripen its color changes to a light green which, later, becomes whitish, then yellowish, and then red, of a light shade at first, and afterwards of a very deep shade. When the fruit is of this last color it is entirely ripe. If not picked at this stage the fruit drops from the tree like any other ripe fruit.

The time of the ripening of the fruit differs in the high and in the low lands, as has just been stated, as the power of the sun shortens considerably, in the latter, the operations of vegetation. While in plantations situated in low localities the fruit begins to ripen in September, and is all ripe in October, in lands situated three thousand or four thousand feet above the level of the sea, the fruit begins to ripen in November and continues to ripen gradually. In December not a single ripe fruit is to be found in plantations situated in the low lands, while in those situated in the high lands ripe fruit is still to be found in February and even in March.

It sometimes happens that in plantations situated as high as four thousand feet above the level of the sea ripe fruit is to be found on the trees all the year round.

This is another advantage of plantations situated in high lands, for when all the fruit ripens in the course of two or three weeks, as happens in the low lands, there is danger of losing a considerable part of the crop for want of hands—which are sometimes very difficult to procure, a danger which is greatly lessened or which does not exist at all when the picking of the fruit may be done during three months, instead of three weeks.

d. Gathering the Crop.—When the fruit is ripe it is to be picked by hand, and with the greatest care, in order not to pick the fruit near by which may not be quite ripe, or injure the branch on which it hangs.

When the trees are very tall, from not having been topped, it will be necessary to use ladders in picking the fruit.

In very large plantations it is necessary to construct cart roads to facilitate the transportation of the fruit to the place where it is to be prepared for market.

Women and children perform the labor of picking the fruit better than men.

The price paid for each measure of fruit picked varies in different localities, being higher, of course, where labor is scarce.

When the coffee-tree is not pruned it grows very tall. I have seen trees seventeen or eighteen feet high, with a radius, at the widest part of the top, of as many as twelve feet, the trunks of some of the largest being as much as five inches in diameter. In such cases the picking of the fruit is more difficult and costly.

The trees are at times so heavily laden with fruit that the branches break down under its weight. To prevent this it is necessary to support them with props.

B. Gathering the Crop in Ceylon.—To each laborer two sacks are given, a small one, which he fastens round his waist, and a large one, which he hangs somewhere near at hand. The first is to hold the fruit as it is picked from the tree, and the second to receive the contents of the first, every time it has been filled.

The trees are divided into rows and one or two rows are assigned to each laborer; so that he does not pick all the fruit of each tree, but only the fruit that is on his side of the tree.

In very hilly ground it is expedient to begin picking the fruit at the most elevated part of the plantation. The reason for this is that the fruit which falls can be more easily picked up, and that it is easier for the pickers to descend with their loads than to ascend with them.

An overseer is set over the pickers so that they may neither leave fruit that is ripe on the trees nor pick unripe fruit.

Care must be taken not to pluck the branch with the fruit from the tree.

A metal check is given to the pickers for each basket which they deliver, and on pay day they are paid according to the number of these checks which they return. This is done in Guatemala also.

The scarcity of hands and the importance of not losing the crop have suggested to the planters of Ceylon an easy manner of conveying the coffee from the trees to the place where it is to be prepared for the market. This consists in placing a galvanized-iron pipe where a stream of water may pass through it to the pulper, carrying the coffee with it. Mr. Sabonadière estimates the cost of such a pipe at from $1250 to $1500 per mile.

The fruit is received in a box of a certain measure, which is so placed that when it is full it can be easily emptied into the tank from which it is conveyed to the pulper. In this way the quantity of fruit received is known.

9. PREPARATION OF THE COFFEE FOR THE MARKET.

Under this head the following subjects will be considered:

A.—Preparation of coffee in Soconusco.

B.—Improvement in the preparation of coffee in Soconusco.

C.—Preparation of coffee in Ceylon.

Each of these points will be considered separately and as briefly as possible.

A. Preparation of Coffee in Soconusco.—Of all the operations relating to coffee the one which in my judgment is least advanced in Guatemala is its preparation for the market. There are not more than four or five estates where the preparation of the fruit is systematically performed and with an adequate saving of time, labor, and money.

I have not seen any estate in which all the operations of preparing the coffee are performed by machinery, that is, in which the ripe fruit is thrown into a general receptacle, from which it passes to others until it comes out sorted and graded, without the intervention of the hand of man, as is the case with wheat and flour, in the flour mills. There are estates, however, in which the operations of preparing the coffee are greatly simplified, the same water-power being used for all of them.

All the operations described below are employed in Guatemala; for in Soconusco not even the most necessary machines are used. So far the estate of El Malacate only has an iron pulper, a wooden retrilla, and a fan. The coffee is generally pulped on grinding stones and bruised in wooden mortars.

The preparation of coffee for the market includes the following operations:

a.—Pulping.
b.—Washing.
c.—Separating the good coffee from the bad.
d.—Exposure to the sun.
e.—Shelling.
f.—Dyeing.
g.—Winnowing.
h.—Sorting the coffee.

Each of these different operations will be treated of separately.

a. Pulping.—The coffee, when it arrives at the place where it is to be prepared for the market, is deposited in a tank full of water, which has a pipe leading to the pulper, into which the water, passing through the pipe, gradually carries it. As a general rule these machines are made of cast iron, and are almost everywhere hand motors, although they might easily be moved by the water used on the plantation.

The pulping machine removes the outer skin from the coffee and separates the two beans which each fruit as a general rule contains, with the exception of the kind called the pea berry, which has a single bean of an elliptical shape. The hull, or pulp, as it was called when treating of fertilizers, is thrown away, when it might be employed with advantage in manuring the ground.

Pulping machines have been in use since the time of Laborie, that is, some eighty years, although they were then constructed of wood; those now in use have not changed essentially in principle.

Mr. Sabonadière mentions the pulping machines which have exclusive privilege in England ; these are the Butler, Wall, Walker, and Gordon machines. The last is the only one I have seen used in Guatemala. Mr. Sabonadière prefers the first.

b. Washing.—The coffee beans, now skinned and separated, when they leave the pulping machine fall into another tank full of water, in which they remain twenty-four hours, in order that they may be freed from a sweet mucilaginous substance of a light color which is found between the skin and the shell of the beans. With this object they are stirred about with a wooden shovel just before being removed from the tank.

c. Separating the Good Coffee from the Bad.—The perfect beans possess a higher specific gravity than water and sink in it; those which float are of poor quality and constitute what is called waste coffee, or coffee of the lowest grade.

In order to facilitate the separation of the perfect from the imperfect beans, a part of the principal tank is divided off, forming a second tank, smaller and lower than the first, so that the imperfect beans may be carried easily into it by the water or by the hand. It is better to construct the dividing wall of the two tanks of the same height as the others, and provide it with a small sluice, which, when opened, will establish a current that will carry the imperfect beans from the larger into the smaller tank. When the beans are thus separated, the process of preparing them for the market is conducted separately.

d. Exposure to the Sun.—When the beans have been pulped and washed they must be thoroughly dried, and this is effected by the action of the sun, which makes this process an exceedingly slow and costly one. A sort of threshing-floor is constructed which is paved with stone and mortar, and on this the coffee is exposed to the sun. The coffee must be taken in every day at sunset, or before, if the sky looks threatening, so that it may not be exposed to the rain or dew. In some estates the coffee is merely heaped up in a corner of the yard and covered with leaves or mats; but in such case it runs the risk of being stolen; and, besides, when the coffee is piled up there is danger of its fermenting, which would injure its quality. The coffee must also be constantly moved about while it is in the yard, in order that the sun may have access to every part of it and not to that only which is on top.

These operations, which are very tedious when the quantity of coffee to be dried is considerable, have to be continued for at least fifteen days, if the weather is fine, to dry the coffee thoroughly. If it is stored before it is perfectly dry, it may rot or at least become discolored, and lose greatly both in quality and price.

When the weather is cloudy or rainy, which often happens in mountainous lands situated at three thousand or four thousand feet above the level of the sea, where the sun is visible only for six or eight hours daily, the operation of drying the coffee is a much slower, and consequently a much more expensive one.

There is no operation in the preparation of coffee which may be so easily simplified as that of drying, performing it by means of artificial heat. Stoves for this purpose have been already invented in Guatemala, but thus far they have not given entirely satisfactory results. I believe, however, that the day is not far distant when some speedy, cheap, and efficacious means of drying coffee, other than the primitive one of exposing it to the sun's rays, will be discovered.

e. Shelling.—After the coffee has been pulped, washed, and dried, there is still another strong covering to be removed from it before it is ready for the market.

The alternate moisture and heat to which this covering is exposed during the operation of washing and drying the bean, causes it to contract and expand greatly, with the result that it becomes loosened from the bean and in many cases breaks, this greatly facilitating its removal.

Various instruments have been employed to facilitate this operation, but the one which has thus far given the best results is the " retrilla." This consists of one or two solid wheels of heavy wood, of from one and a half to two yards in diameter, and from eight to nine inches thick, set vertically, which are made to revolve over a species of circular box lined with wood, and are generally moved by oxen. In some plantations I have seen iron " retrillas," made in England, on the same model as the wooden ones, and moved by water.

The coffee in the husk is put into the box, and the wheel by its weight and its movement removes the coriaceous covering from the bean without breaking it, and loosens another thinner inner covering which resembles the filmy-like skin of an onion. Combined with the wheel is a sort of shovel which serves to move the coffee about.

f. Dyeing.—A bluish color in coffee, being highly esteemed in foreign markets, is given to it artificially on some estates by covering the surface of the wheels which hull the coffee with sheets of lead, which give it the desired color. If the demands of commerce render this color indispensable, some other substance might be employed to give it, which is free from the hygienic objections of lead.

g. Winnowing.—The coffee beans leave the machine mixed with the two coverings above mentioned. To separate them from these the fanner is used, and performs the operation quickly and efficaciously. Some fanners have the additional advantage of sorting the coffee, an operation which will now be described.

h. Sorting the Coffee.—The coffee being now perfectly clean must next be sorted, as the beans differ in size, shape, and color, and some are broken and others whole. As the different kinds of coffee differ greatly in price, it must be sent to market already classified, to obtain the highest price.   Hence the necessity of sorting it.

This operation is performed almost everywhere by hand; but I have seen on some estates separating machines, which consist of various cylinders having holes of different sizes, through which the different kinds of coffee run out, similar, in principle, to the separators of flour in flour mills.   Even when separating machines are employed, however, it will still be necessary to separate by hand the coffee beans of different colors, but there will now be very few of these.

American fanners are also employed, as has been said, in sorting the coffee.

In those estates in which this operation is performed with most care, the coffee is separated into five classes, as follows:

1st. Pea berry, which is considered the best.

2d. First-class, which includes the largest beans, all being of the same size and color.

3d. Second-class, including medium-sized beans.

4th. Third-class, including the smallest beans.

5th. Waste coffee, including beans of a bad color, broken beans, those that floated on the water and all those that cannot be included in any of the preceding classes.

When the operations mentioned have been all performed the coffee may be said to be ready for the market.

B. Improvement in the Preparation of Coffee in Soconusco.—In my opinion, the superior excellence of the Colima coffee, as compared with that grown in Soconusco, consists chiefly in the manner of its preparation.

In Colima the coffee is not first washed, as in Soconusco, thus removing the mucilaginous part of which mention has been made, but is allowed to dry with this substance on it.   Thus the coffee absorbs a considerable part of the substance contained in the mucilage, which improves its aroma and its quality, while the advantages of said substance are entirely lost when the beans are first washed and thus deprived of it.

I believe, therefore, that the quality of Soconusco coffee would be greatly improved by following in its preparation the system followed in Colima, and probably in other places; that is, to allow the coffee beans to absorb, when drying, the saccharine substance which is found between them and their inner covering or shell.

C. Preparation of Coffee in Ceylon.—In the estates of Ceylon coffee is prepared for market in the same manner as in Soconusco, until it remains in the hull; it is then sent to the port of Colombo, where it receives the final preparation.

This is performed in the following manner: When the coffee is ripe, the sooner it is pulped the better, as, if this operation is delayed, the coffee becomes heated, which injures the color of the shell. In very dry weather it is sometimes necessary to sprinkle the coffee lightly with water a few hours before pulping it, as, if it were pulped dry the beans would break and the coffee lose in quality.

The pulping machines are moved in Ceylon by steam.

When the coffee leaves the pulping machine, it passes into large tanks paved and walled with stone, where it is kept until the mucilage remaining on it has fermented sufficiently. The time which it should remain in the tanks depends on the elevation of the plantation above the level of the sea, and the state of the temperature. At an altitude of three thousand feet, the coffee should be kept in the tanks for two days.

The receiving tanks have an opening at the bottom to allow the water to run out, in addition to the sluice through which the coffee passes from the receiving tank into the tank in which it is to be washed. When it is ready to be washed, the water is allowed to run into the receiving tank; the coffee is moved about with long-handled wooden shovels, two feet in length and nine inches in width, until there is sufficient water in the contiguous tank. When the coffee has passed into this tank the water is to be changed several times until the mucilaginous part is entirely removed and the parchment-like hull is of a yellowish-white color.

The tank in which the coffee is washed should be slightly inclined, so that the lighter beans and the husks may be carried to the lower end, where they are collected by means of sieves or baskets. The beans that float are allowed to pass into another lower tank, where all the coffee of inferior quality is collected.

After it has been washed, the coffee in the hull is heaped up on an inclined platform, to allow the water to run off, remaining there until the following morning, or longer, if the weather is wet. If the weather continues wet, the coffee is carried to the storehouse and spread on mats, spreading it out as much as the space will permit, so that the air may dry it. When the wet weather continues long and the storehouses are full, the coffee is allowed to remain on mats, fires being made to dry the air. The coffee is to be moved about continually, in order that it may not become heated; and it should even be sprinkled with water daily. When the wet weather continues very long, there is danger of the coffee being spoiled by becoming heated and germinating.

When the weather is dry and the sun hot, two days will be sufficient to prepare the coffee for sending it to the port of Colombo. When the coffee has been well washed and thoroughly dried immediately after being washed, it is of a light color and very lustrous.

Coffee of inferior quality and waste coffee are dried apart.

When the coffee is perfectly clean the bean assumes a bluish color which afterwards changes to a grayish green.

The final operations of preparing the coffee for market are performed in Colombo, and consist in drying the bean until it becomes very hard, removing from it the parchment-like hull and the pellicle underneath, cleansing it by means of a fanner, sorting the beans according to size and shape, and removing by hand black or broken beans.

The grades of Ceylon coffee are No. 1, No. 2, pea-berry and waste coffee.

Ceylon coffee is sent to market in casks or barrels. The coffee of Soconusco and Guatemala is sent to market in bags.

VI.

PROFITS OF COFFEE CULTURE.

The best manner of showing the profits of coffee culture is to make an approximate estimate of the cost and of the product of a plantation of a given size. Such an estimate, however carefully made, cannot be altogether exact, and at most can only be considered as approximate. It frequently happens, that in the same place and with the same system of cultivation, one planter, because of his greater diligence and aptitude, will raise a crop with much less cost than another. This will be the case with still greater reason when different localities are in question. It frequently happens, also, that unforeseen circumstances will render necessary fresh expenses, which were not calculated upon at first. It is to be observed, too, that even in Soconusco it is remarked that year after year there is an increase in the price of provisions and of the necessaries of life, which will of necessity increase the cost of labor, as well as the other expenses of the plantation. An estimate which, made now, might be approximate, within a year or two would be too low.

The cost, productiveness, and profit of a coffee plantation, in different localities, in order to form a more correct estimate, will now be considered.

1. Cost, productiveness, and net profits of a plantation in Soconusco.

2. Cost, productiveness, and profits of coffee in Barcenas plantation.

3. Cost and productiveness of a coffee plantation in Ceylon.

Each of these subjects will be separately considered.

1. COST, PRODUCTIVENESS, AND NET PROFITS OF COFFEE IN SOCONUSCO.

To proceed in regular order the following subjects will now be considered:

A.—Cost of a plantation in Soconusco.

B.—Productiveness of a plantation in Soconusco.

C.—Profits of coffee in Soconusco.

Each of these points will be considered separately.

A. Cost of a Plantation in Soconusco.—The probable cost of a coffee plantation in Soconusco of, say, one thousand cuerdas, using the utmost diligence and economy, would be as follows, calculated year by year in order to make the calculation with greater facility and exactness:

a.—Value of the ground.

b.—Expenses of the first year.

c.—Expenses of the second year.

d.—Expenses of the third year.

e.—Expenses of the fourth year.

f.—Résumé of expenses.

The expenses of each year will be separately considered.

a. Value of the Ground.—In speaking of the value of the uncultivated lands of Soconusco, it was mentioned that the price of those of Chiapas, according to the tariff of the present biennial,[1] is 25 cents per hectare, or $10.69 per caballeria, and that if two or three caballerias were purchased, the cost would not be more than double that sum. To form a coffee plantation of 1000 cuerdas, two caballerias would be required, to allow ground for the fodder of the animals and other uses ; roads, buildings, patiss, etc. To make an estimate which is rather above than below the cost, the caballerias may be put at a maximum of $50 ; the two caballerias consequently costing $100.

b. Expenses of the First Year.—In the first year the following will be expended in forming the nursery :

Preparation of the Ground.—Three day's labor, one in stubbing, another in hewing, and the third in chopping, for each cuerda, at 25 cents per day's labor, make 75 cents per cuerda. To plant 1000 cuerdas of coffee a nursery of 30 cuerdas will be required, which will cost............ $ 22 50

Seed.—By planting the nursery with seeds much of the cost of buying and transporting coffee plants would be saved, but supposing that the nursery be formed of plants, 175,000 plants, at $2 per thousand, will cost 350 00

Transportation, Planting, and Weeding.—Transporting the plants to the place where the nursery is made, planting them, and eight weedings per year, at $5 per cuerda, will cost for 30 cuerdas................. 150 00

Other Expenses.—Cost of the houses for the laborers, salary of the superintendent, purchase of implements, payment of taxes, expenses of roads, losses in money advanced to laborers, and other incidental expenses, in the first year........... .... 500 00

Total expenses in the first year......................... $1,022 50

[1] The Fomento Department of Mexico publishes every two years a schedule of prices at which public lands are sold, varying in each State.

c. Expenses of the Second Year.—In the second year the young trees are permanently planted, and the following expenses will be incurred :

Preparing the Ground.—Clearing of 1200 cuerdas, as in order to plant 1000 cuerdas, it will be necessary to prepare 1200, to allow for what is lost in roads, houses, and other uses, at 50 cents per cuerda for stubbing and hewing... $ 600 00

Staking.—Planting 104,000 stakes, to plant the same number of coffee trees in 1000 cuerdas of ground, at the rate of 750 stakes for 25 cents.   34 67

Drilling Holes.—Drilling 104,000 holes, at 250 holes for 25 cents........   104 00

Transplanting.—Planting 104,000 trees, at 50 trees for 25 cents........   520 00

Weeding.—Two weedings, the second year, of 1000 cuerdas, at 25 cents per cuerda. Each weeding will cost.................... $250 00
and the two weedings will cost..................................   500 00

Other Expenses.—Repairing and construction of houses, superintendent's salary, purchase of implements, nursery, payment of taxes, roads, laborer's debts, lost debts of runaway laborers, etc.................   650 00

Total expenses for the second year...................... $2,408 67

d. Expenses for the Third Year.—In the third year the expenses of the plantation will be the following :

Weedings.—Four weedings of 1000 cuerdas, at $250 each weeding, will amount in the year to... $1,000 00

Threshing floors.—Construction of 500 square yards of drying floor, at $1.25 the square yard..   625 00

Pulper.—A pulping machine, cost of transportation and of a building in which to set it up...   400 00

Retrilla.—Construction of a retrilla and building for it.................   250 00

Fanner.—Purchase of a fanner.....................................   80 00

Oxen.—Two yoke of oxen to work the retrilla, at $50 each..............   100 00

Picking the Fruit.—Picking the fruit of the first, or trial crop..........   300 00

Other Expenses.—Construction and repairing of houses, superintendent's salary, purchase of implements, nurseries, taxes, roads, debts of laborers in service, bad debts of runaway laborers, etc., etc..............   650 00

Total expenses for the third year........................ $3,405 00

e. Expenses for the Fourth Year.—The expenses for the fourth year will be :

Weedings.—Four weedings, at $250 each $1,000 00

Threshing floors.—1500 square yards of drying floor, at $1.25 per yard...   1,875 00

Machinery.—Fixing the machinery and construction of other buildings...   300 00

Picking the Fruit.—Expenses of gathering the fruit of the second crop...   800 00

Other Expenses.—Expenses for employés, roads, implements, nursery, taxes, debts of laborers in service, bad debts of runaway laborers, etc.   750 00

Total expenses for the fourth year...................... $4,725 00

f. Résumé of Expenses.—The total amount of the expenses incurred in a plantation of 1000 cuerdas in four years is, then, the following :

Value of the ground........ ....$　　100 00
Expenses for the first year..................................　1,022 50
"　　"　" second　"　................................　2,408 67
"　　·　"　third　"　................................　3,405 00
"　　"　" fourth　"　................................　4,725 00

Total expenses for four years...........................　$11,661 17

The total outlay on each cuerda planted with coffee, including buildings, machinery, etc., will therefore be $11.66, and that of each tree, a little more than 11 cents.

B. Productiveness of a Plantation in Soconusco.—The following is an approximate estimate of the yield of a plantation of 1000 cuerdas in Soconusco :

In the third year each plant will yield four ounces of coffee, 104,000 plants will yield 26,000 lbs., which, at a minimum price of 10 cents per lb., will be.. $2,600 00
In the fourth year the yield will be 1 lb. per tree, or 104,000 lbs., which, at 10 cents per lb., are.. 10,400 00

Total yield in the first two years of bearing.............. $13,000 00

That is, $13 per cuerda, or 12½ cents per tree.

C. Profits of Coffee in Soconusco.—

As we have just seen, the yield of a plantation of 1000 cuerdas in the third and fourth years after planting is.............. .... $13,000 00
The total outlay during the four years has been........................ 11,661 17

There remains, then, after the fourth year a net profit of............... $1,338 83

This profit is more or less the equivalent of the interest of the capital invested until the plantation begins to produce fruit ; that is to say, that in four years the capital and its interest are repaid.

The fifth year after the coffee has been planted, or the third year after it has commenced to produce, and in the succeeding years, the yield will be 2 lbs. per tree, or 208,000 lbs., which, at 10 cents per lb., will give... $20,800 00
Deducting the expenses of cultivation, preparing the coffee for the market and improvements during the year, estimated at a maximum of $5 per cuerda, on 1000 cuerdas we have............................... 5,000 00

Net profit of the fifth year and of each year thereafter................. $15,800 00

There is, then, in the fifth year, and in every year thereafter, a profit of 135.49 per cent. on the capital invested during the four first years, which, with its interest, has been already repaid.

Each cuerda will give $15.80 per year, and each tree a little more than 15 cents.

In addition to which, the planter has in his favor the advantage of a possible rise in prices—the price being last year as much as $10 per quintal for coffee on the plantation.

2. COST, PRODUCTIVENESS, AND PROFITS OF COFFEE IN BARCENAS PLANTATION.

Persons who have had experience in coffee culture consider that the foregoing calculations are not exaggerated. Nevertheless, in order to rectify them by presenting, not calculations which may give more or less probable results, but data taken from one of the best managed coffee plantations, situated between the cities of Antigua and Guatemala, belonging to Mr. José Maria Samayoa, I give below the separate items furnished me by its very able manager. The items refer to culture by manzana, which is a lot of land having a square area of 100 varas per side, or an area of 10,000 square varas, that is, 16 cuerdas.

I will divide this subject as follows:

A. Cost of coffee culture in Barcenas.

B. Productiveness of coffee in Barcenas.

C. Profit of coffee in Barcenas.

The three points shall be especially considered.

A. Cost of Coffee in Barcenas.—Each manzana of coffee costs at Barcenas, every four years, as follows:

Nursery and Seeds.—A manzana can contain 1666 trees planted at 2 varas distance from each other, there being three between furrows; the cost will be $12 per thousand plants, and the 1666 trees will cost,........	$20 00
Stakes and Holes.—1666 stakes, and the same number of holes at the rate of $3 per thousand.. ...	5 00
Preparation of the Ground.—Per each manzana.......................	10 00
Transplanting.—1666 trees at $2.50 per thousand.....................	4 17
Weedings.—Three with plow, the first year, after planting, at $1 per manzana...	3 00
Three during the second year, and three during the third year with spade, at $2 each weeding	12 00
Four weedings in the fourth year with spade, at $3 each weeding....	12 00
Other Expenses.—Fencing, etc., in two years, at $1 per year...........	2 00
Total cost...	$68 17

B. Productiveness of Coffee in Barcenas.—A manzana of coffee in Barcenas yields as follows:

The third year after planting the coffee tree, a crop is obtained yielding 3 ounces per tree, or say 312½ pounds, which, at 10 cents per pound, gives	$31 23
In the fourth year after planting, the crop amounts to one pound per tree, or 1666 pounds, which, at 10 cents per pound, gives...............	166 60
Total proceeds.......................................	$197 83

C. *Profits of Coffee Culture in Barcenas.*—

The proceeds from a manzana of coffee at Barcenas is..................	$197 83
The cost of each manzana is..	68 17
There remains a net yearly profit per manzana of..........	$129 66

According to the above data, a cuerda of coffee costs $4.26, and each tree yields a little more than 4 cents, and the proceeds per cuerda are $12.36, and per tree a little less than 12 cents.

One must consider the fact that in the above data no notice has been taken of the cost of buildings, machinery, clerks, preparing the coffee for the market, taking up of the crop, debts of the laborers while on the plantation, and of the runaways and other items comprised in the calculations made above regarding the cost of coffee in Soconusco.

3. COST AND PROFIT OF COFFEE IN CEYLON.

The preceding estimates, made before seeing Mr. Sabonadière's book, are, I think, fully corroborated by the estimate which that writer gives of the cost and profit of 200 acres of ground planted with coffee in Ceylon.

I insert below Mr. Sarbonadière's estimate, taken from his *Coffee Planter of Ceylon* (2d edition, London, 1870), and without further alteration than that of the reduction to dollars and cents of the sums which he puts in pounds sterling, making this reduction on the basis of five dollars to the pound.

Estimated expenditure to plant 200 acres of land with coffee and bring it into bearing :

FIRST YEAR—SEPTEMBER, 1865.

Purchase of 300 acres (2,766 cuerdas) of land at $5 per acre.	$1,500 00	
Survey fees...	205 00	$1,705 00
Nursery or purchase of plants...............		250 00

JANUARY, 1866.

Salary of European Superintendent for one year...........	$600 00	
Allowances...	200 00	
Native Overseer....................	250 00	1,050 00

MARCH TO DECEMBER 31, 1866.

Felling, lopping, and clearing up of 100 acres (922 cuerdas), at $12.50 per acre.................................		1,250 00
Drilling holes in 100 acres, at $6.25 per acre..............	$625 00	
Staking 100 acres at $1.75 per acre......................	175 00	
Planting 100 acres, at $2.25 per acre.....................	225 00	
Filling in holes at $2.25 per acre	225 00	1,250 00
One mile of cart roads.......................	$250 00	
Two miles path, at $75 per mile........................	150 00	400 00
Carried forward....................................		$5,905 00

Brought forward......................................		$5,905 00
Draining 100 acres, at $3.75 per acre.....................		375 00
Weeding to December, ten months, at $4.42⅔ per acre per year		369 00
Permanent Buildings.—Superintendent's House...........	$1,500 00	
Overseer's House................................	300 00	
Stone pillar and shingle houses, 60 by 20, for the laborers...	500 00	
Rice and tool store....................................	125 00	2,425 00
General expenses of transportation........................		180 00
Tools and portable machinery.............................		250 00
Contingent expenses....................................		250 00
Losses in rice..		250 00
Medicines and medical attendance.......................		75 00
		$10,079 00
Loss by exchange on $10,000 at 6 per cent................		600 00
Expenses of the first year............................		$10,679 00

SECOND YEAR—JANUARY TO DECEMBER, 1867.

European Superintendent................................	$750 00	
Native Superintendent..................................	250 00	
Allowances..	180 00	$1,180 00
Felling, lopping, burning, and clearing up of 100 acres at		
$12.50 per acre....................................	$1,250 00	
Holing, staking, and planting of 100 acres, at $12.50 per acre	1,250 00	2,500 00
One mile of road................................... ...	$250 00	
Two miles of path....................................	150 00	400 00
Draining 100 acres at $3.75 per acre, per year		375 00
Weeding of the same for the same time...................	$600 00	
Weeding of 100 acres at 41 cents per month per acre, for		
nine months...	369 00	969 00
Permanent Buildings.—Houses for the laborers, 16 by 20 feet		500 00
General transportation.................................	$250 00	
Tools and portable machinery............................	150 00	
General contingencies..................................	250 00	
Loss by rice..........................	250 00	
Medicines and medical attendance..........	75 00	975 00
		$6,899 00
Loss by exchange on $6,500 at 6 per cent..................		390 00
Expenses of the second year........................		$7,289 00

THIRD YEAR—JANUARY TO DECEMBER, 1868.

European Superintendent..............................	$1,000 00	
Native Superintendent................................	300 00	
Allowances..	180 00	$1,480 00
Topping and pruning....................................	$125 00	
Supplying failures.....................................	125 00	250 00
Carried forward..................................		$1,730 00

Brought forward...................................		$1,730 00
One mile of cart road................................	$250 00	
One mile of path....................................	75 00	
Repairing of roads and drains........................	200 00	525 00
Weeding 200 acres for twelve months at 50 cents per month		
per acre......................................		1,200 00
Permanent Buildings.—Store, 120 by 30 feet, three floors,		
iron roof and stone pillars......................	$5,000 00	
Pulping house, water wheel, and machinery	2,500 00	
Iron pipes for conveying the coffee to the pulper.......	1,250 00	
House for laborers, 60 by 20 feet....................	500 00	9,250 00
Crop Expenses.—Picking, pulping, and curing 400 cwt. at $1.50		
per cwt.......................................	600 00	
Transportation of 1900 bushels parchment to Colombo at		
31¼ cents..	593 75	
Cost in Colombo of curing 400 cwt. at $1.12½ per cwt...	450 00	
Export duty on 400 cwt., at 25 cts. per cwt............	100 00	
		1,743 75
General transportation.............................	375 00	
Purchase of tools..................................	150 00	
General contingencies..............................	375 00	
Loss by rice.......................................	375 00	
Medicines and medical attendance..................	100 00	1,375 00
		$15,823 75
Loss by exchange on $15,000, at 6 per cent............		930 00
Expenses of the third year.....................		$16,753 75

RECAPITULATION.

First year's expenditure........... ....$10,679 00	
Second year's expenditure............................ 7,289 00	
Third year's expenditure............................ 16,753 75	
Total expenditure........................... $34,721 75	
Less value of 400 cwt. of coffee in the London market,	
at $16.75 net per cwt............................. 6,700 00	
Estate Dr. Jan. 1, 1869........................$28,021 75	

Comparing the expenses and the yield of coffee in Ceylon, according to the data supplied by the preceding estimate, with the expenses and the yield of coffee in Soconusco, the total expenses are found to be greater in Ceylon than in Soconusco, notwithstanding the fact that some of the processes of cultivating and preparing the coffee for market cost less there than in Soconusco; while the yield is much smaller in Ceylon than in Soconusco.

Two hundred acres are equivalent to 1,844 cuerdas. Calculating that in each acre there are planted 1200 trees, at a distance of six feet apart, the usual distance in Ceylon, we shall have 240,000 trees, which will give 130¼ trees to each cuerda.

According to Mr. Sabonadière's esitmate, each acre of ground planted with coffee costs, up to the time of bearing, $173.61, which is equivalent to $18.83 per cuerda, or 14¼ cents per tree, while in Soconusco each acre costs $107.50, each cuerda $11.66, and each tree 11 cents.

The causes of the greater cost of coffee cultivation in Ceylon than in Soconusco and Guatemala, are chiefly the following:

1. Higher price of the land, which is estimated in Ceylon at $5 per acre, or $528.77 per caballeria, without the cost of survey, while I have estimated it in Soconusco at $50 a caballeria.

2. The greater cost of the buildings, which in Ceylon are constructed of stone and mortar, with a roof of galvanized iron, and without regard to economy, as their value alone represents almost a third of the total cost of the estate, while in Soconusco they are made of pillars of unhewed logs, with a roof of straw, and at a very moderate cost. The cost of the buildings in Ceylon, according to the preceding estimate, is $10,925, while in Soconusco it does not reach $1,000.

3. The greater number of operations required on a coffee plantation in Ceylon, such as draining, and topping, and pruning the trees.

4. The cost of roads, the cost of the pipes to carry the coffee from the plantation to the pulping house, the loss on exchange in London and the loss by rice, expenses which are either not incurred in Soconusco or are very slight. The cost of roads in Ceylon is $1,325, that of iron pipes $1,250, that of exchange on London $1,920, and the loss by rice $875, making a total of $5,660.

The items which cost less in Ceylon than in Soconusco are the following :

Machinery and implements, for reasons which will be readily understood, cost more in Soconusco than in Ceylon. The same is the case with weeding; the reason of this is, perhaps, that the soil in Soconusco, being more fertile than that of Ceylon, produces more weeds, and vegetation is more luxuriant in the former than in the latter.

A day's wages in Ceylon is seventeen cents (8 pence), but, taking into account the losses by rice, which is sometimes bought at a high price and sold at a low price to the laborers, wages may be estimated at twenty cents per day. The task given to each laborer as a day's work in Ceylon is not mentioned, however, and perhaps this makes up for the difference in wages.

The following table will give an idea of the difference, in the cost of cultivating coffee, between Soconusco and Ceylon.

	IN SOCONUSCO.	IN CEYLON.
Land, two caballerias.............	$100 00	$1,057 54
Manager and overseer for three years..................	1,080 00	3,710 00
Nursery....	522 50	250 00
Clearing the ground, one cuerda.....................	50	1 35½
Staking " "	04	19

	IN SOCONUSCO.	IN CEYLON.
Holing the ground, one cuerda.........................	12	67¼
Transplanting one cuerda.............................	$ 52	$ 49
Weedings, per year.................................	1 00	54
Gathering the crop and preparing it for market per cwt...	2 25	4 11
Medicine and medical attendance for three years.........		250 00
Freight..	150 00	805 00
Implements and machinery, two years.................	950 00	400 00
General contingencies	350 00	875 00
Drainage, per cuerda, two years......................		61 00

Mr. Sabonadière estimates the yield of 200 acres of land at 800 cwt., or 88,270 Mexican lbs., which gives a yield of 441.35 lbs. per acre, or about 48 lbs. per cuerda, or .358 of a pound, which is $5\frac{1}{16}$ oz. per tree.

The yield of a coffee plantation in Soconusco is $1,917\frac{1}{2}$ lbs. per acre, 208 lbs. per cuerda, and 2 lbs. per tree, as has been already stated. Notwithstanding that there are in Soconusco a smaller number of trees in each cuerda, the yield is more than four times greater per cuerda, for while each tree yields in Soconusco 2 lbs. of coffee in the year, in Ceylon it yields only $5\frac{1}{16}$ oz.

But notwithstanding the greater expense of coffee cultivation in Ceylon, as compared with Soconusco, it is still a profitable industry there, for the estimate made by Mr. Sabonadière shows that a plantation of 300 acres of land, of which 200 are planted with coffee, and the total cost of which has been $34,728.75, will at the end of seven years have paid off this sum by its produce, the estate being left free and representing a capital of from $60,000 to $70,000.

VII.

CONCLUSION.

I have endeavored to carry out, to the best of my ability, the object I had in view, in writing this work, that is, to facilitate and extend coffee cultivation in Mexico.

The facts which I have set down will, I believe, show that there are few enterprises that could be undertaken in our country with so much profit as the cultivation of coffee.

The coffee crop of Soconusco, last year (1873), did not reach, it is estimated, 1,500 quintals. The greater number of the plantations already formed, are situated in the low lands, which, as I have already said, are the least suitable for this crop. There seems to be a growing disposition, however, to plant coffee, and new plantations are being formed in the high lands. Persons have even come from other parts to plant coffee in Soconusco. Its production will consequently increase considerably within a very short time.

I have no data on which to base an estimate of the quantity of coffee produced in the other parts of the republic, where this crop is raised; but I imagine that the annual production, in the entire country, is about 100,000 quintals—which is little enough—the greater part of this being raised on the coast of Veracruz. Guatemala alone produces more than 200,000 quintals; and Costa Rica, whose population does not reach 200,000, very nearly 300,000 quintals.

Mexico possesses extensive lands suitable for coffee, which are now uncultivated, and which will make the fortunes of those who shall cultivate them, contributing at the same time to augment the national wealth. The day in which the cultivation of coffee assumes important proportions in Mexico there will be opened up for the country a new source of wealth, of agricultural industry, which will greatly increase its exports, and, as a consequence, its imports, its commercial activity, and even the national revenues, while enriching the planters.

I earnestly hope that this little work may contribute, in some degree, to the realization of these results.

M. ROMERO.

TAPACHULA, *July 18, 1874*

APPENDIX.

In my book on the State of Oaxaca, I published some facts about the causes which affect the climate of that place which I intended to use when I could make a revised edition of my paper on Coffee. But as that is not possible, I think it would be prudent to insert here that memorandum which I think will be of some value to anyone attempting to go into coffee-planting.

The *India-Rubber World*, of New York, of August 15, 1893, published a letter of Mr. F. O. Harriman, Civil Engineer, dated at Jaltipan, in the State of Veracruz, recommending the lands of the Isthmus of Tehuantepec as very well suited for coffee and india-rubber culture. As I was afraid that Mr. Harriman's views were not well grounded, I wrote on September 25, 1893, a private letter to Mr. Hawthorne Hill, the editor of that paper, pointing out what I considered serious mistakes in Mr. Harriman's paper, so that he could correct them editorially if he thought proper to do so. Mr. Hill answered me that the best way to accomplish that end was to publish my letter, and requested my permission to do so, and thinking it might do good to discuss through the press the subject to which my letter referred, I consented to its publication, and it did appear in the issue of The *India-Rubber World* for October 15, 1893. Both Mr. Harriman, from Jaltipan, and his brother, Mr. J. P. Harriman, from Woonsocket, Rhode Island, answered my letter, and I had to write a rejoinder, which put an end to the controversy. In compliance with the intimation I made in the foot-note which appears on page 295 of the foregoing paper, I append the letters published on the subject.

CAUSES WHICH DETERMINE THE CLIMATE OF A LOCALITY.

The climate of any locality consists in the combination of its temperature with the humidity that prevails there. The sun is the source which sends forth heat to the surface of the earth ; when the sun is over the horizon of any locality, that locality receives heat, and when it is below the horizon, that same locality is losing heat through irradiation.

The division of the terrestial globe into five zones, the torrid, the two temperate, and the two frigid, merely gives a general idea of the average temperature of those portions of the earth, because the force of the sun's rays is modified by other diverse causes, which bring about the result that in the same latitude various kinds of temperature may exist.

In order to determine the climate of a locality, various circumstances must be taken into account, the principal ones being the following :

1. *Latitude.*—Generally, latitude determines the temperature of the locality, because the nearer it is to the equator the greater will be the amount of heat that it will receive, and such amount will diminish in proportion as the locality may be far away from the equatorial line. For that reason the line of perpetual snow is low as one approaches the poles ; at the equator it is about three miles, and at the poles it is at the level of the sea : at 20° of latitude it is about 14,000 English feet above the sea : within the tropics its altitude is from 15,000 to 20,000 feet above the sea ; at 30°, about 12,000 ; at 40°, about 10,000 : at 60°, about 4000 ; at 70°, about 2000 : and at 8°, is at sea level.

It is also to be noticed that the line of perpetual snow is higher between the 10° and 20° from the equator than at the equator itself ; this may probably be due to the fact that at the equator the sun only remains 12 hours above the horizon, while near the tropics the longest day is about 13½ hours, and as during that time the sun's rays fall vertically, or nearly so, the heat in summer is greater than on the equator.

2. *Altitude.*—Temperature becomes colder in proportion to the altitude of a place, and the influence of altitude is felt quicker than that of latitude. If we travel from the equator towards the poles along the sea-level, we have to go many kilometers before a change of temperature is noticeable, whilst as soon as we begin to ascend from the level of the sea, a very decided change of temperature is experienced. The ascent of 180 English feet merely, brings about the same change of temperature as travelling one whole degree of latitude, or say, 169¼ English miles, from the equator towards the poles. At an elevation of 15,000 English feet above the level of the sea, we reach perpetual snow in the equator, that being a climate which corresponds along the sea-level to 70° of latitude. For the first 1000 feet of elevation above the level of the sea the temperature descends more than 7°, and higher up about 1° for every 500 feet on an average, and it continues to descend less rapidly in proportion as the elevations become greater.

3. *Location of Mountain Chains.*—If the mountain chains are situated in the northern hemisphere, from east to west, the side that looks to the north is exposed to cold winds, and that looking to the south is sheltered from them, but has the southern winds ; the former, there-

fore, has to be colder than the latter.   That is the reason why Russian Poland, that has no mountains between its territory and the pole, has during winter a temperature as cold as that of Sweden, whilst Hungary, which is protected on the north by the Carpathian Mountains, enjoys a pleasant climate similar to that of Germany.

4. *Proximity or Distance from the Sea.*—The waters of the ocean have a more uniform temperature than the earth, and preserve, for that reason, a proportionate uniformity whenever their influence can be felt, moderating the cold as well as the heat.   A cold wind passing over the surface of the ocean becomes somewhat heated, and in turn a hot wind becomes cooler.   That is why the climate of islands and of countries bordering on the ocean, is more uniform than that of countries situated at a great distance from the sea, and such countries also enjoy more moderate winters, and their summers are cooler.

We may state, for example, that the average temperature of England, which is an island, is about 65° in summer and about 37° in winter, which merely gives a difference of 26°, whilst the average temperature of Pekin, removed from the sea, is 79° in summer and 23° in winter, which gives a difference of 56°.

5. *The Inclination which the Country Bears to the Course of the Sun.*— The angle at which the sun's rays fall on a locality, and consequently its heating power, varies according to the position of the soil of such locality.   When the sun is 45° above the horizon, its rays must fall perpendicularly on the side of a hill looking towards the south, and forming likewise an angle of 45° : whilst the plain below the hill will receive the sun's rays at an angle of 45°.

6. *The Geological Character of the Soil.*—The kind of soil of a locality has a great influence on the climate, principally on account of its greater or less adaptability to irradiate the heat.   Sandy soil is heated easily and quickly, and when the sun's rays do not fall on it it irradiates easily and thereby communicates a portion of its heat to the atmosphere.   Earthy soil, on the contrary, absorbs less easily the heat, and irradiates it more slowly, and so it communicates less heat to the atmosphere.   Marshy lands and forests cool the air.

7. *The Degree of Cultivation of the Soil.*—Cutting or grading and the reclaiming of marshy lands renders warmer the temperature of a locality.   The complete destruction of forests may be fatal to a region because thereby it may be deprived of a protection against certain winds, or diminish humidity in a greater scale, be it through the decrease in the rainfall in places having no vegetation, or because the evaporation of the leaves of vegetable matter ceases.

8. *Prevailing Winds.*—The winds prevailing in a locality have great influence on its temperature.   The winds may be cold or warm, according to the place whence they come and the kind of surface over

which they may pass. In the northern hemisphere, as a general rule, the winds coming from the north are cold, and those coming from the south hot.

9. *The Quantity of Annual Rainfall.*—Rains have great influence over the temperature of a locality, as they render it more or less humid or damp. As a general rule a greater amount of rain falls on islands and on the coast than in districts far removed from the sea, in the mountains than in the valleys, within the tropics than outside of them.

The amount of rainfall in a locality does not depend merely on its latitude, but on other circumstances, as, for instance, the vicinity of high mountains abounding in trees, because elevations as well as vegetation attract clouds impregnated with water, and produce rain. The rainfall also depends on prevailing winds ; when the latter pass over the sea they retain a large quantity of water in the form of vapor, which dampens the atmosphere or converts it into rain.

CONTROVERSY ABOUT THE TEHUANTEPEC LANDS FOR COFFEE.

The *India-Rubber World*, New York, October 15, 1893 :

To the Editor of the "India-Rubber World":

I read with a great deal of interest in a recent number of your journal, Mr. F. O. Harriman's articles on "Rubber-Planting on the Isthmus of Tehuantepec," and I am glad to see that he is so much pleased with his location at Jaltipan. While I think that Jaltipan is a very good location for rubber-planting, and with but one exception agree with everything he says in this regard, I am afraid that he is mistaken in considering that coffee and rubber can grow well on the same ground, or rather, that low hot lands are the best for coffee. In my opinion there is no land hot enough for India-rubber, or, rather, the hotter the temperature the better it is, provided, of course, that it is moist or damp. But not so with coffee, which, in my opinion, requires a temperate climate, where it will not freeze. The mere fact that coffee-trees cannot grow at Jaltipan without shade, shows in my judgment that that zone is not the proper one for coffee-growing, since it requires an artificial reduction of temperature. You can grow pine-apples in St. Petersburg, Russia, but only in a hot-house,—that is, by increasing artificially the temperature,—the only difference being that in one case you increase and in the other reduce the temperature. For commercial purposes, it will not do to change the conditions of nature, as the cost of production will be very much increased when you have to use artificial means to alter the climatic conditions of a place. I have had a great deal of personal experience in coffee-planting, and I am sure that I am right in this view of it, and if necessary, could demonstrate it very clearly.

If Mr. Harriman's estimate about the yield per coffee-tree in Jaltipan is correct, the place must be exceptionally good for coffee-raising. The yield per tree depends mainly on the zone the trees are planted in. When they are planted in the hot zone, the medium yield is from 4 to 8 ounces per tree, and when in the temperate zone about one pound per tree. Isolated trees planted near houses where they have better care and manure, may be found yielding in the hot zone even 8 pounds, but they are exceptional cases, and could not be taken as a basis for the yield of a large plantation. One pound per tree is a very good yield, as an average. The expenses of keeping the plantation and gathering the crop are also smaller in the temperate than in the hot zone.

I do not agree with Mr. Harriman in his assertion that the India-rubber trees require shade while young. If he takes from the woods small plants which have grown in the shade, and transplants them on cleared ground, it is likely that they will not stand the heat, especially as they suffer a great deal from transplanting, even when that operation is done under the best circumstances. But if he sows the seeds in a nursery without shade and they spring up without shade, he will find that they come stronger and stouter, and if he then transplants them to their final location, he will see that they do not need any shade at all, and that the young plants grow more rapidly and stronger without shade.

Very truly yours,

M. ROMERO.

WASHINGTON, D. C.,

September 25, 1893.

The *India-Rubber World*, New York, December (Friday) 15, 1893 :

RUBBER SHADE FOR COFFEE PLANTATIONS.

By F. O. Harriman, C.E.

To the Editor of the " India-Rubber World " :

The communication from Señor Romero in the issue of your journal for October 15th, on the subject of planting rubber and coffee in conjunction, contains ideas so detrimental to the coffee interests of the isthmus district that I feel bound, though not wishing to take issue publicly with Señor Romero, to say something further in the same connection. The eyes of the world are fixed upon the Isthmus of Tehuantepec as a connecting link in the highway of commerce between the Atlantic and the Pacific, and its consequent advantage of soon being within easy reach of the entire world ; and coffee-growing is daily becoming more and more important in the development of this section. As I have tried to point out in your pages heretofore, India-rubber may be made a factor in profitably extending this industry. Hence my continued attention to the subject.

Coffee, wherever planted on the Isthmus of Tehuantepec, and also on the foot-hills and Atlantic plains of the States of Vera Cruz and Tabasco, requires shade ; even the old plantations of the Cordoba and Jalapa districts were shaded to a greater or less extent, and at present, even in these altitudes, much rubber will be found for this purpose. From the *Mexican Trader* Handbook No. 1, *Coffee-Growing in Mexico*, by J. P. Taylor, I quote as follows (page 26):

" *Shade.*—According to Mr. Hugo Finck, the coffee-tree requires shade up to the altitude of from 3000 to 3500 feet above the level of the sea. From 3500 to 5000 feet shade is not absolutely necessary, although the coffee-trees which have it live longer, but their product is less. At Cordoba, Jalapa, and other districts in the State of Vera-cruz, the banana-tree is the favorite one for shade, but, as Mr. Finck says, it is a tree which so rapidly exhausts the soil that coffee-trees beneath it do not bear more than eight or ten years. Mr. Julio Rossignon gives it as his opinion that the method which some planters employ of shading their coffee-trees with bananas is a bad one. The banana, while it maintains humidity in the soil, takes too much of the richness out of the earth. On the other hand, in the return rendered the government by the city council of Jalapa, the banana is recommended as the best tree for shade, on the ground that it has the property of attracting to itself such moisture as may be in the atmosphere, thus bestowing freshness and luxuriance upon the coffee-plant which it covers. There can be no doubt, however, that the banana is selected as a shade-tree chiefly because it bears valuable fruit, which, on the Mexican or inter-oceanic railways, readily realizes from $1 to $1.25 per arroba (25 pounds). Beside the banana, the orange, the lime-tree, aguacate, walnut, mamey-tree, castor-oil plant, the fig, and the rubber-tree, as well as a host of others, are found in the State of Veracruz as shade for the coffee-tree. All the trees specifically mentioned yield more or less valuable fruit, and they are thus desirable on their own account, apart from their shading services."

In the valley of the Coatzacoalcos River, the proper northern part of the Isthmus of Tehuantepec, coffee-growing is no new experiment, having been carried on since the time of the French colonists settling there in 1829–32, and even at present there exist remains of some of these old plantations in the towns of Jaltipan, Soconusco (Santa Ana), Acayucan, Hidalgotitlan, and many places on the banks of the Coatzacoalcos and Uspanapa rivers; but invariably they all are shaded, and of the new plantations, many bearing and shaded by rubber-trees, exactly as good results are given in yield of coffee as when shaded by jonote, coscalite, cocuite, and other shade-trees. In this district the good result is proved by actual experience and existing examples; it is no theory waiting for development. In a plantation thus formed with rubber shade, when the conditions will allow, the cost of production of coffee is not increased, as Señor Romero states, for the rubber forms a greater producing factor than the coffee itself, and the same extension of ground planted in coffee with and without rubber shade-trees, will give more than a double revenue in the former case; or, the capitalized value of the plantation in the former case is more than double what it is in the latter, with hardly an imperceptible difference in cost of forming plantations.

It is not on account of an excessive heat on the isthmus that the shading of coffee is necessary. From the pass of Chivela in the Sierra Madre to the gulf coast the extreme temperature is between 99° and 57° F. In a letter on this subject from Coatzacoalcos, dated August 17, 1880, Mr. Martin Van Brocklin, late chief engineer of the Metropolitan Elevated Railroad Company of New York, and at the time chief engineer of the Tehuantepec Railroad, says : " The thermometer hanging in my office has not been above 85° F. since July 10, when it reached 88°, nor has it been much more than 10° below these figures," and this was during a portion of the hottest season of the year, and Coatzacoalcos is the hottest portion of the northern division of the isthmus.

The shading of coffee is necessary on account of the continued dry southern winds, prevailing during March and April, which, in addition to the sun's rays, will completely bake the ground and exhaust the moisture, and small plants, if not protected, succumb to the combined influence of these elements. The isthmus, on account of the great depression of the Sierra Madre,—only some 900 feet at this point, but rising very abruptly on both sides,—feels the effect of the south winds as no other part of Mexico on the Atlantic slope. Through the effect of the same topographical conditions, by causing a continuous circulation of air currents from ocean to ocean, there is given to this region a cooler and more salubrious climate than is encountered in any other part of Mexico or Central America included within the tropics at the same altitude.

Rubber should be planted from the seed, which falls in April and May, or from young plants from a nursery, at the beginning of the rainy season, in order to be well rooted to resist the effects of the dry season. At the time of planting the prevailing rains are generally severe showers of short duration, with afterwards an almost instantaneous hot sun. Hence, if the young plants are not protected by some light shade, a considerable proportion of the rubber-plants is sure to be scalded. It is true that the rubber afterwards thickens in the trunk quicker in the open, but the coffee must have shade in the dry season, and unless rubber be planted three years before, some other shade is necessary, and low trees like bananas, planted properly, retard the growth of rubber very little.

JALTIPAN, VERA CRUZ, MEXICO
October 30, 1893.

ANOTHER RESPONSE TO SEÑOR ROMERO.

To the Editor of the " India-Rubber World" :

I notice with surprise the criticisms of Señor Romero, in relation to F. O. Harriman's experience in coffee and rubber cultivation on the isthmus of Tehuantepec, as detailed in his article in your edition of August 15th. My brother has had an almost continuous experience in the locality mentioned for over ten years past, and has given the subject an exhaustive study, in connection with the opportunities afforded him through the pursuits of his profession as civil engineer engaged in locating and building the railroad across the isthmus.

That the lands and climate of this locality are unusually well suited to the cultivation of coffee, a number of plantations in the neighborhood, such as Peña Blanca, Villa Alta, and the Boca de Chuniagoa, can testify.

These plantations yield per tree enormously more than those of Cordova and the coffee-producing districts of Oaxaca. On account of the great fertility of the soil, the trees open out so much that they have to be planted three and four yards apart, else in four years they would completely interlace. The trees commence to bear in three years after first setting out, and when in full bearing, in five years, will yield large amounts. At the Peña Blanca plantation, the average crop is 3½ pounds per tree ; it is of a very superior quality, with a little less caricolilla than Cordova or Oaxaca, perhaps, but the yield per tree is very much greater than in those districts, where only from ½ to 1¼ pounds per tree is obtained, and naturally it will be a great deal more advantageous to cultivate plantations in this district.

I fail to grasp the pertinence of Señor Romero's suggestion that " the fact that coffee-trees cannot grow in this locality without shade, shows it is not the proper zone for coffee-growing." This fact is no more conclusive than the fact that a few years ago, when the railroad construction company sent 3000 wheelbarrows to this locality, the native Indians employed there would not use them until they had taken out the wheel and placed a man at each end of the barrow, is conclusive that nineteenth-century ideas are not applicable to labor in this district.

The simple fact that it has been the custom until recently to cultivate coffee only at a higher elevation above the sea-level than this valley, seems to me to offer no valid reason for not accepting the much greater yield of the product attained from richness of soil, etc., here with *shade*, especially when the product of the shade-trees, in seven years from planting, yields a larger profit than the coffee-trees even, and divides the expense of maintenance.

For commercial purposes, it *will* do "to change the conditions of nature," as illustrated by the reclaiming of large tracts of the "great American desert," by artificial irrigation, and the deepening of the outlets of numerous rivers by jetties recently constructed. I see no reason for declining to adopt modern ideas for the cultivation of coffee and rubber in conjunction when the outlook is so promising.

J. P. HARRIMAN.

WOONSOCKET, R. I., *November 9, 1883.*

The *India-Rubber World*, February 15, 1894 :

AN ANSWER FROM SEÑOR ROMERO.

To the Editor of the " India-Rubber World" :

I have seen in your issue of December 15th, a communication from Mr. F. O. Harriman, C.E., dated at Jaltipan, Veracruz, Mexico, on October 30th last, commenting on my letter published in your October number, in which I criticised his former article about his Tehuantepec India-rubber and coffee plantations.

You know very well that my letter was not written for publication, and that I only consented to its insertion in your paper after your solicitation, and because I supposed that the discussion of this important subject would do some good to the public at large, and especially to the coffee and India-rubber industries in Mexico. Far from having any intention detrimental to any of those industries, my well-known interest in both of them made me write my letter, as I think I am the originator and promoter of India-rubber planting in Mexico, and I have given a great deal of my time—at least two consecutive years—to coffee-culture, having started myself a coffee and an India-rubber plantation in the State of Chiapas, in southeastern Mexico.

Perhaps I was too sweeping in my remarks about coffee-planting in the Isthmus of Tehuantepec, due to the fact that my official duties at this capital leave me very little time to consider carefully and maturely other subjects, and that my letter to you was for that reason written in great haste. What I meant to say,—because I am convinced of it by experience and study,—is that hot lands are not the best for coffee, and that as a general rule low lands are hot, and in the Isthmus of Tehuantepec lands are low. As Mr. Harriman says the highest elevation is only 900 feet above the level of the sea, I concluded that they could not be the best lands for coffee.

But Mr. Harriman states in his last letter that the lands on the isthmus are not hot, and as he knows them well and I have only passed through some of them,—never having been at Jaltipan,—his lands may be very good and perhaps the best for coffee, and I sincerely hope they are so, as I have the best wishes for his success, as well as for the success of anybody else who would contribute to the development of the coffee industry in Mexico, which I think is one of the greatest sources of wealth in that country.

As is well known, the temperature of a place depends on several factors, the principal one being its elevation above the level of the sea ; but this factor may be affected or even changed by others, like the currents of air, dampness, etc. The atmospheric conditions of Jaltipan, as described by Mr. Harriman, doubtless may give that place, located 900 feet above the sea-level, a temperature corresponding in other localities to a much higher elevation (say from 5000 to 5500 feet), which I think is the best location for coffee-culture. I am sure, too, that the great currents of air passing through the isthmus of Tehuantepec, which Mr. Harriman describes so well, and which I have experienced while passing through that isthmus, will dry the land, and may make it necessary to use shade for the coffee-trees when they are young and when most of the surface of the land would be exposed to the winds ; but even in that case I should think that when the coffee-trees are grown, and they shade the ground with their own leaves, the yield of the plantation per tree would be increased by pulling down the shade-trees.

I am still firmly of the opinion that as a general rule, recognizing of course that there may be exceptions to the rule itself, but not to its principle, coffee is the product of temperate and not of hot climates,—and that it is better therefore to plant it high rather than low. Mr. Taylor's quotation of Mr. Hugo Finck's opinion, quoted by Mr. F. O. Harriman, to the effect that coffee-trees need shade when planted below from 3000 to 3500 feet, and do not need it when planted higher, I rather think confirms my theory.

I have also read Mr. J. P. Harriman's letter, dated at Woonsocket, R. I., November 9th, published in the same issue of your journal, commenting on my previous communication on this subject. My remarks already made to the other letter will answer his, and I will only add that if coffee-trees yield in Jaltipan or around there 3½ pounds per tree, as he says they average at the Peña Blanca plantations, I would not hesitate in saying that the isthmus lands are the best in the world for coffee-raising, as what I consider the best lands in Mexico for that industry do not average in a large plantation more than one pound per tree per crop, although individual trees may yield considerably more. Nobody will be happier than myself if such is the fact, as I feel such a great interest in the development of that industry in Mexico.

To Mr. F. O. Harriman and his associates, should he have any, I would venture to say,—should they allow me to volunteer my advice,—go on with your plantation and increase it as much as you can, being sure that if the yield is such as expected, you have the best coffee-lands in Mexico, and possibly the best in the world. But should you for any reason be mistaken in that regard, I would advise you still to go on, as a plantation already begun, when the land has been secured and there is sufficient labor, is far better, even in case it has not the best conditions as compared with others which would be only imaginary ones. Coffee production is such a lucrative business that it will yield very large profits, even in case it is not undertaken under the best conditions.

Mr. J. P. Harriman asserts that coffee has heretofore been planted in high lands, and considers that planting it in low lands, which are generally more fertile, shows a great improvement, and mentions in support of his theory an experiment to introduce wheelbarrows in Tehuantepec, the reclaiming of large tracts of the " great American desert " by artificial irrigation, and of deepening shallow rivers by constructing jetties. To my knowledge coffee has been planted so far almost exclusively in the low lands, and it is only recently and in a few places where its culture is more advanced, and experience has shown the advantages of high lands, that these are preferred.

Nobody could deny that men can through industry and labor assist nature very materially in the discharge of its functions, as it is the case in manuring worn-out land, in irrigating arid tracts, which otherwise would be unproductive, etc., but I perceive a great difference between assisting the forces of nature and trying to change them. When a crop is cultivated out of its own natural zone, I think the effort is in the second direction. Even in case of man's industry assisting the forces of nature, I imagine it is better to use land which requires no such assistance. I would make a farm of virgin land, rather than of worn-out land which needs to be manured, and of a moist land needing no irrigation, than of arid land which cannot be productive without irrigation, all other circumstances being equal.

I do not understand the hint to wheelbarrows in Tehuantepec, unless it is to compare me with the native Indians who would not use them until they had taken out the wheels and placed a man at each end of the barrow. I am as firm a believer in progress as Mr. Harriman can be, and I do not think my views on coffee culture are inconsistent with progress, but should I be mistaken I will be glad to acknowledge my error when I am satisfied that I have made any, as I am always open to conviction and I think it is honorable for anybody to recognize his own mistakes.

M. ROMERO.

WASHINGTON, D. C., *December 16, 1893.*

After my paper on coffee culture was writtten, I received a very interesting publication on coffee culture in Brazil entitled *Monographia do Café Historia, Cultura e Producção*, by Paulo Porlo-Alegre, published in Lisbon, in 1879, which contains valuable information on the coffee culture in that country. I am sorry that I have not the time to compare the culture of coffee in Brazil with the way in which it is cultivated in Mexico and Guatemala.

.

INDIA-RUBBER CULTURE IN MEXICO.

INTRODUCTION.

All that I said in the introduction of this book, referring to coffee culture in Mexico, applies to India-rubber culture. When in 1872, I made a long trip of inspection to several of the Mexican States for the purpose of studying the agricultural resources of the country and selecting some branch of it which would be pleasant and profitable to apply myself to, together with a desirable location, and visited Soconusco, I was very much struck with the great future of the India-rubber culture, and I became satisfied that it was the most lucrative branch of agriculture that could then possibly be undertaken.

On that occasion I remained about four months in Soconusco and studied almost exclusively the India-rubber tree, and it seemed to me so promising that I fully made up my mind to undertake a plantation of such trees, and on my return to the City of Mexico, in December, 1872, for the purpose of closing my affairs there and moving my residence to Tapachula, the county-seat of Soconusco, I decided to give to my countrymen the benefit of my studies and experience, or rather surmises about India-rubber culture, and I consequently published a paper entitled, " Importance of India-Rubber Culture in the Future of Mexico," in which I tried to present what I had gathered, and to give a clear idea of the profits of that culture in Mexico, and of the advantages of Soconusco for the same.

My paper on this subject differs from the one on coffee, especially from the fact that when I wrote the latter, coffee raising was an industry already established, and of which one could speak from experience, while India-rubber planting was not in existence anywhere in the world that I knew of, and therefore nobody could lay down with certainty the true principles of the same, and any surmises, however plausible and reasonable, could not be supported by experience.

On returning to Soconusco in 1873 to make there my permanent abode, I purchased a very desirable piece of land, of about 25,000 acres, bounded by the Pacific on the south, and by two large rivers, the Zuchiate on the east, and the Caohuacan on the west, at a distance of about ten miles apart, where a great many India-rubber trees had previously been grown wild and the large ones had been destroyed by the rubber gatherers, a fact showing, in my opinion, that it was the best place for that culture. I planted about 100,000 trees, having to contend with the scarcity of hands, and with the great difficulty of bringing laborers there, because it was somewhat removed from any settlement, the climate warm and productive of intermittent fevers, and there being, besides, a great number of mosquitoes.

In 1875 my trees were prospering and in a very satisfactory condition; but as I had to abandon the place at that time, when the trees developed, the natives tapped them, destroying them as they do with the large wild trees, and I could not therefore have the advantage of the experience drawn from my plantation.

I have not heard of any plantation on a larger scale being made in Mexico, except one on the southern coast of Oaxaca, called "Esmeralda," which I have not seen, and of which I have not reliable information.

Extracts from my paper on the India-rubber culture in Mexico were published in English by the *India-Rubber World*, of New York, in its issue of April 15, 1893.

The demand for India-rubber has increased considerably since my paper was written, while the supply is necessarily diminishing. Every day new applications are being made of that material, as, for instance, tires for bicycles, carriages, and wagons, all of which result in a much larger consumption of that article. In the Pará regions, the main source of the supply, the wild India-rubber trees near the rivers have been destroyed, although new ones are growing up, and it will be more difficult and expensive to go to the interior to tap the trees, so that the wild India-rubber trees are being put to contribution in other regions like Asia and Africa, for the purpose of supplying the demand. The price has consequently increased and a good quality of rubber, such as is produced in Mexico, is now sold at $1 per pound.

The United States Consuls in America, Asia, and Africa sent reports to the Department of State, during the years 1890 and 1891, in answer to a circular addressed by the same, asking for information on India-rubber culture in the tropical regions of the world, and they all were published in a volume of 250 pages (*Special Consular Report on India-Rubber*, 1892), which contains very interesting information on the rubber culture in Brazil, India, and Africa. Unfortunately this information came after my paper had been written and published, for which I am sorry, for had I had such data, I could have enriched my article very materially with important matter ; but I was very much pleased to see that the cardinal points which I laid down about India-rubber culture are the same as those considered the safest in their case.

I saw in the *India-Rubber World* of New York, of March 15, 1894, that a valuable book on india-rubber had been published in Colombo, Ceylon, by A. M. & J. Ferguson, in 1887, entitled *India-Rubber and Gutta-Percha: Being a Compilation of all the Available Information Respecting the Trees Yielding these Articles of Commerce and their Cultivation,*" and that is the first intimation I had of any book on that subject. I am sorry that I have not the time to compare the information contained in that book with my surmises about India-rubber culture.

I am also sorry that my present duties should preclude my revising this paper, which I publish now exactly as it came out over a quarter of a century ago. All I could at present add is that the estimate of the cost of a plantation, while perfectly reliable in 1872, would be subject to serious changes, for the reasons stated in the introduction to *Coffee Culture in Mexico.* In so far as the profits are concerned, I would be still more conservative, and reduce them very materially.

As I am the only one who has written on India-rubber culture in Mexico, and have studied the subject as far as it was possible under the circumstances, I have received frequent calls for my paper on the subject, especially from citizens of the United States, and to satisfy their demands, I have decided to give to the public the following article on the subject, without revising it in any way.

WASHINGTON, D. C., *February 24, 1898.*

THE INDIA-RUBBER CULTURE IN MEXICO.

I.

INTRODUCTION.

It is with a feeling of extreme diffidence that I undertake to write upon a subject on which I can only speak as a layman, inasmuch as neither my few studies nor my habitual occupations have initiated me theoretically or practically in agriculture, botany, chemistry, or any other of the sciences a knowledge of which is necessary to be able to speak intelligently of a branch of agricultural industry that I consider as being destined to attain a great development in Mexico, and to exercise a vast influence upon its future.

My desire in calling the attention of my fellow-citizens to the exploitation of a source of wealth which, I do not doubt, will, in a few years, assure their future, is the sole motive that induces me to write these lines, even at the risk of sometimes falling into an error of more or less importance. I trust that this explanation will serve as an excuse for the inaccuracies which may be found in this paper, and I shall consider my object in writing it attained, if competent and practical persons will kindly point out the gaps or defects that must be in it, so that the subject may be the more clearly explained.

As another excuse for the insufficiency of this paper, however, I think it proper to mention the scarcity of books upon the subject. From the time that my attention was first called to the importance of the culture of the rubber-tree in Mexico, I endeavored to provide myself with such books on this subject as might have been published in Europe and in the United States. I applied to persons in New York, and to the principal European book-stores, but their answers were that they had met with no book treating of the rubber-plant. In some encyclopedias, such as the *Encyclopædia Britannica*, the *New American Encyclopedia*, and other books of reference, I found articles concerning the manufacture of rubber rather than the tree that produces it.

During my recent travels in the Eastern States of Mexico, I endeavored to obtain all the data possible on the subject, so as to supply by the experience of others and my own limited observation what I could find nowhere else. The result of my investigations was not as complete as I could wish, owing to the fact that the rubber-tree not having been cultivated in those localities, no experiments as to its development had been made; and, consequently, there are only conjectures, more or less well founded, concerning it. The summing up of some probable conjectures on this subject is what I shall endeavor to record in this paper.

II.

DESCRIPTION OF THE RUBBER-TREE—BOTANICAL NAME—CHEMI-CAL ANALYSIS—SPECIFIC GRAVITY OF RUBBER—WHEN RUBBER WAS FIRST USED—VULCANIZED RUBBER.

The tree that produces rubber belongs to the family of *Euphorbiaceæ* trees, shrubs, and grass that gives a milky juice. This family is composed of more than fifteen hundred species, which grow principally in intertropical regions.

Its botanical name is *Jatropha elastica*,[1] according to Linnæus; *Siphonia elastica*, according to Persoon; *Siphonia cahuchu*, according to Screber and Wildenow; *Haevea guianensis*, according to Aublet; and *Echites corymbosa*, according to Jacquieu. The trees called *Cecropia*, *Peltada*, *Ficus religiosa*, and *Indica* produce a substance similar to rubber, but inferior to it. The Asiatic rubber-tree called *Ficus* and *Urceola elastica*, grows to a greater size than the American, but its product is inferior in quality to that of the latter.

M. de la Condamine, describing the rubber-trees on the banks of the Amazon River, says that they grow rapidly, are perfectly straight, have branches only near the top, and cover a surface of not more than ten feet.

They have three seeds contained in a pod with three cells, in each of which there is a kernel which, boiled in water, produces an oil that is used like butter.

---

[1] I find in the *Treasury of Botany*, edited by John Lindley, and published in London in 1870, that there are four species of India-rubber: first, *Ficus elastica ;* second, *Siphonia elastica*, which is the one prevailing in Brazil ; third, *Castilloa elastica*, which is the one raised in Soconusco; and fourth, *Urceola elastica*. The *Castilloa elastica* is described as a Mexican tree pertaining to the *Artocarpacea*, which has masculine and feminine flowers on the same branch. The masculine flowers have several stems inserted in a semi-spherical perianth, the feminine flowers consisting in several ovaries contained in a cup.

All the India-rubber trees that I have seen in the United States are entirely different from those which grow in Mexico, and I think that they belong to the *Siphonia elastica* family.

Father Clavijero says that rubber, in Mexican, is called Olliu, or Olli, a word derived from Olquahuitl; that it is a tree of medium size with a smooth trunk of a yellowish color, having long leaves, white flowers, and a yellow fruit, angular in shape, containing kernels of the size of a nut, white and with a yellowish skin. The kernel has a bitter taste and the fruit always grows close to the bark. He also says that it is a very common tree in Guatemala.

I have seen a great many rubber-trees in Soconusco and in the western part of Guatemala contiguous to Mexico and near the sea; but they were nearly all small; the large ones had been cut down for reasons which will be mentioned later. There is a great difference between the size and shape of the leaves of the two varieties; both have them silky and of a deep green; the small trees are very straight, without leaves, except in the upper part, these being large, hanging down from a bough like a stem, and the bark is of a light color.

On the San Carlos farm of Mr. Jeronimo Manchinelli, in the jurisdiction of Tuxtla Chico, in the Soconusco district, I saw three trees that the owner had found growing on the place when he took possession of it, thirty-one years ago, and which he thinks cannot be less than thirty-five years old. They are of an enormous size; I measured the trunk of one of them; it was two metres in diameter, and the space shaded by its foliage had a diameter of at least twenty or twenty-five metres; its branches were also very large, the leaves smaller than those of the smaller trees and their form entirely different from them. Mr. Manchinelli having never extracted any rubber from them, did not know the quantity that each tree could give, but experts calculated that it could not produce less than about fifty pounds a year.

The trunk of the rubber-tree of Soconusco is of a spongy white wood, with large pores plainly visible to the eye.

Very little is known regarding the discovery of the rubber-tree. The French astronomers sent to Peru, in 1735, were the first who called attention to it. It was found afterward at Cayenne by Frisman, in 1751. Dr. Priestly refers to it in the preface of his work entitled *Prospective*, printed in 1770. Various experiments made for utilizing rubber are mentioned in the Memoirs of the Academy of Sciences of France for the year 1768.

Rubber is extracted by making an incision in the bark of the tree from which flows a liquid very much like sap in color and thickness. Exposed to the sun or the fire, the watery part evaporates and the rubber remains. Exposed to the air, it loses its white color and becomes dark.

This liquid is of a light yellow color with a specific gravity of 1012. The rubber separated from the sap rises to the surface like coagulated albumen, and when heated with water, its specific gravity is 0.925, but when pressed out like cream it contains 32 per cent. of the liquid.

From the analysis made by Prof. Faraday, rubber, as it flows from the trees, is composed as follows:

Water with a little free acid..............	56.37
Rubber or *caoutchouc*....................	31.70
Albumen	1.90
Wax..	....
A body of nitrogen soluble in water........	7.13
A substance insoluble in water............	2.90
	100.00

According to the same scientist, rubber already dry contains none of the oxygen which is found in most vegetable products, but is an hydrocarburet consisting of eight parts of carbon and seven of hydrogen, which would require a proportion of 82.27 of carbon to 12.73 of hydrogen for every 100 parts. The quantities found by him were 87.02 of carbon to 12.08 of hydrogen. The same result was obtained in the analysis made by Dr. Ure.

In his *Dictionary of Arts, Manufactures, and Mines*, Dr. Ure observes that rubber, in its liquid state, that is, " cachusina," which is formed by the distillation of the rubber, has less specific gravity than sulphuric ether; while in its fluid condition, it is heavier than the heaviest of all gases.

He remarks also, that the greater part of the rubber imported to Europe came formerly from Pará, in Brazil, but that in recent years great quantities have been received from Java, Penang, Singapore, and Assam.

According to M. de la Condamine, rubber is extracted chiefly during the rainy season, because at that time the trees yield more abundantly than in the dry season.

Mr. Lee Norris, of New York, discovered the means of keeping rubber in its milky form, as it flows from the tree, in hermetically sealed vases; the liquid is first filtered, then well mixed with the eighteenth part of its weight of strong ammonia. When poured on a plane surface and exposed to a temperature between 70 and 100 degrees Fahrenheit, the ammonia that protected it from the action of the oxygen in the atmosphere evaporates and leaves the rubber, which remains white, and in the shape of its container.

Vulcanized rubber, a combination of rubber and sulphur, was first made by Mr. Charles Goodyear, of New York, to whom letters-patent for his invention was granted in February, 1839. Mr. Goodyear made further experiments later on with sulphur, lead, and rubber, but these did not give as satisfactory results as the first ones.

Experiments are at present being made in manufacturing rubber cloth to take the place of water-proof articles which, until now, were composed of glazed linen with a layer of rubber.

III.

IMPORTANCE OF RUBBER AS A RAW MATERIAL.

It is well known that rubber is used as a raw material, in the manufacture not only of water-proof goods, but also of many others which could not be produced as advantageously with any other substance.

Every year it is employed in the manufacture of a great many articles that were not made of that material the year before. It may, perhaps, not be an exaggeration to say, that in course of time it will partially supersede iron. These considerations are sufficient to establish the fact that the demand for rubber, in the markets of the world, far from diminishing, will, in the future, increase considerably.

Thus far, rubber is not the product of a cultivated tree. In every part of the American continent from which it has thus far come, it has been extracted from trees growing wild, and that had not been originally planted by the hand of man. In every locality, also, it is extracted at the cost of the tree itself; either because this is cut down, owing to the belief that the sap is thus more abundant, or because of the frequency with which extractions are made, or of the bad system in use of making them, which injures the trunk and thus kills the tree. Notwithstanding that certain measures to protect it have been adopted in different countries, such as Honduras where a fine of fifty dollars is imposed for every rubber-tree destroyed on government lands, they have proved ineffectual.

The inevitable consequence of this must be that the production will diminish, unless a large number of plantations are soon established, and perhaps even in that case; and as it is not probable that extensive plantations will be made, if only because it would be a new enterprise and for that reason a somewhat risky one, the certain result will be, that the supply in the present rubber districts will decline in proportion as the demand increases.

Now then, it is an incontrovertible principle that the value of an article depends upon the demand which there is for it, on the one hand, and its production, on the other. When the former increases, and the latter diminishes, its value rises in proportion. To-day, the average price of rubber is sixty cents a pound. It is almost certain that within five years it will reach seventy-five cents, and, perhaps, as much as one dollar a pound, owing to the facts above mentioned.

The value of rubber has been quadrupled in Soconusco in less than

ten years; for from eight cents, the price at which it was sold to ex-
porters in 1863, it rose this year (1872) to thirty-five cents a pound;
the cost of transportation to the port of shipment, etc., being at the
expense of the exporter.

Rubber is an article which, even assuming that instead of rising in
price it were certain to retain its present value, or were even to decline
as low as fifty cents a pound, would still yield enormous profits, as will
be seen in the following chapter.

IV.

PROFITS OF THE CULTURE OF THE RUBBER-TREE.

The large profits yielded by the culture of rubber are obvious.
Supposing, for instance, a plantation of ordinary size, containing
about one hundred thousand trees, will give, at the end of a few years
making a low estimate, six pounds of sap a year for every tree ;
that sap, reduced to rubber, would lose about one-half by evaporation, then each tree would yield three pounds net of rubber.

From the analysis made by Prof. Faraday, the sap contains only
forty-four per cent. of rubber, the balance being composed of different substances; therefore, supposing that these evaporate, it will result that from one hundred pounds of sap forty-four pounds of rubber
will remain.   This conclusion agrees with the opinion of Dr. Ure, who,
in his *Dictionary of Arts, Manufactures, and Mines*, says that in reducing the sap to rubber there remains forty-five per cent. of the latter,
the balance of fifty-five per cent. being lost.

The number of pounds of sap furnished yearly by each tree being
reduced to rubber on that basis, two pounds and a half of rubber
would be obtained from each tree, or a revenue of two dollars and a
half per tree, if the price was one dollar a pound; or of one dollar
and twenty-five cents per tree, if the price was fifty cents a pound.   In
the first case, the plantation would give a return of two hundred and
forty thousand dollars a year; and in the second of one hundred and
twenty thousand.   Admitting that this estimate of six pounds per tree
is too high, let it be one-half, one-quarter, or even one-fourth of it,
which would be the minimum yield, as will be seen further on, the returns of the plantation will be one hundred and twenty thousand
dollars, eighty-six thousand dollars, and seventy thousand dollars, respectively, in the first case, that is to say, if the price of rubber was
one dollar per pound; and sixty thousand, forty thousand, and thirty
thousand, in the second case, if the price was fifty cents a pound.

It is to be observed, that sixty cents a pound is to-day the average
price of rubber in foreign markets, and that, taking into account the

expenses of transportation, commission, freight, insurance, and others, including also the profits of the exporter, which may be calculated at thirty per cent. of the price above mentioned, this would be reduced to forty-two cents per pound on the place of production.

As the cost of a plantation of one hundred thousand trees in the State of Chiapas, the best locality for this product, would not probably be more than ten thousand dollars, it results that the profits would really be fabulous.

It must be observed, moreover, that as the yield of every tree will increase annually, there is every reason to believe that a tree twenty years old will give from fifteen to twenty-five pounds of sap.

For the purpose of showing upon what basis the preceding calculations rest, and of giving general data that may be useful to those who would like to go into that business, we will consider in the following chapter, what are the requisite conditions to form such a plantation.

V.

PROPER CONDITIONS TO FORM A PLANTATION OF RUBBER-TREES.

When about to form a plantation of rubber-trees, it is indispensable to ascertain beforehand what are the best conditions for the development of that tree, so that at the least possible expense and in the shortest time, for "time is money," the largest returns may be obtained. The following points, therefore, should be carefully examined:

1. What are the climate and soil most favorable to the development of the rubber-tree?

2. What is the best way to form a plantation, by sowing seeds, transplanting from the nursery, or with cuttings?

3. Should the plantation be exposed to the sun or should it have shade?

4. At what distance must the trees be from each other, so that they shall not interfere with one another's growth, and yet that no land shall be wasted?

5. What operations will the tree require before bearing?

6. How long after planting the seed will the tree begin to bear?

7. What quantity of rubber can each tree produce in a year?

8. What is the best way to extract the rubber from the tree without destroying it?

Unfortunately, it is not possible to answer positively and conclusively every one of the preceding questions. In regard to some of them certain fixed principles, proved by experience, may be laid down;

and, concerning others, one must accept deductions which, in my opinion, are well worthy of consideration.

Before discussing the above questions in detail, I deem it opportune to state, that the principal difficulty to be encountered in dealing with the subject, is the fact that, so far, rubber is in no part of the world, that I know of, the product of cultivated trees, but of wild ones. The largest part of the rubber consumed in the world coming from the Province of Pará, in Brazil, and this rubber being of the best quality, and always obtaining the highest price in the market, it seemed to me that it could be cultivated advantageously.

Happening to be in the city of Tapachula on the 24th of September of the present year (1872), I wrote a letter to the United States Consul at Pará, requesting him to furnish me with detailed information upon almost the very same points enumerated at the beginning of this chapter. The answer, to which I shall refer later, reached me in the City of Mexico. For the present, it suffices for my purpose to quote here a paragraph from a communication upon the subject, addressed to the State Department by Mr. James B. Bond, United States Consul at Para, dated November 5, 1870, which is on page 60 of the *Annual Report on Commercial Relations between the United States and Foreign Nations*, for the year ending September 30, 1870, transmitted February 3, 1871, to the House of Representatives at Washington by the Secretary of State. This paragraph is as follows:

> Rubber is not the product of a cultivated tree : it is extracted from trees in the forests, and the government, in no way whatever, claims anything from those who take them out of national lands. It has been asserted that the trees from which the rubber is obtained are being exhausted in the forests in the immediate proximity to the markets, either because they die or because they give but little sap owing to their being too frequently tapped. But the area of the production is so vast, and the means of reaching the most distant localities increase so rapidly, that no immediate diminution is anticipated. On the contrary, it is possible that it will increase for several years.[1]

From the investigations which I have made, it results that not until a very short time ago did the rubber-tree begin to be cultivated; that the attempts at planting of which I have any knowledge have been on a very small scale and so very few and recently made that they cannot serve for the purpose of this paper.

The principal plantations of which I have any knowledge, are the Zanjón Seco, in the Department of Soconusco, made by D. José María Chacón; that on the farm of San Isidro, the property af Mr. William Nelson, situated in the jurisdiction of Mazatenango, in the District of Suchitepequez, in the Republic of Guatemala, where the rubber-trees

---

[1] This is a retranslation from the Spanish translation of the English original.

are used to shade the coffee- and cocoa-plants; and that of Hatillo, owned by an agricultural society in the State of Veracruz.

I have been told, also, that in Nicaragua and Honduras, some plantations have been formed as experiments, the principal one belonging to Dr. Gauffrau, on the bay of Realejo, near the port of Corinto, in the former republic.

These explanations being made, I shall now proceed to discuss, in regular order, each of the points specified at the beginning of this chapter.

I. CLIMATE AND LAND BEST ADAPTED TO THE CULTURE OF THE RUBBER-TREE.

The fact that thus far rubber is not the product of a cultivated tree, does not preclude the possibility of one answering the question : What climate and land are best suited to its development ?

The best climate is the hottest, and the best land the dampest and the nearest to the seashore or to the low banks of rivers. Wherever rubber-trees are found these conditions are present.

Those of Pará are found on the banks of the Amazon. The rubber land that I have personally examined is in the Department of Soconusco, in the State of Chiapas. Soconusco forms a plain from six to twelve leagues wide, which terminates at the Pacific and ascends gradually and almost imperceptibly to the base of the Cordilleras, where the ascent is steeper, although still gradual. This plain is crossed by numerous rivers which come down from the Cordilleras and empty into the sea. The climate is hotter in the low than in the high lands above the sea-level. One notes the great number of rubber-trees,—all small ones, the large ones having been cut down to extract their sap,—that are in the forests on the plain, and the number increases notably as one approaches the sea, and diminishes in the same proportion as one goes from the shore toward the Cordilleras; even at the base of these mountains, at an elevation of twenty-five hundred feet above the sea-level, and in lands suitable for the culture of coffee, some rubber-trees are found, but they are exceedingly rare.

To establish a plantation it is necessary, before everything else, to select the ground; this should be in the climate best adapted to the development of the tree, as the expenses would be almost the same everywhere; while the trees will grow in much less time under favorable than under unfavorable conditions, and give greater returns when they begin to bear, in the former than in the latter case. In the District of Soconusco alone, there is sufficient land to plant several millions of rubber-trees; and I believe that a great many localities could be found on both sides of the coasts of Mexico, that are equally advantageous for that culture; provided, always, that the plantations are established in the low lands, in a damp climate, and, whenever possible, near the seashore or the banks of rivers. The temperature of the localities in Soconusco where the rubber-tree most abounds is from twenty-eight to thirty degrees Centigrade, or from eighty-three to eighty-seven degrees Fahrenheit. In all cases it would be well to form the plantation in places where the wild trees grow most abundantly, as their presence is the best evidence that the land and climate are favorable to their development.

Dr. Ure states that the Asiatic rubber, or *Ficus elastica*, is found at a very high altitude above the level of the sea.

This tree has, besides, the great advantage of requiring but little labor for its cultivation, which makes its exploitation possible, even on a large scale, in Mexican coasts, which are generally not populous.

2. HOW TO FORM A PLANTATION OF RUBBER-TREES.

In regard to the best method of forming a plantation it must be observed that the rubber-tree not being very delicate, economy of time and money are the first things to be considered. If the land selected be forest land, the first thing to be done is to clear it, should it be thought preferable to have the plantation exposed to the sun; but should the shade be deemed best, the trees already standing will furnish the best and cheapest protection. The soil having been prepared, the planting can begin by sowing the seeds in convenient places, or by transplanting young plants from the nursery or from the forest itself. Sowing the seeds would undoubtedly be the best plan, but it would also be the most expensive and the slowest; the most expensive because it would involve the cost of a double planting, the first in laying out the nursery, and the second in transplanting the young plants from the nursery to the plantation; the slowest, because the time that might be saved by planting saplings would thus be lost.

The method to be adopted will, therefore, depend upon circumstances. Where there are trees already somewhat grown it is preferable to transplant these, because it saves time; where there are large trees, cuttings may be used, and where there are none of either and only seeds can be obtained, the last must be used. It is not necessary that they should be sown in the nursery, as the plant is not delicate and requires no special care, like coffee and some others regarding which experience shows that it is an economy to plant them in the nursery.

On the 16th of September of the present year (1872), being at Tapachula, I made an experiment with Don Sebastian Escobar, a well-known practical agriculturist, thoroughly acquainted with the nature of these lands and enthusiastic in the matter of agricultural progress. We selected a part of the public domain occupied by Señor Escobar, to see whether transplanting could be done by pulling up the small trees, as in that case the roots would come up without any earth around them; or if it would be necessary to remove the soil that covered them; for in the first case, the operation would be quicker and cheaper than in the second. On the land referred to, we saw about sixty small rubber-trees, from eight decimetres to one metre and a half high. We pulled up a few without, and others with the earth covering their roots, and transplanted them at a distance of two metres from each other. We first performed the operation planting some of the trees in the shade, and then planting others in the sun. A short time afterward we noticed that the leaves of the transplanted trees had begun to fade; in the evening of that day, they appeared to be dead. On the day following, they were dry; shortly after they fell off, the branches that remained presenting a not very encouraging appearance. In a week, the trees all began to sprout again; a little later they were covered with luxuriant foliage and not a single one was lost. This is a proof of the endurance of the rubber-tree. The land in Tapachula, where the experiment was made, is not the best kind for the rubber-tree, being somewhat higher than that nearer the shore.

The easiest and most economical way of making such a plantation would be, in the beginning, to combine it with the culture of some product adaptable to the soil, and of a more rapid growth. The land being cleared, it could be prepared for sowing cotton, which generally grows well in the soil suitable for the rubber-tree; and, in sowing cotton, rubber could also be sown at proper distances, or saplings transplanted. The cotton crop being harvested, the rubber would remain without any cost, since the expenses incurred would be only those required for the cotton. This operation could be repeated the year following; and, in this way, the plantation would be gradually enlarged and without additional cost.

There is also another very economical way of planting rubber, and that is, to plant the trees as shade in the coffee and cocoa plantations. I have heard that this operation has been successfully tried in some places. The expenses of a plantation of rubber-trees would not then exceed, in any case, those required for one of coffee or cocoa; but the rubber-trees could not then be planted in the places best adapted for their rapid development and greatest yield, inasmuch as the climate and soil most advantageous for coffee and cocoa are not the best for rubber.

Señor Don José M. Chacón assured me that to have cuttings grow well, the end which is to go into the ground must be pointed, and the slip driven in, probably in order that the soil may adhere the better, and the cutting remain firmly planted.

It is to be observed that in the lands of Soconusco near the shores of the Pacific, seeds and trees somewhat grown are to be found in sufficient quantities to form extensive plantations.

3. THE RUBBER-TREE MUST BE PLANTED IN THE SUN.

As the rubber-tree, so far, grows wild, and is found in the forests of the most fertile lands, where vegetation is very luxuriant, and always in the shade of larger trees, the general opinion of agriculturists in those localities is that, like coffee, it needs shade to grow well. Observation shows, however, that this opinion is inexact. The most superficial observer cannot fail to notice the great difference which there is between rubber-trees growing in the sun and those that are in the shade. The latter have but few leaves, are stunted, and appear withered; while the former have thick foliage, a brighter color, and look much more vigorous. The most careful cultivators in Soconusco, and the very ones who were before of opinion that the rubber-tree required shade for its development, acknowledged before my return from that district that they grew better in the sun.

In this opinion I was soon afterwards confirmed. I deem it proper to state here, however, what Señor Don José M. Chacón told me. Señor Chacón is a very experienced agriculturist, the same who made the plantation of Zanjón Seco. His opinion is that the tree planted in the sun develops more rapidly than it would in the shade, and yields a larger quantity of sap; but this is very soon exhausted, owing to the ardent rays of the sun, which prevent the soil from retaining the necessary moisture. He believes that a tree planted in the sun would yield sap only for two or three years, and would then die for want of sufficient humidity.

With much hesitation, I express the opinion that the reason why some plants require shade to grow better, is that the shade serves to temper the rays of the sun, for I have observed that the lower the temperature of the place where coffee is planted, the less shade it requires, and that it grows better without any shade at all where the temperature is moderate. The rubber-tree being of a kind requiring a very high temperature, it seems to me that the more heat it receives the better will be its development. The humidity of the soil would remain when the trees attained a certain size, for their branches would then meet and give sufficient shade to prevent the rapid evaporation of the ground.

The short time I stayed at Tapachula did not permit me to observe any difference between the growth and luxuriance of the saplings planted in the sun and those that were in the shade. The mere fact that none of the trees planted in the sun had perished, was, in my opinion, a sufficient proof that the rubber-tree requires a sunny exposure, and should be planted without shade.

4. DISTANCE NEEDED IN PLANTING RUBBER-TREES.

The distance apart at which rubber-trees should be planted, is a question which, although apparently secondary, is really an important one. If from a false economy they be planted closer than is proper, the trees will interfere with each other, and will consequently become stunted; while if planted a greater distance apart than is absolutely necessary, there will be a waste of ground and a great increase in the cost of cultivation, besides the cost of fencing, watching, and such other outlays as may be needed, when the plantation is in a state of full development and production. The importance of space is practically illustrated in coffee and sugar-cane plantations: it is seen that on the same land the returns of coffee-trees planted at a distance of three metres apart are double the returns of those growing at a metre and a half or two metres apart from each other. From this it will be perceived how great a difference in the yield of the rubber-tree the distance at which they are planted makes.

The prevailing opinion among the agriculturists of Soconusco, is that a space of two or two and a half metres from tree to tree, on every side, is all that is required. It seems to me that it ought to be much more. If coffee, which is a shrub seldom attaining a height of more than three or four metres, and whose foliage is, at most, three metres in diameter, requires in order to give an abundant crop to be planted at a distance of three yards from tree to tree, is it reasonable to suppose that the rubber-tree, which grows to a very large size, should be planted at the same distance or less ?

In my opinion, planting ought not to be done at a distance of less than five metres, and even this would be too small for trees over thirty years old. The trunks of those on the farm of Mr. Manchinelli, which were of that age, measure, as I have already stated, two metres in diameter, and the circle formed by their foliage is between twenty and twenty-five feet in diameter.

The only objection there can be to leaving a greater space between the trees, and one which may, in some cases, be of sufficient weight to reduce it to less than five metres indicated as the best, is the necessity of economy, inasmuch as the cost of the grove would increase in proportion to the distance apart at which the trees are planted, as will be demonstrated in the following chapter.

5. CARE REQUIRED FOR THE CULTURE OF THE RUBBER-TREE.

The hardiness of the rubber-tree greatly simplifies its culture, and causes this to be proportionately cheap. In the low, hot, and damp lands favorable to its growth, fertility is so great that the labor consists, more than in anything else, in struggling against the luxuriance of the vegetation; and the principal expense is that of the frequent weedings which are necessary to prevent the underbrush and vines from destroying the grove, or causing the trees to grow slowly and to become stunted.

In the lands that are much higher than those favorable to the rub- ber-tree, but less fertile, being less hot and damp, like those that are suited to the coffee-plant, it is necessary to make as many as six weed- ings every year; one every sixty days, in order that the saplings may not be injured or destroyed by the undergrowth and parasites.

The rubber-tree has the great advantage of possessing a vitality superior to that of the weeds or of any other kind of vegetation, and for that reason it does not require the heavy expense of frequent weed- ings. The tree which, without any help from man, can grow in woods full of vines, briers, and other wild plants, can certainly outlive the weeds, for they will not grow more rapidly than it does.

There is no doubt that a grove of rubber-trees requiring to be weeded out only once after having been planted, will grow without that indispensable requirement in the low and fertile lands of the coast; but in that case, the growth of the tree will be slower, because the weeds will share with it the nourishment drawn from the soil; it would therefore be cheaper to weed the grove twice a year, according to the rapidity of the growth of the brush and the means of the owner.

In proportion as the tree grows larger weedings will become less necessary, because its foliage will cover a larger area of ground; and the larger the surface not exposed to the sun the less luxuriant will be the undergrowth. Viewed in this light, a rubber plantation with shade will be more profitable since it will require fewer weedings.

6. TIME REQUIRED FOR THE TREE TO PRODUCE RUBBER.

It is not possible to fix, with any degree of certainty, the time re- quired by the tree before it will yield rubber, which is an important question, for supposing it to be fifteen or twenty years, the enterprise will not offer the same inducement as if it were but five or six years. Six years is a comparatively short period in a man's lifetime, and this is the time required by the coffee- and cocoa-plants to bear fruit. It is safe to say that were it perfectly certain that five or six years were sufficient for the rubber-tree to produce, the number of groves would increase considerably. The importance of this point has led me to give it particular attention.

Superficial observers, in the regions where the rubber-tree is found, believe that the time necessary for its development is not less than from twelve to twenty years. Those who are more experienced and closer observers fix a shorter term. After having heard many and widely differing opinions on this point from agriculturists and studied the question very carefully myself, I am inclined to think that six years, counting from the time the seed was planted, is the period required for the rubber-tree to yield its product, in the soil best suited to its development; for it is quite evident that in less favorable soil, it would need a longer time.

During my recent stay in Soconusco, I was able to satisfy myself by facts of the correctness of the opinion fixing six years for the development of the rubber-tree.

I frequently found trees whose age, owing to their being in a well-known spot, such as the courtyard of a farm, could be ascertained by asking it of the persons who had seen them planted or growing from the seed. This was sometimes difficult, but the difficulty could be removed in every case, and then it appeared that trees from six to eight metres high, with a trunk from six to eight inches in diameter, were three or four years old. This seemed to me conclusive evidence that a tree six years old would have attained the necessary growth to begin bearing without suffering any injury, provided always that it were situated in the best conditions of climate, soil, and cultivation.

Practical and experienced persons in the State of Veracruz have assured me that along its coast, bordering on the Gulf, six years are considered a sufficient period for the development of the rubber-tree.

7. QUANTITY OF RUBBER THAT EACH TREE CAN YIELD.

There is another question not less important than the preceding one; it relates to the quantity of rubber that each tree can yield yearly. There is also a great variety of opinions upon this subject. Many experienced agriculturists are of opinion that the trees can be tapped every two months without injury to them, yielding each time six pounds of rubber, which, in one year, would amount to thirty-six pounds; while there are others who think it imprudent to make more than one extraction every year, and from which not more than six pounds can be obtained. Between these two opinions, there are others differing both as to the number of tappings and the quantity of the yield. Finally, there are some who believe that extracting the sap every two years would give the same quantity as two tappings annually, but the proportion of rubber would be greater.

The information obtained from workmen who, for two years, have been engaged in Soconusco in extracting rubber, to the extent of destroying all the large trees, does not bear upon the question; for, in the first place, the trees used are much older, a great many of them being centenarians; and, in the second place, because they are cut down to obtain the sap. Their statements, moreover, refer to measures of capacity and not of weight, as will be shown later; for they first collect the rubber in gourds and afterwards pour it into jars. But even according to these statements, a tree having attained its proper dimensions in six years, and having had its sap extracted without being cut down, would produce a quantity of rubber weighing not less than six pounds.

It is to be observed, as has been already said, that in order to convert into rubber the sap that flows from the tree after making the incision, it is necessary to let the watery part evaporate, which, according to Prof. Faraday's analysis, which agrees with Dr. Ure's opinion, is as much as fifty-six per cent., the remaining forty-four per cent. being what is properly called rubber. Consequently, the sap coming from the tree must lose at least that quantity before being converted into rubber.

8. METHOD OF EXTRACTING RUBBER WITHOUT DESTROYING THE TREE.

The process of extracting the sap from the tree is also an important point in determining the success of a plantation. In Soconusco a method entirely primitive is used, which causes a great loss of sap, prevents this from being pure, and, what is worse, kills the tree. They begin by cutting down the tree, and then make various incisions across the trunk with a machete, at a distance of three spans (twenty-nine inches) from each other ; this being done, leaves from the tree are placed below the incisions to collect the sap, which is afterward poured into a gourd, and finally put in the jar.

It seems to me that with so ruinous a system, less sap is obtained than if the tree had not been cut down; for I believe that, being no longer in a vertical position, the force of gravity which causes the sap to flow, ceases, and, consequently, the quantity drawn is less than if the tree had been left standing to receive the same number of incisions. When, by chance, they do not cut down the tree, they make only one or two incisions in it at about the height of a man's stature; it is then more difficult to collect the sap by the imperfect means of the leaves. With this process, it frequently happens that earth, dry leaves, small insects, and other foreign substances become mixed with the sap and remain in the rubber, making it impure, causing it to fall into discredit in the market, and greatly reducing its value.

Believing that a more advanced method of collecting the sap was used in Pará, I also made some inquiries upon the subject, to the United States Consul in that province. The information he sent me will be found further on.

It is evident, that to extract rubber properly, a more adequate instrument than a machete is required; and to collect the sap a better receptacle than the leaves used in Soconusco, or the clay used in Brazil. I think it very probable that such instruments, if they are not yet used, soon will be, in view of the need there is for them, and the advances that are being daily made in the manufacture of agricultural implements.

To prevent the tree from dying in consequence of the incisions referred to, it is indispensable to observe two things carefully: first, the incision must not go beyond the bark, for if the woody part is injured, the tree may die; second, such incision should not isolate the lower from the upper portion of the bark, as, in that case, the sap being unable to ascend to the upper part of the tree, this also would cause its death. It is also necessary that the tapping be not too frequent.

There are some who think that to yield a greater quantity of sap, the tree requires several incisions, or a single one in spiral form around its entire length; while others express the opinion, better founded, perhaps, that a single incision made in the lower part is sufficient, as the force of gravity causes all the sap to run down without much injury to the tree.

It is well to be careful, after all the sap is taken out, to heal the wounds made by the incisions, by covering them with wax, woollen stuffs, or clay.

VI.

PROBABLE COST OF A PLANTATION OF RUBBER-TREES.[1]

It seems proper, before concluding this paper, and with the object of furnishing the greatest amount of information relating to the practical points concerning rubber, to present an estimate of the probable cost of a plantation. It must be remarked, that the following data are based upon the present cost of agricultural operations in Soconusco, and were given to me by Señor Don Sebastian Escobar, of Tapachula —an experienced agriculturist, as I have already stated, and thoroughly acquainted with everything pertaining to agriculture in that district.

The cost would vary according to the proximity of the trees, and also, according to whether the soil has been prepared exclusively for planting rubber-trees, and not for anything else, such as cotton, as has been already indicated. Supposing that the plantation is to contain ten thousand trees, and that they are placed at a distance of three yards from each other, applying the measurement used in Soconusco, it will result that a cuerda, the unit of the standard agrarian measure of that district, forming a square of twenty-five yards on each side, or an

---

[1] I have to repeat here what I said in the introduction of this book, namely, that conditions have changed in Soconusco so much since this paper was written, especially in the price of land, labor, taxes, etc., that the estimate of expenses contained in this chapter, while correct at the time it was written, would be now four or five times larger, and that were I to write this paper again, I would make much more conservative the estimate of the rubber produced, which so far was only guesswork.

area of a little over six hundred and twenty-five square yards, will contain eighty-seven trees; a little less than one hundred and forty-one and a half cuerdas being required for the ten thousand trees; and if the trees are placed at four yards apart, fifty-two and a half trees would go in each cuerda and two hundred and fifty-one cuerdas would be required for the ten thousand trees; and if the planting is made at a distance of five yards apart, there will be thirty-six trees in a cuerda, and it will require three hundred and ninety-two and a half cuerdas for ten thousand trees.   In that case, including the price of the land, the cost will be as follows:

Planted at a distance of three yards apart: The value of 141½ cuerdas of land, or a little less than six and a half hectares, at 25 cents a hectare, the price fixed in the tariff of the Department of Fomento, on the 1st of January of the present year, for 1872 and 1873, for uncultivated lands situated in the State of Chiapas, one hundred per cent. for the expenses of surveying, stamped paper, title, etc., at which price a great deal of private land can also be purchased.................. $3 25

Clearing the land, at 50 cents per cuerda....................... 70 50

Planting, at the rate of 25 cents per cuerda........................... 35 25

Removing the weeds, brushwood, etc., for six years, at 25 cents per cuerda for each removal, at $36.25 for five removals...................... 176 25

Total cost................................... .... $285 25

To keep the grove six years, until it is in condition to produce rubber.

If planting is done at a distance of four yards, it will cost :

Value of 251 cuerdas of land, or 11½ hectares, at 25 cents, adding the above charges $5 75

Clearing the land 125 50

Planting.. 62 72

Five removals of weeds in six years 313 75

Total cost... $507 72

Should the grove be planted at a distance of five yards, it will cost :

Value of 392½ cuerdas of land, or 17½ hectares, at 25 cents per hectare, adding the charges indicated..................................... $8 76

Clearing the land 196 25

Planting 98 12

Five removals of weeds in six years 490 62

Total cost... $793 75

The cost of each tree would be, during the six years, including the value of the land :

Planted at a distance of three yards, a little less than three cents each.
Planted at a distance of four yards, a little more than five cents each.
Planted at a distance of five yards, a little less than eight cents each.

It must be remarked that the expenses will not be made at the same time, but gradually during the six years.

The planting of one hundred thousand trees would cost respectively :

$2,852.50, when done at a distance of three yards.
$5,077.50, at a distance of four yards.
$7,937.50, at a distance of five yards.

After six years, the yield will be as follows :

Ten thousand trees, at a minimum rate of six pounds of sap each, will give 60,000 pounds, which, reduced to rubber, supposing that 56% is lost by evaporation, will leave 26,400 pounds of rubber, the cost of which, as calculated by Señor Escobar, is at the rate of three cents a pound. The rubber sold on the place of production at 45 cents a pound, after the deduction already referred to, will give for the 26,400 pounds........$11,880 00
Deducting the expenses of cultivation, at the rate of three cents a pound, according to the information furnished by Señor Escobar........... 792 00

Leaving as a profit for the first year.....................$11,088 00

Considering that the yield of rubber has been calculated at the minimum rate of production, and that it will necessarily increase every succeeding year, to the extent of being three or four times greater than in the first, it is impossible to ignore the great future of that important source of public wealth.

VII.

INFORMATION RELATING TO RUBBER IN THE PROVINCE OF PARÁ, IN BRAZIL.

Considering, as I said before, that as the Province of Pará, in Brazil, is the locality producing the greatest quantity of rubber and of the best quality known, due, in some manner, to the way in which it is extracted, that it might be the product of a cultivated tree, and wishing to obtain all the data possible upon that important branch of commerce, I addressed during my stay in Soconusco the following letter to Mr. James B. Bond, United States Consul at Pará : [1]

[1] My letter and Mr. Bond's answer were written in English, and translated into Spanish, in the Spanish edition of this paper made in 1872. Now they have been retranslated into English from the Spanish translation, and therefore, although their meaning has not been changed, the wording must necessarily be very different from the original English text.

When I published, in the City of Mexico, in December, 1872, my paper on Indiarubber culture, I sent a copy of the same to Mr. James B. Bond, United States Consul at Pará, Brazil, and made further inquiries from him on rubber in Brazil. My letter was received by him in Pará when he was no longer United States Consul there, but was getting ready to return home, and when Mr. Charles M. Travis was fulfilling the duties of that office. Mr. Bond answered my letter in Pará on January 8, 1873, giving me additional information which he had collected while there, and on his arrival in New York he addressed me another letter with a similar purpose, dated February 26, 1873. I also received a letter from Mr. Travis dated at Pará, January 21, 1873, on the same subject, and considering these letters of interest I append them to this paper.

" *James B. Bond, Esq., United States Consul, Pará, Brazil:*

" DEAR SIR :—I beg you to pardon the liberty I take in asking you for some information relating to the culture of the rubber-tree in the Province of Pará, in the Empire of Brazil, that branch of agricultural industry being destined to a great future in Mexico. I will thank you very much if you will do me the favor to furnish me with whatever data you may have upon the following points :

" 1. Is the rubber-tree wild or cultivated in Pará ?

" 2. When forming a plantation of rubber-trees, are the seeds sown, are slips planted, or are saplings transplanted ?

" 3. How long does it take for the tree to produce rubber after being planted ?

" 4. What is the yield of a tree per year ?

" 5. How often is the rubber extracted from the tree ?

" 6. What is the best way to extract the rubber without injuring the tree ?

" 7. How many different kinds of rubber are produced in Pará, and what are their particular qualities ?

" 8. At what distance from each other must the trees be planted ?

" 9. Does the rubber-tree require to be planted in the sun or in the shade for its best development ?

" 10. What climate and soil are most favorable to rubber-trees ?

" 11. What is the height of rubber-trees, and the diameter of the trunks at different ages ?

" 12. What is the estimated value of each tree, and what the cost of extracting the rubber ?

" 13. What is the annual production of rubber in Brazil ?

" I will be very much obliged to you if you will have the kindness to answer in detail, as far as may be possible, each of the preceding questions, addressing your communication to this place, via Panama, by the Pacific Mail steamers, or through the Legation of the United States in Mexico.

" I am, sir, very respectfully, your obedient servant,

" M. ROMERO."

On my return to the City of Mexico, I received the following answer to the above letter :

" NEW YORK, *October 22, 1872.*

" *Señor Don Matías Romero, Tapachula, Mexico:*

" DEAR SIR,—I received your letter of the 24th of September last, and, although I am no longer consul at Pará, having resigned that position last year, and as the new appointee has not yet reached his post, and could not probably answer your questions until well acquainted with that country, I shall give you all the information in my power that can interest you.

" 1. The rubber-tree is a spontaneous product of nature in Brazil, and uncultivated.

" 2. It can grow from seeds, but then, to reach maturity, it will, of course, require a longer time than if propagated by transplanting.

" 3. The time required for the planted tree to be in a proper state to extract the rubber profitably, depends, necessarily, upon the quality of the soil and other favorable conditions for its development. In the localities where it has been extracted for some time, the men employed are using to-day the most slender trees and even the shoots; and I have been assured that this custom, and that of not letting the tree have time to recuperate, has destroyed those that were the most accessibly situated on the river banks.

"But little reliance can be placed on the information obtained from uneducated and unobserving persons like those who are engaged in that trade; when I asked how long it would take for a tree, under ordinary conditions, to reach a vigorous maturity, I was told from ten to fifteen years.

"4. The exact yield that each tree can give has never been known, although I have asked it often of the workmen. It is evident that much must depend upon its size and condition; and, probably, upon the place where it has been growing. It is generally believed that the trees which yield the most, are those whose roots are periodically submerged, but I also have been assured that there is a species of trees which grow in high altitudes and give good sap, though not abundantly. The tree is centenary, and attains great dimensions under favorable circumstances, both as to the locality and age.

"To answer your question to the best of my knowledge, I will say, that many persons have told me that the trees from which no rubber has been previously extracted, yield, in the season, as much as sixteen pounds. Others have given double that quantity, and some only seven pounds when they had been tapped before.

"5. In Brazil rubber is extracted from the trees annually. An earthen vase is fixed to the tree below the incision to receive the sap. The workman who makes this same operation on a certain number of them, collects daily the sap contained in the vases; and, returning to his hut, smokes it in the evening, and during the night, a process which is used to harden it. In the rainy season the rivers rise and generally inundate the places where the works are going on; if that does not happen, the constant rains prevent the clay from adhering to the trees, which, for this reason, are left untouched until the return of the dry season. The information I have been able to obtain leads me to believe, that although incisions are made all over the tree, they do not cause it any serious injury, or, at least, the harm done to it is much slower in its effects. I consider this as a sufficient answer to your sixth question.

"7. Three kinds of rubber are produced in Pará, fine, middling, and ordinary, or *negro head*. The medium is somewhat impure or adulterated, and frequently contains a mixture of smoked and fresh rubber. The ordinary one consists principally of the waste or scrapings taken out of the vases already mentioned, or of pieces which became hard when the sap flowed from the incisions. All this is mixed with the sap, sometimes imperfectly smoked, and sold with all its impurities. The value of rubber varies. The middling quality is generally worth from one to two dollars less than the fine one, per arroba of thirty-two pounds, but little of it is put on the market. The ordinary kind is always in great demand. From last accounts, the difference in the price of one or the other class was from seventeen to twenty-six milreis per arroba of thirty-two pounds.

"8. As no plantations have been made, I cannot tell at what distance the trees ought to be separated. However, as they grow wild, and their value would increase according to their growth and size, I would plant them twenty-four feet apart from each other. To utilize the land between them, I would plant some cacao, which would give sufficient shade to the saplings, and produce a revenue several years before the rubber-tree reaches its maturity. This idea is simply speculative, although confirmed by various opinions of more or less value, which I obtained incidentally.

"10. I am unable to inform you as to the most proper soil and climate for the development of the rubber-tree. It grows in the valley of the Amazon, preferring damp places or those liable to be inundated along the water-course. The species found in the upper Amazon, the Madeira, and Purús rivers, is the most valuable, but it is due, perhaps, to the fact that the particular kind of fuel used to smoke the rubber is more abundant, or, perhaps, because in that region the rubber is sent only after the rising of the rivers ; and for that reason reaches the market in a drier condition.   I doubt whether there is much difference in its intrinsic quality.

" I must say, however, that there are various kinds of trees that produce rubber, or substances very much like it, but more or less inferior to each other in elasticity, and which are not in great demand on the market when they arrive in large quantities.   It has not, as yet, been positively determined if the difference results from the intrinsic qualities or from a distinct care taken in the preparation.   Of that kind is the rubber called Rio Prieto.   I also have received some rubber from Venezuela by way of the Orinoco.   I believe that the tree possesses sufficient vitality to develop itself in climates of very changeable temperatures, from a tropical to a temperate one.

" 12.   The rubber-tree has no value in Brazil ; anybody can go into the forests of the public domain, select and clear a plot of ground, which he can claim afterward as his own, provided he does not abandon it beyond a certain time.   It must not be supposed, however, that the prospector for rubber obtains his plot without trouble : the forest is dense, the jungles are very thick, and the trees do not grow close to each other as in our oak or pine forests, but are scattered, and difficult of access, until paths are made to reach them.   The transportation of laborers and provisions to the place, must be considered as another expense for the exploitation.

" I cannot tell how much the rubber costs to the producer.   This must depend upon the wages of the workmen, the price of their provisions (flour of manioc being the principal article), and other circumstances.   About six or eight years ago, it was said, but I do not know if it was true, that the producer was repaid at a price from 12,000 to 14,000 reis the arroba.   Since then the cost of living in Pará is much higher ; the price of rubber rose to 48,000 reis the arroba, and went down to 22,000 during the last three years.   I believe, though I may be mistaken, that the producer would receive a good price for his rubber, at the rate of 20,000 reis ($10) the arroba.

" I see no reason to think that the production is decreasing.   The majority of the trees are not injured, at least not seriously, by the extraction of rubber made from them.   The forests, at all events, will remain inexhaustible for many years to come. New plantations are being formed gradually as the old ones are exhausted ; and I believe that the closer relations between Bolivia and the valley of the Amazon will furnish to Brazil the only element it needed until now to increase its facilities of production.   In treating this question, many thoughts that are as speculative as practical, arise in one's mind ; but the time is wanting to develop them, and the subject probably may not interest you.   I am, sir,

" Your obedient servant,

(Signed)   " JAMES B. BOND."

VIII.

DATA ON THE RUBBER OF ASSAM, IN ASIA.

In the latest edition of his *Dictionary of Arts, Manufactures, and Mines,* Dr. Andrew Ure gives much important information regarding the rubber of Assam, a province of India, tributary to Great Britain, situated beyond Grafes in the valley of the river Brahmapootra between 25° 45′ and 28° 15′ latitude north, and 90° 35′ and 96° 50′ longitude east of the meridian of Greenwich. I deem it useful to insert here the principal data.

A short time ago, Mr. William Griffith published a report upon the Asiatic rubber-tree called *Ficus elastica*, in which he stated that it was sometimes found isolated, at other times in pairs, and at others in groups of three. It is larger and gives more shade than all the other trees of the forest where it is found; and can be distinguished from them at a distance of several miles by its picturesque appearance, due to the great height and dense foliage of its top. The trunk of one that was carefully measured, had a circumference of 74 feet; the area of its branches a circumference of 610 feet; and its height was 100 feet. On an area of 30 miles long by 8 miles wide, near Ferozpoor, in the district of Chardwar, in Assam, 43,240 trees of that kind were counted.

Lieutenant Weitch afterward discovered that the *Ficus elastica* was equally abundant in the district of Naudwoor, where it is met with on the brow of the hills at an altitude above the level of the sea calculated to be 22,500 feet.

The sap of the *Ficus elastica* of Chardwar is better in the old trees than in the young ones, and more abundant in winter than in summer. It is drawn off by means of incisions in the bark, around the trunk and the branches, as far as the top, and at a distance of one foot from each other. The quantity of the sap increases in proportion to the height of the incisions. The liquid flowing from them is of the same consistency as that of cream and extremely white. Each tree yields forty-two pounds for every extraction; that is to say, every fortnight. The sap contains from four to six tenths of water and from six to four tenths of rubber.

Mr. Griffith affirms that the best kind is obtained from incisions made in the woody parts of the large roots that are a little above the surface. Below the line of the incisions, the inhabitants of Assam dig a hole in the ground in which they put a leaf of the *Phrynium cápitalum* rudely shaped as a vase.

The United Rubber Co. of London has recommended that the sap of the *ficus elastica* be put in bottles of from 1½ to 2½ inches in diameter, and from 4 to 5 inches long; but in Mr. Griffith's opinion, this is the worst way to prepare rubber because it requires more manipulation, causes the rubber to become black in drying, and does not prevent the viscosity of the sap when exposed to the sun. He advises, as the best method, to work it by hand, to wash it in water and to press it.

It has already been shown that the rubber called *Ficus elastica* is inferior in quality to the American species called *Siphonia elastica*; and, for this reason, cannot compete with it.

IX

STATISTICAL DATA RELATING TO RUBBER.

It seems proper to conclude this paper by giving some statistics which will tend to demonstrate the importance of the production of, and trade in, rubber.

The following figures, taken from the article on " Caoutchouc," in *Appleton's New American Encyclopædia*, show the import and export of rubber to the United States, from June 30, 1856, to June 30, 1857.

	1856.	1857.
Import of manufactured rubber....................	$97,796	$180,585
Export of crude rubber.............................	1,045,576	832,058
Total................................	$1,143,372	$1,012,643
Re-export of manufactured rubber....................	$18,379	$62,593
Re-export of crude rubber	120,802	64,491
Export of rubber shoes in 1856, 685,220 pairs ; in 1857, 537,328 pairs..................................	427,936	331,125
Export of other rubber articles	665,602	312,387
Total export from the United States......	$1,232,719	770,596

From January 1, to June 1, 1857, England imported 5433 quintals (cwt.) of rubber, and for the same period in 1858, 9115 quintals (cwt.).

In the article on Pará, in the same Encyclopædia, it appears that the export of rubber from that place, in 1856, was 4,696,829 pounds.

In the report already quoted, on the commercial relations between the United States and foreign nations, for the year ending the 30th of September, 1870, the following data are given (page 65) on the export of rubber from Pará during 1869:

	Quantity.	Value.	Additional value of 40 %.	Total.
To Great Britain (arrobas of 32 pounds)....	158,432	$1,736,490	$694,596	$2,431,086
To the United States (arrobas of 32 pounds).	179,394	2,083,465	833,386	2,916,851
To other countries (arrobas of 32 pounds)..	19,829	221,175	88,470	309,645
Total................................	357,655	$4,041,130	$1,616,452	$5,657,582

In the same report is found the following very important table, showing the annual export of rubber from Pará, from 1851 to 1870:

EXPORT OF RUBBER FROM PARÁ, FROM 1851 TO 1870.

DESTINATION.	1851.	1852.	1853.	1854.
	arrobas.	arrobas.	arrobas.	arrobas.
United States	52,848	49,251	94,201	104,184
England	30,485	45,573	38,243	55,444
France	4,269	9,330	3,446	4,548
Other ports	4,573	9,750	2,213	2,063
Total	92,175	113,904	138,103	166,239

DESTINATION.	1855.	1856.	1857.	1858.
	arrobas.	arrobas.	arrobas.	arrobas.
United States	83,067	71,760	49,923	53,149
England	56,732	65,046	54,397	48,844
France	4,782	9,732	6,784	4,343
Other ports	6,067	592	5,583	8,114
Total	150,648	147,130	116,687	114,450

DESTINATION.	1859.	1860.	1861.	1862.
	arrobas.	arrobas.	arrobas.	arrobas.
United States	85,292	72,195	31,864	54,041
England	55,436	69,903	100,112	93,535
France	5,733	8,378	9,997	8,423
Other ports	2,823	9,682	5,569	13,137
Total	149,284	160,158	147,542	169,137

DESTINATION.	1863.	1864.	1865.	1866.
	arrobas.	arrobas.	arrobas.	arrobas.
United States	82,356	71,260	94,263	106,491
England	118,498	149,352	140,138	154,457
France	4,949	18,547	11,787	21,910
Other ports	4,853	4,811	10,175	11,742
Total	210,656	243,970	256,363	294,600

DESTINATION.	1867.	1868.	1869.	1870.
	arrobas.	arrobas.	arrobas.	arrobas.
United States	134,315	121,908	182,939	....
France	165,519	213,142	180,548	158,432
Total	299,834	335,050	363,487	158,432

The arroba contains 32 pounds.

X.

CONCLUSION.

In my opinion, what precedes is sufficient to demonstrate incontestably the great future of rubber culture in Mexico, and the large profits it would yield after a few years to those who would devote themselves to that industry. It may be affirmed, without any exaggeration, that neither cocoa, tea, coffee, sugar-cane, henequen, indigo, nor any other tropical product, would give the same profits as rubber, and the returns from each of these enterprises are, in reality, equal to those obtained from a rich mine.

When that culture is propagated in Mexico, it will open up a source of inexhaustible wealth that will change the fate of the rubber-growing districts, which, from being poor and miserable as they now are, will become rich and opulent when that plant begins to produce. Anyone in a situation enabling him to make a rubber plantation of greater or less extent may undertake it at once with the full conviction that it is the safest and most lucrative industry. While the coffee, cocoa, sugar-cane, or any other plantation, in favorable years and under good conditions, can give a return of one hundred per cent. on the capital invested in the year, not upon the capital expended in preparing the plantation, including the value of the land, one of rubber will give over one thousand per cent., not alone upon the cost of the extraction, but upon the first capital invested, including the value of the land.

I shall consider my efforts amply rewarded, if the data contained in this paper shall in any way realize the object I had in view in writing it, and which is to create among our agriculturists the desire to plant fields of rubber-trees in suitable localities. By so doing they will be assured of a bright future, and contribute on a large scale to increase the wealth of the country, to promote the welfare and prosperity of places where to-day poverty reigns, and where it can scarcely be said that civilization has penetrated.

I shall be very glad if persons of knowledge and experience in this important branch of public wealth fix their attention upon this subject, and, by their writings, contribute to the great object that I have simply indicated, correct the errors contained in this paper, and supply whatever is lacking to complete it.

MEXICO, *December 12, 1872.*

APPENDIX.

I append now the two letters from Mr. James B. Bond, United States Consul at Pará, Brazil, dated at that city on January 8, 1873, and New York, February 26, of the same year, and a letter from Mr. Charles M. Travis, the successor of Mr. Bond in that Consulate, dated at Pará on January 21, 1873, the two former containing additional information about rubber in that rich Brazilian province, and to which I refer in the foot-note that appears on page 395.

CONSULATE OF THE UNITED STATES AT PARÁ, BRAZIL,
January 21, 1873.

M. ROMERO, Tapachula, Soconusco, Mexico.

DEAR SIR :

Yours of Sept. 24, 1872, was duly received, and not being as well acquainted with the India-rubber tree, its cultivation and production, as my friend Mr. James Bond, ex-Consul of the United States at this port, I addressed him requesting the answers to your inquiries, and such other information as he could give you. I enclose herewith his letter to me, which I hope you will find entirely satisfactory. I would be greatly obliged to you if you would inform me of the result of any attempts that your people make to cultivate the India-rubber tree in Mexico. I can assure you that my motives in wishing this information are entirely for the purpose of a thorough acquaintance with the cultivation and production of India-rubber in the different parts of Central and South America, where the climate may be suitable.

I trust your efforts will be abundantly successful, and that you will do me the favor to communicate with me the efforts being made and the result to introduce into your country that valuable and important article of commerce. If I can furnish you any further information as I become better informed myself, it will be a pleasure to do so. I am, sir, very respectfully,

Your obedient servant,
CHAS. M. TRAVIS, U. S. Consul.

PARÁ, January 8, 1873.

CHAS. M. TRAVIS, ESQ., U. S. Consul.

DEAR SIR :

I have your favor of this date enclosing one from Mr. Romero, in which he asks for information respecting the production of India-rubber in this province.

I answer his questions *seriatim :*

1. The India-rubber tree is of spontaneous growth ; it is never planted or cultivated here.

403

2. The tree will grow from the seed ; the latter part is answered above.

3. It would yield the milk at any period of growth, but of course in quantity proportioned to the size of the tree. As the tree has never been cultivated, no systematic observation has been made in regard to its growth. I should think, however, that a plantation would not be ready for profitable working in less than fifteen years.

4. That depends upon the size and condition of the tree. New trees yield better than those which have been repeatedly tapped. A seringal is considered a good one that will yield eighteen pounds a day per 100 trees. The proprietor of a seringal, if he has good judgment and wishes to preserve his trees in good condition, will give them an interval of repose during the season. It is not safe, if the seringal is to be worked year after year consecutively, to tap the same trees daily for more than three months of the six which make the crop season.

5. Every year during the dry season, which may be said to last six months, varying, however, in term and duration in different parts of the valley.

6. The collector having cleared paths through the forests from tree to tree (which is no light job), goes his rounds in the morning, and beginning as high up as he can reach, makes with a hatchet light diagonal cuts about six inches apart all round the body of the tree. Under each of these he sticks a small cup fashioned of damp clay, a lump of which he carries with him. Each collector is supposed to attend to one hundred trees. As they are often far apart, by the time he has gotten back to his starting-place and taken his meal, it is necessary to go his round again. He empties the little clay cups into which the milk has trickled, and returns with it to his hut. The next day he makes other cuts about six inches below the first and under the spaces left in the first circle, and so on every day. The tree bleeds most abundantly as the cuts descend. Now the smoking process must commence, or the milk will spoil. This is done by means of a nut called urucuri, which burned under a sort of inverted funnel gives a very pungent ammoniacal smoke. A sort of paddle is dipped into the milk and passed through this smoke. Layer after layer is thus smoked and dried, until the weight becomes unmanageable. An incision is then made round the edge, the mould taken out, and the process recommenced until the milk is all secured. It is to the use of this urucuri that the superior quality of the Pará rubber, and particularly that of the Madeira River, is attributed. There are several qualities of rubber-tree, of which at least three are well known to the ordinary worker. One of these called "the white" gives little or no milk.

7. Answered before. They are found scattered through the forest at irregular distances. In some places and in some districts more abundant than in others, but never holding almost sole possession of the ground, like the pine- and the oak-trees in some parts of North America.

8. I should think it would require shade, in early periods of growth, at least.

9. It must be less exclusive in choice of climate than has generally been supposed. Recently it is said to have been found as far south as Rio de Janeiro and Paraguay. It grows abundantly far up the river Purus, in Bolivia, where the climate is temperate, and no doubt would adapt itself to most countries which are free from frost in winter and have a long and hot summer. This, however, is mere conjecture. I have no doubt that it would grow in Mexico, and even in Southern California. Here it is found to flourish best on the river-sides where the roots are periodically overflowed. There is, I am told, an upland tree, but it does not yield so well. Too much dependence, however, must not be placed on such accounts. The workers in rubber are a very ignorant class, not apt to make accurate observations, and the banks of the rivers are almost the only parts of the country that are accessible.

10. The height I do not know. The largest of which I have any account was five feet in diameter ; three feet would probably be a nearer average.

11. The price depends upon the cost and expenses of opening the seringal on public lands. No tax is imposed on the worker. Once opened and worked it becomes the property of the person who has cleared it, and he can sell it to another. The cost of production must, of course, vary with many circumstances and be greater in one part of the country than in another. The producer in many cases sells his product to the country store, sometimes taking merchandise in return. Sometimes they are hired in gangs. The price of *farinha de Mandioca*, which is their main food, must enter largely into any estimate of cost. Taking one year with another, I made an estimate six or seven years ago that 12 cts., or 14 cts. ($6 or $7), p. A. of 32 lbs. would pay wages to the workman. Since then the cost of living has increased, and without being able to make anything like an exact calculation, I should think 20 cts., or $10 p. A. of 32 lbs., would leave good wages, one year with another. The price has ranged much higher than this. The export last year was 370,000 A. of 32 lbs. each.

It must be remembered that the Brazilian arroba is 32 lbs. ; not like the Spanish, 28 lbs.

There are three qualities of rubber :

Fina : The smoked rubber above described.

Entre-fina : Sells for about $1.50 p. A. less than the fina. It has often a layer of coagulated milk unsmoked, or it may have some adulteration or dirt.

Sernamby consists of the thin skin which dries in the clay cups or trickles over and hardens on the tree. These pieces are rolled in a ball and stuck together with unsmoked milk. In the English markets it is called " negro head." It sells usually at a difference from fina of say 10 cts., or $5 p. A.

I may be permitted to say one word in reference to the effect produced upon the condition of the people by the abundance of this valuable natural production.

In my opinion it would be better for the people if the tree did not exist in its native state. As it is not cultivated, the laborer does not see in its yearly growth the increasing fruit of his industry. He is not, therefore, encouraged to industrious habits, or induced to fix his habitation permanently on the soil that has become his own by right of the labor he has bestowed on it, and which, in increasing value, he may transmit to his children. On the contrary, he is tempted to neglect regular labor, to live from hand to mouth as best he may through one-half of the year, looking to the rapid gains of the rubber season for the payment of his debts. The surplus is for the most part dissipated in orgies, and the most of the workmen leave the seringals with little or nothing to show for their work.

This, of course, would not be the case were the tree regularly cultivated after Mr. Romero's idea. It remains to be seen whether such cultivation would compete in cheapness with the natural product. I think it would where land can be had for the asking.

This, I believe, is all I can say to meet Mr. Romero's inquiries. If I mistake not, I have already replied to most of the above questions in answer to a letter addressed me by the Mexican Legation recently in New York.

Very truly,   JAMES B. BOND.

NEW YORK, *February* 26, 1873.

M. ROMERO, ESQ., Mexico.

DEAR SIR :

I have much pleasure in acknowledging receipt of your kind favor of Dec. 21st, and of the *Correo* in which your report is published. I have no kind of objection to the publicity given to the meagre information which I had it in my power to contribute, and write now principally to say that on my recent visit to Pará, from which place I returned three days since, my friend, the U. S. Consul, placed in my hands a letter

from you containing more or less the same interrogatories as those which I had partially
replied to here.   Being on the spot, I was able to refresh my memory in regard to certain details, and I hope you will find the replies more full and more satisfactory than
those which I had previously the pleasure of communicating.   Should you at any future
time get the rubber nut from the Amazon region for plantation in Mexico, be particular
in the selection.   Of the three best-known varieties, that which gives a white porous
wood, to which in your article you make an incidental allusion, is by far the least
esteemed.

The suggestion referred to as made by certain collectors of making a "spiral cut
round the body of the tree," was at one time tried, but it was found so injurious to the
tree that no one follows this method.   Indeed, I think a law was made many years ago
specially to prohibit this practice.

In the letter to Mr. Travis, I give a description of the present system of extraction.

It may be worth while to say that a few years since a French gentleman from
Cayenne employed whisky or rum of a certain proof (18° or 20°, I think, but am not certain) to produce immediate separation and coagulation of the milk.   I have heard of
an herb which in some parts of Central America is used for the same purpose.

I shall be very happy to aid you in the enterprise you are engaged in by furnishing or obtaining information, or indeed in any way by which the prosperity of our sister
republic may be promoted.

I have read your article with much satisfaction, and, if not too much trouble,
would be glad to receive any future contributions on the subject.

I remain, dear sir, yours,   JAMES B. BOND.

The *India-Rubber World*, Vol. XI., No. 6, New York City, March
15, 1894 :

To the Editor of the " India-Rubber World":

Will you be so kind as to give me some information in regard to planting rubber-
trees, the length of time it will take before the tree can be tapped, and the yield of
fluid in Mexico ; also the expense?   References to any literature on the subject will
be gladly received.

EDGAR ZEH, M.D.

WATERFORD, N. Y., February 12, 1894.

[Mr. F. O. Harriman has in Mexico a plantation of rubber-trees which, he estimates, will yield at seven years a larger output of rubber than has ever been gained
from the wild trees of that section.   He has shown to the editor of the *India-Rubber
World* some specimens of goods manufactured from rubber obtained from cultivated
trees four years old.   His advice, however, is not to tap them before six years, after
which he estimates the yearly yield at three pounds.   The Mexican Minister at Washington, a number of years ago, planted some rubber-trees in Soconusco, with the idea
that the trees would yield, after the sixth or seventh year, about three pounds each.
His estimate of the cost of a plantation of 100,000 trees up to the productive age—six
years—was about $8,000.   Mr. Harriman has cultivated rubber and coffee together, so
that his report does not give the cost of rubber culture alone.   This industry is in the
experimental stage, the work which has been done in it being for the most part too
recent to admit of conclusive results.   There is little to be said in regard to it newer
than what is contained in a little book entitled *India-Rubber and Gutta-Percha : Being
a Compilation of all the Available Information Respecting the Trees Yielding these
Articles of Commerce and their Cultivation.* Second edition.   Colombo, Ceylon :
A. M. & J. Ferguson, 1887.   It should be read by any one interested before investing
in rubber-planting.—THE EDITOR.]

INDEX TO GEOGRAPHICAL AND
STATISTICAL NOTES.

INDEX TO ARTICLES ON COFFEE AND INDIA-RUBBER CULTURE.

A

Age of coffee-tree, some think duration depends on shade, 342

Altitude, of various places in Soconusco, 297 ; its effect on climate, 15,000 ft. snow line in Soconusco, 362

Asiatic rubber-tree, grows larger than American, 378

Aublet, his botanical name for rubber, 378

B

Bearing, trees 25 and 30 years, 342

Blossoming (white) of coffee-tree, time of, 343

Bond, Mr. James B., extract from communication to State Department giving information about rubber, 384 ; letters from him in reference to rubber in Brazil, 396–398

Botanical names of rubber-tree, 378

C

Chacón, Sr. Don José Maria, owner of Zanjón Seco rubber plantation, 384 ; opinion about the way to plant rubber cuttings, 387 ; his opinion about rubber planted in Soconusco, 388

Chardwar, rubber, number of large trees in, near Ferozpoor, sap of *Ficus elastica* better in old trees than in young, yield of, 399

Cheapness of coffee-raising, 287 ; made cheaper by raising sugar-cane at the same time, 288

Clavijero, Father, his description of Mexican rubber-trees, 379

Clearing ground for rubber, should be done first, 386

Climate, Soconusco suitable for coffee-raising, 286, 295 ; coffee affected by humidity, 298 ; affected by sun, latitude, and altitude, 362 ; location of mountain chains, 362, 363 ; distance from sea, inclination of country to course of sun, geology of soil, degree of cultivation of soil, 363 ; winds, 363, 364 ; amount of rainfall, 364 ; hot country best for rubber, 385

Coffee-raising in Soconusco, compared with other countries, 286, 287 ; compared with Ceylon, 357–359

Coffee sent to market in casks and barrels, 350

Color of coffee, bluish color which afterwards changes to grayish green, 350

Condamine, M. de la, his description of rubber-trees on banks of Amazon, 378 ; extraction of rubber, 380

Corn, custom in Soconusco to plant at same time with coffee but not best to do it, 314

Cost of coffee in Barcenas, nursery and seed, stakes and holes, preparation of the soil, transplanting, weedings, other expenses, 354 ; of each cuerda, 355

Cost of coffee plantation in Ceylon, 1st year, 355, 356 ; 2d year, 356 ; 3d year, 356, 357 ; total cost and loss, 357

Cost of coffee plantation in Soconusco, of ground, 1st year, 351 ; 2d, 3d, and 4th years, resumé of, 352

Cost of coffee-raising in Soconusco, as compared with Ceylon, 333

Cost, of rubber plantation, of 10,000 trees at distance of 3 yards, 393 ; distance of 5 yards, estimate of 10,000 trees at 3 yards, 4 yards, and 5 yards, of each tree during 6 years, 394 ; of 100,000 trees at a distance of 3, 4 and 5 yards, yield after 6 years, 395

Cost of sugar-cane plantation, 288, 289

Cuerda, number of coffee plants to the, 303, 304

Cultivation of soil, affects climate, reclaiming of marshy land makes temperature warmer, 363

14 DAY USE

RETURN TO DESK FROM WHICH BORROWED

LOAN DEPT.

This book is due on the last date stamped below, or
on the date to which renewed.

Renewed books are subject to immediate recall.

20Jan'57 HK

JUL 24 '67 -5 PM

REC'D LD   LOAN DEPT.

JAN 6   1957   FEB 8 1968 9 4

10May'59B B   RECEIVED

REC'D LD

JUN 3 1959 MAR 21 '68 -5 PM

16 Jan'55 V D   LOAN DEPT.

REC'D LD   REC. CIR.   MAR 22 '78

JAN 4 '65 -12 M   JAN 27 1998

JUL 24 1967 9 4

LD 21-100m-6,'56   General Library
(B9311s10)476   University of California
                            Berkeley

RETURN TO the circulation desk of any
University of California Library
or to the
NORTHERN REGIONAL LIBRARY FACILITY
Bldg. 400, Richmond Field Station
University of California
Richmond, CA 94804-4698

ALL BOOKS MAY BE RECALLED AFTER 7 DAYS
- 2-month loans may be renewed by calling
  (510) 642-6753
- 1-year loans may be recharged by bringing
  books to NRLF
- Renewals and recharges may be made 4
  days prior to due date.

DUE AS STAMPED BELOW

DEC 1 3 2001

FEB 0 8 2007

12,000 (11/95)

www.ingramcontent.com/pod-product-compliance
Lightning Source LLC
Chambersburg PA
CBHW022020110726
47901CB00006B/1600